Rave Reviews for Explore the Virgin Islands!

♥ "Highly recommended." — *Midwest Book Review*

♥ "This is a fantastic guide.... I especially appreciated the easy to follow maps, relevant charts, and inspiring photos. This book allows any traveler to easily plan a memorable vacation experience..... What really think sets this guidebook apart from many others is the wealth of additional information."
— Juanita Watson, *Reader Views*

♥ "Harry Pariser has produced a superb guide to both the U. S. and British Virgin Islands. — Bill Todd, *About.com*

♥ "[This guide includes] recreational activities, balanced with maps, cultural insights, environmental concerns, history, and candid observations. It's definitive — and very welcome in guidebook land."
— Gay Nagle Myers, *Travel Weekly*

♥ "I am amazed at how much new information I could glean from Pariser's book. The book is a treasure trove of the wonderful and unique environment we live in." — Kirk Grybowski, *St. Thomas Source*

♥ "Having lived on St. John for 20 years, it was fun to learn new information about this special island from *Explore the Virgin Islands*. Mr Pariser has hiked the trails and met the people. His book is the most personalized and comprehensive guide I have read. It is a must for anyone visiting St. John. Pariser's most complete guide is unique and fits easily into your beach bag or backpack."
— Anne Marie Porter, St. John, USVI resident and wedding minister.

♥ "Harry Pariser's guide is a great help, with hundreds of hotels (for all budgets), how to get around (ferries, taxis, sailing, chartering), dining options (native and foreign, budget and splurge), and the best spots for bird watching, hiking, golf, tennis, diving, snorkeling, and soaking up the sun."
— *Amazon.com*

♥ "This versatile book will appeal not only to first-time visitors, but to seasoned Virgin Island vacationers as well. Nicely organized and easy to follow. Color photographs and detailed maps round out this comprehensive guidebook."
— *Tammassee.com*

♥ "We rated this series a high four hearts." —

♥ "The fifth edition of *Explore the Virgin Islan* ful and fascinating information.... It's the n when it comes to the Virgin Islands, that's sa
— *Fearless Reviews*

D0916474

Explore the Virgin Islands

SEVENTH EDITION

HARRY S. PARISER

manatee
PRESS

www.savethemanatee.com

Cover set in Avenir. Text set in Sabon and Avenir. Maps set in Avenir. Cover photo (Trunk Bay, St. John) and text design by Harry S. Pariser. All other photos by Harry S. Pariser, except the illustrations and historical photos, some of which are courtesy of The St. Croix Landmarks Society and the Virgin Islands Archives. Photos of fish, lobster, diving, rock iguana, flamingo are courtesy of the BVI Tourism Authority. Photos and maps by the author are available for license: contact the publisher at (415) 665-4829.

Publishing History

First Edition: *Adventure Guide to the Virgin Islands* 1989
Second Edition: *Adventure Guide to the Virgin Islands* 1992
Third Edition: *Adventure Guide to the Virgin Islands* 1994
Fourth Edition: *Adventure Guide to the Virgin Islands* 1997
Fifth Edition: *Explore the Virgin Islands* 2002
Sixth Edition: *Explore the Virgin Islands* 2005
Seventh Edition: *Explore the Virgin Islands*, 2009

Special Sales

Manatee Press titles are available at special discounts for bulk purchases for sales promotions or premiums. Special editions, including personalized covers, excerpts of existing guides, and business imprints may be printed upon demand. For more information contact Manatee Press at (415) 665-4829.

Other Books by Harry S. Pariser

Explore Barbados ISBN 978-1893643567
Explore Costa Rica ISBN 978-1893643550
Explore Puerto Rico ISBN 1-893643-52-2

This guide focuses on recreational activities. As all activities contain elements of risk, the publisher, author, affiliated individuals and companies disclaim any responsibility for any injury, harm, or illness that may occur to anyone through, or by use of, the information in this book. Every effort was made to ensure the accuracy of the information, but the publisher and author do not assume — and hereby disclaim — any liability for any loss or damage caused by errors, omissions, misleading information or potential travel problems caused by this guide, even if such errors or omissions result from negligence, accident, or any other cause.

A Note About Hotel Rates

Please note that most hotel rates in this book apply during the winter season (approximately December 15th through April 1st. At other times, rates may be 20–50% less.

Manatee Press

P. O. Box 225001

San Francisco, CA 94122-5001

(415) 665-4829

fax 810-314-0685

Single-copy orders only: 800-729-6423

www.savethemanatee.com

www.exploreavirgin.com

editorial@savethemanatee.com

bookseller information: Distributed to the trade in the US and Canada by SCB (800-729-6423). Also available through Ingram, Baker and Taylor, Quality, Unique, and Midwest Library Services.

Calling The Virgin Islands

All phone and fax numbers in this book which do not have a prefix are local numbers.

To call the USVI from outside the area code in the USA
Dial 1 + 340 + the number.

To call the BVI
Dial 1 + 284 + the number.

From outside the US
Dial the international code + area code + the number

Table of Contents

free web updates

Charts and Sidebars

■ Maps ■

■ Abbreviations ■

N	North	L	left
S	South	R	right
E	East	ft.	foot
W	West	km	kilometer(s)
pd	per day	mi.	mile(s)
ph	per hour	EP	European Plan (breakfast0
pp	per person	FAP	Full American Plan (all meals)
pw	per week	USVI	United States Virgin Islands
s	single	BVI	British Virgin Islands
d	double	PST	Pacific Standard Time
t	triple	CST	Central Standard Time
OW	one way	EST	Eastern Standard Time
RT	round trip	GMT	Greenwich Mean Time
ha	hectare(s)	DST	Daylight Savings Time

Acknowledgements

Many people helped with this edition including Sophia Aubin (of the fine website vinow. com), Janet Hagbloom, Wendy Snodgrass, Greg Gunter, Kerry Hucul, Sandie Brown Anne Marie Porter, Linda Lohr,, Anthony Finta, Shaun Pennington, Christina Gasperi, George Brown, Gerald Singer was of invaluable help with checking my BVI section. Thanks to Darril Tighe for her help with proofreading and her advice and support. Arthur Koch also assisted with the cover.

About the Author

Mr. Pariser is a writer, artist, photographer, and graphic designer. Born and raised in southwestern Pennsylvania, he is a graduate of the College of Communications of Boston University. Mr. Pariser's first two books *Guide to Jamaica* and *Guide to Puerto Rico and the Virgin Islands* were published in 1986 and 1987. He has also penned guides to Barbados, Belize, the Dominican Republic, and Jamaica.

Mr. Pariser has traveled extensively in Europe, Africa, Asia, Central America, and the Caribbean. He has lived in Japan: in Kyoto, in the historical city of Kanazawa (facing the Japan Sea), and in Kagoshima, a city at the southern tip of Kyushu across the bay from an active volcano.

His articles and photographs have appeared in *The Japan Times, Costa Rica Outlook, Belize First, Caribbean Travel & Life, the San Jose Mercury News, San Francisco Frontlines, Atevo.com, India Currents, JazzReview.com,* among others.

He enjoys painting, cooking, backpacking and hiking, photography, and listening to music— especially jazz, salsa, calypso, and African pop. His other interests range from politics to anthropology to linguistics to cinema, theater, and literature. He lives in the Inner Sunet area of San Francisco. Mr. Pariser received the Society of American Travel Writer's Lowell Thomas Award 1995 Best Guidebook Award (Silver) for his *Adventure Guide to Barbados.* Select articles by him are on the internet:

http://www.HarryPariser.com

Reader's Response Form

Explore the Virgin Islands

I found your book rewarding because _____
_____
_____

Your book could be improved by _____
_____

The best places I stayed in were (explain why) _____
_____
_____
_____

I found the best food at_____
_____

Some good and bad experiences I had were_____
_____

Will you return to the Virgin Islands?_____.

If not, why not? _____
_____
_____

If so, where do you plan to go? _____
_____
_____

I purchased this book at _____

I learned about this book from _____

Please include any other comments on a separate sheet and mail completed
form to Manatee Press or e-mail comments to editorial@savethemanatee.com.

About Manatee Press

Manatee Press was founded in San Francisco, California with the goal of publishing travel guides which inform the reader about history, culture, and the environment of a destination. The manatee's only foe is man, and it has no natural predators. As such, its survival as a species depends upon the human species' willingness to change their interaction with nature as a whole.

Popularly known as the "sea cow," the manatee once ranged in habitat from Florida to Brazil. Europeans swiftly exterminated the creatures in the southern Caribbean. The last sighting in Trinidad was in 1910 when one was harpooned. Manatees move along the ocean floor (at a maximum pace of six mph) searching for food, surfacing every four or five minutes to breathe. Surprisingly, as the manatee's nearest living relative is the elephant, the creature was thought to be the model for the legend of the mermaid Dwelling in lagoons and in brackish water, manatees may eat as much as 100 lbs. of aquatic vegetables per day. Strictly vegetarian, their only enemy is man, who has hunted them for their hide, oil, and meat. Once ranging from South America up to North Carolina, their numbers have dwindled dramatically. In other localities, their tough hides were used in machine belting and in high pressure hoses. Although community education may be the key to stopping hunting, propeller blades of motor boats continue to slaughter manatees accidentally, and the careless use of herbicides is also a threat.

The United States Virgin Islands A to Z

Accommodation — Every type of hotel in most price ranges are available.

Area Code — To dial the US Virgin Islands from outside the islands dial 1-340 and the number. Omit the area code when dialing within the USVI. (The area code for the BVI is 284).

Art and artists — There are a number of art galleries in the main towns on the islands.

Banking — Banks are generally open Mon. to Fri. from 9 to 2:30 PM; also Fri. from 3 to 5:30 PM. ATMs are found at most banks.

Business Hours — Generally from 9–5. Mon. to Fri. Many close on Sun. as do restaurants.

Camping — There is a campground on St. John and tent camping is on St. Croix and Water Island.

Clothes — Informal (except at some resorts)

Car rental — Cars may be rented from companies on the main islands. Expect to spend $40–70 pd with unlimited mileage.

Credit Cards — Generally accepted.

Currency —The US Dollar.

Electricity — 110 Volts AC.

Internet — Access is limited but available at some hotels and internet cafes. But do you really want to be indoors a moment more than is necessary?

Language — English is the native tongue. The local brogue is a variant.

Laundry — Most hotels will do laundry for a fee.

Liquor Laws — Alcohol is available from any store. Rum is cheapest on St. Croix.

Mail — Same level of service as in the mainland US.

Maps — Free maps are probably sufficient for most visitors. A variety of good maps are available at gift shops.

Marriage — The USVI is an excellent place to get married, and many hotels offer packages.

Newspapers — Local newspapers are weekly tabloids but informative. Newspapers from the States are available.

Radio/TV — Many tourist hotels have satellite TV or cable. There are some AM and FM radio stations.

Ruins — The best ruins are found at Annaberg on St. John and along St. Croix's Historical Trail.

Supplies — Foodstuffs are cheapest at supermarkets on St. Thomas and St. Croix. St. John is more expensive. Prices are higher than on the mainland US.

Taxes — Government tax of 8% is added to accommodation. There is no sales tax.

Taxis — Rates are set by the government.

Telephones — Service is good. Pay phones charge 35 cents (per five min.) to call anywhere in the islands .

Theft — Take the same precautions you would in any urban area.

Time — The Virgin Islands operates on Atlantic Standard Time (four hours behind GMT, Greenwich mean time).

Tipping — Tip as you would in the rest of the US.

Visas — Same as for the rest of the US.

Water — Tap water is drinkable everywhere.

THE UNITED STATES VIRGIN ISLANDS

Introduction

Superb beaches, magnificent panoramas, and a near ideal climate are but a small part of what the US Virgins have to offer. World class resorts, hospitable bed and breakfasts, superb snorkeling, kayaking, golf, and historic sites help round out the picture.

These islands (pop. 108,612) have a largely Black population, yet their society is culturally and ethnically a composite of many influences, including Dominicans, Puerto Ricans, downislanders, and refugees from the continental winter.

Set in the Caribbean's NE corner, right at the end of the Greater Antilles, the USVI comprise some 50 islands and cays. The three main islands — St. Thomas, St. John, and St. Croix — are easily accessible from neighboring Puerto Rico.

Like three sisters, each island has its distinct personality and resembles the others only in having beautiful white beaches and offlying coral reefs.

Land And Climate

Located 1,500 mi. SE of New York and 1,000 mi. S of Miami, the United States Virgin Islands are bounded on the N by the Atlantic Ocean and on the S by the Caribbean. Covering 132 sq mi. of land area and volcanic in origin, these islands' well-exposed and only slightly deformed rocks give a nearly complete record of evolution dating back more than 100 million years. Primary growth having vanished long ago, vegetation is largely secondary; there are few streams and water is frequently in short supply. Except on St. John, soils are thin and number among the stoniest in the world. No minerals of any value are found here save salt and blue green stone or blue bitch, an excellent building material.

A ridge of high hills runs almost the entire length of St. Thomas. Although its rocks are chiefly sedimentary, limestone reaching up to the peak of Crown Mountain (1,550 ft.) tells a story of cyclical earthquakes, submergence, and upheavals.

St. John, terminating in a narrow curving neck enclosing a series of bays, rises abruptly

The Virgin Islands

US Virgin Islands Climate		
Month	Avg. temp (F)	Rainfall days
January	77	4.3
February	77	1.9
March	78	2.0
April	79	7.5
May	80	1.3
June	82	2.9
July	84	5.6
August	84	4.1
September	83	6.6
October	83	5.6
November	80	5.4
December	78	3.8

from the sea, with the 1,277-ft. Bordeaux Mountain being the highest point. Coral Bay, on the S side of St. John, is the best harbor in the islands.

St Croix, a fraternal rather than identical triplet, lies 32 mi. to the S separated by 1,000–2,400-fathom trenches. Its topography is quite different from the other islands. In contrast to the steep drops of St. Thomas and St. John, St. Croix has rolling, pastoral hills. The N upland contains 1,165-ft. Mt. Eagle, the S side is a broad coastal plain, while the E end is a rough scrubland.

CLIMATE: Rarely does it rain on these islands. (Average rainfall is only 40–50 in. per year). When rain does come, it usually lasts only a few minutes. May, Sept., and

URL There are a number of sites which help you find local weather and follow storms in the Caribbean:
Caribbean Weather Man
http://www.caribwx.com/clycone.html
Weather Underground
http://www.weatherunderground.com/tropical
The Weather Channel
http://www.weather.com/weather_center/trop_season

Oct. are the wettest months. During the day, temperatures range in the 80s, dropping to the 70s in the evening.

HURRICANES: Cast in a starring role as the bane of the tropics, hurricanes represent the one outstanding negative in an otherwise impeccably hospitable climate. The Caribbean as a whole ranks third worldwide in the number of hurricanes per year. These low-pressure zones are serious business and should not be taken lightly. Where the majority of structures are held together only by nails and rope, a hurricane is no joke, and property damage from them may run into the hundreds of millions of US dollars.

A hurricane begins as a relatively small tropical storm, known as a cyclone, when its winds reach a velocity of 39 mph. At 74 mph it is upgraded to hurricane status. winds may rage as fast as 200 mph and it may range in size from 60–1,000 mi. in diameter. A small hurricane releases energy equivalent to the explosions of six atomic bombs per second.

A hurricane may be compared to an enormous hovering engine that uses the moist air and water of the tropics as fuel, carried hither and thither by prevailing air currents-generally eastern trade winds which intensify as they move across warm ocean waters.

When cooler, drier air infiltrates as it heads N, the hurricane begins to die, cut off from the life-sustaining ocean currents that have nourished it from infancy. Routes and patterns are unpredictable. As for their frequency:

*"June—too soon; July—stand by;
August—it must; September—remember;
October—all over"*

So goes the old rhyme. Unfortunately, hurricanes are not confined to July and August. Hurricanes forming in Aug. and Sept. typically last for two weeks while those that form in June, July, Oct., and Nov. (many of which

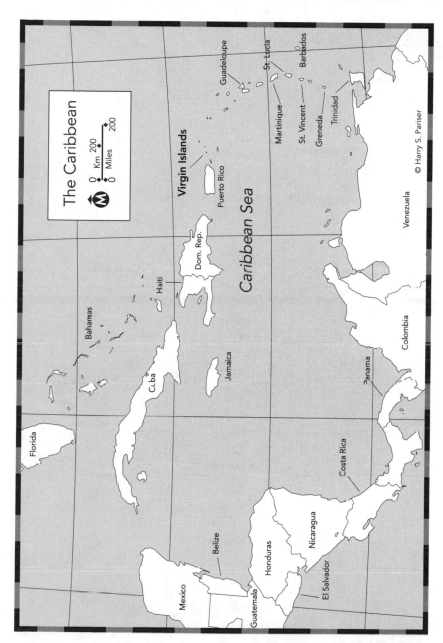

The Caribbean

0 Km 200
0 Miles 200

Guadeloupe
St. Lucia
Barbados
Martinique
St. Vincent
Grenada
Trinidad

Virgin Islands

Puerto Rico

Caribbean Sea

Dom. Rep.

Haiti

Bahamas

Cuba

Jamaica

Florida

Panama

Costa Rica

Venezuela

Colombia

© Harry S. Pariser

Belize

Mexico

Guatemala

Honduras

Nicaragua

El Salvador

INTRODUCTION

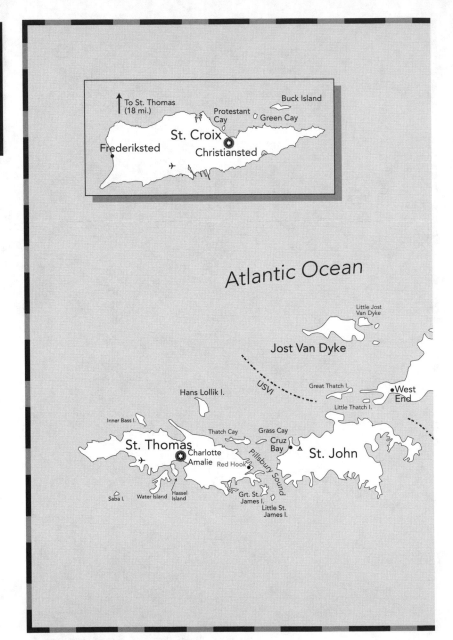

To St. Thomas
(18 mi.)

Buck Island

Protestant
Cay

Green Cay

St. Croix

Frederiksted

Christiansted

Atlantic Ocean

Little Jost
Van Dyke

Jost Van Dyke

Hans Lollik I.

USVI

Great Thatch I.

West
End

Little Thatch I.

Inner Bass I.

Thatch Cay

Grass Cay

St. Thomas

Charlotte
Amalie

Red Hook

Cruz
Bay

Pillsbury Sound

St. John

Saba I.

Water Island

Hassel
Island

Grt. St.
James I.

Little St.
James I.

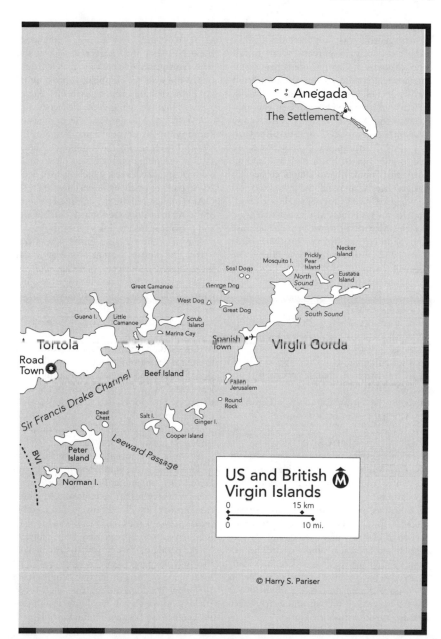

Anegada

The Settlement

Necker Island

Prickly Pear Island

Mosquito I.

Seal Dogs

North Sound

Eustatia Island

Great Camanoe

George Dog

West Dog

Great Dog

South Sound

Guana I.

Little Camanoe

Scrub Island

Marina Cay

Spanish Town

Virgin Gorda

Tortola

Road Town

Beef Island

Sir Francis Drake Channel

Fallen Jerusalem

Round Rock

Dead Chest

Salt I.

Ginger I.

Cooper Island

Leeward Passage

BVI

Peter Island

Norman I.

US and British Virgin Islands

0   15 km

0   10 mi.

© Harry S. Pariser

originate in the Caribbean and the Gulf of Mexico) generally last only seven days.

Approximately 70 percent of all hurricanes (known as Cabo Verde types) originate as embryonic storms coming from the W coast of Africa. Fortunately, though, they are comparatively scarce in the area around the Virgin Islands. Hurricane "season" commences on **Supplication Day** (July 25th) when church services are held to pray against hurricanes) and end on **Hurricane Thanksgiving Day** (October 25) when services again thank the meteorological Commander in Chief for not sending a storm.

Indeed, the islanders must have had a good relationship with the powers that be because a major hurricane did not hit the islands from 1932 until Sept. 1989's Hurricane Hugo. Hurricane Marilyn also struck in 1995; it caused extensive damage, but most of the damage has been taken care of. The most recent hurricane to strike the Virgin Islands was Lenny in July 1999; it caused little damage.

Taino petroglyph

Plant Life

These islands display an amazing variety of plant life, from lichen and mosses to fruit trees and orchids. Considering its tiny area, St. John has an extraordinary diversity of tropical foliage. There are 260 different species of plants, vines, shrubs, and trees. A century old botanical survey of St. Thomas found 1,220 plants in its 32 sq mi. Saint Croix also has a wide diversity of plants: in addition to numerous trees and shrubs, it has 42 varieties of orchids and nearly twice as many types of morning glories.

Trees

Many trees lend a riot of color to the landscape. Native to the VI, the red, yellow, and pink **frangipani** blooms both in gardens and in the wild. Its elliptical, short-pointed leaves have hairy underparts and large, waxy yellow, orange or white flowers.

A native of Madagascar, the orange-red **flamboyant** (Royal poinciana, flame of the forest) flowers during the summer and bears a 20-in. seedpod; its leaf consists of ten or 20 pairs of smaller leaves, which in turn have 20–30 pairs of small, light green leaflets.

Also orange-red are the cuplike blossoms of the **African tulip tree** which catch water and provide watering holes for birds.

A petite yellow bloom with a sweet fragrance, the **ginger thomas** or **yellow elder** is the territorial flower.

The **pisonia** has grey, lumpy trees and roots which resemble poured concrete. Reaching up to three ft. in diameter, they are known locally as "blolly" or "loblolly."

AROMATIC TREES: The **bay rum tree** (*Pimenta recemosa*) produces an oil traditionally obtained through distillation of its leaves and twigs. It is a members of the myrtle family and not related to the bay leaf. It has has small, white flowers and gives off a heady, pungent odor when its dark green leaves are crushed or broken.

There is little incentive to use the poor quality wood of the **wild cinnamon** or canella and their spreading branches with shiny green leathery leaves provide shade. These trees produce small red flowers and inedible red or purple berries. Their smooth gray bark is aromatic and has been used medicinally.

The **gumbo-limbo** photosynthesizes through its perpetually peeling bark. Its local name of "turpentine tree" comes from the pungent odor exuding from their thick, sticky gum which will repel insects and prevent infection. Because its thick, shiny, red-

Two of the best places to see a variety of trees and plants are on the **Reef Bay Trail** in St. John and at the **St. George Botanical Gardens** on St. Croix.

dish-brown bark peels off in scales, it is also known as the "tourist tree."

FRUIT TREES: Famous for its yellow fleshy fruit which has a large pit at its center, the **mango** (*Mangifera indica*) tree has dark green leathery leaves which are pointed at both ends. Introduced from the Asian tropics some four centuries ago, mangos are prized by islanders. If you have never tried one and have the chance to bite in, it is a must.

With compound leaves that have four nearly stalkless leaflets, the **genip** bears small green fruits in grape-like clusters.

A short (generally under 20 ft.) tropical American native, the **sugar apple** has three- to five-in. leaves which are double rowed and alternating. Either round or heart shaped, its distinctive fruit may be eaten raw or used to make a drink or sherbet.

genip

With sharp leaves pointed at both ends, the **soursop** has one of the most distinctive fruits around. While unripe soursop may be cooked as a vegetable, the ripe fruit, which may weigh up to five lbs., can be used in sherbet, drinks, and in preserves.

A S Pacific native, the **breadfruit** has deeply lobed leaves which may reach three ft. It is best known for its fruit; a single tree may bear up to 800 per year, and these can be baked, boiled, roasted, fried, consumed raw, or ground into a high-carbohydrate flour.

PALMS: Known locally as the **teyer** or silver palm, the wild palm is a native which grows in abundance. Its leaves are pleated, almost circular fans which lack a midrib. When exposed in the wind, the soft, silver underside of its leaves gives it one of its names. It has been traditionally used to make brooms. The palms do not regenerate when cut.

Generally found along the coast and widespread in the world's tropics, the **coconut palm,** one of the world's most useful trees, is generally found along the coast and is widespread in the world's tropics.

UNIQUELY NAMED: Colorfully called a "pig turd" in the VI owing to its distinctively shaped pods, the **moca blanca** has light grey bark and smells somewhat like cabbage when cut.

The native **West Indies locust** produces an edible, bad smelling pod whose pulp can be used to make a drink.

Large, symmetrical, strong, and stout, the name of the **sandbox tree** comes from its fruit; the ribbed peel. When seeded and flattened, it was used to sprinkle sand used for blotting ink on parchment. Monkey pistol, its other name, comes from the noise its seedpods make when they split open. Its acrid, milky sap is a skin irritant.

Having yellow green leaves with orange or pink colored stems and small, fragrant white flowers, the **fiddlewood** bears clusters of reddish brown or blackish berries.

One of the most notable tropical trees, the **strangler fig** begins life as an epiphyte, sending down woody, clasping roots which wind themselves around the trunk as they extend into the earth. As the roots grow in size, they meld into a trunk which surrounds the tree. These "strangler figs" most likely kill the tree—not through strangulation but by robbing it of canopy space. They can grow in the ruins of buildings as well.

INTRODUCTION

Mangroves are a vital link in the ecosystem.

Strangler figs are often the only trees left in an otherwise cleared tract of forest.

A native of India, the **painkiller** or **morinda** has five- to 11-in. dark green leaves and small white tubular flowers. Its soft and juicy greenish fruit has a cheese like odor.

With alternating leaves colored blue-green or green, the **seagrape** grows on the shore where it provides shade as well as helps retain sand on the beaches. Resembling grapes in appearance, its fruits may be eaten raw or made into jelly or even wine. Early in the colonial era, the leaves were used as a substitute for paper.

The **fish poison tree** produces pink flowers in March and April. Its scalloped pods and bark contain a poison used by fishermen to stun fish.

OTHER TREES: The **mahogany** is famous for its use in furniture.

In the Caribbean, the **shortleaf fig** is commonly used for fence posts, wood, and fuel. With alternating leaves which are sharply pointed at their ends, it exudes a white latex when parts are cut or broken.

Once believed by slaves to walk at night, the **ceiba** or silk-cotton tree has a distinctively massive grey or grey-green trunk. Known as kapok (which is the name given the tree in Indonesia), the seed pod is filled with many wooly-haired seeds; it was once a major provider of stuffing for pillows, life preservers and the like.

A native of Africa, the **tamarind** (*Tamarindus indica*) has spread over Asia and the Caribbean. It provides shade, and its pods contain a tart, sticky material in which the seeds develop. This is used to make jams and jellies. It is also an ingredient in Worcestershire sauce. Still others include the umbrella

tamarind

tree, false almond, West Indian ebony, West Indian almond, horseradish tree, boxweed, beach maho, black wattle, sweet lime, tan tan, and guava.

MANGROVES: Mangrove forests are found along the coasts. These water-rooted trees serve as a marine habitat, which shelters sponges, corals, oysters, and other members of the marine community around its roots. These organisms, in turn, attract a variety of other sealife. Some species live out their lives in the shelter of the mangroves, and many fish use these roots as a shelter or feeding ground; lobsters use the mangrove environs as a nursery for their young.

Above the water level, the mangroves shelter seabirds and are important nesting sites. Their organic detritus, exported to the reef by the tides, is consumed by its inhabitants, providing the base of an extensive food web. Mangroves also dampen high waves and winds generated by tropical storms.

In the Virgin Islands, mangroves function as hurricane shelters for boats. By trapping silt in their roots and catching leaves and other debris which decompose to form soil, the red mangroves act as land builders.

Eventually, the **red mangroves** kill themselves off when they have built up enough soil, and the black and white mangroves take over. Meanwhile, the red mangroves have sent out progeny in the form of floating seedlings — bottom-heavy youngsters that grow on the tree until they reach six inches to a foot in length. If they drop in shallow water, the seeds touch bottom and implant themselves. In deeper water they stay afloat until, crossing a shoal, they lodge.

Named after their light-colored bark, the **white mangroves** are highly salt tolerant. If growing in a swampy area, they put out pneumatophores (root system extensions). These grow vertically to a height that allows them to stay above the water during flooding or tides and carry on gaseous exchange. Producing a useful wood, the **black mangrove** also creates pneumatophores.

Smaller than the others, the **buttonwood** is not a true mangrove but is found on the coasts where no other varieties are found.

SEAGRASSES: Seagrasses (plants returned to live in the sea) are found in relatively shallow water in sandy and muddy bays and flats; they have roots and small flowers.

Acting as both home and nursery, they host many fish and crustaceans and shellfish which provide food for conch and sea turtles.

Seagrasses are endangered by toxins and boats which rip up seagrass beds with their anchors. They need clear water and sunlight in order to survive.

Seagrasses help to stabilize the sea floor, maintain water clarity by trapping fine sediments from upland soil erosion and stress caused by storm waves and stave off beach erosion.

One species, dubbed **"turtle grass"** (*Thalassia testudinum*), provides food for turtles. Its ribbon-like leaves may reach more than a foot in length. The most common of the grasses, it has deeper root structures.

"Manatee grass" (*Syringodium filoforme*) may be recognized by its leaves which are round in cross section.

Small turtle-grass (*Halophila bailonis*) is characterized by small, rounded leaves which are generally paired. It is often found in deeper waters and appears delicate.

Shoal grass (*Halodule wrightii*) colonizes disturbed areas and can survive in water too shallow for the others.

Other Plants

Plants here have colorful histories, and there may be more to them than first appears. Many plants have had practical uses: while switches for beating slaves were made from the tamarind tree, calabash gourds were perfectly suited for bailing devices, eating utensils, and dishes. Natural herbs and herbal remedies were made from the sandbox, mahoe, and other trees, shrubs, and plants.

Guinea grass, which covers many island hillsides and provides feed for livestock, was originally introduced by mistake. Brought over as birdseed for the governor's pet birds, who rejected it, the seeds were tossed out, and the grass began to proliferate on its own.

INTRODUCTION

Heliconias

Famous worldwide as an ornamental, the heliconia lends an infusion of bizarre color and shape to the island's landscape. The name of these medium-to-large erect herbs comes from Helicon, a mountain in southern Greece believed to have been the home of the muses. There are thought to be around 200–250 species. Relatives within this category include the banana, the birds-of-paradise, the gingers, and the prayer plants.

The family name *Zingiberales* comes from the Sanskrit word *sringavera* which means "horn shaped" in reference to the rhizomes.

Each erect shoot has a stem and leaves which are frequently (although not always) topped by an inflorescence with yellow or red bracts. Each inflorescence may produce up to 50 hermaphroditic flowers. Leaves are composed of stalk and blade and resemble banana leaves. Flowers produce a blue-colored fruit which has three seeds.

Lured by the bright colored flowers and bracts, hummingbirds, arrive to pollinate the blooms. The birds spread pollen as they fly from flower to flower in search of nectar. ■

CACTI: Any visitor to these relatively dry islands will be sure to note the proliferation of cacti and other scrub vegetation. Cacti were classified into a single genera comprising 24 species by Linnaeus in 1737. The name is Greek for "the bristly plant." The oldest fossilized cacti remains are found in Colorado and Utah and date from the Eocene Era some 50 million years ago. Cacti have evolved to suit a hot, dry climate. Their need to reduce surface area—in order to deter evaporation and protect it from the sun's rays—have resulted in flattened, columnular, grooved, bumpy, globe, and barrel shaped plants.

Evolution has transformed their leaves into spines and their branches into areoles—localized regions which carry spines and/or bristles. The stems are responsible for photosynthesis. Shade and light diffusion is provided by bumps, warts, ribs, spines, and hairlike structures. These structures also serve to hinder evaporation and hold dew.

Its thick, leathery flesh stores water effectively and is resistant to withering and can endure up to a 60% water loss without damage. Stomata (apertures) close during the day but reopen at night in order to stave off water loss. Blossoms generally last for only one day, and nearly all depend upon animals for pollination.

VARIETIES: Named after its distinctive shape, the **pipe organ cactus** is generally found in the islands' driest areas. The barrel-shaped **Turk's cap** is capped with red flowers. Its red cap resembles a Turkish fez. The fruit is edible and popular with birds and anoles alike.

With pods resembling a beaver's tail, the **prickly pear** is a small, rapidly-spreading cactus which has innumerable spines and yellow flowers. It may grow up to 15 ft. high. Its edible fruit are reddish purple.

Named for its distinctive shape, the **pipe organ** ("dildo") **cactus** is generally found in the islands' driest areas. This cactus has tall hollow stems which are used for food storage by birds.

The **prickly pear** is a small, rapidly spreading cactus which has innumerable spines and yellow flowers.

CACTI-RELATED PLANTS: The most noticeable of these is the large **century plant** (*Agave Americana*). It has a rosette of thick spiked leaves at its base which, after around a decade, sends up a 10 to 20 ft. stalk and blooms, usually around April or May. Its canary-yellow blooming bulbils are a sight to behold; the plant dies after blooming.

A native of Africa and the Mediterranean, the **aloe** *(Aloe vera)* is a single-stalked succulent renowned for its healing properties. It derives its name from *alloeh*, an Arabic word denoting a bitter, shining substance. It was cultivated in ancient Egypt and, according to a historical tract popularly known as *The Bible* (John:19:39), it was used for embalming.

SHRUBS: The **guana tail** and the hook-sword-shaped **pinguin** (*Bromelia penguin*) are shrubs frequently used as hedges since at least the 18th C.

Century Plant

The pinguin, a type of bromeliad with sharp end spines on its leaves is called the "wild pineapple" locally. The islands indigenous inhabitants are believed to have introduced it. They valued its edible but astringent yellow fruit, which is high in vitamins, and packed specimens in their canoes. Tree frogs use their leaf bases as condos and appreciate their built-in swimming pools.

Turk's Cap

The **four o'clock** is a small shrub with trumpet-shaped purple blossoms which open at four PM each day.

FLOWERS: Brought to the West Indies in the 1700s by the French navigator Bougainville, the **bougainvillea** can be seen cascading over garden walls.

A native of Hawaii, the flowering **hibiscus** comes with apricot, red, pink, purple, or white blossoms.

A vine with yellow flowers which trails along walls and fences, the **cup of gold** is another frequently seen flower.

The **oleander** has a delicate beauty but is deadly if eaten. A variety of **orchids** also thrive here as do **poinsettias**.

FORBIDDEN FRUIT: The **machineel**, said to be the original apple in the Garden of Eden, secretes an acid which may be deadly. If you see some of these trees, stay well away!

Biting into this innocuous-looking yet highly poisonous fruit will cause your mouth to burn and your tongue to swell up. In fact, all parts of this tree are potentially deadly. Cattle, standing under the tree after a torrential tropical downpour, have been known to lose their hides as drops fall from the leaves. Other tales tell of locals going blind after a leaf touched an eye. Slaves wishing to do away with a particularly despicable master would insert minute quantities of juice into an uncooked potato. Cooked, these small doses were undetectable but always fatal if served to the victim over a long period of time.

NAME GAME: Many of the imaginatively named species have colorful stories behind their names: The **"love plant"** was so named because an aspiring suitor would write his lover's name on the leaf; if it remained for a time, it meant that he could count on acceptance of his proposal. And, if the leaf sprouted shoots, then the relationship would flourish.

The **"catch and keep"** sticks to everything it touches, while the **"jump up and kiss me"** is well endowed with small, seductive blossoms.

The trunk of the **"monkey-don't-climb tree"** bristles with thorns, while the **"nothing nut"** is so named because that's exactly what it's good for. The pods of the **"woman's tongue"** tree clatter on and on in the breeze like gossiping housewives.

Other unusually named plants include the "jumbi-bead" vine with its knife-shaped miniature red blossoms, the "stinking toe," "bull hoof," "poor man's orchid," "powder puff," "crown of thorn," "lucky nut," "burning love," and the "lady of the night."

Animal Life

Save for the now-extinct **agouti**, a rodent once considered a delicacy by local Indians, very few land animals existed here before the coming of Europeans. Today, monkeys and wild boars have disappeared, though a few scattered deer still remain.

Introduced in legend rather than fact, werewolves were once hunted by slaves who believed in this European folktale. Perhaps the legend was kept alive in order to cover up for the master when he went on a sexual rampage.

Unique to St. Croix is the husbandry of **Senepol cattle**. More than a half century ago, a Crucian plantation owner named Nelthrop was kicked by a cow. Determined to create a new and improved version, he crossed the African Senegal with the English Red Poll. The result was a new breed that is hairless, shortlegged, requires less water, and is disease resistant.

http://www.senepolcattle.com

The **mongoose** was introduced to kill snakes and rats in 1872. However, mongoose are diurnal, while rats are nocturnal. The two seldom cross paths. It has been eating well: it has just about done in the reptile population as well as many bird species.

First introduced to the Virgin Islands from the eastern US in 1792, **white-tailed deer** have learned to thrive in the VI. Places to see them include Estate Cotton Valley on St. Croix and Estate Nazareth on St. Thomas.

BIRDS: There are over 200 species of birds, including brightly colored wild parakeets, pelicans, and egrets. Since most of the swamps have been drained, the sea bird population has dwindled.

The **brown pelican** ("pilikin bird") is often seen flying in formation. It feeds by plunging its bill into the water and taking in gallons of water into its distended pouch. Great blue herons, reddish egrets, and great egrets are among the other birds.

Prominent among the seabirds, the **brown booby** is so named because, when the birds first encountered seamen, they confidently landed on boats and allowed themselves to be caught; the dummies also allowed their nests to be plundered. Common to the S Atlantic, these brown birds have white bellies. Females may be stouter and with a darker yellow beak.

Brown Pelican (Pelecanus occidentalis)

Faster, Springier Lamb

Lamb has long been a favored dish among Christian carnivores celebrating Easter. However, sheep have long been singularly uncooperative: their breeding cycle does not allow them to reach the preferred slaughter-perfect weight of 110 lbs. by Easter.

Crucian sheep, however, have no such limitation. Non-seasonal and heat-resistant, they are ideal for breeders. The breed is also more resistant to nematode parasites. As they also don't grow wool, they need no shearing, an advantage to the southern producer who is far from the wool market. These woolless sheep are also not as likely to produce meat tasting of lanolin. Consequently, the USDA (whose research produced the findings) is advising southern farmers to try to interbreed the Crucian sheep with their stock. ∎

The **red-footed booby** comes in both white and brown forms. Both interbreed. Their favorite foods are squid and flying fish.

The **brown and white oystercatcher** resides year-round. The locals are impressed by their ability to collect whelk (shellfish)

The diminutive **Audubon's shearwater** flies in flocks just above the surface of the water. Should you hear an eerie howl at night, it may be this bird.

The **red-billed tropicbird** is most often sighted while in flight and may be recognized by its long steamer tail, bright red beak and black markings on a white plumage. Its fave food is squid, and you may see it plunging for these at dusk.

Breeding in winter and spring, the **white-tailed tropicbird** is a related species.

Feeding on small herring and jacks, the brown **noddy tern** arrives in the Virgin Islands in May to nest and remains until Nov. or so.

The **bridle tern** nests in the VI from late April to the end of Sept.

Similar to bridle terns, **sooty terns** may be distinguished by their white stripe which stops over the eye. If they have the misfortune to land in water, their wings may become waterlogged, and they may have difficulty in taking off again.

Roseate terns often choose different islands for their nesting needs (in late May). Do not disturb these birds because they may abandon their nests!

Residing year-round, the **royal tern** is the largest species. They fly in flocks, feeding on herring and anchovies.

The **laughing gull** is a common sight during the summer. These scavengers dine on live fish, crabs, carrion, insects and even the eggs of other birds.

Frigatebirds ("Man-O-War bird," "Weather Bird") reside here year-round, They nest in colonies, and you may see their twig nests in cactus or low trees. The male's most impressive characteristic is his red throat pouch which he will inflate to mark his territory during the breeding months. Watch as frigates snatch food from the surface of the water.

If you're truly lucky, you'll see a **masked booby**. They only frequent Cockroach I. (their breeding grounds), and the area N of St. Thomas. You may sex this white bird with black markings by listening carefully: the females honk but the males whistle.

The **yellow breast** (*coreba flaveola*) was named the "official bird" by the Virgin Islands Legislature in 1970. Also known as the "sugar bird or "bananaquit," it sports a brilliant yellow plumage.

Land birds include hawks, doves, sparrows, thrushes, West Indian crows, wild pigeons, canaries, and several varieties of hummingbirds. The yellow breast is the territorial bird.

REPTILES: The **red-footed tortoise** resembles that box turtle you may have had as a pet as a child.

It is likely that the Indians introduced them as a food source. They dine on fruit, flowers, leaves, and animal matter and may grow as large as 18 in. They are known for their ability to survive without food and water for long periods.

Lizards include several varieties of ground and tree lizards. The anoles are a 300-strong genus of the family *Iguanadae*.

The **crested anole** found on St. Thomas and St. John where it is the most common lizard. Watch for it foraging for insects on the lower trunks of trees.

Smaller than the crested anole, the **barred anole** has three dark patches on its back. It resides on St. Thomas and St. John.

The **grass anole** is called the "*grass lizard*" as it is frequently observed hanging out on Guinea Grass.

The **St. Croix anole** lives only on St. Croix. Whereas the crested anole may jump onto your fingers and feed, the St. Croix anole holds itself aloof.

GECKOS: The family *Geckonidae* is distributed worldwide in areas ranging from rainforest to temperate desert. They have a number of unique characteristics. Most lack eyelids, substituting instead a clear scale which covers the eye. They can "speak." The only vocal lizard, they can bark or squeak. Many have toe pads which enable them to traverse windows and ceilings with aplomb. All feed on insects and various other arthropods.

Watch for fishing bats at work at dusk near the water. They use their sonar to find ripples created by small fish. Their long legs have sharp claws which help them catch fish. They roost in dark rocky crevices near the sea. If you come near a colony, you'll recognize it by the smell!

the vanishing iguana

The tiny **cotton ginner gecko** is found only on St. Croix and its small cays.

The **African house gecko** is a W African native. Known as "woodslave," it is found all over the Caribbean. It is identifiable by its "gek-gek-gek" sound which marks its territory. It is often found in homes where it hides behind pictures, curtains, or furniture and hunts for insects at night.

The **dwarf gecko** can be identified by a dark patch on its shoulders which have two white spots. It forages under fallen leaves.

The **St. Croix ground lizard** lives only on Green and Protestant Cays off the N coast of St. Croix.

red-footed tortoise

The colorful herbivorous **iguana**, whose tail has long been considered a culinary delicacy, is most common on St. Thomas. Male iguanas are larger than females and have more prominent spines, dewlap, and jaw shield.

SNAKES: Smaller than most boas, the endangered **St. Thomas tree boa** loves to hide in piles of rocks or termite nests.

Odder still are the blind snake and the worm lizard. Tan to pink, the **blind snake** is generally smaller than a soda straw and has the feel of a wax candle. It dines on ants and termites which it finds while burrowing. Its sex habits are not known. It has the delightful habit of forcing a small spine, which is at the tip of its tail, into human flesh. This practice has led locals to believe that it stings.

The legless **St. Thomas worm lizard** resembles an earthworm in size and color. It is most often seen in forested areas beneath leaf litter.

CRUSTACEANS, AND INSECTS: Although **centipedes** and **scorpions** live on these islands, they maintain passive, nonaggressive attitudes towards humans unless they are disturbed.

The same goes for the **wasps**, whose nests are a common feature on St. Croix.

The long nosed **termite** builds the gigantic nests which you'll see on St. Croix and elsewhere. They coexist with a healthy tree.

The harmless **hairy tarantula** hides underground in his nest.

A Natural History Guide to Cays of the U. S. Virgin Islands, by Arthur E. Dammann and David W. Nellis, provides a great introduction to the flora and fauna of the region. The superb photography is an added bonus.

INTRODUCTION

ᴪ Humpback Whales ᴪ

Migrating every fall from the polar waters through the passage between Puerto Rico and the Virgin Islands where they breed, these marine mammals may be sighted offshore from Dec. to May. One common place to see humpbacks is between outer Brass and Congo Cays. They travel in pods of three to 15. Humpbacks range in length from 30 to 40 ft. (12–15 m).

Acrobatically inclined, humpbacks leap belly-up from the water, turn a somersault, and arch backwards—plunging headfirst back into the watery depths with a loud snapping noise. When making deep dives, these whales hump their backs forward and bring their tail out of the water.

In addition to diving, male whales love vocalizing. Their moans, cries, groans, and snores are expressed in songs lasting up to 35 minutes. These go on for hours and may be heard by their comrades at distances of 20 miles! The probable reason for the tunes is to attract mates, but little is known about the songs. Up until the time of the first recording in 1952, stories of fishermen hearing eerie songs through their boat hulls were widely disbelieved.

Humpbacks feed on small fish, plankton, and shrimp-like crustaceans—all of which they strain out of water with their baleen. They may devour as much as a ton per day during the feeding season (in the far N) in order to build up blubber for the long trip S to the Caribbean. Distinguished by their very long pectoral fins, scalloped on their forward edges, as well as by large knobs on their jaws and head, humpbacks are black-bodied with a white coloration on their underbelly. Humpbacks have managed to keep their boudoir practices out of the limelight, and no one has ever observed them mating.

Light grey calves are virtually blubberless when expelled from the womb, but still weigh a ton. Mothers move in close to land for nursing. (Never disturb a mother and calf!) A calf feeds off of one or two teats, ordinarily lodged in slits, and down as much as 190 liters (50 gal.) of milk daily. This milk has the consistency of yogurt and has a 40–50% fat content, in contrast to the 2% fat in human milk.

Calves become adults at between four and eight years of age. No one knows how long humpbacks live, and it will probably be the middle of the next century (when the first litter of monitored cows, born in 1975, dies out) by the time that this may be determined. Overhunting during the early to mid-19th C has endangered these marine mammals; they have been internationally protected since the mid-1960s. If you see them, please do not approach too closely. They are not pets!

Sealife

Divers and snorkelers will find a dazzling array of coral, fish, and sponges in all colors of the rainbow.

A kaleidoscope of fish include the doctorfish, grouper, old wife, one-eye, silver angelfish, sergeant fish, marine jewel, and trunkfish.

SEA TURTLES: Sea turtles are some of the most interesting creatures found here. Medium-sized with a length of about three ft. and weighing some 400 lbs., the large-finned, herbivorous **green turtle** lays eggs every two to three years, storming the beaches in massive groups termed barricades. It is readily identifiable by its short rounded head.

One of the smallest sea turtles, at 35 in. or less, the **hawksbill** has a spindle-shaped shell and weighs around 220 lbs. Because of its tortoise shell—a brown translucent layer of corneous gelatin that peels off the shell when processed—it has been pursued and slaughtered throughout the world. It dines largely on sponges and seaweed. Worldwide demand for its shell, which sells for a fortune in Japan, appears to have condemned it to extinction.

With its large head, twice the size of the green turtle's and narrow and bird-jawed, the short-finned **loggerhead** rarely grows longer than four feet. It dines on sea urchins, jellyfish, starfish, and crabs. The loggerhead is threatened with extinction by coastal development, egg gathering, and from hunting by raccoons.

Black with very narrow fins, the **leatherback's** name comes from the leathery hide which covers its back in lieu of a shell. It grows to six ft. in length and weighs as much as 1,500 lbs. The leatherback's chief predator has always been the poacher.

ECHINODERMATA: Combining the Greek words *echinos* (hedgehog) and *derma* (skin), this large division of the animal kingdom includes sea urchins, sand dollars, sea cucumbers, and starfish. All share the ability to propel themselves with the help of tube "feet" or spines.

Known by the scientific name *Astrospecten*, **starfish** are five-footed carnivores which use their modified "tube-feet" to burrow into the sand.

One of the many termite nests found in trees throughout the islands

Sea Turtle Facts

 Sea turtles return to the beach where they were hatched to nest.

 A turtle's sex is largely determined by the the sand temperature. Eggs raised in warmer waters turn female. Not surprisingly, cooler temperatures bring males.

 Sea turtles may take 20–30 years to grow up. Only one of every thousand eggs will result in a turtle which will reach sexual maturity and reproduce.

hawksbill turtle

Sluggish **sea cucumbers** ingest large quantities of sand, extract the organic matter, and excrete the rest. They come in many shapes and colors; the most colorfully named is undoubtedly the *donkey dong*.

Avoid trampling on that armed knight of the underwater sand dunes, the **sea urchin**. Consisting of a semi-circular calcareous (calcium carbonate-built) shell, the sea urchin is protected by its brown, jointed barbs. It uses its mouth, situated and protected on its underside, to graze by scraping algae from rocks.

Surprisingly, to those uninitiated in its lore, sea urchins are considered a gastronomic delicacy in many countries. The ancient Greeks believed they had aphrodisiacal as well as other properties beneficial to health. They are prized by the French and fetch four times the price of oysters in Paris. The Spanish consume them raw, boiled, in gratinés, or in soups. In Barbados they are called "sea eggs," and the Japanese eat their guts raw as sushi.

Although a disease in recent years has devastated the sea urchin population, they are making a comeback. If a sea urchin spine breaks off inside your finger or toe, don't try to remove it: you can't. You might try the cure people use in Now Guinea. Use a blunt object to mash up the spine inside your skin so that it will be absorbed naturally. They then dip the wound in urine; the ammonia

helps to trigger the process of disintegration. It's best to apply triple-antibiotic salve.

Preventing contact in the first place is best. Sea urchins often hide underneath corals, and wounds often occur when you lose your footing and scrape against one.

OPHIUROIDS: A large group (over 1600 species) of echinoderms that includes the brittle stars (*Ophiurida*) and basket stars (*Euryalida*). Brittle stars usually have five arms and may superficially resemble true starfish (*Asteroidea*). Brittle stars have long, flexible arms; its central, armored, disk-shaped body is clearly demarcated from its arms; they wriggle these arms to move.

Basket stars are similar in structure to brittle stars but generally larger. Their forked and branched arms are even more flexible than those of brittle stars.

SPONGES: Found in the ocean depths, reddish or brown sponges are among the simplest forms of multicellular life and have been around for more than a half billion years. They pump large amounts of water through their internal filters to extract plankton.

CNIDARIANS: The members of this phylum — hydroids, anemones, corals, and jellyfish — are distinguished by their simple structure: a cup-shaped body terminating in

Sea turtles still come ashore on some beaches to lay their eggs.

?!¿ Normally the size of a pinhead, the sea jewel (valonia) is the largest single-cell animal in existence. Saclike and round in appearance, it reflects the colors of whatever's nearby.

a combination mouth-anus which, in turn, is encircled by tentacles. While hydroids and corals (covered later in this section) are colonial, jellyfish and anemones are individual. This phylum's name comes from another identifying characteristic: nematocysts, stinging capsules primarily used for defense and capturing prey.

Growing in skeletal colonies resembling ferns or feathers, **hydroids** ("water form" in Greek) spend their youth as solitary medusas before settling down in old age.

Some will sting, and the most famous hydroid is undoubtedly the floating Portuguese Man-Of-War; its stinging tentacles can be extended or retracted; worldwide, there have been reports of trailing tentacles reaching 50 ft.! It belongs to the family of siphonophores, free-floating hydroid colonies which control their depth by means of a gas-filled float. The true jellyfish are identifiable by their domes which vary in shape. Nematocysts reside in both the feeding tube and in their tentacles.

Also known as sea wasps, **box jellies** may be identified by their cuboidal dome from each corner of which a single tentacle extends. Many of them can sting rather fiercely; keep well away. If you should get stung by any of the above, get out of the water and peel off any tentacles. Avoid rubbing the injured area. Wash the area with alcohol and apply meat tenderizer for five to ten minutes.

Solitary bottom-dwellers, **sea anemones** are polyps which lack a skeleton, and they use their tentacles to stun prey and force them to their mouth; they often protect shrimp and crabs who, immune to their sting, reside right by them. Their tentacles

may retract for protection when disturbed. One type of anemones live in tubes which are buried in the murky muck or sand, and their tentacles come out to play only at during the twilight hours.

JELLYFISH: The jellyfish season runs from Aug. to Oct. Most jellyfish are harmless. If you should get stung, get out of the water and peel off any tentacles. Avoid rubbing the injured area. Wash the wound with alcohol and apply meat tenderizer for five to ten minutes.

CRUSTACEANS: The **ghost crab** (*Ocypode*) abounds on the beaches, tunneling down beneath the sand and emerging to feed at night. Although it can survive for 48 hrs. without contacting water, it must return to the sea to moisten its gill chambers as well as to lay its eggs, which hatch into planktonic larvae.

The **hermit crab** carries a discarded mollusk shell in order to protect its vulnerable abdomen. As it grows, it must find a larger home, and you may see two struggling over the same shell. A common sight almost everywhere, these soft-shell crustaceans adopt empty shells (particularly of whelks) as their home, moving house as they grow.

The **kalaloo crab** is a land crab which lives in holes near red mangroves. Locals love to collect them for use in stew.

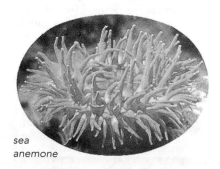

sea anemone

The Conch

The Caribbean's most popularly edible mollusk, the conch (*Strombus gigas*), lives in one of the world's most popular seashells. Although humans have dined on conch for some 3,000 years, they are currently endangered by overfishing and are no longer is found offshore near areas of high human density. Even on the small island of Anegada, a perceptive visitor will note that the newer conch shell piles at the pier are composed of smaller and smaller conch. These are not taken for consumption but to bait lobster traps — another species endangered by overfishing. Closed seasons are in effect in many Caribbean nations, but abuse is still rampant and the mollusk is clearly endangered.

Mother conches lay several spawn masses each season, and each may contain up to half a million eggs. More than 90% of these are eaten during their first three weeks when they swim freely in the ocean.

The Queen Conch's foremost reproductive realm is off the Turks and Caicos whose 99,974-sq.-mi. area (259,000 sq. km) exceeds the conch fishing grounds found in the remainder of the Caribbean. ∎

OTHER UNDERWATER HAZARDS AND CURES: Not a true coral, **fire coral** mimics coral's appearance; it may appear in many forms and has the ability to encrust nearly anything and take its host's form. Generally colored mustard-yellow to brown, it often has white finger-like tips. A cut is quite painful. As with coral wounds, you should wash the affected area with soap and fresh water and apply a triple antibiotic salve.

> *Ah lib on lan' an walk about. But always home in or out. It's the hermit crab (*Coenabita clypeatus*) whom the Virgin Islanders call the soldier crab.*

Found on rocky or coral bottoms, spotted **scorpionfish** are well camouflaged so it's easy to step on them. Although the Caribbean species is non-lethal, their bite can be painful.

The **stingray**, another cleverly camouflaged denizen of the deep, will whip its tail if stepped on — driving the serrated venomous spine into the offender. If this happens, see a doctor.

Bristle worms are fuzzy creatures which have painful-when-touched defense mechanism: their glass-like bristles may break off in the skin and be quite irritating. Apply tape to the skin and attempt to pull the bristles out; reduce the pain with rubbing alcohol.

Tending to bite things thrust at them, **moray eels** can be difficult to dislodge. Once again, preventing bites is best. Always exercise caution before reaching into a crevice!

The Coral Reef Ecosystem

The coral reef is one of the least appreciated of the world's innumerable wonders. This is, in part, because little has been known about it until recent decades. One of the greatest opportunities the tropics offer is to explore this wondrous environment.

A coral reef is the only geological feature fashioned by living creatures, but it is a delicate environment. Many of the world's reefs — which took millions of years to form — have already suffered adverse effects from human activities.

Corals produce the calcium carbonate (limestone) responsible for the build-up of offlying cays and islets as well as most sand on the beaches. Bearing the brunt of waves, they also conserve the shoreline. Although reefs began forming millennia ago, they are in a constant state of flux. They depend upon a delicate ecological balance to survive.

Deforestation, dredging, temperature change, an increase or decrease in salinity, silt, or sewage discharge may kill them. Because temperatures must remain between 68° and 95°F, they are only found in the tropics and, because they require light to grow, only in shallow water. They are also intolerant of freshwater, so reefs cannot survive where rivers empty into the sea.

THE CORAL POLYP: Although corals are actually animals, botanists view them as being mostly plant, and geologists dub them "honorary rocks." Acting more like plants than animals, corals survive through photosynthesis: the algae inside them do the work while the polyps themselves secrete calcium carbonate and stick together for protection from waves and boring sponges. Polyps bear a close structural resemblance to their relative the anemone, which feeds at night by using the ring or rings of tentacles surrounding its mouth to capture prey (such as plankton) with nematocysts (small stinging darts).

Don't Feed the Fish!

Despite the prevalence of the practice, there are a number of good reasons not to feed fish.

! Adding nutrients changes the reef's balance, causing a decline in water quality and clarity.

! Algae eating fish control algae growth, thus preventing them from overgrowing coral.

! Feeding night feeders (such as jacks and snappers) during the day interferes with the relationship between predator and prey and thus the natural balance.

! Human food is human food and may not meet their dietary requirements, thus making them more susceptible to illness.

! Fish fed by divers may become aggressive.

Polyps are able to survive in limited space through their symbiotic relationship with the algae present in their tissues. Coral polyps exhale carbon dioxide and the algae consume it, producing needed oxygen. Only half of the world's coral species have this special relationship and these, known as "hermatypic" corals, are the ones that build the reef. The nutritional benefits gained from this relationship enable them to grow a larger skeleton and to do so more rapidly than would otherwise be possible.

Polyps have the ability to regulate the density of these cells in their tissues and can expel some of them in a spew of mucus should they multiply too quickly. Looking at coral, the brownish algal cells show through transparent tissues. When you see a coral garden through your mask, you are actually viewing a field of captive single-celled algae.

A vital, though invisible, component of the reef ecosystem is bacteria, micro-organisms that decompose and recycle all matter on which everything from worms to coral polyps feed.

Inhabitants of the reef range from crabs to barnacles to sea squirts to multicolored tropical fish. Remarkably, the polyps themselves are consumed by only a small percentage of the reef's dwellers. They often contain high levels of toxic substances and are thought to sting fish and other animals that attempt to eat them. Corals retract their polyps during daylight hours when the fish can see them. Reefs originate as the polyps develop, and the calcium secretions form a base as they grow. One polyp can have a 1,000-year lifespan.

CORAL TYPES: Corals may be divided into three groups. The **hard** or **stony corals** (such as staghorn, brain, star, or rose) secrete a limey skeleton. The **horny corals** (sea plumes, sea whips, sea fans, and gorgonians) have a supporting skeleton-like struc-

Coral Bleaching

Coral bleaching occurs when the anthrozoans, which form the coral, expel their algae, thus declaring a divorce from their symbiotic relationship. These algae, which provide the mascara for the otherwise vanilla coral, provide 90% of the coral's protein.

When coral is heated, their algae lose their abilities to photosynthesize. They take it out on their housemates, the coral, with an assault of free radicals (toxic oxygen-containing molecules). These are created because the algae have no place to put their absorbed light energy.

The coral kick the algae out and then turn white. While they can survive for a while, waiting for more benign conditions to return, they will die if things don't improve.

Ensuing global warming posing problems for the coral reef, along with the divers and snorkelers who come to visit them in their subterranean kingdoms. If ocean temperatures continue to rise, many of our coral reefs will die.

MONITORING OTHER DISEASES: Professor Raymond L. Hayes Jr. has put together a six-page spiral bound set of laminated photo ID cards which illustrate 15 common reef diseases. Each picture is captioned in English and Spanish. The idea is that recreational divers can help document the spread of coral diseases. The set fits right in your BC pocket on your vest. Information about reporting data is included on the back of the card. A set is $10. Send a check to to Dr. Raymond Hayes, Office of Medical Education, Howard University College of Medicine, 520 W St., NW, Washington, DC 20059. Proceeds go to the Association of Marine Laboratories of the Caribbean (AMLC) and to the Global Coral Reef Alliance (GCRA), both of which are nonprofit NGOs.
rhayes@Howard.edu

URL http://coralreef.gov
Action plan on coral reefs
http://www.biogeo.nos.noaa.gov/benthicmap/caribbean Download a map of coral reefs of the Caribbean

ture known as a gorgonin (after the head of Medusa). The shapes of these corals result from the way the polyps and their connecting tissues excrete calcium carbonate; there are over 1,000 different patterns—one specific to each species. Each also has its own method of budding.

Giant **elkhorn corals** may contain over a million polyps and live for several hundred years or longer.

Delicate in appearance only, yellow or purple (depending on diet) **sea fan**, a coral with fanlike branches, is so strong that it will support a man's weight without tearing.

The last category consists of the **soft corals**. While these too are colonies of polyps, their skeletons are composed of soft organic material, and their polyps always have eight tentacles instead of the six (or multiples of six) found in the stony corals. Unlike the hard corals, this group disintegrates after death and does not add to the reef's stony structure. Instead of depositing limestone crystals, they excrete a jelly-like matrix which is imbued with spicules (diminutive spikes) of stony material; the jelly substance gives flexibility. Sea fans and sea whips exhibit similar patterns.

If you have children or are a teacher, the book *The Incredible Coral Reef* is a superb educational tool. It is an "active learning book for kids." The companion volume, **The Incredible Rainforest**, is tremendous as well. http://www.tricklecreekbooks.com

The precious **black coral** is a type of soft coral and is, unfortunately, prized by jewelers. (Don't buy this jewelry!) Its branches may be cleaned and polished to high gloss ebony-black and, in this state, it resembles bushes of fine twigs.

COMPETITION: To the snorkeler, the reef appears to be a peaceful haven. The reality is that, because the reef is a comparatively benign environment, the fiercest competition has developed here. Some have developed sweeper tentacles that have an especially high concentration of stinging cells. Reaching out to a competing coral, they sting and execute it. Other species dispatch digestive filaments which eat their prey. Soft corals appear to leach out toxic chemicals (terpines) that kill nearby organisms. Because predation is such a problem, two-thirds of reef species are toxic. Others hide in stony outcrops or have formed protective relationships with other organisms. The **banded clown fish**, for example, lives among sea anemones whose stingers protect it.

The **cleaner fish** protect themselves from the larger fish by setting up stations at which they pick parasites off their carnivorous customers.

The **sabre-toothed blenny** is a false cleaner fish. It mimics the coloration and shape of the feeder fish, approaches, then takes a chunk out of the larger fish and runs off!

CORAL LOVE AFFAIRS: Coral polyps are not prone to celibacy or sexual prudery. Reproducing sexually and asexually through budding, they join together with thousands and even millions of their neighbors to form a coral. (In a few cases, only one polyp forms a single coral.) During sexual reproduction polyps release millions of their spermatozoa into the water. Many species are dimorphic, with both male and female polyps. Some species have internal, others external, fertilization. As larvae develop, their "mother" expels them and they float off to form a new coral.

EXPLORING REEFS: Coral reefs are extremely fragile environments. Much damage has been done to them worldwide through the carelessness of humans. Despite their size, reefs grow very slowly, and it can take decades or even centuries to repair the damage done in just a few moments.

VIRGIN ISLANDS CORAL REEFS: The islands' coral reefs are a priceless treasure comparable to Yosemite's granite peaks and waterfalls or Yellowstone's geysers. Sadly, development, hurricanes, cruise ships, and abuse by tourists have damaged the reefs in many places.

The most famous excursion is to the reefs lying off of Buck Island, a national monument a few mi. away from St. Croix.

St. John's reefs include Leinster Bay's Waterlemon Cay (an islet in Leinster Bay), and the reef lying off Trunk Bay — which has suffered greatly from abuse and overuse by tourists.

Others include Steven Cay and Fishbowl at Cruz Bay, Johnson Reef on the N coast, and Horseshoe and South Drop on the S coast.

UNDERWATER FLORA: Most of the plants you see are algae, primitive plants that can survive only underwater. Lacking roots, algae draw their minerals and water directly from the sea. Another type of algae, calcareous red algae, are very important for reef formation. They resemble rounded stones and are 95% rock and only 5% living tissue.

History

The original inhabitants of the Virgin Islands were members of the Ineri tribe. Little is known about them and few reminders remain save some archaeological sites. Later joined by the Tainos (Arawaks), both tribes are believed by some historians to have been conquered and enslaved by invading Carib Indians.

DISCOVERY: During Columbus' second voyage, the admiral sighted St. Croix. Christening the island Santa Cruz (Holy Cross), his fleet anchored in Salt River Bay. After putting ashore in a small boat, the island's first tourists made the village rounds. On the way back, Columbus' boat, seeking captives, attacked a canoe full of Caribs, who immediately fled at the strange sight of white men, firing arrows to cover their escape. The Caribs fled inland, leaving behind some Taino slaves whom the sailors "liberated."

Continuing on his voyage, Columbus and his men passed a great number of islands, cluster after cluster, some verdant, others naked and sterile. The islands, seemingly thousands of them, with their combinations of glistening white and azure rocks were, he supposed, filled with jewels and precious stones.

Accordingly, he named the islands Santa Ursula y las Once Mil Virgines (Saint Ursula and the 11,000 Virgins). Prior to sainthood, Ursula was a proper British princess. Engaged to marry a foreign king, she begged a pleasure cruise from her father as a wedding present. This three-year, eleven-ship voyage came to a brutal end when, arriving in Cologne just as it was being sacked

by the Huns, Ursula and her comrades were raped and slain.

COLONIZATION: After Columbus' visit, not much attention was paid to the islands, except in frequent raids by Spaniards, as they carted off natives to slave in Dominican gold mines. These raids led to the complete extermination of the local population.

By 1625 the Dutch and English were settled on St. Croix. Control of St. Croix passed from English to Spanish to French hands.

Finally, a second Danish West India Company, organized by a group of court insiders, was chartered on March 11, 1671, and a decision made to settle on St. Thomas. A little more than eight months passed before the Company had two ships on the way. One was forced to turn back; the other, waylaid by inclement weather, managed to limp into the harbor of what was to become Charlotte Amalie more than six months after the date of departure.

It had been a horrendous voyage for the *Pharoali*: only six of the 239 who had boarded in Copenhagen survived. Other ships followed, some with clergy to provide spiritual guidance. However, of the first priests sent over, most simply couldn't adapt and one had to be sent home for drunkenness. ("Kill devil," as the local unaged rum was called, was potent stuff indeed!)

By 1679 there were 156 whites and 176 slaves on St. Thomas. Tobacco, indigo, cotton, and dyewood were the main exports to Denmark. A series of vile rascals reigned as Danish West India Company presidents. Not having suitable soil for sugarcane cultivation, St. Thomas had become a haven for privateers, pirates, and all manner of shady operators from every part of the Caribbean. There were visits from Bluebeard, Blackbeard (see sidebar), Captain Kidd, and other such "Brethren of the Cloak."

Christopher Columbus

THE SLAVE TRADE: The St. Thomas harbor was renowned for its slave market. Buyers would come from as far away as Curacao and the Carolinas. Saint Croix, purchased from France in 1733, was also a base for the "Triangle Trade." New England ships would buy rum, carry it to Africa, use it to buy slaves, and return to sell the slaves and buy more rum.

Of a total of 123,000 slaves brought over between 1733-82, about 70,000 were re-exported, while the rest were retained. During the severe drought of 1725-26, a number of planters let their slaves starve to death.

St. Croix was purchased from France by the Danish in 1733. The indigenous forests were cut to make room for cane production. The valuable hardwoods were exported to Denmark in cargo schooners which brought back white brick as ballast which was used to build the towns of Christiansted and Frederiksted.

The slave trade was also at a peak during these times, when an imported labor force was essential for the 'development' of the Caribbean and the English colonies as a new

source of income for the European colonial powers. As the American Revolution continued, certain Caribbean islands flourished in the sugar trade and rum production at the cost of the the slaves. It was not unusual for slave populations to be triple the size of those of their European masters during the era that sugar was king.

For a hundred years, the slave trade continued, and the crowns of England, France, Denmark, Holland, and Spain reaped the fortunes of the New World. During this period, St. Croix was one of the richest islands, known for its grand estates, built from cut coral, Danish yellow brick, and indigenous hardwood timber. "Rich as a West Indian," was a phrase of the day, while the wealthy plantation owners attempted to copy the lifestyles of European nobility. Elegant furniture, imported porcelain and fabrics from the Orient, and silver and china from England and France graced their lavish estates and complimented their lifestyles. Conditions for the slaves were quite different, to say the least.

On Sept. 5, 1733, Governor Philip Gardelin announced a new mandate. Among the 18 conditions were: that a leader of a runaway slave revolt should be pinched three times with a red hot iron and then hung; that "slaves who steal to the value of four dollars shall be

Blackbeard

The Caribbean is famous for its hyped-up pirate legacy, and both the US and British Virgins celebrate this with any number of "pirate this" and "pirate that" event. In actuality, pirates like Morgan operated before any of the Virgins were settled, and Spanish galleons did not pass through the Virgin Islands — thus there was no booty to plunder.

However, the Virgin Islands did have its share of brigands. One of these was Edward Teach, a large man whose sartorial signature was a black beard which rode down to his waist and was frequently plaited and adorned with ribbons. A lady's man in the most misogynist sense of the word, Teach had no fewer than 14 wives. Entertainment being sparse, Teach would create his own by shooting bullets around one of his wife's legs, thus creating a dance performance in an area otherwise bereft of cultural events.

Teach was not one to cultivate close male friendships either. A favorite hobby was to randomly shoot a man. He served as the model for Stevenson's Long John Silver, and it is likely the the BVI's Norman Island was the model for his *Treasure Island*. The man is immortalized not only on St. Thomas (where a hotel is named after him) but also in the BVI where he took up residence at Soper's Hole. The offshore islands of Great Thatch and Little Thatch are reputedly named after him. And, now, there is even a beer named after him. ■

Blackbeard hanging from a mast.

pinched and hung"; that a slave who lifts his hand to strike a white or even threatens him with violence would be pinched and hung; a slave meeting a white should step aside until he passed or risk flogging; and all dances, feasts, and plays among slaves were forbidden.

In 1764 Charlotte Amalie was declared a free port for intracolonial trade. Its neutrality attracted privateers of all nations who arrived to sell their booty. In 1815 this trade was extended internationally.

EMANCIPATION: Denmark's King Frederik VI appointed **Peter von Scholten** governor in 1827. An unusual man, versed in Creole and comfortable among slaves, von Scholten lived with Anna Heegard, the granddaughter of a freed slave. Perhaps

Peter von Scholten

under her influence, he began urging freedom for all slaves. In 1847 he implemented the policy of "gradualism," whereby slave children born during the succeeding 12 years were to be free at birth. All slaves would then be free at the end of the 12-year period. Resentment by slaves against the system, however, continued to build.

Receiving word of a planned slave rebellion, von Scholten emancipated the slaves on July 3, 1848, on his own initiative, from Fort Frederik in Christiansted. The rebellion began in Frederiksted before the news reached there. After the news arrived, however, the violence turned into a jubilant celebration.

Brought back to Copenhagen for trial, von Scholten was acquitted. Emancipation led to dire poverty for freed slaves and to labor riots on St. Croix in 1878, during which most of Frederiksted burned.

SALE TO UNITED STATES: During the US Civil War, the danger of having an unprotected Atlantic coastline, coupled with the strategic value of having a Caribbean colony, became clear. Saint Thomas was seen as a Caribbean Gibraltar: a fortress at sea, surrounded by impregnable coral reefs, strategically located, and with harbors eminently suited for naval vessels.

Negotiations, opened secretly by Secretary of State Seward in Jan. 1865, were delayed by Lincoln's assassination, but finally culminated in a treaty signed on Oct. 24, 1867, which provided for the sale of St. Thomas and St. John for $7.5 million, or a half million more than Seward had paid for Alaska.

As a stipulation of the treaty, a referendum among the local populace was held in 1868; a majority of the 12% of the population who qualified for suffrage voted in favor, and the sale was considered by both nations to have been approved. However, although the treaty passed in the Danish Rigsag or parliament, it failed to pass a US Senate divided and impassioned by President Johnson's impeachment.

In the 1890s private American operators, attracted by the possibility of a 10% commission, negotiated with the Danes. Interrupted by the Spanish-American War, negotiations resumed again in 1900, at which time a Standard Oil vice-president joined the group. Boasting that he had 26 senators under his control, he claimed he could deliver a treaty for the price of a Standard Oil depot on St. Thomas.

Meanwhile, with the islands an expensive financial liability, the Danes were hoping to swap them with Germany in exchange for the return of North Schleswig. The Treaty

> **?!** Slaves and freed slaves in the Virgin Islands had their births recorded in a different book from that of the Danes. They were classified as mulatto (equal parts white and African), and sambo (white and mulatto) and placed into other categories such as negro, mestee, quadroon, quintoon, and octeroon.

of 1902, from which any mention of citizenship was deleted, arranged for the sale of all three islands to the US for a bargain basement $5 million.

Although the treaty was passed in the US Senate, it failed by one vote in its Danish counterpart—largely because the US refused to hold a plebiscite. Fresh negotiations dragged on again until the beginning of WWI.

Faced with the prospect of the Kaiser's armies marching into Copenhagen, American naval strategists began to fear for the safety of the Panama Canal and the Danes' strategic islands in the Caribbean. Negotiations began again under President Woodrow Wilson. Seizing advantage of the situation, the clever Danes, reluctant to negotiate at first, pushed the price up five times to $25 million. The US accepted the offer without attempting to bargain, and a treaty was signed on April 14, 1916. At $290 an acre, the islands represent the most expensive US government land purchase in history.

UNITED STATES TAKEOVER: On March 31, 1917, the Stars and Stripes were raised by the US Navy, ending 245 years and six days of Danish rule. Packing up everything moveable-from furniture to the rope belonging to the Government House flagpole-the Danes were happy to leave.

At the time of the US takeover conditions were absolutely abominable. A high death rate was coupled with a high rate of infant mortality. Agriculture was confined to small crops of yams and sweet potatoes. Malaria, typhoid, leprosy, diphtheria, and elephantiasis were widespread. There were four mi. of roads on St. Thomas, no high school, and only 19 elementary school teachers.

The brutality of the slavery system, one of the harshest in the Western Hemisphere, was transformed after emancipation into an almost complete neglect of the poor. As the islands were acquired by the US purely for their strategic value rather than out of any concern for the inhabitants or for economic reasons, the most expedient thing to do was to transfer them to military rule and worry about status, citizenship, human rights, and other such troublesome issues sometime in the future.

Under the Navy, all of the authoritarian local laws remained in force. This surprised locals who, having opted against Danish citizenship, assumed they would automatically be granted American citizenship.

The Navy found a strange world. White Naval officers, many of them from the South, were astounded to find themselves dealing with high-ranking local blacks. Run-ins between locals and intoxicated Marines frequently resulted in violence. A succession of Southern Casears as military governors, hard core supremacists all, fanned the flames.

CIVILIAN ADMINISTRATION: The 14 years of Naval control ended on 18 March 1931 as

Visiting in July 1934, Franklin D. Roosevelt maintained that he was proud of what had been done on the islands.

control passed to the U.S. Department of the Interior and Paul Pearson was sworn in as the first civilian governor. President Hoover, visiting eight days later, declared, "Viewed from every point except remote naval contingencies, it was unfortunate we ever acquired these islands."

Although the Jones Act had granted citizenship to Puerto Ricans in 1917, Virgin

Harry S. Truman visited Drake Seat on Feb. 22, 1948. Here, he is met by Governor William Hastie. He unveiled a plaque at Emancipation Gardens which commemorated the centennial. Truman maintained that "Eventually the UN will succeed, and we will have peace on earth."

Islanders were denied this because the treaty of purchase spoke of citizenship "in" the U.S. as opposed to citizenship "of" the U.S. Citizenship was finally granted in 1927 to most residents, but not until 1932 was this privilege extended to all.

The Basic Organic Act, passed in 1936, gave the vote to all citizens who were able to read and write English and made the U.S. Constitution operative in the Virgin Islands. In addition, all federal taxes collected were to be held for use by local governments in the Islands. Pearson, known as the "Experimenting Quaker," although unpopular with both the left and right, continued as governor under President Franklin Roosevelt.

During the New Deal, the Public Works Administration instituted the Virgin Islands Company (VICO), a public corporation which grew and refined sugarcane, distilled and marketed rum, and controlled water supplies and power production. Rum was produced and sold under the brand name "Government House," bearing a label personally designed by Roosevelt. Unlike its mainland counterparts, VICO (later renamed VICORP) wasn't really such a good idea, as the Virgin Islands are not particularly well suited to sugarcane cultivation.

THE GOVERNORS: President Truman appointed William H. Hastie to be the Islands' first black governor in 1946. He was succeeded by Morris F. Castro in 1950 who, in turn, was replaced by Archie Alexander. Alexander resigned in 1955 under the guise of ill health after allegations of conflict of interest and misuse of government funds had been made against him.

Alexander had been nominated in 1954 by Eisenhower. This wealthy construc-

Vice President Richard M. Nixon visited St. Thomas in 1951. Here, he is accompanied by USVI Governor Archie Alexander. Nixon maintained that St. Thomas was "one of the loveliest places on earth."

Important Dates in USVI History

1493: Columbus discovers St. Croix and the other Virgin Islands.

1625: The Dutch and English settle on St. Croix.

1650: The English are driven from St. Croix by Puerto Rican Spaniards. The French take over from the Spanish.

1651: Chevalier de Poincy, Lt. General of The. French West Indies, buys St. Croix from the bankrupt French West Indies Company.

1653: Ownership of St. Croix is transferred to the Knights of Malta.

1665: Erik Neilson Schmidt, a Danish sea captain, is granted a charter from the Danish king to colonize St. Thomas and is named royal commandant and governor. Saint Croix is purchased from the Knights of Malta by the French West Indies Company.

1666: Schmidt takes possession of St. Thomas only to die 6 months later: he is replaced by Lutheran pastor Kjeld Slagelse.

1667: Saint Thomas is captured by the English, who soon abandon it.

1668: Slagelse and most of the island's Danish inhabitants return home.

1671: Danish King Christian V issues a new charter to the West India and Guinea Company.

1672: Danes, under Gov. Iverson, formally take possession of St. Thomas.

1673: The first consignment of African slaves arrives on St. Thomas.

1674: The king of France takes over St. Croix as part of his dominions from the French West Indies Company.

1681: Taphus (Charlotte Amalie) is founded on St. Thomas.

1684: Saint Thomas formally takes possession of St. John.

1685: Saint Thomas is leased to the Brandenburgh Company to carry on commerce for 30 years.

1691: Saint Thomas is leased to George Thormohlen, a Bergen merchant, for 10 years.

1694: Thormohlen's lease ends in a lawsuit.

1696: French settlers abandon St. Croix.

1716: Export and import duty is reduced to 6 percent *ad valoreum.*

1717: Planters from St. Thomas occupy St John and begin cultivation.

1724: St. Thomas is formally declared a free port.

1726: The first Supplication Day (to pray for "aid against hurricanes") is held.

1730: Taphus is renamed Charlotte Amalie.

1733: Saint Croix is purchased from France by the Danish West Indies Company; slaves on St. John openly rebel.

1734: The St. John insurrection is put down.

1735: Danes formally take possession of St Croix; Christiansted is established.

1751: The town of Frederiksted is established.

1764: Saint Thomas and St. John again granted free port status.

1792: Denmark outlaws slave trade.

1801–2: Britain again occupies the islands.

1804: Much of Charlotte Amalie is swept by fire.

1806: Two more fires devastate Charlotte Amalie.

1807–15: Britain again occupies the islands.

1825: Yet another fire sweeps through Charlotte Amalie.

1826: Another fire on St. Thomas.

1831: Still another fire on St. Thomas.

1848: Slaves on St. Croix are emancipated by Governor-General Peter von Scholten after demonstrations.

1867: A treaty is signed in Denmark for the sale of St. Thomas and St. John to the U.S. for $7.5 million.

1870: The treaty of sale is rejected by the U.S. Senate.

1872: Charlotte Amalie once again becomes the administrative seat of the islands.

1892: Poor economic conditions, coupled with a lack of stable currency, cause a rebellion on St. Thomas.

1898: The U.S. again attempts to purchase the islands.

1902: A second treaty, granting the islands to the U.S. in exchange for $5 million in gold, is signed; it is rejected by the Danish parliament.

1916: Treaty selling the islands to the U.S. for $25 million is signed.

1917: Treaty of sale is ratified and the islands formally become part of the U.S.

1927: US citizenship is granted to most island residents.

1931: Jurisdiction of the islands is transferred from the Navy to the Dept. of the Interior; President Hoover visits the USVI.

1936: The first Organic Act is passed.

1940: Population shows an increase for the first time since 1860.

1946: First black governor of the islands, William Hastie, is appointed.

1950: Morris De Castro, first native-born governor, is appointed.

1954: Revised Organic Act passed.

1956: National Park on St. John approved by U.S. Congress.

1959: The Revised Organic Act is amended.

1968: Passage of the Virgin Islands Elective Governor Act permits the USVI. to elect a governor.

1969: Dr. Melvin Evans, first native black governor and last appointee, takes office.

1970: Dr. Melvin Evans elected governor.

1972: Hon. Ron de Lugo elected as first Congressional delegate from the Virgin Islands.

1989: Hurricane Hugo devastates the islands.

1995: Hurricane Marilyn hits.

tion engineer from Iowa, was the first Republican governor and the second Black governor. His acquaintance with the Virgin Islands consisted of having visited here some ten times, on behalf of the American Caribbean Contracting Company, a group of contractors whose bid on a sewer system failed. During his nomination hearings he had termed Virgin Islanders as "mendicants" and "wards of the state." He maintained that they appeared before Congress in order "to get vast sums of money each year." Alexander asserted that "if the people could tighten up their belts and go to work, they would solve their problem."

It was downhill from there. Alexander was charged with misusing educational funds, bringing his friends in as consultants, using obscene language, and other

Sir Winston Churchill arrived on St. Thomas aboard Aristotle Onassis's yacht Christina *on April 1, 1960. He toured the island with Gov. Merwin who told Lady Churchill that "Magens Bay will not become another Miami Beach. It must be protected for the people."*

offenses. However, the crown jewel which led to his resignation was when he selected his business partner to build the Waterfront Highway while offering him the use of government equipment and the necessary crushed rocks for cheap. Another potential bidder complained about the padded and unfair contract, the bid was cancelled, and he was pressed to resign.

In 1954 Congress passed the Revised Basic Organic Act which established a unicameral legislature and allowed all federal excise taxes collected from rum sales to be returned to the Islands. A succession of governors ruled until President Kennedy — under pressure from his father, who had been a friend of the rum distilling Paiewonsky family—appointed entrepreneur Ralph M. Paiewonsky governor. A bill providing for the direct election of governors direct election of governors became law on Aug. 23, 1968. Selected by President Nixon, Dr. Melvin H. Evans became the last appointed governor on July 1, 1969.

In the first gubernatorial elections, held in Nov. 1970, Cyril King was elected.

On Sept. 6, 1972, five to seven men entered the clubhouse area of the Fountain Valley Golf Course on St. Croix and opened fire. Eight died and four were wounded. Five defendants were sentenced to eight life terms each.

In July 1975, the District Court of the Virgin Islands ruled on the of the Open Shorelines Act, which permitted local access to beaches, to be constitutional. Long overdue, this measure guaranteed Virgin Islanders access to the beaches and to prevent hotels from dumping sewage directly into the ocean. As part of the decision, Bolongo Bay Beach Resort was ordered to remove the fences which blocked access to Virgin Islands beaches.

After the death of his successor Melvin King (no relation) in Jan. 1978, Juan Luis became acting governor and was subsequently elected in Nov. 1978 and re-elected in 1982. In 1986 Democrat and Yale Law School graduate Alexander Farelly defeated State Senator Adelbert Bryan (see "the 1990s" below) of the Independent Citizen's Movement. Tapping the resentment the lower class feels towards the well-to-do, Bryan (a former St. Croix policeman) waged the first real challenge to the status quo in the islands' electoral history.

In Sept. 1989, Hurricane Hugo hit the islands severely. On St. Croix, 70% of the buildings were destroyed or severely damaged, some 150 inmates were freed and went on a crime rampage, and federal troops patrolled the island. The Federal Emergency Management Agency (FEMA) estimated that the USVI suffered at least $400 million worth of damage.

THE 1990s: The 1990s was largely a continuation of what had gone on heretofore. Hurricane Marilyn devastated St. Thomas and damaged other islands in Sept. 1996. In the legislature the colorful figure of Adelbert M. "Bert" Bryan enlivened proceedings in these years. Much of the controversy stemmed over the concept of bringing gambling to St. Croix as a means of enhancing tourism on the island. Bryan introduced an amendment to require that investors in any casino be "aboriginals," i.e. "native" Virgin Islanders—a loaded definition. (The original bill defined "natives" as being individuals born in the Virgin Islands before 1927 and their descendants). Gov. Schneider hoped to issue bonds to the tune of $65 million in order to attract investors and maintained that no casino would be built if such a definition went into effect. He vetoed the amendment. An amendment was finally passed which permitted casino gambling while redefining the definition of "native" Virgin Islanders to those individuals who were born

in the Virgin Islands and to those who were the offspring of Virgin Islanders serving off-islands in the US Armed Forces. (A casino opened in St. Croix in Dec. 1999).

A controversial figure who revels in the limelight, Bryan originally hails from Orlando, FL and was once a police captain. Bryan was caught with chicken wire he had removed from a store during the aftermath of lootings which followed 1989's Hurricane Hugo. Charged with grand theft, Bryan claimed that he was removing the materials for safekeeping from the looters, and he was acquitted in District Court! During the debate over the final amendment to the gambling act (see above) the Senator went around turning off the lights in the Senate Chamber and pulled the plug on the public address system while maintaining that he would prevent a vote to change the definition. The next day the 52-year-old Bryan allegedly shot his son Bryan Jr. on his farm at Upper Love estate. Bryan claimed that his son was coming after him with a machete and that he acted in self defense. The judicial system let him go free. Bryan was reelected.

the 2000s: Democrat Charles Turnbull was re-elected in 2002. In 2006 Democrat John de Jongh was elected by 57.3 and his party won 8 out of 15 seats. In June 2008, Alric Simmonds, a former aide to former US Virgin Islands Governor Charles Turnbull, was sentenced to to eight years in prison. He was convicted on charges of conversion of government property, embezzlement or falsification of public accounts, and grand larceny. He was ordered to pay a $1,248,946.70 in restitution to the USVI government, and he had to turn over all real and personal property as well as forfeit 75% of his retirement income while imprisoned and 25% after his release.

Government

As citizens of the nation and residents of an unincorporated territory under the US flag, at four-year intervals Virgin Islanders elect their own governor, legislature, and a non-voting representative to Congress. The legislature, the backbone of the local government, is a unicameral body of 15 members who are elected to two-year terms. Its main powers and duties derive from the 1954 Revised Organic Act.

Although the system may sound ideal, the realities have been different. In the USVI, politics has always been politics. For years the autocratic legislature has been dominated by the Unity Democrats. Party of the Creoles, it has allowed entry into the political process of only a few Continentals and Puerto Ricans, while the vast number of alien residents remain unrepresented. Party politics are confusing and crossing of party lines while voting is common.

CONSTITUTION: It's been in the works for a while. On Nov. 4, 1981, Virgin Island voters rejected the latest draft of their proposed constitution, the fourth such rejection of a constitution since 1964. The first constitution failed to pass Congress; the second (1972) was approved by Congress only by an insubstantial margin; and the third (1979) was also rejected by the voters.

The latest constitution defined a "Virgin Islander" as one born on, or with one parent born on, the islands—a designation which would have conferred no special benefits. The original draft contained a specification that the governor must be a native. After residents from the States complained, it was removed.

Regarding the modest voter turnout for the election (47%), Judge Henry Feuerzeig—who helped draft and actively campaigned for the constitution—pontificated: "Constitutions aren't sexy. You can't identify with them as you can with a candidate."

Economy

No other Caribbean island or island group has ever undergone such a fast-clipped transformation, ethnic or economic, as did the US Virgin Islands during the 1960s. Although the entire population of the USVI was only 100,000 in the late '70s, the government budget was larger than that of San Juan with its one million people! The islands have the highest per capita income in the Caribbean, about US$14,500 per year (2004 estimate), but they're also plagued by prices higher than Stateside, without wage levels to match.

The presence of continentals, while stimulating to the economy, has served to drive up land values and cause considerable resentment. While the typical native Virgin Islander works for the government, most of the service industry jobs are held by continentals or the down-islanders, disparagingly nicknamed *garotes*, after the tropical bird that flies from island to island—consuming everything in sight before flying home This label was first applied to Antiguans who, arriving to sell fish and provisions, would walk with an exaggerated twitch. Many of these aliens live in inferior housing conditions.

Today, only 45% of the islanders are native born. According to the 2000 census, about 28.7% of families and 32.5% of the popu-

?! USVI Gov. Charles Turnbull sealed the Virgin Islands' Millenium Time Capsule on Dec. 15, 2000 in a 24-sq. in. vault. The stash included local art, US and USVI flags which had been flown at sunset of Dec. 31, 1999 and at sunrise of Jan. 1, 2001, photos, and other memorabilia. It will be opened on Jan. 1, 2100.

INTRODUCTION

lation are below the poverty line, including 41.7% of those under 18 and 29.8% of those 65 or over.

GOVERNMENT: Surprisingly, the largest employer in the USVI is the territorial government. Its more than 13,000 employees give the islands the highest ratio of bureaucrats to taxpayers of any area of the United States. Although the government employs a full third of the working force and receives more per capita in federal funds than any state or territory save the District of Columbia, it has been ponderously slow to deal with practical concerns such as power plants, desalinization plants, and new roads. Stories of corruption are legendary.

The Farrelly Administration had to wrestle with the financial disarray left by his predecessor Juan Luis. Having called the government "a shambles" and proposing to reduce the bureaucracy and turn over certain public services to the private sector, he did little. He was re-elected in 1900, and Roy Schneider became governor in 1994 and was defeated by Democrat Dr. Charles Turnbull, a retired university professor and the son of immigrants from the BVI, in 1998. Turnbull was elected again in 2002 and was followed by John de Jongh in 2006.

However, the problems still continue. Despite the hefty taxes and subsidies, the money just disappears, and the government currently faces a one billion dollar deficit! Problems include nepotism, corruption, incompetence, and increasing violence in the schools.

INDUSTRY: None exists on St. Thomas or St. John. Harvey Alumina constructed a $25 million alumina processing plant on St. Croix's S shore, then sold it to Martin Marietta, who worked the plant for 10 years and then closed it. It adjoins the 1,200-acre Hovensa Refinery, a joint venture between Hess and the Virgin Islands government. Its presence

does not stop the islands' gas prices from being among the highest in the nation.

Completed in 1993, Hess' $1 billion catalytic-cracking unit has increased the refinery's ability to produce high-octane cleaner-burning gasolines which are important in complying with environmental regulations. A second facility was constructed in 2000.

This St. Thomian coalbearing woman shows how dramatically life has changed over the centuries in the Virgin Islands. This woman is dressed in a shirt resembling a Danish flag. This was used as a postcard in the 1880s.

USVI Public Holidays	
January 1	New Year's Day
January 6	Three Kings Day
January 15	Martin Luther King's Birthday
February	President's Day (movable)
March 31	Transfer Day
March/April	Holy Thursday, Good Friday, Easter Monday (movable),
June	Memorial Day (movable), Organic Act Day (movable)
July	Supplication Day (movable)
July 3	Emancipation Day
July 4	U.S. Independence Day
September	Labor Day (movable)
October	Columbus Day, Virgin Islands/Puerto Rico Friendship Day, Hurricane Thanksgiving Day (movable)
November	Liberty Day
Nov. 11	Veterans Day
November	U.S. Thanksgiving Day (movable)
Dec. 25	Christmas Day
Dec. 26	Second Christmas Day

TOURISM: This economic sector is the major income earner. Hotels have increased dramatically over the years as have the number of visitors. St. Thomas alone has some 3,500 hotel rooms. Tourists have been attracted because of the "duty-free" (7% import duty) shopping available, as well as the sense of security offered by islands that are part of the United States.

AGRICULTURE: Almost totally neglected. The only fresh milk available on the islands is found on St. Croix. St. Thomian milk is reconstituted. Obstacles to agriculture include aridity and the high cost of land, which finds more renumerative use in tourism. On St. Croix, Senepol cattle and white sheep are an export item.

TAX HAVEN: Once the USVI was an attractive haven for the mainland's tax evaders. That status changed in 2004 when Congress changed the regulations. The VI government maintains that the changes were too sweeping —forcing out "many legitimate businesses" according to Gov. Charles Turnbull. The Wall Street Journal, writing on the topic in Dec. 2006, maintained that the VI government "spent at least $1.38 million [in 2005] lobbying the federal government on tax-related issues" and paid a "$140,000 fee to hire former Republican Rep. Richard K. Armey" (who is currently a member of the law firm DLA Piper). It also hired PricewaterhouseCoopers who reported that the USVI might lose $80 million should the economic development's tax incentives end. The IRS instituted minor changes to the law in May 2008.

Festivals and Events

With 23 official holidays, Virgin Islanders have plenty of time off-perhaps more than anyone anywhere else in the world! Various public holidays are marked by special celebrations and events peculiar to the USVI.

JAN: New Year's Day features a children's parade in Frederiksted. **Three Kings Day,** which follows on Jan. 6, constitutes the finale of St. Croix's Christmas Festival with a colorful parade of costumed children and adults.

FEBRUARY: The two-day **St. Croix International Regatta** (☎ 773-9531, 773-1048, ext. 11 or 12) usually takes place a week before President's Day More than 30 boats usually attend.
http://www.stcroixyc.com

MARCH: Transfer Day, March 31, celebrates the transfer of the islands to the US in 1917. The Royal Danish Consulate is endeavoring to revive the popularity of the day by staging events on St. Thomas and St. Croix.

APRIL: Easter is marked by church services; outdoor sporting events are held on Easter Monday. Coral World Ocean Park (☎ 775-1555) offers an **Easter Egg Hunt** on St. Thomas around this time.

St Croix holds a **Sports Week Festival** around the beginning of April: Events range from foot racing to tournament tennis to deep sea fishing to underwater photography to name a few of the competitions. The **Rolex Regatta** usually comes in mid-April, as does **St. Thomas' Carnival** which takes place during the last eight days of April.

MAY: The **Half-Ironman Triathalon** (swimming/bicycling/running, ☎ 773-4470) usually takes place on St. Croix on the first Sun. in May. The competition begins with a 1.24-mi. swim from Protestant Cay to Christiansted's boardwalk. From there, they begin a 56-mi. bike ride during which they are challenged by "The Beast," a twisting road which climbs 600 ft. in 7/10 of a mi. The competition ends with a 13.1-mi. race which encircles the grounds of the Buccaneer and terminates in Christiansted.
http://www.stcroixtriathalon.com

 Held during President's Day Weekend in February, the **St. Croix Agricultural Fair** is a great place to sample local food and experience crafts, and lore. Held at the Rudolph Schulterbrandt Agricultural Complex in Estate Lower Love, it's usually open from 9 AM–6 PM; admission is charged. Arrive early to beat the crowds. July's **Mango Melee** at St. George Botanical Garden on St. Croix, is also great fun.

Parades and ceremonies are commonplace throughout the islands on **Memorial Day,** and yacht races are featured on St. Croix.

JULY: A special ceremony marking **Danish West Indies Emancipation Day** takes place in Frederiksted, St. Croix, on July 3, because the proclamation was first read there. All three islands celebrate this day with parades and ceremonies. The one held in **Cruz Bay, St. John,** features a miniature version of St. Thomas' Carnival.

Also in July, many residents of these islands attend services marking **Hurricane Supplication Day** and pray that no hurricanes will visit them.

SEPT: Special festivities are held on all three islands on Labor Day just as they are held on the mainland. **Columbus Day** is also known as **Puerto Rico/Virgin Islands Friendship Day;** a traditional boat trip from St. Croix to the Puerto Rican island of Vieques is made on this day.

NOV: Liberty Day, Nov. 1, commemorates the establishment of the first free press in 1915. **Veterans Day,** Nov. 11, features parades and ceremonies.

The **Virgin Island Charteryacht League Show** (☎ 800-525-2061) takes place in mid-November.
http://www.crownbay.com
http://www.vicl.org

The **Virgin Islands Half-Marathon,** an event organized by the Virgin Islands Pace Runners (☎ 777-0258) generally takes place on St. Croix in Nov. They also hold a race on New Years Day.
http://www.virginislandspace.org
vipacerunner@usvi.net

DEC: The **Charity Golf Classic** takes place on St. Croix in Dec.

St. Thomas holds its **"Miracle on Main Street"** (☎ 776-0100) in mid-Dec. Stores stay open until 9, mocko jumbie dancers parade down the streets, and other features include chalk drawings, a Caribbean Santa, and a parade of lighted Christmas boats along the harbor.

Music

While the Virgin Islands do have deep musical roots, the islands are deeply indebted to their more populous brothers and sisters such as Jamaica and Trinidad for their music. Today, you can hear rock, calypso, reggae, soul, quelbe, steel band music, and disco on the islands.

REGGAE: Originally emanating from the steamy slums of Jamaica, reggae has swept the world and gone international. No one is quite sure exactly from where it appeared, but it appears inseparably linked to the maturation of the Rastafarian movement. Reggae may be defined as the synthesis of electrified African music coupled with the influence of ska, rock steady, and American rhythm and blues. Some give the Wailers credit for transforming reggae into its present format. No sooner had the band gained

An original scratch band circa 1908. Known as **scratch**, **fungi**, or **quelbe**, depending upon geographic location and exact instrumentation, scratch bands are local ensembles which play traditional folk songs. Instrumentation includes a gourd with serrated sides played with a scratcher (the "squash"), the ukelele banjo (a short, four-string version), conga drums played with a stick or mallet, a triangle (the "steel"), and (sometimes) guitar, bass, saxophone, and flute. On St. Croix, *quelbe* music uses a used tail pipe from a car to create a bass sound.

> **?!<** The term scratch band originated because musicians would play any instruments they could "scratch up."

international fame in the early 70s than its members went their own separate ways, with the band's major singer-songwriter Bob Marley changing the name to Bob Marley and the Wailers. By the time of his death from brain cancer at the age of 36 in 1981, Robert Nesta Marley had become an international superstar. His influence remains strong to this day, and no one has yet quite succeeded in filling his shoes.

Although reggae is not strongly developed in the Virgins, there are a few bands playing reggae, and the music (particularly the rapid fire "dance hall" deejay style) permeates the islands.

STEEL BAND MUSIC: This unique orchestra of Trinidadian origin has spread all over the Caribbean. The steel band may have had low-life beginnings — it was a scorned child of the lower classes — but it is now the darling of every tourist board. Some orchestras have grown to as large as 200 members. Although it is often maintained that the instruments are the progeny of African drums, they have much more rhythmically in common with African marimbas. However, in truth, they are far removed from either.

The *pans* — as the individual drums are known — are made from large oil drums. First, the head — along with six in. to a foot of the side — is severed. Then, the top is heated and hammered until a series of large indents emerge. Each of these produces a musical note. Each *pan* is custom designed. The bass *pans* have only three or four notes, while others produce many that carry the melody.

Bands are now divided into three major sections: the "ping pong" (or soprano *pans*) provide the melody using 26–32 notes; the

larger *pans* ("guitar," "cello," and "bass") supply the harmony; and the cymbals, scratchers, and drums add the groundbeat. A contemporary steel drum orchestra in Trinidad generally contains 20 or more *pans*; those found in the Virgin Islands commonly have considerably fewer.

CALYPSO: Perhaps no music is so difficult to pinpoint, and none is quite so undefinable as calypso. Next to reggae, it is the best known music to come out of the English-speaking Caribbean. Its rhythm is Afro-Spanish: sometimes the Spanish elements dominate, sometimes the African. Call-and-response is employed frequently. It *is* strikingly African in the nature and function of its lyrics.

The tunes don't vary a whole lot — there are some 50 or so — but the lyrics must be new! And, without exception, they must also pack social bite. Calypso is a political music, like reggae, and one which, more frequently than not, attacks the status quo, lays bare the foibles of corrupt politicians, and exposes empty programs. The songs often function as musical newspapers, providing great insight into society. Calypso is also a very sexual music — as even the briefest listening will reveal. One of the most frequent themes is the wrath of a scorned woman focused on an unfaithful male partner.

> Steel band music is ubiquitous in the Virgin Islands, and many resorts and hotels feature the steel drum in their entertainment regimen. You can hear the music in concentrated doses during St. Thomas's carnival and at "Music in Steel," an annual concert which takes place the first Friday in December in the BVI. The BVI has a youthful band, the Shooting Stars Steel Orchestra, which frequently performs hither and thither across the archipelago.

ORIGINS: No one can say precisely where or when calypso began, and — although there are many theories — no one knows the origin of the label "calypso." Each island claims it for its own, and certainly all of the islands had music similar in style. In fact, some of them were also called calypso. However, these styles were all influenced by Trinidadian calypso. This was partly because of the popularity of Trinidadian calypso and partly because the same businessman who had the island's calypsonians under contract owned a group of record stores on the other islands.

The famous Trinidadian calypsonian Atilla the Hun (Raymond Quevedo) maintained that it was "undoubtedly African." According to Quevedo, the first calypsos were sung by *gayap* — a group of organized communal workers which has equivalents in W Africa. These work songs — which can be found in every African community in the Americas — still exist. Their more ribald counterparts, which served to spread gossip concerning plantation folk, paralleled modern day calypso. However, it is more likely that they were merely an influence.

The true origins of calypso remain shrouded in mist. Certainly, there are many African elements present in the music, including the use of dynamic repetition, call-and-response patterns, and the rebuking of socially reprehensible behavior — a frequent theme in traditional African songs.

Whatever its roots, calypso seems to have reached its stylistic maturity in the 1870s. It was originally accompanied by rattles, a scraper (called a *vira)*, drums, and a bottle and spoon used like a W African gong.

During the 40s and 50s, calypsonians first began twisting words — executing swift ingenuity — to contrive rhymes that also produced a wide range of rhythmic effects in the vocal line. Lines that vary in length as well as short phrases or cries, juxtaposed between the lines of verses, serve to enliven the music's spirit. Calypso music has incorporated elements of jazz, salsa, Venezuelan, East Indian, and R&B music. But — like all great musical forms — it has been strengthened rather than swamped by their influence.

RISE IN POPULARITY: Calypso was first recorded in 1914, but it was not recognized in the US until American servicemen were stationed in Trinidad during WWII. After the war, the Andrews Sisters pirated and popularized Lord Invader's *Rum and Coca Cola*. Harry Belafonte recorded a calypso album in the 1950s which, because he clearly pronounced the words, made the music more accessible to the rest of the English-speaking world. Lord Kitchener recorded a number of albums in England and Sparrow began pumping them out on the home front. In the 1980s and into the 1990s, a new trend began to emerge. Growing technical advances made musical composition more important, and calypsonians now record with gifted arrangers and the best studio musicians.

Soca, a merger of soul and calypso, has given the music a new level of popularity. It is, in effect, a more danceable and commercial form of calypso. The most famous soca singer is *Arrow* whose *Hot, hot, hot* is set to become a timeless classic. Even the first woman to capture the calypso crown, Calypso Rose, has recorded an album entitled "*Soca Diva*."

THE CALYPSONIANS: As with other contemporary popular styles, the music focuses on the singer. The calypso kings are sexual objects, like the American and British rock stars. One qualification for this position is to be unemployed — the image of the witty iindigent — bordering, but not entering, criminality; another is to be very dashingly and wickedly attractive to swooning women. The calypso singer once lived through donations, like the *griot* musicians of W

Africa. Flamboyant titles—whether it be the Mighty Sparrow or Atilla the Hun—serve to reinforce the high-and-mighty image. Crowned in a tent, he becomes masculine prowess incarnate.

Veteran calypsonian Morris "King Generic" Benjamin was crowned the 2007–2008 Calypso Monarch. He triumphed over competitors were Samuel "Mighty Pat" Ferdinand (the reigning monarch), Alan "King Herrin" Clarke, Jose "TNL" Navarro, Alford Romney, Louis "Qwiz" Richards, Karen "Lady Mac" McIntosh and Kasaun "K-Force" Baptiste.

🦋 The History of Mas 🦋

"The masquerades come from from West Africa and represent ways of people avoiding the evil spirits when they are having their festivities. The Moko Jumbies, for example, would tower over the trees, and if you had a mask up there it would mock the ghosts and perhaps fool them into thinking that either they could not do anything there or that they had been spotted and they might as well leave.

"There are a number of Africans rites of passage which the Christian slaveowners tried to extirpate. But they had a lot of dances, including those in which they would train the body for childbirth. A lot of people see something else in this, but that is what it is about. And we have developed dances out of that such as the *bamboula*, which incorporates a belly roll.

"During the festivities that the Africans would have, they would participate in rituals that the Christians found appalling, but the could not get that out of them. They could not beat it out of them. And they could not train it out of them, so they decided to let it be practiced after Lent, when after a long period of fasting and inactivity they would let the people loose and hold their carnival. And some of the carnivals consisted of *kalindas* or stick fighting. A lot of injuries would result from these, and attempts were made to outlaw them, but it proved difficult.

"These came to be called 'calypsos.' The singers would compete with each other, and they would try to best each other with song instead of sticks. And as time went by we began to see the genesis of carnival, and all of this began in Trinidad. However, all regions of the Caribbean possessed similar traditions. It's amazing because when the West Africans come to visit us during carnival, they're amazed (and so are Virgin Islanders) in the similarities as to how they prepare their food, how they refer to certain things, and that is because they were basically one family. They were separated and are finally together. So when you see the masquerade, you have to think of the West Africa and of the traditions that celebrated Earth and the nature and the naturalness and the spirits that guided them and protected them. Because, when those lights went out, it was just you and whatever was out there, and you had all of those malevolent spirits, so benevolent spirits were a necessity. And, when we play 'mas', we celebrate the benevolent spirits. It's now called mas, and, when they build their costumes, they call it a 'mas camp.' A lot of the designers come from Trinidad, and they call it 'bending wire.'"

—As told to Harry S. Pariser by Anita Davis

Notes

USVI Practicalities

GETTING HERE: The only way to arrive is by air or cruise ship unless you come from Puerto Rico by ferry. Fares tend to be cheaper on weekdays and during low season (mid-April to mid-December).

The islands' gateway city of San Juan, Puerto Rico can be reached by air from everywhere in the Caribbean except Cuba. Even if you don't intend to visit San Juan, it may be necessary to switch planes at San Juan International Airport. (Direct flights are listed below).

From San Juan it's a short hop by small aircraft (such as American Eagle or Cape Air) to either St. Thomas or St. Croix. While discount OW fares are not available, shop around for various RT inter-island fares which may be available. These — like everything else — are cheapest off-season.

Many of the major airlines have contracts with small carriers that service the islands. American Airlines uses American Eagle; this may necessitate a long wait in San Juan. *Be sure to bring adequate snacks with you for the voyage as airlines are notoriously stingy on food these days.*

For St. John, it's best to take a ferry from Red Hook or Charlotte Amalie, St. Thomas. A car ferry runs from Red Hook, St. Thomas

to St. John. The British Virgins may be reached by boat or plane from the USVI.

AIRLINES: Many airlines fly. Schedules are subject to change. *Airlines are listed alphabetically below.*

FINDING AN INTERNET FARE: The best way to select a fare is to go to Orbitz, search for a flight, and then visit the site of the least expensive airline. Many airlines allow you to search for the cheapest fare within a time period of 30 days. If you have a flexible schedule, this is the ideal way to find the lowest fare. Be sure to select your seats and add your frequent flier miles. If you want a window seat, you should obtain one when you book. Bring your own food and/or snacks.

American Airlines (☎ 800-474-4884) flies directly to St. Thomas and St. Croix from Miami and NYC. It also flies from Boston to St. Thomas and into San Juan. For West Coast passengers, it has a flight from Los Angeles to San Juan.
http://www.americanairlines.com

Continental (☎ 800-525-0280) flies non-stop from Newark to St. Thomas and from Newark and Houston to San Juan.
http://www.continental.com

Delta (☎ 800-354-9822) flies direct from Atlanta to St. Thomas and St. Croix and also offers nonstop service from Atlanta to San Juan.
http://www.delta.com

United (☎ 800-538-2929) flies nonstop from Dulles (Washington DC), to San Juan, Puerto Rico. They also fly from Chicago to St. Thomas on Sat. and to San Juan from JFK (NYC) on Sat. and Sun.
http://www.united.com

Try calling a travel agent in the USVI. Sometimes they know where the deals are! Another alternative is to bid on priceline.com. The cheapest airfares are in the late summer.

USAir (☎ 800-428-4322) flies to St. Thomas from Philadelphia and to St. Thomas from NYC, Philadelphia and Charlotte. It offers numerous possibilities for connections.
http://www.usairways.com

FROM EUROPE: In addition to Continental's connecting flights, British Airways, Iberia, BWIA, and Lufthansa all fly to San Juan from where transfers can be made for the VI.

FROM THE CARIBBEAN: LIAT, **American Eagle,** and BWIA service St. Croix and St. Thomas from other Caribbean islands.

FROM PUERTO RICO: Air Sunshine (☎ 888-879-8900) flies from San Juan to St. Thomas, St. Croix, and Virgin Gorda.
http://www.airsunshine.com

Cape Air (☎ 800-352-0714) flies from San Juan to St. Thomas and St. Croix.
http://www.flycapeair.com

Vieques Air Link (☎ 777-4055, 888-901-9247) flies from Vieques to St. Croix.
http://www.vieques-island.com/val

FROM THE CARIBBEAN: LIAT and British West Indies Airlines (BWIA) services St.

Virgin Islands Driving Signals	
Signal	**Translation**
beep beep ▶→	"Thank you" or "Go!"
blowing horn ▶→	"Hello" or "Thanks, go ahead!"
leaning on horn ▶→	"Hurry up" or "Get out of the way!"
stopping ▶→	"We're having a chat with a passing vehicle."
waving hand ▶→	"Slow down" or "Come ahead."

Croix and St. Thomas from other Caribbean islands.

FROM PUERTO RICO: Cape Air (☎ 800-352-0714), **Air Sunshine** (☎ 776-7900, 800-327-8900) and others fly to St. Thomas.

Seaborne Airlines (☎ 340-773-6442, 888-359-8687), a small hydroplane company, flies between Old San Juan and St. Thomas. Rates are around $215–$225 RT.
http://www.seaborneairlines.com

Vieques Air Link (☎ 777-4055, 888-901-9247) flies from Vieques to St. Croix.
http://www.vieques-island.com/val

BY SHIP: **St. John Transportation Services** (☎ 776-6282) has the 95-ft. *Caribe Cay* which takes passengers to Fajardo. Unfortunately, the $1.5-million vessel ran aground in 1995 off of Fajardo. However, it is now running again every other Sunday. It departs Fajardo at 1 PM. Fare is $60 OW, $125 RT.

Innumerable cruise lines stop at St. Thomas, and some may stop at St. Croix. However, cruises are not recommended for the serious visitor as you have but a short space of time to spend on the island itself.

 Don't forget to bring a passport or driver's license with you. FAA regulations--require you to show a government-issued ID (which extends to a social security card or birth certificate) before boarding an airline.

CRUISES: **American Canadian Caribbean Line** (☎ 401-247-0955, 800-556-7450, ❸ 401-245-8303) travels to the three main Virgins as well as to the BVI in a 12-day, 12-stop trip.
http://www.accl-smallships.com

Getting Around

Local taxis — shared or unshared — are expensive. Rate are set, but be sure to decide the price before entering. Look for the "Vitaal Taxi Ambassador" which denotes graduates from a government program.

Inefficient and limited local bus service (both public and private) is available on all three islands. The most helpful are the "dollar bus" on St. Thomas (a pickup truck with a roof and seats), the route from Christiansted to Frederiksted (which passes by key attractions), and the St. John bus which travels between Cruz Bay and Coral Bay enroute to Salt Pond.

Hitching is safest and easiest on St. John. Be sure to use your index finger; a thumb will not work here.

A must for anyone is the "Official Road Map" of the islands available free of charge at tourist information offices. However, be sure to note that the St. John map is wrong regarding the roads around Bordeaux Mountain.

MAPS: The two best **maps** sold are the Virgin Islands Map (1:50,000) produced by **ITMB** (☎ 604-687-3320, ❸ 604-687-5925) of Vancouver, BC and the **Berndtson & Berndtson** map. Contact any good store specializing in travel guides or maps or buy online at **http://www.exploreavirgin.com**

There are also any number of free maps available which are fine for basic navigation but lack detail.

RENTING A CAR: On islands this small, you might expect that it would be difficult to get lost. Signage, however, is extremely poor. Expect to spend $65–$95 pd with unlimited mileage. Weekly rates are available. Rental companies are listed under the individual island sections.

DRIVING: Don't forget that you drive on the left hand side of the road although the vehicles are right-hand drive! There is no "R turn on red," but you can go L on red at an intersection. Left turns at traffic lights are permissible unless marked otherwise. Right hand turns are prohibited against a red light.

Watch for "no turn" signs because there are plenty of one-way streets in town areas. Expect traffic jams during Charlotte Amalie's early morning and late afternoon rush hours. Keep a look out for cars pulled over in the fast lane: locals frequently stop to pick up and discharge passengers without pulling off the road or even using indicator signals!

It is common courtesy here to stop to allow other vehicles to enter from driveways and intersections. It's also the custom to sound your horn when you round a corner. If you see the driver in front of you wagging his or her hand out of the window that means you should slow down or stop.

Always expect the unexpected: some drivers may pull L before turning R and vice versa. You should note that, owing to high jury awards, liability insurance and car insurance is nonexistent.

Tips on Car Rentals

☛ Ask if a weekend rate is available. Determine the least expensive pickup and dropoff times.

☛ Find a gas station near your future dropoff location so you can refill the car and save.

☛ Inquire about discounts available for members of associations.

☛ Ask about the taxes and charges for adding a second driver to the agreement.

Speed limits are 25 mph unless signs say otherwise. On St. Croix, the Queen Mary Hwy. is 35 mph and the Melvin Evans Expressway is 55 mph.

BY PLANE: With the exception of smaller islands such as St. John and Jost Van Dyke, the Virgins, American and British, are well connected by local air service.

The most convenient way to get between St. Thomas, St. Croix, North Sound (Virgin Gorda), and Old San Juan in Puerto Rico, is unquestionably with the **Seaborne Airlines** (☎ 773-6442; ☎ 713-9077, 888-359-8687; Long Bay Road, Charlotte Amalie, US Virgin Islands 00802). It's a convenient way to travel as it eliminates time spent at airports. *However, each passenger may carry only up to 30 pounds of baggage for free; after that, it's $1 per pound You will be charged for your carry on!* Roundtrip fares are around $165–$175 from St. Thomas to St. Croix. One-way fares are $90–$95. Children age two or under are free. Special Internet and weekend fares are offered, as are ferry and seaplane combination packages. Check in 45 min. before your flight.

Internet Hotel Booking

The internet offers unprecedented opportunities for travelers to actively plan and book their trip. *Some of the ways to do this best are:*

➡ Visit the hotel's website. Check the guestbook, photos, specials, packages, and other information. Address questions to the hotel.

➡ See if you can find reviews on other websites. Check for discounts for larger hotels on hotel search engine sites.

➡ See if there are any with-air packages.

➡ If a small hotel, book with them directly if possible to give them needed revenue.

They also offer a "Sea2Sky" ferry-and-air package between St. Thomas and St. Croix as well as other inter-island connections and airline reservations.

BY FERRY: Local ferries run between Charlotte Amalie, St. Thomas and Water Island (from Sub Base) and from Charlotte Amalie and Red Hook, St. Thomas to St. John. Ferries also run between the USVI and Tortola, Virgin Gorda, and Jost Van Dyke in the British Virgins. Details are given in the specific travel sections.

☞ For a complete list of ferries with links to their websites visit:
http://www.vinow.com

Smith's Ferry (☎ 775-7292) operates between St. Croix and St. Thomas on Fri, Sat., Sun. and Mon. Departures from St. Croix (Gallows Bay) are at 7:30 AM and 4:30 PM; arrival is at 9 AM and 6 PM. Departures from St. Thomas is at 9:30 AM and 6:45 PM; arrival is at 11 AM and 8:15 PM. The best place to sit is upstairs on the deck. There's a small cafeteria, but you should bring food or snacks. *This is an excellent way to travel between St. Croix and St. Thomas.*

HITCHHIKING BY YACHT: Hitchhiking by boat through the Caribbean can be easy if you have the time and money to wait for a ride and are at the right place in the right season. Best time to head there is about mid-Oct., just before the boat shows and the preparation for the charter season. Along with those at English Harbor on Antigua, the marinas on St. Thomas (at Red Hook and at Charlotte Amalie) have the greatest concentration of boats and the most competition for work of any island in the Caribbean. Many times it's easy to get a ride from one island to another. Just hang around the docks or pubs and ask. As far as working on yachts goes, it's hard

Know Thy Partner!
Vacation Planning Checklist

Instructions: Photocopy an enlarged version of this sheet (available in PDF format at our website: **www.savethemanatee.com**) and distribute to each person planning the trip and have them fill it in. Check all that apply to each question.

I'm traveling for ❏ business ❏ pleasure ❏ adventure ❏ other
_____

I expect to spend $____ for a room or other_____
I prefer ❏ resorts ❏ camping ❏ rental ❏ B&B ❏ small hotel ❏ other_____
_____

My interests are ❏ parks and reserves ❏ museums ❏ galleries ❏ beaches
❏ water sports (specify_____ ❏ snorkeling ❏ diving ❏ hiking
❏ birdwatching ❏ other _____
I plan to get around by (check all that apply) ❏ rental car (type) _____
❏ local bus ❏ charter bus ❏ taxi ❏ foot ❏ tour ❏ other (describe)_____
I like to travel (check all that apply) ❏ alone ❏ sometimes in a group ❏ leisurely
❏ moderate ❏ fast ❏ breezing through
I expect to spend $ __ daily including $ __ on lodging, $__ on food, $__ on transportation, and $__ on other activities.
I am most interested in visiting/doing (describe in depth below):

PRACTICALITIES

PRACTICALITIES

Meals and Hotels

It's always a good idea to consider your eating habits while booking accommodations. For example, if you eat breakfast, you should think about what you may need or want to eat and when. Check to see when breakfast (or even coffee) will be available.

Many hotels serve a complimentary breakfast which is often continental. Consider whether this will satisfy you or not. Find out what other meals are available and how far it is to other restaurants.

Vegetarians—or those who simply shun meat and fowl—will want to know if the restaurant will have anything for them to eat. Remember, it always pays to inquire before rather than after. ∎

work, low wages, and long hours, and you must have a real love for sailing and the sea. Depending upon whether you are working on salary or for piece work, the salary may or may not depend on how many hours are actually involved. usually you will be engaged in some sort of activity from early morning until late at night. Some boats may be more lax than others, but it generally involves pretty continuous work. Check out *Sail* magazine or *Yachting* for the addresses of charter companies. But it's really unnecessary to write: most people are employed on the spot.

ACCOMMODATIONS: These islands make their living from tourists and housing is tight, so the cost of lodging is correspondingly high —from $80 d to $1500 or more per night. And the 8% room tax along with a frequently applied 10% service charge makes the islands even more expensive!

Note that only high-season rates (generally Dec. to April) are listed in the book. Low-season rates my be as much as 30% less. Internet-only specials may also be lower.

It's cheapest to visit these islands off-season (mid-April through mid-December). Camping (bare sites and rented tents) is available only on St. John and (to a more limited extent) on St. Croix.

It's a good idea to get the **current rates** from the tourist board (☎ 800-372-8784). If they don't list the rates, it's just that the hotels haven't supplied them to the board so use the e-mail, fax, or phone number listed in this book to contact them. Rental agents on the islands are listed in the text.

TRAVELING WITH CHILDREN: The Virgin Islands are as safe as anywhere for children. Where you go will depend upon your offspring's age and interests. The older your child, the more he or she will enjoy the experience.

Just take care that they are not overexposed to sun and get sufficient liquids. Remember to bring whatever special equipment you'll need. Disposable diapers and baby food are available but expensive. Be sure to inquire at your hotel as to extra charges for children and if they'll even be wanted.

Some hotels (including Bolongo on St. Thomas, the Westin on St. John, Chenay Bay and the Buccaneer on St. Croix, and others) have special programs or deals for children. You can save money by dining at local restaurants Finally, keep an eye on the kids while they're in the water. There are no lifeguards.

PLANNING A FAMILY VACATION: Resorts are plentiful in the Virgin Islands but make sure that this is where you want to stay. Your children might enjoy camping at Cinnamon Bay, for example, as opposed to staying in a regular hotel.

Be sure that the resort is suitable for children: beaches should be supervised and play areas must be safe. Hotels with unprotected

The Lowly Roti

One food intrepid travelers will encounter in the Virgins is the *roti*. As anyone who has visited India knows quite well, the *roti* is a pan-fried bread, a form of *chapati*, which was introduced to the West Indies by East Asians, the New World nomenclature for Indians from India. It is the most popular in Trinidad, but you can find it at select shops virtually everywhere. It is something like the American version of the Mexican burrito—a large round bread folded around a center filling. In this case, the filling is generally a spicy curry and might contain seafood, fowl, beef, or just vegetables. Both prawn and vegetable *rotis* are particularly recommended. Ask for an accompanying hot sauce if available. ∎

balconies, busy streets or parking lots, or staircases should be avoided. A suitable resort should have special programs for your youngsters as well as babysitting.

Be sure to budget properly; this involves reading the fine print and calculating what everything will cost you—right down to the taxes and surcharges. It will be an advantage if there are inexpensive restaurants or cooking facilities on the premises.

Ask your children what *they* want and consult with friends and/or relatives with similar tastes. Be sure to allow a couple of months to plan; call up the 800 numbers, check websites, and request brochures.

FOOD: You will find high prices and a dearth of local cuisine, which has been largely supplanted by hamburgers, hotdogs, and Kentucky Fried Chicken. Most restaurant prices reflect the high cost of importing food. Local establishments serve meals which are moderate in price but not inexpensive. There are some food trucks which offer value, and $1 canned beer abounds.

Food A to Z

bush teas Herbal teas

cassava Root used in soup and meat dishes. Sometimes made into a flatbread.

conch Caribbean abalone, conch is fired into fritters, made into cold salad, or stewed. It is beaten before cooking in order to tenderize it.

dasheen Also called *tannia*, this tuber has a rough brown skin resembling tree bark. It is generally cooked in soups or as a side dish.

fungi A light, steamed cornmeal dumpling mixed with chopped okra: the Caribbean mashed potato.

johnny cakes Unleavened fried bread originally known as journey cakes.

kallaloo (callaloo) A stew made with local greens, okra, boned fish, diced pork, and hot pepper.

maubi A drink made from tree bark, herbs and a pinch of yeast.

patés Pastries stuffed with spiced beef or saltfish. A local snack.

plantain A larger, starchier version of the banana. Generally fried or baked.

saltfish A staple in earlier times, this dried fish is generally cod. It is soaked before cooking in order to reduce its salt content.

souse Pig's head, feet and tail stew with lime juice.

sweet potato Pink or reddish-skinned. Its creamy flesh is served as a side dish.

yams White or yellow-fleshed. Different than the sweet potato. Served baked, mashed, or boiled as a side dish.

PRACTICALITIES

0 Explore the Virgin Islands

PRACTICALITIES

Travel Tips: Single-Parent Families

✦ Involve your children in your research and decisions. Talk to them about what you are planning to do.

✦ Try to spend a third of the time on a trip doing things you like, a third on activities you and your child or children like and, a third doing things you both enjoy.

✦ Plan on visiting places that each child is interested in. A school is always a good choice.

✦ Plan your trip in detail in writing. Save a copy afterwards for future reference.

✦ Record any driving or travel directions. Have a child read them to you while driving.

✦ Make a packing list and give a copy to adolescents so they can be in charge of their preparations.

✦ Nutritious snacks and water come in handy whether on a plane or a bus.

✦ Have your children assist with baggage and other tasks such as map reading.

✦ Be sure to thank your children for their help.
— Brenda Elwell, author of *The Single Parent Travel Handbook*.

LOCAL FOOD: Native cuisine vaguely resembles that of Louisiana, with peppers, eggplant, tomatoes, and okra numbering among the standard ingredients.

Local foods that you should definitely try include **fungi** (a light, steamed cornmeal dumpling mixed with chopped okra), **kallaloo** (a stew made with local greens, okra, boned fish, diced pork, and hot pepper), **maubi** (a drink made from tree bark, herbs and a pinch of yeast), **souse** (pig's head, feet., and tail stew with lime juice), **johnny cakes** (unleavened fried bread originally known as journey cakes), **conch salad** (cold salad mixed with pieces of the mollusk) and **patés** (pastries stuffed with spiced beef or saltfish).

Traditional **bush teas** are made from sasparilla flowers and leaves (for head and

Snorkeling Tips

𝕺 You can snorkel and swim for longer periods with confidence if you wear a tee-shirt while in the water.

𝕺 Be sure to make sure that your mask fits before snorkeling. Put the mask on your face, suck your breath in, and inhale through your nose. While you continue to inhale, the mask should stay on you. Try another shape if this does not work.

𝕺 Moustaches, a strand of hair, or suntan lotion may spoil your fit. Moustache wearers should use a bit of vaseline or lip balm to improve the seal.

𝕺 The strap is to prevent the mask from falling off, not to tighten the seal; it should be set up high for comfort.

𝕺 Before submerging you should spit into your mask, coat the lens with your finger, and then rinse; this should have an anti fogging effect. Avoid exhaling through your nose: this may cause fog as well as release moisture.

𝕺 Snorkel only on the outer side of the reef on on low-wind or calm days, bring your own equipment or at least a mask you feel comfortable with (especially if you require a prescription mask).

𝕺 If you're using a kayak, it's a good idea to tie a line to it and carry it around when snorkeling.

chest colds), papaya seeds (for diabetes), tan-tan leaves (for colds), marsh mallow leaves (for prickly heat), and thibbet leaves. The street vendors on St. Thomas sell largely junk food; the ones in Christiansted, St. Croix sell a mixture of junk and nutritious food. Some also sell local food.

There are a few **bakeries** in the main towns where you can buy bread and wonderful local pastries.

A good list of restaurants (in both the USVI and BVI) is found in the "Island Delights" section of *The Daily News.*
http://www.virginislandsdailynews.com

FOOD SHOPPING: If you want to eat well here, you'd better plan on parting with a lot of green. Most food in the supermarkets runs 75% or higher than Stateside on the average, so it's better to bring what you can — especially if you plan to camp on St. John or self-cater.

TIPS FOR VEGETARIANS: Most restaurants will cater to your preferences, and salads are ubiquitous, so you should have no real problems eating, even if you are a vegan. Things like nuts and other specialty items are expensive or unavailable so you might want bring a supply. Restaurants serving vegetarian

food as well as health food stores are listed in the text. If you plan to be dining a lot at your hotel, ask them before booking.

ALCOHOL: Most major brands of U.S and imported beer are available here; comparable prices prevail. **Virgin Islands rum** (notably Cruzan Rum) is quite cheap — at $4 a liter. In 2000, *Caribbean Travel and Life* readers voted it their second favorite rum in the entire Caribbean! Another Cruzan product is Buba Touee, a liquor made of rum, lime, and spices.

DINING OUT: Credit cards are accepted at gourmet restaurants. Cheaper deals are found in the towns. Reservations are recommended at the better restaurants.

Expect to pay at least $10 for a meal at a local restaurant. Entrées at better restaurants run from $20 up, so count on $120 or more for two with wine for a four-course dinner at the better restaurants.

SPORTS: Swimming, snorkeling, scuba, and boating are tops here. The US Virgin Islands is famous for its beautiful beaches, and all are public by law whether built on them or not. All of the better-known beaches rent water sports equipment, have locker and shower facilities, and serve food. The water is warm for diving and visibility is good.

Deep-sea fishing is excellent for blue marlin as well as for dolphin, sailfish, tuna, wahoo, skipjack, and kingfish. The islands

PATE JOHNNY CAKE BUSH TEA

Local food is the thing to try. This sign is from Frederiksted, St. Croix.

As with nearly everything in life, some of the best things may be found where you are. Hovering over a small area while snorkeling may reveal a cornucopia of delights, rather like having your own private undersea aquarium. Shallow water is ideally suited to this. Take care not to touch but to watch intently. The rewards are there.

PRACTICALITIES

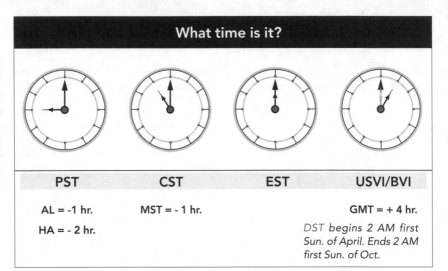

What time is it?

PST	CST	EST	USVI/BVI
AL = -1 hr.	MST = - 1 hr.		GMT = + 4 hr.
HA = - 2 hr.			*DST begins 2 AM first Sun. of April. Ends 2 AM first Sun. of Oct.*

are legendary for boaters because of their sheltered anchorages, fantastic weather, and incomparable beauty.

The best spot for **surfers** is Hull Bay on the N coast of St. Thomas, where the waves are most vicious during the winter months.

Windsurfing is also good, with St. Croix being the place for beginners. Specifics on all of the above-from beaches to windsurfing-are detailed under the individual islands in the travel section.

Scuba and snorkeling are outstanding. The best way to appreciate these is to combine a trip to the USVI with one to the BVI. St. Croix's most famous snorkeling spot is Buck Island, a national monument. It has numerous dive sites as do the other two Virgins. St. John is the best island for snorkeling. Diving and snorkeling spots for all the islands are detailed under their individual introductory chapters.

Kayaking expeditions (along with day trips) are offered St. John's

Kayaking expeditions (along with day trips) are offered St. John's **Arawak Expeditions** (☎ 693-8312; 800-238-8687; Box 853, Cruz

Bay). They run introductory half-day trips ($50) as well as full-day trips ($90) which visit remote parts of St. John and head over to surrounding islands. Accommodation is camping. Five-day kayaking and camping trips are also available as is an "adventure week" trip. An adventurous five-day trip explores the BVI with stops at Peter Island and Norman Island before crossing the Sir Francis Drake Channel to the West End of Tortola and heading N to Jost Van Dyke before returning to St. John. There is also a five-day expedition to Anegada (around two per year; generally in April) cost around $1200 pp.

http://www.arawakexp.com
info@arawakexp.com

 If you are on a cruise, don't believe everything your cruise director tells you. Cruise ships have alliances with shops and tours, and these can be quite lucrative for all concerned. If they tell you that you should shop only at "approved shops," on Main Street, Charlotte Amalie, don't believe them!

Shopping Tips

● *Know your prices.* Do research on the local prices for the goods you wish to buy.

● *Buy what you need.* Don't feel compelled to buy because you are here.

● *Know the differences.* Gold that is 24 karats in the US and Canada is marked 999 in items of European manufacture; 18 k gold is 750, and 14 k gold is 585.

● *Shipping is available.* But make sure you understand the liability coverage and costs involved.

● *Remember* that rum is cheaper in St. Croix than anywhere else in the US and British Virgin Islands.

Deep Sea Fishing

Fish	Location	Season
Blue marlin	*100 fathom edge*	
All year; July-Oct. best.		
White marlin	100 fathom edge	
All year. Spring		
Sailfish	*Offshore* Oct. to April;	
Dec. and Feb. best.		
Wahoo	*Offshore* All year. Sept.	
to May.		
Allison tuna	*Offshore*	All year.
Dolphin (fish)	*Offshore*	
Spring, Fall, and Winter; Spring is best		
Kingfish	*Reef-banks*	
All year; Spring is best.		
Tarpon	*Inshore*	
All year; Spring is best.		

Kayaking tours are also offered on St. Thomas and St. John, and many hotels and companies offer rentals. All are listed in the specific chapters concerned.

MOUNTAIN BIKING: Bike Water Island (☎ 714-2186) offers three-hr. tours of Water Island (off of St. Thomas) for $60 pp including transport, guide, and water.
Arawak Expeditions (☎ 693-8312; 800-238-8687; Box 853, Cruz Bay) offers mountain biking on St. Thomas.

FISHING: The Virgin Islands have a number of contests which attract fisherfolk from all over the world.
The **USVI Open/Atlantic Blue Marlin Tournament** (☎ 888-234-7484, 340-775-9500), generally held in mid-Aug., is held on St. Thomas.
http://www.usvi.net/bsa

The **Virgin Island Game Fishing Club** (☎ 775-9144) runs the **June Moon** Big Marlin Fishing Tournament and the **July Open**. The June Moon hunts marlin residing in the North Drop, 20 mi. off of St. Thomas. Entering its fourth decade, the July Open is a world-renowned event.
The annual **Bastille Day Kingfish Tournament** is held by the Northside Fishing Club (☎ 774-6827) on St. Thomas.
St. Croix's **Golden Hook Fishing Club** (☎ 719-9208) runs the Golden Hook Challenge in August and the Wahoo Tournament in November.

ADVENTURE TOURS: On the Loose (☎ 800-688-1481) offers an environmental and cultural tour in which you stay at Maho Bay Camp and mix with the locals.
http://www.otloose.com

URL http://www.usvi.net/gamefishing
Gamefishing

⊂ The United States Virgin Islands on the Internet ⊃

The numbers of websites devoted to the United States Virgin Islands have grown in recent years. Many are listed in this book. Others can be found through search engines. Here is a list of just some of the more interesting and useful ones.

General

http://www.exploreavirgin.com Information, photo essay, message boards, mailing list

http://www.usvitourism.vi Official government tourism site. Streaming videos.

http://www.usvi.net Virgin Islands information

http://www.gov.vi The Virgin Islands government

http://www.vigov.net/vigov Political Links

http://www.vibj.com *The Virgin Islands Business Journal*

http://www.vinow.com Excellent Virgin Islands website (news, podcast, info)

http://www.wtjx.org Channel 12

http://www.usvi-on-line.com Information including travel forums

http://www.usvi.edu University of the Virgin Islands

http://www.onepaper.com/virginvoices *Virgin Voices* newspaper

http://www.entreevi.com Restaurant guide

St. Thomas

http://www.virginislandsdailynews.com *USVI Daily News*

http://www.stthomassource.com *St. Thomas Source*

http://www.innparadise.com St. Thomas and St. John hotels

St. John

http://www.stjohntradewindsnews.com St. John's newspaper

http://www.stjohnsource.com *St. John Source* (online newspaper)

http://www.stjohnusvi.com Good general website

http://www.nps.gov/viis Virgin Islands National Park

http://www.stjohnlinks.com St. John links

St. Croix

http://www.gotostcroix.com

http://www.stcroixsource.com *St. Croix Source (online newspaper)*

http://www.visitstcroix.com *St. Croix guide*

http://www.ecani.com Photo tour of St. Croix

http://www.visitstcroix.com Comprehensive coverage of St. Croix

Web Surfing Tips

➥ Always search for a site twice if it is not found the first time. (Hit the "reload button.")

➥ If a site is down, try a variation of the hotel or organization's name: It may have gotten its own domain.

➥ Visit **www.savethemanatee.com** or **explorevirgin.com** for updates and info.

➥ When visiting Virgin Islands websites, check for links to other useful sites.

SHOPPING: Shops are open Mon. through Sat. from 9 AM–5 PM; they close for official holidays. Hotel shops close at 9 PM. These islands still maintain the minimal import duty of 7%, which has made them into a "duty-free shopper's paradise." Charlotte Amalie and Christiansted are the two main shopping centers. High overhead and avarice have made the Virgins less competitive with San Juan and even the mainland, but watches, gold, crystal, and liquor are still relatively good values. There are also more unique souvenirs including cheap Cruzan rum and local artwork and crafts.

AMERICAN CUSTOMS: Returning American citizens, under existing customs regulations, can lug back with them up to $1,200 worth of duty-free goods. Items sent by post may be included in this tally, thus allowing shoppers to ship or have shipped goods like glass and china. Over that amount, purchases are dutied at a flat 5% on the next $1,000. Above $2,200, duty applied will vary. Joint declarations are permissible for members of a family traveling together. Thus, a couple traveling with two children will be allowed up to $4,800 in duty free goods. Undeclared gifts (one per day of up to $100 in value) may be sent to as many friends and relatives as you like. Obtain a Customs Form 225 if you've placed a special order. One gallon (or five fifths; six if the sixth is a local product) of liquor may be brought back as well as five cartons of cigarettes and 100 cigars. Pre-1881 antiques, unset gems, and local handicrafts are also duty free. Plants in soil may not be brought to the mainland but most fruits can. For any questions contact the Customs Bureau (☎ 774-2510) or the USDA (☎ 776- 2787).

URL WIVI (96.1 FM) programs new wave, country music, Grateful Dead, reggae, heavy metal, and classical.
http://www.pirateradiovi.com

WSTA (1130 AM),St. Thomas, offers daily news and carnival music.
A list of stations:
http://tinyurl.com/yp595k

Metric Conversion Chart
1 inch = 2.54 centimeters
1 foot = .3048 meters
1 mile= 1.6093 km
1 km = .6214 miles
1 acre = .4047 hectares (ha)
1 sq. km = 100 ha
1 sq. mi. = 2.59 sq. km
1 ounce = 28.35 grams
1 pound = .4536 kilograms
1 quart = .94635 liters
1 US gallon = 3.7854 liters
1 imperial gallon = 4.5459 liters

PRACTICALITIES

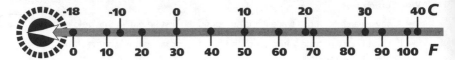

CANADIAN CUSTOMS: Canadian citizens may make an oral declaration four times per year to claim C$100 worth of exemptions. These may include 200 cigarettes and 40 fl. oz. of alcohol. In order to claim the exemption, Canadians must have been out of the country for at least 48 hours. A Canadian who's been away for at least seven days may make a written declaration once a year and claim C$300 worth of exemptions. After a trip of 48 hours or longer, Canadians receive a special duty rate of 20% on the value of goods up to C$300 in excess of the C$100 or C$300 exemption they claim. This excess cannot be applied to liquor or cigarettes. Goods claimed under the C$300 exemption may follow but merchandise claimed under all other exemptions must be accompanied.

GERMAN CUSTOMS: Residents may bring back 200 cigarettes, 50 cigars, 100 cigarillos, or 250 grams of tobacco; two liters of alcoholic beverages not exceeding 44 proof or one liter of 44 proof-plus alcohol; and two liters of wine; and up to DM300 of other items.

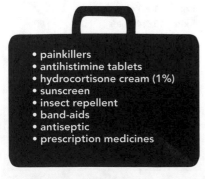

- painkillers
- antihistimine tablets
- hydrocortisone cream (1%)
- sunscreen
- insect repellent
- band-aids
- antiseptic
- prescription medicines

MONEY AND MEASUREMENTS: Monetary unit is the US dollar; measurements are the same as those used in the States. The islands operate on Atlantic Standard Time.

BROADCASTING AND MEDIA: Local TV, largely consisting of recycled pap from the States, is available for those addicts who positively must watch. Cable (with HBO, MTV, and CNN) is generally available at hotels.

The main newspaper on St. Thomas is **The Daily News**, formerly owned by billionaire and controversial local businessman Jeffrey Prosser. Its off-island coverage is poor. Headlines in the *Daily News* have read "Navarrete soars to top in spelling bee." The paper won the 1995 Pulitzer Prize for its investigative reports on links between the crime rate and corruption in the criminal justice system, but that was before Prosser's takeover. Many reporters and editors have left after his takeover, but the paper bankruptcy forced the paper's sale to PA's Times-Shamrock inn May 2008.
http://www.dailynews.vi

St. John has the monthly **Tradewinds**, and several competitors, while St. Croix has the **Avis** which is an echo of *The Daily News*.

The **San Juan Star** is available on St. Thomas and St. Croix. Mainland newspapers are available but exorbitant. There

Don't wait for people to say "good morning" to you. Say it to them, even if they are not looking at you. It will go a long way for you.

PRACTICALITIES

are innumerable free publications of various kinds. A particularly nice on is the new biannual ArtFusion Magazine.
http://www.artfusionmagazine.com

VISAS: All visitors from abroad (except US citizens and Canadians) require a US visa. It's best to obtain a multiple-entry visa and, if possible, do so in your own country, because US embassies and consulates tend to be persnickety about issuing visas to citizens of countries other than the one they're stationed in.

HEALTH: Good but expensive medical care is available. But if you have a serious illness, you should fly to Puerto Rico or the mainland. Make sure you have adequate health insurance. Hospitals and clinics are located in or near the island's main towns (see individual sections for listings).

CONDUCT: Many people do not appreciate having their pictures taken without their permission. Racial tension and animosity (largely found on St. Thomas) do exist, so do nothing to make the situation worse. Going shirtless, wearing only a swimsuit, or wearing too short shorts is illegal on streets.

Traditional Virgin Islands culture is polite to the extreme, with an emphasis on saving face: to be accused of being "rude" is worse than being called "lazy" or "shiftless," though this has begun to change dramatically in recent years.

Inquiries are usually prefaced by a "Good Morning," "Good Afternoon," or "Good Night." These simple courtesies go a long way. Don't rush an answer either. Locals will answer you at their own pace.

On St. Croix remember to respect private property while visiting ruins; be sure to ask permission first. All beaches in the USVI are public by law from the vegetation line down to the water. Expect to be charged ($1–3), however, if you use private facilities like lounge chairs or changing rooms. And remember that you are sharing the beach. Don't litter or make excessive noise.

PERSONAL SAFETY: Saint Thomas and St. Croix have very high crime rates which have been exacerbated by the drug (chiefly crack) problem. Getting mugged on these islands (St. Thomas in particular) is a very real possibility, so exercise caution while walking around the streets at night. It's better to go with someone, especially if you are a woman. Too many cruise ship passengers have caused too much resentment by flashing too much money around. Try to avoid this and keep valuables safely locked up—or, better yet, leave them at home.

Facts About Jet Skis

▼Jet skis account for 40% of all boating injuries.

▼Jet skis traverse shallow and sensitive inshore waters, areas where ordinary water craft can not go.

▼Jet skis have caused injury and/or death to manatees, seal pups, nesting loons and other species.

▼Jet skis discharge as much as a third of their raw gas and oil mixture into the water. Each year jet skis spill the equivalent of four Exxon *Valdez* tankers full of raw petrochemicals into US waters. A two-hour ride may emit enough to cover an eight acre pond. The oil byproducts also damage the environment.

▼Jet skis have been banned from Canada to the Florida Keys. They are banned in the VI National Park.
http://www.bluewaternetwork.org

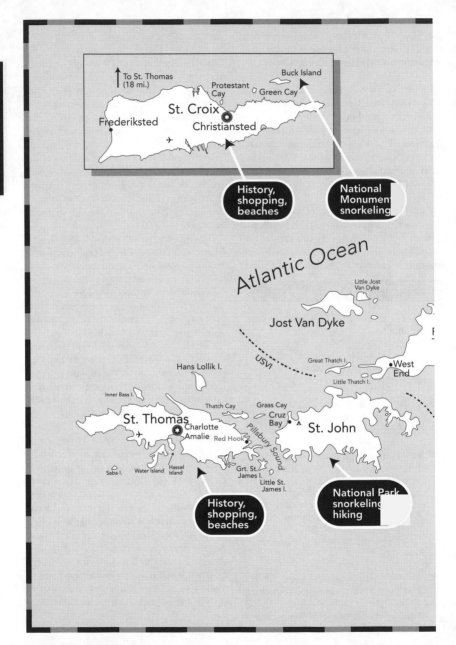

To St. Thomas (18 mi.)

Buck Island

Protestant Cay

Green Cay

St. Croix

Frederiksted

Christiansted

History, shopping, beaches

National Monument snorkeling

Atlantic Ocean

Little Jost Van Dyke

Jost Van Dyke

Great Thatch I.

West End

USVI

Little Thatch I.

Hans Lollik I.

Inner Bass I.

Thatch Cay

Grass Cay

Cruz Bay

St. Thomas

Charlotte Amalie

Red Hook

Pillsbury Sound

St. John

Saba I.

Water Island

Hassel Island

Grt. St. James I.

Little St. James I.

History, shopping, beaches

National Park snorkeling hiking

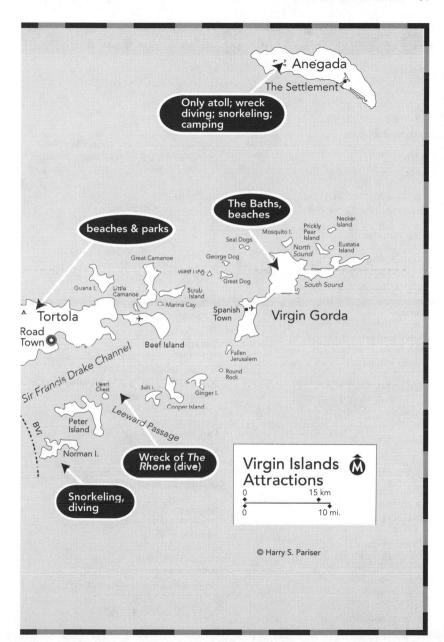

Anegada

The Settlement

Only atoll; wreck diving; snorkeling; camping

The Baths, beaches

beaches & parks

Necker Island

Mosquito I.
Prickly Pear Island

Seal Dogs

North Sound

Eustatia Island

Great Camanoe

George Dog

West Dog

Great Dog

South Sound

Guana I.
Little Camanoe

Scrub Island

Marina Cay

Spanish Town

Virgin Gorda

Tortola

Road Town

Beef Island

Fallen Jerusalem

Round Rock

Sir Francis Drake Channel

Pearl Chest

Salt I.

Ginger I.

Cooper Island

Leeward Passage

BVI

Peter Island

Norman I.

Wreck of *The Rhone* (dive)

Virgin Islands Attractions

0   15 km
0   10 mi.

Snorkeling, diving

© Harry S. Pariser

USVI Tourism Offices

Atlanta
225 Peachtree St., N.E., Suite 760
Atlanta GA 30303
☎ 404-688-0906
Fax 404-525-1102
usviatl@aol.com

Chicago
500 N. Michigan Ave., Suite 2030
Chicago IL 60611
☎ 312-670-8784, Fax 312-461-8788
usvichgo@earthlink.net

Los Angeles
3460 Wilshire Blvd., Suite 412
Los Angeles CA 90010
☎ 213-739-0138, Fax 213-739-2005
usvi_la@msn.com

Miami
2655 Le Jeune Rd., Suite 907
Coral Gables FL 33134
Fax 305-442-7200, Fax 305-445-9044
usvimia@aol.com

New York
One Penn Plaza, Suite 3525
New York, NY 10119
☎ 212-502-5300, Fax 212-465-2324
usviny@aol.com

Washington DC
444 North Capitol St. N.W, Suite 305
Washington DC 20001
☎ 202-624-3590, Fax 202-624-3594
usvidc@sso.org

Puerto Rico
60 Washington St.
Ste. 1102, San Juan
Puerto Rico 00907
☎ 787-722-8023
Fax 340-722-8023
ncumpiano@usa.net

St. Croix
PO Box 4538, Christiansted, St. Croix
US Virgin Islands 00822
☎ 340-773-6449
Fax 340-778-9259

Custom House Bldg., Strand St.,
Frederiksted, US Virgin Islands 00840
☎ 340-773-0495

St. John
PO Box 200, Cruz Bay, St. John
US Virgin Islands 00830
☎ 340-776-6450

St. Thomas
PO Box 6400,
Charlotte Amalie
US Virgin Islands 00804
☎ 340-774-8784
Fax 340-774-4390

Canada
2810 Matheson Blvd. East, Suite 200
Fax Mississauga, Ontario L4W 4X7
☎ 416-622-7600, Fax 416-236-0439
smelnyk@travmarkgroup.com

Denmark
Park Allé 5, DK-8000, Arhus C.,
Denmark
☎ 86-181933
Fax 86-181934
usvi@danskvestindiskturist.dk

England
Power Road Studios
114 Power Road
Chiswick, W4 5PY, London
☎ 020-8994-0978
Fax 020-8994-0962
domn@destination-marketing.co.uk

In the US: **1-800-372-8784**

It isn't that locals are dishonest or try to help criminals. There are a lot of convenient alleyways for thieves to run to; police are insufficient in number, and they have a very real fear of recrimination. In fact, it's not unlikely that the thief has a relative on the police force. It would be advisable, if you're going out for dinner on the island of St. Thomas, to travel by cab and make an appointment for the driver to pick you up afterwards. Avoid the waterfront between town and the St. Thomas marina—especially the area around the housing projects. The Savan area (W of Market Square and N of the Holiday Inn) is another area to avoid. Stay off of Back Street. after dark. If camping on St. John, don't leave valuables in your tent. Never, never leave anything in an unoccupied vehicle.

ENVIRONMENTAL CONDUCT: Dispose of plastics properly. Remember that six pack rings, plastic bags, and fishing lines can cause injury or prove fatal to sea turtles, fish, birds, and other marine life. Unable to regurgitate anything they swallow, turtles and other sea creatures may mistake plastic bags for jellyfish or choke on fishing lines. Birds may starve to death after becoming entangled in lines, nets, and plastic rings. And all of these objects take hundreds of years to decompose and can do a lot of damage in the interim.

If you should see someone capturing or harming a sea turtle or taking eggs contact the **Bureau of Environmental Enforcement** (☎ 774-3320, St. Thomas; ☎ 773-5774, St. Croix) or the **National Marine Fisheries Law Enforcement Division** (☎ 774-5226). All of these activities are illegal.

Remember that the parks and reserves were created to preserve the environment. Refrain from carrying off plants, rocks, animals, or other materials. Buying black coral jewelry also serves to support reef destruction and turtle shell items come from an endangered species. On St. John remember not to feed the donkeys or leave food within their reach.

UNDERSEA CONDUCT: Respect the natural environment. Take nothing and remember that corals are easily broken. Much damage has already been done to the reef through snorkelers either standing on coral or hanging onto outcroppings. Take care not to touch!

☺ Virgin Islands Dos and Don'ts ☹

- ▸ *Don't* condescend to locals. *Do* treat the local people with the same respect you would like to be treated. Allow them the courtesy of answering at their own pace.
- ▸ *Do* try local food and try to patronize local restaurants as well as gourmet bistros.
- ▸ *Don't* make promises you can't or don't intend to keep.
- ▸ *Don't* just stay lounging around your hotel. *Do* get around and explore, but don't over-extend yourself and try to do too much. There's always the next visit.
- ▸ *Do* try to conserve energy by switching off lights and a/c when you leave your hotel room. *Don't* dump your garbage at sea or litter in town.
- ▸ *Don't* remove or injure any coral, spear fish, remove tropical fish, or annoy turtles or touch their eggs. *Do* not feed fish. *Don't* wear jewelry while swimming or diving. *Don't* stand on anything other than sand. *Do* show respect for the underwater environment. *Don't* swim in rough surf.
- ▸ Most locals don't smoke, and it is considered rude to smoke around them.

PRACTICALITIES

Keep the Beach Turtle Friendly

Here is a short list of things you may do. In addition, hotel owners may prohibit the use of pointed-end drink stands and mimimize beachfront lighting.

 Leave native beach vegetation in place. Hawksbills hanker for beaches with green. Plants stave off erosion.

 Remove your garbage. Garbage will contaminate beach sand, and bacteria or fungus may infect sea turtle eggs. Garbage may also hinder hatchlings seeking to make their challenging waddle from egg to waves.

 Never, ever drive on a beach. Cars compact the sand which makes it harder for the sea turtles to dig out from or into sand. Vegetation is also destroyed.

 Make sure your beach chair is stacked in a pile, high and dry and as far from the edge of the beach as possible. Turtles, in order to safeguard their nests, lay eggs above the high water mark.

In order to control your movement under water, make sure that you are properly weighted prior to your dive. Swim calmly and fluidly through the water and avoid dragging your console and/or octopus (secondary breathing device) behind you.

While diving or snorkeling resist the temptation to touch fish. Many fish (such as the porcupine) secrete a mucous coating which protects them from bacterial infection. Touching them removes the coating and may result in infection and death for the fish. Also avoid feeding fish, which can disrupt the natural ecosystem. In short, look, listen, enjoy, but leave only bubbles.

BOATING CONDUCT: In addition to the behavior patterns detailed above, always exercise caution while anchoring a boat. The single most serious threat to the marine resources of the VI comes from cruise ship anchors. Improperly anchoring in seagrass beds can destroy wide swathes of the grass, which takes a long time to recover. If there's no buoy available, the best place to anchor is a sandy spot, where you will cause relatively little environmental impact. Tying your boat to mangroves can kill the trees, so you should do so only during a storm.

In order to help eliminate the unnecessary discharge of oil, maintain the engine and keep the bilge clean. If you notice oil in your bilge, use oil-absorbent pads to soak it up. Be careful not to overfill the boat when fueling.

Emulsions from petrochemical products stick to fishes' gills and suffocate them, and deposits in sediment impede the development of marine life. Detergents affect plankton and other organisms, which throws off the food chain balance.

When you approach seagrass beds, slow down because your propeller could strike a sea turtle. Avoid maneuvering your boat too close to coral reefs. Striking the reef can damage both your boat and the reef. Avoid stirring up sand in shallow coral areas because the sand can be deposited in the coral causing polyps to suffocate and die.

If your boat has a sewage holding tank, empty it only at properly equipped marinas. Avoid using harsh chemicals such as ammonia and bleach while cleaning your boat; they pollute the water and kill marine life. Use environmentally safe cleaning products whenever possible.

Boat owners should avoid paint containing lead, copper (which can make mollusks poisonous), mercury (highly toxic to fish and algae), or TBT. Finally, remember that a diver-down flag must be displayed while diving or snorkeling.

Virgin Islands Vocabulary	
Aright	Hi. Goodbye. Thank you. Yes.
A yu	everyone
Cheez-n -bread	exclamation, denotes surprise
Chook	to tick or prick. Also to fool
Chupse	sucking of teeth indicating disbelief or displeasure
Crucian	St. Croix native
Dem	plural of one, i.e "those"
Eh eh	exclamation indicating surprise or concern. "Well, me God" generally follows.
Fig	Banana
Gongolo	Millipede
Irie	All right. Happiness (Rastafarian expression)
Jammin	Dance
Jumbi	Ghost or spirit
Limin'	Kicking back
Maun'in	Good morning
Me son	Any man
Ol' Conch	A tough or stubborn person
Psst	Male expression directed towards any female
Shake ya ras	Hurry up
Soon come	Just a moment (i.e. sometime today)
Tanks	Thank you
Waya mean?	What are you talking about?
Wa' sup?	What's going on?

GETTING MARRIED: It is a simple matter to marry here. Simply pick up the relevant papers from any USVI Department of Tourism office, mail them around three weeks prior to your trip, and pick up a license from the Territorial Court.

WEDDINGS AND HONEYMOONS: Many resorts offer special packages. Specializing in weddings on all three islands, On St.

John, **Anne Marie Porter** (☎ 693-5153, 888-676-5701, cell 626-4658) performs nondenominational weddings and wedding vow renewals (price includes certificate and consultation). Ann Marie comes highly recommended, and she doesn't take commissions from hotels and car rental firms unlike many other "reverends." She has special services for gay couples, will gear a ceremony to meet your needs, and can also advise on locales. Anne Marie also offers a free vow renewal service on Trunk Bay Beach each Valentine's Day.
http://www.re-marryyourmate.com
http://www.stjohnweddings.com

Fantasia Weddings (☎ 777-6588, 800-326-8272) offers wedding planning services.
http://www.fantasiaweddings.com

Caribbean Style (☎ 715-1117, 800-593-1390) offers wedding planning.
http://www.cstyle.co.vi

Weddings the Island Way (☎ 777-6505, 777-6550, 800-582-4784) provide seven different packages including such services as live steel band music and a helicopter ride to an uninhabited isle. They have a number of plans available starting at $375.
http://www.weddingstheislandway.com

On St. Croix, **Seaside Weddings** (☎ 773-9607) offers ceremonies from $495 up.
http://www.seasidewed.com
seasidewed@islands.vi

Daytrippin'
What to take on a day trip? Water, money, swim suit, towel, sunscreen, reading material, camera and film, snorkeling gear (if not provided), shoes if hiking), snack food.

WHAT TO TAKE: Bring as little as possible, i.e., bring what you need. It's easy just to wash clothes in the sink and thus save lugging around a week's laundry. Remember, simple is best. Set your priorities according to your needs. If you're planning to do a lot of hiking, for example, hiking boots are a good idea. Otherwise, they're an encumbrance and tennis shoes will suffice. With a light pack or bag, you can breeze through from one hotel to another easily. Confining yourself to carry-on luggage also saves waiting at the airport. See the chart for suggestions and eliminate unnecessary items.

PHOTOGRAPHY: Film isn't particularly cheap here so you might want to bring your own. Bring enough memory cards if you are shooting digital. Avoid photographs between 10 and 2 when there are harsh shadows. Photograph landscapes while keeping the sun to your rear. Set your camera a stop or a stop and a half down when photographing beaches in order to prevent overexposure from glare. A sunshade is a useful addition. Keep your camera and film out of the heat. Avoid exposure to salt water at all costs. Replace your batteries before a trip or bring a spare set. Finally, remember not to expose your fast speed exposed film to the X-ray machines at the airport. Hand carry them through. If working with digital photography, be sure to bring sufficient flash cards.

UNDERWATER PHOTOGRAPHY: The Fuji Waterproof and the Kodak Weekender are the low end way to go for snorkelers; scuba diving shutterbugs will need to move up to an Ikelite or use Ikelite's Aquashot, a housing which supplies a flash (mandatory for shots deeper than 20–30 ft.). The Aquashot will go down as far as 125 ft. If possible, try to get close (within four ft.) and shoot your subject from the side or above. Avoid stirring up sediment, and, by all means, avoid touching or otherwise damaging your subject.

Services and Information

Mail service is not the most reliable in the world. In fact, 6,000 advertising circulars, magazines, and packages arrived in Puerto Rico on Nov. 5, 1985 from Jacksonville, Florida via the Commonwealth's shipping line. Trailer Marine Transport, which was supposed to transport them to St. Thomas, forgot completely about them for the next 2.5 years. They were finally delivered in March of 1988! Things are improving however. *Be sure to label letters "VI" and not "USVI."*

Zip codes for *St. Thomas* are: 00802 (Charlotte Amalie street addresses), 00801 (Sugar Estate, Boxes 7001-12440), 00803 (Veteran's Drive, Boxes 1701-5686), and Emancipation Garden Station (00804, Boxes 0001-1694, 6001-6880). *For St. John*: Boxes 0001-8310 are 00831, and Cruz Bay street addresses use 00830. *For St. Croix:* 00821 (Christiansted, Boxes 0001-1786), 00822 (Downtown Station, Christiansted, Boxes 2501-4622), 00823 (Sunny Isle, Christiansted, Boxes 4951-8710), 00824 (Gallows Bay Station, Christiansted, Boxes 24001-16610), 00851 (Kingshill, Boxes 0001-3032), 00841 (Frederiksted, Boxes 0001-3569), 00820 (Christiansted street addresses), 00810 (Frederiksted street addresses), and 00851 (Kingshill street addresses).

PHONE SERVICE: Innovative, the local phone company, is notorious for its bad service and high basic service charges (around $26/month). It costs 35 cents to call any of the three islands via pay phone for five minutes; no warning will sound so keep a check on your watch if you don't want to be cut off in mid-sentence. Amazingly, you have to pay 25 cents to dial an 800 number! A rise in the cell phone population has lead to a decrease in pay phones that function. **https://www.innovativetelephone.com**

Area code for the islands-is *340*. *Puerto Rico* is *787* and *939* and the *BVI* is 284.

(As bad as Innovative is, WAPA — the Water and Power Authority — is worse. Their extortionate charges are a major reason hotels are so expensive here.)

AT&T Direct operates throughout the USVI and the BVI. **AT&T Calling Centers** are found at the Buccaneer Mall (across from Havensight on St. Thomas) and at Sion Hill Shopping Center on St. Croix.

Cell phones (Cingular, Sprint) work from most places if you have roaming.

The phone book is searchable online: **http://www.viphonebook.com**

For information about local events, be sure to pick up current copies of *St. Thomas This Week* and its St. Croix equivalent. There are a seemingly unlimited number of other publications, most of which are chock to the brim with advertisements.

INTERNET: There are quite a number of sites relating to the USVI on the internet. (See chart for partial list). Internet cafes

PRACTICALITIES

Clothing
socks and shoes
underwear
sandals, thongs, windsurfing sandals
T-shirts, shirts (or blouses)
skirts/pants, shorts
swimsuit
hat
light-jacket/sweater

Toiletries-
soap
shampoo
towel, washcloth
toothpaste/toothbrush
comb/brush
prescription-medicines
chapstick/other essential toiletries
insect-repellent
suntan-lotion/sunscreen
shaving-kit

toilet paper
nail clippers
hand lotion
small mirror
glasses/contact lenses/sunglasses

notes

are found in the main towns, and access is available through some hotels. The cheapest access is found at the local libraries.

ORGANIZATIONS: If you've been impressed with the natural beauty of places like Salt River and Jacks Bay on St. Croix and wish to keep them that way, you may want to contribute to the **St. Croix Environmental Association,** Box 3839, Christiansted, St. Croix, USVI 00822. They sponsor some great hikes on St. Croix. Student membership is $10, individual $25, and family $40.
http://www.seastx.org
sea@viaccess.net

Membership ($15 individual, $25 family) in the **Friends of National Park** (Box 11, St. John 00831) offers you a chance to directly participate in the preservation of this fantastic area. They also publish The *Virgin Islands National Park News*, a free bi-annual tabloid which offers an entertaining pastiche of information; it's issued by the Friends of the National Park. Other valuable work includes soliciting volunteers and working on the boat mooring system. *Their tours are great!*
http://www.friendsvinp.org

The Nature Conservancy's program in the USVI aims to protect high quality lands and waters as well as its biodiversity and to establish cooperative conservation, stewardship and science programs with federal and territorial governments. For more information and to contribute ($25 for membership) contact Carol Harris Mayes, Program Director, The Nature Conservancy, 14B Norre Gade, Upstairs, Charlotte Amalie USVI 00802.
The **Community Foundation of the Virgin Islands** (☎ 774-6031) operates a number of programs, scholarships, and awards.
http://www.fdncenter.org/
  grantmaker/cfvi
dbrowncfvi@att.global.net

To become a tax deductible member of the **St. George Village Botanical Garden of St. Croix** (☎ 772-3872) send $25 to Box 3011, Kingshill, St. Croix 00851-3011.

VOLUNTEERING: Earthwatch (☎ 617-926-8200) sends paying volunteers out to assist researchers working in the field. Costs are tax deductible, except for airfare. Write 680 Mt. Auburn St., Box 430-P, Watertown MA 02272 or c all 1-800-693-0188.
http://www.earthwatch.org

Caribbean Volunteer Expeditions (☎ 607-962-7846; Box 388, Corning, NY 14830) offers occasional volunteer expeditions to the Virgin Islands. Past trips havefocused on history and archaeology. Trips are from one to two weeks in duration and cost from around $300–$800 pw not including airfare.
http://www.cvexp.org
ahershcve@aol.com

Maho Bay Resort (☎ 800-392-9004) offers work exchange programs during the summer months.
http://www.maho.org

ACTIVISM: Whether you're a visitor or a resident, it is important to make known your concerns on social or environmental issues. Be sure to state your opinion clearly, include examples and key information, and include a return address. Write Dr. Charles Turnbull, Governor, Government House, St. Thomas 00801; The Honorable Donna Christiansen, US Rep. to Congress, US Representative to Congress, US House of Representatives, Washington, DC 20515. Letters to The Legislature should be sent to The Honorable Almando Liburd, VI Legislature Building, St. Thomas 00801.

St. Thomas

Most populous and popular of all the United States Virgin Islands, St. Thomas measures three by 13 miles. A self-styled "American Paradise," it hosts one million tourists a year; only 51,181 souls are permanent residents.

Flanked by the Atlantic to the N and the Caribbean to the S, the land is hilly and rugged. Hills, running up to 1,500 ft., give incredible views.

Charlotte Amalie (pronounced Ah-MAHL-ya) is the the Virgin Island's commercial and political center. The town is very much a cruise ship town, and they dominate its landscape and small downtown area. For most visitors it is a small town, but Crucians find it crowded and urbanized, while St. Johnians regard a trip to St. Thomas as a 'trip to the city.' The town still has its historical heritage remarkably intact, and you may visit some of its old homes (and even stay in them!). It's hard not to fall in love with the stone staircases, ("stair steps") and, among the seemingly syndicated morass of shops, some gems are well worth visiting. There are plenty of good restaurants in all price ranges in town, and

many of them serve local food. A number of good coffee houses offer internet access, but the nightlife is mainly at the island's resorts.

Although commercialized, the island still retains substantial charm. There are a number of popular attractions, two of the most popular of which are Coral World Ocean Park and Magens Bay. And there are many knockout views from all over the island. You can go kayaking, diving, fishing, windsurfing, snorkeling and find spas, tennis courts, golf courts, and, last but not least, child care. If at times St. Thomas may seem overbearing, just remember that, throughout its history, St. Thomas has always been a place where money and property have come before human beings.

TOPOGRAPHY: This 32-sq-mi. island has been largely denuded; no primary forest remains. The visitor will find steep roads and, in Charlotte Amalie, innumerable staircases or "step streets."

HISTORY: Arriving in 1666, the first Danish settlers found an abandoned island. To guard the harbor, Fort Christian was constructed in 1674. First known as "Tap Hus," the town was renamed Amalienborg (later Charlotte Amalie) after the Danish queen in 1691. In 1755, after the dissolution of the Danish West India Company and purchase by the Danish government, the capital was transferred to Christiansted, St. Croix. A series of fires between 1804 and 1832 destroyed two-thirds of the town before a strict building code was enacted.

In 1837, a Lutheran Church census discovered at least 140 nationalities on St. Thomas. Most residents spoke two or more languages; church services were given in three languages and newspapers were print-

ST. THOMAS

ed in several. During this period, Charlotte Amalie was the third largest city in the Danish realm. After the emancipation of slaves in 1848, the island was transformed from an agricultural community into a supply depot for blockade runners and privateers from the South, as well as for the US men of war that chased them. Capital status was restored to Charlotte Amalie in 1871.

During the last quarter of the 19th C, St. Thomas became a coaling depot for European steamship companies. When the US Navy took possession of the island in 1917, they dredged a large channel between St. Thomas and neighboring Hassel I. to allow them an alternate escape route in case of attack.

Since the end of WW II, tourism has become the chief "industry" of St. Thomas.

Island-Wide Practicalities

Arrival and Transport

ARRIVING BY AIR: From San Juan a beautiful flight takes you past Icacos, flying directly over Culebra with Vieques in the background. Houses on St. Thomas look like white dots on a patch of green moss. The aircraft main terminal, to the W of Charlotte Amalie has been attractively remodeled.

From the airport to town, a van will cost you $7, or $6 pp if you share, plus $2 per bag. [Larger bags (30"x20") may be charged up to $4.] For rates to destinations other than Charlotte Amalie see the chart later in this chapter. *Don't let them overcharge you!*

It is not practical to take a bus because the schedule has been cut way back and the bus does not come into the terminal. If you have strong legs and little luggage, however, you may go out to the main road and wait for the VITRAN (around $1; exact change) or for a "dollar taxi" or "safari" (a pickup truck with seats and a roof). Be sure to ask

if it is a "dollar bus." *Otherwise, they may try to charge you the taxi rate.* Rides are $1 for short trips. Examples are anywhere in town, between the University of the Virgin Islands and the Hospital (Schneider Regional Medical Center), points between the Hospital up to Pricesmart (a discount warehouse), and traveling from one point to another in the "country" (the used to describe the middle and east end of the island). The fare rises $2 for more extended, cross-island trips such as traveling from the Hospital to points beyond PriceSmart, and traveling from PriceSmart and beyond to anywhere in town. If proceeding directly to St. John, you must travel from the airport to town and then take the ferries from Charlotte Amalie to Cruz Bay or take a bus or taxi to Red Hook and then the ferry on to St. John.

ARRIVING ON A CRUISE: There are two cruise ship piers. If your ship arrives while a few others are docked, you may be shuttled in by small boat. If arriving at the West Indian Company Dock, it's best to take the taxi shuttle into town. From the Crown Bay pier, the road to town is along a hot and heavily-trafficked main road so you may wish to take a taxi.

GETTING AROUND: The only local bus service, VITRAN (☎ 774-5678) runs to various locations all over the island. However, service cutbacks have limited its usefulness. The privately-run "dollar" buses (which charge $2 for longer distances: see the previous "arriving by air" section for details) may

 The Reefer (a ferry) will take you out to the beach at Frenchman's Reef. This is a great way to get to a beach if staying in town.

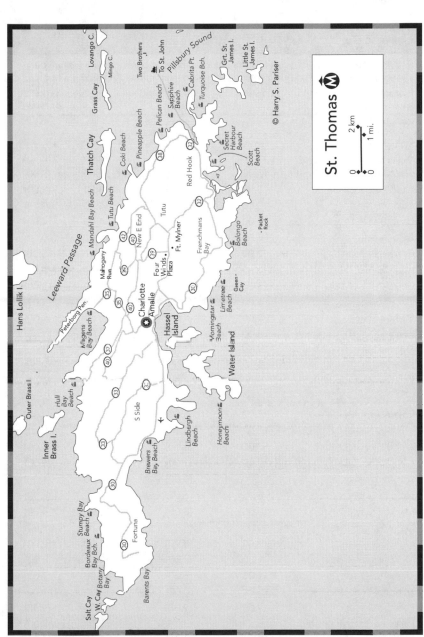

ST. THOMAS

St. Thomas Ⓜ

© Harry S. Pariser

0   1 mi.
0   2 km

Lovango C.
Mingo C.
Grass Cay
Two Brothers
To St. John
Pillsbury Sound
Cabrita Pt.
Turquoise Bch.
Grt. St. James I.
Little St. James I.
Pelican Beach
Sapphire Beach
Secret Harbour Beach
Scott Beach
Pineapple Beach
Coki Beach
Red Hook
Packet Rock
Thatch Cay
Mandahl Bay Beach
Tutu Beach
Tutu
Bolongo Beach
Frenchmans Bay
Ft. Myhner
Four Winds Plaza
New E End
Leeward Passage
Mahogany Run
Charlotte Amalie
Green Cay
Limetree Beach
Hars Lollik I
Peterborg Pen.
Magens Bay Beach
Hassel Island
Morningstar Beach
Water Island
Outer Brass I.
Hull Bay Beach
S Side
Lindbergh Beach
Honeymoon Beach
Inner Brass I.
Brewers Bay Beach
Stumpy Bay
Bordeaux Beach
Fortuna
Salt Cay
W. Cay Botany Bay
Barents Bay

42
40
40
40
37
35
35
33
33
30
30
30
32
38
39
30
32
35

ST. THOMAS

🚐 Taxi Fares on St. Thomas 🚐

The first rate shown in each column is for one passenger. In parentheses is the rate per passenger if more than one are traveling to the same destination. Luggage is $2 per piece.

Location	Town	extra person	Airport	extra person
Airport Terminal	7.00	(6.00)		
Amer. Yacht Harbor	13.00	(10.00)	15.00	(11.00)
Anchorage	15.00	(10.00)	18.00	(12.00)
Blackbeard's Castle	5.00	(4.00)	8.00	(7.00)
Bluebeard's Castle	5.00	(4.00)	8.00	(7.00)
Bolongo	10.00	(8.00)	12.00	(9.00)
Carib Beach Hotel	7.00	(6.00)	4.00	(4.00)
Coki Beach	12.00	(9.00)	14.00	(10.00)
Compass Point	12.00	(9.00)	14.00	(10.00)
Coral World	12.00	(9.00)	14.00	(10.00)
Cowpet Bay Village	15.00	(10.00)	18.00	(12.00)
Crown Bay Dock	5.00	(4.00)	5.00	(4.00)
Drake's Seat	7.00	(5.00)	9.00	(7.00)
Elysian Resort	15.00	(10.00)	18.00	(12.00)
Emerald Beach Hotel	7.00	(6.00)	4.00	(4.00)
Four Winds (Tutu)	9.00	(7.00)	11.00	(8.00)
Frenchman's Reef	8.00	(6.00)	10.00	(8.00)
Frenchtown	4.00	(4.00)	7.00	(6.00)
Havensight Mall	6.00	(5.00)	8.00	(7.00)
Hull Bay Beach	12.00	(8.00)	15.00	(10.00)
Island Beachcomber	7.00	(6.00)	4.00	(4.00)
Island View Guest House	9.00	(7.00)	8.00	(6.00)
Lindbergh Bay	7.00	(6.00)	4.00	(4.00)
Mafolie Hotel	8.00	(6.00)	10.00	(8.00)
Magens Bay	10.00	(8.00)	12.00	10.00
Magens Point Resort	10.00	(7.00)	12.00	(9.00)
Mahogany Run	10.00	(8.00)	13.00	(10.00)
Morningstar Beach	9.00	(8.00)	10.00	(8.00)
Mountain Top	11.00	(8.00)	12.00	(9.00)
National Park Dock	13.00	(10.00)	15.00	(11.00)
Paradise Point	9.00	(7.00)	11.00	(9.00)
Paradise Point Tramway	6.00	(5.00)	8.00	(9.00)
Pavilions and Pools	13.00	(10.00)	15.00	(11.00)

🚐 Taxi Fares on St. Thomas 🚐				
Location	Town	extra person	Airport	extra person
Point Pleasant	13.00	(10.00)	15.00	11.00)
Red Hook	13.00	(10.00)	15.00	11.00)
Ritz Carlton	15.00	(10.00)	18.00	(12.00)
Sapphire Resort	13.00	(10.00)	15.00	(11.00)
Seaborne Seaplane	4.00	(4.00)	7.00	(6.00)
Secret Harbour	15.00	(10.00)	18.00	(12.00)
Wyndham Sugar Bay Resort	12.00	(8.00)	9.00	(3.00)
Yacht Haven Grande	4.00	(4.00)	7.00	(6.00)

ST. THOMAS

be caught to locations such as Coral World Ocean Park and Sapphire Beach.

Buses leave the Market Square for **Red Hook** ($1) hourly from 8:15 AM to 5:15 PM and return from 7:15 AM to 5:15 PM.

FERRIES: A harbor shuttle (the *Reefer*, ☎ 693-8500, ext. 145) operates between the vicinity of Charlotte Amalie waterfront's Yacht Haven Marina (near Havensight) and Frenchman's Reef Hotel. It takes 15 min., the fare is $6 OW, and it runs from the waterfont at every hour on the hour from 9 AM–5 PM. It returns every hour on the half hour, 8:30 AM–4:30 PM. (It does not run on Suns. from June–Nov.).

Ferries (☎ 690-4159; $5 OW, $10 RT) run to Phillip's Landing on **Water Island** from Crown Bay Marina (Sub Base) at 6:30, 7:15, 8, 10:30, noon, 2, 3:15, 4:15, 5:15, and 6 from Mon. to Sat.; 8, 10:30, noon, 3 and 6 PM on Sun; and additional ferries run some evenings. The ferry returns at 6:45, 7:30, 8:15, 10:45, 12:15, 2:15, 3:30, 4:30, 5:30, and 6:10 from Mon. to Sat. and at 8:15, 10:45, 12:15, 3:15, and 5:15 on Sun. and holidays. **note:** These times are subject to change. Check www.vinow.com for current times. (Ferries to other islands are listed at the end of this chapter).

TAXI SERVICE: Other island destinations are reachable only via expensive shared meterless taxis. (Recent prices are included in chart). Suitcases are $2 each; $1 is charged per min. of waiting time after the first five minutes; RT fares are double plus additional for waiting time; between midnight and 6 AM there is an extra charge of $2 pp. A two-hr. island tour by taxi is $50 for one or two and an additional $25 pp thereafter. A three-hr. taxi tour is $60 and $30 respectively. For complaints call Mr. Kenrick Robertson at the Taxi Commission (☎ 774-0828) from Mon. to Fri, 8 AM–5 PM. Be sure to have the offending taxi's license plate number.

OTHER: Hitching is possible, but locals are not as accommodating as their St. Johnian neighbors.

Numerous guided tours (ranging from helicopter tours to kayaking) are also available and many are listed later in the text.

RENTING A CAR: Cars (around $40 pd for a compact with unlimited mileage) can be rented on a daily or weekly basis.

A $2.50 pd tax is imposed on car rentals, and there are extra charges for those rented at the airport. Gas runs around $4/gal. There are a large number of rental companies. Note

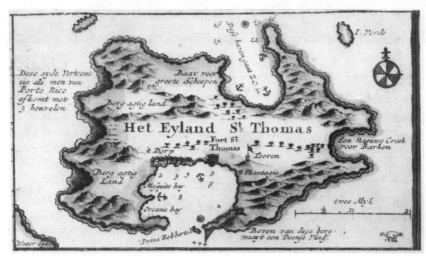

Old Map of St. Thomas (1707) by Gerard Hulst van Keulen

that you may not be able to take your rental car to St. John; ask before renting.

Amalie Car Rental (☎ 774-0688, ☏ 774-0788, 888-568-3535) is in Crown Bay.
http://www. amaliecar.com
amaliecar@islands.vi

Avis (☎ 800-331-1212, 774-1468, 774-4616), is located on St. Thomas as well as St. John. They have six locations on St. Thomas.
http://www.avis.com

Budget (☎ 800-626-4516, 776-5774, 774-5774) has five locations.
http://www.budgetstt.com

Cowpet (☎ 775-7376) is at the Sub Base.
http://www.cowpetautorental.com

Dependable (☎ 774-2253, 800-522-3076) offer a 12% discount if you book via the net. They're "three minutes from the airport."
http://www.dependablecar.com
dependable@dependablecar.com

Discount (776-4858, 877-478-2833) offer free island-wide pickup and drop-off. They also rent **scooters**.
http://www.discountcar.vi
http://www.discountscooterrental.vi

St. Thomas Taxi Service	
Dial a Ride (disabled)	☎ 776-1277
East End	☎ 775-6974
Independent Taxi	☎ 693-1006
Islander Taxi	☎ 774-4077
Sunflower Bliss	☎ 777-7343
24-hr. Radio Dispatch	☎ 693-0496
VI Taxi Radio Dispatch	☎ 774-7457
VI Taxi Association	☎ 774-4550
Wheatley Taxi/Tours	☎ 775-1956

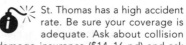 St. Thomas has a high accident rate. Be sure your coverage is adequate. Ask about collision damage insurance ($14–16 pd) and ask what the deductible is. Avoid driving at rush hour and on Main Street.

E-Z Car Rental (☎ 775-6255, 800-524-2027) is on the East End.
ezcar@viaccess.net

First Rent-a-Car (☎ 776-3730, 690-6467) rents compacts, mid-size vehicles, and minivans.
http://www.firstrent-a-car.com
firstrent@earthlink.net

Hertz (☎ 800-654-0700, 774-1819, 774-0841, 774-1879, 774-0841) is at the airport.
http://www.hertz.com

Thrifty (☎ 776-1500), by the airport, has a wide variety of models.

Zip Rentals (☎ 715-1501) is in the East End but offer pick up or drop off everywhere on the island.
http://www.ziprentalsvi.com

Tropical Scooter (☎ 714-7408, cell: 643-1295) rents scooters for around $55 pd. They're next to Modern Music across from Havensight.

DRIVING: Park in town in the municipal parking lot to the E of the fort which is 50cts/hr., $4 pd (6 AM–6 PM). Illegally parked vehicles can be ticketed ($25).

Expect late afternoon traffic jams in town. (St. Thomas could be the first island in the Caribbean to experience gridlock!) Unless otherwise noted, speed limits are 20 mph in town and 35 mph everywhere else.

Narrow roads race up and down hillsides; one of the best views to be had is from Rte. 30 just above Havensight.

Queens Quarter in Charlotte Amalie circa 1890s

St. Thomas Accommodations

The island is an expensive place, especially in season. The demand for rooms is just tremendous, so there are few deals. Hotel owners will tell you that their costs (especially water) are so high that "I even charge my relatives." Those on a budget would be better off avoiding this island and pitching a tent in the campsite at Cinnamon Bay, St. John. (which, at 35 smackers, is hardly cheap either!). Guesthouses are the next least expensive alternative, and, they are *the* place to stay on this island, if you want to get to know it a bit.

RENTAL AGENTS: McLaughlin Anderson Vacations, Ltd. (☎ 776-0635, 800-537-6246, ✆ 777-4737; 100 Blackbeard's Hill, St. Thomas 00802) has an excellent selection of villas in St. Thomas, St. John, Tortola, and Virgin Gorda.
http://www.mclaughlinanderson.com
nancy@mclaughlinanderson.com

Calypso Realty (☎ 774-1620, ✆ 774-1634, 800-747-4858) rents and sells villas.
http://www.calypsorealty.com
calypso2@viaccess.net

Charlotte Amalie Accommodations

note: All street and route mailing addresses should be completed with 00802. Other villa rentals are also listed in the accommodations sections. Wheretostay.com is a good place to check for guests' reviews of hotels on the island.

GUEST HOUSES AND SMALL HOTELS:
Bellavista Bed & Breakfast (☎ 714-5706, 888-333-3063), 2713 Murphy Gade, is an upscale bed and breakfast set on Denmark Hill. Proprietor Wendy Snodgrass offers luxury accommodation with an imaginative flair. She also has one of the nicest

small-inn websites you'll find anywhere. Wendy has put a tremendous amount of creative effort into her quite attractive rooms ("Bamboushay" is the nicest and most expensive), and you'll also find a pool and dining and living rooms. You can also make friends with Wendy's dog and cat. Enthusiastic Wendy will recommend restaurants and attractions.

Wendy is famous for her two-course breakfasts which include good coffee, frappes, yogurt or handmade granola, and dishes such as ginger pancakes with mango sauce, and banana Swiss waffles. Wendy also provides complimentary bottled water, nightly turndown service, spa robes, luxury linens and fresh flowers. Visitors can relax by the pool and sunbathing deck while they enjoy the beautiful panoramic view and tropical gardens. Rates for the four-bedroom property begin at $155 d during the summer season and $175–$245 d per night during the winter season. Rates vary according to the room booked. In addition, families or large groups have the opportunity to rent the entire inn for special full house rates of $695 nightly during the summer season (and $790 during the winter season (three night minimums).
http://www.bellavista-bnb.com
mail@bellavista-bnb.com

Villa Santana (☎/✆ 776-1311), near the crest of Denmark Hill, stands on the site of a historic villa built in the 1850s by General Antonio Lopez de Santa Anna during his third exile from Mexico. Destroyed in 1986, the home itself has not been rebuilt but a six-unit country villa has taken the place of ancillary buildings such as the wine cellar and pumphouse. Units have names like "La Casa de Piedra" and "La Terraza." Rates run around $135 d and up.
http://www.villasantana.com
info@villasantana.com

Miller Manor (☎ 774-1535, ☏ 774-5988, 888-229-0762; Box 1570, St. Thomas 00804) is another guest house nearby which features similarly personalized service. This is a good place to stay if you want to be a bit away from the fray and have a good view of things. Rooms have phones, TV/VCR, free coffee and complimentary videotape rentals are included. All-year rates run around $95–$160. Weekly rates are available during the off season. A 10% energy charge is added.
http://www.millermanor.com
moreinfo@millermanor.com

Ramsey's Guesthouse (☎ 774-6521, ☏ 776-7874; Estate Thomas 14 P-6, St. Thomas 00821) is run by a local family and provides Virgin Islands-style hospitality. Rates run from around $80–100 d with the highest rates being for suites which have balconies and kitchens. Rooms have phones and TVs. Morning coffee or tea is offered, and you may use the kitchen. The guesthouse is set in the hill above Pueblo in the direction of Sub Base. Call for directions.
http://www.ramseysguesthouse.com
ramseysguesthouse@yahoo.com

The Crystal Palace (☎ 777-2277; 8 AM–10 PM AST only: 866-502-2277) is a B&B set in the ancestral home of the Lockharts, one of St. Thomas's best known families. Upstairs is a homey living space with antique furniture galore that the family shares with guests. Breakfast is served on a splendid balcony commanding a harbor view. The atmosphere is clean, comfortable, and relaxed. Proprietor Ronnie Lockhart presides over it all and will make you feel right at home. He'll point out the birds nesting in chandeliers, and a wall which dates from the 1800s. This is neither a historical museum nor a snobby inn. Downstairs, there are five a/c and fan-equipped rooms;

two with twin beds and communal baths; one with private bath and a double bed. They are gay friendly. Rates run around $120 d and up.
http://www.crystalpalaceusvi.com
ronusvi@aol.com

A small locally-run establishment, Midtown Guest House (☎ 776-9157, 779-8826), 1B Commandant Gade, is near Emancipation Gardens. This is another good choice if you are on a budget: it has a central location and friendly management. Rooms have TVs (free HBO) and phones. Rates run around $80 d.
http://www.midtownguesthouse.com

The 15-room Bunker Hill Hotel (☎ 774-8056, ☏ 774-3172), up the street at 7A Commandant Gade, has two pools. Its a/c rooms have cable TV and phone and start at $115 d. A full breakfast is included.
http://www.bunkerhillhotel.com
info@bunkerhillhotel.com

Hotel 1829 (☎ 776-1829, ☏ 776-4313, 800-524-2002; Box 1567, St. Thomas 00804) is a National Historic Site. Originally completed in 1829, it was built by a French sea captain for his bride. The highly attractive 12 a/c rooms have bar, phone, and satellite TV. There's a small pool. Rates start at around $105 d and up with continental buffet breakfast. Superior, deluxe, suite, and penthouse suite accommodations are also available. They are gay friendly but do not accept children under 12 or pets. There's no elevator, but there're plenty of steps.
http://www.hotel1829.com
hotel1829@islands.vi

Not to be confused with the bed and breakfast, the Bellavista Scott Hotel (☎ 714-5500), Estate Thomas in the back of Pueblo, is run by a friendly local family.

Convenient to the main part of town, it is down low which means less of a breeze and no views. However, the a/c 26 mini-suites are large, have cable TVs, and include a separate bedroom and a kitchen with electric range. Superior and two-bedroom deluxe suites are also available. Rates start from around $125 d and up. The hotel also has **Jamaican Me Crazy**, a good restaurant, and a large pool.
http://www.bellavistascott.hotel
bellavista@viaccess.net

NEAR TOWN: At 4 Raphune Hill, the homey 14-room **Villa Blanca** (☎ 776- 0749, 800-231-0034, ☏ 779-2661; Box 7505, St. Thomas 00801) has great views from attractive rooms with private balconies, cable TV, small kitchenette, a/c and fans. It also has a pool and honor bar and free wireless internet. Originally the home of Dodge automobile heiress C. C. Dodge, it was last renovated in 1998, and is now named after affable owner and manager Blanca Smith, who speaks both English and Spanish. Packages are available. Rates start at around $135 d plus a 10% service charge.
http://www.villablancahotel.com
info@villablancahotel.com

Serene **Galleon House** (☎/☏ 774-6952; ☏ 774-6952; 800-524-2052; Box 6577) is centrally located. Amenities here include breakfast, pool, sun deck, complimentary snorkeling equipment, cable TV/HBO, phones in rooms, and a choice of fans or a/c. Their private veranda rooms (queen or twin beds) offer views of the city and harbor. Rates run from around $85–$160 d.
http://www.galleonhouse.com
info@galleonhouse.com

Located to the N of town in the hills, 15-room **Island View Guest House** (☎ 774-4270, 800-524-2023, ☏ 774-6167;

Box 1903, St. Thomas 00803) offers rooms with fans (optional a/c in deluxe rooms), and twin, queen, and king beds. An efficiency and a two-bedroom efficiency is also available. Facilities include TV, fax machine, laundromat, pool, and complimentary breakfast. A shuttle is in the planning stages. Room rates (not including 15% service charge) run around $80–$140 d; more expensive rooms have private baths. Weekly rentals are available.
http://www.islandviewstthomas.com
info@islandviewstthomas.com

Set 800 ft. above town, 23-rm. **Mafolie Hotel** (☎ 774-2790, ☏ 774-4091; 800-255-7035; 7091 Estate Mafolie, St. Thomas 00802) offers complimentary continental breakfast, RT transport to Magens Bay Beach, pool with deck, and a good restaurant. Sleeping four, its mini suites have wicker furniture, cable TVs and refrigerators. Prices range from around $130 d. It has received mixed reviews on wheretostay.com.
http://www.mafolie.com
mafolie@st-thomas.com

The **Bolongo Inn at Villa Olga**, (☎ 715-0900, 800-524-4746), next to the Oceana restaurant at the end of Frenchtown, is a pleasant 12-room inn with swimming pool which is now run by owners of Bolongo Bay Beach Resort. All rooms have a/c, cable TV and phone. Its elevated sundeck has a harbor view. It's a short walk to town, and dining is quite convenient. Rates run from around $125 d.
http://www.bolongobay.com/VillaOlga.html
villaolga@bolongobay.com

At **Home in the Tropics** (☎ 777-9857, ☏ 774-3890; P.O. Box 6877, St. Thomas, VI 00804-6877), a comfortable guesthouse, is set on Government Hill. Rooms have a/c, ceiling fans, safe, cable TV, hair dryer, and

WiFi. Shared guest areas include pool, living room, dining room, and covered gallery (with views) in front of the house. This area has an honor bar. Rates start from US$185 d.
http://athomeinthetropics.com
info@athomeinthetropics.com

The **Green Iguana Guesthouse** (☎ 776-7654, 800-464-8825, code 7333) has four condos and four rooms for rent. Good views and Texas management. Each room has a phone (with your own number and answering service) and basic kitchenette and laundry access is included. It is right in back of Blackbeard's Castle, and you may use their pool. It's ten-minutes down the stair steps to Government Hill. Rates range around $135 d.
http://www.thegreeniguana.com
info@thegreeniguana.com

LARGER HOTELS: Right on the waterfront, the **Holiday Inn Windward Passage** (☎ 774-5200; 800-524-7389; Box 640, St. Thomas 00804) has 139 rooms and 11 suites. Facilities include a/c, cable TVs, balconies, and phones. Multi-beach shuttle service and buffet breakfast are included in the rates. Seafront rooms command great views. It has a good restaurant in the courtyard. This is a great place to stay for Carnival, while on business, and if you like being just blocks away from shopping. Rates range around $220–$550 d plus a 10% service charge. Suites are more.
http://www.holidayinn.st-thomas.com
reservations@holidayinn.st-thomas.com

The 184-room red-roofed **Bluebeard's Castle** (☎ 774-1600, ☻ 774-7925, 800-524-6493; Box 7480, St. Thomas 00801) is set next to a tower constructed in 1679 by Carl Baggart as a lookout to protect the town from attack. Rooms are equipped with refrigerators, cable TVs, and a/c or fans. There are two gourmet restaurants with nightly entertainment and dancing, a waterfall-fed

ST. THOMAS

Charlotte Amalie's waterfront today.

pool, tennis, and a fitness center. There's also an executive conference center and banquet facilities. This is the place to go for activity, not seclusion. It's around ten min. downhill to Main Street. Complimentary travel to Magens Bay Beach is included. Prices start at around $200 s or d for standard rooms. http://www.extraholidays.com

Accommodations East of Charlotte Amalie

MARRIOTT RESORTS: The island's two Marriott Resorts, **Frenchman's Reef** and **Morningstar Beach** (☎ 776-8500; 800-621-1270, Box 7100, St. Thomas 00801), are interlinked. Facilities include five restaurants and three lounges, tennis, two pools, Jacuzzi, shops, exercise room, unisex salon, and the USVI's largest conference center.

All told there are 504 rooms and suites, including 98 at the more expensive Morningstar. All offer a/c, cable TV, phone, and mini-bar. A full range of water sports including scuba and deep-sea fishing are available. The resorts are connected to town by *The Reefer* ferry. Room rates vary tremendously depending on the season, whether they are all-inclusive, and on the number of people involved. Least expensive (around $200 pp) is for three nights in a triple during the off-season for the "Sun, Sand, and Free" program which includes some amenities (such as a sunset cruise) but not meals. Wedding (☎ 800-FOR-LOVE) and honeymoon packages are available, as is a "Caribbean Diving Adventures" package.

☞ Smoking is forbidden within the hotel, and the entire hotel has Wi-Fi. http://www.marriottfrenchmansreef.com

East End St. Thomas Accommodations

The Bolongo Beach Resort (☎ 775-1800, 800-766-2840, ℮ 775-3208; 7150 Estate Bolongo, St. Thomas 00802) is a casual beachfront resort with 65 a/c rooms on the beach. All rooms have microwave, minifridge, hair dryer, iron and ironingboard, in-room safe, balcony, and one queen or two double beds. Its "European plan" includes use of kayaks, aqua tricycles, windsurfers, sunfish, sailboats, snorkel equipment, and anintroductory scuba lesson. Bolongo's "All Inclusive Plan" also includes all meals (a la carte dining) all drinks and all gratuities. "All Inclusive" guests staying seven nights will also receive a day sail to St. John and a sunset cruise. Facilities include a pool with swim-up bar, beach volleyball, tennis courts, and the St Thomas Diving Club, a 5 star PADI facility. Its two restaurants are **The Lobster Grille** (Caribbean inspired menu, seafood and continental cuisine) and **Iggie's** (casual seaside dining). Wifi access is at the pool bar and in the guest lounge. Children (12 and under) may stay for $10 on the European plan, and a discounted meal add-on is charged for the "All Inclusive Plan." Rates range from $300 pn (European plan) to $539 pn (all inclusive) for winter travel. The **Bolongo Bay Condominiums** (☎ 775-1800, 800-766-2840, ℮ 775-3208) are a set of studios and two-bedroom condos with full kitchens. Set at the end of the beach, they command an ocean view. Up to six can sleep in the two-bedroom. Rates are around $270 (studio) and $370 pn (two-bedroom). Honeymoon packages, wedding packages and dive packages are available. http://www.bolongobay.com info@bolongobay.com

Bluebeard's Beach Club and Villas (☎ 775-4770, ℮ 714-6144; 800-524-6559) have 74 time-share units (a/c and fan), pool,

and restaurant. Despite the name, it is on a relatively secluded part of the S shore, and the time-shares are offered for nightly or weekly rental.
http://www.extraholidays.com
bbcresorts@islands.vi

Near Bolongo Bay, eight-unit **Watergate Villas** (☎ 775-1540, ☏ 779-6109, 800-524-2038; Rte. 6, St. Thomas 00802) has pools, beach bar, snorkeling equipment, and diving. Rates run around $155–$320. A 10% surcharge is added.
http://www.st-thomas.com/paradise
 properties
paradise@st-thomas.com

Hilltop and private **Secret Harbour Villas** (☎ 775-2600, ☏ 775-5901, 800-524-2250; 6280 Estate Nazareth, St. Thomas 00802) offers studio, one-, two-, and three-bedroom units. Each has a kitchen, a/c, phone, TV, balcony, and maid service. On the premises are a Jacuzzi, pool, tennis courts, and workout center. These facilities are shared with Secret Harbour Beach Resort which has 20% higher rates. Rates start at $130/studio and range up to $355/two-bedroom during the peak season.
http://secretharbourvi.com
info@secretharbourvi.com

Secret Harbour Beach Resort (☎ 775-6550, 800-524-2250; 6280 Estate Nazareth, St. Thomas 00802) offers the same facilities and has a dive shop, watersports, and a/c full suites with private balconies or terraces. Four units for the disabled were added in 2000, and the resort is ADA-compliant. Its small beach has snorkeling opportunities. Rates start at around $300 for a studio suite for two.
 ☞ Both Secret Harbours have great views and sunsets.
http://secretharbourvi.com
info@secretharbourvi.com

Set near Red Hook and managed by **Antilles Resorts** (☎ 800-524-2025, 773-9150, ☏ 778-4004) as well as **Paradise Properties** (☎ 800-524-2038, 770-1540, ☏ 779-6109), the 80-unit **Anchorage Beach Villas** (☎ 773-9150, ☏ 775-4202, 800-524-2025, 800-874-7897; Rte. 6, St. Thomas 00802) features studios and one- or two-bedroom a/c villas with kitchen, living/dining room, telephone, cable TV, and maid service. It has a beachside restaurant, pool, tennis, snorkeling equipment, and diving. Rates start at around $370 for one to four persons. A 10% service charge is applied; it's $30 for each additional person.
http://www.antillesresorts.com
reservations@antillesresorts.com
http://www.st-thomas.com/
 paradiseproperties
paradiseproperties@att.worldnet.net

Run by Paradise Properties, **Cowpet Bay Village** (☎ 775-6220, ☏ 775-4202, 800-524-2038; Rte. 6), on Cowpet Bay Beach, has from one- to four-bedroom villas. Rates run around $375 pn (for one to four in a two-bedroom) and up with a 10% surcharge.
http://www.st-thomas.com/paradise
 properties
paradiseproperties@att.worldnet.net

Done up in Italian Renaissance style, the 150-suite **Ritz Carlton Hotel** (☎ 775-3333, ☏ 775-4444, ☎ 800-241-3333) overlooks St. John. It lost its roof and both of its restaurants from Hurricane Marilyn in 1995 but reopened in Dec. 1996 as a Ritz-Carlton property. Barack Obama vacationed here in March 2008. It includes the Palm Terrace Restaurant, four tennis courts, fitness center with aerobic workouts, complimentary watersports, private catamaran, and beach bar. In addition to the landscaped gardens, there's a lagoon where you can birdwatch. Rooms have private balconies, digital safe, minibars, radios, cable TVs, room and

bath phones, hair dryers in bathrooms, and climate controls. Rates run from around $760–$2,000 d.
http://www.ritzcarlton.com

The **Elysian Beach Resorts** (☎ 775-1000, ☏ 778-0810, reservations: 800-438-6493; Box 7480, St. Thomas 99801) have 140 timeshare rooms with a/c (12% energy surcharge) at a beachside location. Rates start at around $175–$235 d.
http://www.extraholidays.com
http://www.elysian.us/guestbook

Set on Sapphire Beach, **Sapphire Beach Resort & Marina** (☎ 775-6100, ☏ 775-2403, 800-524-2090, 800-874-7897; Box 8088, St. Thomas 00801) offers private suites and villas in a total of four categories. Rooms have private balconies, kitchens, and satellite TVs. Boardsailing, snorkeling, sunfish sailing, cocktail hour, rum bottle, and children's activity program are complimentary. There are also restaurants, four tennis courts, a quarter-acre pool, and a 67-slip marina. A variety of wedding packages are available. Rates range from around $330 (winter) EP. Suites can accommodate four, villas can hold six, and there is a charge of $30 for each additional person. Children under 12 stay and eat free. Confusingly, the property also includes 43 units which are managed by **Antilles Resorts** (☎ 800-524-2025, 773-9150, ☏ 778-4004).
☞ Keep in mind that Antilles has no on-site office, so make sure that someone will be on-property to check you in. Also, Antilles does not share Sapphire's children's program.
http://www.sapphirebeachresort.com
sbrsalesdir@sapphirebeachresort.com
http://www.usvi.net/hotel/sapphire
http://www.antillesresorts.com
reservations@antillesresorts.com

Set near the beach of the same name, **Sapphire Village** (☎ 773-9150, ☏ 778-4009, 800-524-2025; Rte. 6, St. Thomas 00802) is managed by **Antilles Resorts** (☎ 800-524-2025, 773-9150, ☏ 778-4004) as well as **Paradise Properties** (☎ 800-524-2038), 770-1540, ☏ 779-6109). Sapphire Village overlooks Sapphire Beach Resort, a hilltop location which offers spectacular vistas. Each condominium includes a small kitchen and private balcony. There's a restaurant, two pools, and the beach is a short walk. Rates run around $150–$180 d.
http://www.antillesresorts.com
reservations@antillesresorts.com
http://www.paradisepropertiesvi.com
paradiseproperties@vipowernet.net

Located on Rte. 6 at 6400 Estate Smith Bay (a mi. W of Red Hook and adjacent to Sapphire Bay) the condo complex **Pavilions and Pools** (☎ 775-6110, ☏ 775-6110, 800-524-2001; Rte. 6, St. Thomas 00802) is spread over two hilly acres. It offers a daily shuttle into town. A manager's cocktail party is held each Tues., and a restaurant is open nightly for dinner (except Tues. and Fri.) The congenial and caring staff prompt many visitors to return. There are two types of pavilions — the 1,400-sq.-ft. "International" and the 1,200-sq.-ft. "Caribbean." Both feature a small private swimming pool, a/c and fans, living and dining area, rattan furniture, fully-equipped kitchen, and sunken garden shower. The fully-equipped kitchen has a gas range. Some rooms are handicapped accessible. It's an easy walk to the breezy beach. Rates run from around $250–$275 d.
http://www.pavilionsandpools.com
vacation@pavilionsandpools.com

Located on Rte. 6 at 6600 Estate Smith Bay, **Point Pleasant Resort** (☎ 775-7200, ☏ 776-5694, 800-524-2300) offers 128 recently remodeled a/c units with kitch-

ens, satellite TV, radio, and great views from private balconies. They range from junior suites to two-bedroom suites which sleep six. There are three pools and two restaurants (Agave Terrace and Fungi's on the Beach), and two beaches are nearby. Iguanas populate the gardens. Toilet water is recycled. Free WiFi is offered in the lounge. Expect to walk a bit, and it is best suited to self-sufficient guests. Rates run around $260–$400 d.
http://www.pointpleasantresort.com
reservations@antillesresorts.com

On Sapphire Beach and managed by Paradise Properties (☎ 800-524-2025) and by Antilles Resorts (☎ 800-524-2038), **Crystal Cove Villas** (☎ 775-0111, ✆ 779-6109; Rte. 6, St. Thomas 00802) has studios and one- and two-bedroom a/c villas with kitchen, living/dining room, telephone, cable TV, and maid service. The premises have a salt water pool, cable TV, beachside restaurant, and watersports. Prices start from around $200 for a two-bedroom.
http://www.antillesresorts.com
reservations@antillesresorts.com
http://www.st-thomas.com/
  paradiseproperties
paradiseproperties@vipowernet.net

Pineapple Village Villas (☎ 775-5516, 800-992-9232, ✆ 800-874-1786) offers garden bedrooms and suites which have phones, cable TV, a/c and fans, plus kitchenettes or kitchens. On the grounds of the former Grand Bay Palace (whose rooms are slated to become Wyndham timeshares). Rates run around $150-$200 EP plus $35 for each extra person. A 10% service charge is added.
http://www.pineapplevillas.com
pineapplevillas@worldnet.att.net

The nearby 14-unit **Pineapple Rooms and Villas** (☎/✆ 777-6275, 800-479-1539)

runs from $200 for a studio suite. It offers both single rooms or a villa with any number of bedrooms up to four king beds with four baths ($650). It is also on the grounds of the former Grand Beach Palace (which is slated to be converted to Wyndham timeshares).
http://www.stayusvi.com
stayusvi@aol.com

The 300-room **Wyndham Sugar Bay Resort & Spa** (☎ 777-7100, ✆ 777-7200, 800-WYNDHAM) is at 6500 Estate Smith Bay. It has three interconnected swimming pools with waterfall, seven tennis courts (including a stadium court), the $1.5-million Journeys Spa, restaurants, nightclub, bars, watersports center, a ballroom and more than a dozen conference rooms. Following the land contours, the rooms and suites nestle into the hillside. Rates start at around $500 d.
www.wyndhamsugarbayresort.com
reservations@sugarbayusvi.com

Northern St. Thomas Accommodations

Located on Magens Bay Road, secluded and intimate **Magens Point Resort** (☎ 777-6000, ✆ 777-6055, 800-524-2031) has a pool and lighted tennis courts. All other sports are nearby. Within walking distance of the beach which it overlooks, its a/c hotel rooms feature phone, TV, and balcony. Junior and full suites also have queen size sofa bed, living room, and kitchenette. Its restaurant offers Italian and seafood dishes. Dining, golf, and honeymoon packages are offered, and rates run around $225–315. A $3 pp pn energy surcharge is added. It has decidedly mixed reviews on wheretostay.com.
http://www.magenspoint.com
info@magenspoint.com

Southwestern St. Thomas Accommodations (Near the Airport)

This area has a few hotels. While the location is very convenient for arrival and departure, jet noise can be a distraction.

Set on Lindbergh Beach, the **Island Beachcomber Hotel** (☎ 774-5250, 800-982-9898 /742-4276, ☏ 774-5615; Box 2579 VDA, St. Thomas 00803) offers 48 a/c rooms with refrigerator, phone and cable TV. Use of water rafts, snorkeling gear, and chaise lounges is complimentary. The Garden Restaurant is on the premises. Rates start at $140 d for standard rooms. A 10% service charge is added.
http://www.islandbeachcomber.net
islandbeachcomber@hotmail.com

Next door, three-level, four-building, 90-rm **Best Western Emerald Beach Resort** (☎ 777-8800; ☏ 776-3426, 800-233-4936; 8070 Lindbergh Bay, St. Thomas 00802) has a pool, restaurant, water sports, and tennis. Attractive a/c rooms are in four, pink, three-story buildings; they have balconies, marble bath, in-room safe, and phone. Superior rooms run for around $245–$305. A 7.5% service charge is applied. Dive packages are offered in conjunction with Sea Trade Ltd. Food trucks are nearby for the budget conscious and/or adventurous. The hotel is very popular with guests.
http://www.emeraldbeach.com
reservations@emeraldbeach.com

Nearby, the **Best Western Carib Beach Resort** (☎ 774-2525, 800-792-2742, ☏ 777-4131; 70-C Lindbergh Bay) is around 2.5 mi. from downtown and on Lindbergh Beach. It has 69 ocean-view rooms from around $135 CP plus 5% service and tax. Tasteful rooms have a/c, refrigerator, and cable TV. It has pool, beach, watersports, and tennis. A free shuttle is included.
http://www.caribbeachresort.com

St. Thomas Dining and Food

You won't go hungry here. Food can be pricey, especially in the gourmet restaurants. There aren't a whole lot of places (other than fast-food greasepits) where you can eat well for less than $10. Generally, a meal in a local restaurant costs this much. For a relatively complete list of current dining, together with opening hours and credit cards accepted, check the "Weekend" section of Friday's *Daily News*.

NOTE: In describing restaurant prices in this section, *inexpensive* refers to places where you can dine for $15 pp and under including a drink, appetizer, and dessert. *Moderate* means $20–$30; expensive is $31–$50, and *very expensive* means over $50 pp a meal.

VEGETARIAN DINING: Restaurants are growing in number, and it is easy to find veggie fare all over. You can find items for a pierside picnic at the Open Pit Barb-b-Que, a mobile food stand on the Waterfront which also serves sides of macaroni and cheese and potato salad. It's across from the Firstbank during lunch and across from the Lottery Building after 5 PM.

Rootsie's Ital (☎ 777-5055) is a tasty Rastafarian takeout which serves lunches. Rootsie cooks all his food in clay pots; dishes are tastefully spiced with local herbs. Bowls of vegetables range in price from $4–8. It is at 36 Kronspindsens Gade behind and just a block or two up from the Windward Passage Hotel near the Labor Dept.

INEXPENSIVE IN-TOWN DINING: *Also see "local food" next.*

Bobby's Hardwood Grill (☎ 777-6054), Drakes Passage and Trompeter's Gade, is a popular breakfast and lunch spot.

On the waterfront and right in the town center, the **Green House** (☎ 774-7998) serves three meals per day and features entrées such as mango banana chicken. It has entertainment nightly.

On the Waterfront, inexpensive **Bumpa's** (☎ 776-5674) serves breakfast and lunch.

Inexpensive **Coconuts** (☎ 774-0099), Dronningens Gade, serves American dishes and seafood lunches.

Jen's Island Café and Deli (☎ 777-4611), 43–46 Norre Gade, is a great choice for a quick breakfast, lunch, or dinner or to stay and linger to write postcards during the hours the locals are enslaved in their offices. You can use the a/c to cool off or sit outside. Happy hour specials, salads, wraps, local dishes, and homemade bread are offered.

Inexpensive **Palm Passage Restaurant,** Palm Passage, serves Italian lunches. It also serves *espresso*, *cappucino*, and *afogado* (vanilla ice cream and *espresso*) drinks.

Set behind Banco Popular on the Waterfront, **Taco Fiesta** (☎ 774-6600) serves bush tea ($1), breakfasts (from $3.50 for a breakfast *burrito*), *burritos* (tofu, $5; mahi mahi, $8), salads, and sides. It has daily specials and is open daily from 6 AM–10 PM.

The nearby **Giggling Gecko** (☎ 774-7777) offers inexpensive breakfasts and salads, sandwiches, and burgers for lunch.

Pita Express (☎ 777-4072), an inexpensive sandwich shop, is in Palm Passage. It has a few tables but is more of a takeout joint. Whole wheat pita pockets and grilled eggplant sandwiches are amongst the specialties. They also offer quiche and salads. They will deliver from 11 AM–3 PM for a surcharge.

OTHERS: Mercury Cafe, 3435 Dronnigen's Gade, serves gourmet coffee, wine and offers "open air casual dining." It's open for all theee meals, and dinner features dishes such as lobster pasta.

The **Kokopelli Cafe** (☎ 715-5280) is what you might expect to find in the Market Square East, a shopping center. Pizza, salads, sandwiches, and gourmet coffee are offered. A play area allows parents to have a respite from the rug rat blitzkrieg while laying down some action on the video gaming consoles.

A/c **R&J's Island Latte** (☎ 777-8100), Raadets Gade at the waterfront, serves coffee drinks, dessserts, and sandwiches and wraps. They have wireless internet.

LOCAL FOOD: In the Royal Dane Mall, inexpensive **Gladys' Cafe** (☎ 774-6604) serves a varied breakfast and lunch as well as local specialties such as saltfish and dumplings or conch and *fungi*. This is an excellent place to sample local food in an atttractive atmosphere with friendly service. It's open Mon. to Sat. from 6:30 AM–4:30 PM.

Popular with locals and visitors alike, **Cuzzin's Caribbean Restaurant and Bar** is set in an a/c 200-year old building on Back St. It offers moderately-priced local dishes such as *conch creole*, as well as local drinks (sea moss!) and good appetizers. Lunch is served 11 AM–4 PM from Mon. to Sat. and dinner is served from 5–9:30 PM, Tues. to Sat.

For Trinidadian dishes, try the **Ideal Restaurant** on Garden St. (near the PO). This is the place to go for great *roti*!

Another alternative is **Mamie's House of Roti,** Princesse Gade, owned and run by the Sooklal family. Their specialty is "dal puri" which chef Myroon Sooklal has been making for decades.

The **Negril Café and Cocktail Lounge** (☎ 774-4830, 866-465-3062), 6A Commandant Gade, is open daily from 11:30 AM and offers such *irie* dishes as *ackee and saltfish*, vegetarian lasagna, and stewed peas "our way."

At the Bellavista Scott Hotel, **Jamaicamecrazy** (☎ 774-5500, ext. 127) serves three meals daily. The food is 100%

authentic, and this is your chance to try such classics as ackee and saltfish ($17), steamed fish ($24), and various jerk, *ital*, and vegetarian dishes.

Other inexpensive places downtown serving West Indian food include **Red Snapper,** Back Street (2 Gullets Gade) and **Diamond Barrel,** 18 Norre Gade.

MORE FORMAL IN-TOWN DINING: Amalia (☎ 714-7373), Palm Passage, an open-air gourmet Spanish restaurant with a pleasant atmosphere, is open for lunch and dinner from Mon. to Sat. *Tapas, sangria,* and Spanish wines, and homemade desserts are among the features here.

Amici's (☎ 776-5670), Riises' Alley, is an attractive open-air restaurant which serves salads, pizzas and sandwiches. It's open daily 11 AM–3 PM.

Popular and colorful, **Virgilio's** (☎ 776-4920), Back Street, seats about 40, has brick walls, and serves gourmet Italian cuisine. Entrées run from $20 to around $40. You will find a wide variety of pastas and sauces to choose from, and desserts are super as well. They have a takeout window.

Beni Iguana's (☎ 777-8744), Havensight, sells a variety of sushi including rolls.

Tavern on the Waterfront (☎ 776-4328), 30 Dronnigen's Gade, serves gourmet lunches and dinners including seafood. Entrées run around $10–$20. The owner is an expat Romanian; believe it or not, an Arbys was once housed in this building.

Hervé (☎ 777-9703) is a Government Hill gourmet restaurant which serves lunch and dinner. Expect sparkling settings complimenting an innovative mix of Caribbean and European delicacies. This is a popular choice.

The **Banana Tree Grille** (☎ 776-4050) offers gourmet evening meals (great views) at Bluebeard's Castle. Dishes include seafood delights such as tempura lobster tail as well as gourmet deserts and specialty coffee drinks. Entrées run around $15–$25. Dinner only.

The **Room with a View Wine Bar and Bistro** (☎ 774-1600, ext 9530) at Bluebeard's Castle serves great dinners; light meals are served from 10 PM–1 AM.

Pilgrim's Terrace (☎ 777-1016), Mafolie Hill, offers unique appetizers (Thai vegetable tofu wrap, $8), salads, soups (change daily), and dishes such as grilled or fried king fish and curried tofu linguini pasta. They will deliver.

FRENCHTOWN DINING: Craig and Sally's (☎ 777-9949) is a popular choice which serves gourmet seafood and other dishes such as "smoked mozzarella and tomato salad" with main courses such as "jumbo shrimp *fresca*." Great wine list.

Open-air and on the dock in Frenchtown, **Hook, Line, and Sinker** (☎ 776-9708), 62 Honduras, offers burgers and daily specials. Its best known dishes include *bouillabaisse* and almond-crusted yellowtail. It also serves breakfasts as well as Sunday brunch.

Popular with residents, **Bella Blue** (☎ 774-4349) is a gourmet restaurant with a cheerful Mediterranean decor. Formerly known as Alexander's, it now offers French, Italian, Greek, Middle Eastern, and Spanish fare ranging from "pink peppercorn tuna" ($26) to "sundried tomato pesto" ($16). It's open for lunch and dinner from Mon. to Sat.

Behind Bella Blue, **Epernay** (☎ 774-5348) offers sushi, pasta, seafood, appetizers, dessert, and other dishes.

Oceana Restaurant and Wine Bar (☎ 774-4262) serves delights such as oyster, crab, and avocado salad, sea bass, and great desserts. Everything is homemade and frequently homegrown.
http://www.oceana.vi

YACHT HAVEN GRANDE DINING: Three60 (☎ 775-8225) offers 360-degree views. Its cuisine combines Caribbean, Latin, and Asian influences, and it has a good wine and cocktail list. **Grande Cru** offers drinks and light Mediterranean-style dishes. **W!kked** serves three meals and offers a tropical menu. **Fat Turtle** has BBQ items and a "bubble wall" of built-in drink dispensers.

SUB BASE (CROWN BAY MARINA)/CONTANT DINING: To the W of town, this is a popular area for dining.

Inexpensive **Chester Chicken**, a West Indian fast food restaurant at Contant, serves three inexpensive meals daily. A Sunday brunch is offered.

Inexpensive to moderate **Tickles Dockside Pub** (☎ 776-1595) three meals daily. Veggie burgers, seafood, salads, sandwiches, and soups and chowders are among the dishes offered.

The **Lechon King** (☎ 777-4014), Crown Bay Land Fill #17, serves *mofongo*, veggie burgers ($7), and grilled mahi mahi ($18). It's open Tues. to Sat. from 11 AM–10 PM.

Victor's New Hideout (☎ 776-9379) serves West Indian lunches and dinners. Seafood dishes include island conch, lobster, grouper fillet, breaded shrimp, and king fish. Entrées range from $12–$30. They will host wedding receptions and other events.

Inexpensive **Arian's** (☎ 776-1401), Sub Base, serves three West Indian and American meals daily.

Near the airport, the **Island Beachcomber** (☎ 774-4250) serves moderate American and West Indian dishes.

In the Emerald Beach Resort nearby, **The Palms** (☎ 777-8800, ext. 5300) has three meals a day. An attractive circular bar and restaurant, its lunch and dinner entrées are Mediterranean influenced and include *pizzetas* (thin crusted pizza) and *bouillabaisse*, the house specialty.

Arthur's Cafe (☎ 775-4049), Cowpet Bay, offers seaside dining at the Anchorage

Condominium Complex. Dishes range from a grilled mahi mahi sandwich ($9) to shrimp parmesan ($17) to salads.

HAVENSIGHT/LONG BAY DINING (FROM CHARLOTTE AMALIE): Delly Deck (Havensight Mall) has American food; The Gourmet Gallery in Havensight has sandwiches. It also has a branch at Crown Bay Marina (Sub Base). The **Pizza Amore** (☎ 774-2822), Al Cohen's Plaza, serves slices and whole pies.

Out at Havensight, the **Great Wall** (☎ 776-3566) serves inexpensive to moderate Chinese food for lunch and dinner.

In Barbel Plaza, **Little Bo Peep** serves West Indian breakfasts and lunches.

EAST OF CHARLOTTE AMALIE: Limetree Beach Bistro (☎ 774-0370) is an open-air restaurant overlooking the beach. It serves all three meals, and dinner choices include such selections as seafood bisque, conch fritters, coconut shrimp, lobster, yellowtail, and snapper.

Family-run **Randy's Bar and Bistro** (☎ 775-5001, 777-3199) is set at the top of Raphune Hill on Rte. 38. Lunch and dinner are served daily except Sun. Seafood and salads are special here. Purchase wine from their neighboring business (wide variety) and pay a $5 corkage fee to have it with your meal.

In the Marriott Frenchman's Reef, the **Sunset Bar & Grill** (☎ 776-8500) serves lunches. **Windows on the Harbour** serves breakfast buffets, seafood buffets, and brunches on Fri. and Sun. The resort also has **Caesar's Ristorant, Presto Deli** (open 24 hours daily.) and the **Captain's Café**.

In **Frenchman's Reef** (693-8500), moderate to expensive Caesar's offers Italian dishes. It is open for lunch daily and dinner daily (except Wed.).

The **Havana Blue** (☎ 715-2583), Morningstar Beach, serves international fusion dishes.

Set atop Watergate Villas on Bolongo Bay, inexpensive to moderate **David's** (☎ 777-3650) serves seafood and daily specials in a casual atmosphere.

Mim's Seaside Bistro (☎ 775-2081), at Watergate in Bolongo Bay, serves lunch and dinner; all-you-can-eat shrimp is offered on Thursdays. Its "signature dish" is lobster in curry sauce.

The **Lobster Grille** (☎ 775-1800, ext. 2553), Bolongo Bay, serves fresh seafood. lobster, meat, and pasta dishes. It's open Tues. to Sat. from 6 PM. The informal **Iggies** here offers casual fare like burgers, sandwiches, BBQ and nightly specials plus a West Indian Buffet Carnival Night every Wed. Seven TVs will please spots fans, and karaokeis offered every Thurs. and Sat. from 8pm – midnight. At the **Ritz Carlton**, the casual **Café** (☎ 775-3333) offers dinners as does the **Dining Room**, and there are several casual restaurants as well.

NORTH OF CHARLOTTE AMALIE: At Estate Elizabeth, gourmet **Sib's Mountain Bar and Restaurant** (☎ 774-8967) serves American and Caribbean cuisine including all-you-can-eat chicken and ribs.

EAST END/RED HOOK DINING: There are plenty of places to eat on the eastern side of the island.

COMPASS POINT: Patrick's (☎ 715-3655), Compass Point Marina off of Rte. 32, offers a wide variety of gourmet dishes ranging from seared tuna steak and mussels marinara to *ensalada Andaluza* (served with your choice of protein or Portabello mushroom).

Schnitzel Haus (☎ 776-7198), Benner Bay (next to Fish Hawk Marina at Estate Frydenhoj on Rte. 32), serves German food (including vegetarian dishes and German beers) Mon. to Fri. for dinner.

At Secret Harbour, **Blue Moon Cafe** (☎ 779-2262) offers gourmet lunches and dinners to beachgoers. You might dine on fried calamari for lunch and twin lobster tail ($41), seafood pasta ($26.50), or grilled tuna served with mango soy sauce and wasabi mashed potatoes ($25) for dinner. This terrace restaurant has a very relaxed atmosphere and overlooks the sandy beach.

Tamarind by the Sea here serves seafood, pasta, and meat dishes for dinner nightly.

Robert's American Grille (☎ 714-3663), 6800 Estate Nazareth, serves dinner from Tues. to Sun. as well as a Sunday brunch. Entrées range from curried vegetable stew ($15) to seafood pasta ($20–$25) to Cruzan BBQ shrimp with grits ($23).

AMERICAN YACHT HARBOR AND RED HOOK: **Caribbean Saloon** (☎ 775-7060) is on the top floor at the American Yacht Harbor. It serves lunch and dinner and offers a "Happy Hour," a special late-night menu (10 PM–4 AM). It has live music on some nights. Entrées run from around $10–$30. Dishes range from vegetarian stir fry ($13) to mahi mahi ($20) and twin lobster tails ($37).

Burrito Bay Deli (☎ 775-2944), American Yacht Harbor, serves inexpensive burritos and smoothies.

Off the Hook (☎ 775-6350) serves salads (smoked salmon, $12), yellowtail snapper filet ($24), St. Thomas fish stew ($23), potato gnocchi ($16) and other unique dishes. They have a children's menu.

The Deli can fix you up with an inexpensive box lunch or serve you breakfast or a salad.

American-style breakfast and lunch are found at **The Three Virgins.**

Doubling as a fish retailer, the **Fish Shack** serves three meals daily.

Whale of a Tale (☎ 775-1270) serves seafood and pasta from 5 PM. Entrées run around $25.

Inexpensive Irish pub **Molly Malones** serves three meals daily.

At Red Hook, moderate to expensive **Frigate East Restaurant** (☎ 775-6124) serves fresh fish, steaks, and teriyaki dishes for dinner daily. They have a children's menu and salad bar.

Señor Pizza (☎ 775-3030), in Red Hook across from the St. John ferry, offers NY-style pizza.

Duffy's Love Shack (☎ 779-2080) is a well-known bar with exotic drinks such as Revenge of Godzilla. Lunch and dinner (food up till midnight!) are served. It's open daily from 11:30 AM to 2 AM. Its "happy hour" runs weekdays 4-7 PM.

The **XO Bistro** (☎ 779-2069), Red Hook Plaza, serves gourmet light fare (pizzas and baked Brie). It hosts music some evenings.

Latitude 18° or **Alex's Restaurant** (☎ 779-2495), Vessup Point Marina across the bay from the St. John ferry dock, serves a selection of *mezza* (Mediterranean tapas) for $15 as well as individual items. They also serve garlic-crusted tuna, linguini in a tomato basil sauce, and other entrées. It has live music some nights.

East End Café (☎ 715-1442) serves US and Italian dishes along with daily seafood specials. Meals are accompanied by live music on Sat. evenings. It's open for lunch and dinner daily.

Only open for dinner, moderate to expensive **Agave Terrace** (☎ 775-4142)

is at Point Pleasant Resort, Smith Bay Rd. (Rte. 38). It has a good wine list. Specialties include lobster chinola, lobster angelina, pasta, salads, and a wide selection of vegetarian dishes. A steel band plays here Tues. and Thurs. evenings.

Also at Point Pleasant Resort, **Fungi's On the Beach** (☎ 775-4142) offers *kallaloo*, johnnycake, local microbrews and crowd pleasers such as pizza. According to your interests, you may watch bikinis, yachts, or iguanas as you dine.

The Lookout Lounge is open inside the restaurant, and the resort's inexpensive **Bayside Cafe** offers up paper-plate cuisine (grilled items) as well as fruit drinks.

TILLETT GARDENS: **Jack's**, at Tutu Gardens, offers American-style dishes—namely deep-fried items. They also serve a veggie burger and offer unique sauces such as "scorned wench." Free WiFi is in the garden.

SMITH BAY: Inexpensive **Pizza Plus** serves pizza plus chicken and ribs, **Lake's Chicken Fry** also serves seafood, **Super Pool Barbeque** offers BBQ chicken and West Indian food, and popular, elegant, and expensive **Romano's** (☎ 775-0045) serves Northern Italian and Continental cuisine for dinner (6:30–10:30 PM). It shows the work of owner/artist Tony Romano. **http://www.romanorestaurant.com**

Carol's Roti Plus offers inexpensive but hearty food at Smith Bay.

Toad and Tart (☎ 775-1153), Smith Bay, serves English pub-style fare.

NORTH SIDE DINING: At Mahogany Run, **Old Stone Farmhouse** (☎ 777-6277) is just what the name suggests, an old country home transformed into an ultra-gourmet restaurant. An international dinner menu is served Tues. through Sun. Dishes range from Prince Edward Island mussels steeped in Blackbeard's Ale and coconut milk to

> If you're on Magens Bay Rd., be sure to stop by **St. Thomas Dairies**. The dairy does not produce milk. However, its Udder Delight continues to serve milk shakes, cones, and cold juices. Try one of the shakes made with exotic liquors.

Most Romantic Places to Kiss

St. Thomas may be a bit more congested than elsewhere, it still has some good spots.
➤ At the top of the Paradise Point tramway.
➤ On Honeymoon Beach on Water Island
➤ On the grounds of the Ritz Carlton
➤ At Magens Bay Beach

hummus-crusted swordfish with pesto, to red curry grilled tofu with glass noodles and seared plantains. Sushi, desserts, and salmon *paillard* are specialties. Great tasting menus.

At Magens Bay Beach, **Magens Bay Cafe and Pizzeria** serves breakfast and lunches.

Hull Bay Hideaway (☎ 777-1898) offers daily fish and lobster specials. The "pan seared catch of the day" is $18. They have a children's menu.

Indigo Bar & Restaurant (☎ 776-0474), overlooking Magens Bay, offers international gourmet dishes, daily specials, and a Happy Hour which runs from 4 PM to dusk.

Food Shopping

BAKERIES AND SNACKS: A&F Bakery (☎ 776-5145) is at 7-8 Curacao Gade.
The Daylight Bakery is at 57 Prindsens Gade and at 10 Norre Gade.
Weekes & Weekes Bakery is at 3 Gamble Gade.
Bachman's Bakery is at Wheatley Center.
The Farmers Bakery is in Vitraco Park.

MARKETS AND SUPERMARKETS: There're plenty of these. If shopping in one, check your receipts after purchase: mistakes do happen! Along the harbor, a pickup truck sells fruit and vegetables.

At Long Bay, the **Natural Food Grocery and Deli** (☎ 774-2800) serves vegetarian food (veggie burgers and vegan platters) as well as meat and cheese.

In Crown Bay Marina and at Havensight, **Gourmet Gallery** stocks caviar, wine, and other delicacies. Stock up here for your picnic.

At Sub Base, Estate Thomas (a mi. N of Havensight), and at Four Winds Plaza (across from Tillett Gardens), **Pueblo** is one of the islands' largest chains.

Plaza Extra is in in United Shopping Plaza and Tutu Park Mall.

Useful St. Thomas Phone Numbers

Air Anguilla	778-9177
Air Center Helicopters	775-7335
Ambulance	922
American Airlines	800-474-4884
American Eagle	693-2560
American Express	774-1855
Antilles Helicopters	693-7880
Cape Air	800-352-0714
Caribbean Air	774-7071
Chamber of Commerce	693-0100
Continental Airlines	777-8190
Decomp. Chamber	776-2686
Delta Airlines	800-221-1212
Dial-a-Ride	693-2043
Directory Information	913
Fire	921
Hospital	776-8311
Hospitality Lounge	693-9493
LIAT	774-2313
National Park	693-6201
Native Son (ferry)	774-8685
Police	915
General Post Office	774-1950
Speedy's Fantasy (ferry)	774-8685
Smith's Ferry	775-7202
Tourist Information	774-8784
USAir	774-7885
United Airlines	800-241-6522
Vieques Air Link	777-4055

National Food Discount is next to Pueblo at Home Gas Station, Estate Thomas.

Cost-U-Less is set a mi. E of town at Hogensborg which is on Rte. 38, .25 mi. W of the Rte. 39 intersection. It mostly sells in quantity.

Quality Plus is at Four Winds Plaza.

Price Smart (☎ 777-3430) is off of Weymouth Rhymer Hwy. at Fort Mylner.

Compass Foods is at Compass Point.

Gonzi's Seafood and Mini Mart is at 105 Smith Bay.

Red Hook Market is at Red Hook Shopping Center, and **Marina Market** (same owner as the famous wine and spirits shop in Cruz Bay) is in Red Hook. It has good quality produce.

St. Thomas Entertainment & Events

ENTERTAINMENT: St. Thomas has the greatest variety of nightlife found on any of the Virgins. Unfortunately, because of the crime here, it's recommended that you take a taxi to and fro.

To find out what's going on specifically check the "Weekend" supplement to the Thursday *Daily News.* The *Island Trader* also features a "Creative Loafing" section which is updated weekly. Call up for directions and cover charge.

PERFORMANCES: The open-to-the-stars 1196-seat amphitheater at **Reichhold Center for the Arts** (☎ 693-1559) has plays and performances.
http://www.reichholdcenter.com

The **Pistarckle Theater** (☎ 775-7877), Tillett Gardens in Tutu is the island's only professional theater company. Performances range from "The Nerd" to "Harriet's Return." They also run a summer camp. The company's name means "a great confusion,"a word which likely derives

from *spetakel*, a Danish word with the same meaning.
http://www.pistarckletheater.vi

Set at the Antilles School in Frenchman's Bay, **the Prior-Jollek Hall** (☎ Carol Malo: 776-1600) opened in 2007. It hosts performers such as the Moscow Piano Quartet.

MUSIC/DANCING: The Green House has DJs nightly except Sun.

Island Blitz (☎ 776-3004) in Contant is an entertainment complex offering sports bar, wine and champagne bar, dance club, an. It is open from Mon. to Sat. noon–2 AM and Sun. from noon–4 AM.

HOTEL ENTERTAINMENT: Many of the hotels have disco and/or live music. Check the *Island Delights* section of the St. Thomas *Daily News.*

CINEMA: Market Square East (☎ 776-3666) has seven cinemas.

EVENTS: Chief among these is **Carnival.** Revived in 1952, it is usually held during the last eight days of April. The parade, which takes place on the last day, features the King and Queen of Carnival, Mocko Jumbi ("imaginary ghosts") mounted on 17-ft.-high stilts, and local contingents of steel and calypso bands, dance troupes, and floats. A Children's Parade is held the day before. Events are held inside compact Lionel Roberts Stadium (near Blackbeard's

 To head to Havensight Mall, it's easiest just to hop on one of the taxis returning cruise ship passengers to the ship. You'll hear the cry "back to the ship" as they round them up on Main St.

Hill). There is one night of calypso revues featuring the best of the Caribbean's calypso singers (from the Mighty Gabby of Barbados to Swallow from Antigua), a Latin/Calypso Music Night, a Calypso Revue, a Steelband Jamboree (featuring steel band competitions), and the selection of king and queen.

At night action centers around the food stalls with a special "food booth day" as a traditional part of the festivities. In 1993 a tumultuous controversy centered around this day when the governor—in response to the deficit—refused to allow government employees to take their traditional day off with full pay so they could sample the food booth goodies. If you're staying over on St. John, you can take special late night ferries back after events.

For more information contact the **VI Carnival Committee** (☎ 776-3113).

The legal holiday of **Martin Luther King Day** in Jan. is generally marked by a march, ceremony, and music at Emancipation Gardens.

Every **St. Patrick's Day** local Irish residents hold a parade.

On March 31, the anniversary of **Transfer Day** (cession of the islands from the Danes to the US) is marked by several public ceremonies.

French Heritage Week generally takes place in Frenchtown and on the Northside during the second week of July.

Twice per year the **"Arts Alive"** fair (see sidebar) takes place at Tillett Gardens in Tutu.

St. Thomas Shopping

Know your Stateside prices before arriving if you intend to save money on duty-free goods. (for limits see "shopping" in the Introduction.) The island's shopping areas are in town and at Havensight Mall where the cruise ships dock. Others include resort gift shops, shopping centers, and Mountain Top. The free "Shopping Map" is a good guide to businesses. But the most fun way to shop is just to go browsing.

☞ A tee shirt purchased in St. Thomas became the center of a major controversy in 2007 when Joe Winiecki of Largo, Fla. boarded a Southwest flight in Columbus, Ohio, donning a fictional fishing shop T-shirt reading "Master Baiter." A Southwest steward ordered Winiecki, who was seated in the aircraft, that he must either change his shirt, turn it inside out, or disembark. He changed under protest, but management later apologized.

CRAFTS AND UNIQUE ITEMS: Local crafts are uncommon but still can be found.

A great place to stop by is **Native Arts and Crafts** which you will find just past the Visitors Bureau Information Center.

Captain's Corner has stores on Dronningens Gade (Main St.), the Waterfront, at Havensight (two locations), at Mountaintop, and in Cruz Bay, St. John. It sells a wide variety of items, including voodoo masks, model ships, and hot sauces and spices.

Down Island Traders on the waterfront, sells a variety of teas, spices, and unique fruit jellies.

Tradewinds Shop, 30 Dronningens Gade (Main St.) on the waterfront, sells items ranging from larimar to hook bracelets.

On the waterfront at Raadgets Gade, the **English Shop** sells crystal and china.

S&S Antiques (☎ 774-2074), 25 Main St. (Dronnigens Gade), carries a great variety of antiques.
http://www.sosantiquesvi.com

Opened in May 2008, the **Afro-Caribbean Drum Center** (☎ 227-1646) sells beads and all manner of drums and is open Mon.–Sat. from 11:30 AM – 3:30 PM. It's located at

#1 Snelge Gade: enter between Subway and Cuzzins along Trumpeter Gade: turn L at the Bambini mural.

☞ Owner Jammin' Jerry Z provides 45 min. tours ($15 pp for drummers, $3 pp for spectators) which demonstrate Afro-Caribbean drumming and offer a hands-on introductory lesson. http://www.acdrumcenter.com

Ifa Ase, 21 Bjerge Gade, is an "Afrocentric" store which also has events. The name comes from combining the Rasta phrase for natural "ital" with the Yoruban word "ase," (pronounced "ashay") which means personal empowerment.

Botanica San Miguel, 33 Princesse Gade, sells an assortment of candles, balms, and the like which are employed in the rituals of Santeria, a religion which has its roots in West Africa's Yoruba culture.

In the Al Cohen building across from the entrance to Havensight Mall, **Coin D'Oro** imports gold jewelry, necklaces, silver, crystal, and pens. Reggae fans may want to check out the **Reggae Lounge** here.

CLOTHING, SHOES, AND LEATHER: Near the park and across the street, **Zora the Sandalmakers**, 34 Norre Gade, sells a variety of handmade sandals and bags.

SNORKELING GEAR: Mask and Fin (☎ 774-7177), 42 Norre Gade, sells gear.

CAMERAS AND ELECTRONICS: **Boolchands** has stores at Havensight and on Main St; they also sell linen and lace.

With stores at 33 and 35 Main St. and at Havensight, **Royal Caribbean** is one of the largest camera and electronic stores.

JEWELERS: There are innumerable jewelry shops. Impoverished window shoppers and the well-heeled alike may feast their eyes

on the gems and jewelry displayed. *Shops below are listed alphabetically.*

Housed in an attractive old building on Dronningens Gade (Main St.), **A. H. Riise** sells jewelry and other goods including Javanese and Balinese handicrafts.

Alpha Jewelers, 17 Dronningens Gade (Main St.) sells jewelry, watches, and gems.

Part of a worldwide chain, **Amsterdam Sauer**, 14 Dronningens Gade (Main St.), carries a variety of gems including topaz.

Ballerina Jewelers, 6-7 and 7A Dronningens Gade (Main St.), stock a variety of items

Boolchands has stores at Havensight and at 31 Dronningens Gade (Main St.) sells jewelry and gems.

One of the largest of the island's jewelry shops, **Cardow** has a good selection of diamonds and emeralds. Their two shops on Main St. are right across from each other.

Cartier, the famous jeweler, is on Dronningens Gade (Main St.).

Columbia Emeralds, Royal Dane Mall, have a wide variety of gems and watches.

Dazzlers, Havensight Mall, sell jewelry along with perfume and other items.

Diamonds International, on Dronningens Gade (Main St.) next to Drake's Passage, offers gold jewelry and a wide selection of loose diamonds, rubies, emeralds, sapphires, topaz, and amethysts which may be matched with the setting of your choice. Other stores are at the Grand Galleria, the Wyndham Sugar Bay Resort, and at Havensight Mall.

Empire Jewels, 22 Dronningens Gade (Main St.), stock a large collection of gems.

Gemstone House and **Gemcasa**, Royal Dane Mall and Store Tvaer Gade, offer an abundance of set and unset gems.

Grand Jewelers, 7 Dronningens Gade (Main St.), is a family-owned diamond and unset gem store.

Coffee Break Time

While shopping on St. Thomas there are a number of places where you can take a coffee break:

Beans, Bytes & Websites (☎ 776-7265), *Royal Dane Mall*

Little Switzerland Internet Café (in town)

Frenchtown Deli & Coffee Shop

Calypso Cafe (in back of the A. H. Riise Mall).

H. Stern jewelers has two jewelry (and one watch) stores on Dronningens Gade (Main St.), and stores in the Frenchman's Reef, Bluebeard's Castle, and at Havensight.

House of Rajah, 32 Raadets Gade, sells watches and jewelry.

Set inside A.H. Riise on Dronningens Gade (Main St.), the **Ilias Lalao Unis** counter offers a variety of handcrafted Greek designs.

Imperial Jewelers, 10 Dronningens Gade (Main St.), stock loose and set stones.

Jewels, on the Waterfront and at Havensight, sell watches and jewelry including the designs of David Yurman.

The four branches of **Little Switzerland** offer jewelry, watches, crystal, and other luxury items; one faces Emancipation Park between the waterfront and Main St. The other three are on Main St. and in Havensight.

Lucky Jewelry, 17 Dronningens Gade (Main St.), specializes in blue, pink, and carnary diamonds.

Nita's Jewelry, Drake's Passage and Trompeter Gade, sells rubies, sapphires, watches, and other items.

Omni Jewelry, 7A and 14A Dronningens Gade (Main St.), sell color diamands as w ell as other gems and jewelry. They are also at Havensight.

Touch of Gold, 25A Dronningens Gade (Main St.), sells Skagen watches and other jewelry.

Trident Jewels and Time, 9LB Gade (Main St.), sells the Hidalgo line of mix and match stackable rings and bracelets.

HANDBAGS: Longchamp Boutique, 2 Dronningens Gade (Main St.), sells Longchamp bags.

The Crystal Shoppe, in A. H. Riise on Dronningens Gade (Main St.), sells a wide variety of name-brand products.

PERFUME: Tropicana Perfume Shop, 2 Dronningens Gade (Main St.), has a good selection.

LINENS: Boolchands has stores at Havensight and at 31 Dronningens Gade (Main St.). They feature Battenburg lace and hand-embroidered goods.

Linen House, Inc. has stores at 7-A Royal Dane Mall, on Main St., and in Palm Passage.

Mr. Tablecloth, 6 Dronningens Gade (Main St.), sells everything you need for your tables as well as bed linen.

Omni Linens, 14A Dronningens Gade (Main St.) and at 5332 Raadets Gade and Havensight, sells linen as well as jewelry.

TOYS: Grandpa's Korner Emporium has a great selection. It's at International Plaza and at Tutu Park.

RECORDS: International Records & Tapes is at 3 Store Strade which is down the street to the W from Parrot Fish.

Another good record store is **Modern Music** which is in Nisky Center, Havensight.

 Set at Lockhart Shopping Center one block up from the cruise ship dock, and at Tutu Gardens, **Kmart** has about the lowest alcohol prices.

ALCOHOL: You can take advantage of liquor-tasting bars to get plastered even if you don't intend to buy any liquor. If you do intend to buy some, shop around for the lowest liquor prices. A large number of stores on and around Main St. sell booze.

The **Virgin Island Brewing Company** has a store inside the International Mall just off the Waterfront in Royal Dane Mall. Another is at International Plaza.

GRANDE GALLERIA: This new complex of shops has some interesting stores including the **Belle Femme Boutique.**

HAVENSIGHT MALL: Located alongside the West Indian Company Cruise Ship Dock, the **Havensight Shopping Mall** has a concentration of more than 40 shops along with a bank and restaurants. You can find nearly everything — clothes, jewelry, watches, leather goods, candies, crystal, luggage — you might want to buy. Many of the shops here also have a branch in town.

ART GALLERIES: Gallery St. Thomas, upstairs at #1 Main St., offers a wide variety of works by different local artists. Watch for the building with blue shutters which is a block N of the PO. You can also see works from this gallery at Bella Blu, a Frenchtown restaurant.
http://www.gallerystthomas.com

The **Virgin Islands Council on the Arts** (☎ 774-5984), 5070 Norre Gade, hosts exhibits.

The **Jonna White Art Gallery,** Palm Passage off of Main St., highlights her distinctive large-size art.

Bambini-Swayne Gallery is across from the Synagogue and features the work of Ellen Swane and Vincent Roy Bambini. **Cloud Nine** is nearby.

Mango Tango, an art gallery, is at Al Cohen's Plaza on Raphune Hill and at Yacht Haven Grande.

On Rte. 38 across from Four Winds Plaza (where you get off if arriving by bus) and set between Point Pleasant and the (closed) Grand Beach Palace, Tillett's Gardens houses the **Tillett Art Gallery and Craft Studios** which contains a variety of silk screen fabrics, enamelware, stained glass, and pottery — all of which are designed on the premises. **http://www.tillettgardens.com**

This drawing of a St. Thomian woman is by Camille Pissarro (1830–1903), an important member of the French Impressionist group of painters, who was was born in St. Thomas. His father was a French Jewish merchant, and his mother was of Creole origin. Pissarro departed St. Thomas for Venezuela before settling in France in 1855. He moved to England during the Franco-Prussian war. Later, he became a fervent anarchist.

Kilnworks Pottery and Fine Crafts Gallery, Smith Bay, sells a variety of work including Peggy Seiwert's Caribbean cloud pastel vases as well as sculptures, enamels, and watercolors.
http://www.kilnworkspotteryvi.com

OUTLYING SHOPPING: Opened in June 1993, **Tutu Park Mall** features a K Mart (cheap booze!) and 20 or so other stores and restaurants. It's next to the **Four Winds Shopping Plaza** (Pueblo, Western Auto, drugstore, SDA vegetarian restaurant) and across from **Fort Mylner Shopping Plaza** which has expanded as Rte. 32 has been altered.

Market Square East has a Cost-U Less, a movie theater, and a World Gym.

St. Thomas Information and Services

INFORMATION: *St. Thomas This Week* is the most useful of the free publications; single copies ($3) are available by mail by writing Box 1627, St. Thomas 00804. There are also a near infinite number of other free handouts including the *USVI Playground* and *What to Do St. Thomas St. John*.

Staffed with tourism secretaries, the **Hospitality Lounge**, is housed in an old building along Post Office Alley and near the waterfront. You can pick up a lot of useful information here.

Be sure to read *The Daily News* while on the island; the Friday edition has an extremely useful "Weekend" section. Founded in 1930, the paper won a 1995 Pulitzer Prize for public service for an exposé of corruption in the islands' criminal justice system. Billionaire Jeffrey Prosser took over the paper in 1998, but bankruptcy forced the paper's sale to PA's Times-Shamrock in May 2008.
http://www.virginislandsdailynews.com

The **St. Thomas/St. John Hotel Association** (Box 2300, St. Thomas 00803) can be reached at 774-6835.

INTERNET ACCESS AND PHONE: The Virgin Islands Public Library and Archives, Main St. between Gutters Gade and Queen's Quarter, are open Mon. to Fri. 9 AM–9 PM. A quiet place to pass the time, it offers internet access for a fee ($2 ph).

Other places offering **internet service** include **Little Switzerland Internet Café** (☎ 776-2100) in town, **Beans, Bytes & Websites** (☎ 776-7265), Royal Dane Mall, the **Offshore Bar** (☎ 779-6400) at the Port of Sale Mall (near the cruise ships), the **Frenchtown Deli & Coffee Shop**, and the **Cyber Cafe** in Red Hook.

The offices of the **Island Resources Foundation** (☎ 775-6225, Box 33, St. Thomas 00802) are at Red Hook.

SERVICES: There are five **post offices.** One is at Emancipation Gardens on Main St. in downtown Charlotte Amalie near the fort. Another is at 100 Veteran's Drive in Frenchtown (around 20 min. on foot from the town center along the waterfront). A third is at Havensight. The fourth is at 9630 Estate Thomas. A fifth is in Tutu Park Mall.

The Calling Station (☎ 777-8205) is at Al Cohen's Mall in Havensight. Look for the white horse.

HEALTH: The **Schneider Regional Medical Center** (☎ 776-8311) is in Sugar Estate.
http://www.rishospital.org

Red Hook Family Practice (☎ 775-2303) offers 24-hr. care at Red Hook Plaza.

Doctor's Choice Pharmacy (☎ 777-1400) is at Wheatley Center and has a branch on Main St.

VIDEO: Island Video (☎ 774-6165) is at Four Winds is in Nisky Center.

St. Thomas Video and CDs is in Al Cohens Plaza Bldg. at Havensight.

LAUNDRY: **La Providence Laundromat** (☎ 777-3747) is in Tutu Park on Rte. 38.

Imaginatively named **Lost Sock Laundromat and Dry Cleaner** (☎ 775-1931) is at Four Winds Plaza.

Four Star Laundromat (☎ 774-8689) is at 68 Kronsprindsens Gade.

BANKING: **Banks** are open Mon. to Thurs. 9 AM–2:30 PM, Fri. 9 AM–2 PM, 3:30–5 PM.

Bank of Nova Scotia has bank branches with ATM services at the following locations: Waterfront, Havensight, Nisky Center, Red Hook, and Tutu.

Banco Popular has bank branches with ATM services at the following locations: Altona, Hibiscus Alley, Ft. Mylner, Sugar Estate, and Red Hook.

Firstbank has has bank branches with ATM services at Waterfront, Red Hook, FirstBank Plaza, and at several other places.

☞ Don't forget that you can use your ATM or credit card at a US Post Office and get up to $50 cash back.

BOOKSTORES: The comprehensive **Dockside Bookshop** (☎ 774-4937) is inside Havensight Mall. It should be selling copies of this book, so recommend it to any guidebook-needy friends you meet here.

The Island Newsstand is at the airport.

SPAS: Most of the large resorts have health clubs and spas.

Lé Face by Zina (☎ 774-7283), Crown Bay Marina, offers a range of treatments.

The Look spa (☎ 776-8672) is a full-service spa set in the Mariona Building in Frenchtown which offers services ranging from manicures to facials to massages. They offer special "bridal party rates."

Main St., Charlotte Amalie circa 1900.

St. Thomas Attractions	
1	Mountaintop, Estate St. Peter, Fairchild Park
2	Mahogany Bay Golf Course
3	Drakes Seat
4	Coral World
5	Tillett Gardens
6	Kayaking Tour
7	Charlotte Amalie (historic sites)
8	Hassel Island
9	Water Island
10	Paradise Point, Havensight

St. Thomas Beaches	
A	Hull Beach
B	Magens Bay Beach
C	Coki Point Beach
D	Water Bay (Pineapple Beach)
E	Sapphire Beach
F	Great Bay Beach
G	Cowpet Bay Beach
H	Secret Harbour Beach
I	Bolongo Bay Beach
J	Frenchman Bay Beach
K	Limetree Beach
L	Morningstar Beach, Bluebeards Beach
M	Honeymoon Beach
N	Lindbergh Beach
O	Brewers Bay Beach

Knot's Away Spa (☎ 775-7905) is offers facials, tinting, massages and other services at American Yacht Harbor .

Gym Sweeny and Sea Grape Spa (☎ 777-4422) is at the Elysian Resort near the Ritz Carlton and Cowpet Bay. They offer spa treatments and fitness training.

OTHER: Mom's Day Care Center (☎ 495-0526) at 394-325 Anna's Retreat takes care of kids (two mos. to 12 years) from 6 AM–6 PM (including two meals and baths).

Charlotte Amalie

Many of the 51,181 St. Thomians live in this small but attractive town. Although cruise ships rather than slavers visit the harbor these days, the smell of history is still in the air. The shops lining the streets running parallel to the harbor were originally pirate warehouses.

As a reminder of the colonial past, street signs affixed to corner buildings are in both English and Danish, and cars drive on the left side of the streets. The three main streets are **Dronningen's Gade** (Main St.), **Norre Gade** (North St.), and **Vimmelskaft's Gade** (Back St.).

A series of interlocking alleyways (converted into shopping malls) runs from Dronningen's Gade (Main St.) down to Veteran's Drive, a four-lane thoroughfare which parallels the waterfront.

By all means, avoid downtown when the cruise ships unleash their passengers and it becomes a struggle just to walk.

☞ For more information on cruise ships, see the special report "Cruise Control" which is available on the Ocean Conservancy's website: **http://www.oceanconservancy.org**

Charlotte Amalie Sights

Best way to see this town is on foot when only a few cruise ships are in the harbor. Among its most charming features are its stone stairways, known as "stone steps," which were constructed because the steep hillsides rising behind the town made road building problematic. If you can ignore the touristic, salesminded atmosphere that prevails downtown, there's plenty to see. You're sure to find your own attractions in addition to the ones listed below.

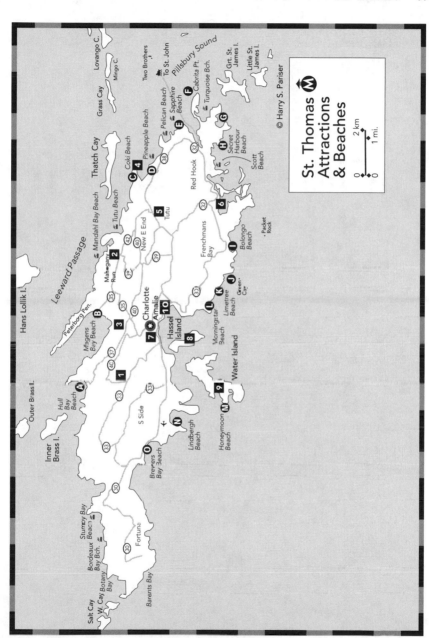

St. Thomas
Attractions
& Beaches

© Harry S. Pariser

0   2 km
0   1 mi.

Hans Lollik I.

Leeward Passage

Outer Brass I.

Inner
Brass I.

Salt Cay
W. Cay   Botany
Bay
Bordeaux
Bay Bch.
Stumpy Bay
Beach

Barents Bay

Fortuna

S Side

Brewers
Bay Beach

Lindbergh
Beach

Water Island

Honeymoon
Beach

Hull
Bay
Beach

Magens
Bay Beach

Peterborg Pen.

Charlotte
Amalie

Hassel
Island

Morningstar
Beach

Limetree
Beach

Green
Cay

Frenchmans
Bay

Bolongo
Beach

Packet
Rock

Thatch Cay

Mandahl Bay Beach

Tutu Beach

Coki Beach

Mahogany
Run

New E End

Tutu

Red Hook

Lovango C.

Mingo C.

Grass Cay

Two Brothers

To St. John

Pillsbury Sound

Pineapple Beach

Pelican Beach

Sapphire
Beach

Cabrita Pt.

Turquoise Bch.

Grt. St.
James I.

Little St.
James I.

Secret
Harbour
Beach

Scott
Beach

ST. THOMAS

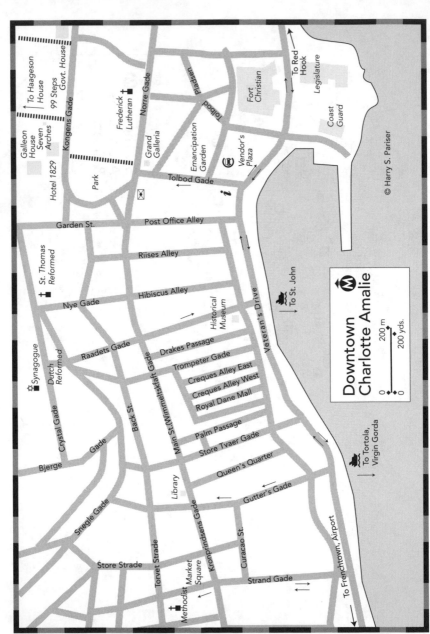

© Harry S. Pariser

To Haageson House
99 Steps
Govt. House
Galleon House
Seven Arches
Hotel 1829
Park
Kongens Gade
Frederick Lutheran
Norre Gade
Pladsen
Tolbod
Grand Galleria
Emancipation Garden
Vendor's Plaza
Fort Christian
To Red Hook
Legislature
Coast Guard
Tolbod Gade
Garden St.
Post Office Alley
Riises Alley
St. Thomas Reformed
Hibiscus Alley
Nye Gade
Historical Museum
Veteran's Drive
To St. John
Synagogue
Dutch Reformed
Raadets Gade
Drakes Passage
Trompeter Gade
Creques Alley East
Creques Alley West
Royal Dane Mall
Crystal Gade
Back St.
Main St. (Wimmelskaft Gade)
Gade
Palm Passage
Store Tvaer Gade
Queen's Quarter
Bjerge
Library
Gutter's Gade
To Tortola, Virgin Gorda
Snegle Gade
Kronprindsens Gade
Curacao St.
Torvet Strade
Store Strade
Methodist
Market Square
Strand Gade
To Frenchtown, Airport

Downtown Charlotte Amalie

0 200 m
0 200 yds.

ST. THOMAS

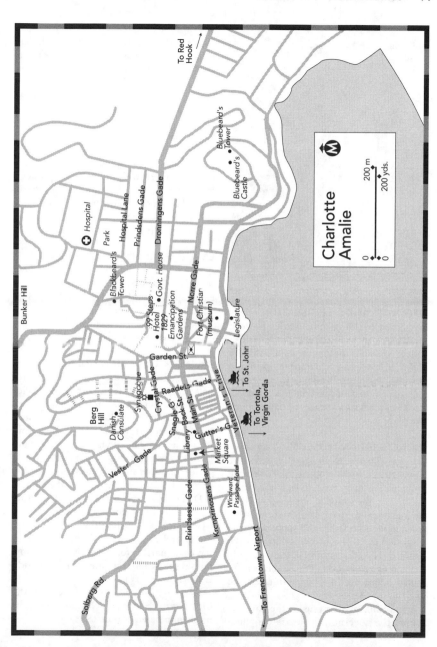

Charlotte Amalie

200 m
0
200 yds.
0

To Red Hook

Bluebeard's Tower

Bluebeard's Castle

Bunker Hill

Hospital

Blackbeard's Park

Hospital Lane

Prindsens Gade

Dronningens Gade

Blackbeard's Tower

99 Steps

Hotel 1829

Govt. House

Norre Gade

Emancipation Gardens

Fort Christian (museum)

Legislature

Garden St.

To St. John

Berg Hill

Danish Consulate

Synagogue

Crystal Gade

Raadets Gade

Snegle G.

Back St.

Main St.

Library

Gutter's

Veteran's Drive

To Tortola, Virgin Gorda

Vester Gade

Market Square

Windward Passage Hotel

Princesse Gade

Kronprinsens Gade

Solberg Rd.

To Frenchtown, Airport

Haagesen House.

VIRGIN ISLANDS LEGISLATURE: This lime-green building with white shutters, constructed in 1874, served as the Danish police barracks before housing the US Marines. It became a school in 1930 and then the legislature building in 1957. For a unique glimpse of local politics in action, check out the heated, virulent debates which take place inside.

FORT CHRISTIAN MUSEUM: *Enter along Veterans Drive.* Built shortly after the arrival of the first colonists, this imposing landmark, in neoclassic style, is the oldest building on the island. Completed in 1672, the masonry ramparts and bastions were added in the 18th C; the fort was completely renovated in 1871 when Charlotte Amalie regained its status as capital. It is currently undergoing renovation . (The displays highlighted below are likely to be found there when it reopens).

A building of many uses, the fort has housed the governor, the artisan commu-

nity, and in times of natural disaster during its early history, the entire population. It has also served as the local branch of the Lutheran Church, as a site for pirate executions, and as a jail. The small museum once occupied a few fluorescent-lit cells in the basement; it has now been brought up to the main level and expanded. Note the archaeological artifacts, shells, old mahogany furniture, and display of household utensils, including a hollow glass rolling pin which could be filled with water to keep dough from sticking. The museum outlines Virgin Island history from the Carib era to the present day. There are many historical photos as well as an entire room devoted to herbs.

EMANCIPATION PARK: These small public gardens near the fort mark the spot where Governor von Scholten proclaimed the emancipation of the slaves on July 3, 1848. A bell on the SW corner is a replica of the United States' Liberty Bell, and the statue is of King Christian IX.

FREDERIK LUTHERAN CHURCH: One of the most beautiful architectural treasures on St. Thomas, Frederik Luthera is the oldest church on the island and the second oldest Lutheran building in the Western Hemisphere. It is located uphill from Emancipation Park along Norre Gade. Built in 1793, it was renovated in 1826 and 1973.

Bethania Hall, which serves as the Parish Hall, stands adjacent to the church. A Danish manor, it was built as the private residence of one Jacob S. Lind in 1806.

The building nearby, which once housed the Grand Hotel, dates from 1840. Once the headquarters for the social elite, it now houses shops and restaurants in the **Grande Galleria**, a courtyard.

Farther down Norre Gade is the **Moravian church** which dates from the nicely numbered year of 1888.

The 99 Steps

HAAGENSEN HOUSE: Set right off the 99 Steps, Haagensen House is run by the St. Thomas Historical Trust. It displays an outstanding collection of antiques from Barbados, St. Croix, and St. Thomas. You'll also find Danish, English, Japanese and US porcelain. (The Buffalo plates are the most valuable). The kitchen has a brass bedwarmer, and every child that walks in assumes is a popcorn maker! The Haagensens —the slave owners who owned the property —had nine children. The patio commands great views. A walking tour chiefly designed for cruise-ship tourists (☎ 776-1234, ✆ 693-4321, 800-344-5771) now runs from Blackbeard's Castle to Villa Notman (the former Hotel Boynes), to the Villa Brittania, to Haagensen House, and then down to Hotel 1812.

GOVERNMENT HOUSE: Now the official office of the elected USVI governor, this elegant brick-and-wood, three-story mansion stands atop the hill on Kongens Gade. It was built in 1867. Stand in the small park across the road and view the impressive architecture and the black limos parked outside.

Farther up the same street to the W is **Hotel "1829"** which is a good example of 19th C architecture. It is the end point for the Haagensen House tour.

CROWN HOUSE: Climb either of the two step streets along Kongens Gade to reach here. Now privately owned, this 18th C mansion once functioned as the governor's residence. This mostly stone two-story house has a Dutch-gambrel hipped roof. Peter von Scholten lived here when he was governor of St. Thomas in 1827.

SEVEN ARCHES MUSEUM: This 19th C Danish craftsman's house (☎ 774-9295), restored in traditional style by Barbara Demaras and Philbert Fluck, is the only private home on the island open for viewing. This is a good place to take a refreshing break from your shopping. Originally there was a staircase between the first and second

The entrance to the synagogue.

floor. Now, however, the second floor is a museum, and the couple live on the first. Barbara is an accomplished painter, and she enjoys meeting interesting people.

Nearly all of the furniture is from Barbados; a few pieces come from Haiti, and the bed is from the VI. The Royal Copenhagen porcelain is from Barbara's parents.

From the second floor you can see a nightblooming cactus on a structure which used to be the servants' quarters for the house next door. Watch for the iguanas which have trained Philbert to feed them hibiscus flowers from the lovely small garden below.

Be sure to check out the comments in the guest book and add your own. Admission is $7. It's open Mon. to Sat. from 10 AM–4 PM and on Sat. and Sun. from noon–4 PM. Knock for admission. To get here, pass Government House, then Moron House, and then turn L at the Lt. Governor's office. The entrance is a short walk up the step street to the L.

99 STEPS AND BLACKBEARD'S TOWER: The step street perpendicular to Blackbeard's Tower is the 99 Steps, most famous of the town's step streets. As you climb, count to see how many there actually are. Note the multicolored bricks: they arrived here as ship's ballast; the yellow ones are from Denmark, the reds come from England, France and Spain.

SYNAGOGUE OF BERACHA VESHALOM VEGIMULTH HASIDIM: This house of worship is on Crystal Gade. Take the stairs up to the entrance. Rebuilt in 1833 on the site of previous synagogues, this building was constructed in a mixture of Gothic Revival styles. The congregation was founded in 1796 by settlers arriving from Curacao and St. Eustatius.

Still in use today, it's the oldest synagogue on the island and the second oldest in the Western Hemisphere. All furnishings date from 1833. Its six Torahs (Old Testament parchment scrolls hand-lettered in Hebrew) remain hidden behind the mahogany ark's doors, but you can see the Spanish 11th-C menorah (candelabra used in the celebration of Chanukah).

There are two explanations for the sand on its floors. One is that it commemorates the exodus of the Jews from Egypt. The other is more complex. During the Spanish Inquisition, Spanish Sephardic Jews were compelled to practice in secret. Sand muffled the sound of their prayers and other movements; this custom was brought with them when they emigrated to the Caribbean, and similar sand floors may be found in other Caribbean synagogues. Today, its 300 members is largely composed of recent immigrants. This congregation celebrated its 200th anniversary in 1996 and was named a National Historic Landmark in 1997. The synagogue is open Mon. through Fri. from 9:30 AM–4 PM. Worship services are held on Fri. evenings.

http://www.onepaper.com/synagogue hbrewcong@islands.vi

MARKET SQUARE: The site of what was once the largest slave market in the Caribbean, **Market Square** is located along Kronprindsens Gade near the library. Here, locals sell a vast variety of fruit and vegetables ranging from tannia to okra to cassava. There's even a dreadlocked dude who offers up fresh squeezed sugarcane juice; a pair of "Black Jews" bear witness against imposters in Israel. The market's unique curved roof was imported from Europe. It has been recently refurbished.

ALTON AUGUSTUS ADAMS MUSIC RESEARCH INSTITUTE: The Alton

Augustus Adams Music Research Institute (☎ 774-6707), 1-B Kongens Gade, is a branch of the Black Music Research at Columbia College in Chicago. This resource center containing computerized archival material on Virgin Islands and Caribbean music opened in 2003. The institute is housed in the ancestral abode of Alton Augustus Adams (1889–1987) who was the first black bandmaster in the US Navy as well as the composer of the Virgin Islands march. The institute is attempting to revive interest in forms of traditional music such as quelbe, the official music of the Virgin Islands. It's open Tues. through Fri. from 9 AM–3PM.
http://www.cbmr.org

PARADISE POINT: Set atop Flag Hill and overlooking town, this shopping area, restaurant, and bar can be reached by road.
The **St. Thomas Skyride** (☎ 774-9809) is open daily. It takes visitors from opposite the Havensight Mall up to this 700-ft. lookout point. This is best experienced if you've never taken a chairlift before; otherwise, it's not all that remarkable for the premium price of transport ($19 adults, $9.50 children 6–12). This is a cruise-ship-passenger tailored attraction if there ever was one! A small collection of shops and a restaurant is set at the top. they've also added the Skyjump (9 AM–5 PM), a safer version of bungee jumping, and offer a rental apartment and cottage as well as wedding and other packages. (It is generally closed when cruise ships are not in port).

BUTTERFLY FARM: One of a chain of such operations, the Butterfly Farm at Havensight Mall by the Cruise Ship Dock shows visitors the life cycle of the butterfly.
http://www.thebutterflyfarm.com

Town within a town, this small community in the SW part of Charlotte Amalie is home to one of the smallest but most conspicuous ethnic groups in the Virgin Islands —descendants of the French Huguenots. Also known as "Careenage" because old sailing boats careened here for repairs, the brightly painted houses have immaculate, packed-dirt yards. These days Frenchtown is visited mainly by patrons of its fine restaurants.

HISTORY: Centuries ago, Protestant French Huguenots, fleeing religious persecution in Catholic France, were among the earliest settlers in the Caribbean. They arrived on several islands, including miniscule St. Barths (St. Bartolemy). In 1848, two members of the La Place family migrated to the site of Frenchtown and to sleepy Hull Bay along the N coast. Emigration began in force between 1863–1875, when economic conditions on St. Barths worsened and many sought to flee that tiny, rocky wart of an island.

THE PEOPLE: Some 1,500 strong, the "Frenchies" are a tough people renowned for their fishing abilities. The two French communities speak different dialects of archaic West Indian French and retain their cultural distinctions; there has been intermarriage and sociability between them.
Traditional dress was unique and resembled that found in their native Brittany. Women's heads were adorned with the *caleche,* the traditional shoulder-length headdress; men wore black and calico shirts, had their denim trousers rolled halfway up their legs, and went barefoot. Retaining this style of dress after arrival caused the locals to poke fun of them. In return, the vitriolic French spat out "cha cha" which means "go to the devil."
Ironically, the locals began to refer to the community as "Cha Cha Town," a name

which sticks to this day. There has been no love lost between the French and the local blacks—each side regarding the other with derision. Long the lowest socioeconomic class in the USVI, the French have emigrated in droves to the mainland in recent years where they readily assimilate. Today, they have moved up the economic ranks on St. Thomas.

EVENTS: Traditional events such as St. Anne's Day, Bastille Day, and the Christmas Day parade are still observed. Father's Day is a big celebration here..

THE FRENCH CIVIC ORGANIZATION MUSEUM: Housed in a yellow building next to Joseph Aubain Ballpark in Frenchtown, the three-room **French Civic Organization Museum** (☎ 714-2583) opened in July 2004. This very special collection of French relics chronicles French

influence in the Caribbean. Locals have donated more than 275 heirlooms ranging from a carved mahogany bed frame to several 80-year-old meat hooks to a 60-year-old toaster. Other items include fishing nets, mahogany furniture, antique accordions, and tambourines. A computer stores the genealogies of local families. A traditional house is next door to the museum. Admission is free: it's open Mon. to Fri. 9 AM–6 PM (closed noon–1 PM for lunch.

Hassel Island

This small island guarding Charlotte Amalie harbor is one of the most important historic sites in the USVI. Today, the National Park Service manages 90% of its 135 acres.

Today, there are a few hiking trails. They run to all of the sights. Be sure to see the fortification at **Cowell's Point** which was restored by the British in 1801 and named after the colonel to whom St. Thomas surrendered.

The Frenchtown waterfront

GETTING HERE: For ferry ($3) information call 693-9500, ext. 445 or 775-6238.

HISTORY: Activities ranging from agricultural to commercial to military have gone on here. Originally a peninsula attached to St. Thomas, Hassel Island became an island in the 1860s when the Navy cut through and dredged the narrow connecting isthmus in order to allow docking ships easier access to the harbor.

During the early 1800s, steamships would stopped at Hassel to transfer cargo and take on fuel, and the island had two working marine railways, three coaling docks, and a floating drydock. Fort Willoughby was constructed during the 1801 and 1807 British occupations of the island. A US Naval Station was located on Hassel Island from 1917-31; it was reactivated during WW II but abandoned thereafter.

Much of the island was acquired during the 1930s by the Paiewonsky family, chiefly in order to provide water for their rum distilleries. During the 1970s, Gov. Ralph Paiewonsky (1906-1991) wanted to develop the island but his conservationist brother Isidor (1894-2004) opposed the move. Lucrative offers, including one of $3 million from Reverend Sun Myung Moon, were turned down. Finally, the two brothers compromised by selling the land to the Department of the Interior for incorporation in the USVI National Park.

ST. THOMAS

Water Island

Fourth largest of the US Virgins (2.5 mi. by 1.5 mi.), **Water Island** is the oldest centerpiece of the Water Island Formation, a geological configuration consisting of 70 million year old lava flows. It's named for the freshwater ponds that once proliferated here. Its highest point is some 300 ft., and there are many irregular bays and peninsulas. The island today is largely a community of retirees. Residents have built and maintain the road system and provide for their own fire protection and garbage collection.

GETTING HERE: Ferries (☎ 690-4159) run to **Water Island** from Crown Bay Marina (Sub Base) at 6:30, 7:15, 8, 10:30, noon,

Called "Cha Chas" by the locals, St. Thomas Frenchmen sell baskets and hats in front of what is now the Old National Bank Building in Market Square, Charlotte Amalie in 1927.

and 2, 3:15, 4:15, 5:15, and 6 PM from Mon. to Sat.; 8 and 10:30 AM, noon, and 3 and 5 PM. on Sun and holidays. Additional ferries run some evenings ($10). The ferry returns at 6:45, 7:30, 8:15, and 10:45 AM, and 12:15, 2:15, 3:30, 4:30, 5:30, and 6:10 PM from Mon. to Sat. Sun. and certain holidays it runs at 8:15 and 10:45 AM and at 12:15, 3:15, and 5:15 PM. Rates are $5 OW, $9 RT; children are $3 OW, $5 RT. The first two luggage items are free; it's then $1for each additional item. Weekly, monthly and commuter passes are available. Tickets are sold on board by the captain. NOTE: These times are subject to change. Check vinow.com for current schedule.

HISTORY: Although there is not evidence of any permanent settlement, the island's first visitors were Arawaks. In the post-Columbian era, it became a popular hangout for pirates, who would shelter in its bays to await quarry.

The island's name comes from its fresh water ponds, where windjammers would refill their water casks. The earliest Danish land title known for the island dates from 1807, and the British may have granted it to Italian emigrant Joseph Daniel during their occupation (as part of the War of 1812–14) as a reward for his services as a shipyard owner.

In any event, it remained in his family's possession until 1905 when, under coercion, they sold it for $21,000 to the West Indian Co., Ltd. Their idea was to rent the property to foreign governments to use for maneuvers. This became unfeasible following the US purchase in 1917, and the island remained undeveloped.

In 1944, the US government purchased the island for $10,000 and began constructing an army base. Construction ceased right after the end of WWII, and it was given over to the Chemical Warfare Division who tested poison gases on pigeons and goats here. The army leased the island to the St. Thomas Development Authority. Aspiring retirees Walter and Floride Phillips, arriving in March 1951, saw the possibilities for development. The island was transferred to the Dept. of the Interior in 1952 and a 20-yr. lease signed with Water Island, Inc. which gave the VI corporation the opportunity to renew automatically after 20 yrs; the extension expired at the end of 1992. Control over the island passed into the hands of the local government in 1996; the remains of the old hotel here were demolished in 1998.

SIGHTS: Partially an artificial creation, **Honeymoon Beach** is the main attraction here. There's also a small botanical garden. Water Island has its very own one-room schoolhouse: The Virgin Valley Learning Center was begun in October 2002 by Robyn Bitterwolf and Cindy Wortman; most of its students come from St. Thomas.

PRACTICALITIES: Pirates Ridge Deli has an all-you-can-eat pizza on Friday nights. **Heidi's Honeymoon Grill** (☎ 777-5288) is open only on Sat. night. for gourmet dinners but is open daily for lunch. She sets up a movie screen on Mon. nights.

There are a number of villas. A good list is here:
http://www.vinow.com/waterisland/ accommodations_wi/

Providence Point Cottage and Apartment (☎ 777-8800, 800 233-4936) has a private dock, a small private beach, and a private pool.
http://www.water-island.com

Turtle Hill Vacation Home (☎ 641-1888) is a roomy two-bedroom with panoramic views.
http://www.turtlehillwaterisland.com

Villa Terra Nova (☎ 850-624-4948) is a breezy two-bedroom, two-bathroom private home with ocean views.
http://www.villaterranova.com

Virgin Islands Campground (☎ 776-5488, 877-502-7225) offers upscale accommodation in cabin tents. Facilities include hot tub, free WiFi, a communications room (with TV), shared kitchen and bathhouse, snorkeling equipment, and bike rental. Rates run around $135 for four in a cabin; a more expensive efficiency apartment holds two.
http://www.virginislandscampground.com
info@virginislandscampground.com

Water Island Adventures (☎ 714-2186, 775-5770) offer bike tours which are popular with cruise passengers.
http://www.waterislandadventures.com

Around St. Thomas

Although Charlotte Amalie is the island's heart, there are a number of other settlements and scattered points of interest. There's nothing here as spectacular as some of the sights and attractions on other Caribbean islands, but the views are great.

BEACHES: With more than 40 beaches on this small island, there's plenty of territory to explore. Beaches are open to the public because private property begins only above the high tide mark. Remember to take the usual precautions while visiting: Never leave anything of value in your car or unaccompanied on the beach. And be sure to use plenty of suntan oil: the sun is hot!

☞ Nudity and toplessness are frowned upon (and are illegal).

Following is a list of prominent beaches running counter clockwise from Charlotte Amalie. Set to the SE off Rte 30, the very accessible **Morningstar Beach** is a family beach with beige sand and occasional surf. All of the amenities are found here: snorkel gear, small sailboats, sailboards, tennis courts, etc. It lies behind the luxurious Frenchman's Reef hotel and the Morning Star Beach Resort. You may take "The Reefer" Ferry to get there. (See "getting around.")

Off of Rte. 30, the **Bluebeard's Beach Club and Villa** nearby is palm-lined and tranquil. Most of its visitors are staying at the hotel. Ask to see the iguanas.

Bolongo Beach has a high per-capita population of honeymooners. You can generally find a volleyball game in progress. Scuba and snorkel equipment are for rent.

Scott's Beach is next. Small but attractive, it's for strong swimmers only, as the water gets deep a short distance from the shore and the waves are feisty. To get here take Rte. 32, turn at Compass Point, and the beach is on the L. Enter through the restaurant.

The secret is out about **Secret Harbour Beach**. Secret Harbour Beach Resort is here, along with diving and snorkeling rentals, and restaurant/bar; sunsets are magnificent, and palm trees shade the sand. Picnicking is prohibited. It's accessed by Rte. 322. You should turn R just before the St. John ferry dock, follow the road, make a sharp R, and then a sharp L.

Circled by the Elysian Resort, the Cowpet East/West, and The Anchorage condos, **Cowpet Beach** has windsurfer rentals. It has a beachside restaurant at The Anchorage and food and drink and rentals at the Elysian.

Great Bay Beach has high winds and (accordingly) great windsurfing and kiteboarding. Equipment rentals are available.
http://islandsol.net

Vessup Beach, reached by rough Rte. 32 (Red Hook Rd.), has tables, grills, and little shade. It has a windsurfing operation.

Sapphire Beach is noted for its reef populated with fish and its waves peopled with suntanned windsurfers. Sunday afternoons there's a band and a party-down atmosphere. Sailboards, snorkel gear, small sailing craft, and lounge chairs are for rent. TV and film commercials have been filmed here, but it is not generally crowded. The **Sapphire Beach Resort** stands here. To get here take Rte. 38 to the signed turnoff and follow the road.

Lindqvist (Lindquist) Beach is on the east end not far from Sapphire Beach and Red Hook. Lindquist, part of Smith Bay Park, is a public beach run under the Magens Bay Authority. A $2 admission fee is charged for visitors age 13 and above. There are security guards, lifeguards, and trash bins; bath houses and a concession stand are planned. Following years of legal disputes, the VI government purchased the 21.5-acre parcel in Smith Bay surrounding Lindquist Beach for $8.9 million in November 2006.

Also known as **Pineapple** and **Renaissance, Water Bay Beach** is located in Smith Bay. You must enter through the resort. Pineapple Village Villas and others are here as well. It's accessed via Rte. 38 (Smith Bay Rd.).

Small **Coki Beach,** reputed to have the island's best snorkeling, lies next to Coral World Ocean Park at the NE end via Rte. 388. It becomes crowded when cruise ships are in port. There's a great view of Thatch Cay offshore. Lockers are available in Coral World Ocean Park; theft on this beach is rife.

Visitors may find **Mandahl Beach** disappointing: sand is scarce, the access road is rough, and there are a large number of sea urchins. Frenchies moor their boats in the lagoon here. Fisherman fish on the beach and from rocks.

☞ If you visit Mandahl Beach, you may want to check out the Buddhist temple under construction nearby. The **Nirvana Temple** (☎ 714-2700 or 998-2700) is the project of acupuncturist and physician Dr. May Trieu, a Vietnamese immigrant. **http://nirvanatemple.org**

Magens Bay, off Magens Rd. (Rte. 35), is on nearly every list of the world's best beaches. It's flanked on one side by Peterborg, which has luxurious villas of the wealthy, and palm groves are set to the back. This magnificent mile-long horseshoe of sand was given to the local government in 1946 through the beneficence of publishing tycoon Arthur Fairchild. It is the only beach which charges admission ($4 per person; $2 residents; children under 12 are free; parking is $2). Facilities include changing rooms, toilets, and a refreshment and gift center. This crowded beach is superb for people watching. The arboretum at the rear of the beach is being restored after abandonment by the local Rotary Club. Be sure to visit.

From here you can proceed through dry forest filled with lignum vitae, genip, cashew, and other woods to the **Peterborg Peninsula** which encloses the N side of the bay. The 6.67-acre patch of prime beachfront property at the E end of Magens Bay, designated for reserve status, is still unprotected because it has only forked over $600,000 of the selling price. The 20th Legislature appropriated the funds on Oct. 13, 1994, but the remainder of the $1.8 million sale price has yet to be paid. This means that the land could be sold to commercial interests and developed! In 1997, Merril Lynch donated 50 acres of surrounding land at the base of the peninsula to the Nature Conservancy. They currently control 311 acres.

 If you're thinking of combining chartering and staying in a luxury resort, **Regency Yacht Vacations** (☎ 800-524-7676) offers land and sea charter packages.

The **Nature Conservancy** is offering a **Magens Bay hike** ($60 pp) through **Virgin Islands Ecotours** (☎ 779-2155).

Once the site of Larry's Hideaway Campgrounds, **Hull Bay** still has Frenchie fishermen hauling in their catch. Snorkelers and (under appropriate conditions) board and body surfers abound. Imbibe at the **Northside Hideaway** bar which has the island's sole horseshoe pitch.

Follow Rte. 37 to the bottom of the road and make a sharp R onto the beach. One of the less frequently visited beaches, **Stumpy Bay** has plenty of surf and few people. To get here drive a mi. down a road off Rte. 30 W and then walk a half mi. to the beach.

Accessible by bus from Charlotte Amalie, mellow **Brewers Beach** lies off Rte. 30 near the University of the Virgin Islands. It has no facilities save some snack wagons. Owing to its W End location, the sunsets are fantastic.

For a quick dip after arriving or before departing the island, **Lindbergh Beach,** named after the famous flier who landed here during his world tour in the 1920s, is conveniently located across the street from the airport. Accessed by Airport Rd., it stretches from the Emerald Beach Resort past the Island Beachcomber Hotel and has a smooth, sandy bottom. Carnival parties and political rallies are held here.

ESTATE ST. PETER GREATHOUSE AND BOTANICAL GARDENS: Here you can find some 500 varieties of plants and trees which are identified on a nature trail running through the three landscaped acres. **The Greathouse** (☎ 774-4999/1724, ✆ 774-1723) has an amazing kitchen. The estate was once a large banana plantation. Open Mon. to Sat. from 9 AM–3 PM, it charges $10 admission ($5 residents, $2 students and church groups).

Suckerfish in Coral World.

Mountain Top on the North Side, is a heavily tourist infested viewpoint but, at 1,500 ft. (450 m), it is the island's highest point. It has a/c shopping and international stores.

The US Army renamed St. Peter Mountain, the island's highest, "Signal Mountain" and constructed their communications facility here. The cell phone antenna tower here is built on underground bunkers. Mountain Top originally served as the NCO and enlisted men's club, and the military invited Conrad Graves in as piano player. Taking advantage of the bananas on the St. Peter's plantation, Graves developed the famous recipe for the banana daiquiri which rules as Mountain Top's chief attraction.

CORAL WORLD OCEAN PARK: Once merely an underwater observation tower for marine life, **Coral World Ocean Park** (☎ 775-1555) has blossomed into a multifaceted enterprise, bringing aquarium, marine zoo, and sea trekking under one roof. It has two restaurants and two gift shops. Coral World isl ocated near Coki Beach on the island's NE and provides a good way for non-divers to view underwater sea life. Guided tours are led daily from 3 PM. From the two-level deck, observe life on the sea floor as well as the circling sharks, barracudas, and stingrays above. Tanks outside hold stingrays, sharks, turtles, birds, and other creatures. Marine Garden Aquariums has 21 saltwater tanks featuring zoological curiosities such as purple anemones and fluorescent coral.

Perhaps the best part is the seahorse collection which provides you a chance to view these elusive, scarce, and exotic creatures. Under the seahorse release program, seahorses are hatched and raised here and then released.

Coral World is open daily 9 AM–5 PM; Thurs., Fri., and Sat. until midnight; $18 adult admission, $9 children. Locals are given a hefty discount. Check around for a discount ticket in publications before you go here.
http://www.coralworldvi.com

OTHER SITES: Just on the edge of town atop Denmark Hill sits **Catherinegberg**, a mansion built around 1830 in modified Greek Revival and classical Georgian styles. It's closed to the public).

Restored **Nisky Memorial Mission**, which dates from 1777, stands along Harwood Highway.

Set at 1,200 ft (360 m), **Fairchild Park** offers views of both N and S coasts. Publishing tycoon Arthur Fairchild donated the park to the "people of the Virgin Islands" in 1946. His home **Louisenhoj**, a giant 'castle,' is closed to the public.

Valdemar Hill is a lookout point on Skyline Drive. Tour buses stop here.

St. Thomas Tours, Excursions, and Charters

LAND TOURS: There are a large number of basic tours around the island.

The **VI Taxi Association** (☎ 774-4550) offers a variety of tours.
http://www.vitaxi.com/id2.html

Fun Water Tours (☎ 775-7245) runs a variety of tours including trips to Tortola.
http://www.virginislandsshoreexcursions.com

Serenity Tours (☎ 714-4396) offer customized transport and tours for individuals and groups.
http://www.usviserenity.com

Flamon's Taxi & Island Tours (☎ 775-0335, cell: 513-4041) offer a wide variety of tours, including walking tours.
http://www.therealdealusvi.com

ST. JOHN TOURS: Most of these are listed under the St. John section.

For package tours to St. John call **Tropic Tours** (☎ 774-1855, 800-524–4334) whose "Island Safari Running" departs at 9 AM, Mon. through Sat.
http://www.tropictoursusvi.com

To hike the **Reef Bay Trail** (see St. John section) with the Park Service (☎ 776-6201), take a 9 AM ferry from Red Hook; the bus departs at 9:45 on Mon. and Wed.

FOR THE DISABLED: *Tropic Tours* (☎ 774-1855); can arrange tours for those in wheelchairs. **DIAL-A-RIDE** (☎ 776-1277) offer transportation assistance. **Aqua Action** (☎ 775-6285) and **Admiralty Dive Center** (☎ 777-9802) offer scuba for the disabled.

Accessible Adventures (☎ 344-8302) now offers tour services for the disabled on St. Thomas.
http://www.accessvi.com

⚓ Sir Francis Drake ⚓

Throughout history, the world has often been governed by prelates, officials, and brigands. Often, there has been a considerable overlap of roles between the three occupations. Even today, in the contemporary "First World," many brigands are lionized rather than jailed. So should come as no surprise that a coarse and lowly pirate might have become a "Sir" in 16th-century Britain.

Francis Drake was born in Tavistock, England to a Protestant family, and they were driven out of Devon early in his childhood following a Catholic uprising. They relocated to an old ship off the coast of Kent. Drake's father became a dockyard preacher, while the young Francis soon aspired to be a sailor. Drake's earliest experience was on a vessel which plied the coasts, and his first opportunity to hit the high seas came after a slaver hired him. He became acquainted with the lay of the land of the Spanish Main (the wealthiest portion of the Spanish New World empire—defined as the land lying between the Isthmus of Panama and the Orinoco River), and his instructor was fellow pirate and later comrade-in-arms John Hawkins.

Having witnessed firsthand the weakness of the Spanish Empire, Drake had found his career niche and continued activities that today might be characterized as international terrorism covertly funded by foreign governments. Some of his expeditions were paid for by Queen Elizabeth (who reaped a portion of the financial awards, thus building on the generational trust fund which forms the current Queen's wealth today). The Queen summoned him to a top-secret audience in 1577 where she engaged him to plunder the Spaniards and also to search for a Northwest Passage. Drake and four other ships set off later that year; only Drake's was to return. The others faced mutiny and shipwreck. Drake captured several galleons before returning in 1580 via the California coast and the rest of the world. His ship arrived back in the motherland packed with plunder equal to a year's national income and brandishing the achievement of having been the first British craft to circumnavigate the world.

The next time Hawkins and Drake teamed up John Hawkins became the procurer, buying cannon-equipped craft which could outspeed and conquer Spain's unwieldy galleons, and Drake became an admiral. He headed out in 1585, sacking Santo Domingo, Florida's St. Augustine, and held Cartagena (present-day Columbia) for ransom. This expedition hurt the Spaniards but returned little in the way of pecuniary dividends for the pockets of the project's backers.

Operation "Singeing the Beard" departed in 1587; Drake was on a mission to destroy the Spanish Armada in its berth in Cadiz. However, the time had passed for this, and Drake engaged the fleet off the coast of England in July 1588. The defense team, led by Drake as Vice-Admiral (an apt character reference) and Lord Admiral Howard at the helm, succeeded in routing the Armada. This proved to be the highpoint of his career.-

His 1589 expedition — formulated with the intention to return the King of Portugal to the throne and thus weaken the influence of Spain's monarchy proved in the end to be one of those ill-conceived, bumbling Iran Contra/Bay of Pigs style deals, and it ended in failure. Drake's subsequent retirement lasted for five years until the Queen Mother decided to give the Hawkins-Drake duo a second wind and sent them off to the West Indies to teach Spain a thing or two.

At Guadeloupe, the Spanish learned from a captured English vessel that the fleet was headed for San Juan and dispatched five galleons off to carry the warning and provide for a defense. Having learned that their intentions had been discovered and their advantage of surprise thus forfeited, the English docked at Virgin Gorda; they may have been trying to fool the Spanish. Late in the evening of November the Fourth they sailed out of Virgin Gorda, taking the present-day Sir Francis Drake Channel, to arrive at San Juan's entrance at daybreak.

It was too late: the harbor had been blockaded. Drake was routed, and he sailed South to Panama — this time without Hawkins, who had died in the Virgin Islands after an illness. His Panamanian venture proved similarly unproductive, and Drake must have realized that his career was on the rocks. Within a month's time, he sickened and died while off of the Honduran coast.

In the end, his adventuring-proved to be the historical catalyst leading to Britain's empire, and part of the reason why one may visit the British Virgin Islands today. It is on such men that the existence of present-day Western 'democracies' has been based, and it is the rationale for his virtual deification.

Present-day visitors may stop at Drake's Seat on St. Thomas, a viewpoint from which Drake is said to have been able to watch for vessels sailing through what today is known as the Sir Francis Drake Channel, while his ships lay in wait at Magens. ■

HELICOPTER/AIR TOURS: The Air Center (☎ 775-7335) offers tours for around $110/pp on up; 10 min. ($50 pp;) and half hour ($110) tours, as well as half-day excursions for couples to uninhabited Hans Lollik. http://www.aircenterhelicopters.com

DIVE SITES AND SNORKELING: There are 34 or so dive sites here within twenty min. by boat from the shore. Most sites are 25–85 ft. deep. Expect to spend around $60 for a one-tank dive and $75 and up for a two-tank dive.

One of the most popular sites, the *West Indian Transport Shoal* was sunk intentionally in 1984. It houses corals, nurse sharks, stingrays, and a colorful menagerie of fish.

Visibility often reaches 150 ft. in the vicinity of *Sail Rock*, nine mi. from St. Thomas harbor.

Farther still is *Saba Island* with three different dive sites. The SE Reef (**8**) ranges from 20–50 ft. and is for intermediate divers. Huge boulders rest on the sea floor, and there is a natural archway as well. Pillar coral is also found as are Creole wrasse.

Grain Wreck, the unmarked site of a 450-ton cargo ship sunk in the 1960s as an exercise for the Underwater Demolition Team, is restricted to experienced divers. At 70–110 ft., you can find rays, turtles, and sharks here.

Apparently sunk during WWII, the **Barges** lie in 40 ft. and house nurse sharks

The Hans Lollick Controversy

The 500-acre uninhabited Hans-Lollik island, set two mi. N of St. Thomas, is the center of a dispute between developers Tamarind Resort Associates of Dallas and the USVI government. The developers maintain that the government's denial of a Coastal Zone Management permit has effectively prevented them from using their property and that the government has reneged on its promise to permit development here. Tamarind's latest plan calls for a 150-room luxury resort, 160 single-family homes, 365 condos, shops, restaurants, and a heliport.

In March 1998, the Third Circuit Court of Appeals upheld the CZM commission and halted the project. The developers may still come back with a new proposal for the 500 acres or sell it for around $10 million dollars, but for the interim, Hans-Lollik will remain undeveloped. ∎

and other fish. The wreck of the **Warrick** (1816) rests on **Packet Rock.**

French Cap Cay, a rocky underwater promontory, is surrounded by myriad varieties of sealife. In addition to a beautiful pinnacle, it features fire and pillar corals. Farther offshore than most, French Cap Cay is less frequently dived. This intermediate to advance dive runs from 40–75 ft. and has a slight current. Visibility may be up to an astonishing 200 ft.

Explore **ledges** (**11**) which cut as deeply as 20–25 ft. into the rock. Angelfish, groupers, and turtles are among the residents here. It is set 25 min. from Compass Pt. and 40 min. from E End.

The Pinnacle (**12**) is a small seamount near French Cap's S tip. Watch for eagle rays here as well as tube and barrel sponges. Visibility is generally marvelous.

Tunnels, reefs and huge boulders comprise **Cow and Calf** (**7**), the top dive spot on the island and one well suited to nov-

ice divers and snorkelers. Depths here range from 25–40 ft. Legend has it that a nearsighted seaman mistook the rocks for migrating humpback whales, thus the name. An "H"-shaped coral tunnel network is set at the W end of the "cow." Two divers can fit at a time, and the corals here are spectacular. Watch carefully for horse-eye jacks on the borders of the rocks. There is some surge present.

Set some 2.5 mi. S of St. Thomas, Capella Island has **Capella Reef** (**10**) off of its S side. This 30- to 70-ft. novice-to-intermediate dive has good visibility (up to 80 ft.) and great reefs. Swim through ravines comprised of large igneous blocks. This area is still recovering from 1989's Hurricane Hugo but remains worthwhile.

Several dive spots on the N coast are near **Thatch Cay**—where a series of underwater tunnels allow divers to swim —and near the wreck of **General Rodgers** (**2**). This 42–65.-ft.z intermediate dive is set almost directly off of the (closed) Grand Beach Palace Resort. The 120-ft. Coast Guard vessel was sunk by the Dept. of Planning and Natural Resources with the intention of creating a reef formation. Residents include barracuda, bristleworms, hydroids, hogfish, and snapper. A second, smaller craft is nearby.

The Tunnels (**1**) here is a novice dive (watch out for surge!) which is relatively shallow at 40 ft. You'll find arches and canyons at the bottom, and residents include blue tang, black coral, and tarpon.

Another good spot is **Carval Rock** (**5**). Set at a depth of 20–70 ft., this advanced site is visited by dive boats from both St. Thomas and St. John. Dangerous currents can be present at times, and there are always some currents present. Soft corals carpet the ocean floor with resident basketstars. Follow a passageway at the base of the rocks to the SW, where two cuts, smaller and larger, lead to a school of tarpon. (Do not try this route if there is a surge!) Coral-covered ravines and dramatic precipices mark the N side. Boats anchor on the S side.

Both novice and experienced divers frequent **Congo Caye** (**4**) which is set around three mi. NE of St. John. Congo Caye has reefs, rocks, as well as huge undersea boulders and lava archways which rise up to 30 ft. (9 m) below the surface. Rays and tarpon reside here.

Situated SE of St. Thomas, St. Thomas's Buck Island has the ruins of the coral-encrusted **Cartenser Senior** (**9**), a WWI cargo vessel. It was moved from the place where it had first sunk after divers formed an underwater picket line to stave off imminent destruction by the Corp of Engineers. It was relocated to the vicinity of Buck Island, but Hurricane Alan moved it again. Sponges and corals have since dug in their heels, and Christmas tree worms brighten it up. This novice 25–35-ft. dive is quite popular, and fish — not being quite as dumb as their reputation makes them out to be — have caught on to the fact that there are frequent feedings here. Snapper, parrotfish angelfish, and sergeant majors are frequently in attendance. Snorkelers can also view the boat.

Little St. James (**6**) is a shallow dive which is good for novices. It has majestic pillar corals and ledges set down 15–40 ft. These house schools of goatfish and grunts. Other marine life includes lobster, angelfish, lizardfish, and featherdusters. The water is almost always calm.

Set on the S side of **Grass Cay**, **The Mounds** (**3**) are a collection of around 20 pinnacles with star and pillar corals which are frequented by the occasional eel and turtle.

At **Hans Lollick, The Pinnacle** (**14**) is 40 ft. in diameter and 65 ft. in height. You can find tarpon and rays here.

Coki Beach (**13**) is a great night dive area; you might see octopus, oval squid, and moray eels.

St. Thomas & St. John Dive Sites	
1	The Tunnels
2	*General Rodgers* (wreck)
3	Grass Cay
4	Congo Cay
5	Carval Rock
6	Little St. James (ledges)
7	Cow and Calf Rocks
8	Saba Island (Southeast Reef)
9	*Cartenser Senior* (wreck)
10	Capella Reef (S side of Capella I.)
11	French Cap Cay (deep ledges)
12	French Cap Cay (The Pinnacle)
13	Coki Beach (night dives)
14	Hans Lollick (The Pinnacle)

INSTRUCTION: There are a large number of qualified dive operators. A partial list:

The **AAA St. Thomas Diving Club** (☎ 776-2381) is at Bolongo Bay. **bill2381@viaccess.net**

Admiralty Dive Center (☎ 777-9802, 888-900-DIVE) is at the Windward Passage downtown. It offers daily two-tank dives, night dives, repairs, rentals, and packages for around $80 for a two-tank, two-location reef dive. **http://www.admiraltydive.com admiralty@viaccess.net**

Aqua Action at Secret Harbour (☎ 775-6285) also runs dives to the *Rhone*. Owner Carl Moore also teaches scuba to the disabled. He is a certified instructor of the Handicap Scuba Association. **http://www.aadivers.com AquaAction@islands.vi**

Blue Island Divers (☎ 774-2001) work out of Crown Bay Marina. The co-owners met in Saudi Arabia (of all places!) and their operation is a long-held dream. **diveinusvi@att.global.net**

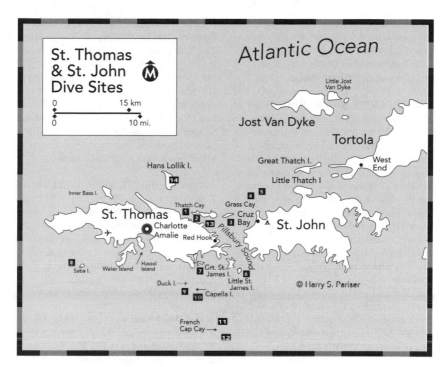

At Coki Beach, the **Coki Beach Dive Club** (☎/✆ 775-4220) specializes in beginners and offers tours, rentals, and night dives for those certified; four-day PADI and NAUI certification courses are available.
http://www.cokidive.com
pete@cokidive.com

The **Chris Sawyer Diving Center** (☎ 775-7320, 800 882 2965, ✆ 775 9495) is another operation worthy of note. They run four-hour morning and two-hour afternoon dives to the *Cartenser Sr.* A variety of packages are offered as are night dives and visits to the wreck of the *Rhone* (see description in the BVI section). They are at Compass Point Marina, 41-6-1 Estate Frydenhoj, St. Thomas USVI 00902.
http://www.sawyerdive.vi
sawyerdive@att.global.net

Dive In! (☎ 775-6100, ext. 2144, 800-524-2090, ✆ 777-9029) is at Sapphire.
http://www.diveinusvi.com
bpachta@att.global.net

The **VI Diving School** (☎ 774-8687, ✆ 774-7368) offers group instruction and PADI certification. It's at 9200 Long Bay Road, Vitraco Park Building 2, Bay 1.
Underwater Safaris (☎ 774-1350, ✆ 777-8733) are at Havensight.
http://www.scubadivevi.com
uws@diveusvi.com

SNORKELING TOURS: Homer's Incredible Night Snorkel Adventure (☎ 774-7606, 866-719-1856) is run by Homer Calloway who takes guests on an exciting night snorkel using flashlights. It departs Mon. through Sat. at 5:30 PM

and returns at around 9 PM. Friday nights Homer hosts a BBQ at Hull Beach followed by a snorkel tour. The tour is around US$38 pp and the tour plus BBQ is US$89 pp.
http://www.nightsnorkel.com

THE ATLANTIS SUBMARINE: One of the most unusual activities available on the island is an underwater voyage on the Atlantis Submarine. The brainchild of Canadian Dennis Hurd, this US$3 million recreational sub is one of a small fleet deployed at tourist concentrations throughout the world; the others are at Kona and Honolulu (Hawaii), Catalina Island (near Los Angeles), Grand Cayman, Barbados, and at Guam. Before you depart, a videotape supplies orientation. After your voyage, you return to the center where a dive certificate is awarded.

It's located in Havensight Mall, Bldg. VI, Bay L. To book, call 776-5650 or-800-253-0493 stateside. It costs $89 for adults and $49 for children; night dives are additional.
http://www.goatlantis.com

SEA EXCURSIONS: The new Yacht Haven Grande, constructed after a hurricane destroyed the original, lives up to its name. Its marina can accommodate up to 50 megayachts of 450 ft. and longer), and the retail center has some 32 shops, a health club and spa, four restaurants, as well as a set of 12 upscale condominiums. A 70-room boutique hotel is in the works.
http://www.yachthavengrande.com

Most trips average around $60 for a sunset sail, $90 for a half-day sail, and $135 for a full-day sail.

Alaunt Charters (☎ 771-8044, 866-DAYSAIL), Red Hook, offers sails aboard the 53-ft. ketch *Alaunt* to St. John and Jost Van Dyke.
http://www.alauntcharters.com

Captain Nautica's "Great Beaches Getaway" (☎ 715-3379) takes you to Trunk Bay, Waterlemon Cay, and Honeymoon Beach for snorkeling. This full-day trip (9AM–4 PM) includes continental breakfast and restaurant lunch and one drink. It leaves from the American yacht Harbor in Red Hook. It costs around $100 for adults, $65 for children under 12. They also offer a "Best of the BVIs."
http://www.captainnautica.com

Departing from Frenchtown, the **Dancing Dolphin** (☎ 774-8899; Box 6957, St. Thomas 00803), a 50-ft. catamaran, offers Tues. half-day trips to Turtle Cove and Buck Island; afternoon sees a sail, snorkel, and sunset dinner cruise. Every Thursday they offer a full-day champagne sail to St. John and a sunset champagne cruise.
http://www.thedancingdolphin.com

The Daydreamer (☎ 775-2584), a 43-ft. trimaran, has day sails to St. John as well as a sunset cruise and a sail to Jost Van Dyke); dinner cruises are also available.
http://daydreamervi.com

Pam and Brian do offer personalized trips aboard the *Fantasy* (☎ 775-5652, 513-3212).
http://www.dayssilfantasy.comt

Heavenly Days (☎ 775-1800), Bolongo Bay Beach Club, is a 53-ft. catamaran which offers a six-hour sail to St. John with complimentary bar. Private charters and a once-weekly two-hour "Harbor Cocktail" cruise are also offered.

High Pockets (☎ 715-2812) offers daysails around St. Thomas and St. John with a maximum of six guests.
http://www.sailhighpockets.com

Ike Witt Charters (☎ 771-2600), Red Hook, promises entertaining sails.
http://www.ikewittcharters.com

"Jester" (☎ 513-2459) is a 38-ft. sloop which sails with a maximum of six guests-from Point Pleasant Resort in Water Bay. BBQ lunch, two snorkel spots, sunset sails, and St. John and BVI trips number among Capt. Jim Kozar's offerings.
http://www.sailjester.com
jester@islands.vi

The Kon Tiki Raft is a three-hour harbor tour ($29 for adults) which departs daily between I and 2 PM; there's a glass bottom, a beach stop, calypso music, limbo, rum punch, and unlimited soft drinks.

Limnos Charters (☎ 775-3203) have a 53-ft. craft which offers a 70-mi. day cruise to visit The Caves at Norman Island, passing by Salt I. and Ginger I. on the way to Virgin Gorda, then returning to St. Thomas or St. John. A continental breakfast, picnic lunch, and open bar are included.
http://www.limnoscharters.com

Personable Captain Maxine takes up to six to St. John aboard the sloop the Lou (☎ 775-7467).
http://www.sailwithcaptainmax.com
seamax@islands.vi

Magnum Charters (☎ 779-2244), East End, offers day trips to Anegada, Culebra, and Vieques.
The New Horizons II (☎ 775-1171, 800-808-7604), a 60-ft. custom ketch, offers full-day sails and sunset sails. One trip goes to The Baths, Marina Cay (lunch), Guana Island and to Jost Van Dyke. They also offer a gourmet Sunset Dinner Cruise ($85) departing from Sapphire Marina; they board at 5 PM.

St. Thomas Itineraries

If you have 3 days: Spend one day in Charlotte Amalie (shopping and sights), a day seeing the island, and a day visiting St. John or on a sea excursion.

If you have one week: Spend one day in Charlotte Amalie (shopping and sights), one day touring St. Thomas, three days at the beach or on excursions, and two days on St. John (hiking and beaches).

The 50-ft. yawl Nightwind (☎ 775-4110/6666) runs from Red Hook to St. John.
http://www.sailyachtnightwind.com

The Pirate's Penny and the Stormy Petrol (☎ 775-7990) are two yachts which run trips to Virgin Gorda.
Operating out of Red Hook at 82 Red Hook Center, Rafting Adventures (☎ 779-2032) explores the BVI and St. John on speedy 27-ft. deep-V inflatables; half- or full-day trips are available. They also have week-long camping trips.

Rumbaba Charters (☎ 650-1659, evenings: 777-2155), American Yacht Harbor, will take you to St. John. A picnic lunch is served on the boat or on the beach. They offer half-day and full-day and sunset sails.
http://www.rumbabacharters.com
info@rumbabacharters.com

Treasure Isle Cruises (☎ 775-9500, 888-253-2347) will arrange all manner of tours.
http://www.treasureislecruises.com

Scubadu (☎ 643-5155), a catamaran with kayaks and float mats, offers daysails as well as sunset dinner cruises.
http://www.sailvi.com

ST. THOMAS

Sundance (☎ 779-1722), a 44-ft. cutter departs from slip #12 on 'A' Dock, American Yacht Harbor, Red Hook, at 9. It takes a maximum of six guests.
http://www.sundance44.com

Treazzure (☎ 690-2735) is a 60-ft. ketch which offers day sails with a continental breakfast, a gourmet lunch, water toys, and a 17-ft. inflatable dinghy.
http://www.sailingvirginislands.com

The *True Love* (☎ 513-0655), a schooner built in 1926 and fully restored in 2003, featured in the 1956 movie "High Society." It now offers a day sail to St. John ($120 pp) which includes a continental breakfast along with a gourmet lunch. Charters are also offered.
http://www.sailtruelove.com

The *Winifred* (☎ 775-7898, 771-1020) will take you out for a day sail; lunch, snorkeling, and glass-bottom-boat viewing are on the agenda. Guests are limited to six. It departs from "D" dock at the American Yacht Harbor.
http://www.sailwinifred.com
winifred@sailwinifred.com

YACHT CHARTERS: *VIP Yacht Charters* (☎ 866-847-9224) offers a wide variety.
http://www.vipyachts.com

RENTALS: Rent a 21-, 25-, or 27-ft. motorboat from **Nauti Nymph** (☎ 775-5066).
http://www.nautinymph.com
www.st-thomas.com/nautinymph.com

See An Ski (☎ 775-6265) offers powerboat rentals with (optional) captains.
http://www.seeski.com
seeski@viaccess.net

For Virgin Gorda trips contact **Transportation Services, Inc.** (☎ 776-6282; Sun. and Thurs.) or **Native Son** (☎ 774-8685; Sun. and Wed.). The latter also runs to Tortola.
http://www.nativesonbvi.com

DEEP-SEA FISHING: Worldwide Fishing, a website, offers a number of St. Thomas options if you search.
http://www.worldwidefishing.com
David Pearsall (☎ 640-7423, 774-7306) operates Peanut Gallery Fishing Charters. Departures are from the Crown Bay Marina "D" Dock.
http://www.fishingstthomas.com

At Piccola Marina on Red Hook Rd., **St. Thomas Sport Fishing** (☎ 775-7990) offer fishing charters.
The *Fish Hawk* (☎ 775-9058; 54 Frydenhoj, St. Thomas 00802) is at Fish Hawk Marina at East End Lagoon.
The *Ocean Quest* (☎ 776-5176) offers inshore light tackle fishing.
Black Pearl Charters (☎ 775-9982), Sapphire Marina, offers half- to full-day trips for 1–6 p. The *Phoenix*, a 46-ft. classic Rubovich (☎ 775-6100), is also geared towards Sapphire Resort guests.
At Sapphire Bay, the **Charterfishing Fleet** (☎ 775-3690) offers a variety of charters in 36- to 46-ft. boats. At Red Hook, these include the *Abigail* which is a 43-ft. Custom, and *El Zorro 11,* a 31-ft. Innovator.
The *Marlin Prince* (☎ 693-5929) operates fishing charters.
http://www.marlinprince.com
captain@marlinprince.com

The *Peanut Gallery* (☎ 775-5274), a 28-ft. catamaran, offers deep-sea fishing. The *Peanut* also will take you inshore for fishing.
http://www.fishingstthomas.com

BOATING AND SAILING CHARTERS:
The island's boating center is at Red Hook. For fishing boats see above.

Fanfare Charters (☎ 715-1326, 877-715-1373 are located in Red Hook and claim to have the lowest prices in the Virgin Islands.
fanfare@viaccess.net
www.fanfarecharters.com

Paradise Connections (☎ 774-1111, 877-567-9350) offers all-inclusive yacht charters for around $1300 pp, pw.
http://www.paradiseconnections.com

Waters Edge Sports (☎ 771-7356), American Yacht Harbor, has gourmet day sails (two to six people)to the BVI for $1500–$1,900. They also offer fishing and power boat rentals.
http://www.wemarine.com

KAYAKING: One of the best adventures on St. Thomas is offered by **Virgin Islands Ecotours** (☎ 779-2155) at the Marine Sanctuary and Mangrove Lagoon. You arrive at 9 AM to receive an orientation and then board your kayaks for the 2.5-hr. trip. Proceeding through the lagoon you land on a beach at Cas Cay, a 15-acre wildlife sanctuary, for a brief guided snorkeling session. You'll learn lots about the ecosystem. Cruise ship passengers may even learn the difference between mangroves and mango trees. Alternatively they offer an "eco-tour" to Cas Cay. Here you hike for 45 minutes and snorkel in the adjacent lagoon or relax on the beach. They also offer a special birthday party for children which comes complete with treasure hunt. Virgin Islands Ecotours are at Estate Nadir which is off Rte. 32 on the way to Red Hook.
http://www.viecotours.com
info@viecotours.com

Kayak Safaris (☎ 792-5794) offers all-inclusive five-to-seven-night tours to out of the way locations.
http://www.kayaksafaris.com

SEA TREKKIN': Coral World (☎ 775-1555, ext. 247) offers the only opportunity to explore the sea floor for non divers. The process is an adventure in itself, a throwback to the days before plastic and high tech paved the way for mass marketing of dive adventures. You climb down a stairwell, have a helmet placed on your head, and sink. The heavy helmet becomes weightless underwater, and you listen to narration through speakers as you explore the deep along a trail. There is none of the danger of scuba, but you still are able to experience underwater nature in a direct fashion. The disadvantage is that you have to keep your chin up, literally, which does curtail the view a bit. Your friends and admirers can watch you from Coral World's underwater exhibition chamber.

Explore the Virgin Islands author Harry S. Pariser was the first outsider to test the waters with the gear in the fall of 2000. A couple was married here in Jan. 2001. Presumably, the bride was kissed after emerging from the water although they may have rubbed helmets as an expression of intimate devotion.

SNUBA: At Coki Beach and over at Trunk Bay in St. John, **Snuba** (☎ 693-8063) is a type of snorkeling using an air source contained on a flotation raft that follows your every move underwater.
http://www.visnuba.com

SURFING: The only spot is at **Hull Bay** which gets rough during the winter months.

WINDSURFING: The best windsurfing is found at the E end (in locations such as Sapphire and Water Bay (also known as Renaissance and Pineapple) beaches) during the middle of the day when winds are high.

While Morningstar to the S offers the gentlest winds, Hull Bay on the N is the roughest.

INSTRUCTION: Schools are located at Pt. Pleasant and at Sapphire Beach resorts.

West Indies Windsurfing (☎ 775-6530, cell: 998-4658, 9 Nazareth, Vessup Beach) offers **kiteboarding** and windsurfing lessons and rentals. Easterly winds prevail here; a large hill to the E shelters Vessup. Owner John Phillip originally hails from Morgantown, West VA.

PARASAILING: Call **Caribbean Parasailing** (☎ 771-3938, ten locations) if riding on a sail 500 ft. in the air is your cup of tea.

Blue Dolphin Watersports (☎ 771-1138, 777-4226) also offers parasailing, as does **Caribbean Watersports and Tours** (☎ 775-9360) .

St. Thomas Sports

GOLF: The only 18-hole course is at **Mahogany Run** (777-6250, toll free: 800-253-7103) on the island's N coast. Challenging and naturally lush, the course tests control as opposed to power. Its course record is 66 strokes; it's rated at 70.1, the total yardage is 6,022, the longest hole is 564 yds., and the shortest is 153 yds. Rates for two run from around $130 to $170 for 18 holes; this includes cart rental but not clubs. http://www.mahoganyrungolf.com

TENNIS: Six **public courts** are free of charge: two each at Crown Bay (Sub Base), Bordeaux, and at Long Bay. Those at the Sub Base are open until 8 PM on a first-come, first-serve basis.

The major hotels also have private courts with private lessons available.

Bluebeard's Castle (☎ 774-1600, ext. 196), has two lighted courts open to 11. Non-guests pay $3 pp per court.

The **Bolongo Bay Beach and Tennis Club** (☎ 775-1800, ext. 468) has four lighted courts open to 10 PM it is open to non-guests and members for lessons and use ($10/hr.).

Bluebeard's Beach Club (☎ 774-8990) has two courts which are lighted until 9. Lessons are $16/30 min., and non-guests pay $6/hr. per court.

Sapphire Beach Resort and Marina (☎ 775-6100, guest services) has four courts; lessons are $16/30 min., and court rentals are $10/hr. per court.

Marriott's Frenchman's Reef (☎ 776-8500, ext. 6818) offers four lighted courts which are open until 9 PM; non-guests are charged $10/hr.

The **Mahogany Run Tennis Club** (☎ 775-5000) has two lighted courts open until 10. Charges are $8/hr. per court until 6 PM and $10 thereafter.

The **Ritz Carlton** (☎ 775-3333, ext. 58) has three courts for $60/hr. Reservations necessary.

The **Wyndham Sugar Bay Beach and Racquet Club** (☎ 777-7100, ext. 2007) has seven courts including a stadium court (holds up to 250); all are lit until 11 PM, and there's a pro shop and non-hotel guests pay $9 ph.

HORSEBACK RIDING: Head over to St. John and the **Carolina Corral** (☎ 693-5778 in Coral Bay on the island's E end. http://www.st-john.com/trailrides

BOWLING: St. Thomas has an ultramodern six-lane bowling alley and youth center which opened in 2000. The **VICM Youth Center** (☎ 714-3071) is run by Christian Youth Ministries. Charges are round $9 ph day and $16 ph evening. It's at 105 Bolongo Bay which is at the base of Donkey Hill. http://www.vichristianministries.org

HORSERACING: The Clinton Phipps Racetrack (☎ 775-4355, Rte. 30 at Nadir 42) has scheduled races with betting which are extremely popular with locals.

From St. Thomas

Ferries are a convenient way to get around the islands. The $10 million Urman Victor Fredericks Terminal, a new terminal, opened at Red Hook in Oct. 2007. The 9,500-sq.-ft. facilty includes shops, bar, food vendors, and a waiting area. Other ferry departure points are along the waterfront in Charlotte Amalie. To get to the ferry from Red Hook, you can either take a local bus, taxi, or a shuttle bus. Get off when you see the 7-11 convenience store.

Ferry times listed below are accurate at time of publication. For current information about schedules call the ferry lines or see the schedule in *St. Thomas This Week.*
http://www.stthomasthisweek.com

FOR ST. JOHN: Ferries run on the hour (6:30, 7:30 AM, 8 AM to midnight) between Red Hook, St. Thomas, and Cruz Bay, St. John ($6.10 OW, 20 min.).

Another runs six times daily (9 AM–5:30 PM) between Charlotte Amalie, St. Thomas, and Cruz Bay, St. John ($11.10 OW, 45 min.). Departures are at 9, 1, 3, and at 5:30.

CAR FERRIES: Three car ferries (RT $42–$50; 25 min.) currently run (from Red Hook to Cruz Bay). Try to arrive a half hour prior to departure. Uniformed fee collectors levy a $3 "port fee" on each car, small and medium SUV, and motorcycle. Pick-up trucks, vans, and large SUVs are charged $6.

Boyson (☎ 776-6294) runs from 6:30 AM–7 PM. Boyson departs every hour on the half hour from 6:30 AM to 6:30 PM.

Love City Car Ferries (☎ 779-4000) depart at 7, 9, and 11 AM and at 1, 3, 5, and 7 PM. *The 7 PM ferry is not available on weekends.*

FROM ST. JOHN: It returns at 6:15, 8, and 10 AM, and noon and 2, 4, and 6:15 PM.

Global Marine runs the ferry *Tug Life* (☎ 775-6279) Times are 6:15, 8, and 10 AM, and noon, 2, 4, and 6 PM. On Saturdays and Sundays there is no 6:15 AM ferry.

FROM ST. JOHN: It returns at 7:15, 9, and 11 AM, and at 1, 3, 5, and 7 PM. On Sat. and Sun. there is no 7:15 AM ferry.

FOR ST. CROIX: American Eagle (☎ 800-327-8900) flies daily (25 min.). **Air Sunshine** (☎ 776-7900, 800-327-8900) also flies as does **Cape Air** (☎ 800-352-0714). http://www.airsunshine.com http://www.flycapeair.com

The most convenient way to get between St. Thomas and St. Croix by air is with the **Seaborne Airlines** (☎ 773-6442; ✆ 713-9077, 888-359-8687; Long Bay Road, Charlotte Amalie, US Virgin Islands 00802). It's a convenient way to travel as it eliminates time spent at airports. However, each passenger may carry only up to 30 pounds of baggage for free; after that, it's $1 per pound You will be charged for your carry on! Roundtrip fares are around $165–$175. One-way fares are $90–$95, Special Internet and weekend fares are offered, as are ferry and seaplane combination packages. Check in 45 min. before your flight.

BY FERRY: Operators of the **St. Croix Ferry** have changed many times here over the years.

VI Sea Trans (☎ 776-5494) runs a ferry (90-min.) between the Marine Terminal in Gallows Bay near Christiansted, St. Croix and the Marine Terminal in Charlotte Amalie (next to Seaplane Terminal) on St. Thomas. Arrive a minimum of 45 minutes prior to departure; a photo ID is required. Rates are $50 OW, $90 RT. It departs Fri., Sat., Sun., and Mon. at 7:30 and 4:30pm

and returns on Fri., Sat., Sun., and Mon. at 9:30 AM and 6:30 PM.
http://www.goviseatrans.com
caribbean.fastferry@gmail.com

FOR TORTOLA: Air Sunshine (☎ 776-7900, 800-327-8900) and **Cape Air** (☎ 800-352-0714) fly.
http://www.airsunshine.com
http://www.flycapeair.com

FROM CHARLOTTE AMALIE BY FERRY: Called Tortola Wharf by locals but officially dubbbed the Edward Wilmoth Blyden Marine Terminal, the ferry depot is to the W of town along the Waterfront.

For the West End and Road Town ($40 RT, 45 min. to West End, 1.15–1.5 hrs. to Road Town), *Smith's Ferry Services* (☎ 775-7292) and *Native Son* (☎ 774-8685) depart from Mon. to Fri. for West End and Road Town daily from 8 AM to 5:30 PM. Sat., Sun., and Wed. schedules are different from the other days.
http://www.nativesonbvi.com

The Road Town Fast Ferry (☎ 777-2800) is a high-speed catamaran ($55 RT, 50 min.) which departs Charlotte Amalie at 8:40 AM, noon, and 4:15 PM from Mon. to Sat. and on Sun at noon and at 4 PM. Children's fares are discounted, and packages and discount fares are offered.
http://www.roadtownfastferry.com

Inter-Island Boat Services (☎ 495-4166 on Tortola) runs from Cruz Bay to West End from Mon. to Sat. at 8:30,11:30, and 3:30, with an additional trip on Fri. at 5; and on Sun. at 8:30,11:30, and 4:30.

FROM RED HOOK BY FERRY: *The Road Town Fast Ferry* (☎ 777-2800) is a high-speed catamaran ($55 RT, 35 min.) which departs Red Hook at 8 AM, 11 AM, 2:45, and 4:15 PM from Mon. to Sat. and on Sun at noon and at 4 PM. Children's fares are discounted, and packages and discount fares are offered.
http://www.roadtownfastferry.com

Native Son, Inc. (☎ 774-8685; $40 RT, 30–45 min.) and *Smiths Ferry* (☎ 775-7292) both head to West End, **Tortola** daily at 7:45, 8, 11:15, 2:55, 3:15, 5, and 5:30.
http://www.smithsferry.com

FOR JOST VAN DYKE: Ferries ply between Red Hook (Tortola) Cruz Bay (St. John) and Great Harbour. *Inter-Island Boat Services* (☎ 776-6597) departs **Red Hook** at 8 and 2 and **Cruz Bay** at 8:30 AM and 2:20 PM on Fri., Sat. and Sun.

FOR SAN JUAN, PUERTO RICO: **American Eagle** (☎ 800-327-8900) flies daily. **Seaborne Airlines** (see "FOR ST. CROIX" on previous page) flies from St. Thomas to Old San Juan.

FOR FAJARDO: Vieques Air Link (☎ 777-4055, 888-901-9247) flies daily.
http://www.vieques-island.com/val

FOR ST. CROIX: American Eagle (☎ 800-327-8900) flies nonstop daily.
http://www.airsunshine.com

FOR VIRGIN GORDA: The **Bitter End Yacht Club** (800-872-2392) can arrange charter flights. **Seaborne Airlines** (☎ 773-6442; ✆ 713-9077, 888-359-8687; Long Bay Road, Charlotte Amalie, US Virgin Islands 00802) flies to North Sound.

Transportation Services (☎ 776-6282) and *Inter-Island* (☎ 776-6597) depart from Red Hook at 8 on Tues., Thurs., and Sat. ($40 RT, 1 hr. 45 min.).

St. John

Although only a 20-min. ferry ride away from Red Hook on the E tip of St. Thomas, St. John seems worlds removed from its neighbor. More than any other Virgin, St. John is someplace special. Seasoned Caribbean travelers call it the most beautiful island in the Caribbean, and no one who visits can fail to be romanced by the loveliness of its scenic charms and the friendliness of its inhabitants.

This small island has numerous near-deserted beaches with wonderful snorkeling, spectacular and sedate hiking trails, plantation ruins, and coral reefs teeming with life. Set amidst a pristine sea, the island is contoured like a maple leaf. More than half of the island's area has been placed under the aegis of the National Park Service. Though the smallest of the "natural area" National Parks of the United States, St. John nevertheless brings together, within its 9,500 acres of land and 5,650 acres of surrounding water, a natural ecosystem which is amazingly varied and spectacularly beautiful.

St. Johnians range from New Age folks heavily into hugs, affirmations, and past-life regressions to retired millionaire CEOs, to a tight community of locals who are mostly all related to each other. A community of (largely) illegal aliens from the Dominican Republic are the most recent arrivals on the scene.

St. John is no longer a slacker's paradise. Living costs here have skyrocketed, and many locals work more than one job just to make it. Despite surface appearances, life here can be stressful, but residents have the incredible advantage of living in a pristine natural environment, one whose incredible wealth never fails to astound and amaze visitors. However, the bohemians have not totally vanished: a plot of some thousand marijuana plants was found in the Esperance area in 2001. Some locals are fighting back against unbridled development.

The island is compact, yet vast. Visiting St. Thomians find themselves wide-eyed at a road which seems to go on without end (or signs of habitation) for miles. And it would take weeks to visit all of the snorkeling spots and explore the hiking trails. Your time here will be too short but very sweet.

The off-season can be wetter but is considerably less touristed. Many cruise ship passengers visit the island on day trips, which means that the best known beaches can be crowded, but there are plenty of alternatives.

Accommodations range from camping to posh resorts, and there is plenty of gourmet dining around, as well as quality excursions (sailing, diving, kayaking) around St. John and the BVI.

↪ A new book, *Keep Left!*, highlights life on St. John:
http://www.keepleftbook.com

TOPOGRAPHY: Geologically complex, St. John is comprised of multi-million-year-old rock formations which have been rearranged via erosion, changes in the water level, and faulting. Rising steeply and quickly from the shore, St. John's ridges climax in three peaks: 1,193-ft. Camelberg, 1,147-ft. Mamey, and the 1,277-ft. Bordeaux. Its terrain ranges from moist subtropical forests on the NW slopes to the arid wasteland and salt ponds found on the E end.

FLORA AND FAUNA: There are over 800 species of plants. Gallery moist forests are widespread in the central mountains and surroundings. Most trees in these forests are evergreen, but some, such as the hog plum and the kapok are deciduous. (The kapoks were used to make canoes). The gallery semi-deciduous forest is limited to smaller guts and ravines found within watersheds on the East End and on the SE corner uplands. Mangrove communities are found at Leinster Bay, Hurricane Hole (on the N side of Coral Bay), and at Lameshur Bay on the island's S coast.

More than 160 species of birds have been recorded in and around the park and, of these, over 25 nest on the island. Species include the Zenaida dove, gray kingbird, green-throated carib, bananaquit, pearl-eyed thrasher (trushee on St. John), American oystercatcher, Antillean crested hummingbird, Green coated Carib hummingbird, and the sandpiper.

Used for local transportation until the 1950s, some 400 feral donkeys now freely roam the hills. They have caused extensive ecological damage, resulting in the near extinction of certain species of trees.

Other mammals include the mongoose, deer, and pigs. There's also a variety of bats, the only mammals indigenous to the islands, ranging from fruit-eating bats to the fish-eating bats found near the harbors.

History

Taino Indians, existing in frugal harmony with the island's resources, inhabited St.

John for 1,000 years They had already departed by the time the first Europeans arrived. Given by the Spanish, the island's name refers to St. John the Apostle, as opposed to St. John the Baptist, after whom San Juan, Puerto Rico was named.

Before the Danish West India and Guinea Company acted to take control of St. John in 1694, the island had only been visited infrequently. It was not until 1717 that the first company-operated plantation was established at Estate Carolina in Coral Bay. Settlers hoped that this area, with its fine harbor, would soon rival Charlotte Amalie in importance.

At first, their optimism appeared justified; St. John became one of the most productive spots in the whole region. By 1733, 15 years after taking possession, 101 plantations were under cultivation. Seven-year tax exemptions had attracted 208 whites, who controlled 1,087 black slaves. Danes were overwhelmingly outnumbered by Dutch.

SLAVE REBELLIONS: St. John was used as a training ground where slaves were "broken in" before being shipped to the more sophisticated plantations of St. Thomas. A large number of the slaves were members of the Amina tribe; to these proud tribesmen, tilling the land was women's work and considered degrading. Akamboos, many of whom had been sold to Coral Bay planters, were equally rebellious.

In 1733, Philip Gardelin, the new governor of St. Thomas and St. John, issued an 18-point manifesto. Under its terms, punishment — ranging from amputation, to beatings, and to pinching the skin with a hot iron — were prescribed for all types of infractions. Slaves were forbidden all dances, feasts, and plays; any slave caught in town after curfew faced being beaten and locked in the fort. That very same year the island was beset by a hurricane, a long drought, a plague of insects, and a fall storm.

Refused rations by their owners owing to scarcity, the half-starved slaves struck decisively for freedom. At dawn on Sun. Nov. 13, 1733, slaves entered Fort Berg carrying the customary load of wood. Whipping out cane knives concealed in the wood pile, they sliced open all of the soldiers save one who had scurried under a bed. They then fired two cannon shots that were the prearranged signal to hundreds of slaves to rise up in revolt. All across the island, marching bands of slaves ransacked great houses and burned cane fields. Whole families of settlers were wiped out. Within a few hours, the slaves controlled the entire island.

SHORT-LIVED FREEDOM: By late December, the rebels had been forced into waging a guerrilla war in the hills. The British sent 70 men from Tortola, but they withdrew after being ambushed, as did a similar force dispatched from St. Kitts in February. In order to help the Danish, the French sent two warships from Martinique which arrived in April.

Finding themselves hopelessly outnumbered in mid-May, the rebels held one last feast in a ravine near Annaberg, then — according to the story — committed ritual suicide en masse. Forming a circle, each shot the one next to him until the last one shot himself. When the planters arrived, they found seven guns — all broken to pieces save one — a symbol that the struggle would continue until freedom had been won. While the ruined settlers chose to relocate, others soon arrived, and St. John became a prosperous colony once again.

This lasted until the Napoleonic Wars, when British troops occupied the island in 1801 and again from 1807–13. This second occupation served to depress the economy.

Plaiting fish pots on St. John.

ST. JOHN

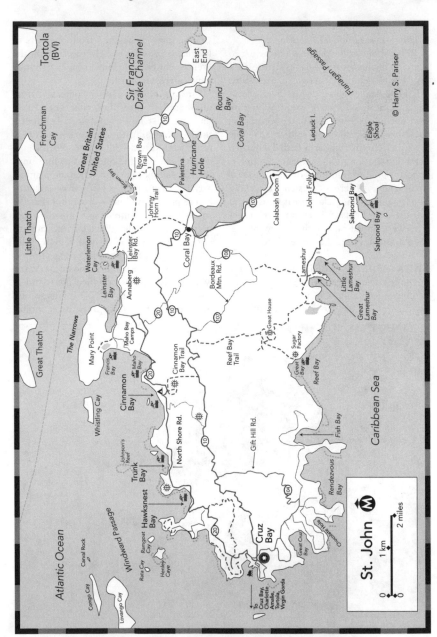

© Harry S. Pariser

Tortola
(BVI)

Frenchman
Cay

Little Thatch

Great Thatch

Atlantic Ocean

Windward Passage

Congo Cay

Carval Rock

Rata Cay

Henley
Caye

Lovango Cay

Sir Francis
Drake Channel

Great Britain
United States

Brown Bay

Brown Bay
Trail

Waterlemon
Cay

Leinster
Bay

The Narrows

Mary Point

Francis
Bay

Maho Bay
Camps

Maho
Bay

Cinnamon
Bay

Whistling Cay

Johnson's
Reef

Trunk
Bay

Hawksnest
Bay

Ramgoat
Cay

North Shore Rd.

Annaberg

Leinster
Bay Rd.

Johnny
Horn Trail

Coral Bay

Palestina

Hurricane
Hole

Calabash Boom

Johns Folly

Saltpond Bay

Saltpond Bay

Leduck I.

Eagle
Shoal

Round
Bay

Coral Bay

East
End

Flanagan Passage

Bordeaux
Mtn. Rd.

Great House

Lameshur

Little
Lameshur
Bay

Great
Lameshur
Bay

Reef Bay
Trail

Sugar
Factory

Great
Bay

Reef Bay

Fish Bay

Cinnamon
Bay Trail

Gift Hill Rd.

Caribbean Sea

Rendezvous
Bay

Cruz
Bay

Great Cruz
Bay

Chocolate Hole

To
Cruz Bay,
Charlotte
Amalie,
Tortola,
Virgin Gorda

St. John

0   1 km

0   2 miles

10

10

20

104

107

108

20

20

10

The perfection of the sugar beet and the 1848 emancipation resulted in falling profits. Many planters were already facing ruin when a new variety of sugarcane was introduced from Java at the end of the 19th century. After another short-lived burst of enthusiastic activity, the sugar balloon burst again, and the island wandered off in a somnolent stagger, which the transfer to American ownership in 1917 left unchanged.

Islandwide Practicalities

GETTING THERE AND GETTING AROUND: Catch the hourly ferry from Red Hook, St. Thomas ($6.10 OW), or from Charlotte Amalie ($11.10 OW) to Cruz Bay. (Reduced rates for locals with ID, and children, and there is a $2 charge for bags handled by the crew.) Car ferries also operate. See "From St. Thomas" for schedules. The island is also accessible by ferry from Tortola and Virgin Gorda.

The ferry dock is located right in the center of town. (The Caneel Dock is at Caneel Bay). It's easy to walk anywhere in town. To visit other parts of the island, take local transport (which can be expensive), hitch, or rent a car or jeep. A few collective taxis ($2–3 pp) run to places like Caneel and Cinnamon.

A public **bus service** (☎ 776-6346) has been operating since 1998 and is the best value on the island. A $1 fare will take you from Cruz Bay all the way to Salt Pond.

Useful St. John Phone Numbers	
FirstBank	776-6881
Connections	776-6922
National Park Service	693-6201
Native Son (ferry)	774-8685
Post Office	779-4227
Smith's Ferry	775-7202
Speedy's Fantasy (ferry)	774-8685
Tourist Information	776-6450

Service is hourly and ends after dusk. *However, be warned that it can be irregular.*

If **hitching**, stand on the outskirts of town and use your forefinger to point in the direction you want to go. (St. Johnians consider using your thumb to be rude, and you won't get a ride that way). Also, don't try to hitch if there are more than two of you standing together.

TOURS: Island tours (two hrs., $30 for two; $12 each for three or more) are available by taxi. Sea excursions, including snorkeling are listed in the appropriate sections below.

St. John Island-Wide Accommodation

Because of the small land area and the island's extreme popularity, St. John is an expensive place to visit, although not necessarily more expensive than the other islands. The most reasonable accommodation is out at Coral Bay and in campsites. If planning an extended stay on the island, remember that housing is expensive and difficult to find. If you want to buy a house here, count on shelling out around $750,000! One home in Peter Bay went for $2 million in 2000. Another Peter Bay home was selling for $9.5 million in 2008.

NOTE: All street addresses should end with St. John 00830, and all PO Boxes with St. John 00831. All phone numbers are in area code **340** unless otherwise specified.

Outlying accommodation is lised in Maho Bay, Coral Bay, and other sections.

CRUZ BAY ACCOMMODATION: In the center of town, **The Inn at Tamarind Court** (☎ 776-6378, ✉ 776-6722, 800-221-1637; Box 350, St. John 00831) is conveniently

URL http://www.stjohnusvi.com
General web site for St. John.

located in town, around three blocks from the ferry pier. Breakfast (superb coffee and croissants) is included. There are 20 simple yet comfortable a/c rooms. The bar/restaurant is set in a courtyard and is a local hangout. Rates run around $75 d (standard) to $150 (apartment) per night.
http://www.tamarindcourt.com
tamarind@attglobal.net

St. John Inn (☎ 693-8688, ❸ 693-9900, 800-666-7688) is a small hotel near the Tamarind but more secluded. Rooms have names such as "Golden Gate" and are small but homey. Uunpainted hardwood cabinets house a TV/VCR unit. (Tapes are available for rent for $5). Most of the units have private baths and some have kitchenettes. You may choose to use either the fan or a/c. Rooms have phones. Rates run from around $160–$185 d plus tax.
http://www.stjohninn.com
info@stjohninn.com

Garden by the Sea Bed and Breakfast (☎/❸ 779-4731) is a ten minute walk from downtown. Attractively furnished rooms have neither TVs nor phones but do have elephant-bamboo canopy beds, Caribbean colors and ceiling fans; some have East Asian-style fountains. Breakfast is served on the open deck which faces the harbor. Rates start at $275 d with breakfast, and its few rooms are frequently booked well in advance.
http://www.gardenbythesea.com
info@gardenbythesea.com

The **Hillcrest Guesthouse** (☎ 776-6774, cell: 998-8388) rents suites from $250 s or d (or $1,500 pw). Its homespun and absolutely unforgettable website will tell you everything you want to know about this property. Sample excerpt: "The accommodations are secure, ask my pet dogs, Gigi, Belle Starr,

St. John Taxi Fares

Official rates from Cruz Bay. Round-trip fares are double the one-way fare plus $1 per minute waiting charges after the first five minutes. Two-hour island tours are $50 for one passenger; $25 per person for two or more. Three-hr. tours are $70 for one passenger, and $35 per person for two or more.

Destination (from Cruz Bay to)	1 person	2 or more (each)
Annaberg	18.00	9.00
Caneel Bay	6.00	5.00
Chocolate Hole	7.00	6.00
Cinnamon Bay	9.00	7.00
Coral Bay	16.00	9.00
Gallows Pt.	5.00	4.00
Maho Bay	18.00	9.00
Reef Bay Trail	9.00	7.00
Trunk Bay	8.00	6.00
Westin	6.00	5.00

known as 'Belle', and my newest member, Taj Mahal, known as 'Taj', and Yum Yum, my siamese cat. They keep an eye on things. We live on the second floor and the suites are located on the third floor." Wi-Fi is free for guests, it's nonsmoking, and they are associated with the Windy Level Restaurant on Centerline Rd.
http://www.hillcreststjohn.com
hillcrestguesthouse@yahoo.com

Just on the edge of town, 11-rm. **Estate Lindholm** (☎ 776-6121, ❸ 776-6141, 800-322-6335) is a bed and breakfast offering rooms with cable TV, phone, refrigerator, and microwave oven. A small fitness facility

and pool complete the grounds. It appeals to Westin resort types who want something a bit more intimate. Continental breakfast is included. It is a stiff hike up and down the hill from town, so a car would be an asset here. Rates run from around $320 d.
http://www.estatelindholm.com

ULTRA-LUXURY RESORTS: Billing itself as "the smaller friendlier hotel," **Gallows Point Suite Resort** (☎ 776-4634, 800-323-7229, ✆ 776-6520; Box 58, St. John 00831) offers oceanview and harborview loft and garden suites set on a secluded peninsula just five min. on foot from Cruz Bay. Each comfortably-equipped suite has a kitchen, living room, and a private porch area. The large tiled bath has a shower in a garden like area. Although furnished according to each owner's peculiar tastes, assets generally include TV, stereo, blender, microwave, dishwasher, pots and pans, and a wall safe. There's also a small pool by the sea with good snorkeling off the rocky beach. Service lives up to the hype, and you get a briefing when you check in. Early risers can score a photocopy of faxed news from *The New York Times.* Rates for lofts run $335–$675 d. Rates include transport to and from the pier. Children under five are not welcome here.
http://www.gallowspointresort.com
information@gallowspointresort.com

Located a short drive from town at Great Cruz Bay, the **Westin Resort and Villas St. John** (☎ 693-8000, ✆ 779-4500, 800-808-5020) has 285 luxuriously appointed guest rooms, suites, townhouses, and 48 villas. It provides tennis, complimentary water sports, pool, spa, an exercise studio, and restaurants (24-hr. room service). **Chloe and Bernard** here is one of the island's top (and top priced) restaurants. It's open evenings, reservations are recommended, and it is known for its steak and seafood dishes.

The Westin's 34 acres of gardens overlook a 1,200-ft. white sand beach. Rates run around $719–$849 d during the winter. Disabled access is available. Its main competitor in terms of exclusivity, Caneel Bay, is described under a separate section later on in this chapter.
http://www.westinresortstjohn.com
stjon@westin.com

IN CORAL BAY: Coral Bay accommodation is listed under the "Coral Bay" section.

CAMPING: "Camping" is available at Cinnamon and Maho Bays (see "accommodation" under respective sections), but only Cinnamon Bay has bare sites where you can pitch your own tent. In-depth reviews of these are provided in the appropriate sections.

HOUSES AND VILLA RENTALS: As there are only a few hotels and guesthouses on the island, rentals are increasingly becoming the way to go for visitors. We list these in alphabetical order for convenience. For others check the latest issue of the *Tradewinds,* St. John's weekly rag. The best way to select oe would be to check its website and contact the ower with questions. Many have a one-week minimum.
    Aerie (☎ 779-4183) is a charming, completely-equipped garden cottage.
http://stjohnhouserentals.com/Aerie.htm
dmicheletti@earthlink.net

    Artistic Villas (☎ 776-6420, 800-253-7107, Box 349, St. John 00803) are run by potter Donald Schnell and his wife Deborah. **Villa Bougainvillea** and **Gift Hill Villa** are three-bedroom luxury houses which are tastefully furnished and offer great views. They also have a property right on the beach. Rates run around $195–$335 pn.
http://www.artisticvillas.com
info@artisticvillas.com

Renting for around $138-$195 pn, **Battery Hill** (☎ 776- 6152, 800-416-1205; Box 458) is a set of eight a/c two-bedroom villas with a pool and kitchen and near a beach. **Park Isle Villas** (☎ 693-8261, ☎ 800-416-1205) is another choice.
http://www.batteryhill.com

Catered To (☎ 776-6641, 800-424-6641, ☻ 693-8191; Box 704, Cruz Bay 00831), offers a variety of private homes which may have pools. Rates run from around $3,100 pw on up.
http://www.cateredto.com
cateredto@cateredto.com

Cloud Nine (☎ 693-8495, ☻ 779-4383, 866-683-8496) offers villa rentals from around $4,000 pw.
http://www.cloud9villas.com
info@cloud9villas.com

Carefree Get-Aways on St. John (☎ 779-4070, 888-643-6002) offers home rentals and property management.
http://www.carefreegetaways.com

Caribbean Villas & Resorts (☎ 776-6152, 800-338-0987, ☻ 779-4044, Box 458, Cruz Bay 00831) has a wide selection of villas on St Thomas and St. John. Rates run from around $1,400 pw and up.
http://www.caribbeanvilla.com
info@caribbeanvilla.com

Caribe Havens (☎/☻ 776-6518, Box 455, St. John 00831) offers 13 homes from around $1,200 pw.
http://www.caribehavens.com
info@caribehavens.com

A set of one-bedroom luxury condos with cable TV and a/c, **Cruz Bay Villas** (☎ 776-6416, 888-228-8784; Box 656) rents for around $135-$175 d.

http://www.cruzbayvillas.com
info@cruzbavillas.com

Coconut Coast Villas (☎ 693-9100, ☻ 779-4157, 800-858-7989) has rentals in waterfront cottages from $170 d pn and up; an extra person sharing is $25 pp.
http://www. coconutcoast.com
info@coconutcoast.com

Destination St. John (☎ 779-4647, ☻ 715-0073, 800-562-1901; Box 8306, Cruz Bay 00831) offers rentals from $1,500 pw and up.
http://www.destinationstjohn.com
info@destinationstjohn.com

Estate Zootenvaal (☎ 776-6321) offers furnished homes on a private beach from $275 pn for a one-bedroom house. Their website, which includes an oceanic sound-track, has complete details.
http://www.estatezootenvaal.com
robinclair@estatezootenvaal.com

Gardenia (☎/693-8495, ☻ 479-4383, 866-693-8495) is a studio apartment which sleeps four and rents for around $1,015 pw. It has Jacuzzi, spa, and a/c.
http://www.cloud9villas.com
info@cloud9villas.com

Great Caribbean Getaways (☎ 693-8692, 800-341-2532) is run by Pam and John Reddinger.
http://www.greatcaribbeangetaways.com
info@greatcaribbeangetaways.com

Island Getaways (☎ 693-7676, 693-7676, ☻ 693-8923, 888-693-7676) offers a variety of rentals from around $1,400 pw up to $8,000 pw.
http://www.islandgetawaysinc.com
kathy@islandgetawaysinc.com

Lavender Hill Estates (☎ 914-725-7800, 800-725-7800; Box 8306, St. John 00830) are a set of condos located near Cruz Bay; they have a pool, kitchen, and TV; units have a/c in the master bedroom. Rates run around $365 pn for a one-bedroom and $535 pn for a two-bedroom.
http://www.lavenderhill.net
gary@lavenderhill.net

Lime & De Coconut (☎ 508-627-5702) rents villas with ocean views from $1,300–$15,000 pw.
http://www.lime-coconut.com
islands@lime-coconut.com

McLaughlin Anderson Vacations, Ltd. (☎ 776-0635, 800-537-6246, ☏ 777-4737; 100 Blackbeard's Hill, St. Thomas 00802) represent many villas here.
http://www.mclaughlinanderson.com
villas@att.global.net

Private Homes for Private Vacations (☎ 776-6676, Mamey Peak) manages, rents, and sells.
http://www.privatehomesvi.com

St. John Properties (☎ 693-8485, ☏ 776-6192, 800-283-1746) has 20 or so private homes and apartments. Rates run around $800 pw and up.
http://www.stjohnproperties.com
info@stjohn.properties.com

Three one-bedroom a/c units, **Samuel Cottages** (☎/☏ 776-6643) have kitchens and decks and are near town. They rent for about $125 pn, $600 pw.

Sea Turtle Villa (☎ 677-2486, 888-800-6445, ☏ 677-9216) rents for $3,000-$4,000/wk. Commanding a great view, it offers all the amenities including a pool.
http://www.seaturtlevilla.com
reservations@seaturtlevilla.com

Serendip Vacation Apartments (☎ 776-6646, 888-800-6445; Box 273, St. John 00830) have ten units in two buildings. Each has a twin bed in the bedroom, a living room with twin studio beds, kitchen, and great views of Cruz Bay. Rates run around $1,020 pw and up.
http://www.serendipstjohn.com
serendipcondo@viaccess.net

Sea Cay Villa (☎ 776-4070, 888-643-6002, ☏ 774-6000; Box 272, St. John 00831) is a three-bedroom home with sundeck and private pool overlooking the S shore. It rents for around $4,200 pw.
http://www.carefreegetaways.com

Sea View Vacation Homes (☎ 776-6805, 888-625-2963, Box 644, Cruz Bay 00831) offers weekly rentals of luxury homes.
http://www.seaviewhomes.com
seaviewhomes@islands.vi

Star Villas (☎ 776 6704, ☏ 776-6183, 888-897 9759; Box 599, Cruz Bay 00831) offers one- and two-bedroom villas in or near Cruz Bay or Johnson Bay. Rates run around $150–$350 pn during the winter.
http://www.starvillas.com
bobmail@viaccess.net

Suite St. John (☎ 776-6969, 800-348-8444) offers homes in a number of locales. They offer suites in the Gallows Point Resort, rent Cinnamon Bay Estate, and rent suites at Lavender Hill Estates.
http://www.suitestjohn.com
gallowspt@aol.com

Vacation Vistas (☎ 776-6462, Box 476, Cruz Bay 00831) offer homes ranging from cottages to luxurious villas. Rates start at around $2,400 pw.
http://www.vacationvistas.com
lisa@vacationvistas.com

Villa Safari (☎ 776-6862) is a secluded villa on a white sand beach which rents for around $6,000–$8,000 pw depending upon the number of people.
http://www.st-john.com/safari
tpusvi@attglobal.net

A set of one- to five-bedroom homes with great views, **Windspree, Inc.** (☎ 693-5423, ☉ 693-5623, 888-742-0357; 7 Freemans Ground, St. John 00830) rents for around $1,400–$5,000 pw.
http://www.windspree.com
windspre@viacess.net

St. John Dining, Food, and Entertainment

Food is expensive on St. John because so little is grown here and food items must be imported via St. Thomas. Your choices are to a) buy everything in the markets, b) travel to St. Thomas and shop for food, c) bring food with you, d) dine out or e) some combination of the above.

DINING: There are so many places to eat here that one would need weeks to visit them all.

Set just above town, towards the beginning of the North Shore Road and next to Estate Lindholm, **Asolare** (☎ 779-4747) offers a blend of SE and E Asian gourmet cuisine. There are two seatings (5:30–6:45 and at 7:30–8:45) taken each evening. Appetizers include "Kampuchea shrimps ravioli" ($9) and "lemongrass steamed mussels" ($9); main courses range from "grilled salmon *confit*" to "*maguro nori* tuna."
http://www.stjohnrestaurants.com/asolare.htm

Set in the Lemon Tree Mall, the **Lime Inn** (☎ 776-6425, 779-4199) has been doing its thing for nearly two decades now; it remains one of the most popular local restaurants, and many locals dine here regularly. In addition to

appetizers (grilled shrimp, $7.95), soups (clam chowder, $4), and salads (Greek salad, $5.95), entrées include "shrimp Dijon" ($15.95), lobster, pasta, and "the fresh catch of the day."

At Meada's Shopping Plaza near the pier, **JJ's Texas Coast Cafe** features moderate Tex-Mex dishes; catfish is served on Fri. nights. Breakfasts include bagels, fruit plates, and omelettes.

Cafe Roma (☎ 776-6524) has good pizza as well as seafood, veal parmigiana, and baked pastas. They have pizza ($12.50 for cheese) and pies. They're one of the oldest and most popular of all the town's restaurants.

Fred's, is one local food spot. For really good and reasonable local food ($7–8 for a large plate) try **Hercules,** a modest establishment run by a St. Kitts native which is down the road towards the harbor from the Tamarind Inn. Vistors are wild about his *pates*. The more adventurous can try bull foot soup (cows feet and vegetables) for breakfast.

Cap's Place has conch fritters for $1 as well as other reasonable food. It is right in the center of town, on the corner across from the post office, and is something of a hangout for local Dominicans.

Upstairs at Wharfside Village, the **Paradise Cafe** serves light food.

Offering a nautical decor, the **Fishtrap** (☎ 693-9994), next to the Raintree Court mini mall, offers gourmet seafood. Entrées start at $18 (for which you get "sesame tuna and stir-fried vegetables in a garlic chili sauce on steamed rice.)
http://www.thefishtrap.com

Across from the Fishtrap, **Sosa's Restaurant** serves delicious inexpensive meals. The Dominican atmosphere is about the closest you can come to visiting the Dominican Republic without going there.

Woody's Seafood Saloon is near FirstBank; it opens for lunch and stays open late. It is a popular watering hole with locals and tourists alike. It offers seafood from $7, making it one of the more affordable places. Dishes range from vegetarian primavera to rock lobstertail to shrimp tempura. Country schlock star Kenny Chesney is reputed to hang here. Don't be surprised if you see the occasional dude or dudette in a ten-gallon hat who are here to try to catch a glimpse of him.

Happy Fish (☎ 776-1717), an a/c sushi restaurant located on the second floor of the Marketplace, serves tasty (but not inexpensive) sushi: rolls start at $5. In addition to the expected beer and sake, they serve some 30 different martinis, a number of which are Asian themed.

The immensely popular **Waterfront Bistro** (☎ 777-7755), is set right on the water at Wharfside Village. It's the only true beachfront restaurant on St. John other than those at Caneel Bay and the Westin. Like these two, it offers elegant seaside dining (gourmet dishes, an extensive wine list). It's open for lunch and dinner, and reservations are recommended.

The **Banana Deck** (☎ 693-5055) is a two-story open-air complex near the shoreline. It has an open-air kitchen, a pool table. It offers several daily specials; there are generally two fresh fish dishes, two pasta dishes, and two vegetarian dishes.

La Tapa (☎ 693-7755) offers *tapas* (Mon. to Fri. 4:30-6:30 PM) ranging from smoked salmon to brie to marinated olives; all for $2.50 each. Entrées ($18–$36) include paella and "tuna Basquaise."

ZoZo's Ristorante (☎ 693-9200, closed Sun.) serves appetizers (eggplant tower, $8), salads (orange salad, $9), pastas ($15–21), and entrées such as *zuppe de pesce* (lobster, mussels, shrimp, and calamari in a white wine seafood broth).

On the road to Mongoose from town, **Morgan's Mango** (☎ 776-8141) offers Caribbean cuisine. Appetizers and salads

reflect the whole range of the archipelago's cuisine (flying fish from Barbados, Cajun shrimp from New Orleans), and entrées include a vegetarian plate ("Morgan's loves vegetarians!"), as well as seafood dishes such as "Voodoo Snapper" from Haiti, and an extensive assortment of mixed drinks. A grill night, each Fri. night, features live music and a meat and seafood grill.

Rumbalaya (☎ 714-6169), Wharfside Village, serves casual Caribbean and American-style dishes; it has a children's menu.

Ocean Grill (☎ 693-3304), Mongoose Junction, serves lunches and dinner in an open-air courtyard. Its "inspired eclectic menu" draws from traditional Caribbean ingredients and employs fresh local ingredients including organic produce. A Sunday Brunch is served.

The Tap Room (☎ 998-1333), above Ocean Grill in Mongoose Junction, serves drafts of St. John Brewers' Virgin Islands Pale Ale. Soak up the a/c or sit on the patio. http://www.stjohnbrewers.com

The **Sun Dog Cafe** (☎ 693-8340), at Mongoose, serves a wide range of dishes including salads, pizza, sandwiches (fresh veggie wrapper, $6.50) and "the mighty mahi taco" ($9.50). Thursday evening is sushi night.

The Paradiso (☎ 776-8806), upstairs at Mongoose, serves a wide range of dishes.

Ronnie's Pizza serves pizza and has a salad bar. It's in Boulon Center.

Satyamuna (☎ 774-3663), a Mediterranean vegetarian restaurant on the second floor of the Market Place, offers delights such as lasagna and spinach pie in filo dough. It's run by the affable Giuliana and Ofer.

One alternative to the restaurants is to picnic on bread, cheese, and other such digestible commodities sold at local shops and bakeries.

ST. JOHN

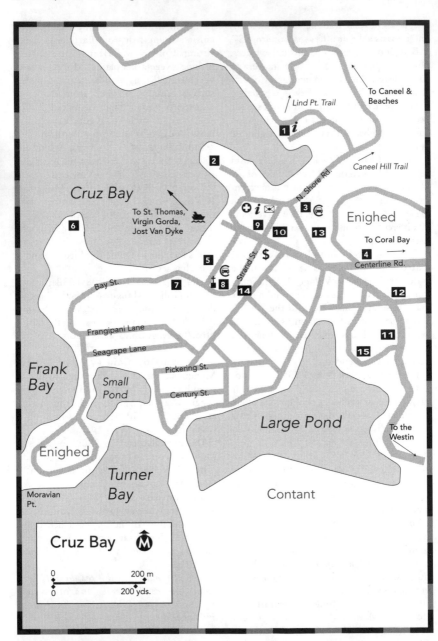

To Caneel &
Beaches

Lind Pt. Trail

1 *i*

Caneel Hill Trail

Cruz Bay

2

N. Shore Rd.

To St. Thomas,
Virgin Gorda,
Jost Van Dyke

✚ *i* ✉

3 🚌

Enighed

9

10 **13**

To Coral Bay

6

5

$

4

Centerline Rd.

Bay St.

🚌
† **8**

7

Strand St.

14

12

Frangipani Lane

11

Seagrape Lane

15

Pickering St.

*Frank
Bay*

*Small
Pond*

Century St.

Large Pond

Enighed

To the
Westin

*Turner
Bay*

Moravian
Pt.

Contant

Cruz Bay ◉**M**

0		200 m
0		200 yds.

Cruz Bay	
1	National Park HQ/Park Information
2	The Battery
3	Mongoose Junction
4	Tamarind Court
5	Wharfside Village
6	Gallows Pt. Resort
7	Stone Terrace (closed restaurant)
8	Raintree Court
9	Connections
10	Cafe Roma
11	Library
12	Marketplace/Starfish Market
13	Lime Inn
14	St. John Inn
15	The Lumberyard

C&D Bakery is at 17-35 Enighed in the Lumberyard.

OUT OF TOWN: Out on Centerline Rd. (Rte. 10) and the junction with Bordeaux Rd. (Rte. 108), **Le Chateau de Bordeaux** (☎ 776-6611; dinner reservations required) is set by a beautiful overlook. It's about 20 min. from town. Modest yet intimate and expensive, it offers gourmet cuisine such as saffron pasta, West Indian seafood chowder, and yellowtail tuna. There are two seatings (5:30-6:45 and at 7:30–8:45) taken each evening. Expect to spend at least $60 pp. Be sure to sit next to the window. It is a great place to watch a full moon rise.

Other restaurants of note are out at Caneel Bay and near Coral Bay and are described in the text.

MARKET SHOPPING: Very expensive, so try to bring what you can with you. If you're planning on cooking your own food at the campground and staying a while, it may be worth going over to St. Thomas to shop (as many of the locals do) because the few local stores have a minimum selection of goods at maximum prices. In any event, when buying canned or bottled goods be sure to check the expiration date.

Dolphin Market is an attractive supermarket which is less expensive than Starfish.

Just down the road and set in the imposing Marketplace building, the ultramodern, upscale **Starfish Market** (☎ 779-4959) has quality merchandise at high prices. It's open 7:30 AM to 9 PM. It shares its building with the sister **Starfish Gourmet and Wines**, Baked in the Sun Bakery and Kaleidoscope Video.

Pine Peace Market (☎ 693-8725), along South Shore Road around a half-mi. from town, is the most affordable market but is not good for fresh produce.

There are several other places on the outskirts of town as well as in Coral Bay. Maho and Cinnamon Bays have expensive commissaries.

ENTERTAINMENT: For its size, Cruz Bay has amazingly vibrant nightlife. With a plethora of local guys around, tourist gals won't be lonely long. To find out what's happening where on the island, check local tree trunks and utility poles, as well as the bulletin board across from the bank. At night, it's easy to walk around and see what's on. Bands (mixing reggae, calypso and other rhythms) play regularly (generally Wed. and Fri.) at **Fred's** (☎ 776-6363).

A **Sunday Jazz Jam** takes place at the Beach Bar, near the ferry dock in Wharfside Village, from 4:30–7:30 PM. For more information call Steve Simon at 693-8834. If you have a chance, don't miss an opportunity to see a performance by the **Love City Pan Dragons**, a children's troupe who practice in a building near the Inn at Tamarind Court and on the way to the Cruz Bay Inn.

Finally, don't miss the nightly audio-visual display put on by the moon, stars, and crashing surf.

Events, Shopping, Information, and Services

EVENTS: St. John's own Reverend Anne Marie Porter conducts **Valentine's Day Marriage Vow Renewal Service** (☎ 888-676-5701) every Feb. 14th at 5:30 PM on Trunk Bay beach. Anne Marie, known as the barefoot minister, welcomes locals and tourists alike to this celebration of love. Each participating couple receives a lovely marriage reaffirmation certificate and long stemmed rose.
http://www.vivows.com

St. John's Fourth of July Celebration commemorates the emancipation of slaves on July 3, 1848. Not as large as the one on St. Thomas but equally intense in atmosphere, it is the grand finale to Carnival festivities that begin in early June. During the week preceding the 4th of July, festivities reach their climax and activities include live bands playing in the "Village," a food fair, J'ouvert, (see below), the Fourth of July parade, and fireworks. (Sometimes the 4th of July Parade is celebrated on the 5th, depending on what day of the week the holiday falls. Emancipation Day in the USVI is celebrated on July 3rd).

Constructed along the waterfront, Carnival Village has live bands, handicrafts, food and drink stalls as well as games and pony rides for children. Calypso and reggae bands from all over the Caribbean ride through town on the back of trucks. Celebrations begins in earnest at 4:30 AM on July 4 when St. Johnians depart their homes in costume for the "*j'ouvert*" (French for "opening" or "break of day") festivities. The parade is the highlight of the festival,

Most Romantic Places to Kiss

St. John has a lot of great places.

➤ At the lookout at Lind Point

➤ In the ruined windmill at Christ of the Caribbean.

➤ At the petroglyph pond on the Reef Bay Trail.

➤ Along Lameshur Beach

and its highlight is the moko jumbie dancers who hop, skip, and do acrobatics on stilts. They are followed by the Carnival Queen and various floats. Evening fireworks climax the celebration.

The **St. John Arts Festival takes place during Feb**. Participants have included the 73rd National Guard Army Band and the St. John Quadrille Dancers.
http://stjohnartsfestival.org

The **8 Tuff Miles Race**, a footrace between Cruz Bay and Coral Bay which runs through the park, is held every Feb.
http://www.8tuffmiles.com

The **"Love City" Triathalon,** first held in 1999, is held in Sept. It involves a half-mi. swim, a 14-mi. bike ride, and a four-mi. run. Starting point is Big Maho Bay with a swim.
http://www.8tuffmiles.com

The **St. John Blues Festival** takes place in Cruz Bay and Coral Bay each March.
http://www.stjohnbluesfestival.com

SHOPPING: The island's mellowness extends into its stores. About the only time these shopkeepers get upset is when they find that a customer has shoplifted an item. While the selection found on St. Thomas isn't available, neither does the "buy, buy,

buy" atmosphere prevail. The bulk of the shops are run largely by transplanted continentals and offer attractive, moderately priced goods.

Shell Seekers, near the dock, sells a variety of books and periodicals among other items. **Sparky's,** nearby, offers free delivery of alcohol to the airport. **St. John Spice** is another special shop.

MONGOOSE JUNCTION SHOPPING: Designed by architect Glenn Speer, Mongoose Junction evokes the feel of sugar plantation buildings. The island's foremost shopping complex, it was inaugurated in 1987, and continues to expand. Its distinctive masonry design incorporates stone and coral, drawing inspiration from the island's 18th-century plantations. The first building you see coming from town houses **Big Planet** (adventure gear), **Little Planet** (kid's adventure gear), and the **Paradiso** restaurant.

The next building houses **Jewels** (jewelry, watches), and **Bamboula** which offers a wide range of goods including fabrics, CDs and cassettes, and books. It has a wider range of local artists than any other store and is open nightly until 9:30. You can also find a number of other shops here. The **Bougainvillea,** a boutique, serves swimwear as well as jewelry and other accessories. They have another branch at the Westin. Under the same management, the **Island Fancy** is an art gallery and children's clothing shop which sells books and gifts. **Caravan Gallery** sells jewelry and special gifts. **R & and I Patton** design silver and gold jewelry. **Bajo El Sol** sells work by local artists including prints and crafts. While shopping here, you can stop for a brew at **The Tap Room,** the island's only microbrewery.
http://www.mongoosejunctionstjohn.com

WHARFSIDE VILLAGE SHOPPING: To the R of the ferry dock along the road, this attractive complex contains some 30 stores. On the second floor, **Cruz Bay Gift Emporium**

sells local and continental newspapers as well as magazines, books, and other goods. **Arawak Silver Works** offers other unusual items. **Palm Jewelers,** sell hook bracelets and other jewelry. **The Cruz Bay Clothing Company** sells swimwear and other clothes and gifts. **The Cruz Bay Photo Center** offers film processing and sells cameras. **Dreams and Dragonflies** sells jewelry, clothing, and other unique items. **Shae Design** sells the jewelry of Shaneen Broomfield. **Freebird Creations** sells unusual jewelry, tribal masks, and watches. **Galeria del Mar** is a Caribbean fine art and crafts gallery which has ceramics, glassworks, and sculpture. **St. John Kids** is another unique store.

RAINTREE PLAZA: This has a number of small shops with a large variety of goods.

LEMON TREE MALL: Here you'll find shops including **Pink Papaya** which stocks Haitian painted tinware and other handicrafts and colorful household items.
http://www.pinkpapaya.com

ELSEWHERE: Out in Frank Bay, **Coconut Coast Studios** (☎ 776-6944) exhibits the watercolors of and other work by Elaine Estern.

The **Artists Association of St John** (AASJ) sells its wares upstairs at The Lumberyard.
http://www.stjohnarts.com

The main shopping outside of town is found at the **Westin** and at the **Caneel Bay Gift Shop** which carries a line of clothes and other items.

The **Donald Schnell Studio,** on the upper level at Amore Center, features hand-blown and stained-glass items.

BOOKS: The friendly **Book and Bean** (☎ 779-2665) is at the Market Place. In addition to a small selection of books, they also sell fair trade organic coffee as well as magazines.

INFORMATION: The **tourist office** is near downtown next to the post office. Be sure to obtain *The St John Guidebook* and the accompanying map. Both are useful for shopping and dining.
http://www.stjohnguidebook.com

The local newspaper, *Tradewinds*, will come in handy.
http://www.stjohntradewindsnews.com

Its competitor is the *Virgin Voices*, a tabloid which focuses on lifestyles.
http://www.virginvoices.com

The *St. John Times* is another alternative.
http://www.stjohntimes.com

A good source for news about the island is:
http://www.newsofstjohn.com
Another useful online source is:
http://www.stjohnsource.com

Open daily from 8 AM–4:30 PM, the **National Park Service** (☎ 776-6201) office, right on the bay and near the ferry, is perhaps the best source of information on the island. Don't procrastinate! Make this your first stop. Folders, maps, and an excellent selection of books are available. Ask for information about any of an incredible number of activities including nature hikes, history walks, and snorkel trips. They also present films and talks at Cinnamon Bay campground. Information can be obtained in advance by writing directly to National Park Service, 1300 Cruz Bay Creek, St. John, USVI 00830.
http://www.nps.gov/viis

While on St. John, be sure to obtain a copy of *The Virgin 1sland News*, a free bi-annual tabloid which offers an entertaining pastiche of information; it's supported by the **Friends of the National Park** (Box 111,

St. John 00831; ☎ 779-4940); memberships are $15 individual and $25 family. They do other valuable work including soliciting volunteers and working on the boat mooring system. They also offer special trips such as a cultural history tour on board a boat as well as an offshore snorkel trip.
http://www.friendsvinp.org

SERVICES: Telephones are located at the public ferry dock and across from the **post office**, which, in turn is near the tourist information office. **note:** The Post Office will be moving in 2005 or so.

First Bank (☎ 776-6881) operates a small branch **bank** near the Lutheran church. It has an ATM which functions when it has good digestion. **Scotia Bank** (☎ 776-6552), in the Marketplace, also has an ATM. Also, don't forget that you can use your ATM or credit card at a US Post Office and get up to $50 cash back.

The beautiful, carpeted two-story **Elaine lone Sprauve Library,** a reconstruction of the Enighed Estate great house, stands just above town. Special cultural programs are often held here. It has newspapers and inexpensive (but slow) fee-based internet access.

Next to Woody's town and inside the Quiet Mon Pub, the **Cyber Celtic Cafe** (☎ 779-4799) offers internet access for $10/hr. Out at The Marketplace, **Surf da Web Cyber Cafe** (☎ 693-9152) offers high-speed access ($12/hr.), wireless access, and other services.

Set on Southshore Road are **Paradise Laundromat** and **Paradise Laundry Service.**

Chelsea Drug Store is in the Starfish Market complex.

Virgin Islands Communications (Connections) (☎ 776-6692) offers a variety of services including typing/word processing, laminating, laundry drop off, answering service, mailing service, photocopies, and outgoing phone calls at direct dial rates (in air conditioned privacy).

Video rentals are available at **Kaleidoscope Video** in the same complex as the Starfish Market.

Anne Marie Porter (☎ 693-5153, 888-676-5701) performs nondenominational weddings and wedding vow renewals. Anne Marie is a lovely lady who is very caring and helpful. She can guide you to a hotel suited to your needs and offers four different services (depending upon your needs) as well as a free pre-wedding consultation. Unlike others, she does not take commissions from rental car agencies and hotels.
http://www.stjohnweddings.com
http://www.remarryyourmate.com

Other wedding planners include:
http://www.usviwedding.com
http://www.elegantweddingsand events.com
http://www.islandstyleweddings.com
http://www.lovecityweddings.com
http://www.waywardsailor.net

RENTALS: It isn't necessary to rent a car if you're willing to do some walking, as local transport (and charter taxis) run all along the North Shore Rd. and head past and/or into Caneel, Trunk, Cinnamon, and Maho. And a new bus runs hourly (or thereabouts) all the way to Salt Pond.

Where a car does come in handy is when visiting areas such as the East End and Lameshur Bay which are more remote. However, a one-or two-day rental should be sufficient unless you are staying well out of town.

Car rentals include: **Best Rent A Car** (☎ 693-8177, night: ☎ 775-0815), Centerline **Conrad Sutton** (☎ 776-6479), **Delbert Hills** (☎ 776-6637/7947, 800-537-6238), **Cool Breeze Car Rental** (☎ 776-6588), **Hertz/Varlack** (☎ 693-7580), **Spencer's Jeep Rentals** (☎ 693-8784, 888-776-6628, ✆ 776-7118), **St. John Car Rental, Inc.**

(☎ 776-6103), and **O'Conner Car Rental** (☎ 776-6343).

Gas runs about $4–5/gal. The only **gas stations** are in Cruz Bay and in Coral Bay, so be sure to fill up regularly. In Cruz Bay, the E & C station is down the South Shore road across from the basketball courts. Stations are open from 7 AM–8 PM Mon. to Sat. and from 7 AM–4 PM on Sun. Both may be closed on holidays.

PARKING: In town, the public parking lot by the tennis courts is most likely place for day parking. Move your car at night when other spots should have opened up. Parking is getting harder and harder in town. Tickets are freely given here so be careful.

TOURING BY CAR: Don't try to do too much. St. John is deceptively small. If you're into views, the best ones are found on the L along Centerline Rd. towards Annaberg so it's best to head this way and return along the North Shore Rd. You should allow at least two days if you really want to get around. One full day could be spent driving the North Shore–Centerline loop, and on second you might explore the East End and dip down to the island's S. Without a car you can still take a taxi or the bus to select locations, explore trails near your hotel (if any), and swim, snorkel, dive, and kayak.

While driving, be aware that pedestrians, cows, pigs, and chickens all have the right of way. The recent construction boom has meant that previously unsurfaced roads have been surfaced. That means you can drive faster than before, but it is dangerous to do so. A seatbelt law is in effect. Foreigners do not require an international driving license.

HEALTH CARE: In case of emergency, a doctor can be reached 24 hours a day by calling the **Police** (☎ 776- 6262). At 3B Sussanaberg, the **Myrah Keating Community Health Center** (☎ 776-6400, ✆ 779-6400) can be reached at 922 during an emergency. **Cruz Bay Family Practice (☎ 776-6789)** offers 24-hr. service at Boulon Center.

For dental care contact **St. John Dental** (☎ 693-8898) in Boulon Center. http://www.nycenterfordentistry.com

Chelsea Drugs (☎ 776-4888), a small but friendly pharmacy, is in The Marketplace as is **Health Care Connection** (☎ 776- 8989), which offers health care services.

EXERCISE: **The Gym in Paradise** (☎ 777-0600) is at The Marketplace.

St. John Watersports, Excursions, and Tennis

Friendly **St. John Adventures Unlimited** (☎ 693-7730) is located in the a/c shop to the R of the entrance to the Gallows Point Resort. They can give you the lowdown on all of your options and will book everything from a massage to a horseback ride for you. http://www.stjohnadventures.com

BEACHES: St. John has 39 beaches. The best are on the North Shore Rd. These include Caneel Beach, Cinnamon Bay Beach, Hawksnest Beach, Gibney's or Little Hawksnest Beach, Jumbie Beach, Trunk Bay Beach, Peter Bay Beach, Cinnamon Bay Beach, Maho Bay Beach, Francis Bay Beach, and Waterlemon Beach.

You can supplement a visit to a beach with a hike; trails such as *Cinnamon Bay Nature Trail* are right near the beach. The more adventurous can visit the S shore area. *When at the beach, give others some space. This isn't New Jersey, and locals especially enjoy their privacy.*

The **most crowded beaches** are Trunk Bay (which charges $4 admission), Cinnamon Bay, Caneel Bay, and Little Maho.

Maho Bay has shallow water for quite a ways out, so it is great for young children.

Drunk Bay is best for beachcombing but poor for swimming.

WATERSPORTS: Call **Low Key Watersports** (☎ 669-8999, 800-835-7718) at Wharfside Village for parasailing or sea kayaking as well as diving (four different wreck dives, night dives, and certification courses) and snorkeling. http://www.divelowkey.com lowkey@viaccess.net

Featuring a wide variety of diving excursions and snorkeling trips, **Cruz Bay Watersports** (☎ 776-6234, ✆ 776-8303, 800-835-7730) has a free snorkeling map. They also offer excursions to Jost Van Dyke on Tues, Thurs., and Sat. http://www.cbw-stjohn.com

Various rentals are available at **Cinnamon Bay** and **Maho Camps**. Sunfishes are also at Maho. **Noah's Little Arks** (☎ 693-9030) rents dinghies for around $65 per half day and $110 per full day.

SEA KAYAKING: Although a number of operations offer sea kayaking, the main company with trips is **Arawak Expeditions** (☎ 693-8312, 800-238-8687; Box 853, Cruz Bay). They run introductory half-day trips ($50) as well as full-day trips ($90 pp with lunch) which visit remote parts of St. John and head over to surrounding islands. An adventurous five-day trip explores the BVI with stops at Peter Island and Norman Island before crossing the Sir Francis Drake Channel to the West End of Tortola and heading N to Jost Van Dyke before returning to St. John. They also offer kayak rentals and mountain bike tours.

St. John Ecotours (☎ 643-6397) offers a full-day kayak trip to Hurricane Hole. http://www.stjohnecotours.com

BOAT EXCURSIONS: Most of these are in the $70 range for a day sail. **Connections** (☎ 776-6922) arranges sailing trips and trips to Jost Van Dyke. (They have an office in the town center). *Note that St. Thomas operators may also be willing to pick you up.*

Calypso Charters (☎ 777-7245, 998-5564, 693-7328) offers half- and full-day sails to Jost Van Dyke, Waterlemon Cay, and other locations. They also have half- and full-day dinghy rentals.
http://www.calypsovi.com

The motor yacht **Cinnamon Bay** (☎ 776-4037, 998-3219) offers public cruises as well as private charters around the island and to Norman I. and Virgin Gorda.
http://www.motoryachtcinnamonbay.com

Cloudbreak Charters (☎ 626-2709, 244-5592) offers day trips, fishing and water taxi services aboard a 28-ft. Carolina Classic.
http://www.stjohnboatcharters.com

Gypsy Spirit II (☎ 344-2111), a Coronado-27, offers sunset sails, full moon sails, and Sun. three-hour sails.
http://www.vi-fun-n-sun.com/gypsy.html

Hurricane Alley (☎ 776-6256, ☎ 693-9841) offers half-day, sunset and full-day sails, as well as trips to Jost Van Dyke ($115 pp) on three different boats.

Long Distance (☎ 513-1386, 779-4994) offers half- to full-day sails on a 40-ft. Pearson. They offer guided snorkeling.
sailboatlongdistance@hotmail.com

> *i* • Definitely visit the **National Park Visitor's Center** to take advantage of their brochures, tours, and other information.

The Outlaw (☎ 771-3747) is a Baltic yacht with two staterooms which provides charters for groups of up to six. They offer half- and full-day sails, sunset sails, BVI trips, and overnight and weekly charters. A full-day sail is $800, and you may circumnavigate St. John.
outlaw_stj@pocketmail.com

Departing from the Park Service, a six-hr. three-stop round-island snorkeling trip runs on Wed. aboard the *Sadie Sea* (☎ 690-4651, 776-6572) There's also a two-stop, three-hr. snorkel tour (Mon. and Wed., 9 AM) and a night snorkel tour ($55). Check with the Park Service for current details of any trip.
http://www.sadiesea.com

Serena Sea (☎ 776-6725) offers a three-hr. tour from Coral Bay which takes you to Hurricane Hole, Round Bay, and Flanagan Island on board a wooden yacht. Departures at 9 AM and 1 and 5 PM.

The Right Reverend Philip G. Chalker, the **Wayward Sailor** (☎ 776-6922) offers sails and snorkeling aboard his yacht. He can also marry you or renew your wedding vows.
http://www.bookitvi.com/wayward.htm
wayward@bookitvi.com

The White Wing (☎ 776-6922) offers a number of different excursions to the BVI including a dinner cruise to the *William Thornton* at Norman Island. They also offer some innovative St. John nautical adventures. All rates are private charter and run around US$70 pp on St. John, more to the BVI. Two-day "mini cruises" start at around $550.

SCUBA RENTALS/TRIPS: In town, **Cruz Bay Water Sports** (☎ 776-6234; Box 252, St. John 00830) and out at Cinnamon Bay visit **St. John Water Sports** (☎ 776-6256; Box 252, St. John 00830).

SNORKELING: Snuba (☎ 776-8063) will take you "snubaing" at Trunk Bay for

$57 including park fee. (Snuba is a type of snorkeling using an air source contained on a flotation raft that follows your every move underwater.)
http://www.visnuba.com

St. John Ecotours (☎ 643-6397) offers an "East End Cruise" which combines a hike along Leinster Bay with a snorkel cruise of St. John's East End) and a "Natural Adventure Combo," an early morning hike along the Cinnamon Bay Trail combined with a Congo Cay boat and snorkeling tour.
http://www.stjohnecotours.com

BOATING CHARTERS: Contact **Connections** (☎ 776-6922) for information concerning boat charters. **Ocean Runner** (☎ 693-8809) rents 20-, 22-, or 25-ft. hydrasport powerboats.
http://www.oceanrunner.vi

RIDING: The **Carolina Corral** (☎ 693-5778) at Coral Bay offers rides ($45/hr.) on beaches, mountain roads, and during the full moon.
http://www. st-john.com/trailrides

FISHING: There is no deep-sea fishing allowed in National Park waters. Consult with the park service for further details as to where other fishing is permitted. **Red Hook** (see "St. Thomas") is a center for sport fishing.

Bite Me (☎ 693-5823) offers fishing trips ranging from a half- to full day.
http://www.bitemechartersvi.com

Gone Ketchin' (☎ 714-1175, cell: 998-2055) is a 25-ft. cabin boat which offers beginning to advanced sport fishing.
http://www.goneketchin.com

World Class Anglers (☎ 779-4281; Box 8327, Cruz Bay 00831) offers half- and full-day trips; ask for Capt. Loren Nickbarg.

TENNIS: In **Cruz Bay**, two courts are near the fire station and lighted until 10.

The **Westin** (☎ 693-8000) offers six lighted courts which are open until 10; non-guests are charged $15/hr.

Caneel Bay (☎ 776-6111, ext. 234) has 11 courts; lessons ($30/30 min.) are offered to non-guests, and use of the courts is $10 pp.
mcdonald@viaccess.net

HIKING TOURS: The **Friends of the National Park** (Box 111, St. John 00831; ☎ 779-4940) offer hikes, snorkels, bird-watching, and other activities. Every month sees different activities, and this is a highly recommended way to experience the island. Pick up a brochure at the ranger station.
http://www.friendsvinp.org

DISABLED TOURS: **Disabled visitors** are now offered tours through the **St. John Community Foundation**: (☎ 693-7600).

St. John Underwater

DIVE SPOTS: Most dive excursions head for points off the N coast as well as to the E end of St. Thomas. They can take you to the **West Indian Transport Shoal** (see St. Thomas), and the *RMS Rhone*. (see "Rhone National Marine Park" in the BVI travel section. A diving site map is included in the St. Thomas section). TIPS: Off of Caneel Bay, you can see spotted eagle rays; avoid feeding them. Owing to the rougher water, the S coast is seldom snorkeled or dived.

Carvel Rock and the dropoff by **Congo Cay** are two popular sites.

 If swells prevent swimming at the North Shore, you can head to Salt Pond and Lameshur where you are guaranteed calmer waters.

ST. JOHN

Moorings on St. John

Be sure to obtain a copy of the free full-color **Mooring & Anchoring Guide** *from the National Park Service. The National Park Service maintains moorings at these locations:*

- ⚓ Francis Bay
- ⚓ Greater Lameshur
- ⚓ Hawksnest
- ⚓ Jumbie Bay
- ⚓ Leinster Bay
- ⚓ Lind Point
- ⚓ Little Lameshur
- ⚓ Maho Bay
- ⚓ Rams Head
- ⚓ Reef Bay
- ⚓ Salt Pond

Eagle Shoal, a lovely coral grotto housing nurse sharks and stingrays, has numerous crevices.

Offshore from Cruz Bay, **Steven Cay** features sea fans, mountain and star corals, and large numbers of triggerfish and angelfish.

Others include Fishbowl at Cruz Bay, Johnson Reef on the N coast, and Horseshoe and South Drop (a fairly narrow ridge of seafloor cracks and fissures which is a good place to spot large fish)

A well developed reef structure between Grassy Cay and **Grassco Junction** offers seven towers around which turtles, octupi, and stingrays gather.

SNORKELING SPOTS: Superior snorkeling is found at Trunk Bay, Jumbie, Peter Bay, and Waterlemon; other locations include the East End (Hanson Bay, Long Bay, Brown Bay, Privateer Bay, and at Haulover on the Drake's Passage side).

From Cruz Bay you may walk to and then snorkel at **Salomon Beach, Honeymoon Beach,** and **Caneel Bay.**

Between the first two is a headland which has brain coral the size of basketball as well as other species. The W side of Honeymoon has snorkeling in water 10 ft. or less in depth. It boasts a variety of pillar, elknorn, and other corals. There are also fringes of reef near the shoreline to the E of Honeymoon and W from Salomon. Landlubbers will want to arrive at hours other than 10 AM–3 PM (when tour boats arrive) so they can have the area all to themselves.

Caneel's main beach has a small area of fringing reef off the NE end. You'll find gorgonians, hard corals, and finger corals. Watch for sea urchins here.

Hawksnest Bay offers shallow reefs which are a bit shallow—some of which is too shallow, in fact, to snorkel above. This reef has been damaged in the past by storms and development, but it is under recovery. Watch for elkhorn coral. The best area is off the E side.

Jumbie Bay has a shallow reef to the R which extends across cliffs to Trunk Bay. Deeper water hosts brain coral. To the L, there is a bit of coral.

Trunk Bay has a heavily used underwater trail. (Admission $4). This beach can be very crowded between 10 AM–4 PM.

Windy but offering good visibility, **Cinnamon Bay** has a ledge area between the beach and Cinnamon Cay. Watch for invertebrates. Rest in sandy spots before snorkeling around the cay. (Gorgonians congregate at its rear). On the W end, in the direction of Little Cinnamon, is a section of besilted reef which has a portion of an airplane propeller. The E end has dead coral but fish galore. Watch for coral heads scattered through other areas.

Sheltered **Maho Bay** has seagrass beds which green sea turtles know and love.

Park Rules and Regulations

➤ Fires are permitted only on grills in designated picnic areas.

➤ Pets must be kept on leashes and are prohibited from entering picnic areas, beaches, or the campground.

➤ Fishing is prohibited in swimming areas.
➤ Camping is prohibited outside the campground.

➤ Cans should be placed in recycling bins.

➤ Boats longer than 210 ft. are not allowed to anchor within park waters, and those ranging from 125-210 ft. may anchor only in Francis Bay, in sandy areas and in depths greater than 30 ft.

➤ Boaters must use moorings in Reef Bay, Greater and Little Lameshur bays, and in Salt Pond Bay.

Watch for them in early morning or late afternoon. A bit of coral and fish may be seen offshore near the rocky tips of the bay.

Francis Bay is a good place to snorkel for beginners; head to your L in the direction of Maho. Hardier souls will appreciate the rocky section at the other end. Sea turtles, jacks, and tarpon also inhabit these waters.

Leinster Bay offers snorkeling halfway to Waterlemon Beach. Hurricane Bertha turned some of the coral heads here on their side, but they are still alive. Watch for parrotfish. Leinster Bay's **Waterlemon Cay** (an islet) is a long swim but has great snorkeling. Traverse the unofficial trail that runs along the E shoreline to get closer in. (Watch for coral while exiting). Orangish-brown cushion sea stars live here.

You must hike or take a boat to **Brown Bay**. Explore coral and seagrass here. Head out to the L to find a thick fringing reef; it heads toward Waterlemon Cay. A short swim to the R finds a reef where gorgonians have set themselves up. Watch for conch,

baby fish, and even turtles in the seagrass beds directly offshore.

Set on the N side and sometimes confusing to find, **Haulover Bay** has good snorkeling off of the reefs to the L. On its E end, Haulover Bay has a narrow, short, hard-to-find trail which terminates in a rocky beach. Snorkel straight out to find large coral. However, the water is deep and the wind is often strong, so weaker swimmers should confine themselves to the area on the R. The Coral Bay side offers smoother swimming but less coral and more urchins.

Set on the SE, **Salt Pond Bay** has a sun drenched beach with good snorkeling along its L around the point. If you swim out to the boat moorings, you can find a set of rocks which has some great coral formations. Watch for sea turtles. You may also hike to Ram Head from here.

Little Lameshur Bay has a small cluster of coral offshore to your R. A great reef is found out at the tip of **Yawzi Point**. Head out from the rocky beach which is to the L ¼ of the way down; this is faster than swimming from the beach at the end.

You may snorkel in seagrass in **Chocolate Hole** which is two mi. from Cruz Bay along Rte. 104. Watch for conch and rays. This is a good alternative when there are N swells.

You may snorkel in a mangrove environment at **Princess Bay**.

The Virgin Islands National Park

Practically synonymous with the island itself, the Virgin Islands National Park is the island's most valuable resource. Remember that this is a trust held in perpetuity and one which visitors years hence will wish to find in the same shape it is today. Act accordingly.

THE MAKING OF A NATIONAL PARK: In 1939, a National Park Service study compiled by Harold Hubler recommended that a park be established on St. John; the plan was forgotten after the onset of WW II.

Cruising around the Caribbean for six years after the war, multimillionaire philanthropist Laurence Rockefeller (1910–2004) determined that the island had "the most superb beaches and view" of any place he had ever seen, and that St. John was "the most beautiful island in the Caribbean." He quickly bought up nearly half the island during the early 1950s and established an exclusive resort at Caneel Bay on the grounds of a ruined sugar plantation.

Discovering Hubler's report, Laurence transferred the property into his Jackson Hole Preserve Corporation, a nonprofit tax writeoff. Jackson Hole then offered to donate 5,000 acres, provided they retained franchise rights to the park area.

Legislation signed into law by President Eisenhower on Aug. 2, 1956, authorized the federal government to accept donations of up to 9,500 acres (9,485 acres on St. John and 15 acres on St. Thomas). No local opinion was sought before a government bill was introduced in Congress in 1962 which would have authorized $1.25 million to acquire another 3,300 acres of St. John by condemnation—whether the owners acquiesced or not! This sum was contingent upon a Rockefeller offer to provide matching funds. Even the government administrator for the island first heard of the plan over the radio, and he, like other islanders, was outraged. The bill passed (without the condemnation clause) and Laurence withdrew his offer of matching funds.

In 1976 the park was included in the initial network of biosphere reserves designated by the United Nations, and a Virgin Islands Biosphere Research Center was completed in 1986. The park's popularity has grown dramatically over the decades: it now receives some 1.2 million visitors per year.

The Virgin Islands Land Trust announced in Sept. 2007 that it had acquired a majority interest in the 420-acre park inholding Estate Maho Bay for $19 million. Eighteen acres of property located away from the beach will be retained and used to pay for the property. The remainder will be donated to the national park. The additional acreage for Maho Bay Campground, whose lease will expire in 2012, may or may not be able to be acquired by the trust.

Formerly paid for entirely by your taxes, congressional budget cuts have forced the national parks down the road of making a buck. The Pentagon and the CIA do not need to pay their own way, but the parks now charge "user fees." There is a $4 pp fee for access to Trunk Bay and to Annaberg Ruins; children under 17 are free. Cruise ships are charged a mere $2 per passenger. Annual passes are $10 ($15 for families) which is worthwhile for frequent visitors.

☞ Call the park service (776-6201) for information on the frequent cultural demonstrations that take place here from Tues. to Friday.

BOATING: Park waters are subject to regulations designed to help preserve the environment. The N and S offshore areas were added to the park in 1962. Altogether, there are 26 anchorages around the island. Overnight stays in park waters are limited to 14 days per year, and boats are not to be left unattended for more than 24 hours.

Charts and maps, along with a complete list of park regulations, are available at the Cruz Bay Visitor's Center.

For excursions and charters see "Islandwide Practicalities" earlier in this chapter.

HIKING: A total of 22 trails—from brief walks to two-hour jaunts—are probably the most under-utilized of all of St. John's resources. Most are steep and rocky, so they give maximum exercise for the time involved. In just a short time, you climb from 700 to 1,200 ft. above sea level, where you get a very different view of the island. Trees creak in the wind and shy feral donkeys scatter when approached. Although NPS tours are available (see "Islandwide Practicalities"), the best way to go is on your own. If you do go with the park service, be sure to book trips well in advance if possible.

The "Trail Bandit" sells inexpensive trail maps: **http://www.trailbandit.org**

ENVIRONMENTAL CONCERNS: The development of the island has had severe environmental consequences. A 1994 research project launched by Colorado State University researchers found that unpaved roads are sending sediment into the coral reefs. Accordingly, they recommended that roads should be paved if possible, and new construction should be curtailed.

The *Wind Spirit*, an ultramodern craft operated by Wind Star Cruise Line, caused extensive damage to a coral reef. On Oct. 9, 1988, the boat was heading towards an authorized mooring in Francis Bay when a crewmember lowered the two-ton anchor too soon. The ship slowed down, almost halted, and then proceeded, leaving a huge stream of coral sediment in its wake as it dragged along the sea floor.

Although the ship failed to report the incident, it was observed and the government filed suit. (The cruise line—which uses that old "eco" line in publicity—failed to settle). As a consequence, the National Park Service filed a lawsuit in Nov. 1990. The trial was held in 1994, and $300,000 was awarded (to the US government, unfortunately, *not* the Park Service) in 1996. The boat left a 400-foot-long and ten-foot-wide scar.

To date, the area remains largely barren of coral. The damage may take hundreds of years to rectify or the reef may never recover. A second ship, the *Seaborn Pride* paid $50,000 to the Park Service after accidentally dropping anchor off of Caneel Bay in 1990 and damaging the reef.

The past few years have seen rampant speculation and development driven by low interest rates coupled with tax incentives for millionaires. This has resulted in sky-rocketing rents for St. Johnians and totally amazing prices for real estate. It has meant the defacement of island hillsides with what local architect Glen Spear terms "wedding cake houses." Sadly, there is a lack of leadership willing to deal with these problems.

According to the non-profit National Parks Conservation Association (NPCA), which released a 48-page "state of the parks assessment" in 2008, the park is threatened by development. Senior Marine Program Coordinator Jason Bennish maintains that "The park is at serious risk from development on properties within the boundaries of the park" which poses "a big problem." "Development is incompatible within the park and you get fragmentation. You basically end up with gaping holes in the middle of the park."

"Another big problem from development is the threat to water quality," Bennish asserts. "Often with large scale development that is not done in an ecologically sound manner, you have sediment runoff. All dirt and sediment from loosened soil and construction ends up in the bay and threatens the health of the marine area."

Cruz Bay

Cruz Bay, once a relaxed and small town, has become an increasingly busy place. New condos are under construction in town; the Enighed Pond has been dredged to construct a cargo port; and an increasing number of vehicles ply the tiny town's roads. Shoppers throng to the ultramodern but aesthetically pleasing Mongoose Junction shopping center. The impressive Starfish Market complex caters to residents and visitors alike. In and around town, there are also a number of other shops, a wide range of restaurants, a small park, and a ranger station for the national park.

NOTE: For accommodations, food, and services in Cruz Bay see "Islandwide Practicalities" earlier in this chapter.

SIGHTS: St. John's Administration Building, known as **the Battery,** was built on the foundation of an 18th-C fortification. Near the pier stands the **Nazareth Lutheran Church.**

Gallows Point, directly across from the harbor and now the sight of numerous developments, served a gruesome purpose in its time.

Farther out of town, along Centerline Rd. (formerly known as "Konge Vej"), stands the **Bethany Moravian Church.** Note the renovated 18th-C Parish Hall, the vaulted cistern behind it, and the two Dutch ovens inside the small house to the rear.

Near a large green water tank, a short paved road to the L leads to the ruins of **Estate Catherineberg** (Hammer Farms). One of the earliest plantations on St. John, it was restored in 1986. Here you'll find a beautifully rebuilt windmill which is one of the most impressive ruined structures in the Caribbean. It is only one of two USVI sugar mill ruins featuring barrelled vaulting; the other is in Smithfield, St. Croix.

Back in town, the **bandstand** in the park was built in 1992 under the auspices of the St. John Community Foundation.

The **date palm** in front of the tourist bureau was transplanted from in front of Oscar's Convenience Store in March 1993.

In another direction, the now gunless **Lind Battery,** allegedly constructed in a single night by the English during either their 1801 or 1807 assaults, can be reached by the Lind Point Trail (see "hikes" below).

NEAR CRUZ BAY: **The Pastory Gardens** (☎ 777-3147), around a mile from town along Centerline Rd., offer an 18-hole "executive putting course" and the Compass Rose Restaurant and Bar.
http://www.pastorygardens.com

An unusual sight in the island's center, a **"smoothie stand"** is located in a vehicle which got stuck on Centerline Road. This is the type of thing that characterizes St. John.

HIKES AROUND CRUZ BAY: The *Lind Point Trail* (1.1 mi., one hour) connects the NPS Visitor Center with Caneel Bay Plantation. Just before the descent to Caneel Bay, the trail reaches an overlook at Lind Point. You enter the trail right in back of the ranger station where an open trail traverses pillar cacti, night blooming cacti, and tan tan, to reach a beautiful overlook facing Cruz Bay harbor. This is a great place to come for the sunset but bring a flashlight.

Solomon Beach is next, and then you can get to **Honeymoon Beach** right next door by heading around in back of the NPS-owned house (the former presidential suite of Caneel) and following the road. At Honeymoon, you may find all sizes and shapes of frog people who have disembarked from yachts and boats and are working on their snorkeling skills.

The *Caneel Hill Trail* (2.4 mi., two hours) joins Cruz Bay with the Northshore Rd. entrance to Caneel Bay via Caneel Hill and

 St. John offers a much greater number of snorkeling sites than either St. Thomas or St. Croix. You can easily swim from most of the beaches.

ST. JOHN

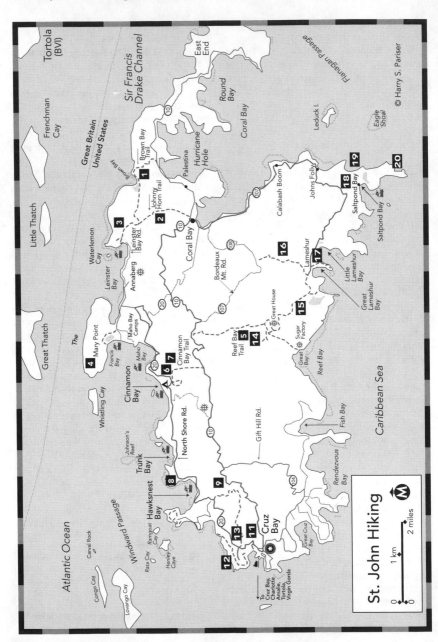

St. John Hiking

0 1 km
0 2 miles

© Harry S. Pariser

Margaret Hill. These two trails are interconnected by the **Caneel Hill Spur Trail** (0.9 mi., 40 min.) which crosses Northshore Rd. at an overlook of Cruz and Caneel Bays. Be sure to stop and see Caneel Bay and its beach; the size of the place is incredible. At the main beach, you might find very tame egrets and pelicans at the far end.

Caneel Hill (719 ft.) has a wooden tower, and **Margaret** has a large rock outcrop.

From here you can proceed to beautiful **Hawksnest Beach** on a curving road. (Look for glow worms at night).

Also known as Oppenheimer Beach, **Gibney's** or **Little Hawksnest Beach** may be reached from a small parking area. This is not a NPS beach; it was purchased from the Gibney family by A-bomb inventor Robert Oppenheimer. His daughter left it to the "Children of St. John" in her will. There's good snorkeling offshore, and another sandy beach is over to the R. You may see dogs and horses here as park rules do not apply. **The Gibney Beach Cottages** (☎ 777 6826) consist of a one-bedroom suite and a two-bedroom cottage. Both have ceiling fans, full kitchens, and hammocks. Rates are $3,000 pw (summer) and $5,000 pw (summer). http://vivacations.com/villas/gibney-villas

A gem of a small beach, **Jumbie Beach** is nearby and down a trail. Its name means "ghost," and it's believed by some that the spirits of dead slaves walk here. Snorkel in the offshore reefs here.

Interlocking Centerline and Northshore roads and joining the Caneel Hill trail over a portion of its route, the relatively unfrequented **Water Catchment Trail** (0.8 mi., 30 min.) has a deep-forest feeling to it.

About three mi. from town along Centerline Rd. is the shortest hike on the island; it takes 10 min. to get to the top of Peace Hill, once home to the island's strangest sight, the **Christ of the Caribbean**. Set amidst the ruins of the Denis Bay Plantation with its sugar mill tower, the armless but enormous concrete statue which once stood here was donated to the Virgin Islands National Park in 1975. It was built in the 1950s on the orders of a certain Col. Wadsworth, a transplanted mainlander, who dubbed the area **"Peace Hill"** and dedicated the statue to "inner and outer peace." If you didn't know what it was, you might have assumed it was some kind of Minoan deity. Legend has it that, when one arm broke off by accident, the Colonel ordered the other arm broken.

St. John Hiking Trails	
1	Brown Bay Trail (1.2 mi., 2 hours)
2	Johnny Horn Trail (1.5 mi., 2 hours)
3	Leinster Bay Trail (0.8 mi., 30 min.)
4	Francis Bay Trail (0.3 mi., 15 min.)
5	Reef Bay Trail (2.5 mi., 2 hours)
6	Cinnamon Bay Trail (1.2 mi., 1 hour)
7	Cinnamon Bay Self-Guiding Trail (1 mile, 1 hour)
8	Peace Hill (Christ of Caribbean)
9	Water Catchment Tr. (0.8 mi., 30 min.)
10	Turtle Point Trail (0.5 mi., 30 min.)
11	Caneel Hill Trail (2.1 mi., 2 hours)
12	Lind Point Trail (1.5 mi., 1 hour)
13	Caneel Hill Spur Trail (0.9 mi., 40 min.)
14	Petroglyph Trail (0.3 mi., 15 min.)
15	Lameshur Bay Tr. (1.8 mi., 1.25 hours)
16	Bordeaux Mountain Trail (1.2 mi., 1.5 hrs.)
17	Yawzi Point Trail (0.3 mi., 20 min.)
18	Salt Pond Bay Trail (0.2 mi., 15 min.)
19	Drunk Bay Trail (0.3 mi., 20 min.)
20	Ram Head Trail (0.9 mi., 1 hour)

In better days, Jesus appeared to be standing on stilts like some carnival participant. Brought to earth by 1995's Hurricane Marilyn, the statue once lay in repose on the ground, but it has now disappeared. The Wadsworth family declined to rebuild the statue, and the Park Service dissuaded a private funding effort.

However, the breathtaking 360" views and the ruined sugar mill with its exposed colony of bees make this site a must. As an added bonus, a path leads down to **Denis Beach**, a small but wonderful beach which is a favorite of locals. Note that the sugar estate ruins and adjacent property off the beach are in private hands. Please respect this.

Hawksview Estate near here (☎ 690-0394) rents out for $12,000–$18,000 pw. **http://www.hawksviewestate.com** **info@hawksviewestate.com**

Christ as he once stood on Peace Hill

Around the Island
Caneel Bay

Caneel Bay (☎ 776-6111, ℮ 693-8280, 888-767-3966) is where good American politicians are sent on holiday. Located about one mi. down the road from Cruz Bay, this elite resort, whose name comes from *kaneel*, (the Dutch word for cinnamon), is a place at which a select few of the well-connected and well-heeled may relax.

Insulated from the plebeians by the surrounding parkland, this 166-room oasis of Florida-style architecture is set on 171 acres including gardens (with more than 350 species of plants), tennis courts, and seven beaches. There's even a "Self Centre" operated by a follower of New Age Guru Deepak Chopra. The only luxury missing is golf.

Although much of its original posh status has been lost to Little Dix, another former Rockresort in the neighboring British Virgins, it has attracted prominent guests, including the late President Richard Nixon. More recently, Harrison Ford, Judy Collins, Mel Brooks, Michael J. Fox, Brad Pitt, Angelina Jolie, Alan Alda, William Hurt, and Michael Jordan have stayed here. Bill Clinton was refused hospitality because it was felt that his presence might impinge on the privacy of other guests.

Because of the nature of its clientele, it has been said that Caneel Bay is for "the newly wed or the nearly dead." Worthy of note on the grounds are the ruins of the Durloe Plantation, which have been transformed into a bar and gift shop.

PRACTICALITIES: Rooms run from $450–$1,400 during the winter. A 10% service charge is added. Room rates include guest room, use of sunfish, windsurfers, snorkeling gear, unlimited use of the ferry to St. Thomas, as well as special weekly activities. The **Caneel Beach Grill Terrace** serves popular gourmet buffet breakfasts and

lunches while **The Equator** serves gourmet dinners; many of the entrées are based on the dishes of tropical cultures. Sunsets here are awesome. Rates for visitors arriving for meals include RT fares on a private boat from Red Hook or regular transport from Charlotte Amalie.
http://www.caneelbay.com
caneelbay@att.global.net

FROM CANEEL BAY: An elite-priced ferry ($75 RT) runs to Charlotte Amalie, St Thomas. It is only for guests. The *Lind Point Trail* (1.5 mi., one hour) goes back to Cruz Bay. *Turtle Point Trail* (0.5 mi., 30 min.) begins at the N end of Caneel Bay. (Register at the front desk at the main entrance before using this trail.) Farther down the main road to the E is Hawksnest Bay and Peace Hill.

Peter Bay

Peter Bay is one of the few places where housing developments have been possible on St. John. And, with accordingly high prices, it has attracted a large number of wealthy individuals. Peter Bay has possibly the highest concentration of alpha males in the world. When they are not filing lawsuits over property lines, they are insulating themselves behind a/c comfort. Its most famous resident was country schlock singer Kenny Chesney. His trust sold his home here for $4.4 million in 2007. Another property, Stoneridge, a seven-bedroom home, was for sale for $14 million in 2008).).

There are also a few other expensive villa rentals here. The **Botanical Villas** (☎ 715-0548), 17-1 Estate Peters Bay, offers a set of lovely villas in pastel colors.
botanicalvillas@yahoo.com

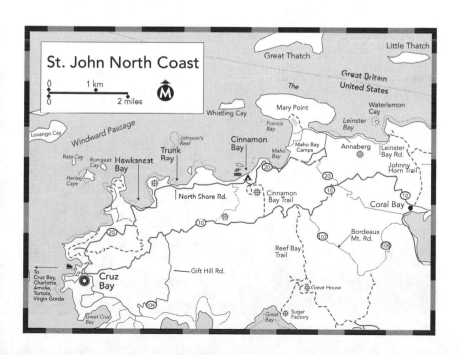

Trunk Bay

Most popular and famous of all the island's beaches, **Trunk Bay** is named after the "trunkback" or leatherback turtle (which may reach eight ft. and weigh up to 1,000 pounds)–though it's rarely seen around here these days. Another large creature, the cruise ship tourist, has moved in instead. Hundreds of cruise ship passengers may arrive at once. An hour in the water, and they're on their way. Trunk Bay is not the place to come for solitude and seclusion. As many as 1,500 people (!) may visit here on a single day including a large number of power boats, which not infrequently damage the coral with their anchors. For a more solitary visit, you might want to vist this beach at hours other than between those of 10 AM and 2 PM, the hours of greatest congestion. The parking lot can be a circus during this time period.

Lockers and snorkeling equipment are available for rent here. A small snack bar (burgers, seafood salad, beers, and ice tea) is also present along with BBQ pits.

SNORKELING TRAIL: Identified by orange markers, it's no longer quite the mecca for snorkelers that it used to be. The coral has been damaged by boat anchors, souvenir hunters, and careless swimmers. Friendly fish still greet you underwater, however, and tiny "ghost crabs" still spook the beach. Watch out for sea urchins.

The beach gained additional notoriety when actress Renee Zellweger married musician Kenny Chesney here in 2005; the marriage was annulled at the end of that year. Part of the Scenic American Landscapes series, a 94-cent US postage stamp released in May 2008, features Trunk Bay.

Cinnamon Bay

Cinnamon Bay, a small but pretty beach has an outlying coral reef with lots of fish, a campground, and rewarding walks in the vicinity. Despite the name, no cinnamon grows here; the Danish mistook the smell of the bay rum trees for cinnamon. To get here

Catherineberg, a restored sugar mill, is one of a number of ruins on St. John.

take either one of the large taxi-buses ($7) from town, hitch, or walk.

ACCOMMODATIONS: There are 10 bare sites, 40 erected tents, and 40 cottages available. Up to six people in two tents may occupy the bare sites ($27 per night for two; add'l persons $7). Picnic table and charcoal grill are provided. Canvas tents (10 by 14 ft. with concrete floor) with camp cots, two-burner propane gas stove, and utensils, are $80 d during the high season; $17 extra third person). Cottages ($110–$140 d during the high season; $17 extra third person) measure 15 by 15 ft., have concrete walls and floors, two screened walls, four twin beds, picnic table and grill, ice chest, propane gas stove, water container, cooking and eating utensils. Linen is changed weekly, and a deposit is required.

Make reservations well in advance by contacting **Cinnamon Bay Campground** (☎ 693-6330, ✆ 776-6458, 800-539-9998; Box 720, Cruz Bay, St. John, USVI 008310. **http://www.cinnamonbay.com**

FOOD: Best to bring as much of your own as possible. The commissary only has a limited and expensive supply of goods, so it's better to shop in St. Thomas beforehand or even to bring food from the mainland. The snack bar and the Tree Lizards Restaurant serve food. Local music is featured on some nights. Cookouts on Sun. nights provide a good opportunity to socialize with fellow campers.

SERVICES AND PRACTICALITIES: Upon check-in (2–8 PM daily), you will be provided with a map of the campground. If arriving before that time, you may use camp facilities. Site assignments will be posted for those arriving after 8 PM. Check-out is 11; luggage may be left in the office. There are four bath houses; water should be conserved. Pay telephone service is available near the registra-

tion desk. Campground office numbers are 776-6330/6458, and 776-6111, ext. 260. The bus schedule is posted near the registration desk. Films are shown Sun. nights after the cookouts. Snorkel sets, scuba tanks and underwater cameras may be rented.

Bring plenty of insect repellent to combat mosquitos, the most ferocious animals on the island. If you should see any donkeys do not feed them or place any food within their reach. Do not pet them (they can kick and bite without warning) and keep your children well away from them.
http://www.cinnamonbay.com
cinnamonbay@rosewoodhotels.com

HIKING: This is a good place to base yourself for hiking on the island.

The *Cinnamon Bay Self-Guiding Trail* (one mi., one hour) passes by native tropical trees and the ruins of a sugar factory. The trailhead is a few yards E of the entrance road to the campground.

A hundred yards E of the entrance road, *Cinnamon Bay Trail* (1.2 mi., one hour) begins 100 yards E of the entrance road into Cinnamon Bay Campground. This forested trail runs along an old Danish plantation road uphill to Centerline Road. The Reef Bay trailhead is 0.9 mi. E of this junction along Centerline Road.

Still farther, along a path hemmed in by hogplum trees, is the **old Danish cemetery**. Tombstones here were sized according to the deceased's station in life. Look for thrashers, anis, quail doves, golden orb spiders, and the low-flying zebra butterflies.

Also along this trail you may see "starvation fruit," which resembles a mushy white potato, and Teyer palms, St. John's only indigenous palm species, which is readily recognizable by its fan-shaped fronds-formerly used to make fish traps, brooms, fans, and building roofs.

The unmaintained *America Hill Trail* goes to the ruins of the America Hill Great

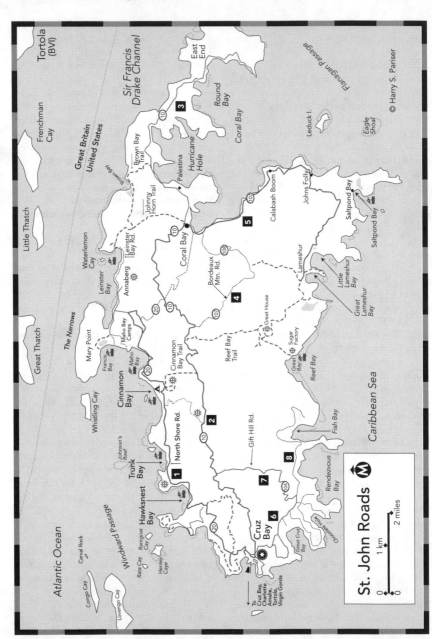

ST. JOHN

Tortola (BVI)

Frenchman Cay

Little Thatch

Great Thatch

Whistling Cay

Lovango Cay

Congo Cay

Carval Rock

Rata Cay

Henley Cays

Ramgoat Cay

Atlantic Ocean

Windward Passage

Johnson's Reef

The Narrows

Mary Point

Francis Bay

Maho Bay Camps

Maho Bay

Cinnamon Bay

Trunk Bay

Hawksnest Bay

North Shore Rd.

Cinnamon Bay Trail

Sir Francis Drake Channel

Great Britain
United States

Brown Bay

Brown Bay Trail

East End

Round Bay

Coral Bay

Palestina

Hurricane Hole

Johnny Horn Trail

Waterlemon Cay

Leinster Bay

Leinster Bay Rd.

Annaberg

Coral Bay

Bordeaux Mtn. Rd.

Great House

Reef Bay Trail

Calabash Boom

Johns Folly

Leduck I.

Eagle Shoal

Flanagan Passage

Saltpond Bay

Saltpond Bay

Lameshur

Little Lameshur Bay

Great Lameshur Bay

Sugar Factory

Great House

Reef Bay

Gift Hill Rd.

Fish Bay

Rendezvous Bay

Chocolate Hole

Cruz Bay

Great Cruz Bay

Caribbean Sea

To Cruz Bay, Charlotte Amalie, Tortola, Virgin Gorda

St. John Roads

0 — 1 km
0 — 2 miles

🚗 St. John Roads at a Glance 🚗

St. John has a lot of alternatives. You should note that (unless you want to rely on the bus) you'll need to rent a car if you wish to go to destinations other than the beaches lining North Shore Rd. Many taxi drivers may be reluctant to take you even as far as Coral Bay.

➤ North Shore Rd. (Rte. 20) 1

Beginning in Cruz Bay, this is the road to take to the best beaches. It's Federally maintained and thus in better shape than the other roads. It connects with Centerline Rd. near Annaberg. It is the road to take for **beaches** (Caneel Beach, Cinnamon Bay Beach, Hawksnest Beach, Gibney's or Little Hawksnest Beach, Jumbie Beach, Trunk Bay Beach, Peter Bay Beach, Cinnamon Bay Beach, Maho Bay Beach, Francis Bay Beach, and Waterlemon Beach); **hiking** (Lind Point Trail, Caneel Hill Trail, Margaret Hill Trail, Water Catchment Trail, Peace Hill Trail, Cinammon Bay Trail, America Hill Trail, Maho Goat Trail, and Johnny Horn Trail); and **ruins** (Caneel Bay, Peace Hill, Cinnamon Bay, Annaberg).

➤ Centerline Road (Rte. 10) 2

This 13 mi. stretch of road heads to Coral Bay and the East End. As it is set on a ridgetop, it affords spectacular **views** (such as the one from Chateau Bordeaux). It provides access to **trails** (Water Catchment Trail, Margaret Hill Trail, Cinnamon Bay Trail, and Reef Bay Trail), North Shore Rd., and Bordeaux Mountain Road.

➤ East End Road 3

This continuation of the road stretches from Coral Bay to the East End. The last portion of this spectacular road is dirt. It passes by **trailheads** (Johnny Horn Trail, Brown Bay Trail) and **beaches** (Princess Bay Beach, two beaches both named Haulover, Hansen Bay Beach, Long Bay Beach, and Privateer Beach) This is a route you will long remember.

➤ Bordeaux Mountain Rd. (Rte. 108) 4

This paved road heads around to Coral Bay and may be used to access the **Bordeaux Mountain Trail.**

➤ Salt Pond Road (Rte. 107) 5

This begins past Coral Bay and then turns into Lameshur Rd. The paved road ends to the S. After this you must use a four-wheel-drive and even this can be tricky after it rains. Be sure to ask around in Coral Bay if you go along this stretch, and keep in mind most rental car contracts prohibit travel along this portion of the road. It passes by a number of **trails** (Drunk Bay Trail, Ram Head Trail, Bordeaux Mountain Trail, Lameshur Trail, and Europa Bay Trail) and **beaches** (Johnson Bay Beach Friis Bay Beach, Salt Pond Bay Beach, Drunk Bay Beach, Ram Head Trail Beach, Great Lameshur Beach, Little Lameshur Beach, and Europa Bay Beach).

➤ South Shore Road (Rte. 104) 6

This road heads from Cruz Bay to the S. It climbs a stretch of road known as Jacob's Ladder (past the Hyatt) and terminates at the intersection of **Gift Hill Road** 7 and **Fish Bay Road** 8. The former climbs to the top of Gift Hill before intersecting with Centerline Rd. near the island's garbage dump (the scene of a fire extinguished in Sept. 1992). Beaches off the South Shore Road include Great Cruz Bay Beach, Chocolate Hole Beach, and Hart Bay Beach. Fish Bay Rd. heads ('natch enough) to Fish Bay. **Beaches** running off from here include two beaches named Dittlif, Klein Bay Beach, and Reef Bay Beach. (At Fish Bay you may access the Ditliff Point Trail).

House. As the ruins are dangerous, the NPS has stopped maintaining the trail. The trailhead is off to the L from the main trail; watch for a signless metal post.

Maho Bay Camps

Maho was the second campground on the island, opened in 1974. Designed with ecological conservation in mind, a series of tent cottages built on wooden boardwalks preserve the natural ground cover to prevent erosion; insecticides are not used here, and taps and communal toilet facilities are specially constructed to conserve water. The resort won the Green Globe Commendation Award in 2000 for its environmental conservation policies.

Seeming more like tree houses than tents, all 114 of these three-room, 16-by-16-ft., canvas cottages have completely equipped dining and cooking areas. Propane stove, ice cooler, and electric range are supplied. The living room readily converts to a second bedroom. The bedrooms have reading lamps and can be completely sealed off.

Although farther from shore, the hillside tents are cooler during the daytime and have fewer bugs. Everything you need is supplied, and there's a small but complete commissary. Prices for goods are high.

Inexpensive breakfasts and dinners are served at the restaurant. The "Help Yourself Center" has toys, books, and groceries left by departing guests. Snorkeling equipment is available for rent. The "Art Gallery" displays artwork made in classes using recycled materials and kilnfired. Rates are around $130 d with $15 per add'l person.

Maho's success has spurred owner Stanley Selengut to develop other alternatives. **Harmony** is a new "environmentally correct" set of buildings that offers guests more traditional amenities — such as in-room baths with hot-water showers. Set on the hill next to Maho Bay, its four two-story villas are made almost entirely from recycled products. Rafters and floor girders are wood scrap composites; the bathroom tiles are made from crushed old light bulbs; the insulation foam is manufactured from recycled milk jugs; the deck floor is made with recycled newspaper; doormats are made from recycled car tires.

Despite what one might expect given this description, the rooms, which are decorated with native art, are quite attractive. And views from the balconies are nothing short of spectacular.

Harmony's 12 self-catering units, housed in four two-story buildings and perched on the ridge above Maho Bay Camps, are totally "off the grid." Water is collected on roofs and stored in cisterns. Electricity is provided by solar power. As a guest, you may monitor their electricity and water use closely. Rooms are also equipped with personal computers which have customized software that enables you to convert current and voltage to watts, check weather reports, and make suggestions for energy conservation. Waste water is also recycled. Guests are requested to fill out questionnaires concerning their energy consumption.

High season rates and lodging at Harmony runs around $215–$230 a night per couple for a bedroom studio and $225–$240 a night per couple for a living room studio. Add'l persons are $25 pp, pn.

The 54-acre **Estate Concordia**, on the island's S tip, is a Maho Bay offshoot project. It has nine luxury units with swimming pool (around $150–$225) and 25 16'-by-16' cottages, which are called "Eco-tents," are $155–$185 pn; $15 add'l person. The units hold up to six, and are operated by solar or wind power, have composting toilets and full kitchen facilities. Five units have disabled access. There's easy access to Concordia's pool, a white sand beach at Salt Pond Bay, and to Ram's Head hiking trail.

For information on Maho, Harmony, or Concordia, write to Maho Bay Camps, Box 310, Cruz Bay, St. John, USVI 00830 (☎ 776-6240) or to Maho Bay Camps, 17-A E 73rd St., New York, NY 10021 (☎ 800-392-9004, 212-472-9453). http://www.maho.org

HIKING: At the W end of the Mary Creek paved road, the *Francis Bay Trail* (0.3 mi., 15 min.) passes through a dry scrub forest, and past the Francis Bay Estate House to the beach.

At **Francis Bay** you can see and even swim with sea turtles. This is a pretty place to spend some time. At one end of the beach, pelicans cavort across the water, dive bombing in search of fish. Near the main entrance you might see a lady sashaying up and down the beach, totally absorbed by her personal stereo. Or you might meet a pretty Argentinean on extended holiday. The trail behind the beach passes by a lagoon with piles of driftwood along its sides.

At **Mary's Point**, the rocky and precipitous hammer-headed peninsula set near the trail's beginning, you can see nesting brown pelicans, an endangered species.

Several hundred slaves are said to have leaped to their deaths from Mary's Point during the 1733 slave revolt rather than face recapture. Local legend maintains that the water here turns red each May.

NEAR MAHO: Maho has **Little Maho**, a small beach. Kayaks, sunfish, windsurfers, and snorkeling equipment is available for rent.

Better is the NPS-run **Maho Bay Beach**, the best portion of which is at its far end. The nearest beach to a road on the entire island, it has shallow water and is well protected so the beach may be calm when other beaches on the North Shore are experiencing swells. There are a few picnic tables. Snorkeling is good offshore in the seagrass; you may be able to spot sea turtles.

Annaberg Ruins

The attractive ruins of **Annaberg**, a 510-acre sugar plantation, date from around 1780 and sit atop a point overlooking Leinster Bay. Structures here have been spruced up rather than restored, and a self-guiding tour takes you through what was once one of the 25 active sugar-producing factories on St. John. You might imagine yourself back in the 18th C, when the entire surrounding area was covered in sugarcane. Walk through the former slave quarters, the ruins of the village, the remains of the windmill, horsemill, boiling bench, and oven. Drawings of schooners and a street scene, which may date back to Dutch times, decorate the small dungeon. The estate was run by overseers, which is why no great house was ever built. Fruit trees on the property were planted by Carl Francis, a cattle farmer, who lived here during the early 1900s. A free "Folk-life Festival" is held here in Feb. in commemoration of Black History Month.

VICINITY OF ANNABERG: From here it's a nice—albeit very long — walk, via two interconnecting paths, to Coral Bay. First follow the *Leinster Bay Trail* (0.8 mi., 30 min.), actually the remains of an old Danish road, along the shoreline of Leinster (Waterlemon) Bay to pebbled **Waterlemon Beach** with its crystal-clear water. **Waterlemon Cay** (excellent snorkeling with coral reefs) is off in the distance. Don't try swimming here unless you are absolutely certain of your abilities.

At **Leinster Bay**, you'll find a mangrove preserve. Herons nest in the buttonwood

?!< Waterlemon Cay is named after a plant which lives here, the *Passiflora laurifolia* which produces the bellapple, a local fruit. Locals call the islet "Jewel Cay."

Archaeology on St. John

Owing to the protected nature of much of its land, St. John is a wonderful place for archaeologists. The National Park's legal requirement to preserve and to protect cultural and historical aspects of land before any excavation and/or building may transpire entails that archaeologists are called upon as a matter of course to document and record any historical findings in the area.

The discovery of a midden—an area whose soil is composed of shell, pottery, and bone (i.e. a garbage dump from antiquity)—is an exciting find for a researcher. Modern techniques—including the use of computers and videotaping—allow them to document the past as never before. Archaeologists believe that Tainos migrated from the Lesser Antilles around 700 BC, and a midden found at Cinnamon tells parts of the tale.

Other bits of history—both ancient and more contemporary— have been uncovered at plantation ruins at Annaberg, Cinnamon, Catherineberg and Reef Bay. Searching the shallow soil which rests atop bedrock, archaeologists have found pottery, carvings (including Zemis, carved deities), and human remains. Pottery uncovered at Cinnamon Bay, when classified by type and style, reveals when things were prosperous and when difficulties set in. Other artifacts discovered at sites include tobacco pipes, clay pots fired by slaves, and wine and gin bottles. A midden at Mary's Creek yielded the remains of parrots; once common in the island, they were wiped out by hunting. More discoveries are certain to result in the future. ■

and yellow spaghetti vine. The latter covers trees and bushes and looks as if someone had scattered gallons of spaghetti with tomato sauce. The trail follows the ridges S to the paved road running past the Emmaus Moravian Church in Coral Bay.

The unmaintained **Brown Bay Trail** (1.6 mi., two hours) starts from the ridge saddle 0.6 mi. along the Johnny Horn Trail. Branching to the E, it descends through a hot and open valley covered with dry thorn scrub before running along Brown Bay, then ascends across the ridge above Hurricane Hole before terminating at the East End Rd., 1.3 mi. E of Emmaus Moravian Church.

NOTE: The useful **A Field Guide to Native Trees and Plants of East End St. John** by Eleanor Gibney and Doug White ($30) is good to bring along while exploring this area. Read about the author here: http://en.wikipedia.org/wiki/Gibney_Beach

Coral Bay

Quiet streets and a relaxed atmosphere mark the site of the best harbor in the US Virgin Islands and a burgeoning boating center. More than two centuries ago Admiral Nelson claimed Coral Bay was large enough to hold most of the navies of Europe. (It is still sufficient for a modern fleet.)

Although it was the site of the first Danish settlement on the island, the village never grew to the size or prominence hoped for. Originally named Crawl Bay, after the cattle enclosures found here, it was changed to Coral Bay later on.

Coral Bay has a few shops and restaurants, a horseback riding facility, and Coral Bay Organic Gardens, a farm run by Hugo and Josephine Roller, which grows organic vegetables sold to Cruz Bay restaurants.

Small though it may be, Coral Bay has its problems, as shown by the fact that Guy H. Benjamin School declares itself to be a "Drug

trees here, and bitterns, gallinules, lesser and greater yellowlegs, and black-necked stilts can be sighted as well.

Next follow the ruins at the other end of the bay to the beginning of the historic **Johnny Horn Trail** (1.8 mi., two hours). The trail climbs a ridge framed by cactus

Free School Zone." The improved road is allowing people to speed and cause accidents.

Sedimentation problems resulting from runoff from the new access roads to villas constructed above the town, coupled with the dumping of sewage from boats in the harbor, has been wreaking havoc with the marine environment. The Coral Bay Association for Marine Planning (CAMP) is a new organization of boat owners here which is dedicated to improving the marine environment.

SIGHTS: First to greet the visitor is the **Emmaus Moravian Church.** Constructed during the late 1700s on the site of the Caroline Estate, this large yellow building stands at the edge of town. Judge Sodtmann and his 12-year-old daughter were murdered on this spot during the 1733–34 slave revolt; local legend maintains that a *jumbie* (spirit) appears as a ram each and every full moon to haunt the premises. It is definitely a Kodak Moment. The windmill nearby is another relic of the vanished estate.

Further to the N past the Moravian cemetery is the beginning of the path to the top of Fort Berg Hill which sticks out into the harbor. At the top are the ruins of Fort Berg, which slaves captured and held during the 1733–34 revolt (see "History" earlier in this chapter).

English Battery, at the foot of the fort, was built during the occupation of 1807–14; a few rusty cannon are still lying about.

Not a "sight" but worthy of note, the **John's Folly Learning Institute** (Barbara Thompson, ☎ 714-7134) offers learning and training opportunities for local youth in the areas of culture, technology, science, and the environment.

EVENTS: The **St. John Blues Festival** takes place each March. The main event is a concert at Coral Bay's ball court.
http://www.stjohnbluesfestival.com

Coral Bay also has what might be the world's smallest **Labor Day parade,** a lively event which is not to be missed.

PRACTICALITIES: Keep Me Posted in the Cocoloba Shopping Center, offers Internet access for $8/hr. It hosts the **Syzygy Gallery.**
http://www.syzygyartgallery.com

Billing itself as "A Pretty OK Place," **Skinny Legs Grill** (☎ 779-4982) serves food (burgers, dogs, and sandwiches) and is the local hangout bar; it has live music.

Island Blues, a music-oriented bar, offers food and four TV screens.

Sweet Plantains Restaurant (☎ 777-4653) is a bit further on along the opposite side of the road. Jamaican-Americans Prince and Rose Adams serve delicious West Indian fusion cuisine.
http://www.sweetplantains-stjohn.com

Outside town towards the S, **Shipwreck Landing** has a good selection of food, and **Miss Lucy's** (☎ 693-5244, 7 mi. S) has good local food and legendary "full moon parties" with fish and roast pig and local veggie dishes such as okra and fungi for $10. Sun. brunch is also served from 1–2, and lunch

Steering around goats is one of the delights of St. John driving.

ST. JOHN

If you'd like to visit the East End area, Wesley Easley, the "singing" taxi driver, can also take you on a private tour of this area. He can point out useful plants and herbs. Wesley (☎ 776-6282) is famous for his singalong renditions of "Who Drives the Bus," and he won the "Best Tour Guide of the Season" award from Princess Cruises in 1999.

and dinner are offered Tues. through Sat. The late owner, Miss Lucy, made local feminist history by becoming the first female taxi driver on the island.

Love City Mini Mart is at Estate Carolina to the S.

SERVICES: **Connections** here (☎ 776-6922) offers long distance and local calls, copies, and fax service. **Kaleidoscope** rents videos.

On the waterfront, **Crabby's Watersports** (☎ 714-2415) offers trips to the BVI by sail and motor and snorkel and kayak tours and rentals.

http://www.crabbyswatersports.com

The **Carolina Corral** (☎ 693-5778) offers horseback rides.

http://www. st-john.com/trailrides

From Coral Bay

TO THE EAST: A dramatic winding and curving road, surrounded by cactus-covered bluffs, leads to **Round Bay** at the E end of the island.

There is an excellent view of Tortola to the L before reaching **Hurricane Hole** to

Coral Bay during the 1800s.

the R where ships still shelter during hurricanes. This area is comparatively undeveloped and relatively few people live at this end of the island. There's no public transport, so drive yourself, hitch or walk. You can eat at **Vies Snack Shack** (conch fritters and other delicacies) or the **End of the Road Stand.**

The area is even becoming popular with Asian visitors. At Estate Zootenevaal, 17 Chinese were picked up in March 1996. Robin Clair, the manager, passed 16 men and one woman who were "neat, clean, and smiling" and carried their clothes in plastic bags. The close-lipped PRC nationals claimed they came from Cuba but more likely were dispatched from St. Maarten.

ACCOMMODATION: Hospitable **Mrs. Vies** (☎ 693 5033) runs a campground and has simple wooden bungalows. The bungalows rent for around $40 d and have two single beds. Sheets are provided, and their electricity is solar powered. The six camping sites have platforms with tents, foam mattresses (no sheets), ice chest, gas lamp, gas stove. Hanging solar shower bags are provided. They rent for around $25 d plus $10 for each add'l person. It costs about $20 to take a taxi out here, but Mrs. Vies recommends that you rent a car, and she relishes campers who are able to bring their own tent for their bare sites. She is open from Tues. to Sat. There's a small beach.

This is not a place to stay for resort-type yuppies but rather is a haven for those who wish to experience Caribbean style hospitality—right down to the conch fritters and the crowing roosters. Using the area as a base, you can also explore this gorgeous less frequented side of the island. Or you can just chill out and discover the USVI as it used to be.

TO THE SOUTH: From the junction before Coral Bay, take the road (concrete with bits of imbedded shell) along the mangrove-lined coast, which smells strongly of brine. The next town is **Calabash Boom** where there's a health clinic.

The *Salt Pond Bay Trail* (0.2 mi., 15 min.) begins 3.6 mi. S of Coral Bay and leads to Salt Pond Beach. (Don't leave valuables in your car).

From the S of the beach, turn to the E and follow the ***Drunk Bay Trail*** (0.3 mi., 20 min.) along the N of the salt pond to Drunk Bay Beach. Most of the year this bleak and rocky beach ("drunk" means "drowned" in Dutch creole) is swept by 30-mph trade winds. The seaside lavender bay pea vines, which cover the sandy soil, prevent sea erosion. At the far end of Drunk Bay, **Ram Head,** the oldest rock on the island (dating from the Lower Cretaceous Period over 90 million years ago), overlooks a 200-ft. precipice.

Follow **Ram Head Trail** (0.9 mi., one hour) to a blue cobble beach and on to the top. The view features patches of coastal hedege in the foreground. *Setaria setosa,* a native grass, flourishes on the coastal cliffs. Wild goats and feral donkeys may be sighted in this area.

Back on the main road, sandwiched on a peninsula between Great Lameshur and Little Lameshur Bays, is **Yawzi Point Trail** (0.3 mi., 20 min.). Years ago people afflicted with yaws (a contagious tropical skin disease resembling syphilis) were forced to live here in order to avoid spreading the disease.

The *Lameshur Bay Trail* (1.8 mi., 1.25 hours) connects Lameshur Bay with Reef Bay trail through open forest.

A rock side trail, 1.4 mi. before the Reef Bay junction, leads to dramatically silent, pea-soup-colored **Europa Pool** (watch your footing). Look out for the Reef Bay Great House which has been recently restored.

ST. JOHN

Little Lameshur Bay features a few boats and snorkelers; donkeys and mongoose can be seen nearby.

From Little Lameshur Bay, the sunny *Bordeaux Mountain Trail* (1.2 mi., 1.5 hours) climbs 1,000 ft. right up to the top of Bordeaux Mountain (1,250-ft.), highest point on the island. Gently sloping and beautiful, it has stone seats by the side of the trails which overlook Europa and Lameshur Bays.

You generally share this blissfully serene trail only with the birds and breeze. There are magnificent views of the British Virgins from here. This trail dates from the time when donkeys laden with bay leaves would descend to the still at Lameshur Bay below. The oil was extracted by boiling in seawater, and then shipped to St. Thomas where it was used to produce St. John's Bay Rum, a famous cologne. From the top, the paved road connects with Centerline Road and another (much rougher and steeper) runs to Coral Bay, but you'll probably want to come back down again rather than follow it on.

NOTE: The road down to Lameshur via Rte. 107 is extremely steep, although navigable, and you may wish to think twice before taking the plunge.

The only accommodation down here is at Estate Concordia which offers both "Eco-tents" and luxury units. See "Maho Bay" for details.

The **US Virgin Islands Environmental Resource Station** (VIERS, ☎ 776-6721, ✆ 776-6645; PO Box 250, St. John 00831) offers lodging and meals to students, researchers and "eco minded" tourists. The field station of the University of the Virgin Islands, most of VIERS' buildings are two-room cabins, including eight dorm-style guest rooms for students (six beds), five single bed rooms for individual researchers, three one-room efficiencies, and three two-room efficiencies (some with private toilets and showers), classroom, library, museum, dining hall, and water-side science lab. Visitors wash dishes and do light chores in groups Rates are US$76 per person per night which includes three meals daily. One- and two-room efficiency cabins are available for "eco-tourists" at a rate of about $124 per night (they can join the meal plan for $38 per person per day). VIERS has a very popular volunteer program. The station is a five minute walk to Lameshur Bay and a short walk to Lameshur Bay and Reef Bay Trails. In the mainland, contact Clean Islands International (☎ 410-647-2500, 888-647-2501).

http://www.islands.org
viers@islands.vi

Reef Bay Trail

The most popular hiking trail on the island, the *Reef Bay Trail* begins five mi. E of Cruz Bay and takes two hours to negotiate. Formerly a wagon road, it was still the best road on the island as late as 1950. An incredible abundance of nature, much of it annotated by the National Park Service, grows along the sides of the trail. Descending through both wet and dry forests, the trail passes the remains of no fewer than five sugar estates, their stubbles of masonry foundation nearly consumed by strangler figs and wild orchids.

Built of red and yellow imported brick, basalt rock, and brain coral, this attractive mosaic is still held together by local mortar of lime made from seashells, sand, molasses, and goat hairs. Stone rocks, laid over the road, act as culverts which divert the torrential rainfall.

Along the path, you may see wild pigs, donkeys, or even a hermit crab clatter across the road. The laundry pool along the gutter

 Be sure to bring plenty of water and something to munch on when going on the *Reef Bay Trail*. There is no supply of drinkable water on the trail.

Dayhiking Checklist

✔ Water (two quarts)

✔ Binoculars

✔ Windsurfing sandals

✔ Food/snacks

✔ umbrella

✔ swim trunks

✔ small towel

✔ camera

St. John Itineraries

If you have 3 days: Spend one day in Charlotte Amalie (shopping and sights), and two days on St. John.

If you have 5 days: Spend one day in Charlotte Amalie (shopping and sights), and four days on St. John (hiking and beaches).

If you have one week: Spend one day in Charlotte Amalie (shopping and sights), one day touring St. Thomas, and five days on St. John (hiking and beaches). Or take an excursion to St. Croix, Tortola, or Virgin Gorda.

of the trail was formerly a meeting and gossiping place for housewives.

About 100 ft. away from a mango tree on the trail stand the remains of the wattle-and-daub **Old Marsh House** which was swept away in the Oct. 1970 floods.

ESTATE PAR FORCE: These ruins are right on the trail. Built before 1780, it was remodeled in 1844. All that remains of the estate are the corral, sugar factory, and horsemill. In lieu of an expensive windmill, horses circumnavigating the 80-ft. grinding stone supplied power to grind the cane.

PETROGLYPH TRAIL: Beginning 1.7 mi. down the Reef Bay Trail, it takes 15 min. to reach this quiet, peaceful, and secluded pool which teems with life, including wild shrimp. Situated below a small waterfall, chiseled petroglyphs were believed to be the work of indigenous Indians. Alternative, if less likely, theories have emerged. In 1971, a Ghanaian ambassador visiting the site, noted the resemblance of one of the symbols to an Ashanti one meaning "accept God."

More recently, the double spirals have been found to be identical with those on Libyan tombstones dating from 200 A.D. Symbols of purification, these were decoded by Dr. Barry Fell, the world's leading epigrapher; the symbols mean "plunge in to cleanse and dissolve away impurity and trouble; this is water for ritual ablution before devotions."

REEF BAY ESTATE HOUSE AND SUGAR PLANTATION: Last stop on the trail. Made of local stone, the great house was originally stuccoed and painted. Its hilltop location enabled it to take full advantage of sea breezes. Actually a functional dwelling as recently as the 1950s, it has been under restoration during 1990s.

Reef Bay Sugar Factory is about .75 mi beyond the great house on the main trail. The

Environmental Travel Suggestions

℮ Turn off your room lights, fan, and a/c when you go out.

℮ Reuse your bath towels.

℮ Take local transport or walk if you can.

℮ Reduce purchases of bottled water.

℮ Carry a water bottle. (Remember that VI tap water is safe to drink).

steam-operated flywheel, standing along the S wall of the boiling platform, operated until 1916. It is a magical spot, almost haunted. You may lunch on the picnic table here and use what the park service regards to be toilets. You might see a hermit crab puttering about inside, an anole marking its territory, or a mongoose make tracks for the bush. Surf crashes ominously in the distance.

FROM REEF BAY: Either climb back up to Centerline Rd. or retrace your steps and take the Lameshur Bay trails to reach the main road leading back to Coral Bay. You will have to hike a bit to get one, but you should be able to get a bus up until sunset, from Salt Pond Bay but you can expect a long wait so bring reading material.

From St. John

The only way to get anywhere is by ferry. These run to St. Thomas and to the British Virgin Islands. You a ferry from Cruz Bay to Red Hook and then on to Charlotte Amalie by bus.

NOTE: *Times may shift so be sure to reconfirm before your departure date.*

FOR ST. THOMAS: A ferry ($6.10, 20 min.) runs on the hour to Red Hook from 6 AM–10 PM daily; an additional ferry is at 11:15. Beer is served on board. (Some of these may not run July–Nov.)

A **ferry** to Charlotte Amalie ($11.10, 45 min.) runs at 7:15, 9:15, 11:15, 1:15, 2:15, 3:45, and 5:15. (Some of these may not run July–Nov.)

Three **car ferries** also operate to St. John. See the "From St. Thomas" section for details.

FOR JOST VAN DYKE: Transportation Services of St. John (☎ 776-6282/6597) operates a ferry (originating in Red Hook)

The petroglyphs, found along the Reef Bay Trail, have been a tourist attraction for quite some time. This photo dates from the 1890s.

on Fri., Sat. and Sun. at 8:30 AM and 2:20 PM. RT is $50 for the 45 min. trip.

FOR FAJARDO, PUERTO RICO: St. John Transportation Services (☎ 776-6282) has a a twice-monthly ferry departure on Thurs. (5 PM, St. John; 6 PM, St. Thomas) which returns on Sundays at 1 PM. $125 RT. Transport to Condado is included.

FOR ST. CROIX: You must take a ferry to Charlotte Amalie, St. Thomas and then fly with **Seaborne** (the seaplane shuttle) to downtown **Christiansted** or with American Eagle (☎ 800-327-8900), or **Cape Air** (☎ 800-352-0342/1714, 800-635-8787) to the airport. Another alternative is to take the ferry from Charlotte Amalie to Christiansted,. St. Croix.
http://www.flycapeair.com

FOR TORTOLA: West End-bound ferries ($35 RT, 30 min.) leave daily at 8:30 and 11:30; from Mon. to Sat at 3:30; Fri. at 5 PM as well; and Sun. at 4:30 PM as well. Call 693-6597/6282 to check schedule. It's not necessary to have a RT ticket. The ferry leaves from the pier directly in back of the customs building. Follow it along to the L and then around. The best seats are topside on this beautiful, panoramic ride. Sea gulls glide in the wind; cacti arc from the sides of cliffs. On the way you pass by cays covered with tropical forest, much as the whole area was before the coming of Europeans. The other option is to return to St. Thomas and fly (see "From St. Thomas").

FOR VIRGIN GORDA: Transportation Services of St. John (☎ 776-6282/6597) operates a ferry on Thurs. and Sun. morn-

 ## Who Was Robert Oppenheimer?

If there is one figure in recent decades who epitomizes the moral contradictions faced by scientists whose developments may produce unintended consequences, it is Robert Oppenheimer, the father of the Atomic Bomb. Oppenheimer maintained that "Our science has concentrated on asking certain questions at the expense of others, although this is so woven into the fabric of our knowledge that we are generally unaware of it. In another world, the basic questions may have been asked differently."

Named as the director of the Manhattan Project in 1942, he coordinated the world's first explosion of a nuclear bomb on the Los Alamos plateau in New Mexico on July 16, 1945. He recited a passage from the *Bhagavad Gita*: "I am become death, destroyer of worlds." Within a month, two Japanese cities—Hiroshima and Nagasaki—were bombed. He earned the Presidential Medal of Merit in 1946 and was named the director of Princeton's Institute for Advanced Study and served as chairman of the General Advisory Committee of the Atomic Energy Commission from 1947 to 1952. After he opposed the development of the hydrogen bomb, he fell out of favor. His security clearance was revoked in 1953. President Lyndon Johnson reinstated his security clearance in 1963, and he was presented with the AEC's Enrico Ferme Award. Oppenheimer retired from Princeton in 1966; he died of throat cancer the next year.

In his later years, Oppenheimer spent a lot of time sailing on St. John, and a beach is named after him. ∎

ings at 8:30 AM with a 3 PM return; RT (1.75 hrs. each way) is $50. The location is the same as that for Tortola above. It may leave early at times, so be there well beforehand. The other option is to return to St. Thomas and fly (see "From St. Thomas").

FOR JOST VAN DYKE: Transportation Services of St. John (☎ 776-6282/6597) operates a ferry (originating in Red Hook)

on Fri., Sat. and Sun. at 8:30 AM and 2:20 PM. RT is $50 for the 45 min. trip.

FOR FAJARDO, PUERTO RICO: St. John Transportation Services (☎ 776-6282) has a a twice-monthly ferry departure on Thurs. (5 PM, St. John; 6 PM, St. Thomas) which returns on Sundays at 1 PM. $125 RT. Transport to Condado is included.

St. Croix

S t. Croix (pronounced "Croy") is separated from the other two United States Virgins not only by distance but in other ways as well. With around 53,234 residents (compared to the 51,181 found on St. Thomas). it is comparatively spacious and less developed. This cosmopolitan island strikes a comfortable balance between the commercialism of St. Thomas and the tranquility of St. John.

Although the last island to fall under Danish contol, St. Croix retains the strongest Danish influences of the three. You will feel a true sense of living history here. The island's two towns, Frederiksted and Christiansted, retain 18th-C. architecture, and ruined sugar estates and windmills dot the countryside. There are a few small museums as well as a "historical trail" you can explore with a car. The large Puerto Rican (and growing Dominican) population add a stimulating Latin element.

But the main way in which the island differs from St. Thomas and St. John is through the diversity of its economic base. Whereas the other two American Virgins operate almost solely on their tourism 'industries,' St. Croix offers a modern West Indian soci-

ety in which, as a visitor, you may participate and thus come closer to experience life as the locals here lead it.

The island is spacious enough that you won't get island fever, but compact enough that you can get around quite a bit in just a few hours. Attractions range from historical sites and ruins to spectacular vistas to great diving and sailing trips. It offers artists and craftmen, beaches, spas, numerous restaurants, and a casino.

Towards the end of the 18th C, there were approximately 114 cane-crushing sugar mills and 14 oxen mills. Today, you see their remains wherever you drive, and the island retains the Danish land survey which accords the plots the names given by a planter or plantation owner from the days of yore. Fountain Valley, a 4,085-acre holding formerly owned by the Rockefellers, covers a tenth of the island's land area and includes Davis Bay Beach and Carambola Golf Course.

Covering another 1,600 acres on the S coast in the center of the island, HOVENSA runs one of the world's largest-capacity oil refineries; it produces 700,000 barrels per day. The largest of the island's Senepol cattle ranches, Fritz Lawaetz's Annaly Farms spreads across 5,000 acres near the island's NW corner.

The two towns of Christiansted and Frederiksted have preserved their historical past without selling their soul and becoming Disney enclaves. They have a surprisingly large number of good restaurants relative to their size and have a number of shops which sell unusual arts and crafts.

There's a bit of shopping and nightlife scattered elsewhere around the island, and a pilgrimage along the "historical trail" will reveal some gorgeous vistas and dramatic vantage points near gorgeous beaches. Pack a picnic lunch and enjoy!

ST. CROIX

ST. CROIX

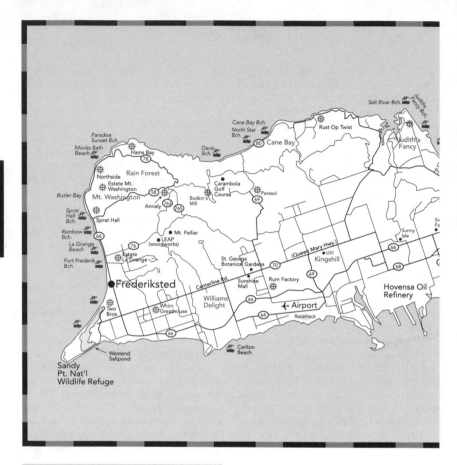

The Land and Its History

Largest and most fertile of all the US Virgin Islands, St. Croix offers a wealth of scenic beauty, including a small 'rainforest' (actually a tropical wet forest) in the NW end of the island. St. Croix, 28 mi. long by seven mi. wide, is 84 sq mi. in area, or more than three times the size of St. Thomas. The island is still subdivided into large former sugar plantations with names like "Barren Spot," "Wheel of Fortune," "Lower Love,"

"Hard Labor," "Profit," "Work and Rest," and "Humbug." These plantation boundaries were delineated by the Danish West India and Guinea Company in the 18th C and remain virtually unchanged to this day.

This comparatively flat and spacious island is blessed with an abundance of vegetation. While the tropical forests of the W adjoin the arid scrublands of the E, the hills of the N contrast sharply with the long, even plateaus of the S which feature arid scrubland, salt pond, and coastal mangroves.

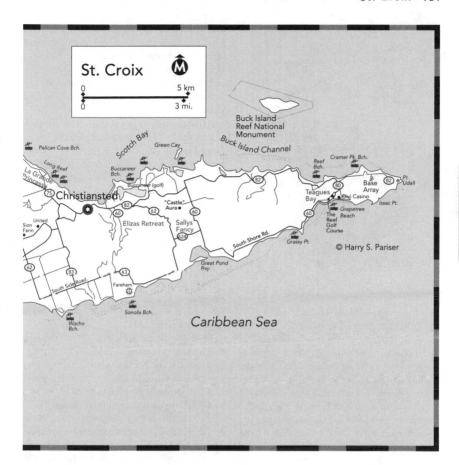

Although water has always been in short supply, the flat S plain is well suited to sugarcane (unlike the other, almost entirely mountainous islands); however, economics have dictated the demise of sugarcane production here. The N is frequently lush and verdant, though the S may be brown and desolate during the drier seasons. The E end is quite dry.

HISTORY: Between the time Columbus and his men were attacked by Indians at Salt River in November 1493 and the time the island was first settled in 1631, the native inhabitants had disappeared, presumably conscripted to work in the gold mines of Santo Domingo. The Indians had called the island "Ay Ay," and Columbus called it Santa Cruz — the name which stuck.

Viewed by the superpowers of the time as a small pearl to be fought over, ownership of the island was disputed among English, French, and Dutch settlers. It is said to have borne the flags of seven nations. These (in

The caravels of Columbus invade in 1493.

order) are: Spain, Holland, England, France, the Knights of Malta, Denmark, and the US.

When the dust of disputation settled in 1650, France had control; ownership was transferred the next year to De Poincy, a leading Knight of Malta. In 1653 he deeded his title to the Knights of Malta. The island was then sold to the French West India Company in 1665. Twelve years later, the French monarchy took possession of the island from the bankrupt Company, and in 1695, Louis XIV ordered it abandoned.

The island was left to unofficial squatters until 1733, when it was sold to the Danish West India and Guinea Company which, two decades later, sold the island to the Danish government after it too nearly went bankrupt.

?! Much of St. Croix's European legacy is derived from the Scots and Irish who were initially overseers on the plantations. Danes never arrived in sufficient numbers to have an important cultural influence other than in architecture.

DANES AND ENGLISH: Arriving Danish settlers found that large tracts of land had already been cleared by the French. For a time thereafter, St. Croix became one of the richest sugar islands in the Caribbean. Within 20 years, there were 1,000 people and 375 plantations.

Arriving from neighboring islands, English sugar planters soon outnumbered the Danes five to one. This one-crop prosperity lasted for 80 years, during which time cane production swelled from 1.5 million pounds in 1755 to 46 million in 1812. By 1796, more than half of the island was planted in sugarcane.

In 1802 there were 30,000 slaves, but the slave trade was abolished the next year. Briefly captured by the British in 1801, the island was held by them again from 1807–15 during the Napoleonic Wars. The island's prosperity collapsed with the development of the beet sugar industry and the US foreign sugar tariff of 1826. Slaves were emancipated in 1848.

Further setbacks followed. Part of western Christiansted burned in 1866, an earthquake and tidal wave hit the island in 1867, the capital was moved back to Charlotte Amalie in 1871, drought prevailed from 1871–1877, and a labor riot occurred in 1878 and 1892. It was almost as though someone had it out for the island, which continued its decline after the US purchase in 1917. The island's fortunes were only reversed following the post-WW II growth in tourism. Devastation again struck the island with Hurricane Hugo on Sept. 17, 1989 when 90% of the buildings were damaged or destroyed and 22,500 people were left homeless. The island had almost recovered when it was hit by Hurricane Marilyn in 1995.

These days, St. Croix is getting busier. Current population (2000 census) is 53,234. The new casino has meant expanded facilities at the E end of the island including an improved road to Pt. Udall. Up until the

ST. CROIX

Knights of Malta

The Knights of Malta have a long and colorful history. They played an important role in the Caribbean as pirates and slave traders. Not true knights in the medieval sense of the word, the Knights of Malta were a religious order of the Roman Catholic Church who were originally known as the Order of St. John of Jerusalem. In 1651, Philippe de Lonvilliers de Poincy, the French Governor of St. Kitts, deeded St. Croix to the Knights of Malta. They proved themseves to be inept administrators, and the French West India Company bought the island from the Knights in 1665. The Knights lost their French holdings in 1798 after Napoleon expelled the religious orders from Malta.

Today, the Knights are headed by Great Chancellor Bailiff Ambassador Count Carlo Marullo di Condojanni, Prince of Casalnuovo. Count Marullo presides over the "government" of the Sovereign Military Hospitaller Order of St. John of Jerusalem, of Rhodes and of Malta. While it is recognized as a state by the Vatican and maintains diplomatic ties with some 87 nations (which have included Cuba, Modolva and Afghanistan), it lacks both citizens and territory. (There is also another branch of the order which is affiliated with the Russian Orthodox Church.)

Count Marullo's order identifies itself as "SMOM" on license plates and administers dozens of hospitals and clinics throughout the world via its membership fees and contributions. Nations such as Burkina Faso, Bolivia and Lithuania recognize SMOM postage stamps. King Juan Carlos of Spain and former Italian Premiers Francesco Cossiga and Giulio Andreotti number among the 12,000 knights worldwide. Its 2,300 American members pay $2,000 to join and then $1,250 per year. The organization dreams of being recognized by the UN.
http://www.tnominfo.org

crash in late 2000 at least, 'dot commie' millionaires and other digerati were buying up property like there was no tomorrow.

Practicalities

INFORMATION: The Dept. of tourism has offices in Government House in Christiansted and in the old Customs House in Frederiksted. The *St. Croix Avis* is the local daily. There are a variety of free brochures including *St. Croix This Week*. Two useful websites are:
http://www.gotostcroix.com
http://www.visitstcroix.com

ARRIVING BY AIR: Henry E. Rohlsen Airport is seven mi. from Christiansted on the S coast. The recently renovated airport has a Danish colonial feel to its design. Pick up information at the **tourist office counter.**

Shared taxis to Christiansted cost $16 for one or two, $9 pp if three or more, *plus $1 per piece of luggage after the first.* (Chartering the taxi is a flat $36). Shared taxis to Frederiksted cost $12 pp for one or two, $6 each for three or more, *plus $1 per piece of luggage after the first.* (Chartering the taxi is a flat $24).

☞ If you come via the seaplane from St. Thomas, you will land in downtown Christiansted; the ferry also docks nearby.

ARRIVING BY FERRY: The ferry should leave you at Gallows Bay.

ISLAND ORIENTATION: Elongated St. Croix is traversed by a number of main roads; smaller ones branch off. Locations are chiefly identified by their old estate names.

The airport is in the island's SW, the small town of Frederiksted lies to the W of it, and Christiansted faces a bay to the NE near the /middle of the island. Owing to the lack of

Useful St. Croix Phone Numbers	
Ambulance	922
American Airlines	800-474-4884
American Express	773-9500
Cape Air	800-352-0714
Chamber of Commerce	773-1435
Continental Airlines	800-231-0856
Delta Airlines	800-221-1212
Fire	911/ 772-9111
Hospital	778-6311
Island Center	778-5271
LIAT	774-9930
Police	911/ 772-9111
Seabourne Airlines	773-6442
Tourist Information	773-0495
USAir	800-622-1015

water, among other factors, the area to its E, which is narrower and drier than the W, is comparatively sparsely populated. The lushest area is the "Rain Forest" in the NW, which offers hiking and horseback riding.

It takes around an hour to drive between the two main towns. Allow a couple of days to really explore the island, more if you want to stop and savor.

GETTING AROUND: It's both pleasant and easy to walk around either town. Shared taxi vans ($2.50; $3 after dark) run somewhat regularly along Centerline between Christiansted and Frederiksted. (Rates are fixed by the local government, are posted in the taxis, are featured in *St. Croix This Week* and are available from the tourist bureau and the police department). Keep in mind that rates are set for a two-person minimum and that a double fare will apply for just one passenger. A $2 charge applies for suitcases and liquor boxes. A waiting charge of 25 cents per min. (after the first ten min.) is

added, and roundtrip fares are double single fares plus waiting charges.

Taxi stands in Christiansted are on King St. (down the street from Government House) and in Frederiksted by Fort Frederik. You may stop by and make arrangements to be picked up later in the day. *Complaints, questions?* Call the Taxi Commission at 773-2236.

BUS SERVICE: Cheaper than shared taxis, the **public buses** (☎ 773-1290, ext. 229; $1; senior discount of 55 cents for 55 and up) run less frequently. Nevertheless, they are a comfortable way to get around on the main route between Christiansted and Frederiksted. They depart Christiansted for Frederiksted six times daily from 6:30 AM–6 PM; departures from Frederiksted have a parallel schedule; allow two hours (plus waiting time) for the round trip. For more information call VITRAN (☎ 778-0898).

Taxi Service	
Taxi stands are found in Frederiksted (by Fort Frederik) and in Christiansted (on King St., near Government House and Market Square). **Limousine Service** is available at 778-5466. Complaints may be lodged with the **Taxi Commission** (☎ 773-2236).	
Airport	
St. Croix Taxi Association	778-1088
Christiansted	
Antilles Taxi Service	773-5020
Caribbean Taxi & Tours	773-9799
Cruzan Taxi Association	773-6388
Golden Rock Taxi	778-7007
St. Croix Transit Tours	772-3333
T'Bird Taxis & Tours	773-6803
	514-4600
Frederiksted	
Discovery Tours	772-4492
Frederiksted Taxi Service	772-4775

🚐 Taxi Fares on St. Croix 🚐

The first rate shown in each column is for each passenger. In parentheses is the rate per passenger if more than two are traveling to the same destination.

Destination	Airport		Christiansted		Frederiksted	
Airport Terminal	16.00	(9.00)	10.00	(5.00)		
Butler Bay					11.00	(6.00)
Buccaneer Hotel	20.00	(10.00)	9.00	(5.00)		
Cane Bay Plantation	22.00	(11.00)	24.00	(11.00)		
Carambola Beach Resort	20.00	(10.00)	30.00	(12.00)	27.00	(12.00)
Chenay Bay Beach Resort	13.00	(6.50)	8.00	(4.00)	24.00	(12.00)
Christiansted	13.00	(7.50)			20.00	(9.00)
Cormorant Beach Club	13.00	(7.50)	10.00	(5.00)	20.00	(9.00)
Cotton Valley	24.00	(11.00)				
Divi Carina Bay Resort	24.00	(12.00)	18.00	(9.00)	30.00	(15.00)
Frederiksted Town/Pier	12.00	(6.00)	24.00	(11.00)		
Gallows Bay			6.00	(3.00)		
Green Cay Marina	22.00	(11.00)				
Hovensa Oil Refinery Gate	12.00	(6.00)				
Salt River Marina			22.00	(11.00)		
Shoy's Estate	20.00	(10.00)				
St. Croix Yacht Club	20.00	(10.00)				
St. George Botanical Gardens	10.00	(5.00)				
Sprat Hall Plantation	17.00	(9.00)			10.00	(5.00)
Sunny Isle Shopping Center	12.00	(6.00)	10.00	(5.00)		
Whim Museum	10.00	(5.00)			9.00	(5.00)

STREET ORIENTATION: This can be extremely confusing! In Christiansted and Frederiksted, street numbers start numbering on one side of the street, then cross over at the end of the street, and are then numbered back down in the other direction on the other side. Christiansted's street numbers begin at the waterfront, run inland to the old town limits, and then return on the other side of the street. Frederiksted's numbers begin either at the town's northern limits or at the waterfront on the W. The main streets, and those paralleling them, have long blocks. Cross streets have short ones. Corner plots generally take their number from the main streets, though the building's entrance may be around the corner.

CAR RENTALS: Expect to spend about $40 pd in summer, with unlimited mileage, and in winter $40–$50. Gas (around $4 per gallon) is additional. Rental companies include **Centerline Car Rentals** (☎ 778-0450, 888-288-8755), **Judy**

ST. CROIX

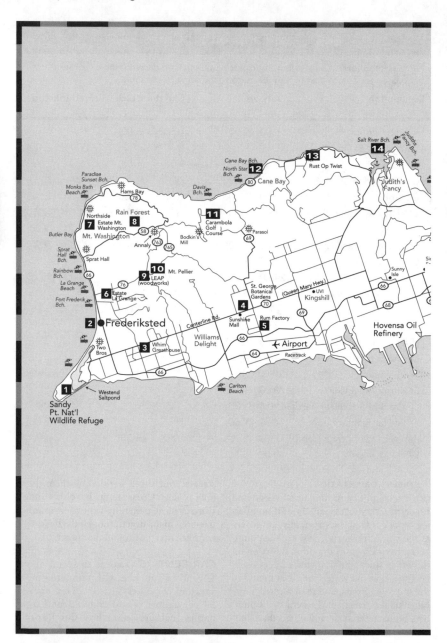

Paradise
Sunset Bch.
Monks Bath
Beach
Hams Bay
78
Northside
Rain Forest
7 Estate Mt.
Washington
8
Butler Bay
Mt. Washington
58
Sprat
Hall
Bch.
Sprat Hall
763
Annaly
765
Rainbow
Bch.
La Grange
Beach
9 10 Mt. Pellier
LEAP
(woodworks)
Fort Frederik
Bch.
76
Estate
6 La Grange
2 ● Frederiksted
Centerline Rd.
Williams
Delight
Two
Bros
3 Whim Greathouse
66
1
Westend
Saltpond
Sandy
Pt. Nat'l
Wildlife Refuge
Carlton
Beach

Davis
Bch.
North Star
Bch.
Cane Bay Bch.
12 Cane Bay
80
13 Rust Op Twist
Salt River Bch.
Judith's
Fancy Bch.
14
Judith's
Fancy

11 Carambola
Golf
Course
Parasol
69
Bodkin's
Mill

St. George
Botanical
Gardens
(Queen Mary Hwy.)
70 Kingshill
● UVI
Sunny
Isle
66
4
Sunshine
Mall
Rum Factory
5
69
68
Hovensa Oil
Refinery
66
64 Racetrack
← Airport

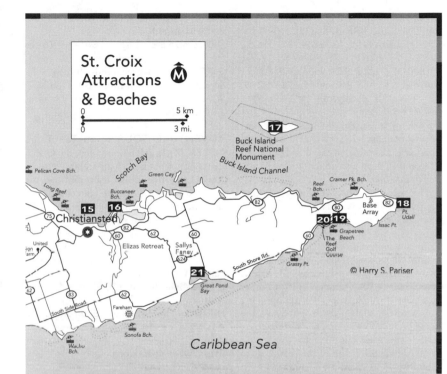

🌊 St. Croix Attractions & Beaches 🌊

1 Sandy Point National Wildlife Refuge

2 Frederiksted (historic town, shopping)

3 The Whim Plantation Museum

4 St. George Botanical Gardens

5 Cruzan Rum Distillery

6 Estate Little La Grange (museum)

7 Estate Mt. Washington

8 Rain Forest (hiking, horseback riding, mountain biking)

9 LEAP (woodworking)

10 Mt. Pellier (bar), Mt. Victory

11 Carambola (hotel, golf course)

12 Cane Bay Beach (diving)

13 Rust Op Twist (ruins)

14 Salt River (historic site, kayaking)

15 Christiansted (historic town, shopping)

16 Buccaneer Resort (beach, golf course)

17 Buck Island (snorkeling)

18 Point Udall (scenic lookout)

19 Divi Bay Casino & Resort

20 The Reef (golf)

21 Great Pond Bay (birdwatching)

ST. CROIX

of Croix (☎ 773-2123), **Olympic-Ace** (☎ 773-800, 888-878-4227, ℮ 773-6870), **Midwest** (772-0438), **Hertz** (888-248-4261, 778-1402), **Avis** (☎ 800-331-1212, 778-9355, 778-9365), **Budget** (☎ 888-227-3359, 713-9289, 778-4663), and **Skyline** (☎ 719-5990, 877-719-5990).

Parking in Christiansted is found near Fort Christiansvaern by King's Wharf; paid parking is available on the W side of town at Strand St. *Note that street parking is limited to two hours.*

The island's only two-way divided highway, the **Melvin H. Evans** (named after the former governor), runs from Sunny Isle Shopping Center W to one mi. before Frederiksted.

Centerline Road (Queen Mary Highway) runs from Christiansted to Frederiksted. Its speed limit is 30–40 mph. Limits on other roads are 35 mph, with 20 mph applying in towns. On Melvin Evans Highway, the speed limit is 55 except when approaching traffic lights (then it is 30 mph).

☞ To tour the E end of the island, drive E on Rte. 82 to Point Udall and then return via Rte. 60. Most fun of all is to explore the rougher roads in the NW portion of the island using a four wheel drive vehicle.

LAND TOURS: Taxis will give you a tour. For information contact the **St. Croix Taxi Association** (☎ 778-1088, 773-9799).

In the Pan Am Pavilion, **Island Attractions** (☎ 773-7977) can arrange trips.

St. Croix Safari Tours (☎ 773-6700, eve.: 773-9561, 800-524-2026), offers tours in a 25-passenger open-air bus. Stops range from Carambola to Salt River. It is narrated by a local expert. It departs King St. at 10 AM and returns to the waterfront at 3 PM.

A similar operation is run by **The Travellers Tours** (☎ 778-1636) and leaves from the Old Customs House in Christiansted.

Desmond's Eagle Safari Tours (☎ 778-3313, cellular 771-2871, ℮ 773-1672), a green-and-white vehicle, departs at 9:40 from Mon. to Sat. on King St. next to the Government House; it returns around 2 PM.

ADVENTURE TOURS: Tan Tan Tours (☎ 773-7041, cell: 473-6446), 31 Queen Cross St., offers a fantastic jeep tour to the Annaly Bay tidepools for around $60 pp. You head down a very rough road to this set of tidepools which are sheltered from the ocean. This is a great way to visit this beautiful spot, and the only way to get here besides hiking in. They also offer a great West End Scenic Tour ($110 pp) and an East End Sunrise Tour ($50 pp).
tantour@viaccess.net

HIKING: The St. Croix Environmental Association (☎ 773-1989) has once monthly hikes.
http://www.seastx.org
sea@viaccess.net

WATER SPORTS AND EXCURSIONS: *For sailing, diving, and other operations on the island, see Frederiksted)*

Windsurfing, snorkel-gear rental, and kayaking are offered at The Beach Shack (☎ 773-7060; Box 4230, Christiansted 00822) at the Hotel on the Cay.

Big Beard's Adventure Tours (☎ 773-4482) has trips to Buck Island with

Wheel Coach Services (☎ 719-9335, ℮ 719-1414) offers special transport for the elderly and disabled. Vans are equipped with lifts and tour staff are trained as emergency medical technicians and are versed in CPR.

beach BBQ. They also have a tour booking agency near their shop in Pan Am Pavilion.
http://www.bigbeards.com
info@bigbeards.com

Captain Carl Holley (☎ 277-4042) can take up to six on his *Mocko Jumbie*. Children are welcome.
http://www.fishwithcarl.com
fishwithcarl@yahoo.com

Mile Mark Watersports (☎ 773-2628), located next to the King Christian Hotel's lobby and on the waterfront, offers excursions including the trip to Buck Island (see "Buck Island") as well as fishing charters.
Kite St. Croix (☎ 773-9890) is *the* place to go for kiteboarding.
http://www.kitestcroix.com
info@kitestcroix.com

DIVING: The Diverse Virgin program allows you to purchase six or more prepaid trips which can be used at a number of different operators.
http://www.diversevirgin.com

Anchor Dive Center (☎ 778-1522, 800-532-3483) has operations in Salt River.
http://www.anchordivestcroix.com

N2 The Blue (☎ 772-3483, 888-STX-DIVE) offers custom dive adventures. They share a building in Frederiksted with the Coconuts Bar & Restaurant.
http://www.n2blue.com
info@n2blue.com

Located at 40 Strand St. in downtown Christiansted, **Dive Experience** (☎ 773-3307, 800-235-9047) is a PADI five star IDC facility. In addition to dive pack-

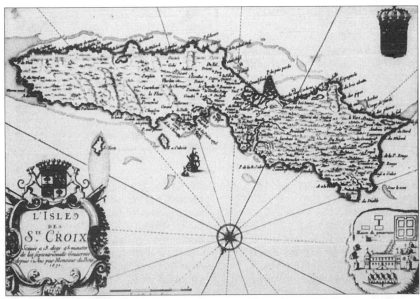

Map of St. Croix from 1671

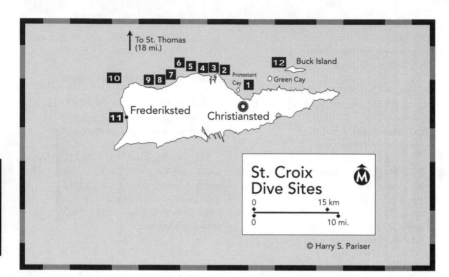

To St. Thomas (18 mi.)

6 5 4 3 2

10 9 8 7

Protestant Cay 1

12 Buck Island

Green Cay

Frederiksted

11

Christiansted

St. Croix
Dive Sites

0   15 km
0   10 mi.

© Harry S. Pariser

ages ($200–$425), CPR and Medic First Aid courses are also offered.
http://www.divexp.com
divexp@viaccess.net

On the boardwalk at 59 Kings Wharf, **Dive St. Croix** (☎ 773-3434, 800-523-DIVE) is the only dive company authorized to dive off of Buck Island and offers a variety of diving and certification courses as well as rental and repairs for scuba equipment. They also have a branch at Colony Cove's beach shack.

St. Croix Ocean Recreational Experiences/VI Divers (☎ 773-6045, 773-6045, 877-773-6045), 1112 Strand St., is another operator.
http://www.scorevi.com
score@viaccess.net

Operating out of the Caravelle Arcade, **St. Croix Ultimate Bluewater Adventures** (☎ 773-5994, 877-STX-SCUBA) offers two-tank dives and has a great store.
http://www.stcroixscuba.com

	St. Croix Dive Sites
1	The Barge
2	Little Cozumel
3	Salt River Canyon (East Wall)
4	Salt River Canyon (West Wall)
5	Rust-Op-Twist
6	Jimmy's Surprise
7	Cane Bay Drop-off
8	West Palm Beach
9	*Northstar Wall*
10	Butler Bay (wrecks)
11	Frederiksted Pier
12	Buck Island

BEACHES: The island has many wonderful beaches, but you should take care to leave nothing of value in your car while visiting them. Near Christiansted heading E is the **Buccaneer Beach**. (You may use the shower facilities at the Buccaneer Hotel). Blessed with a steady breeze, this beach's chairs and towels are rented for $4. Admission to the property for non guests is charged.

Others are **Shoys Beach, Reef Bay Beach** (windsurfing; Duggan's Reef, Teague Bay off Rte. 82), and **Cramer Park Beach.**

Nearer to town, **Hotel on the Cay's beach** is open to public use, but you must take a ferry to get there. Round the E point is **Isaac Bay,** a difficult to access beach.

Farther on are secluded **Grapetree Beach** (a thousand-foot stretch of sand off South Shore Road/Rte. 60 at the island's E tip) and **Jack's Bay Beach** (which is owned by the nature conservancy and has marked trails.

To the W of Christiansted are **Hibiscus Beach** (good snorkeling), **Pelican Cove** (snorkeling at the reef and the home of the **The Palms**), **Judith's Fancy, Salt River,** and **Cane Bay** (excellent snorkeling and diving; sea turtles underwater).

Davis Bay Beach (bodysurfing) is the home of the Carambola Beach Resort.

La Grange Beach and **West End Beach** (great snorkeling) are just outside Frederiksted.

Rainbow Beach (calm waters and good snorkeling; Rte. 63), **Sprat Hall Beach** (and accompanying guesthouse/museum; Rte. 63), and all-rock **Monk's Bath** (Veteran's Road) lie farther to the north. The island's most beautiful beach, **Sandy Point Beach** (weekend-only hours at times) lies to the S of Frederiksted. **Turtle Beach** is a beautiful beach on Buck Island off the N coast.

DIVE SITES: Although the island is almost entirely circled by coral reefs, the most accessible stretches with the largest variety of lifeforms are those off Christiansted coast. Good diving is found off of Cane Bay, Northstar, and Davis Bay.

Set off of the beach of the same name, **Cane Bay Drop-Off (7)** is set some 100-150 yds. offshore. It's a good beach dive, but operators run trips here as well. The wall's rim is set at 40 ft. and is marked by

a spur and groove formation with amazing brain corals and a wide variety of sealife.

Highlighting a coral pinnacle, **Jimmy's Surprise (6)** boasts tube sponges, moray eels, and queen angelfish. This advanced dive leads to its base, an area some 70-80 ft. in diameter. Watch for barrel sponges interspersed between spectacular gorgonians. Fish such as grouper and angels dig it down here.

Named after the sugar estate, **Rust-Op-Twist (5)** is a spur and groove formation set between Jimmy's and Cane Bay Drop-off. Down at 70-80 ft. it is a novice dive on the spot of a former fish farm. Currents feed the sealife here. Dive into the current and then ride it back home.

West Palm Beach (8) is a novice dive site set between Northstar and Cane Bay. Follow a spur and groove formation to a vertical wall at 35-40 ft. From here a slope leads down to 50-60 ft. where it plunges further. Angelfish, orange elephant ear and other sponges, and butterfly fish are among the species you may see here.

Northstar Wall (9) is a light to moderate dive which extends from 50 to 130 ft. It may be reached from either boat or beach. Entrance is a bit under a mi. W of Cane Bay. Watch for sea urchins while entering, You must first swim out 200 yds. Watch for anchors along the wall. A Danish one is embalmed on a sand shelf down around 60 ft.

Set at the mouth of the river of the same name, **Salt River Drop-off** actually consists of two sites which are the east (3) and west (4) sides of an underwater canyon known as **Salt River Canyon**. While the E wall is more sloping and hosts schools of fish, the W wall begins at 30 ft. (9 m) and swiftly drops to 90 ft. (18 m), after which it plummets to 1,000 ft. (300 m). Its caves and crevices house black coral forests, tube sponges, and a variety of coral as well as sting rays and other fish. Schools of barracuda are in the area. The "west wall" is one of the island's most famous dive sites.

Cup corals and pillar corals are found at **Little Cozumel (2)**. This 40-70 ft. intermediate-level site is E of Salt River Canyon. Two small walls run from 40 ft. down to 70 ft. and host a wide variety of coral. Barracuda, grouper, and snapper may be seen.

Butler Bay (10) has a few shipwrecks: *Rosaomaira*, a 177-ft. steel-hulled freighter; *Suffolk Mae*, a 140-ft. trawler; and the *Northwind*, a 75-ft. tugboat sunk in 50 ft. of water. It's an intermediate dive, but novices may visit the shallower wrecks. Refloated here after sinking, the *Rosaomaira* is the deepest of the trio. Sponges, corals, and angelfish have adopted her. The *Suffolk Mae* washed up in Frederiksted in 1984 and was sunk here. Only the hull and deck remain. The *Northwind* hosts a variety of creatures, as does the *Virgin Islander*, a 300-ft. barge sunk in 1991 in 70–80 ft. These wrecks are a 20 min. boat ride from Frederiksted and around an hour from Christiansted.

The **Frederiksted Pier (11)** is a great day or night dive. To get into the water, you have to walk to the end of the pier and then jump, a prospect which may appear daunting. (The less brave may descend by ladder). It's a virtual natural history museum: You might see rays, brittle stars, Christmas tree worms, frogfish, trumpetfish, and arrow crabs. Your best chance of spotting a sea horse is at night.

Intentionally sunk in order to attract fish, **The Barge** is on a reef just outside Christiansted. Resting in 70–90 ft., it is a novice dive. Fish expect to be fed here and will let you know it. Yellowtail, barracuda, and coneys are among the residents.

Lang Bank is a full day trip but is a virgin reef. Dolphins and wahoo can be found here.

You can dive off of **Buck Island (12)**, but it won't challenge experienced divers. However, the spots are beautiful. One cut is

---

Most Romantic Places to Kiss

St. Croix is a truly romantic island.

➤ At Point Udall at dusk

➤ Along Sandy Point Beach

➤ In the windmill at Estate Op Twist

➤ On the grounds of St. George Village Botanical Gardens

---

set in 35 ft. and offers coral caves; a second is larger. There is no current, which is an advantage for novices.

FISHING AND BOATING: You can fish from shore at Hams Bay. The best sport fishing is found off of the N coast at Lang Bank. Wahoo, dolphin (the fish), and kingfish are the biggest catches.

The Golden Hook Fishing Club (☎ 778-5738, ext. 223) promotes saltwater game fishing while stressing the importance of conservation.
http://www.fishstx.com

Jones Maritime Company (☎ 773-4709, 866-760-2930) offers instruction on its craft as well as sunset cruises aboard the *Rodeo Clown*. It has its office at 1215 King Cross St.
http://www.jonesmaritime.com

FISHING CHARTERS: The **Ruffian** (☎ 773-0289; Box 24370, Gallows Bay 00824) is a 41-ft. Hatteras.

The **Day Dreamer** (☎ 773-2628) Mile Mark Charters, 59 Kings Wharf, Christiansted 00820) is a catamaran.

Stress Buster Fishing Charters's **Stress Buster** (☎ 713-5317, 863-698-2701) is a 28' center console rigged for fishing.
http://www.stressbusterfishingcharters.com

Captain Harold Price (☎ 244-4232) or 340-626-6198 offers six- ($450) and 8-hr. ($600) charters aboard the *Unreel*, a 34-ft. a/c Mainship.
http://www.virginislandsoutfitters.com

Fantasy Sportfishing (☎ 773-2628), 59 King's Wharf, uses a 38' Bertram Special Edition for its expeditions. They have a one-wk. fishing school.
http://www.caribbeanseaadventures.com

Captain Carl Holley, (☎ 277-4042), at the Silverbay Dock in Christiansted Harbor, runs the *Mocko Jumbie*, a 36' Hatteras.
http://www.fishwithcarl.com

St. Croix Inshore Fishing Charters (☎ 514-6078), operates a 17-ft. Key West Flats boat which fishes for shook, tarpon, snapper, bonefish, ladyfish, and permit.
http://www.stcroixinshorefishingcharter.com

TENNIS. Four free and lighted public courts are located in Canegata Park in Christiansted and two are in Frederiksted across from the fort. The **Buccaneer Hotel** (☎ 773-2100, ext. 736) has eight courts, two of which are lighted. Non-guests pay US$16 pp, ph.

Other locations (around $5 ph) include **The Reef Club** (☎ 773-9200), **Chenay Bay Resort** (☎ 773-2918), **Villa Madeleine** (☎ 773-8141), **Sugar Beach** (☎ 773-5345), and **Antilles Resorts at Mill Harbour** (☎ 773-3840).

GOLF: The Reef (☎ 773-9200) charges $12 for nine holes plus $8 for a cart or, for 18 holes, $20 and $15 for a cart. It also offers club rentals, practice range, and special summer rates. Spacious and challenging, this 3,100-yd. course is set in a valley below Reef Villas in Teague Bay.

The Buccaneer Hotel (☎ 773-2100, ext. 738) charges around $30–65 pp for non-guests, $15 per cart pp for its 18-hole course. Hilly and attractively landscaped, it is rated at 67, its record is also 67, it has a total yardage of 5,685, its longest hole is 513 yds., and its shortest is 127 yds.

Designed by Robert Trent Jones, the **Carambola** (☎ 778-5638, pro shop; 800-228-3000) course which is ranked among the world's ten best resort courses. It charges non guests around $95 with cart for 18 holes and around $70 with cart for nine holes. (These rates can change with the season). Situated in a valley with streams and ponds, it is rated at 72.7 and has a record of 66 strokes; its longest hole is 593 yds., and its shortest hole is 139 yds. It is associated with the hotel at Davis Bay, a couple of mi. away and on the other side of the ridge.
http://www.golfvi.com

HORSEBACK RIDING: Paul and Jill's Equestrian Stables (☎ 772-2880/2627, $50 for two hrs.) are just outside Frederiksted. Jill takes you on a nature tour of the rainforest, matching you with a horse of your choice. Unlike most horse rides where you climb up on sagging Old Blue who seems to have one foot in the pot at the glue factory, Jill's horses have character, spirit, and personality. Moreover, you have the opportunity to trot and canter as well as walk. (Don't worry if you're a beginner; Jill is very patient. But don't overestimate your riding skills either.)

A variety of trails takes you through the rainforest, past the island's only dam, and up to plantation ruins for a view. On the way, Jill points out colorfully named natural features (like the "monkey no climb tree") and wildlife. For the ride, wear long pants or slacks, and shoes (for protection). Saddlebags for cameras are provided. Unless you're staying in Frederiksted, it's best to come here on the day that you rent a car as the RT taxi fare for two may be comparable anyway. Advance reservations (for the morning or afternoon ride; $75 pp) are required. There are no rides on Sundays. http://www.paulandjills.com

Equus Rides (☎ 778-0933) ride along the North Shore. Rides begin at Off the Wall Restaurant at Cane Bay Beach. Sunset and moonlight rides are also offered.

PLANTATIONS AND RUINS: This may be the island's most attractive feature. Certainly, if you get bored with the beach (or get burnt), exploring these is an alternative. More than 150 sugarmills whirled over the island for more than 100 years. They were replaced in turn by the steam mills which died with the sugar industry.

Judith's Fancy, NW of Christiansted and near St. Croix by the Sea (a hotel which was closed in 1996), is one of the most picturesque ruins on the island.

Sprat Hall, a French plantation on the W coast above Frederiksted, has been transformed into a B&B.

The **Heritage Trail** (see sidebar) is a great new development, and **Rust Op Twist,** a former sugar plantation which has been turned into a historical site, is one of the best places to stop on it.

BIRDING: There are more than two dozen excellent sites around the island including Salt River on the N coast; Great Pond and Long Point on the S coast; and the Southgate Pond Nature Preserve, Coakely Bay Pond, and Altona Lagoon—all to the E of Christiansted. Birds that nest on St. Croix include the egret, common ground-dove, Wilson's plover, smooth-billed ani, the green-backed heron, the common moorhen, and the pied-billed grebe.

St. Croix Heritage Trail

The **St. Croix Heritage Trail** is one of the Caribbean's most remarkable attractions. Established in 1999, it is still growing and expanding.

Traversing the entire 24 miles of St. Croix, the "trail" provides a format and framework with which to explore the island and its culture.

Some of the more significant sites include the Whim Plantation Museum, St. George Village Botanical Garden, and Fort Frederik.

For more information call the Landmarks Society (☎ 772-0598) at the Whim Plantation.
http://heritagetrails.stcroixlandmarks.org
info@stcroixheritagetrail.com

HIKING:Ras Lumumba Corriete a Dominica-born naturalist and expert on the flora and fauna of St. Croix, is highly recommended by Bruce Wilson of Mt. Victory Camps. He runs **Ay-Ay Eco Hikes and Tours** (☎ 277-0410, 772-4079).

The **Estate Adventure Nature Walk,** across the road from the Agriculture and Food Fair grounds in Estate Lower Love, is a short trail which takes you through different types of vegetation. Birders should walk it in the morning. A trail guide is by the entrance.

Christiansted

Christiansted, the larger of the two towns on the island, is by far the most fascinating town in the US Virgin Islands. It strikes a

?!☜ St. Croix has the ruins of more than 100 sugar mills and the largest concentration of baobab trees in the Caribbean. Imported from West Africa, they were considered sacred by native Africans.

⚑ Christiansted's Intelligent Design ⚑

T he main thing that Christiansted has to offer is its authentic historical atmosphere: the town is so well preserved that parts were designated a national historical site in 1952. You'll notice blocks of pastel pink, yellow, and brown colonnaded buildings with high-peaked roofs and an attractive fort, government buildings, and other buildings.

Christiansted's design was the concept of a single man. Frederik Moth, the island's first Danish governor, who was governor-to-be in 1734. Moth plotted streets and subdivisions, and he later developed building codes and regulations. The bulk of development was under the auspices of the Danish West India and Guinea Company and took place in the mid- to late-1700s. Strand Gade, the first street, was laid out in May 1735.

The discriminatory building code, cited above and instituted in 1747, had the incidental effect of preserving the town's old houses for posterity. New buildings were required to be of wood or masonry and to have tile (later switched to shingled) roofs. Buildings had to be in a straight line, and buildings (except on Strand Gade) had to have masonry footings or foundations. Thatched roofs were banned from the town center. Building height was limited to two to three storys. The owners built out above the sidewalks, thus creating the delightful archways that greet today's visitors.

Today's Christiansted Historic District covers six blocks, with most important structures centered on King's Wharf, King St., and on Company St. With a little imagination, you can try to picture life here as it once was. Stop in the fort and Steeple Building and have a look around. ■

balance between Charlotte Amalie's rabid commercialism and Cruz Bay's laid back atmosphere. (Only the shallowness of the town's harbor has saved it from the cruise ships and a St. Thomian fate).

Downtown has a pleasant Danish colonial feel and offers everything from gourmet restaurants to art galleries to informal eateries and a brew pub. It takes about a day to even start to explore it. Despite the small area, there's plenty to see. Shops are largely individual and memorable, especially the jewelry crafts shops.

A boardwalk now runs along the wharf area. When extended, it will stretch from the seaplane terminal to Gallows Bay. Farther up from the harbor, the St. Croix Foundation began renovating the seedy Sunday Market Square (formerly known locally as "Times Square") in 2004. Market

St. roadway features a row of mahogany trees, granite curbs, period lighting, and underground utility lines.

Out on the way to Gallows Bay, an atmosphere of pleasant lassitude prevails, with chickens clacking amidst tamarind trees, the smell and crackle of fish frying coming from open windows, and boats with peeling paint careened next to the side of houses. It's as if rural Maine had been transplanted to arid Arizona. Farther on, it's been developed as a business area with shops, delis, coffee houses, and small businesses including a bookshop.

HISTORY: Founded in 1734 as a planned community (see sidebar) by the Danish West India and Guinea Company, Christiansted was made the Danish colonial capital in 1755. Christiansted was built on the site of Bassin, a

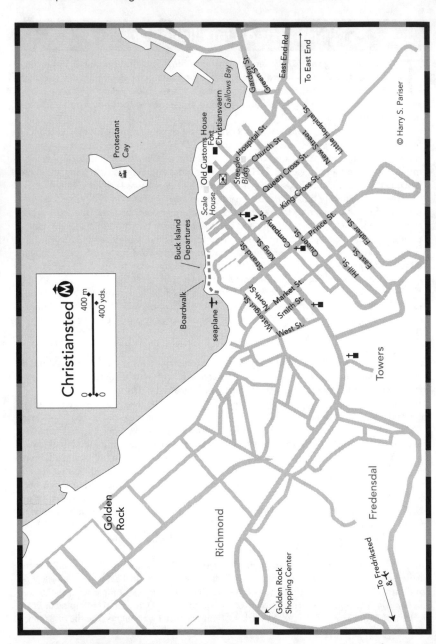

Christiansted

400 m
400 yds.

© Harry S. Pariser

Protestant Cay

Buck Island Departures

Boardwalk

seaplane

Old Customs House
Scale House
Fort Christiansvaern
Gallows Bay

Steeple Bldg.
Hospital St.
Church St.
Queen Cross St.
King Cross St.
Company St.
Strand St.
King St.
Queen St.
Prince St.
New Street
Little Hospital St.
Fisher St.
East St.
Hill St.

Garden St.
Green St.

East End Rd
To East End

Waterguit St.
North St.
Market St.
Smith St.
West St.

Towers

Golden Rock

Richmond

Fredensdal

Golden Rock Shopping Center

To Fredriksted &

It's your responsibility as a visitor to make a greeting first. A pleasant 'Good Morning,' 'Good Afternoon,' or 'Good Night' will gain you a warm response.

French settlement consisting of a few squalid huts. Before that, it had probably been inhabited by the Dutch. The town prospered during the last quarter of the 1700s, especially after it superceded Charlotte Amalie as the seat of government in 1775.

"Prosperity" was certainly a limited phenomenon by today's standards. At the beginning of the 1800s, some 5,000 or so inhabitants lived here, their lifestyle subsidized by slavery. King Sugar's decline in the 1820s and thereafter brought somnolence

and an end to expansion: the town today fits within its 18th C. boundaries, with only a bit of expansion along the highway and at Gallows Bay. The town's historic buildings were brought together under the Christiansted National Historic Site, a unit of the National Park Service, in 1952.

ORIENTATION: The Boardwalk faces the water and runs from the King Christian Hotel. The Wharf area (along with the ferry to Protestant Cay) are behind the Scalehouse at the end of this street. The Custom House and Government House are back away from the water along this street, and the Fort is behind the Custom House and across from the Steeple Building. Company St. (Companiets Gade) and

Fort Christiansvaern as depicted in 1837.

Steeple Building

the Gallows Bay PO and on to other shops. Fort St., at the intersection of Lobster and Anchor Way, leads to Chandlers Wharf (shopping), and Gallows Bay Market Place.

Christiansted Sights

Christiansted is a lovely town to walk around in. Try to pick a quiet time to explore. Allow a morning for this walking tour.

⚡ Be aware that street parking in town is limited to two hrs. The speed limit is 20 mph.

SCALEHOUSE: Built in 1855–1856, scales stand in the entryway here. Imports and exports were weighed in and inspected in this building.

DANISH CUSTOMS HOUSE: Begun in 1751 and completed in 1840, this elegant building is currently empty. It served as a Customs House throughout the Danish period.

FORT CHRISTIANSVAERN: One of the best-preserved 18th C forts in the Caribbean, this fortification is *the best* preserved of Denmark's five West Indies forts. Built from Danish bricks brought as ballast in sailing ships, Christiansvaern was constructed from 1738 to 1749; the walled stable yard to the E of the citadel was added in 1840.

It remained the military hub of the island until it was converted into the police headquarters in 1878. Painted yellow ochre, it has been restored to its 1840 appearance. Standing at the edge of the harbor, there are no outerworks. Enter through the wooden gate flanked by masonry columns. Pick up the self-guiding pamphlet at the Visitor's Center. Enjoy the great views from the water battery. Open Mon. to Fri, 8 AM–4:45 PM; Sat. and Sun. 9 AM–4:45 PM; $3 admission (ages 16–62).
http://www.nps.gov/chri

Queen St. (Dronningens Gade) run parallel to King St. (Kongens Gade), as does Strand St. (Strand Gade), which runs behind King St. and intersects with some major shopping areas: Caravelle Arcade, the Pan Am Pavilion, Comanche Walk, and Kings Alley. From the Fort and the Steeple Building, Hospital St. (Hospital Gade) leads to Lobster St which runs into Anchor Way, which leads to

Christiansted's Fort Christiansvaern in 1770.

Fort Christiansvaern as it appears today.

ST. CROIX

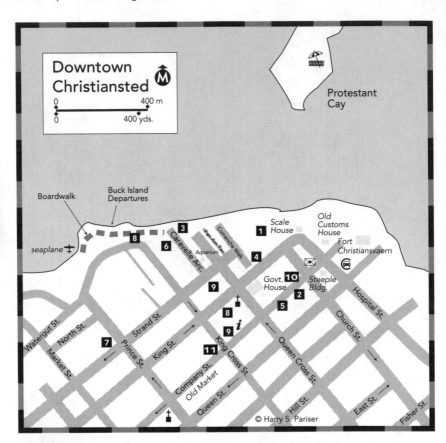

Downtown Christiansted

0 — 400 m
0 — 400 yds.

Protestant Cay

Boardwalk

Buck Island Departures

seaplane

Scale House **1**

Old Customs House

Fort Christiansvaern

3

8

6

Caravelle Arc

"Pan-Am Pav"

Comanche Walk

Aquarium

4

9

Govt. **10** House

Steeple Bldg.

2

8

5

Hospital St.

Watergut St.

North St.

Market St.

Strand St.

Prince St.

King St.

7

i

9

11

King Cross St.

Company St. Old Market

Queen St.

Queen Cross St.

Church St.

Hill St.

East St.

Fisher St.

© Harry S. Pariser

STEEPLE BUILDING: This very attractive and photogenic structure was built from 1750–1753. Called The Church of Our Lord of Sabaoth, it was the first Lutheran church on the island. Its classic Georgian steeple was added in 1793–96. Since 1831, when it was taken over by the government, it has been used as a military bakery, hospital, and school. Its roof was removed in 1841–1842, its walls were extended, and two other walls were lowered. Completely restored in 1964, it formerly housed a museum but is now being reinterpreted as a Lutheran Church. Open Mon. to Fri, 8 AM–4:45 PM; Sat. and Sun. 9 AM–4:45 PM. Free admission with paid admission to fort.

DANISH WEST INDIA AND GUINEA COMPANY WAREHOUSE: Completed in 1749, it was used to house the auction yard, offices, and personnel for the Danish slave trading company. After 1833 it became a military depot and then the telegraph office. It now houses the park headquarters. While visiting, try to imagine slaves being auctioned off here.

Downtown Christiansted	
1	King Christian Hotel
2	Company House Hotel
3	Caravelle Hotel
4	Breakfast Club
5	Apothecary Hall, Luncheria
6	Kings Alley Hotel
7	Pink Fancy Hotel
8	Holger Danske
9	Queen Cross Strreet
10	Bacchus
11	Kendrick's
12	Brew Pub

GOVERNMENT HOUSE: Government House, King St. at the corner of Queen Cross St., is the island's landmark public building. Renovated in 2000, it once housed both the governor as well as the administrative offices. A two-story townhouse — ostentatiously Baroque in design — stands at its core.

Built in 1747, it was acquired in 1771 for use as the governor's residence. In 1828, the neighboring home of a merchant-planter was acquired by Governor-General Peter von Scholten, and a link was built between the two dwellings a few years later. The flanking wings were added about 1800, and a third story followed in 1862.

After passing through security, you may walk through the iron gates to the second-story reception hall where there's an attractive iron staircase. (Ask the security guard for entry). The departing Danes had left nothing in the ballroom save the mahogany floor. In 1966, the Danish government donated the period reproduction furniture found there now, including the crystal chandeliers and gilt mirrors. The four antique chairs in the antechamber were donated by Queen Margarethe of Denmark during her 1976 visit. (Visitors are permitted to enter when there are no events underway. You must pass through security).

☞ Government House now houses the Tourism Office.

THE LUTHERAN CHURCH: This was built in the early 1740s as the Dutch Reformed church and then acquired by the Lutherans after they vacated the Steeple Building in

Christiansted as it appeared in the 19th C.

1831. The tower over the front porch was added in 1834.

PROTESTANT CAY: Out across the harbor and popularly known as "The Cay," it is the home of the **Hotel on the Cay**, as well as the blue-green St. Croix ground lizard, exterminated by the mongoose and now found only here and on Green Cay. Its name derives from the the late 1600s when non-Catholics, refused burial on the main island, were interred here. A ferry runs every ten min ($3 RT if you are not a guest of the hotel).

ST. CROIX ARCHEOLOGICAL MUSEUM: If you are fortunate enough to arrive here when it is open, the **St. Croix Archeological Museum** (☎ 692-2365, 773-9595), 6 Company Street in **Apothecary Hall**, is well worth a visit. Artifacts here found on St. Croix date back as far as 2000 BCE. A wide selection of tools (shell and stone tools, flaked tools, and various shell implements) are among the items on display. The free museum is open on Sat., 10 AM– 2 PM.

Also here is the recreated **Apothecary Shop** in **Apothecary Hall** which has finishing touches right down to the rocking chair and the fine collection of original bottles and vials on the shelves.

OTHERS: Constructed from limestone blocks, the **St. John's Anglican Church** on King St. dates from 1849–1858; it was first established in 1772. It's done in the Gothic Revival style prescribed for Anglican Churches worldwide. A few years younger (1852) and a bit farther down the road stands the **Friedensthal Moravian Church**. Founded by Moravians in the 1750s in order to evangelize and train enslaved Africans, it dates from 1852–1854.

Just **outside the town** are a number of ruins including the Estate Richmond (near Bassin Triangle), the old Danish Prison, Estate Orange Grove, and Estate Hermon Hill (at Questa Verde and Hermon Hill Road). Jacobsberg Ridge (within walking distance nearby) commands an excellent view.

Villa Rentals

As on St. Thomas and St. John, renting a house is a comfortable way to visit the island.

Bidelspacher Rentals, 3 North Grapetree Bay, Christiansted (☎ 773-9250, 773-9040) represents "The Reef" condos (one and two bedrooms) on Teague Bay and two- and three-bedroom homes on the East End.
http://www.bidelspacher.com
requestinfo@bidelspacher.com

CMPI Vacation Rentals (☎ 778-8782, 800-496-7379), under Tutto Bene restaurant, rents private villas.
http://www.enjoystcroix.com
cpmi@fordrealestatellc.com

Island Villas (☎ 800-626-4512 ☏ 772-2958, 800-626-4512), 340 Strand St. in Frederiksted, offers everything from studios up to five-bedroom residences.
http://www.stcroixislandvillas.com
carol@stcroixislandvillas.com

Vacation St. Croix (☎/☏ 778-0361, ☏ 778-5491, 877-788-0361), 1142 King St., offers rentals from $2,500 d pw.
http://www.vacationstcroix.com
marti@vacationstcroix.com

Christiansted Accommodations

Except for Hotel on the Cay (which has a small beach), none of the hotels here have a beach. The advantages to staying in town are a good selection of restaurants, social life, and shopping.

Centrally located at 44A Queen Cross St., the pink with blue trim two-story European-

style **Hotel Caravelle** (☎ 773-0687, ☏ 778-7004, 800-524-0410) has 43 attractive a/c rooms with phone and cable TV with HBO. Other amenities include pool, restaurant, and watersports. It has the highest occupancy rate on the island. Rates run $140–$160 d. It has mixed reviews on tripadvisor.com
http://www.hotelcaravelle.com
elsie@hotelcaravelle.com

Holger Danske (☎ 773-3600, ☏ 773-8828, 877-465-4373) charges $120 d and up. Set right on the boardwalk, it has attractive but small rooms with a/c, balcony or patio, and phones; some have efficiencies. It has a pool as well as the Angry Nate's Restaurant. Open daily, it serves seafood and international dishes. Entrees start at $16.
http://www.holgerhotel.com
holgerdan@aol.com

St. Croix's Hispanic-owned **Dorado Inn (Hotel) Bar & Restaurant** (☎ 692-5188), 17 Company St., specializes in Latin and local food and seafood. Rates range from $75–$110 d.

The 35-unit **King's Alley** (☎ 773-0103, ☏ 773-4431), 57 King St., has a set of 12 new suites (furnished with Danish West Indies furniture and custom-designed batiks). A/c and fan-equipped rooms (recently refurbished) have balconies (on upstairs rooms), phones, and cable TV. All rooms have king or twin beds. Refrigerators are available upon request. Rates range from $110–$170 d. A restaurant should be open by 2009. Read the reviews at tripadvisor.com before booking.
harborwalk@att.global.net

Now owned by Danes, the 39-rm. **King Christian Hotel** (☎ 773-6330, ☏ 773-9411, 800-524-2012; Box 24467, St. Croix 00824)

has a pool. It's conveniently located by the waterfront at 59 King's Wharf. The hotel's "superior" rooms feature two double beds, a/c, color cable TV, telephone, refrigerator, room safe, bathroom w/shower, separated dressing area, and balcony. The "minimum" rooms feature private bath, a/c, telephone and one double or two single beds. Ask about their dive packages. Rates run around $100–$135 d.
http://www.kingchristian.com
info@kingchristian.com

At 18 Queen Cross St., the **Breakfast Club** (☎ 773-7383, ☏ 773-8642) is a bed-and breakfast which offers seven tastefully-decorated rooms with kitchenettes, mahogany beds, and fans. A full breakfast is included. All-year rates run around $60 s, $75 d; rates include government tax. A Sunday Brunch (reservation only) is held from 11 AM–1 PM.
http://nav.to/thebreakfastclub
tchapin@islands.vi

The Company House Hotel (☎ 773-1377, 2 Company St., was restored in 2007. Its 27 a/c rooms (which include one suite) feature refrigerator, phone, color cable TV with free HBO, and a pool. Rates run around $70.80 d including taxes and continental breakfast. It has a conference room. It is a sister hotel to King Christian.
http://www.companyhousehotel.com

At #1 Strand St., **Club Comanche** is currently under renovation.
At 27 Prince St., **Pink Fancy** (☎ 773-8460, ☏ 773-6448; 800-524-2045) is a white-and-pink colored historic landmark which dates from 1780. It was first lovingly restored a century later. This is a place best suited for those into hanging out and getting to know people. The Pink Fancy has a pool and is within easy walk-

ing distance of the seaplane shuttle and the ferry service to the Hotel on the Cay and its beach.

Amenities in the hotel's 12 large and comfortable rooms (which have names such as "Sweet Bottom") include kitchenettes, breakfast, a/c and fans, cable TV, radio, and phone. A simple buffet-style continental breakfast is served by the pool. The rooms start at $140 d for the winter season; deluxe rooms are $185 d, have a three-night mini-mums, and include a continental breakfast. Their informative web site gives full details.
http://www.pinkfancy.com
info@pinkfancy.com

Set on a seven-acre island just offshore, 55-rm. **Hotel on the Cay** (☎ 773-2035, ☞ 773-7046, 800-524-2035; Box 4020, Christiansted 00820) offers Christiansted's only beach. Their Harbormaster Restaurant, set right on the beach and just below the pool, serves breakfast and lunch and hosts a W Indian BBQ complete with steel band, mocko jumbies and other traditional entertainment.

The hotel has a pool, tennis courts and water sports. Honeymoon, convention, dive, and group packages are available as are an innumerable number of activities ranging from a scavenger hunt to sand volleyball. A/c rooms have balconies, ocean views, TV, and kitchenettes (with microwave, refrigerator, toaster and coffeemaker). Ground level rooms are wheelchair accessible. Rooms run around $130 d; tax, a 7.5% service charge, and a $2 pp energy charge are added to this. It is also a timeshare. The disadvantage of staying here is that the ferry ceases running between 1 and 6 AM (unless you make prior arrangements). The advantage is that you have a small but good beach with snorkeling. You also might birdwatch, and perhaps spot the endangered ground lizard which resides on this island.

http://www.hotelonthecay.com
hotc@viaccess.net

HEADING SOUTH: Set on the south coast, **Longford Hideaway** (☎ 773-5912, ☞ 773-2386, 800-377-2987) is a romantic and attractive cottage set inside a working cattle ranch. Visit the excellent website put together by owners Valeria and Chicco Gasperi. It charges around $125 d or $630 pw.
http://www.longfordhideaway.com
longfordhideaway@att.net

Accommodations near Christiansted
HEADING WEST: Also on the same hill (at 56 Estate Hermon Hill), **Carringtons Inn** (☎ 713-0508, ☞ 719-0841, 877-658-0508) opened in late 2000. Owner-operators Claudia and Roger Carrington, originally from Guyana but long-term residents of the States, will lend a personal touch to your stay. Their five comfortable rooms come with a/c, fan, phone refrigerator, coffee maker and with either queen- or king-sized beds. These rooms have been creatively furnished and sport names such as "Flamboyant" (the largest room: great for honeymooners!) and "Frangipani." A large pool, comfy TV lounge area, and great views are distinct pluses. Internet, fax, and copier access is available. Claudia and Roger provide a hearty breakfast repast which usually includes items such as French toast, juice, fruit, and yogurt. Rates run around $100–$165 d. Tennis and a gym are within walking distance; town is a good walk. You may want a car if staying here.
http://www.carringtonsinn.com
info@carringtonsinn.com

The secluded **Suite Birds of Paradise** (773-1364, ☞ 773-1364, 800-695-8284), 4027 Herman Hill, has but two rooms and a suite, Rooms feature cable TV, coffee maker, hair dryer, iron, voice mail, and a kitchen.

At 32451 Estate Golden Rock, **Sugar Beach Condo Resort** (☎ 773-5345, ℰ 773-1359, 800-524-2049) offers 46 units bordering a 500-ft. stretch of beach. Each one-, two-, or three-bedroom central-a/c-and-fan equipped suite has a private balcony with great views and a breeze. Its pool lies by a ruined sugar mill tower. Watersports are available. Rates run from $188–$385 (plus tax and service) for studios to four-bedrooms.
http://www.sugarbeachstcroix.com
sugarstx@viaccess.net

Set one mi. W of Christiansted at 3280 Golden Rock, **Club St. Croix Beach and Tennis Club** (☎ 773-4800, ℰ 778-4009, 800-524-2025) is a 54-condo beachfront resort whose rooms include kitchens, a/c, cable TV, and phone. Facilities include poolside restaurant and bar, and three tennis courts. Rates run around $175/unit.
http://www.antillesresorts.com
reservations@antillesresorts.com

Fronting a palm-lined beach, the 44-rm. **Hibiscus Beach Hotel** (☎ 773-4042, ℰ773-7668, 800-442-0121), 4131 Grande Princesse, has a restaurant, bar, and pool. Rooms feature phone, in-room safe, a/c and fans, balcony or patio, and TV. Rates run around $190 d. Golf and dive packages are offered.
http://www.hibiscusbeachresort.com
info@hibiscusbeachresort.com

At 4126 La Grande Princesse, **The Palms at Pelican Cove** (☎ 718-8920, ℰ 718-9218, 800-548-4460) has a great gourmet restaurant (excellent presentation), bar, pool, tennis, snorkeling, and nearby golf. The 34 deluxe rooms are set in a white concrete building and spread across 12 acres. They

have a/c, fans, and balcony or patio. Rates run around $190 d in season. It was formerly known as the Comorant Beach Club.
http://www.palmspelicancove.com
info@palmspelicancove.com

The **Inn at Pelican Heights** (☎ 713-8022, ℰ 713-8526; 888-445-9458), 3D and 3E Estate St. John, commands a view of Pelican Bay. Its suites have full kitchens, fans and a/c, cable TV, and patio. Breakfast is included in the rates (from around $140 d). Packages are available. There is a pool on the property.
http://www.innatpelicanheights.com
info@innatpelicanheights.com

The 16-rm. **Kronegade Inn Hotel** (☎ 692-9590, ℰ 692-9591; 11-12 Western Suburb at the edge of town) has rooms for around $70–120 d.; it has full kitchens and living areas, your choice of a/c or fans, and phone and TV. Check out the reviews on tripadvisor.com before booking.
http://www.kronegadeinn.com

Remax Rentals at Mill Harbour (☎ 773-8372, ℰ 773-1579; 877-657-8372), 3220 Golden Rock, runs around $225 d. Rates rise according to the number of people, an d weekly, and monthly rates are available.
http://www.stcroixislandconnection.com
tryayay@viaccess.net

Next door at 3200 Golden Rock, **Colony Cove** (☎ 773-1965, ℰ 773-5397, 800-524-2025) a luxury all-suite, 60-unit beachfront resort, faces a palm-lined beach. Attractive two-bedroom, two-bath suites have kitchen, dining and living room, a/c, phone, cable TV with free HBO, and private balcony. Facilities include pool, tennis, windsurfing, snorkeling, and scuba. One of the resort's best features is its gardens, with a variety of local plants and herbs.

Although the beach is not impressive, the snorkeling is. Be sure to swim out to the tires, which attract a wide range of fish. Prices run from around $235 d ($20 per extra person) in season. Units may hold up to five. Daily housekeeping is 10% of room rate; a midweek cleaning is complimentary. A variety of packages including golf at Carambola, honeymoon, and diving are also available.

Bookings here are also available through management company Antilles Resorts (☎ 800-524-2025, 773-9150, ☏ 778-4004).
http://www.antillesresorts.com
reservations@antillesresorts.com

Villa Margarita (☎ 713-1930, ☏ 719-3389, 866-274-8811), 22 Salt River, is a getaway next to Salt River Bay National Park and within walking distance of the marina. This tranquil inn's three suites have kitchen, open-air balconies overlooking the ocean, cable TV and VCR, phone, fax, and Internet access. It charges around $140–$210 d.
http://www.villamargarita.com
info@villamargarita.com

Set at Cane Bay Beach, the intimate and informal **Cane Bay Reef Club** (☎ 778-2966; 800-253-8534; Box 1407, Kingshill) has a large pool and nine two-room suites with overhanging balconies. The Carambola golf course is nearby. Rates range around $150–$250 d.
http://www.canebay.com
cbrc@viaccess.net

Set next to Cane Bay Reef Club, **Waves at Cane Bay** (☎ 778-1805, ☏ 778-4945, 800-545-0603, Box 1749, Kingshill 00851-1749) features 11 studios and one villa. All are equipped with kitchen, ocean-view balconies, radio, fan, and cable TV. Most have a/c. Facilities include a gourmet

restaurant, natural grotto pool and a PADI dive center. Rates run around $140–$155 d.
http://www.canebaystcroix.com
info@canebaystcroix.com

Fronting 'Davis Bay Beach, the **Carambola Beach Resort** (☎ 778-3800, ☏ 778-1682, 888-503-8760) has 26 six-rm. buildings which resemble small villas. Each of the 121 rooms includes a/c and fan, bath radio and there is a spa, pool and beach. There are also three restaurants and one bar. Units rent from around US$275 on up.
http://www.carambolabeach.com
info@carambolabeach.com

HEADING EAST: Just outside of town, **Schooner Bay Condominiums** (☎ 778-7670, ☏ 773-4740) rent for around $1,100 pw. The attractively-furnished two- and three-bedroom suites have tile floors, rattan furniture, a nice kitchen, and TV with VCR. Balconies overlook the harbor, and there's a laundry room, two pools (one of which is popular with children), hot tub, and tennis courts. It's a short walk to Gallows Bay and downtown Christiansted.

The 46-rm. **Tamarind Reef Hotel** (☎ 773-4455, ☏ 773-3989, 800-619-0014) is set near the Green Cay marina and has recently been refurbished. It is near two beaches with good snorkeling (but no surf). Rooms have a/c, TV, phone, refrigerator, coffee maker, iron and ironing board, and hair dryer; 19 rooms have kitchenettes. It offers personalized service. Rates are around $200–$300; a 10% service charge is applied. Free use of kayaks is offered.
http://www.usvi.net/hotel/tamarind
reservations@tamarindreefhotel.com

The Buccaneer (☎ 773-2100, ☏ 778-8215, 800-255-3881, Box 25200, Gallows Bay, Christiansted 00824) has a country club setting with 138 rooms set on 340 landscaped acres along with three beaches, two pools, an 18-hole golf course, eight tournament tennis courts (two lighted), health spa, watersports, shopping arcade, and an 18-station, two-mi. jogging/ parcourse track. Dating from 1948, it is one of the few Caribbean resorts that are still in the hands of the Armstrongs, the original owners. And Elizabeth Armstrong, the general manager, has shown a commendably strong commitment to support the Buck Island Reef Sea Turtle Research Program.

The property has been an estate since 1653, and the ruins of a sugar mill can be seen. A wide variety of accommodations — from standard to ficus suite — are offered. You're taken around the grounds in a complimentary van, and a taxi shuttle to town also runs. Rates run around $340–$990 d. A variety of packages are offered, and an "Elope To A Wedding in Paradise" service is also offered. In the UK call 0-45383-5801 or ℰ 0-45383-5525.
http://www.thebuccaneer.com
mango@thebuccaneer.com

Near Green Cay Marina and providing the privacy of "gardenview" and "oceanview" cottages scattered through 30 acres, **Chenay Bay Beach Resort** (☎ 773-2918, ℰ 773-6665, 866-226-8677; Box 26000, Christiansted 00824) offers 50 attractive efficiency cottages with kitchen, a/c, and fan. Facilities include a children's program, infinity edged pool, spa, restaurant, tennis, kayaks, floating mats, children's playground on the beach, complimentary use of snorkeling equipment, and grocery shuttle. Family cottages are available. Rates run from around $159-309/unit. Beachfront bar and grill, The Shores, offers classic cuisine with a Caribbean flair. There's a small beach here and the water remains shallow for a considerable distance from shore
http://www.chenaybay.com
reservations@islandone.com

Set 3.5 mi. E of Christiansted, **Estate Tipperary** (☎ 773-0143, ℰ 778-7408; 501 Tipperary #10 on Southgate Rd.) is a three-bedroom, two-bath private home which has a Jacuzzi, pool, and housecleaning service. Rentals start at $1,750/wk for 1–4. Write Mrs. Beverly Bell Collins, Salt Box Farm, 1 Wright Lane, Westford, MA 01886.
http://rentalo.com/1717/
privatevacation.html

Set on Grapetree Beach, the **Divi Carina Bay Resort** (☎ 773-9700, ℰ 773-6802, 888-464-3484; 25 Estate Turner) opened in late 1999. It has 126 oceanfront rooms, 20 oceanview villas, and proximity to the **casino**. Rooms have patio or balcony, kitchen or kitchenette, and TV. Facilities include a gourmet restaurant, tennis courts, fitness room, basketball courts, pool and ping pong tables, and watersports center. Rates run around $250 d and up.
☞ The Divi Carina has "The Links," an 18-hole miniature golf course as well as a driving range and club house.
http://www.divicarina.com
http://www.carinabay.com

CAMPING: The island has two traditional campsites. Both are E of Christiansted and would require a car to be practical.

Cramer Park, on the East End, has free camping. There is a catch, two of them in fact: there's no fresh water and the flush toilets may not be functioning. Easter Weekend is packed here. You'll see an amazing collection of SUVs parked, batteries of speakers booming out pounding reggae, stacked cases of beer, and fish frying.

In the Greatpond area, stands the **Boy Scout Camp** which has tent rentals. Compared to the other two, it's a bastion of convenience with showers, restrooms, refrigerators, electrical outlets, and boat rentals. Baresite camping is $10 pp, pd. Tent and mattress are additional. For more information write: **Boy Scouts** (☎ 772.0934), Box 1353, Frederiksted, VI 00840.

Mt Victory Camp (☎ 772-1651), off of Creque Dam Road in the Rain Forest, offers platform-camping in a comfy and homey atmosphere. Tent camping is available by request. For more details, see the Frederiksted "Accommodations" section.

Christiansted Dining and Food

If you have money to spend and like to dine well, Christiansted (as well as the island as a whole) is an excellent place to be. There are also a number of lower-priced places for those who can afford only around $12 a meal or so.

NOTE: In describing restaurant prices in this chapter, *inexpensive* refers to places where you can dine for $15 and under, including a drink, appetizers and dessert; you may in fact pay more. *Moderate* means $16–$25, *expensive* means $26–$40, and *very expensive* means over $40 a meal.

LIGHT DINING: Takeout is available from vendors near the wharf and by the marketplace as well as at all of the less expensive eateries.

One inexpensive to moderate restaurant serving West Indian and Continental lunches is **Harvey's** (☎ 773-3433) at 11B Company St. It has a vegetarian plate for $6.

The French Press (☎ 773-6912), Company St., serves pressed sandwiches, homemade soups, imported French cheese, and fresh baked pastries on Tues. to Fri. from 11:30 AM–3 PM.

Singh's Fast Food (☎ 773-7357), 23B King St., is open for lunch and early dinners (closes at 8 PM). The place to go for *roti*!

Cora's Snack Bar (☎ 713-9888), 32 King St., serves good local dishes.

At 45 King St., **Kim's Restaurant** (☎ 773-3377) is both unpretentious and

popular. This is a good place to get introduced to local food.

Nearby and across from Government House, **Lalita Juice Bar & Tea Room** (☎ 719-4417), in the KALIMA Center 54 King St. offers organic smoothies, sandwiches, soups and salads. Breakfast and lunch are served. It also offers wireless internet, a sauna, and aromatherapy.

Inexpensive **Brady's,** 15 Queen St., also serves West Indian food three meals daily. Their fish sandwiches make a great light lunch.

For reasonably priced Mexican-American food, try the inexpensive **Luncheria** (☎ 773-4247) inside Apothecary Hall at 6 Company St. (off of Queen Cross). It has vegetarian selections (including lard-free refried beans) as well as low-cal dishes, whole wheat tortillas, and superb frozen margaritas.

Another good choice here is **Cafe Christine,** the choice of professionals for weekday lunches. Its menu changes daily, and it shows work by local artists.

Set in the Caravelle Hotel Arcade bordering the waterfront, **Rumrunners** (☎ 773-6585) serves three meals daily (7 AM–10 PM) and offers daily specials. Appetizers are huge, and the fried onions are especially popular.). Dishes range from conch fritters (lunch) to local island lobster and veggie selections (dinner). Sunday brunches offer mimosas and bloody Marys. Happy hour is 4–6 PM daily. Secure parking is offered. **http://www.rumrunnersstcroix.com.**

Right on the boardwalk, the **Fort Christian Brew Pub** (☎ 713-9820) serves light meals downstairs and evening seafood and US-style dinners upstairs in its dining room. Brewed on the premises, it features several microbrews; its beer is bottled in the States.

Paradise Cafe (☎ 773-2985), Queen Cross St. at 53B Company, is an a/c restau-

ST. CROIX

rant serving three inexpensive meals from Mon. to Sat. It offers daily specials, breakfasts (banana, strawberry, or banana pancakes), soups/salads, sandwiches (tuna melt, veggie), and fresh fish or steak specials. Dinner specials run around $15.

The Avocado Pit (☎ 773-9843) is a deli set next to the fort. Granola, fresh fruit, and yogurt are on the breakfast menu. It closes at 5 PM.

On the waterfront next to Stixx, **Shannanigans** (☎ 713-8110), a great place for breakfast and lunch, is popular with locals.

L&M Restaurant (☎ 713-0321) Queen Cross Street, is open for breakfast and serves local food for lunch.

FORMAL DINING: Try and get hold of the St. Croix Restaurant Association's booklet *Dining in St. Croix* if it's available. Expect to spend around $20–30 pp or more for dinner including tip.

A popular restaurant open for lunch and dinner from Mon. to Fri., expensive "Nouvelle American" **Kendrick's** (☎ 773-9199), King Cross St., serves pasta and a variety of dishes ranging from BBQ roasted salmon to shrimp *saltimbocca*. Dine in casual attire upstairs or formally downstairs.

Open for lunch and dinner, the inexpensive to moderate **Bombay Club** (☎ 773-1838, reservation suggested), 5A King St., serves a wide variety of dishes, including pasta, quiche, sandwiches, and seafood. Lunch specials are reasonable, and it is a favorite of many locals.

Bacchus (☎ 692-9922), upstairs on Queen Cross St. between Strand and King Sts., is a gourmet restaurant offering a fine wine list and seafood and other dishes. Entrées include "sea scallops with cream and herbs" and "eggplant Napoleon." They will cater to dietary restrictions, and they offer nightly fish and lobster specials. Desserts are tasty.

Set in the Pan Am Pavilion at 39 Strand St., the informal **Stixx Bar and Restaurant** (☎ 773-5157), a popular and informal, inexpensive to expensively priced watering hole, serves three meals daily and features a special entree nightly. Lobster and a Sun. brunch number among the specialties. And don't miss the crab races on Fri. at 5:30 PM!

Parrot Cove (☎ 773-6782), 1102 Strand St (upstairs at Queen Cross), serves continental dishes for lunch and dinner (773-6782); open 7 days a week 11 AM–2 AM.

Harbormaster (☎ 773-2035, ext. 450) at the **Hotel on the Cay** offers a Tues. night beach BBQ with entertainment.

Savant (☎ 713-8666), 4C Hospital St., is an excellent mid-range a/c restaurant which has a varied menu — from seafood to Mexican to Asian variations. Open for dinner daily save Sun. Call for reservations.

Moderately-priced **Dee Anna's Restaurant** (☎ 719-5499), 55 Company St., is set in a historic courtyard and quite popular with visitors.

Zebos Wine Bar and Restaurant (☎ 692-2864), Strand St., is open daily until 2 AM. Dinner is served from 6–10 PM.

Dashi (☎ 773-6911), located in the Caravelle Arcade off Strand St., serves sushi and Asian dishes.

GALLOWS BAY DINING AND FOOD: At Gallows Bay Market Place, the attractive **Anna's Café** (☎ 773-6620) is a good place for a light meal.

The **Golden Rail Cafe** (☎ 719-1989), set in the St. Croix marina, offers breakfast, lunch and dinner daily. Feast on a daily special and take in the scenery.

Moderate **Tutto Bene** (☎ 773-5229), in the Boardwalk Building on Hospital St. in Gallows Bay, specializes in Italian cuisine. Its name means "everything good," and the menu changes daily. It's extremely popular with locals and visitors alike. Pizza, roasted garlic, jumbo prawns, and linguine shrimp basilico are among the yummy offerings. A post-meal apertif is on the house. For non-smokers, the downside to this place is its lack of a clearly-defined nonsmoking area. Be sure to call for reservations. http://www.tuttobenerestaurant.com

The Case Place (☎ 719-3167), Chandler's Wharf, offers Caribbean-inspired dishes such as conch, lobster, seafood special, and even veggie burgers for lunch and dinner. They offer "safe parking." http://www.thecaseplacevi.com

The inexpensive **No Bones Café** (☎ 773-2128), 127 Flag Drive, is around the corner from Computer Solutions in Gallows Bay. It serves inexpensive lunches; dinners feature dishes such as "Spencer's shrimp" ($16.95) and "Five Peppers Any Way" ($11.95–$15.95), depending upon ingredients). They have an an "all you can eat and peel" shrimp night on Sat.

Anything Goes (☎ 773-2777), across from the hardware store in Gallows Bay, serves subs, sandwiches, veggie dishes, daily specials, and sushi on Saturdays.

A veritable carnivores' heaven, **Cheeseburgers in Paradise** (☎ 773-1119) is 3.5 mi. E of town on the way to Duggan's Reef on the E End. You'll find the occasional Jimmy-Buffett-style acoustic guitar performance held under the stars here. It advertises that it's a "local characters' hangout" and that "funny stories abound."

HEADING FARTHER EAST: The **Tamarind Reef Hotel** has the **Deep End Bar** (☎ 773-4455) which serves light lunches and offers weekend afternoon beach parties.

The **Buccaneer** has **The Terrace Restaurant** which serves breakfast and dinner daily. Its menu offers Euro-Caribbean

---

St. Croix Hip Weekend Itinerary

After a day's exploring, hit the crab races at Stixx at 5:30 PM on Friday. Then dine at **Blue Moon** (in Frederiksted: live jazz), at the South Shore Cafe, or at an in-town bistro. (If it is the third Friday of the month, check out Sunset Jazz on the Frederiksted waterfront.)

On Saturday morning go **snorkeling** at **Buck Island**. Later on, have **dinner** at Tutto Bene, Bacchus, Truffles, or another gourmet restaurant. Then **go dancing** at **Club 54** but don't arrive before 11 PM at the earliest.

On Sunday, pack a cooler and bathing suit and embark on an **island tour**; head to the South Shore Cafe or to the Marina Bar known as **Golden Rail** for brunch. ∎

---

fusion dishes. It also has the beachside **Mermaid** and the **Grotto Grill**.

The **Cultured Pelican** (☎ 773-3333), Coakley Bay, serves Italian dishes such as manicotti stuffed with ricotta, pizzas, and calzones. This restaurant is a great place to have a romantic sunset dinner. Also check with the management to see if the

 Don't miss Christiansted's **crab races** held every Monday at Kings Alley at 5 PM, on Wed. at the Hotel on the Cay at 4 PM, and at Stixx at 5:30 PM on Friday. Here, you may purchase a crab for $2. Purchasers of speedier crustaceans (hermit crabs to be exact) will be rewarded with prizes such as a sailing trip to Buck Island of a RT ticket on the seaplane shuttle to St. Thomas. This event is suitable for children of all ages.

ST. CROIX

Crucian Christmas Fiesta

A traditional Christmas Festival, the **Crucian Christmas** is held annually during the end of December and the beginning of January. First off, the Prince and Princess are crowned, and then Miss St. Croix is selected. A one-day Food Fair is presented at the Christiansted and Frederiksted markets. This is followed by the opening of the Festival Villages a few days later. These serve food and have nightly entertainment from local bands playing calypso and quelbe tunes. Guavaberry liquer and coquito are the beverages of choice, and local culinary specialties such as *benye* (a fried banana fritter) and *pasteles* are sold. The Children's Parade and the Adults' Parade top off the festival in January. For more specific info on dates contact the St. Croix Festival Committee (☎ /19-3379). ∎

Caribbean Dance Company has a performance scheduled here.

Inexpensive to expensive, seaside **Duggan's Reef** (☎ 773-9800), Teague Bay, serves seafood, curries, and pastas. Dishes range from conch tempura to teriyaki salmon to to Irish Whisky lobster to Caribbean-style blackened fish. It has a Sun. brunch and offers low calorie and low cholesterol items; veggie pasta is also prepared by request. The large portrait here is of Frank Duggan during his service in Vietnam in 1969; the many Massachusetts sports pennants pay homage to owner Frank Duggan's roots. It's open for dinner nightly from 6–9:30 PM.

Featuring waterfront dining with a wide variety of dishes, **The Galleon** (☎ 773-9949), Green Cay Marina at Estate Southgate, offers seafood (fresh island fish and lobster), pasta, steak, lamb, and other dishes for dinner. Black bean soup, salads, and pastas are also served. Dishes include "vegetable ravioli" and "shrimp calypso." It has piano performances most evenings. The

Deep End, also here, offers cocktails and light snacks. as well as vegetarian dishes; its grill is open all weekend.

The very casual **Island House** (☎ 773-2918) at Chenay Bay features American/ Caribbean cuisine for lunch and dinner. Entrées range from "vegetable alfredo" ($17) to crab stuffed grouper ($23). Evening events here range from a Mexican night to a West Indian buffet.

At the old dairy on Rte. 62, the **South Shore Cafe** (☎ 773-9311) serves gourmet dining at "casual prices." Dishes include vegetarian specialties, seafood, and Italian entrées made with handmade pasta. They also brew their own beer. Medium-priced and casual, this is the type of place that you would expect to find in the Caribbean.

The **Divi Carina Bay Resort and Casino** (☎ 773-9700) offers dining in a number of small restaurants, the most elegant being the Starlight Grille.

Hot Wheels Racing

Sunday is the big day here for racing. Some 200 young men may assemble in the parking lot at Junie's Barbeque in Estate La Reine. Souped up vehicles with names like Arachnarod and Phantastique are at their command. However, these cars are miniature, and they race on a wood and metal two-car track. Many of the competitors are father and son teams, just as they are on Puerto Rico where the fad originated.

Races are divided into metal and plastic car races. Each car pays a $1 entry fee which finances trophies and a monthly award of a bike or Walkman. ∎

ST. CROIX

OUTLYING FOOD AND MARKET SHOP-PING: Very little food is found in the town's open air market except on Saturdays. **Stop N' Save Super** stands at the intersection leading to Gallows Bay.

Pueblo, the VI's major supermarket chain has a store at Golden Rock Shopping Center just outside town at the beginning of Rte. 75 (Northside Road). Other locations are at Ville La Reine (Kingshill).

The Sunny Isle Shopping Center also has **K Mart,** sporting goods stores, Office Max, Radio Shack, bookstores, a drugstore, a bank, and food court.

Plaza Extra is at United Shopping Plaza at Peter's Rest and at Esteate Plessen on Centerline Rd. **Cost-U-Less** is just to the E.

Head to **Princesse Seafood** (☎ 773-3710) for fresh fish; it's run by a retired chef. It's closed Sun. to Tues. It's at 12A La Grande Princesse on Rte. 75 next to F&H Paint and before the Nissan dealership.

ISLAND BAKERIES: Thomas Bakery, 33 King St., sells good wholewheat rolls and loaves as well as pastries; they also sell juicy Trinidadian gossip rags such as *The Bomb* and the *Daily Express.*

Open daily, **Star Fish Patisserie,** (☎ (778-3474), Peter's Rest, is across the road from United Shopping Plaza).

Pastry Hut (☎ 772-2465), near Sunshine Mall on Centerline Rd., is open daily save Sat. Shop here for pastries, breads, and health foods.

The Centerline Bakery is outside of Frederiksted.

Other bakeries are found in Fredriksted.

HEADING W.: In Princess Plaza, a few min. drive to the W of town, the a/c **Salud! Bistro** (☎ 719-7900; reservations suggested), serves creative Mediterranean cuisine amidst a romantic atmosphere. It offers nightly spe-cials such as fresh fish, a good cocktail and wine list, and live flamenco music. **http://www.saludbistro.com**

Due W of town, the inexpensive to moderate **Breezez** (☎ 773-7077), at Club St. Croix in Golden Rock, offers a vari-ety of sandwiches, salads, stir fries, *fajitas,* and other specialties. They serve breakfast, lunch, and dinner daily and have a Sun. brunch with "lobster Benedict."

At 17 La Grande Princesse on North Shore Rd., inexpensive **2 Plus 2** (☎ 773-3710) offers shrimp, chicken, and meat dishes; there's also entertainment with DJs.

Fronting Pelican Beach, the moderate to expensive **The Palms** (☎ 778-8920) at has dancing under the stars Fri. evenings, Sunday brunch, and lunch and dinner daily. It serves gourmet international dishes.

Elizabeth's Restaurant (☎ 719-0735), Palms Resort, offers an eclectic range of gourmet dishes. It's open for three meals daily and offers a Sunday brunch.

Set at Mill Harbour and Colony Cove to the W, the inexpensive to moder-ate **Serendipity Inn Beach Restaurant** (☎ 773-5762) serves lunch and dinner (fresh catch of the day; $10 Fri. night BBQ) daily as well as dishes like Cruzan pancakes or coconut shrimp.

Off of Rte. 70 at marker 1.5 in Estate Whim, inexpensive to moderate **Villa Morales** (☎ 772-0556) offers a range of fish and meat entrées served in traditional Spanish and West Indian style. Weekly lunch specials (stew goat, roast pork) are served, as is *paella.* Some have termed their fare as "Cruzarican."

At Sunny Isle Shopping Center, inexpen-sive to moderate **China Jade Restaurant** (☎ 778-1996) serves Chinese food including all-you-can-eat buffets on Sat. Locals say it has the best Chinese food on the island.

On Hess Rd. at 114 Castle Coakley, moderate **Gertrude's** (☎ 778-8362) offers Caribbean lobster, broiled snapper with papaya salsa, and other delicacies. They also serve salads, stir fries, and vegetarian pasta. Three meals are served; it's closed Sun.

Junie's Restaurant (☎ 773-2801), 132 Peter's Rest, serves West Indian fare including such seafood dishes as conch ($12), salt fish and dumplings ($12), buttered shrimp ($15), and lobster ($20–$40). It is open daily (specials 10 AM–4PM) and offers live entertainment on Fri. and Sat. evenings. It also has a conference room and will cater parties.

Tracey's Restaurant (☎ 719-1469), 55 Cassava Garden at Hess Rd. in Peter's Rest, serves hearty, homecooked breakfasts as well as a wide variety of dishes for lunch and dinner.

Columbus Cove (☎ 778-5771) is at Salt River Marina; it serves three meals daily from 8 AM–9 PM. They also serve daily specials, have a Tues. night "homemade pasta" evening, and offer Sat. and Sun. brunch. This is a meeting place for the kayaking trip here.

Full Moon at Cane Bay (☎ 778-5669) is across from the beach of the same name. Open daily, it offers dishes such as conch fritters and mahi mahi sandwiches. Pizza and fish and lobster dinner. Sat. afternoons generally feature live entertainment and an all-you-can-eat nights. Full moon parties feature a reggae band.

The **Waves at Cane Bay** (☎ 778-1805) is open all seven nights and offers entrées ($20–$25 range) such as seafood jambalaya and shrimp calypso. You can impress your date by starting off with the roasted garlic appetizer—a whole roasted garlic bulb served with brie and French bread.

Lobster Reef Cafe (☎ 719-9094), in La Vallee E of Cane Bay, serves a wide variety of inexpensive dishes daily from 11:30

AM–9:30 PM. They also have a children's menu and daily Happy Hour.

The Carambola Beach Resort has the Saman Room (seafood gumbo and other dishes). The hotel has a "Champagne" Sun. brunch (11AM–2 PM) with "free flowing champagne" and steel band music as well as a Fri. night "Pirate's Buffet" from 7–9 PM.

Off the Wall (☎ 778-4771) is a great little beach bar with food and entertainment. Stop by on Friday nights when they have free appetizers and watch the sunset.

Other dining is listed under Fredriksted.

Christiansted Nightlife, Events, and Shopping

ENTERTAINMENT: The town's nightlife is neither bland nor extraordinarily exciting. Many restaurants and hotels have an assortment of tourist-oriented nightlife ranging from steel bands to country music to limbo dancing. **Moonraker** (rock, hip hop, and karaoke.), **Club 54** (late night reggae), and the bars and restaurants around **Kings Alloy** are places to watch for entertainment.

Dining entertainment may be offered some restaurants. Also, keep an eye out for their other events (ruin rambles, wine tastings, and gala parties). Check *This Week in St. Croix*, the *Avis*, and Friday's "Weekend" section in the *Daily News* for details.

Back up on Company St., Latin music battles the pulsating sounds of reggae pouring from competing bars as vehicles and pedestrians cast long shadows on the pavement.

OUTLYING ENTERTAINMENT: *Frederiksted's entertainment is listed under that town's section.*

Outside of town, there's plenty of live music going on during the weekend. **Two Plus Two** (☎ 773-3710), at 17 La Grande Princesse on Northside Rd just ¾ mi. past the intersection with Rte. 74, offers calypso and reggae on the weekends and disco weeknights.

Also outside of town in Kingshill, **Mid-Land** (☎ 778-0979) has a reggae scene on weekends with plenty of friendly locals. It's a place to go for the adventurous.

Gertrude's at Estate Coakley (Hess Rd. at 114 Castle Coakley) has a dance band Fri. evenings.

MOVIES: Films are shown at the **Diamond Twin Cinemas** (☎ 778-5200) and six-screen **Sunny Isle Theater** (☎ 778-5620) at Sunny Isle.

OTHER DIVERSIONS: **Horse races** are held once a month at the track near the airport. A real fashion show, it's well worth your time to check one of these out.

The **Divi Carina Bay Casino** opened in late 2000. A free shuttle service operates from Christiansted and Frederiksted. Other routes are available. Check with your hotel for current times. It attracts a largely local clientele and has live bands performing.

More casinos may be opened in the future at other locations, but they have a monopoly for now.

☞ **Drag racing** takes place around the Divi Carina and at other locales.

http://www.cdravi.com

PERFORMANCES: Cultural programs are offered at the Estate Whim Greathouse by the **Landmarks Society** (☎ 772-0598). Also check to see if anyone is performing at 600-seat **Island Center.**

The **Caribbean Community Theater** (☎ 778-1983), #18 Estate Orange Grove, performs plays such as "Play It Again Sam," at their new theater on the road between the Easterly Building and Long Reef Apartments in the Orange Grove area.

http://www.cct.vi

EVENTS: Starting before Christmas Day, the **Crucian Christmas Festival** (see sidebar) culminates on Three Kings Day, Jan. 6. Festivities include calypso contests and

 The Saint Croix Landmark Society (☎ 772-0598) hosts a series of art and craft fairs with food, dubbed **"Starving Artists Day,"** several times per year. There is a small charge, and entertainment may include mocko jumbies.

other entertainment, the crowning of kings and queens, horse racing, and children's and adult parades.

The **Valentine "Jump Up"** takes place in Christiansted in early to mid-Feb. It features live music and discounts at stores and restaurants.

The **St. Patrick's Day Parade** is held in March. Crucians love any excuse to party, and everyone is "Irish" for a day. The Lost Dog Pub generally wins the contest for the best float. One year's version featured a 15-ft.-tall volcano surrounded by palm trees along with a live band and 20 frenzied dancers.

The annual **Agricultural and Food Fair** takes place here during President's Day Weekend (usually in mid-February). It includes storytelling, crafts demonstrations, and other activities. You may learn how to weave fishnets or make pottery.

The **Sports Week Festival** is held during the beginning of April with the **70.3 Ironman Triathlon** following on the first Sunday in May. The competition begins with a 1.24-mi. swim from Protestant Cay to Christiansted's boardwalk. From there, they being a 56-mi. bike ride during which they are challenged by "The Beast," a twisting road which climbs 600 ft. in $\frac{7}{10}$ of a mi. The competition ends with a 13.1-mile race which encircles the grounds of the Buccaneer and terminates in Christiansted.

http://www.stcroixtriathalon.com

The **Emancipation Actitities** (☎ 772-1000) are held the days before the 4th of July in Buddhoe Park in Frederiksted; music, art and food are featured.

The **St. Croix Coral Reef Swim,** is held in Oct. Swimmers swim the five mi. from Buck I. to the Buccaneer Hotel's Mermaid Beach. http://www.swimrace.com

SHOPPING: Not nearly as big a commercial center as St. Thomas, St. Croix nevertheless has a wide selection of duty-free goods including famous Cruzan Rum. Locally made bracelets are a popular item with visitors and locals alike. King St. and Camagniets Gade (Company St.) are the main shopping areas. We have listed the shops in this order: Caravelle Arcade, Pan Am Pavilion, Kings Alley, Kings Wharf, Strand St., King Cross St., Queen Cross St., King St, Company St., and Gallows Bay.

☞ Be sure to check out the "Artwalk," which features openings at a number of stores and galleries. It's usually held the first Thursday of the month from Oct. through June.

CARAVELLE ARCADE SHOPPING: **Violette's Boutique** (☎ 800-544-5912 for brochure/orders) sells a variety of duty-free luxury items.

PAN AM PAVILION: **The Gold Shop** has been selling handcrafted jewelry here since 1970.

Many Hands, in business for three decades, sells original art including prints, watercolors, **ceramics,** hand painted note cards, baskets, and Christmas ornaments.

St. Croix Cutlery sells knives, binoculars, and other items.

The Purple Papaya offers sarongs, tee-shirts, liquor, and other items.

Cane Bay Dive Shop East sells snorkel and dive gear and assorted gifts.

Steele's Smokes & Sweets sells chocolates including handmade fudge as well as everything a smoker could need or want.

KINGS WHARF: **Mile Mark Boutique** sells novelty items, swimsuits, and tee shirts.

Dive St. Croix offers dive items, tee shirts, as well as rental and repairs for scuba equipment.

KINGS ALLEY WALK: **Hotheads** sells a wide variety of swimwear and accessories.

The Caribbean Bracelet Company sells a variety of bracelets.

QUEEN CROSS STREET: **Yellow House Gallery,** 3A Queen Cross St., exhibits work by local artists. (**Watch Your Step Studio** is upstairs). http://www.judithkingart.com

The Natural Jewel and **The Jewelry Factory** show a wide range of jewelry.

Soaps and Scents sell a wide range of bath and body care products.

Set next to the Caravelle Hotel, **Centipede** sells swimwear, shoes, and accessories.

STRAND STREET: At Strand and King Cross **Trends** sells jewelry, handbags, and other accessories.

Set across from the Caravelle on Strand St., the **Royal Poinciana** sells exotic perfumes, local condiments, and cosmetics.

Dive Experience, 40 Strand St., sells scuba gear and other items.

Crucian Gold sells original and highly distinctive gold jewelry.

Tesoro offers an amazing collection of crafts and other items in two shops which face each other. Owners Ed and Candy travel the Caribbean in search of wares. It has good prices on its dolls, steel drum art, and baskets.

The Royal Poinciana sells Caribbean-flavored spices, scents, art, notecards, coffee, local jams, and other items.

The Coconut Vine, 1111 Strand St., sells clothing and gifts.

KING STREET: **Tradewinds,** 53 King St. across from Government House, sells a variety of crafts and jewelry.

At 54 King Street, **Danica Art Gallery** (☎ 719-6000) is owned and run by island artist Danica David and exhibits work by him and by other island artists.
http://www.danicaartvi.com

Twin City Coffeehouse and Gallery (773-9400), 1022 King St., exhibits local artists. It also serves light food, breakfast all day, and a gourmet lunch. It has WiFi, an internet cafe, and is open Mon. to Sat, 7 AM–3 PM.

QUEEN STREET: **Taller Larjas**, at the corner of 20A Queen and Market Sts., shows island artists in a homey environment.

COMPANY STREET: The **Mitchell-Larsen Studio** offers glass art made on St. Croix.

Across the street, **Little Lizards** sells clothing, crafts, and accessories.

Owned by talented craftswoman Sonya Hough, **Sonya's**, 1 Company St., is in a townhouse across from the Steeple Building. **Christiansted Gallery** is upstairs and sells work by local artists.

At 3 Company St., **Nelthropp and Low** offers a wide variety of handmade and custom designed gold and silver jewelry as well as gold and silver sculptures and crystal.

Small Wonder, 4 Company St., sells hand painted St. Croix sweatshirts for children.

Gone Tropical, 5 Company St., sells a wonderful variety of handicrafts including crafts from Bali.

Designworks, 6 Company St., sells local art, furniture, household products, and some books.

Burnin' House Boardshop, 51 Company St., sells all manner of skateboards and surf boards.

Island Tribe of St. Croix, 55 Company St., sells batik clothing for women of all sizes. **Cache of the Day**, same address, sells cards. **D&D Contemporary Fine Art Photography**, also here,

Danish West Indian Furniture

Danish West Indian furniture is a Caribbean standout. Stylish, distinctive, and classical, this large, boldly -proportioned furniture has traditionally been crafted from tropical hardwoods. It has gained international recognition only in recent years. The furniture is neither signed nor dated, as household inventories did not distinguish between imported and locally-made furniture. Verification is something of an art form dependent upon examination of design, workmanship, and materials.

Under the reign of King Sugar, newly rich planters furnished hundreds of Crucian greathouses with this furniture. As imported furniture soon rotted, craftsmen were needed to repair it. No European furniture craftsmen were present, so it appears that freed slaves made the local furniture. They originally copied European models, then later incorporated African zoomorphic decorative motifs as well as plant and animal motifs.

In addition to mahogany, the favored wood, other indigenous woods such as sabicu, thibet, satinwood, bulletwood, purpleheart, and Spanish cedar were also employed. The most expensive piece of furniture was a four-posted bed. The stout posts support mosquito netting, and most of the early bedposts have rope-twist turnings on the upper sections and ring and flattened ball turnings or stylized pineapple carving lower down. The finely carved headboards were set with turned spindles. A caned rocking chair was another popular item as was the planter's chair.

Following emancipation in 1848, craftsmen began to move to towns. The neoclassical style remained dominant. Sadly, by the time of the US purchase in 1917, furniture production had ended.

Today, St. Croix Landmarks Society sells reproductions.
http://www.stcroixlandmarks.org

has a wonderful selection of work by various photographers.

ib Designs, Company St. near Queen Cross St., sells Whelan Massicot's jewelry including his famous "infinity bracelet." The name is short for "Island Boy."

AT GALLOWS BAY AND CHANDLER'S WHARF: **Karavan West Indies** offers a wide range of gifts and collectibles ranging from woodcarvings to beads, original jewelry, ceramics, and local artwork.

Traveller's Tree sells a variety of handicrafts and home furnishings.

The major bookstore in town (and on the island) is **Undercover Books & Gifts** (☎ 719-1567) which has a small selection.

Artist Betsy Campean (☎ 719-2246) has her studio at Gallows Bay Frame behind Caribbean Printing. Call for hours or to make an appointment.

OUT OF TOWN: The **Walsh Metal Works Gallery** (☎ 773-8169) is behind the Coca-Cola plant in Peters Rest. Devoted to promoting emerging artists of the Virgin Islands, it has openings and artist talks, and hosts an annual African Market. It's open from Mon. to Fri. from 10 AM–4 PM and by appointment.
http://www.walshmetal.com

ALCOHOL: Cruzan Rum tends to be cheaper here than on the other islands. A liqueur, Buba Touree, is locally manufactured and combines rum, lime juice, and spices.

At Sunny Isle Shopping Center, **K Mart** has around the lowest alcohol prices. However, you can also find an extensive selection in any shopping center, and stores in the towns offer a good selection, so it's not necessary to go out of your way.

Information, Services, Health, and Diving

INFORMATION: A **tourist information service** (☎ 773-0495) is located at 53a Company St. between Queen Cross St. and King Cross St.

The **National Park Service** gives out information inside the fort and has a great shop in the Old Danish Scalehouse.

The local **Chamber of Commerce** (☎ 773-1435) is in Orange Grove. They can answer your questions regarding investment, government, business, trade, and trends.

Be sure to obtain *The St. Croix Guidebook* and the accompanying map. Both are useful for shopping and dining. Other publications, such as the **St. Croix Explorer** and the **St. Croix Happenings**, are useful as well.
http://www.stcroixguidebook.com

NEWS: For the inside scoop read the *St. Croix Avis* daily. (It can also be found on St. Thomas but can be hard to find there).

The most useful of the local free publications is **St. Croix This Week** which is easy to find. (Single copies may be ordered for $2 from Box 4477, Christiansted 00822-4477). Another useful publication is the *Prestige Guide*. Although it's not much in terms of hard news, the **St. Croix Avis** offers a good deal of information on events, as does the *Daily News*.

RADIO: Stations worth listening to include WJKC Isle 95 (95 FM: urban/reggae music), WMNG Mongoose (104.9 FM; adult contemporary music, news WVIQ Sunny (99.5 FM news, Adult contemporary music), and WSTX 97X (970 AM: news, local talk shows, Caribbean and adult contemporary music),

☞ Roger W. Morgan, owner of WYAC-FM 93.5, runs the "Free Speech" program from 9–noon weekdays. Morgan is known for having instituted an unsuccessful attempt to recall four St. Croix senators after the senate voted itself a 31% pay hike. In retaliation, senators targeted by the recall wrote an official letter to the FCC requesting the agency disallow the station's transfer. The effort failed. Listen live: **http://www.paradise935fm.com**

ONLINE: Michael Dance has an informative blog about St. Croix: *http://stcroixblog.massagestcroix.com* So does artist Bonnie Luria: *http://bonnieluria.wordpress.com* The **St. Croix Source** is the best source for online news about St. Croix. **http://www.stcroixsource.com**

LAUNDRY: Tropical Cleaners and Launderers (☎ 773-3635), 16-17 King Cross. St., are open from Mon. to Sat, 7:30 AM–6 PM.

Du-N-Save (☎ 778-0336), 1-A Clifton Hill in Kingshill, is open Mon. to Fri. from 8AM to 10 PM and Sat. and Sun. from 4 AM to 10 PM.

Prince Street Laundry, across from the Pink Fancy, is a good choice in the downtown area.

HEALTH CARE: Emergency service (24 hours) is available at the **St. Croix Hospital** (Juan Luis Hospital, ☎ 778-6311, emergency 911, ☎ 778-5500), 4007 Estate Diamond, on Peppertree Rd. (Rte. 79).

The **People's Drugstore** (☎ 778-7355) is at Sunny Isle.

Golden Rock Pharmacy (☎ 773-7666) has been recently remodeled.

Located in Beeston Hill, the **Rehabilitation Center** offers physical therapy and health management.

The **Frederiksted Pharmacy** (☎ 778-8888) is at Apothecary Hall.

Caught a cold? No problem!

SERVICES: The **Tourism Office** (☎ 773-6449) is located in Government House; enter on the Queen Cross St. side. It's open Mon.–Fri. from 8 AM–5 PM; it's closed holidays.

Florence Williams Public Library King St., is open Mon. to Fri. 9–5, Sat. 10–3, and should be offering internet access for a $2 ph fee. Other access (around $10 ph) is offered by **Surf the Net** (☎ 692-7855), 1002 Strand St. in PanAm Pavilion ($16/hr.); and at **A Better Copy** (☎ 692-5303), 52 Company St.

The **Post Office** (☎ 773-3586) is located on Company St. next to the Old Market. Hours are Mon. to Fri. from 7:30 AM–4:30 PM. Islandwide, **other post offices** are located at Gallows Bay, Estate Richmond (near Christiansted on Rte. 75), Kingshill, in Sunny Isle, and in Frederiksted.

There are a number of **banks** in town including the Bank of Nova Scotia, First Bank, and First BanCorp. Bank of St. Croix is in Gallows Bay.

ATMS are found (among many other places) at the Pueblo at Golden Rock and in Villa La Reine; K-Mart in Whim; Sunshine Supermarket in Estate Cane; the First VI Bank (King St.); the Banco Popular (Golden Rock); the Bank of Nova Scotia; and at

Saving the Endangered St. Croix Ground Lizard

An effort is underway to reintroduce the St. Croix ground lizard (*Ameiva polops*), a black lizard which grows to about three to four inches and has narrow parallel stripes of brown, black and white. Alternating rings of bright blue and black adorn its tail. Fewer than a thousand St. Croix ground lizards survive. All remaining specimens reside on three offlying cays: Protestant Cay, Ruth Cay and Green Cay; Green Cay was designated a national wildlife refuge in 1977 in order to protect the species.

Once widespread along Buck Island's coast, the lizard became endangered in the 1900s following the introduction of the Indian mongoose, proceeded by an influx of dogs and cats and a boom in coastal development. These factors, which prevent the lizard from being introduced to the main island, are absent on Buck Island, but these same factors prevent National Park Service from successfully reintroducing the endangered lizards to St. Croix. Accordingly, a plan has been set in place to introduce the lizard to Buck Island, a federally protected area that, in the words of the park service, "will reduce the likelihood of the lizard's extinction." Following

the approval of the 2008 plan, the NPS and U.S. Fish and Wildlife are expected to jointly collect 60 St. Croix ground lizards from the Green Cay refuge and relocate them at Buck Island. The lizards would then be marked and released into temporary enclosures in set forest proximate to the beach and would be watched for months, a strategy it is hoped will ensure their survival and adaptation to the park.

The project is termed a "reintroduction" because the ground lizard is believed to have thrived here until the small Indian mongoose was brought in in 1912. In the following decades, ship builders cut down the majority of the island's trees, burned its vegetation and introduced non-native plants and animals.

The lizard's reintroduction was set in place by a 1984 US Fish and Wildlife Service Recovery Plan designated Buck Island Reef National Monument as a suitable location. Subsequently, the mongoose population has been eliminated, tree rats have been controlled, and a non-native plant control program has been established. The project's ultimate goal is to have the St. Croix ground lizard reclassified from threatened to endangered. ■

other locations. Frederiksted has ATMs at two places on Strand St. First BanCorp and the Scotia Bank.

Also, don't forget that you can use your ATM or credit card at a US Post Office and get up to $50 cash back.

An **American Express** office is located at Southerland Tours in Caravelle Arcade.

For video rentals, try the **Blockbuster Video** (☎ 778-0800) at Ville La Reine.

SPAS: **Tropical Therapy** (☎ 773-5333) in Gallows Bay offers acupuncture, massage, waxing, and other therapies and services.

The Denovo Spa (☎ 773-2440) is at 227 Golden Rock.

Finally, out in Frederiksted, the **SandCastle on the Beach** (☎ 643-0203) offers massage and spa services ranging from a "Citrus Body Polish" to a "Moor Mud Treatment."

YOGA AND MASSAGE: Kripalu Yoga is taught by **Tina Henle** (☎ 773-0372) who also offers massages. Other masseuses include Shelly (☎ 653-7278), Jake Sheehan (☎ 773-0566), and Aziyza (☎ 771-0399) who offers "Thai Stretch Therapy."

Buck Island Concessioners

Milemark, Inc. (☎ 773-2628) Sail or motor half-day or full day; glass bottomed boat available. King's Wharf.

"Charis" (☎ 773-9027) One six-passenger sail vessel, half or full day, available.

"Diva" (☎ 778-4675) One six-passenger sail vessel w/motor, half- or full-day, available.

Big Beard Tours (☎ 773-4482) Sail or motor, half or full day, available.

"Teroro II" (☎ 773-3161, ☏ 773-4041) One 42-ft trimaran sail w/motor, 36-ft. trimaran, Green Cay Marina, half- or full-day available.

RENT A MOM: Kat and Pat's **P. M. Services** (☎ 773-5443) offer everything from limo service to home cooked meals to babysitting. Custom packages are available. **pms@viaccess.net**

The Caribbean Dance School (☎ 778-8824), 5 Church St., holds classes in gymnastics, self defense, yoga, jazz, ballet, etc.

GYMS: The a/c **VI Family Sports & Fitness Center** (☎ 778-5144) has freeweights, basketball court, 25-m heated pool, coed sauna, and steam room, climbing wall, and classes ranging from aerobics to yoga. Short-term rates are available.

Buck Island Reef National Monument

Comprising 880 acres in total, **Buck Island Reef** is the only underwater National Monument in the US. Its center, the 180-acre Buck Island, lies two mi. off the N shore of St. Croix. Some 30,000 people visit this seductive nymphet of an island every year. Proclaimed a national monument in 1961, the island has been uninhabited from the 1750s. The story of its name is a convoluted tale which has been frequently misrepresented. The earliest evidence is a French map dating from 1667 which shows the island called Ile Vert ("Green Island"); the Dutch settlers called it Pocken-Eyland because of the Pokholz (*Lignum vitae*) trees, which gave it its greenery.

A small island to the W, now known as Green Cay, was called Ile a Cabritz (Goat Island). In the early Danish period, the names for the cay and the island were transposed in a mapmaking error. Thus, Buck Island should really be known as Green Cay and vice versa!

Today, visitors are permitted onshore only from 8 AM to 5 PM daily. Dramatically reforested since the goats' departure, the island today is as close to nature now as it's been in 150 yrs. Even though the spectacular stuff is really underwater, it's worth a visit just for the island itself. More than 40 species of birds flutter around the 62 species

Buck Island Reef National Monument

of trees, and the island is a rookery for frigate birds and pelicans. A nature trail (takes one hour) runs along the top of the mile-long island; follow the trail to the top of the island for a spectacular view of St. Croix. The beaches here (on the SW and W coasts) are superior to any on St. Croix.

Watch out for the machineel trees on the W coast and the touch-me-not which has yellow needles hidden under its green leaves. The National Park Service is currently aiming to exterminate invasive non-native plant species on the island. Of the island's 228 plant species, there are 19 invasive species, and, around ten of these threaten to overrun the native plants

UNDERWATER: Originally a simple fringing reef, a magnificent barrier reef stretches 2,000 yards along the eastern half of the island. Its effect is one of sheer fantasy. Swim past the elkhorn coral that marks the entrance to the reef and follow the markers on the bottom to find your way along the 30-min. underwater trail. While underwater, check out the rainbow gathering of fish, including the queen angelfish, the foureye butterflyfish, the smooth trunkfish, and the French and blue angelfish. Others include the yellowtail, spadefish, red snapper, tilefish, trumpetfish, and several varieties of parrotfish. Fish here are so naive and trusting that they'll eat right out of your hand.

While you're investigating the downstairs branch of this living natural history museum, note the primitive multicellular animals. Most primitive of all are the sponges, which come in all shapes and sizes. A dinosaurian prototype of the starfish, the flexible, multi-

armed crinoid anchors itself to crevices with its central, white, root-like pedestal.

One of many reef organisms capable of producing sounds underwater, the spotted drum (*Equetus punctatus*) produces a continuous discordant and eerie symphony of snaps, pops, grunts and scraping noises.

GETTING HERE: Access is limited to private and chartered boats. Concessioners are licensed by the NPS and must meet strict standards. Expect to pay at least $50 for the 5.5-mi. sail. (A full-day sail is more). A variety of all shapes and sizes of boats (including catamarans, yachts, native sloops, trimarans and glass-bottomed boats) leave from Christiansted's King's Wharf and Green Cay Marina.

One of the best operators is **Mile-Mark Charters** (☎ 773-BOAT) which has both sail and motorboat trips from $35 and up. Don't worry if you have never snorkeled before or even if you can't swim. They've handled people from Nebraska who've never even seen the sea before! If you're unsure of your abilities just wear a flotation cushion and hold on to the life preserver towed by the guide.

A popular boat is Capt. Heinz's *Teroro II* (☎ 773-3161/4041), a 42-ft. trimaran.

Big Beard (☎ 773-4482) is also well-equipped and has a good reputation.
http://www.bigbeards.com
info@BigBeards.com

NOTE: When planning your trip, consider your priorities. For example, do you wish to sail or motor, do you want a glass bottomed boat or not, and how long do you want to spend on the island? All tours stop at the underwater nature trail for around 45 min. The differences between the trips lie in other particulars. You should ask if the boat will dock at Buck Island or merely anchor offshore. If you want to hike the nature trail, allow for an hour ashore.

 Tours to Buck Island may not include water, so buy your own supply in advance.

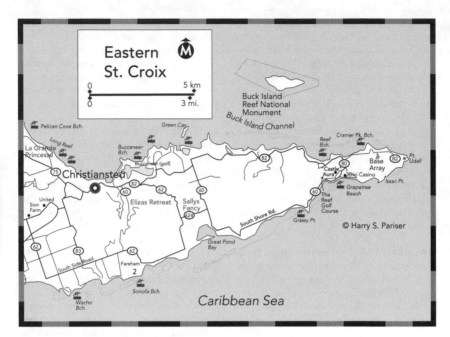

PRACTICALITIES: If you plan on snorkeling, hiking, fishing or picnicking, pack appropriately. Although there is a well-equipped picnic area, no food is available on the island, so bring your own. Beware of sunburn, cuts from coral, spiny sea urchins, jellyfish, fire coral. Never reach into a dark hole, lest you be savaged by a moray eel. White floats are placed around the trail area in case you need to rest. Maneuver your boat slowly through park waters. For further information contact Superintendent, Christiansted National Historic Site (☎ 773-1460), Box 160, Christiansted, St. Croix, VI 00820. http://www.nps.gov/buis

Heading East From Christiansted

The farther east you go, the fewer people you find and the drier the vegetation becomes. Take Hospital St. (Rte. 82) E out of Christiansted. Once the island's main

industrial port during the 1960s, **Gallows Bay** is now part of the town's tourist area.

Solitude Gas Station, informally known as Smokey's, the last gas station out this way, is at Solitude. Smokey's wife Camella operates a *roti* stand here. People will drive all over the island to eat here, and some folks will even come all the way out here to pick up a *roti* before going to the airport.

Buccaneer Hotel ($6 pp for use of beach facilities) lies to the E past Altona Lagoon. Beaches in this area have been given names by the hotel like "Mermaid," "Whistle," and "Grotto." Farther on is **Shoy's Beach** or **Punnett's Bay** where leatherback, hawksbill, and green sea turtles nest. Just ahead of this is the turnoff for **Green Cay Marina** (☎ 773-1453, ✆ 773-9651), Estate Southgate, a full-service yacht harbor.

The 20-acre **Green Cay**—a National Wildlife Refuge for the St. Croix ground lizard (otherwise eradicated by the mongoose) and a rookery for herons and pelicans—lies just offshore.

The **Southgate Pond Nature Preserve**, established in 2000, has some 96 species including 26 which are considered threatened or endangered in the USVI.

The story is that a visiting birdwatcher, plagued with a flat tire, happened upon the property, discovered that it was available and due for development, and plopped down the 827,697 clams necessary to preserve the land. He or she remains anonymous by choice, but the action shows that the mega-wealthy can use their money to make a difference when they choose! Nesting sea turtles and endangered birds will be eternally grateful.

The 100-acre tract extends from Green Cay Marina to Chenay Bay Beach Resort and from the eastern third of the salt pond E and from the beach to East End Rd.

On the left hand side coming from town, **Southgate Farms** (☎ 514-4873) is set right across from Cheeseburgers In Paradise. It's open Wed. (3–6 PM) and also on Sat. (9–noon). Farmer/local artist Luca Gasperi sells fresh organic vegetables, herbs, salad greens, baked goods, and paintings.

☞ For a local experience, you can visit Luca's studio by appointment. His work ranges from tranquil watercolors to huge acrylics to sculptures using found objects. His works invariably deal with the themes of environmental conservation and the preservation of sustainable agriculture. http://www.lucagasperi.com

Next site on down the main drag (East End Road) is **Chenay Bay Beach Resort** with its white sand beach. Miss Bea Road leads to normally deserted **Prune Beach.**

Hog Bay's beach lies near Coakley Bay Beach condominium.

Solitude Valley Road leads to **Solitude Country Store** near the ruins of Estate Solitude. The secluded coves of Coakley, Solitude, and Yellowcliff are along this stretch.

Duggan's Reef, a restaurant and beach area, lies just past Teague Bay. The condos here resemble nothing so much as a set of gigantic personal computers in search of a corporate office.

Along this stretch, you'll see a structure which appears to be a castle. No, you're not imagining things. The structure belongs to Nadia Farber, widow of Long Island industrialist Sid Farber. Her **Castle Aura** is an imposing stucco and marble structure of Moorish design. The Bulgarian-born countess is said to wear only caftans with color-coordinated turbans. She uses a white lace parasol to shield the heat and is an enchanting conversationalist. At one point she planned on establishing Community Aura, a hillside development whose charm would enhance that afforded St. Croix by her castle. The plan did not materialize. She has her name on the Contessa Nadia Farber Emergency Department at the John T. Mather Memorial Hospital, Port Jefferson, Long Island, where she also resides, and she has been featured on the TV program "Lifestyles of the Rich and Famous."

Smuggler's Cove has a white sand beach and picnic area.

Next is **Cramer Park** which has a campground (no fresh water and the flush toilets are frequently out of order), and a coral sand beach. The only shade here is provided by seagrape trees and palms.

The remainder of the island's eastern portion—extending from here 1.5 mi. to Point Udall—is still relatively pristine. A path heading E traverses hilly terrain covered with cacti-some of them reaching the height of trees. You may also ascend to the top of 672-ft. **Sugar Loaf Hill,** but permission from the property owner is required. You can follow other paths to white sand beaches whose waters provide good snorkeling. **Boiler Bay** (named for the large algae-covered rocks lying offshore) is next.

The other beaches in this area (like beautiful East End Bay, Issacs Bay, and Jacks Bay) are best reached on foot. To reach **Issacs Bay** and **Jacks Bay** you should park on the righthand side of the road (going towards Point Udall) and walk around ten minutes or so down to the beach. As elsewhere, be sure to leave nothing of value in your car. Leaving it unlocked (with an alarm on and a steering-wheel "club," if available) is preferable. You should have these gorgeous beaches virtually to yourselves on a weekday.

Point Udall is said to be the easternmost point in the United States. (It's not; that distinction belongs to Wake I., a US military-occupied possession in the South Pacific). The reason to come to this 226-ft. point is the view. A nifty monument with a brass plaque and flagpoles now makes the spot official. On a clear day, you may see as far as Saba, 90 mi. to the east. A beautiful new road leads down to the point. From here, hike down to the sea along the paths. Exercise care. To reach the S coast, it's necessary to reconnoiter to Rte. 60 (Southshore or Southside Road).

Set less than a mi. from Point Udall, the 82-ft., 260-ton **radio telescope** (☎ 773-4448) is used to explore quasars, pulsars, radio galaxies, molecular clouds, galactic nuclei, black holes, and other unexplored spots in the cosmos. The National Science Foundation funded the $5 million construction cost. The telescope is part of a chain of ten identical radio receivers known as the Very Large Baseline Array which stretch from the Virgin Islands to Hawaii. It is the easternmost of all the receivers, and it is also the lowest in altitude; most are on mountaintops. You can view a picture of the Milky Way as recorded at 4.25 gigahertz.

If you are interested in radio astronomy, it's well worthwhile to call to reserve a tour, or even to stop by when you are in the neighborhood. Of particular note is the hydrogen laser atomic clock which tells time to with an accuracy of one second per million years. This correlates the data with the other computers in the array. **http://www.nrao.edu**

St Croix East End Marine Park (STXEEMP, ☎ 773-3367), the Virgin Islands' first territorial marine park, encompasses an approximately 60 sq. mi. area. This "shoreline" park, extends for some 17 mi and runs from the high-tide line to the three-mi. limit. It has four different types of managed areas within its boundaries: recreation management areas (2.8%), no-take areas (8.6%), open-fishing areas (81.6%), and a turtle preserve (7%). It offers wonderful free public interpretive tours, some of which include snorkeling. Call or check the top-notch website for the schedule. The headquarters for the park are at Canp Arawak. **http://www.stxeastendmarinepark.org**

At **Grapetree Bay** stands the remains of the Hurricane Hugo-devastated Grapetree Bay Hotel and what appears to be a fine white sand beach. In fact the sand was dredged from Turner Hole to the west. Despite the construction of an expensive barrier, currents periodically sweep the beach naked of sand-revealing the beach's true nature! A trail from near the hotel ruins leads to **Jacks Bay** and its white and pink sand beach. Climb Pentheney, the hill behind Grapetree, for the view. note: a new hotel is scheduled to be built here.

On a spit extending into the ocean, **Grassy Point** has one of the island's most scenic views. Surf pounds onto the rocks.

Straight ahead to the W, **Rod (or Red) Bay** has good snorkeling but no beach.

Amidst the ruins of Estate Great Pond stands **Camp Arawak,** a campsite (see "camping" under "accommodations") and a grassy beach. The headquarters for the East End Marine Park are also here. **Great Pond Bay** itself has fantastic birdwatching and a nature trail.

Originally named after its developer-owner Paul Golden, the Wyndham St. Croix Golf Resort and Casino may be slated for construction here. It will include a golf course, casino, conference room, and 605 hotel rooms. There was considerable community opposition to the rezoning of this area by community activists including newspaper columnist Olasee Davis. Large areas of concreted turf will affect the hydrology of the Great Pond and may result in increased erosion and runoff which would damage coral reefs, as the second-longest barrier reef in the Caribbean lies offshore. Fertilizers used on the golf course might also result in runoff which might kill reefs. The US Dept. of Fish and Wildlife maintains that lighting from the resort could endanger sea turtle nesting on the beach and that federally-listed bird species, such as the Least Tern, might flee the pond's W end as a result of construction noise. In 2004 the Department of Planning and Natural Resources' Coastal Zone Management Division reported that the plans fail to meet many required environmental standards mandated under the Virgin Islands Coastal Zone Management Act.

To return to Christiansted from this point, you can take Rte. 60 N and Rte. 82 (East End Rd.) across or you can continue along Rte. 624 and then take Rte. 62 N which merges with Rte. 624.

Further along Rte. 62, Estate Foreham's ruins contain the Boy Scout Camp (see "camping" under "accommodations"); the entrance to the Great Pond nature trail is nearby.

Machenil Bay, along the S coast heading W, has a fine white sand beach.

From **Ferrall (or Fisherman's) Point** nearby one can hike along to Halfpenny Bay, Spring Bay, and Foreham Bay.

Southside Road terminates to the W at **Cane Garden Bay,** an interesting hiking and birdwatching area with salt ponds and salt flats. Heading along the S coast, you may see reddish-brown grazing Senepol cattle and dairy cattle.

Along The Northwest Coast

Palm fringed **Little Princesse Beach** is off Rte. 75 past Golden Rock. The 25-acre **Little Princesse Estate** (☎ 773-5575), 52 Estate Little Princesse, is administered by the Nature Conservancy. The estate was first owned by Frederick Moth who became the first governor of the US Virgin Islands. Although not spectacular, this is a fun place to visit. It's fun to explore the grounds and view the sugar mill ruins. If you're fortunate, Assistant Land Steward Richard Gideon will show you around the grounds. He gives a great tour. On the trails, you'll see ironwood, a giant termite mound, remains of the original greathouse and overseer's house, and a solar power plant. You'll likely be accompanied by the property's three dogs: Princess, Poppy, and Piglet. Plans are to plant 1,200 trees using 16 native-tree species here. The invasive species here are also to be eliminated. **http://www.tnc.org**

Further on are the ruins of **Estate La Grande Princesse** with Pelican Cove's white sand beach (where the Palms Resort, one of the island's premier properties, is located).

Rte. 751 passes Estate St. John on to the so called "French Ruins" or "Maltese Ruins" of **Estate Judith's Fancy** which are now part of a private home.

ST. CROIX

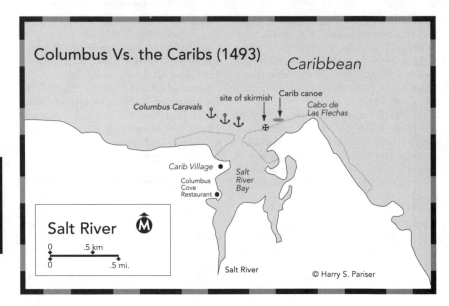

Columbus Vs. the Caribs (1493)

Caribbean

site of skirmish
Carib canoe
Columbus Caravals
Cabo de
Las Flechas

Carib Village
Columbus
Cove
Restaurant
Salt
River
Bay

Salt River

0   .5 km

0   .5 mi.

Salt River

© Harry S. Pariser

The road ends at **Salt River Bay** (good surfing and snorkeling). Offshore lies the wreck of the freighter *Cumulus*, which went aground on the reef in October 1977 with a cargo of stolen cars bound for down-island. Back on Rte. 80 lies **Sugar Bay**, with its mangroves and swamp ferns.

Salt River National Historical Park and Ecological Preserve

Salt River is is the principal sight on this coast. It is thought (judging from the descriptions in the log entries) that some of Columbus's men landed here. The Cape of Arrows here was supposedly named by him after crew members attacked the Caribs, who retaliated. The area was the administrative center during both the English and French rule in the mid-1600s.

In 1965, the five-acre landing site was purchased by the VI Government and placed in the National Register. In 1978 it was designated a "Significant Natural Area" and an "Area of Preservation and Restoration" under the VI Coastal Zone Management Act.

In 1979, a 690-acre site, including the entire shoreline but excluding the Cape of the Arrows, was made a Natural Landmark; this area included the major mangrove stands in Sugar and Triton Bays.

Made a National Historical Park and Ecological Preserve in 1992, Salt River may also become a World Heritage Site and a National Marine Sanctuary. A 288-room luxury hotel, 300 condos, and a 157-boat marina were once slated for construction here. The permit was renewed in 1993, but a judge declared the extension of the coastal zone management permit to be invalid in 1994, thus saving the reserve. Today, the ruins of a hotel—a different one built during the mid-1960s—serve as a reminder of the folly of unbridled development.

SIGHTS: The parking area's asphalt covers the island's premiere archaeological site, which dates from 350 AD —one of the few

Indian ball courts found in the Caribbean. The petroglyph-incised stones were carted off to a Copenhagen museum in 1923. Just keep in mind when you get out of your car that you are standing on sacred ground. A **Visitor's Center** opened in 2004. Hike W along the beach to find a tidal pool.

Set on the estuary's SE end at Triton Bay, a 12-acre mangrove reserve is administered by the NPS. Donated by the Nature Conservancy, it is one of the few remaining lagoons. (Krause Lagoon on the S coast was dredged out in order to facilitate the ports for the oil refinery). Including 45 acres of white and black mangroves fringed by red mangroves, this area supports the highest diversity of birdlife known in the VI.

These mangrove forests provide a critical habitat for the North American land birds who migrate and winter here. Of the 108 bird species, 17 are locally endangered and three (the brown pelican, roseate tern, and peregrine falcon) are federally endangered.

There are also seagrass beds offshore and a giant wild fern garden is along the coast; the endangered least tern nests on a peninsula off the bay's E shore.

ACCOMMODATION: Villa Greenleaf (☎ 719-1958, ✆ 772-5425, 888-282-1001) is the sister establishment of a Maine B&B. The five suites run around $305 and up; rental car, golf, and dive packages are offered. It is set on Rte. 79 (off Rte. 75 in Montpelier). Their beautiful website has pics of the rooms alog with full information.
http://www.villagreenleaf.com
info@villagreenleaf.com

ACTIVITIES: Salt River Dropoff is an excellent dive site (see "dive sites"), and the Salt River Marina, on the bay's W side, is the home of **Anchor** (☎ 778-1522), a dive operator who also offers marine excursions into the mangroves.

Caribbean Adventure Tours (☎ 778-1522, 800-532-3483) offers guided kayaking trips.
http://www.stcroixkayak.com
info@stcroixkayak.com

FROM SALT RIVER TO THE WEST. From **Michael's Hill**, Estate Clairmont Road just off from its junction with North Shore Road (Rte. 80), commands an impressive view. **Estate Clairmont** is a private home. Rte. 73 leads S to the ruins of Estate Belvedere, Estate Lebanon, Estate Little Fountain, Estate Mon Bijou, and (on Rte. 707) the ruins of Estate Slob and Estate Fredensborg.

Cane Bay is one of the island's top dive sites, and **Cane Bay Beach Bar** here is a good place to take a break. **Cane Bay Club** offers digs here.

Heading W from the junction of Rte. 80 with Rte. 69, a road leads on to **Davis Beach.** Davis is small but attractive.

Closed for years after Hugo, the former Rockresort of **Carambola** is now the **Carambola Beach Resort** and is famous for its golf course (a couple of mi. away and on the other side of the ridge).

A 360-degree panorama of the island can be had from a hill NW of secluded **Bodkins Mill,** accessible on foot from Scenic Road.

A rough hike leads to **Annaly Bay** with its tidepools. [**Tan Tan Tours** (☎ 773-7041, cell: 473-6446) do a great trip here]. Rte. 78, Scenic Road West, continues on along a rough road to the lighthouse at **Ham's Bluff.** A steep, overgrown path leads along **Furnel Ridge** to the N shore.

The **Bottle Garden** [in Grove Place on the E end of Rte. 76 (Mahogany Rd.)] is a remarkable collection of different bottles and cans in the company of totem-like plastic dolls, toys, and other artifacts. A radio plays in the background.

Rte. 78 terminates in Hams Bay. S of the junction of Rte. 78 with Rte. 58 lies the **"Rain Forest"** (see below) which is really a secondary tropical forest. Routes 765, 763, and 75 traverse it. Rte. 58 leads to US Navy-constructed concrete **Creque Dam**. The **Mt. Victory** ruins, site of the wonderful **Mt. Victory Camp** (see Frederiksted's "accommodations section"), are on the way to it.

Along Rte. 63 heading N lie **Sprat Hall** (a B&B) and then **Butler Bay**, a nature preserve and an excellent birding spot, which has a small beach and an inland (sometimes waterless) waterfall. The ruins here are worth visiting .

A bit further on lies the so-called **Monks Baths** or Malta Baths whose construction local legend attributes to the Knights of Malta during their occupation (1653–1665) of the island. It is more likely that they are of natural origin.

Enroute To Frederiksted

Queen Mary Highway (Centerline Road) extends the entire way from Christiansted. Comparatively inexpensive shared taxis (around $2.50, $3 after 6 PM) run this route from early morning until around 9 PM. To catch one you should stand by the corner of the FirstBank in Christiansted.

ISLAND CENTER: Aptly located in the center of the island off Queen Mary Highway (Centerline Rd.) a half mile N of Sunny Isle Shopping Center, **Island Center** (☎ 778-5271), a ten-acre complex, contains

Things looked quite different out on the island during the era when King Sugar ruled. This photo dates from the 1890s.

> Contact the **St. Croix Landmarks Society** (☎ 772-0598) to see if they are holding one of their candlelight concerts which, as one might expect, feature musicians playing by candlelight. You can also ask about tours of the island's ruins which happen from time to time. Whim Greathouse hosts the society's annual antique auction which takes place each March.

a 1,100-seat amphitheater (600 seats under a canopy and 500 in the open) which showcases cultural events. You might be able to see the Caribbean Dance Company, the African American Dance Ensemble, or the Michigan Banjos here.

SUNNY ISLE SHOPPING CENTER: An oasis of American mall culture, the Sunny Isle Shopping Center, at the junction with Rte. 66, has mainstays such as K Mart, Foot Locker, Wendy's, and the like. Note the strange looking sausage trees which flower during the summer. **United Shopping Plaza** is on Queen Mary Hwy. (Centerline Rd.) about a mile to the east.

ST. GEORGE VILLAGE BOTANICAL GARDEN: The island's premier gardens (☎ 692-2874) are located off Centerline Rd. about four mi. W of Frederiksted. Enter through the stone gates along a road flanked on either side by rows of royal palms, the trees grown by Hebraic kings in the Garden of Babylon.

Originally a 150-acre estate during the 18th–19th C, this garden contains the ruins of a great house, rum factory, lime kiln, baker's and blacksmith's shops, and a stone dam. You'll find a giant *coco de mer* (sea coconut) by the entrance to the Great Hall, and there a few trees of African origin stand within the garden.

The garden had its beginnings as the clean up project of a local garden club in 1972.

Known to have archaeological remains since the 1920s, it was discovered to be the site of the island's largest Arawak village (inhabited from 100–900 AD) in 1976. After the sugar production ceased in 1919, the area became a cattle ranch until the 1950s. Currently privately funded and managed by staff rather than volunteers, the 16-acre garden complex has a library (open on Thurs. or by special request) and a variety of ongoing projects, including collecting samples of the plants that Spanish explorer Gonzalo Fernández de Oviedo presented to Queen Isabella in 1536. It is now a Center for Plant Conservation, one of only 25 in the entire US.

Be sure to visit the garden with its pre-Columbian crops (maize, cassava and sweet potatoes) and the old cemetery. The flowers and foliage here are truly wonderful. Note the opuntia and the aloe on which kids have carved their names. The rainforest area (which provides nice but short hiking) is the only area irrigated. In late afternoon, it must be one of the most peaceful tourist spots in the Caribbean.

Concerts are occasionally held here on Sundays. The annual **Quadrille Ball** is also held here. This is also a great place to have a wedding catered.

The gardens are open daily from 9 AM–5 PM except Christmas; $8 admission; $6 for seniors; $1 for children.
http://www.sgvbg.com

ESTATE WHIM PLANTATION MUSEUM: Located two mi. off Centerline Rd. and on Rt. 70 (Queen Mary's Highway) near Frederiksted, this large sugar estate com-

> Best time to visit **St. George** (unless you have allergies) is in February when many plants are in bloom. Be sure to pick up the walking tour guide.

plex (☎ 772-0598) was originally known as St. John's Rest. Restored by the St. Croix Landmarks Society, it was owned by an eccentric Dane named Christopher MacEvoy, Jr.

The comparatively small one-story European-design estate house is oval-shaped with a large number of windows. Built around 1794, its yard-thick walls are made of cut stone and coral held together with lime-and-molasses mortar. A moat surrounds the building; it is dry and was intended to keep the building cool as well as to supply light to the basement storehouse.

Antiques (both Crucian and imported) fill its interiors. Note the planter's chair with its footrack and bootjack. A tired owner would have slaves pull the boots from his swollen feet. To the rear, the cook house and attached museum contain displays of sugar production artifacts, a pot-still for making rum, engravings, weapons, and the tomb-stone of Anna Heegard, the famous mistress of Governor-General von Scholten.

Reconstructed with numbered blocks brought from Nevis, the windmill fairly represents the ones in use during the island's sugar heyday.

Displays include the ruins of the sugar processing factory, the Scottish steam engine, and the watchhouse. There's also a gift shop which has a good selection of books, prints, watercolors, and crafts. (Whim now even has its own line of furniture).

Hours are subject to change, but it's generally open Mon. to Sat. from 10 AM–4 PM; $10 admission with guided tour (every half-hour); $4 for children 5–12; free for children under 6. (Grounds-only admission is $5 for adults).

http://www.stcroixlandmarks.com
landmark@viaccess.net

A restored great house, Whim is the USVI's premier plantation-era architectural landmark.

OTHERS FROM WEST TO EAST: The **USDA Experimental Forest** (mahogany) lies off Rte. 708 to the N of Queen Mary Highway (Centerline Rd.).

Estate Greathouse, just past the junction of Rte. 708 with Queen Mary Highway, contains a-monument (placed here 80 years ago by a biographer) to "Rachel Fauwett Levine," Alexander Hamilton's mother. Hamilton himself lived here from age 10 to 18, over 200 years ago. His mother's bones lie at some unknown spot on the estate. Her real name, despite what is engraved, was Rachel Lawcett Lavien. This greathouse is under consideration to be added to the National Park Service; however, it is not certain whether Hamilton ever lived here.

The **other monument** here is to Dutch sailors who died during a yellow fever epidemic in 1886 when the great house had the unenviable function of serving as an isolation ward. Nearby is an antique Danish bell. (The greathouse itself is private property and off limits).

The **Lawaetz Family Museum** (☎ 772-1539; $10 admission, $4 children, 6–12; $5, senior and students) combines a museum with a walking trail in Estate Little La Grange. This self-guided trail, which extends through the garden and orchards, introduces you to local vegetation. The museum will introduce you to turn-of-the-century Danish life. The home has been owned by the Lawaetz family since 1896, and they (or other docents) regularly guide visitors around. Tours (reservations recommended) are held every half-hr. from 10 AM–4 PM. It's open from Tues., Thurs. and Sat. from 10 AM–4 PM during the winter season and

usually Tues., Thurs. and Sat. from 10 AM–3 PM, during the summer season. It's closed on major holidays.

Farmer Carl Lawaetz raised crops and cattle on Estate Little La Grange's 400 acres. The only furnishings remaining from when the home was purchased is the carved and painted wooden Indian, which—bow and arrow poised—still stands guard over a doorway. Wife Marie arrived in 1902. Her paintings, photographs, and sewing are on display in the home. All seven Lawaetz children were born in the four-post mahogany bed in the nearby master bedroom, and Carl died here in 1945 and Marie in 1964.

The home/museum is a five min. drive from Frederiksted. Head N along the seashore on Rte. 63, turn R on Rte. 76 (Mahogany Rd.) and then drive 1.5 mi. to the museum which will be on the R side of Rte. 76. Watch for the sign.
http://www.gotostcroix.com/lawaetz landmark@viaccess.net

The cleared ruins of **Estate Spanish Town** lie inside the grounds of the fomer VIALCO aluminum refinery.

Villa La Reine Shopping Center (and Kingshill Post Office) are on Rte. 75 heading N near its junction with Centerline.

☞ **Farmer's Market** operates every Sat from 6 AM on to early afternoon right across the road from the Villa La Reine Shopping center. Many farmers sell fruits

Western St. Croix. Sandy Point National Wildlife Refuge is in the southwestern corner of the island.

Residents love **Armstrong's Ice Cream**, and it makes a great pit stop. It is on Centerline Rd. near Frederiksted.

Giant Trees of St. Croix

Although many contemporary Virgin Islanders do not realize it, they have long had a relationship with large trees, one which predates their ancestors passage from the slave ships from Africa. The largest tree in the USVI is the 300-year-old baobab at Eatate Grove Place which stands 53-ft. high and has a circumference of 55 ft. During the 1878 plantation uprising, it served as a meeting point for rebels. The island's fledgling labor movement met here in the early 20th C. Labor activist David Hamilton Jackson (1848–1946) gave many of his speeches here. Legend has it that people sought shelter from hurricanes in the tree's hollow center and women are reputed to have given birth there.

The baobab is an African native, and the tamarind, another African native, provides the only important spice of African origin. Dubbed "The Emperor" by local Rastas, the large tamarind at Estate Bethlehem is some 300 years old. A larger one is at Whim Great House. Jumbies (spirits) are believed to assemble beneath the tamarind. (Information from Prof. Robert Nichols, author of *Remarkable Big Trees in the U.S. Virgin Islands, An Eco-Heritage Guide to Jumbie Trees and Other Trees of Cultural Interest*.). ∎

and vegetables. Sample whatever happens to be in season. Get here early. Many vendors also sell produce along Centerline Rd. (Rt 70/Queen Mary Highway).

The **La Reine Chicken Shack** (☎ 778-5717), **Estate La Reine**, is a good place to sample local dishes and ambience.

Fredensborg Pond, the island's largest freshwater marsh, stands near the old water mill of Estate Fredensborg, off Rte. 707 and near the **Bethlehem Old Works**. The pond is not in a safe area to visit. The Old Works are being restored by Farmers in Action.

On Centerline Road near the College of the Virgin Islands, **The VI Government Agricultural Station** (open Mon. to Fri., 8AM–5 PM) has experimental hybrid crops like mangoes, bananas, etc. The annual **Agricultural and Food Fair** takes place here on President's Day in mid-February. It includes storytelling, crafts demonstrations, and other activities. Near the station lie the ruins of **Estate Lower Love.**

Near the **airport** stand a **miniature mill** and stone house of contemporary construction.

The Cruzan Rum Distillery (☎ 692-2280), located S off of Rte. 64 (West Airport Rd.) is constructed amidst the ruins of Estate Diamond, offers tours ($4) of its facilities It's open Mon. to Fri. from 9 AM–11:30 PM and 1–4:15 PM. Closed on holidays.

The factory features a sugar mill which has been converted to a water cistern. The seven flags of St. Croix fly in front. Approximately 95% of its product is shipped to New York, where it is bottled. Cruzan rum is made more traditionally than other rum and is one of the island's great shopping values. (Some varieties are aged for up to 12 years). The tour shows you the processing process with vast vats churning dark liquids around and warehouses holding casks. It first became a distillery in 1934 and, as cane production on the island is a thing of the past, it now uses molasses from El Salvador and the Dominican Republic. An informative video shown in the showroom, starts your tour.

Dating from the last century, the ruins of **Estate Hogensborg** stand to the N of Queen Mary Hwy. about a mile before Whim Greathouse. It's not the safest area.

West End Saltpond (great birdwatching) and **Sandy Point National Wildlife Refuge,** a fine three-mile stretch of sand, lie along a bumpy road off Rte. 661 to the S. Although there's little in the way of snorkeling, visibility is superb, and the beach is unfrequented. If you want to explore, birdwatch, and get away from the crowds, this is definitely the place.

Sandy Point is the most important location in the US for regular nesting of the leatherback sea turtle. The turtle, which measures over six ft. long and sometimes weighs more than 1,000 pounds, is the largest living turtle species. In 1984, the US Fish and Wildlife Service purchased the 398 acres in order to protect the sea turtles. The beach has been continually monitored since 1981, and nesting females are logged and tagged. Poachers are being deterred, and nests facing destruction by natural beach erosion are being relocated. A BBC documentary on the leatherback turtle was filmed here in 1996.

Although they are geared towards the education of locals, visitors (who are members of the St. Croix Environmental Association) may join **tours** here (☎ 773-1989). Earthwatch runs expeditions to this beach.

Nesting turtles clamber ashore (Feb. through July) in the dead of night. Each mother digs a large pit and deposits a cache of 80 golf-ball-sized eggs, which she then buries. If you go to see these turtles, don't disturb them before they've settled, or they'll haul themselves right back into the sea again. (Green and hawksbill turtles also nest here). Least terns also nest here, and brown peli-

cans, Caribbean martins, American oyster-catchers, and white-tailed tropicbirds may also be seen. The beach is open only on Sat. and Sun. from 10 AM–4 PM and is generally closed from Mother's Day though Labor Day (leatherback nesting season).

At West End Saltpond, you can also see birds including black-necked stilts, herons, bananaquits, black-faced grassquits, and white-crowned pigeons. Brown pelicans, terns, and white-cheeked pintails also nest here. The beach plays host to a tall orchid (in hues of brown, lavender, and ochre) — which is known locally as the Sandy Point orchid, although it is indigenous to the entire Caribbean.

Closed entirely during some parts of the year, and now **only open on weekends**, the reserve closes at 7 PM, and visitors are urged to leave nothing of value in their locked cars. Put the alarm on and use a "club" if available. As they may puncture eggs, items such as beach umbrellas and volleyball nets are prohibited on the beach. Fires are also forbidden, as are dogs and horses.

Frederiksted

Located on the W coast of the island, **Frederiksted** has great views and an impressive colonial legacy. Its tree-lined streets still exhibit a wide variety of colo-

Frederiksted in 1770

ST. CROIX

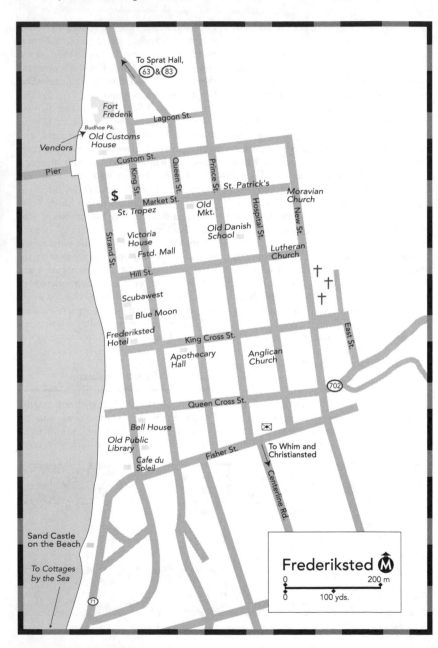

To Sprat Hall,
63 & 83

Fort
Frederik

Lagoon St.

Budhoe Pk.
Old Customs
House

Vendors

Pier

Custom St.

King St.

Queen St.

Prince St.

St. Patrick's

Moravian
Church

New St.

$

Market St.

St. Tropez

Old
Mkt.

Hospital St.

Lutheran
Church

Strand St.

Victoria
House

Fstd. Mall

Old Danish
School

Hill St.

Scubawest

Blue Moon

Frederiksted
Hotel

King Cross St.

East St.

Apothecary
Hall

Anglican
Church

702

Queen Cross St.

Bell House

Old Public
Library

Cafe du
Soleil

Fisher St.

To Whim and
Christiansted

Centerline Rd.

Sand Castle
on the Beach

To Cottages
by the Sea

71

Frederiksted M

0   200 m

0   100 yds.

nial architecture. Frederiksted is so quiet and peaceful that it's difficult to believe this town ever burned during riots (in 1878).

In the past, cruise ship passengers have seen most of this town only in their peripheral vision as they were speedily bused to Christiansted. These days they tend to linger longer.

The rebuilding of its cruise ship pier, now known as the **Ann E. Abramson Pier**, has brought changes to the town, and it's well worth a walk around. It has a highly relaxed atmosphere in comparison with Charlotte Amalie, the US Virgin Island's other cruise ship stop. At present, however, very few cruise ships are visiting.

HISTORY: Frederiksted was established on October 19, 1751 and named for King Frederik V. Danish surveyor Jens M. Beck designed its plan: two areas (each four blocks long by three blocks long) were to face each other across a lagoon. The settlement grew slowly. There were exactly two houses in 1755 and still only 314 residents by 1766.

The same restrictive building codes were applied here as in Christiansted with similarly fortunate consequences for today's visitor. Some of the original shoreline warehouses in town were destroyed by the 1867 tidal wave or the fire (caused by labor riots) of Oct. 1–2, 1878, in which the commercial part of the town burned to a crisp. The majority of the remarkable restorations and reconstructions date from after this era, a period when the Victorian gingerbread style prevailed.

Frederiksted Sights

There's quite a bit to see around town. But much of it is just savoring the atmosphere. Go out for an early morning or evening stroll and take things in. Catch the pier at sunset, go out snorkeling, horseback riding, or diving.

FORT FREDERIK: Originally built to discourage smuggling, Fort Frederik was begun in 1752. and completed in 1760, this quiet but imposing structure has played an important role in the island's history. From here, the flag of the new American republic was saluted for the first time by a foreign power in 1776.

According to local legend, an American brigantine was in port here when independence was declared. When a homemade Stars and Stripes was hoisted, the fort, ignoring the rules of neutrality, returned the cannon fire. The British and Danish archives tell a different tale. They relate that the ship was already flying American colors and the ship fired a salute. The fort responded in kind which was the custom. In any event, this was the first salute to an American ship. Here, also on July 3, 1848, Governor General von Scholten read the proclamation emancipating the slaves. Restored in 1976, the fort houses a museum (open Mon. to Fri. 8:30 AM–4:30 PM; $3 admission).

THE OSCAR HENRY CUSTOMS HOUSE: Located S of the fort, this late 18th C structure was badly damaged by 1989's Hurricane Hugo but has been fully repaired and now houses the tourist office. The bronze bust of General Buddhoe, hero of the emancipation, stands out front.

VICTORIA HOUSE: Located a block or two S of the Customs House, this private home with elaborate gingerbread, a local landmark, is an excellent example of Victorian architecture. Most of the house was consumed in the flames of 1878 and rebuilt thereafter.

BELL HOUSE (OLD FREDERIKSTED PUBLIC LIBRARY): Stands two blocks farther S at Queen Cross St. Bell House was once owned by a man named Bell who, appropriately enough, decorated the stairs with those charming chiming objects. It currently houses the Athalie Petersen Public Library.

OLD DANISH SCHOOL: This is about 1¼ blocks away on Prince St. Designed in 1835 by Hingelberg, a famous Danish architect in his time and renovated during 2008, it now houses government agencies.

ST. PATRICK'S CATHEDRAL: On Prince and Market Sts., this building is a mid-19th C reconstruction of the original 18th C cathedral. Built with locally-cut coral stone, it was completed in 1848 by Father Timothy O'Ryan, an Irishman from Galway. The monument inside the gate to the right memorializes sailors killed when a tidal wave tossed the USS *Monongahela* into Strand St. in 1867.

OTHERS: The small **Caribbean Museum Center for the Arts** (☎ 772-2622) is on Strand St. and open Mon. to Fri., noon–6, PM, Sat. 10–4 PM
http://www.cmcarts.org

Largely deserted, the **open air market-place** dates from 1751.

The cemetery of the **Holy Trinity Lutheran Church** (on the hill between Hospital and New Sts.) exudes a simple charm amidst panoramic surroundings. There are wooden grave markers and tombs topped with artificial flowers. The church itself dates from 1792.

Frederiksted pier is a great place for diving. With its plume worms, octopi, sponges, giant puffer fish, and large numbers of miniscule red, yellow, and orange sea horses, this dock is frequently called the most interesting "pier dive" in the Caribbean.

The Vincent F. Mason, Sr. Coral Resort is S of town off of Rte. 63 (Veteran's Parkway, about 1.5 mi. from town). The white sand beach here has mild surf, and you can both snorkel and dive here. The Old Frederiksted pool has been renovated, and the new park has tables, grills, parking and restrooms.

Frederiksted Accommodations

Located at 442 Strand St. near the cruise ship dock and facing the waterfront, the **Frederiksted Hotel** (☎ 772-0500, ✆ 719-1272) is a modest local hotel. It has a small pool and a local courtyard restaurant which serves breakfast.

Room amenities include a/c, phone (with voicemail and dataport), cable TV, and radio. Rooms are basic but comfortable and are popular with expat workers and tourists alike. There's good snorkeling offshore. Rates start at $110 s and d. Special rates are offered for long term rental.
http://www.frederikstedhotel.com
info@frederikstedhotel.com

Set a half-mi. from Frederiksted, the 21-rm. **Sand Castle on the Beach** (☎ 772-1205, ✆ 772-1757, 800-524-2018; 127 Estate Smithfield, Frederiksted 00840) faces directly onto a perfect beach. Renovated in 2003, it now has a fitness center with personal trainers, spa, massage service, as well as its gourmet **Beach Side Café** (see mention below). There are two pools; the smaller and more secluded is clothing optional. Suites have full kitchens, and all of the simple rooms have kitchenettes. Overhead fans, TV and VCR, hairdryer, and iron with ironing board number among the amenities. Rates run around $140 d CP (for a studio with kitchenette) to $300 CP (to house four in a two- bedroom courtyard villa). It caters to a largely gay clientele, but anyone would feel welcome here.
http://www.sandcastleonthebeach.com
info@sandcastleonthebeach.com

ST. CROIX

Set quite near Sand Castle and also on the beach, **Cottages by the Sea** (☎/℮ 772-0495, ℮ 772-1753; 800-323-7252; Box 1697, Frederiksted 00841-1697) has 20 spread-out 16 simple cottages with cable TV, fans and a/c, private patios, and kitchens. Paneled rooms have rattan furniture and colorful spreads. Rates start at $125/unit. They also rent kayaks, bicycles, and scooters. Be warned that the place is quite dog friendly, and many guests bring their dogs here.
http://www.caribbeancottages.com
vacations@caribbeancottages.com

The Virgin Islands Sustainable Farm Institute (473-3115; P.O. Box 1007, Frederiksted) at Mt. Victory Remainder on Creque Dam Rd. has the goal of providing "a model of a working educational farm enterprise that integrates sustainability in education, environment, and community through quality instruction in agroecology, natural resource management, and farm tourism." It offers tours such as the Organic Farm Taste Tour ($35), which takes place on Sundays, as well as "slow food" and "bush skills naturalist" workshops. They have hardwood cabanas, treehouse, and a yurt. Rates range from $60-$150 d (with a two-night minimum). A luxurious and private hillside villa ($500 pn, 2-4 person,). Management says that "We specialize in nourishing, tasty foods: homegrown bananas, mangoes, pineapple, tomatoes, coconut, hot peppers, eggplant, salad greens, papaya, and passionfruit, which you can enjoy three times a day served (daily meal plan $35) at our open air community center kitchen. Wi-fi is offered." It has a university-accredited study abroad program.
http://www.visfi.org
info@visfi.org

Mt Victory Camp (☎ 772-1651, 866-772-1651) is a great place to stay. It's run by Bruce Wilson (a local whose family moved to St. Croix when he was a teenager) along with his wife Mathile, a Haitian-born agronomist. A stay here is a unique experience. Screened-in platform tents and bungalows have electricity, two beds (or more) with linens, mosquito nets, a kitchen with sink, two cooking burners, ice chest, pots and pans, and utensils. Solar heated showers and toilets round out the features. Unlike other campgrounds, the units are habitable all through the day because the breeze wafts through. All construction here has been done with local timber (which are not arsenic treated). Bruce breeds the red-footed tortoise, and one camping bungalow, constructed with West Indian almond, even has a few in residence. So far, there are three tent platforms which rent for $85 pn and will hold two adults and two children. Two larger bungalows rent for $95 each. You may also pitch your own tent here for $30 pn for two persons. Evening campfires are fun. The grounds have gardens, and WiFi coverage is extensive. and there are hiking trails as well as ruins.

☞ Mt. Victory has the remains of one of eight schools built around 1840 in accordance with von Scholten's edict proclaiming compulsory education for all children. It is now a historical site.
http://www.mtvictorycamp.com
mtvictory@unitedstates.vi

Frederiksted Dining and Food
LOCAL FOOD: The inexpensive **Motown Bar & Restaurant,** 19 AB Strand St., serves West Indian food.

The Lost Dog Pub, 14 King St., is a watering hole in Frederiksted famous for winning the best of show at the annual St. Patrick's Day parade. The bar in the front serves pizza, and an attractive restaurant sits behind. It is one of those places where everybody knows everyone else.

Set right next to the Lost Dog, the **West End Grille** (☎ 772-2160), 16A King St., features island cuisine with daily speicals such as boiled fish with *fungi*, fried king fish, along with sides such as plantains, tostones, and johnny cake. It's open for lunch and early dinners from Tues. to Sat.

Serving three meals daily, **Pier 69** (☎ 772-0069), 69 King St., has live entertainment Fri. and Sat. from 10 PM and on Sun. nights from 7 PM. Owner Mary Moorhead is a good source for information.

Open 11 AM–7 PM, **UCA Headquarters** serves Rasta fare including sea moss and tamarind juice. A very *ital* place to stop!

Vegeria on King St. is a vegetarian restaurant which does lunches.

Set to the N of town, the inexpensive **Rhythms at Rainbow Beach** (☎ 772-0002), 1A Prosperity, serves West Indian and American dishes for lunch and dinner.

☞ Rhythms at Rainbow Beach always has music on Sunday afternoons and is very popular with locals and visitors alike.

GOURMET DINING: Featuring quiches, crepes, brochettes, and the like, the 19th-C atmospheric, moderate to expensive **Le St. Tropez** (☎ 772-3000), 67 King St., is open for lunch and dinner and is one of the island's nicest French restaurants. Entrées range from *poisson du marché* to *scampi pescatori*.

At 17 Strand St., right down the street from the Frederiksted, the **Blue Moon** (☎ 772-2222), set in historic Victoria House, offers dishes ranging from shrimp gazpacho to salmon Wellington. Jazz is featured on Fri. and Sat. nights, and you'll be surprised by the quality of the local talent. Sunday brunch and sunset are other times to come.

Coconuts on the Beach (☎ 719-6060), at 72 La Grange just N of the pier, serves Tex Mex food on the beach. Sunsets are spectacular.

Aqua West (☎ 719-2186,) above Turtles Deli in Prince Passage, is a waterfront restaurant serving international dishes. It has special events such as wine tasting, and sushi.

A street in Frederiksted as it appeared in the 19th C.

Set at Sand Castle On The Beach, the **Beach Side Café** (☎ 772-1205) presents a monthly wine dinner ($75 pp including gratuity) which presents a five-course gourmet tour of a certain region or continent (such as Australia). It offers daily specials, has Saturday night live jazz, and is open (at hours which vary according to the season) for lunch and dinner.

Sunset Grill (☎ 772-5855), right on Sprat Hall Beach, serves upscale island fare for lunch and dinner from Wed. through Sat. (On Sunday, they offer a huge buffet brunch from 11 AM–3 PM; entertainment follows). The menu includes vegetarian dishes. Chaises on the sand sport beach umbrellas, and there's a nice raft in the sea with chaise lounge. They also have great full moon parties.

MARKET SHOPPING: As is the case with its Christiansted cousin, the **outdoor market** (dating from 1751), located on the appropriately named Market St. at Queen, doesn't have a great deal to offer.

☞ Many stores stay open until 1 PM on the first Friday of the month.

There are a number of **small corner stores** which the locals have dubbed "Arab One," "Arab Two," and "Arab Three."

Several other small stores are in town.

A **fish market**, located at the junction of Strand St. and Rte. 702, is most active on Wed. and Sat. mornings around 9.

The island's only seaside deli, **Turtles** (☎ 772-3676), 625 Strand St., serves fresh baked bread and everything else you might suspect. It's highly recommended by locals.

GALLERIES: Cultural Creations of the Virgin Islands (☎ 773-2284), 66 King St., sells crafts, books, spices, clothing, sauces, and other items. It's housed in the historic Brow Soda factory. Open daily.

ENTERTAINMENT: A free **"Sunset Jazz"** concert series (☎ 719-3672) is held the third Friday of every month from 5:30–7:30 PM. at Veteran's Park on the waterfront. And, as previously mentioned, the Blue Moon has jazz on Friday. There are a few other clubs around.

Attracting a crowd in their 20s and 30s, the **Rainbow Beach Club** (☎ 772-0002) at Rainbow Beach to the N of town, has a West Indian BBQ on the beach with reggae, a beer drinking contest, and volleyball on Sun. afternoons. They throw a popular beach party with live music every Sunday afternoon. The world's largest underwater wedding took place here on Sept. 13, 2003 when the loving couple, accompanied by over 100 well wishers, were married by a priest in ten feet of water.

On Sun. at 6, the **Domino Club** at 48 Montpelier (see "outlying sights" to follow) offers a one-man calypso band.

Mt. Victory Camp (☎ 772-1651) hosts a fantastic pig roast which serves local seafood and food dishes as well in season. There's generally a live band, and this is a great opportunity to mix with the locals. People say that you find the "best mix of people" here. It starts around 3 PM and keeps going for quite a while. To get here, take Rte. 58; it's around two mi. from town.

Queen Street, the red light district, has Domnican prostitutes plying their wares outside of honky tonks decorated with Christmas lights. It can be a dangerous area later on in the evening.

SERVICES AND INFORMATION: A **Dept. of Tourism office** (☎ 773-0495) is located inside the Customs House.

The **Althalie Petersen Library** (☎ 772-0315), housed in the historic Bell House (see "Sights"), offers Internet access and an interesting collection of books.

Internet access ($12/hr.) is also available at **Awakening Community Efforts**, a red-and-white building on Strand St.

The Caribbean Dance School (☎ 778-8824), 11 Strand St, offers classes in yoga, jazz, and ballet.

Laundromat **Simply Suds** (☎ 772-3011) is at 68 Queen St.

DIVING: The Diverse Virgin program allows you to purchase six or more pre-paid trips which can be used at a number of different operators.
http://www.diversevirgin.com

N2 The Blue (☎ 772-3483, 888-STX-DIVE) offers custom dive adventures. They share a building in Frederiksted with the Coconuts Bar & Restaurant.
http://www.n2blue.com
info@n2blue.com

Offering a complete range of aquatic sport activities including boat, pier, and beach dives, **ScubaWest** (☎ 800-352-0107), 12 Strand St. near the pier in Frederiksted, rents snorkeling equipment, diving instruction, and sportfishing. A weekly calendar of events is posted at the wharf.
http://www.divescubawest.com
adventure@divescubawest.com

EVENTS: A special ceremony takes place in town on July 3, **Danish West Indies Emancipation Day.**

TOURS: The **St. Croix Environmental Association** (☎ 773-1989) offers hikes in the rainforest and at other locations.

SHOPPING: The rebuilding of the cruise ship dock has meant an increasing revitalization of town. However, as cruise ship traffic has been limited, shops have had a hard time here.

Vicinity of Frederiksted

The most interesting stop in town is actually outside it and to the N on Rte. 76. **LEAP Woodworking** (☎ 772-0421) produces an

St. Croix's Rain Forest area has sugarcane work ruins and a wealth of flora.

assortment of cutting boards, clocks, and other items. All are reasonably priced considering that they're crafted from the island's native wood. Mahogany, thibet, and saman are used, but the wood comes from trees cut down by a new road project or a new property development. On the way you'll pass three gigantic statues carved from wood (by David Boyd and Jeffrey Barber), reminiscent of the guardians found in in front of Japanese temples. Inside the enormous workshop pavilion, Willie "Cheech" Thomas, wearing a pair of blue noise retarding phones around his ears and a dust mask, will show you around. It's generally open Mon. to Fri. but you might want to call first.

THE MT. PELIER DOMINO CLUB: A short ride from town up Rte. 76 from LEAP, this bar is one of the W side's foremost attractions. It features a team of beer swilling pigs: Miss Piggy and Tony and their two rapidly growing youngsters. Although they love their Old Milwaukees, the owners have switched them over to Sharp's, a non-alcoholic brew. The switch was made after Miss Piggy's kids came out of the womb and started shaking with DTs, and, in any event, they don't pass out as quickly so the bar can do more business. To try it out, pick up a brew, pay the feeding charge, and offer it to any pig that pokes his head out of the pen. The pig will chomp down on it, and beer will run down his or her face as the can is chomped and swilled. The monument nearby is to Buster, the original beer drinking pig, who died after he was fed poisoned sponges by a malevolent youth. Fried fish and johnny cakes are also on sale, as are $15 tee shirts. A 'Buster Memorial Jam' is held every March. Natch' it features a pig roast.

Also out of town, one mi. N, is **Estate Mt. Washington Plantation** (☎ 772-1026), which offers mahogany reproductions, fabrics, and antiques. It's open Sat. from 10 AM–4 and weekdays by appointment.

THE RAIN FOREST: The "Rain Forest" is situated N of Frederiksted, the island's NW corner. Although lushly covered with tropical vegetation, it is actually a tropical dry secondary forest. It receives only 40 in. of rain whereas a true rainforest receives upwards of 80.

The best road for exploring is **Mahogany Rd.** (Rtes. 76, 763, 765), named after its stands of majestic mahogany trees over two centuries old. Along this road you can also find gumbo limbo, samaan (rain tree), and silk cotton trees. While strap and swamp ferns grow along gullies and guts, a variety of fruit trees — ranging from mammee apple to mango and breadfruit — can be seen near the remains of former estates such as Estate Prosperity.

More remote areas (four-wheel-drive recommended) are accessed by the narrow and winding **Scenic Rd.** (Rte. 78), **Western Scenic Rd.** (63/78), and the **Creque Dam**

St. Croix Itineraries

If you have 3 days:
Spend one day in and around Christiansted (shopping and sights), one day on Buck Island, and one day touring the island (beaches and sights).

If you have 5 days:
Spend one day in and around Christiansted (shopping and sights), one day on Buck Island, one day on the east of the island, and two days around the island (beaches and sights).

If you have one week:
Spend one day in and around Christiansted (shopping and sights), one day on Buck Island, one day on the east of the island, and four days around the island (beaches and sights). Or take a day excursion to St. Thomas or Virgin Gorda.

Rd. (Rtes. 58/78). A number of unmarked footpaths lead off the roads. Exercise caution.

The Scenic Rd. heads E via pink-and-white cedar forested hills which have steep, sometimes hard-to-follow paths leading up its sides. It continues E to **Eagle Ridge**, from where you can ascend flat-topped **Mt. Eagle** (1,165 ft., 334 m) and the antennae-and-radio-dish-topped **Blue Mtn.** (1,096 ft., 334 m), the highest points on St. Croix. A more direct approach to this area is from the E end of Scenic Rd. between Canaan Rd. (Rte. 73) and River Rd. (Rte. 69).

Beginning at Hams Bay on the NW, the **Western Scenic Rd.** is described in "Along the Northwest Coast," above. From the W coast, **Creque Dam Rd.** intersects the Sprat Hall Estate before reaching the lush Creque Dam and Rain Forest, where you can find mahogany, turpentine, white cedar, and silk cotton trees.

From St. Croix

FOR ST. THOMAS: Cape Air (☎ 800-352-0714) flies.
http://www.flycapeair.com

The most convenient way to get between St. Croix and St. Thomas by air is with the **Seaborne Airlines** (☎ 773-6442; ✆ 713-9077, 888-359-8687; Long Bay Road, Charlotte Amalie, US Virgin Islands 00802). It's a convenient way to travel as it eliminates time spent at airports. However, each passenger may carry only up to 30 pounds of baggage for free; after that, it's $1 per pound. You will be charged for your carry on! Roundtrip fares are around $165–$175. One-way fares are $90–$95. Special internet and weekend fares are offered, as are ferry and seaplane combination packages. Check in 45 min. before your flight.

BY FERRY: Operators of the **St. Croix Ferry** have changed many times here over the years.

VI Sea Trans (☎ 776-5494) runs a ferry (90-min.) between the Marine Terminal in Gallows Bay near Christiansted, St. Croix and the Marine Terminal in Charlotte Amalie (next to Seaplane Terminal) on St. Thomas. Arrive a minimum of 45 minutes prior to departure; a photo ID is required. Rates are $50 OW, $90 RT. It departs Fri., Sat., Sun., and Mon. at 7:30 and 4:30 PM and returns on Fri., Sat., Sun., and Mon. at 9:30 AM and 6:30 PM.
http://www.goviseatrans.com
caribbean.fastferry@gmail.com

FOR ST. JOHN: You must fly or ferry to St. Thomas and take a ferry.

FOR TORTOLA: American Eagle (☎ 800-327-8900) flies as does **Air Sunshine** (☎ 776-7900, 800-327-8900) and **Cape Air** (☎ 800-352-0714)
http://www.airsunshine.com
http://www.flycapeair.com

FOR VIRGIN GORDA: Air Sunshine (☎ 776-7900, 800-327-8900) and **Cape Air** (☎ 800-352-0714) fly.
http://www.airsunshine.com
http://www.flycapeair.com

BIA (☎ 778-9177, ✆ 772-5932) offers charter flights to Virgin Gorda.

FOR VIEQUES: Vieques Air Link (☎ 777-4055, 888-901-9247) flies from Vieques to St. Croix.
http://www.vieques-island.com/val

FOR SAN JUAN: Air Sunshine (☎ 776-7900, 800-327-8900) flies via St. Thomas. **Cape Air** (☎ 800-352-0714) flies directly.
http://www.airsunshine.com

FOR ANGUILLA: American Airlines flies direct.

THE BRITIJH VIRGIN IJLANDJ

Introduction

Peaceful and quiet, the British Virgin Islands offer solace to the traveler weary of the commercialism and despoiled atmosphere of the Caribbean's larger islands. Incredible scenery lies both above and below the water. Although these islands are the premier yachting destination in the Caribbean, their beautiful beaches and hiking trails are attractive to landlubbers as well.

NOTE: Much of the information in the USVI Introduction (flora and fauna, etc.) also apply here. If you are only visiting the BVI, be sure to read this section as well.

The Land

Comprising the eastern portion of the Virgin Islands archipelago, these islands, like their neighboring American cousins, are primarily volcanic in origin. (A notable exception is Anegada, which is a limestone and coral atoll.) Grouped for the most part around the Sir Francis Drake Channel, and lying 60 mi. E of Puerto Rico, these 50 or so islands, cays, and rocks date from eruptions that took place 25 million years ago.

Altogether, the islands comprise 59 sq miles of land area, with Tortola, the largest and most rugged, taking up 21 of these. Most are uninhabited; the largest inhabited islands are Tortola and Anegada. Rivers are nonexistent and, owing to the aridity of the climate, water is in short supply. The only notable mineral deposit is the salt on Salt Island.

Orchids

The British Virgin Islands have 16 native species of orchids. Found on the North Sound in Virgin Gorda and in Tortola, the Christmas Orchid (*Epidendrum ciliare*) gets its name because it flowers in December and Jan. This attractive yellow bloom is specially adapted to store water, a prerequisite for survival in its environs. The Ground Orchid (*Habenaria monorrhiza*) is a white flower which blossoms in the spring. A West African native, the reddish Tall Ground Orchid (*Eulophia alta*) is the BVI's most distinctive bloom.

Orchids were named by Dioscorides, a Greek physician who, noting the similarity of the tubers of one species he was examining to male genitals, named the species "orches." Nearly all orchids are pollinated by insects or hummingbirds, and it is believed that many may only be pollinated by a single specific bird. Aside from their aesthetic value, orchids are of little economic importance. They were once thought to have medicinal properties, but these claims have largely proven false, and not a single species is currently used in modern medicine. Their only valuable product is vanilla, an extract obtained from the cured unripened pods of various species belonging to the genus *Vanilla*. ∎

BVI INTRODUCTION

The British Virgin Islands A to Z

Accommodation — Every type of hotel in every price range is available. Campgrounds are found on Tortola, Jost Van Dyke, and Anegada. The nicest hotels tend to be small, intimate affairs. Many are owned by locals.

Area Code — To dial the British Virgin Islands from outside the islands *dial 1-284 and the number.* Omit the area code when dialing within the USVI. The area code for the USVI is 340.

Art and artists—There are a small number of fine artists and craftspeople in the BVI. However, most crafts for sale are imports.

Banking —Banks are generally open Mon. to Fri. from 9 AM–1 PM; also Fri. from 3 PM–5:30 PM. ATMs are scarce.

Business Hours —Generally from 9 AM–5 PM, Mon. to Fri. Many close on Sun. as do restaurants.

Camping—There are campgrounds on Tortola and Jost Van Dyke.

Clothes—Informal (except at some resorts) is the rule. You won't need much if any in the way of warm clothing.

Car rental—Cars may be rented from companies in the larger islands.

Credit Cards—Generally accepted.

Currency—The US Dollar.

Departure tax—$5 sea; $20 air.

Driving — Driving is on the left, the opposite side as in the mainland US. Valid drivers licenses are required, and a special BVI permit ($10) is also needed. A credit card is required to rent a vehicle.

Electricity —110 Volts AC

Internet— Access is limited but available at some hotels and internet cafes. But do you really want to be indoors a moment more than is necessary?

Language—English is the native tongue and variants range from the Queen's English to the local brogue.

Laundry—Most hotels will do laundry for a fee. Save by bringing some detergent and washing a few small items yourself.

Liquor Laws— Alcohol is available from any store.

Mail—Expect it to take around a week to the States. Rates are higher than US rates.

Maps—Free maps are probably sufficient for most visitors. A variety of good maps are available at gift shops.

Marriage—The BVI is a good place to get married, and many hotels have packages.

Newspapers— Local newspapers are weekly tabloids but informative. Newspapers from the States are available.

Radio/TV—Many tourist hotels have satellite TV or cable. There are a a few AM and FM radio stations.

Ruins—Nothing outstanding. However, the terrestrial national parks are well worth visiting.

Supplies—Foodstuffs are cheapest at supermarkets in Roadtown, Tortola. Prices are quite high. Bring specialty items with you or you may have to do without.

Taxes — Government tax of 7% is added to accommodation. There is no sales tax.

Taxis — Rates are set. Be sure to know what these are.

Telephones — Service is good.

Theft — The islands are safe, but sensible visitors always take precautions.

Time — The Virgin Islands operates on Atlantic Standard Time (four hours behind GMT, Greenwich mean time).

Tipping — Tip as you would in the States.

Visas — Stays of up to six months are allowed.

Water — Tap water is drinkable everywhere.

CLIMATE: Really fine! Set within the tradewind belt, temperature on these islands rarely drops below 70 degrees F at night; daytime temperatures range between 80–90 degrees F throughout the year. Rain, and water in general, is scarce. (The Climate Chart in the USVI "Introduction" also applies here.) February through August tends to be fairly dry, but May is often rainy. Sept. through Dec. can be quite wet. Rainfall in Jan. is intermittent.

FLORA AND FAUNA: Basically similar to the US Virgin Islands. Specific exceptions are treated in the travel section text.

History

Columbus sailed by the British Virgin Islands on his second voyage in 1493. In the early 1500s the Spaniards settled for a while on Virgin Gorda to mine copper and, stopping in on Tortola, gave it its name (meaning "turtle dove").

At first, few migrants were attracted by Tortola's steep hills. Unsettled and unclaimed, it remained the province of buccaneers who utilized its hidden caves as hideouts. The first actual settlement on Tortola was by pirates at Soper's Hole, West End. The Dutch began the first permanent settlement on Tortola in 1648. A mixed band of pirates drove out the Dutch in 1666 and, in turn, invited the English to come in. Soon after, however, the French took the island, but the British recaptured it in 1672. A migration of Anguillans followed.

With the exception of the islands already taken by Denmark, the British gradually began to occupy all of the unclaimed islands remaining in the Virgin Islands group. Before the end of the 17th C, the planter class had achieved a degree of prosperity. (Planters here, however, never made the fortunes their counterparts did on the flatter, wetter islands such as St. Croix and Barbados). Crisis followed crisis in the 18th C as the European nations brought their chess game to the Caribbean.

By 1720, the population was 1,122 whites and over 1,500 blacks. The Virgins (including Anguilla) were given their own lieutenant governor under the British-regulated Leeward Islands government. Along with Anguilla, and St. Kitts and Nevis, the Virgins were incorporated into the separate Leeward Islands Colony in 1816.

More than half the white residents fled in 1831 after discovery of a slave plot which, had it succeeded, would have resulted in the murder of them all. An 1853 revolt began in Road Town and spread all over Tortola and nearby islands. Tortola was reclaimed by the bush and remained largely wild for decades.

In 1872, the islands were placed by Britain under the Leeward Islands Administration and admitted as a crown colony. Severe hurricanes in 1916 and 1924 caused extensive damage.

The Legislative Council was abolished in 1902, and the governor-in-council became the sole legislative authority. A presidential legislature for the islands was established in 1950 with elected and appointed members. On Dec. 31, 1959, the Office of the Governor of the Leewards was abolished; the administrator on Tortola became the Queen's Representative. The 1967 constitution granted the islands a ministerial government, and a few years later, after the de-federation of the Leewards Island Colony, the Virgins were set up as a separate colony.

three others pled guilty in 2004 and are serving prison terms.

The BVI adopted a new constitution in 2007. The name of the Head of Government changed from Chief Minister to Premier; the Premier is elected in a general election in tandem with other members of the unicameral 13-seat Legislative Council. The Premier nominates an Executive Council which the Governor then "appoints." David Pearey has served as Governor since 2006, and Ralph T. O'Neal has served as Premier since August 22, 2007.

Government

One of the most stable governments in the Caribbean, the BVI are a self-governing Dependent Territory (read: colony) with a governor appointed by the British queen. When asked where the British Virgin Islands were, Sir Winston Churchill is said to have replied that he had no idea, but he should think that they were as far as possible from the Isle of Man.

As the British Empire continues to contract, the symbolic importance of these islands has grown. Queen Elizabeth II has seen fit to arrive here by royal yacht twice during a ten-year period, and Prince Andrew visited in 2000 to dedicate the Royal BVI Yacht Club. The current governor is Mr. David Pearey.

The island's chief minister is elected by the locals. Residents seem unconcerned with independence and content at present with the status quo. These islands were once seen as being the least important place in the British Empire. The Virgin Islands Party ruled from 1986 until June 2003 when a corruption scandal (revolving around the construction of the new airport) unseated it in favor of Chief Minister Orlando Smith and his National Democratic Party. Former Financial Secretary Allen Wheatley and

Economy

Until very recently the British Virgin Islands had known nothing but a subsistence

Sugar Cultivation

The Dutch brought sugarcane in the early 17th C to Sopers Hole. Most of the cotton fields were turned to sugar by the early 18th C, and a 1796 map shows 104 plantations. Plantations had around 150–200 slaves who lived in their own set of huts. Rocky soil and steep slopes made cultivation challenging and less productive than elsewhere.

Cane would be planted before the approach of the rainy season. Slaves would put cuttings into holes, and terraces had to be built and reinforced with stones. Bundles would be carried by mule or cart to the mill.

The abolition of slavery in 1834 heralded the begining of the end of King Sugar's harsh rule, and the fields began returning to scrub. The hurricane of 1837 destroyed 17 sugar mills, and a drought prevailed until 1847. Production had ground to a virtual standstill by 1860, and the hurricanes of 1867 and 1871 destroyed the remaining mills. Although cane continued to be cultivated, peasant farming and animal husbandry took over. ∎

✖✖✖ Important Dates in BVI History ✖✖✖

1493: Columbus sails by the British Virgins. Some of present-day Virgins included in grant to Earl of Carlyle.

1648: Dutch buccaneers settle Tortola.

1668: English buccaneers expel Dutch.

1680: Planters from Anguilla begin to settle Tortola and Virgin Gorda; deputy governor and council selected.

1685: English settlements on Tortola and Virgin Gorda raided by Spaniards.

1718: Spanish attack Tortola and attempt settlement.

1774: British House of Assembly commences meeting in Road Town, Tortola.

1802: Road Harbour (present-day Road Town) becomes a free port.

1803: Last public slave auction held on Tortola.

1808: Slave trade abolished by Britain.

1816: Along with Anguilla, St. Kitts, and Nevis, the Virgins are incorporated into the separate Leeward Islands Colony.

1834: Slavery abolished on British islands.

1853: Revolt begins in Road Town and spreads all over Tortola and nearby Islands; cholera outbreak reduces population by approximately 14%.

1872: Islands placed under Leewards Island Administration; admitted as a separate colony.

1905: Government Savings Bank established.

1922: First hospital opened.

1943: First secondary school opened

1949: Demonstrations held throughout the islands demand representative government and closer association with the US Virgin Islands.

1956: Leeward Islands Federation dissolved; BVI commissioner becomes administrator

1959: First issue of first newspaper (*Tortola Times*) published.

1966: Queen Elizabeth II and Duke of Edinburgh visit.

1967: New constitution granted.

lifestyle. Tourism—responsible for more than half of the $20 million GNP—has brought a measure of prosperity The tourism boom began in the mid-60s, with the construction of the Rockresort at Little Dix Bay on Virgin Gorda, and today the islands are the yachting capital of the Caribbean, with 13 yacht marinas, some 300 bareboats and around 100 charters. More than 200,000 visitors arrive annually, and some 67% of these stay on these "floating hotels."

The islands have a standard of living second in the Caribbean only to the US Virgin Islands. And they have gained the benefits of financial shoulder-rubbing with their wealthier neighbor, without contracting its serious problems.

Since the 1940s, thousands have migrated to the USVI, relieving population pressures and transferring savings back home. After the collapse of the plantation system in the 19th C, the planters left and either sold the land cheaply or gave it to their former slaves. As a consequence—in contrast to other Caribbean islands where a small elite control the land—the common people of the BVI largely own their own turf. Most goods are imported. There is no industry

Steel band music is ubiquitous in the Virgin Islands, and many resorts and hotels feature the steel drum in their entertainment regimen. You can hear the music in concentrated doses during St. Thomas's carnival and at "Music in Steel," an annual concert which takes place the first Fri. in Dec. in the BVI. The BVI has a youthful band, the Shooting Stars Steel Orchestra, which frequently performs hither and thither across the archipelago.

to speak of, save for tourism and offshore company registration, and agriculture is largely confined to garden plots.

IBCs: One major revenue source these days is the result of the International Business Company (IBC) legislation passed in 1984 which gives locally-registered companies tax incentives. Multinationals have been flocking in droves to register here because of the zero-tax provisions, low-cost incorporations, and limited regulation. More than 600,000 businesses have signed up, employing 1,600 people. The islands are currently the largest source of investment for Hong Kong, and millions of dollars from the Peoples Republic of China are laundered here, in Bermuda, and in the Cayman Islands.

This has made for some surrealistic news stories. For example, Rimbunan Petrogas Ltd, a Malaysian company incorporated in the BVI, signed a contract with a deal for offshore oil and gas exploration in 2007 with the Myanmar Oil and Gas Enterprise, a company owned by the totalitarian Burmese government. Capital flight investigators maintain that a large percentage of the money sent illegally from the mainland goes to the BVI, Bermuda and the Cayman Islands before returning via Hong Kong.

However, a number of companies using the BVI operate honestly. An example of this is a 2005 transaction by Chen Tianqiao,

British Virgin Islands Fast Facts

Here are some facts about some of the major islands. Population figures are approximate.

Tortola Main island. Capital of Roadtown. Pop. 23,908. Marinas, government services, resorts and hotels. Camping at Brewer Bay.

Beef Island Connected by bridge to Tortola. Airport, ferries to Last Resort, Marina Cay and North Sound. Good beach, windsurfing school, restaurants, stores.

Peter Island Luxury resort with gourmet restauran and t. Great beaches. 4.5-mi. long; set five mi. S of Tortola. Ferry from Roadtown.

Virgin Gorda The Baths is a famous landmark. Good snorkeling. Pop. 3,000.

Norman Island The Caves offer great snorkeling. Floating restaurant *William Thornton* offers meals.

Jost Van Dyke Small hotels and restaurants, camping. Four mi. NW of Tortola. Mountainous, four-mi. long. Inns, restaurants, camping, rentals, moorings. Pop. 200.

Anegada Northernmost island. Eleven mi. long. Flat coral atoll. Set. 15 mi. N of Virgin Gorda. Pop. 200. Deserted beaches, great snorkeling, bone fishing, deep-sea fishing, wrecks, small hotels and restaurants, camping.

China's second-richest businessman. Shanda Interactive Entertainment, Tianquiao's online game company purchased a 19.5 percent stake in Sina Corp, China's leading Internet news portal, for $196 million in a stealthy operation which legitimately used four BVI shelf companies as cover. On the other hand, American multimillionaire Walter Anderson was convicted in 2007 of

The British Virgin Islands is, after Hong Kong. the largest source of foreign direct investment in China. The British Virgin Islands injected $5.78 billion into China during 2006.

hiding up to $450 million offshore: much of that was in the BVI. He was sentenced to 108 months in prison.

One controversy making international news has been the dispute between the government of the British Virgin Islands and Consolidated Water (CWCO) over ownership of a desalinzation plant. It has constructed another $8 million desaliniza-tion plant at Bar Bay for which the only potential customer is the BVI government. Investors worry that the shares may tank (because earnings will take a hit) if the situation is not resolved in the company's favor.

Festivals and Events

Regattas, regattas, and regattas. For current information on major yachting, angling, and rugby events in the BVI, write to the **BVI Yacht Club** (☎ 494-3286), PO Box 200, Road Town, Tortola, BVI. Also, be sure to obtain an annual calendar of events from the Tourist Board.
rbviyc@surfbvi.com

JANUARY: The **Bud Open Windsurfing Games** (☎ 495-4559) are held. The BVI Yacht Club also holds the **Pusser's Juice Reef Cup** (☎ 494-3286) this month. The **Malibu Long Board Shoot-Out** takes place in mid-January.
http://www.go-hiho.com

The **Governor's Cup** takes place towards the end of the month and is sponsored by the **Royal BVI Yacht Club** (☎ 494-3286).

FEBRUARY: Around Valentine's Day, the **Sweetheart's of the Caribbean Schooner Race** (☎ 494-9262) is held at the West End.

The BVI Botanic Society holds an annual **Horicultural Society Show** (☎ 494-3134) this month or in March.

MARCH: Foxy's Music Festival (☎ 495-9258) is also around this time. A wide variety of musical styles of bands play at Foxy's on Jost Van Dyke.
http://www.foxysbar.com

Farmer's Week (☎ 495-2532), generally held during the last week of March, features donkey rides and local crafts and festivals.

Now into its second decade, the **BVI Spring Regatta,** third leg of CORT (Caribbean Ocean Racing Triangle, involv-ing Puerto Rico and St. Thomas), usually takes place from the end of March through the beginning of April. It is preceded by Puerto Rico's Copa Velasco Regatta and then followed by St. Thomas's Rolex Cup Regatta, and many racers compete in all three. Festivities take place at the Regatta Village which is generally on Nanny Cay.
http://www.bvispringregatta.org

APRIL: The **Virgin Gorda Easter Festival** (☎ 495-5181) is a food and music festival.

The **Spanish Town Fisherman's Jamboree** (☎ 495-5252) is sponsored by the Fischer's Cove Beach Hotel.

MAY: The **BVI Music Festival** (☎ 495-3378) takes place at the end of each May.
http://www.bvimusicfest.com

JUNE: Generally held from late July through early Aug., the **Hook-In-Hold-On Windsurfing Challenge (HIHO)**, with 12 point-to-point windsurfing and sail-boat races, is sponsored by The Moorings (☎ 494-0447, 800-535-7289, ☎ 494-6488).
http://www.go-hiho.com

VISAR Waterworld (☎ 494-4357) is held the first week in June.

The **Carrot Bay Log Boat Regatta**, usu-ally held in June, offers two log boat races along with a parade, dinghy racing, bicycle racing, and other activities. This is the brainchild of Egbert Donovan, owner of the Shell Museum, who enjoyed the sport as a child so much that he wanted to share the tradition.

Boats are generally crafted from "spirit of turpentine," a local hardwood. The mast, boom, and support beams are fashioned with a lighter wood, and sails are made from cut plastic. The longest is around a yard. You may see log boats at Egbert's museum in Carrot Bay.

Held at the end of June, the **Highland Springs HIHO** involves team competition. **http://www.go-hiho.com**

The **Lewmar Pursuit Race** (☎ 494-3286) is also held this month.

JULY: July First is **Fishermans's Day** (☎ 468-3701, ext. 5555). In mid-month, the **Match Racing Championships** (☎ 494-3286) are sponsored by the BVI Yacht Club.

AUGUST: Held from late in the month before, the **BVI Emancipation Festival** (☎ 494-3134) features traditional steel band, calypso, soca, and fungi music. It commemorates the emancipation of the islanders from slavery on Aug. 1, 1834. August Monday, August Tuesday, and August Wednesday are official holidays, but the entire festivities consume two weeks. Boldly decorated booths are erected at the Festival Village in Road Town, which serves for headquarters for the events, and traditional food and drink and carnival rides are available. Nightly entertainment takes place on a central stage. Sunday sees an Emancipation Service held at the Sunday Morning Well. It is preceded by a Freedom March. On August Monday, a grand parade with marching bands and floats moves down the waterfront road. The Miss BVI or "Queen Contest" is also held. The win-

BVI Public Holidays	
1 Jan.:	New Year's Day
March:	Commonwealth Day (movable)
April:	Good Friday (movable) Easter Monday (movable)
May–June:	Whit Monday
June:	Sovereign's Birthday (movable)
1 July:	Territory Day (movable)
Aug.:	Festival Monday, Festival Tuesday, Festival Wednesday (movable)
21 Oct.:	St. Ursula's Day (movable)
14 Nov.:	Birthday of Heir to the Throne
25 Dec.:	Christmas Day
26 Dec.:	Boxing Day

ner moves on to the Miss Universe Pageant. Pole plaiting is a recently revived tradition.

The **BVI Yacht Club** (☎ 494-3286) sponsors the **BVI Gamefish Tournament** each August as well as the **Anegada Sailing Race. Foxy's Wooden Boat Regatta** (☎ 495-9258) takes place each late Aug. to early Sept. It's held on Jost Van Dyke and features lots of great ships. **http://www.foxysbar.com**

SEPTEMBER: The BVI Yacht Club (☎ 494-3286) hosts the **September Warm-Up Race**, and the Long Bay Beach Resort (☎ 495-4242) hosts the **Fall Caribbean Art Festival**.

OCTOBER: Airline companies compete in the **Interline Regatta**, a nine-day sailing event held annually; it's sponsored by **The Moorings** (☎ 800-535-7289).

The same month finds the **Captain's Fishing Tournament** and the **Virgin's Cup/**

William Thornton which is sponsored by the BVI Yacht Club (☎ 494-3286). The **Women's Sailing Week** and **The Defiance Day Regatta** are both sponsored by the Bitter End Yacht Club (☎ 800-872-2392), as are the **Fast Track Sailing Festival** and the **Pro-Am Regatta**.

Halloween is marked by the **Annual Halloween Costume Ball** held at the Long Bay Resort (☎ 495-4252).

NOVEMBER: The **Charter Yacht Show** (☎ 494-6017) is held in November as is the **Round Tortola Sailing Race** which is sponsored by the BVI Yacht Club (☎ 494-3286). The **Karibik Trophy** brings a Teutonic migratory onslaught of some 200 German sailors on 30 yachts; it takes place over a two-week period. Its sponsor is the KH & P Yacht Charter Company of Germany.

The **Tri-BVI Triathalon** (☎ 494-2359) is run by the BVI Cycling Federation. http://www.bvicycling.com

DECEMBER: Held in the first half of the month, the **CAT BVI** (☎ 494-0337) is a grand prix catamaran contest.

The **Music in Steel** (☎ 494-4134) concert, held the first Fri. of the month, spotlights local steel bands.

This same month the **BVI Charter Yacht Society** (☎ 800-298-8139) holds its annual boat show, the **Commodore's Race** (☎ 494-3286) takes place as does the **Gustav Wilmerding Race** (☎ 495-4559).

The **Scratch/Fungi Band Fiesta** highlights *fungi* band performances.

While the Long Bay Resort (☎ 495-4252) hosts the New Year's Eve Ball, **Foxy's Gala New Year's Eve Party** (☎ 495-9258) is held at Foxy's Tamarind Club on Jost Van Dyke. http://www.foxysbar.com

---

Tips on Travel to the BVI

➜ It may be cheaper to fly via St. Thomas rather than via San Juan. It will likely prove less expensive still to take a ferry over from St. Thomas and St. John.

➜ If you are traveling in a group and headed to Virgin Gorda, it may be more economical (or at least more convenient) to charter a plane. Traveling light will make things easier.

➜ Remember that Sept. and parts of Oct. are the quietest time which may work to your advantage if you are solitary. Rates also tend to be lower then.

➜ Jost Van Dyke is busiest on weekends, when there is an influx of daytrippers from St. Thomas.

➜ If you want to avoid hordes of cruise ship passengers (disgorge schedule: twice weekly, Nov. to April), check the paper for the schedules. Avoid visiting Sky Bar & Restaurant and Cane Garden Bay on these days.

Practicalities

GETTING HERE: The BVIs are a bit difficult of access which is what gives them a good portion of their charm. The easiest — but most expensive — way is to fly from San Juan or St. Thomas to Tortola or Virgin Gorda. (If you're flying from the US or Canada, you'll have no choice but to change planes in one of these two places). Most flights arrive at Terrence B. Lettsome

---

Remember to bring munchies and/or food with you, as most of the major airlines (including American) are either not serving meals or (pathetically!) are selling them. Items for sale are usually overpriced, and vegetarian and/or other special-need food items are often not offered at all. Sandwiches, nuts, and fruit are good choices.

International Airport on Beef Island, a small island linked to Tortola by a new bridge.

Another alternative is to fly to Virgin Gorda, or (*the cheapest alternative*) is to take ferries from St. Thomas and St. John to Jost Van Dyke, Virgin Gorda, and Tortola. (A late ferry from St. Thomas is planned). Or you can fly to Tortola's Beef Island Airport (EIS) and then take a ferry to Virgin Gorda.

No discount air fares from Puerto Rico or the VI are generally available, but you may get a discounted ticket by making an advance purchase or buying a RT ticket. As carriers have changed frequently in the past, be sure to check with your travel agent or online.

FROM PUERTO RICO: American Eagle (☎ 800-327-8900), **LIAT** (☎ 495-1197, 495-2577, 888-844-5428; USVI/PR: 866-549-5428; Antigua: 268-480-5601/2), **Air Sunshine** (☎ 495-8900, 800-327-8900), and **Cape Air** (☎ 800-352-0714, 800-635-8787) fly to Beef Island Airport, Tortola (EIS).

FROM ST. THOMAS: LIAT (☎ 495-1197, 495-2577, 888-844-5428; USVI/PR: 866-549-5428; Antigua: 268-480-5601/2) flies from St. Thomas to Tortola.

Seaborne Airlines (☎ 773-6442; ✆ 713-9077, 888-359-8687) offers a convenient flight between downtown St. Thomas and North Sound on Virgin Gorda. **http://www.flyseaborne.com**

FROM ST. CROIX: Air Sunshine (☎ 495-8900, 800-327-8900) flies daily to Beef Island, Tortola.

Fly BVI (☎ 495-1747) offers charters. **http://www.fly-bvi.com**

FROM GREAT BRITAIN: British Airways flies to San Juan, Puerto Rico and local flights connect from there to Beef Island.

BVI Driving Tips

🚗 Watch your map. Road signs are scarce and turns can come up fast.

🚗 Watch for mirrors on hills and curves. These will help you to see oncoming traffic.

🚗 With automatics, if you feel you need more power, turn off the a/c while going up steep hills.

🚗 If you find the inveterate tailgaters troublesome, pull over to let them pass.

🚗 Livestock encounters mean you must slow down.

🚗 Roundabouts mean that you enter a circle and then exit at the road of your choice. Turn L into and out of the circle and drive clockwise while navigating the roundabout.

🚗 Caution should be the rule. Locals may speed but you should not!

Another possibility is to fly to the US and enter via the USVI. **Air 2000** (☎ +44 2392 222226) have started a weekly charter flight from Gatwick to St. Thomas.

BY SEA: Ferries run from St. Thomas to Tortola, Virgin Gorda, and Jost Van Dyke. Boats from St. John leave for West End, Tortola, and occasional daytrips for Virgin Gorda are available. Round trips are discounted but will limit your travel options as you must return with the same line.

For a list of ferries with links to their websites see:
http://www.bvitourism.com/ GettingAround/Ferries/

CRUISES: A cruise ship pier was built in 1993 and some larger ships call at Tortola.

American Canadian Caribbean Line (☎ 401-247-0955, 800-556-7450, ✆ 401-245-8303) travels to the three main

Virgins as well as to the BVI in a 12-day, 12-stop trip.
http://www.accl-smallships.com

GETTING AROUND: There is little local transport other than expensive shared taxi service available on Tortola and Virgin Gorda; rates are fixed by the local government. Settle the price before you get in.

Scato's Bus Service (☎ 494-2365) operates a local "bus" service on a pickup truck with canopy. Service is irregular.

A beautiful but strenuous way to see the islands is on foot. Slopes are incredibly steep, but views are magnificent.

Other alternatives include renting a car or using your thumb. Hitching is easy: both locals and visitors are usually happy to get riders, but it can be difficult to find a ride after dark.

HELICOPTER RENTAL: Island Helicopters (☎ 495-2538, 24 hours: 499-2663; PO Box 2900, East End, Tortola) will take you anywhere within reason. For emergency medical transfers call 284-499-2663.
http://www.helicoptersbvi.com
info@helicoptersbvi.com

CAR RENTALS: Rates are around $55–$75 per day plus gas ($4.50/gal.) with unlimited mileage; off-season rates are lower. A 5% tax is added. It doesn't take long to drive around any of these islands so, if you want to economize, it might be better to rent a car for just a day and see the sights. A BVI license ($10 for temporary permit) is needed; it may be obtained, upon presentation of a valid foreign driver's license, from either the Traffic and Licensing Dept. in the Hodge Bldg. near the roundabout or from the rental companies. Depending upon the agency, you must be either 23 or 25 to rent a vehicle. Bicycles also need a permit: $5! They also need a license plate.

Yacht Chartering Tips

⚓ Study up before you go.

⚓ Book early to prevent disappointment.

⚓ *Book late* if you are less particular and hope to score a last-minute bargain.

⚓ Expect *to spend* around $1,500–$1,800 pw to charter a 30- to 50-ft. sailboat with an experienced captain.

⚓ "Bareboat" chartering means you do all of the work. Costs are lower.

⚓ "Crewed" means that you have help. Try to find a crew that matches your personalities and needs.

⚓ If you book off-season, you may be offered "free days" as an incentive.

⚓ All of the BVI are within easy reach of each other, which makes sailing here perfect for beginners.

⚓ More adventurous sailors can head for St. Croix or Anegada.

⚓ Remember that — while you may be able to do that seven-day itinerary in three days —the point is to relax!

⚓ Taking the ferry from St. Thomas across to Tortola saves you money and gets you in the mood.

⚓ Be sure you know how to set your anchor.

⚓ If you don't like to cook or can't, hire a cook.

⚓ Don't overpack. All you need is a few tee shirts and several bathing suits and a pair of shorts for venturing ashore.

⚓ Cancellation insurance insulates your pocketbook in the event of an unexpected cancellation.

If you have a credit card which offers car insurance, be sure to know which types of vehicles it covers. Make sure that your credit card has a $1000 limit available, an amount required for pre-authorization as a guarantee for damages against the deductible.

Although the majority of vehicles have the driver's seat on the L, driving on the L-hand side of the road may cause you problems at night when oncoming lights tend to direct to the R, reflecting in the eyes of the driver, much as having brights on would.

NOTE: most of the rental companies are listed under the appropriate part of the travel sections. Other rentals are also noted.

DRIVING: The maximum speed limit is 30 mph which decreases to 10–15 mph in residential areas. Driving is on the L-hand side, and roads are narrow and winding.

BICYCLES: The **Last Stop Sports** (☎ 494-5064, ✆ 494-0593) at Nanny Cay rents bikes with helmets ($20 pd, $120 pw) as well as kayaks and surfboards http://www.laststopsports.com info@laststopsports.com

Sailing and Yacht Charters

If you're a typical visitor, this will be one of if not *the* reason you're coming here. The combination of good weather, protected waters, and good anchorages not too far apart has served to help build the island's yachting industry. Pioneers, such as the Mooring's Charlie and Ginny Carey, have built the business from the bottom up during the past three decades or so.

Be prepared for a few discomforts: hand held showers situated right next to the toilets are standard fare. Try to plan your itinerary at least six months in advance if you're interested in peak times like February, March, Easter, Thanksgiving, and Christmas. The poorest conditions for sailing run from the end of August through the middle of October. Bring dramamine in the unlikely event that you get seasick.

You can expect to spend between $1,500–$2,000 pp for an eight day/seven night cruise with all meals, alcohol, and use of sports equipment included.

BVI Snorkeling Spots

The British Virgin Islands is one of the finest places to snorkel in the world. This is largely because environmentally conscious individuals have worked to preserve the reefs.

Tortola Smuggler's Cove has a reef just offshore. Cane Garden Bay and Brewers Bay also have reefs, but they are farther offshore.

Peter Island White Bay offers good, shallow snorkeling.

Virgin Gorda There's good snorkeling at Devil's Bay, The Baths, at Mountain Point (to the N of The Baths), and on The Dogs to the W.

Norman Island The Caves offer great snorkeling as does Benures Bay, a cove on the NE shore. Another spot is Sandy's Edge to the W and at The Indians.

Jost Van Dyke Good snorkeling at White Bay. Snorkel out along the rocks at the W end or anywhere along the outer edge. Green Cay and Sandy Spit are other spots.

DEFINITIONS: Bareboat charters come without crew; you may hire a skipper. **Crewed charters** supply a crew. Guests sit back and relax. These are generally reserved through a broker. Food, crew, and amenities are included. **Sailing schools** offer nautical training in a charter environment.

QUALIFICATIONS: Most boats are heavy displacement vessels with a lot of momentum. You should have adequate experience skippering this type of boat as well as a good basic comprehension of inboard engines. Although requirements vary in their specifics, aspiring captains of smaller boats should have experience of regularly skippering at least a 25-ft. sailing boat. Applicants customarily fill out an application which includes a resume of sailing experience. Generally, you must agree that the charter company retains the right to place an instructor/guide on your boat at your expense should it prove necessary after a trial run. Another alternative is to pre-book a skipper for all or part of your holiday.

CHARTERING: There are a large number of charter operations. Most offer day sails as well, and skippers are generally available for bareboats.

At Seacow Bay, **Barecat Charters** (☎ /☻ 495-1979, 800-296-5287) offers 32-ft. and up catamarans.
http://www.barecat.com
lynne@barecat.com

In Joba Marina, **BVI Yacht Charters** (☎ 494-4289, ☻ 494-6552, 888-645-4006; Box 3018, Road Town) rents 32–50-ft. bareboats with skippers available.
http://www.bviyachtcharters.com
charters@bviyachtcharters.com

Catamaran Charters (☎ 494-6661, 800-262-0308, ☻ 494-6698; Box 281, Road Town) rents 37–65 ft. catamarans.
http://www.catamaranco.com
charter@catamaranco.com

Nanny Cay's **British Virgin Islands Charter Yacht Society** (☎/☻ 494-6017, 877-211-5268; Box 3512, Road Town) offers all-inclusive charter yachts, power or sail, from 40–85-ft. and accommodating 2–12. *It has a wonderful web site.*
http://www.bvicrewedyachts.com
mail@bvicrewedyachts.com

Charterportbvi (☎ 494-7955), #6 Christopher Bldg., Village Cay Marina, rep-

resent, around 60 boats.
http://www.charterportbvi.com
yachting@charterportbvi.com

Chocolat Blanc Day Sail (☎ 496-6600, ☻ 496-7319; Box 3018, Road Town) offers short and long-term charters.
http://www.chocolatblanc.com
chocblanc@surfbvi.com

From Fort Burt Marina, **Conch Charters, Ltd.** (☎ 494-4868, ☻ 494-5793, US: 800-521-8939, Canada: 800-463-6625; Box 920, Road Town) offers a number of 3-to-51-ft. fully-equipped bareboat sailing yachts.
http://www.conchcharters.com
ask.us@conchcharters.com

In Nanny Cay, *Endless Summer II* (☎ 494-3656, ☻ 494-4731, 800-368-9905; Box 823, Road Town) offers a 72-ft. Irwin with four staterooms.
http://www.endlesssummer.com
info@endlesssummer@com

In Nanny Cay, **Horizon Yacht Charters** Ltd. (☎ 494-8787, ☻ 494-8989, 877-494-8787; Box 3222, Road Town) offers sailboats and motor launches.
http://www.horizonyachtcharters.com
info@horizonyachtcharters.com

Set at the Mariner Inn at Wickham Cay II on the E side of Road Town, the **Moorings** (☎ 494-2331, Box 139, Tortola) offers 39- to 51 ft. sloops as well as a variety of sloops and ketches. In the US, write 19345 US

 Sheppard Powerboat Rentals (☎ 495-4099), **King Charters** (☎ 494-5820), **M&M Powerboat Rentals** (☎ 495-9993) and **Power Boat Rentals** (☎ 494-5511) provide the chance for you to skipper your own craft from island to island. (Pick a calm day for this).

Hwy. 19 N, 4th Fl, Clearwater, FL 33764 (☎ 727-535-1446, 888-952-5420).
http://www.moorings.com

North South Yacht Vacations (☎ 494-0096, ✆ 494-6958, 800-387-4964; Box 281, Road Town), Inner Harbor Marina, offers 34-ft. and 45-ft. sail and power boats. Both crewed and bareboat charters are available, and they operate a sailing school.
http://www.nsyv.com
northsouth@nsyv.com

In the Inner Harbour Marina, **Regency Yacht Vacations** (☎ 495-1970, 800-524-7676, ✆ 768-7811) operate fully-crewed sail or power 45- to 200-ft. craft. They also represent Northrop and Johnson.
http://www.regencyvacations.com
info@regencyvacations.com

At Road Reef Marina, **Tortola Marine Mgt. Ltd.** (☎ 494-2751, 494-2751, ✆ 494-5166, 800-633-0155; Box 3042, Road Town) rents 30 to 51-ft. sailboats, a 37-ft. trawler, and 39-ft. catamarans.
http://www.sailtmm.com
charter@sailtmm.com

The **Trimarine Boat Co., Ltd.** (☎ 494-2490, ✆ 494-5774, 800-648-3393; Box 362, Road Town) operates two trimarans. They offer diving and snorkeling.
http://www.bvidiving.com
cuanlaw@surfbvi.com

Based in Florida, **Virgin Island Sailing Ltd.** (☎ 800-382-966, 941-966-9387) offers sail packages and crewed charters.
http://www.visailing.com
tom@visailing.com

Promenade Sail Dive Charters (☎ 499-2756; ✆ 866-388-0770; Box 2249, Road Town) has a 65-ft. trimaran in Village

> If you're interested in charter yachts, you should obtain the informative *A Guide to Crewed Charter Yachts* which is obtainable from the Tourist Board. It includes information on boats available through the Charter Yacht Society (☎/✆ 494-6017, 800-298-8139; Box 8309, Cruz Bay, VI 00831).

Cay Marina which offers fully-crewed sailing and diving charters for from two to twelve guests.
http://www.yachtpromenade.com
saildive@yachtpromenade.com

Virgin Traders (☎ 495-2526, ✆ 495-2678, 888-684-6486, Box 993, Road Town) offers 44–64-ft. luxury motor yachts.
http://www.virgin-traders.com
cruising@virgin-traders.com

At Frenchman's Cay, **Voyage Charters** (☎ 410-956-1880, ✆ 410-956-6619, 888-869-2436) has a number of catamarans.
http://www.voyagecharters.com
info@voyagecharters.com

Yacht Connections Ltd. (☎ 494-7956, ✆ 494-8009, 800-386-8185) have 40- to 200-ft. craft which accommodate from two to 20. They have a branch (☎ 44 0 1590-671-667) in the UK also.
http://www.yacht-connections.co.uk
yachting@surfbvi.com

At Trellis Bay on Beef Island, **Wanderlust Yacht Vacations** (☎/✆ 494-2405, 800-724-5284), offer a variety of craft.
http://www.wanderlustcharters.com
wanderlust@wanderlustcharters.com

OTHERS: Ann-Wallis White (☎ 410-263-6366, ✆ 410-263-0399) repre-

⚓ British Virgin Islands Popular Anchorages ⚓

⚓ **Soper's Hole** At the W end of Tortola. Deep and sheltered, it has complete facilities.

⚓ **Road Town** There are a number of marinas here. You can also anchor at Brandywine Bay and Maya Cove just past Road Harbour.

⚓ **Deadman's Bay** On the E tip of Peter Island and a short sail from Road Town. Anchor in the extreme SE corner and watch for swells (especially in the winter). Marina available.

⚓ **Beef Island** Anchorages at Trellis Bay and out at Marina Cay. Marinas available.

⚓ **Salt Island** Moorings at Lee Bay (near the wreck of the Rhone) and at Salt Pond Bay. Both are rough and recommended for day use only.

⚓ **Cooper Island** Moorings at Lee Bay and Salt Pond Bay. Restaurant and other facilities available.

⚓ **Virgin Gorda** Moorings at The Baths, North Sound, and other locations. Marinas available at North Sound and in The Valley.

⚓ **The Dogs** On good days the best anchorages are on the bay to the W of Kitchen Point (George Dog) and off the S side of Great Dog.

⚓ **Jost Van Dyke** Anchorages at little Harbour, Great Harbour, and White Bay. While Little and Great are easy to enter, you must enter White Bay through a channel in the reef's center. It is subject to winter swells.

⚓ **Sandy Cay** Moorings offshore of this uninhabited island set to the E of Jost Van Dyke. Watch for swells.

⚓ **Norman Island** Moorings near the entrance to The Caves and at The Bight.

⚓ **Pelican Island and The Indians** Near The Bight off of Norman Island. Moorings offshore. Rainbow Canyon and other dive sites are nearby.

BVI INTRODUCTION

sents a number of boat owners and offers crewed charters at competitive prices.

NOTE: **Day sails** are listed under Tortola or Virgin Gorda in the travel section.

SAILING SCHOOLS: The **Offshore Sailing School** (☎ 800-221-4326, UK: 0808-234-4681) is at Prospect Reef.
http://www.offshore-sailing.com
sail@offshore-sailing.com

PROVISIONING: You may allow the charter company to provision you, provision yourself, or have an independent contractor provision you. Charter companies will either provision you for all meals or only some of them (thus allowing you to dine offshore). Be sure to ask for a sample menu.

Although a large number of items are available at shops and markets in the VI, many specialized items may not be found everywhere (or you may not have time to shop for them).

Camping in the BVI

Despite its reputation as one of the Caribbean's most expensive destinations, the BVI has a large number of small campgrounds. Camping makes a visit very affordable for the less well-heeled. And some places even have tents available. You can cook your own food (a considerable savings, given the high cost of dining out) and be much closer to nature than you would be otherwise. Theft is generally not a problem, but you should exercise caution anyway. There are two campgrounds: one on Tortola and one on Jost Van Dyke. Virgin Gorda and the other islands have none. ∎

MOORINGS: One important aspect of nautical travel around the BVI that visitors should be aware of is the system of moorings. This system was begun by the Virgin Islands Dive Operators Association, with funding from the Canadian government and with the full support of appropriate BVI governmental agencies. The number of moorings has grown to over 120 with a total of 250 permanent moorings projected. Each mooring consists of a stainless steel pin which is cemented into the bed rock; its eyehook is attached to a polypropylene rope which is about 10 ft. longer than the water's depth.

A half-pound lead weight is attached to the top of the cord; this keeps the extra cord from floating to the surface during slack periods at low tide. A plastic-filled mooring buoy is attached to this; it has a 15 ft. polypropylene rope with an eye splice at its end. This ingenious rig was invented by Dr. John Halas of Florida's Key Largo National Marine Sanctuary.

Buoys are color coded as follows: **red buoys** denote non-diving day use; **yellow** are restricted to commercial dive boats; and **white** are for dive use only on a first come,

first serve basis. There is a 90 min. limit on the white buoys.

No vessels over 55 ft. or 35 tons may use the buoys. You must attach to the pennant eye and make sure that there is no chafing with your boat. If the configuration provided proves incompatible, it is your responsibility to attach an extension line to the pennant eye. All buoys are used at your risk, and neither the government nor the National Parks Trust bears any responsibility for losses or injuries. All users of moorings must have legally met BVI Customs and Immigrations requirements and hold a valid National Parks Mooring Permit. Despite what one might conveniently hypothesize, a dinghy tied to a buoy indicates a reservation; it is not permissible to untie the dinghy, tie up your craft, and then tie the dinghy to your boat, as some opportunists have done. Setting a dinghy adrift is likewise prohibited.

If you are impressed by the buoy system and wish to support it, you may contribute to the Friends of the National Park Trust (see "organizations").

MOOR-SEACURE: Moorings have proven so popular that they have been installed at a number of islands by MOOR-SEACURE (☎ 494-4488). These include the Last Resort at Trellis Bay (Tortola), Marina Cay, Cooper Island, Anegada Reef Hotel, Cane Garden Bay (in front of Rhymer's, Tortola), Sopers Hole Marina (Tortola), Vixen Point, Biras Creek, Abe's By the Sea (Jost Van Dyke), and Harris (Jost Van Dyke). There is a fee to use these moorings.

Other Practicalities

ACCOMMODATIONS: Although these islands have intentionally geared themselves towards tourism for the wealthy and the super rich, some good values include campsites on Tortola, Anegada, and Jost Van Dyke. There are a few places to stay on the islands for under $100 d. Lower priced options include The Jolly Roger (West End, Tortola), Paradise Suites and the Seaview (Road Town).

A **7% hotel tax** applies to all accommodations save campsites, and a 10–15% service charge frequently is applied. (Tipping may be expected on top of this).

In the States a number of travel agents represent hotels and resorts in the BVI. One prominent agent is the **Caribbean Information Office,** Ltd. (☎ 800-621-1270, ✆ 708-699-7583).

bvisland@caribbeans.com

PROPERTY MANAGEMENT FIRMS: Renting your villa is an increasingly popular option. **Areana Villas** (☎ 494-5864, ✆ 494-7626; Box 263, Road Town) offers a variety of rentals.

http://www.areanavillas.com
info@areanavillas.com

British Virgin Islands Villas (☎ 494-2442, ✆ 494-1701) represents villas, resorts, and hotels.

http://www.britishvirginvillas.com
tranquille@surfbvi.com

Hawk's Nest (☎/✆ 495-1677; Box 926, Road Town) have rentals from $600 pw.

http://www.hawksnestbvi.com
info@hawksnestbvi.com

Nail Bay Resort and Villas (☎ 494-8000, 800-871-3551, ✆ 495-5875; Box 69, Virgin Gorda) offers one- to three-bedroom villas.

http://www.nailbay.com
info@nailbay.com

Priority Property Management (☎ 495-5201, ✆ 495-5723; PO Box 25,

---

A Traditional BVI Christmas

Although largely a thing of the past, a traditional Christmas is hallmarked by the production of guavaberry liqueur. Soaked in rum and spices, this concoction brews for six weeks until syrup is added. Locals would search for a fishing rod tree which would be transformed into a BVI Christmas tree.

From early Dec., carolers would arrive at homes from around 9:30 PM to 2 AM. They would visit every home right through New Years. Visitors would be given delights such as tarts or a small sum of money. ∎

Virgin Gorda) offers one- to three-bedroom units from $2,000 pw.

http://www.priorityproperty.com
info@priorityproperty.com

Purple Pineapple (☎ 495-5201, ✆ 495-5723, 877-787-7530) offers one- to six-bedroom units.

http://www.purplepineapple.com
reservations@purplepineapple.com

Tropix Property Management (☎ 495-6362, ✆ 495-6647) manages luxury villas on Virgin Gorda.

http://www.tropixbvi.com
info@ tropixbvi.com

FOOD: If you're on a tight budget, be aware that high prices largely prevail. In the restaurants, if you're from New York City, you'll pay the equivalent of home. Ask to see the menu before you sit down.

There are many reasonable places to eat, but fast food chains (thank goodness!) are banned, and even local places are hardly cheap ($1 for a watery cup of coffee!).

Small stores sell groceries on the islands. The only supermarkets are on Tortola.

BVI Conduct

If you would like to be well accepted by British Virgin Islanders, learn to speak in their manner.

☞ While greeting, ask about their health.

☞ Ask them to "Please repeat" rather than saying "What," if you do not understand something.

☞ Remember to ask before taking a photo. (Children love to have their photos taken but adults can be camera shy).

☞ Things (such as restaurant meals) may take a long time because the pace of life is slower. Learn to groove with it!

Fungi Music Revealed

Fungi, along with "scratch," is the term for the local folk music; a similar form is known in Jamaica as 'mento'; other West Indian islands have similar musical traditions. Many resorts have *fungi* musicians play. Or attend the annual Scratch/Fungi Music Festival held each Dec. Tortola's North Shore Shell Museum also has a *fungi* band play some nights. Check the *Limin Times* for other venues.

There are also a few other local artists.

Former Irish nurse and Nevis native Watts Pemberton produces music which combines Celtic, calypso, rumba and pop influences.

http://www.carijam.com

Other groups to watch out for include The Shooting Stars, a steel band; local calypsonians such as Benji V; and bands such as Caribbean Ecstasy. ∎

The *BVI Restaurant and Food Guide* is a good resource which is published in magazine form annually. It's online at:
http://www.bvirestaurantguide.com

SHOPPING: At one time there was not much to buy in the BVI, but the number and quality of shops have increased in recent years, but many goods are still imported from the other Caribbean islands. On Tortola, there are a number of some souvenir shops, but, unlike before, items are becoming more sophisticated: Balinese and Indonesian imports, fine jewelry, books, African tribal art. There are even a few local condiment manufacturers and some people cast ceramic dishes from molds and paint them. However, the best buy remains the duty-free alcohol (one liter) allowed by US customs.

Some alternative souvenirs include the postage stamps and sets of mint coins offered by the General Post Office in Road Town on Tortola, Sunny Caribbee's line of Caribbean seasonings and artwork.

MONEY: The US dollar reigns supreme here. Because of the physical proximity and economic ties with the USVI, the dollar was made the official currency back in 1962.

Credit cards are now as universally accepted as they are in the US Virgins. Some businesses may impose a 5% surcharge if you pay by credit card.

Measurements are the same as in the United States. Time here is permanently Atlantic Standard Time

MEDIA: The 10,000-watt **ZBVI** (780 AM) broadcasts weather reports every half-hour from 7:30 AM–6:30 PM.
http://www.zbviradio.com

The FM stations are **ZROD** (103.7), **Z Bold** (91.7), and **The Heat** (94.3).

The only newspapers are the weekly *Island Sun*, the weekly *Beacon* and the *BVI Standpoint*. Both are brief but informative and must-reads for those who wish to clue in on what's going on.

A free guide, *Limin' Times* highlights TV and entertainment. Pick one up at Bobby's Supermarket in Road Town, which also has a wide variety of imported newspapers.

VISAS: Residents of most countries do not require a visa, but a passport is required for entry. Visitors are given one-month entry stamps but may stay for up to six months (with renewals each month), provided they have return or onward tickets, sufficient funds (as judged by the customs official), and prearranged accommodations. (In practice, the last two are seldom required for shorter stays).

"Rastafarians" and "hippies" were once required to apply for "special approval" for entry. (This law was repealed in Aug. 2003.) Fido is welcome only if the Department of Agriculture (☎ 495-2532, ✆ 495-1269) gives its permission in advance. Jetskis (thank goodness!) are banned.

Cruising permits are required for all charter boats. They are available from the **BVI Customs Department** (☎ 494-3475, 468-3701, ext. 2533).

HEALTH: In Road Town is 50-bed **Peebles Hospital** (☎ 494-3497), eight doctors, two dentists, and two visiting eye specialists. (A new hospital is set to open in 2010; it will be directly above the current location).

The **B&F Medical Complex** (☎ 494-2196/4139/5313) is in the Mall Bldg. at Wickhams Cay I. There is only one doctor on Virgin Gorda. There's no decompression chamber (for divers) in the islands.

The **Bougainvillea Clinic** (☎ 494-2181, ✆ 494-6609), Russell Hill, offers general health services as well as plastic surgery.

Eureka Medical (☎ 494-2346, ✆ 494-6755), Medicure Heath Center in Road Town, also offers medical care.

Dr. Ron Hash (☎/✆ 494-4271), McNamara Rd. in Road Town, is a **chiropractor**. He also visits Virgin Gorda. chiron@surfbvi.com

CONDUCT: People here are among the most friendly and hospitable in the whole

BVI Phone Numbers	
Air Anguilla	495-1616
American Eagle	494-2559
Bobby's Cinemax	494-2098
BVI Hotel Assoc.	494-3514/ 494-2947
BVI Taxi Association	494-2322
Customs	494-2601, ext. 3475
Directory Assistance	119
Federal Express	494-2297
	494-4712
Fly BVI	495-1747
Immigration	494-3701, ext. 4961
Inter-Island Boat Services	495-4166
LIAT	495-1187
National Parks Trust	494-3904
Native Son (ferry)	495-4617
North Sound Express	494-2746
Peebles Hospital	494-3497
Peter Island Ferry	494-2561
Police	494-3822
Port Authority	494-3435
Roadtown Fast Ferry	494 2323
Smith's Ferry	494-5240
Speedy's Fantasy (ferry)	495-5240
Tourist Board	494-3134

Caribbean. Keep in mind, however, that the local culture is still highly conservative, so be sure to dress conservatively (e.g., confine your bathing suit to beach areas) and adopt a suitable demeanor. Some people may be sensitive about having their picture taken so try to ask; children, as in most places, are generally gleefully cooperative.

There's less theft here than in the USVI, and theft was the last thing on anyone's

British Virgin Islands Internet Sites

Information about the BVI is growing by leaps and bounds. The place to start is **www. bvitourism.com**. *or, for official government information visit* **bvi.gov.vg**. *Here is a small sample of other alternatives.*

http://www.exploreavirgin.com Information from the author of this book.

http://www.britishvirginislands.com General guide

http://limin-times.com Entertainment guide.

http://www.islandsun.com A BVI newspaper

http://www.bvibeacon.com The BVI's other newspaper

http://www.caribwx.com Weather info

http://www.bvigovernment.org. Local news and vacation guide

http://www.fly-bvi.com Sightseeing, photography, and inter-island BVI flights

http://www. capeair.com Capeair

http://www.bestofbvi.com British yacht and villa reservations. Great beach photos.

http://www.blytmann.com/anegada.htm Shipwrecks

http://www.anegada.com Anegada and chartering

http://www.bviwelcome.com *The Welcome* magazine online

http://www.bviguide.com BVI government

http://www.ultimatebvi.com General guide

http://www.wheretostay.com BVI hotel evaluations

http://www.bvihcg.com British Virgin Islands Conservation Group

mind a few years ago. These days, however, petty thievery is on the increase and reasonable caution is advised.

SERVICES AND INFORMATION: For information about the area, either the superbly informative and free bimonthly magazine *The Welcome* or the annual *Tourism Directory* is a must. Obtain a copy of the Tourism Directory before arrival by calling the tourist company at (800) 835-8530. But if you're going soon, let them know. While you have them on the line, specifically request the *Bonanza Vacations Packages* brochure as well as the useful *Intimate Inns* pamphlet.

The Welcome is online at:
http://www.bviwelcome.com
Also recommended is:
http://www.bvitourism.com

Banks On Tortola, the Bank of Nova Scotia, Banco Popular, First Caribbean, and FirstBank have varied opening hours but are generally open Mon. to Thurs from 8:30 or from 9 AM to 3 PM and on Fri. from 9 AM to 4 PM, or as late as 5:30 PM.

The **BVI Hotel and Commerce Association** (☎ 494-3514, ☻ 494-6179) assists visitors who are in need of finding accommodation or a business, or who wish to start a local business.

TELEPHONE SERVICES: The provider is Cable and Wireless, a monopoly whose main office is on Main Street in Road Town. **International phone calls** may be made from inside. To call islands from the US, dial 284 (the area code) + 49 (BVI code) + the remaining five digits.

▩ British Virgin Islands Tourist Board Offices ▩

BVI
The British Virgin Islands Tourist Board
P.O. Box 134, Road Town, Tortola
☎ 284-494-3134
✆ 284-494-3866
http://www.bvitourism.com
bvitourb@surfbvi.com

USA
New York
The British Virgin Islands Tourist Board
370 Lexington Avenue
New York, NY 10017
☎ 212-696-0400
☎ 800-835-8530

Atlanta
3390 Peachtree Rd., NE
Ste. 1000, Lenox Towers
Atlanta, GA 30326
☎ 404-240-8018
✆ 404-233-2318
bviatlanta@worldnet.att.net

UNITED KINGDOM
BVI Tourist Board
15 Upper Grosvenor Street
London, W1K 7PJ
☎ 44 (0) 207 355 9585
✆ 44 (0)207 355 9587
http://www.bvitourism.co.uk
infouk@bvitouristboard.com

GERMANY
BVI Information Office
c/o Travel Marketing Romberg TMR
Schwarzbachstr, 32
D-40822 Mettmann Bei Düsseldorf
☎ 49-2104-28-66-/1
✆ 49-2104-91-26-73
g.romberg@travelmarketing.de

ITALY
AIGO Communications
Piazza Caiaizzo 3
20124 Milano, Italy
☎ 011 39 02-667-14374
✆ 011-39-02-669-2648
staff@aigo.it

Pay phone cards (available in a number of denominations) simplify dialing. Certain phones now will only use these pay phone cards. Coins are not accepted in these phones. The cheapest way to call internationally is to use a US or international calling card. US cell phones have been known to connect to towers on St. John from certain areas of the islands. However, be sure to check your cell phone rates before "roaming" because local charges are extortionate.

At other pay phones, which also offer digital readouts, local calls are 25 cents and only quarters are accepted. Information is 119. The phone book may be searched online at: http://www.britishvirginislandsyp.com

INTERNET SERVICE: Internet service is available at a few locations everywhere. Some hotels offer Wifi and/or terminal access. However, the charges are high: around $20 ph.

Wireless "wi-fi hotspots" can be accessed at ten anchorages for a hefty daily or weekly fee. http://www.bvimarinewifi.com

POSTAL SERVICES: Road Town's **GPO**, on Main Street, is open Mon. to Fri. 9 AM–4 PM, Sat. 9–noon.

Post offices are found on Tortola at East End, West End, Cane Garden Bay, Carrot Bay; on Virgin Gorda at The Valley

British Virgin Islands Parks

© Harry S. Pariser

BVI Parks and Reserves

1. Botanical Gardens. Queen Elizabeth II Park
2. Sage Mountain National Park
3. Mount Healthy National Park
4. Diamond Cay (Jost Van Dyke)
5. Wreck of the *Rhone* National Park
6. Gorda Peak National Park
7. West Dog Bird Sanctuary
8. The Baths
9. Devils Bay, Spring Bay
9. Fort Point
10. Fallen Jerusalem Island
11. West Dog Island
12. Dead Chest Island
13. Prickly Pear Island

and North Sound; and on Jost Van Dyke and Anegada.

Rates on letters (per ½ oz.) are 55 cents for US/Canada, 60 cents for UK/Ireland, 75 cts for Europe, and 75 cents for Asia, Africa, and Australia. Postcards are 35 cents for US/Canada, 40 cents for UK/Ireland, 40 cents for Europe, and 50 cents for Asia, Africa, and Australia.

GETTING MARRIED: You will need to spend a minimum of three days on the island before you may apply for a marriage license. Register at the Registrar's Office (☎ 494-3492; Box 418, Road Town); it's open 9 AM–3:30 PM, Mon. to Fri.; 9–noon, Sat. You will need to supply your names, occupations, and the names of two witnesses. Fees are $35 (for an office wedding) or $110 plus travel expenses (if the wedding is performed off-premises.)

After organizing the date, you must apply for a license at the Attorney General's Chambers (☎ 494-3701). Fees (paid in postage stamps!) are $110 if you've spent between 3–14 days in the territory and $50 if you've been here 15 days or more.

Proof of identity and proof of marital status (original or certified copies of Decree Absolute for divorced spouses or a death certificate for deceased spouses) is required

If you would like a church wedding, you must arrange this with the minister and bans must be published for three consecutive Sundays prior to the wedding.

The registrar will only perform weddings on Mon. to Fri. from 9 AM–sunset and on Sat. from 9 AM–noon; he takes the day off every Sunday. For further information, contact the **Registrar's Office** (☎ 494-3701, ext. 5001, 5002, 5003).

ORGANIZATIONS: The offices of the **National Park Trust** (☎ 494-3904, 494-2069, ☺ 494-6383) are on Fishlock Rd. It is devoted to conserving natural and historic areas, protecting endangered or important species, and increasing public awareness. The organization won the 1996 Ecotourism Award given by *Islands* magazine. If you wish to send a tax deductible donation, make the check payable to ECNAMP and address it to National Parks Trust, Ministry of Natural Resources, Box 860, Road Town, Tortola, British Virgin Islands. Individual membership is $20, and family membership is $30.

Ex-Exxon tanker captains, Dow Chemical CEOS, and others may partially atone for their environmental sins by donating $1,000 or more and becoming benefactors.
**http://www.bvinationalparkstrust.org
bvinpt@caribsurf.com**

Virgin Islands Search & Rescue (Box 3042, Road Town) also needs donations to continue its valuable work of saving lives of those lost at sea. Tax-free US contributions may be made.

Kids and the Sea (☎ 494-4209) is a nonprofit organization which instructs the young about safety at sea and how to handle small craft, dive, swim, etc.

Sports

DIVING AND SNORKELING: This subject is detailed in the sections on individual locations. Diving and snorkeling's environmental impact has been limited here by the smaller numbers of visitors. Expect to pay around $70 for a one-tank dive and more for a night dive.

Here's an alphabetical listing of the most prominent sites:

Alice in Wonderland — **13** Less than 100 yards from Ginger I., SE of Tortola, this site offers profuse cornucopia of corals.

Anegada Reef — **19** Home of a number of shipwrecks including the *Rocus.*

Angelfish Reef — **6** A sloping reef set off the W edge of Norman Island. It's 90 ft. down to the bottom where you can find a large school of angelfish.

Blond Rock — **4** Resembling a natural amphitheater, this spot lies submerged in 12 ft. of water. Accessible only in calm water, it lies between Dead Chest and Salt Island. Lobsters, crabs, fan corals, and fish live here and love it. Its name comes from its yellowish dunce cap of fire coral. As there is heavy swell and strong current, it is best suited to the experienced. The environs (half-cave, half-open) evoke feelings you won't find elsewhere. The dive range is 10–60 ft.; this is an intermediate-level site.

Brenner's Bay — A good beginner spot, accessible by dinghy from Norman Island.

Brewers Bay Pinnacle — Located 200 yards from the W of the Bay, it houses stingrays and tarpon. A small cave lies on the E side of the bay.

The *Chikuzen* — Located six miles to the N of Beef Island, at a depth of 75 feet, this 246-ft. refrigerated vessel, sank in 1981. Numerous species of fish (including sting rays) live here.

Chimney — Set off of the N side of the W Bay of Great Dog. A canyon with an underwater arch and many small residents. Walls are covered with colorful coral. Avoid this site when there is a N swell.

Cockroach Island — An intermediate dive site, marked by a rocky pinnacle, is set 100 yds. off the SW corner. Lush corals and abundant sealife. An angelfish-inahbited ridge runs from the pinnacle's base towards Cockroach. Strong surface current.

George Dog — A 25–30 ft. dive.

Ginger Island — Site with large coral heads, wonderful visibility, and petable stingrays.

Great Dog Island — A reef to the S side extends E and W; there are a number of dive locations found here.

Great Harbour — This is directly across from Road Town Harbour and is a large protected bay to the N of Peter Island. It has a large number of colorful sponges.

The Indians — Four large rocks whose tips protrude near Pelican Rock. Soft and hard corals prosper in the canyons and grottoes of these formations. You'll find sea fans, elkhorn, brain, and other corals here. Exceptionally calm, this site is suitable for both scuba and snorkeling.

Invisibles — Set one mi. E of Necker Island, this site offers "peaks" whose summits are from four to 70 ft. below the surface. This area has plenty of marine life, including nurse sharks. Can be rough. An intermediate or advanced dive.

Joe's Cave — Near West Dog Island, this cathedral-like cave has colorful occupants ranging from eels to tarpon. This is a 20-30 ft. intermediate dive. It is named after the

British Virgin Islands Dive Sites	
1	Carrot Shoal (Peter I.)
2	Dead Chest West (Peter I.)
3	Painted Walls (Peter I.)
4	Blonde Rock
5	The Caves (Norman I.)
6	Angelfish Reef (Norman I.)
7	Rainbow Canyon (Norman I.)
8	Ringdove Rock (Norman I.)
9	The Indians (Norman I.)
10	Santa Monica Rock (Norman I.)
11	Wreck of the *Rhone* (Salt I.)
12	Dry Rocks West (Cooper I.)
13	Alice in Wonderland (Ginger I.)
14	The Chimney (Norman I.)
15	Joe's Cave (Norman I.)
16	Cockroach (Norman I.)
17	The Baths (Virgin Gorda)
18	The Aquarium
19	Anegada dive sites/*Rocus* wreck
20	*Chikuzen* wreck (Beef I.)

first dive operator to run trips here. Avoid this area when there is a N swell.

Little Camanoe — A 30-ft. reef dive is set off of the NE tip. Marvelous coral overhangs.

***Marie L*, The *Pat*, and the Barge and Grill** — A sunken modern cargo boat and tugboat. The first two, set off of Cooper Island's Manchioneel Bay, lie side by side at 45–90 ft. This is an intermediate dive. The Barge and Grill is a bit to the N.

Markhoe Point — Set off the SE edge of Cooper Island, this sheer rock wall plunges around 70 ft.; you may find nurse sharks here.

Painted Walls — A series of submerged rocks (off the SW point of Dead Chest I. It forms 20-50 ft. canyons. The site's name comes from the colorful sponges, algae, and corals that cover the rocks' surfaces. Great visibility. You might see angelfish or barracuda here. It's an intermediate-level site. The second canyon has a tunnel which leads

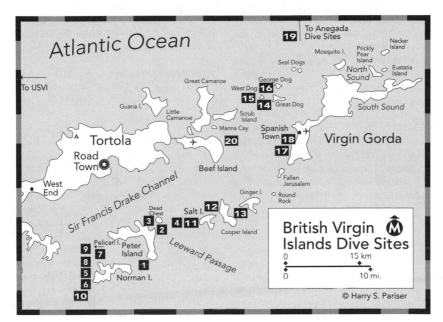

Atlantic Ocean

To USVI

Tortola

Road Town

West End

Sir Francis Drake Channel

Guana I.

Great Camanoe

Little Camanoe

Marina Cay

West Dog **16**

15

14 Great Dog

Scrub Island

Spanish Town **18**

17

Seal Dogs

George Dog

To Anegada **19** Dive Sites

Mosquito I.

Prickly Pear Island

Necker Island

North Sound

Eustatia Island

South Sound

Virgin Gorda

Beef Island

Fallen Jerusalem

Dead Chest

Ginger I.

Round Rock

Salt I. **12**

3

2

4 11

13

Cooper Island

Leeward Passage

Pelican I.

9

7

Peter Island

8

1

5

6

10

Norman I.

20

British Virgin ⓜ
Islands Dive Sites

0   15 km

0   10 mi.

© Harry S. Pariser

to a shallow reef and patches of coral garden. Be sure to turn over rocks to find the brittle starfish.

The *Rhone* — The remains of the 310-ft. two-masted steamer which now lie at depths of 20-80 ft. Viewed in the crystal-clear water, it's a veritable underwater museum and is one of the most famous dive sites in the entire Caribbean. Its **anchor** is outside Great Harbour off Peter Island at a depth of 55 ft. (It can be hard to find; a guided tour is recommended). As the stem is in shallower water, it's more suitable for snorkelers, as is the Rhone Reef. There is a fringing reef located to the S of the wreck, which has two coral caves at a depth of 25 ft., as well as colorful marine life.

Scrub Island — A reef is found off the N shore of this small island off of Tortola.

Seal Dog Rock — This "rock" extends down to 60 ft.; for experienced divers only.

A cultivated pearl among the natural varieties, the ***Fearless***, a 97-ft. 300-ton ship, is the BVI's newest dive site. A former mine sweeper which never saw naval action, the ship served as Triton's machine shop at Nanny Cay. When it began to sink at the dock, it was donated to the BVI Dive Operators Association who then anchored and sank the boat off Peter Island. Although the boat was apparently already sinking, she refused to go down when she arrived at her intended gravesite and tons of water had to be pumped into her hold before she sank. The craft has now been joined by The ***Willie T***, a bar and restaurant anchored off of Norman Island.

Santa Monica Rock — Another underwater pinnacle lying about a mile from Norman Island in the direction of St. Croix. Its location makes it an ideal site to see spotted eagle rays, nurse sharks, and barracudas.

Van Ryan's Rock — This is off Collision Point on Virgin Gorda and has lobsters, turtles, many fish and corals.

Visibles — A set of caves and canyons which reach 70 ft. Nurse sharks and moray eels live here, and many fish species spawn here.

REGULATIONS: You may not remove any marine or terrestrial plant, animal or historical artifact. Fishing without a license is prohibited. Dispose of garbage only at correct garbage disposal points. Building fires and waterskiing are prohibited activities within park waters.

DEEP-SEA FISHING: The BVI are some of the world's richest sport fishing grounds. Spearfishing is prohibited. Charters operate on Tortola, Virgin Gorda, and Anegada. Wahoo, dolphin (the fish), tuna, and kingfish abound. The world's record Atlantic blue marlin (1,300 lbs.) was caught here.

Great deep-sea fishing spots include the **Sea Mount**, a volcanic island that rises 2,000 ft. from the seabed and is 20 mi. E of Virgin Gorda; the **Saddle**, an area NE of Jost Van Dyke which drops off to 1,000 ft.; and the section beyond Anegada's Horseshoe Reef.

The **BVI Yacht Club** sponsors a number of annual tournaments including the Game Fish Tournament, which coincides with the August Festival, and the Charity, Easter, and Ladies' tournaments. Permits are required: contact the **Fisheries Division** (☎ 494-3429) for information.

SURFING: The best surfing is found at Cane Garden Bay and at Apple and Carrot beaches on Tortola. It is best during the winter months.

WINDSURFING: Known as "boardsailing" here. Many resorts provide or rent equipment. **Boardsailing BVI** (☎ 495-2447, 494-0422, 800-880-SURF; Box 537, Long Look), at Beef Island's Trellis Bay, provides lessons and rentals. they also have a branch at Nanny Cay (☎ 494-0422), and they also rent kayaks. Windsurfing cruising, a new type of windsurfing, is being popularized here. Owing to technological advances, long boards and sails have been lightened, making it feasible to windsurf from island to island. In one day you can windsurf from Tortola across the Sir Francis Drake Channel, go to Anegada (15 mi.), or to North Sound (10 mi.).
http://www.windsurfing.vi
jwright@surfbvi.com

HORSEBACK RIDING: Shadow's Stables (494-2262) on Tortola takes you on trips to Cane Garden Bay or up Mt. Sage. **Mr. Thomas** (☎ 494-4442) also offers good trips. This is an atypical way to see the island

Traveling Around the BVI

Tortola

Ferries from St. John to St. Thomas ply along beautiful coasts and past romantic, deserted islets to reach the very attractive island of Tortola. Although development has made an impact here (most of the British Virgin Islands' 10,000 population resides on Tortola), there is little of the sprawling concrete architecture that has spoiled the majesty of St. Thomas.

Protected from heavy traffic by a bypass, the administrative capital Road Town (pop. about 1,500) retained its small-town flavor well into the 1980s. Sadly, it has been over-whelmed (through lack of organized planning) by a flood of concrete boxes, many of which are downright ugly. These days, the once-calm town is now beset by traffic jams most weekday rush-hour mornings and afternoons. There's also a new cruise terminal out in the middle of nowhere; shops may be eventually be built near it.

Although crowded compared with the recent past, the remainder of the island has only been touched by a well-disguised and harmoniously built hotel and/or villa here and there.

Split lengthwise by a ridge of sharply ascending hills, Tortola is studded with islets, coves, sandy beaches, and bays. Sugarcane cultivation having ceased long ago, much of the land has been reclaimed by nature. If you look carefully, however, you can sill see the outlines of what once were fields.

In addition to sugar, Tortola supplied Britain with Sea Island cotton—more than a million pounds of it by 1750. Cotton declined as cheaper green-seed cotton from the American South became available, so local Sea Island cotton was supplanted by sugar, which declined in turn.

Travel here is steep but sweet. The paved concrete roads are embossed with the criss-cross impressions of rake heads. These roads shoot sharply up hills giving way to majestic panoramas before descending in curves to the bold blue bays below. Sky World, a restaurant above Road Town, offers a 360-degree panorama.

Practicalities

GETTING HERE: The **Road Town Fast Ferry** (☎ 494-2323, St. Thomas: 777-2800), a high-speed catamaran ($55 RT, 50 min.), departs at Charlotte Amalie at 8:30 AM, noon, and 4 PM from Mon. to Sat. and on Sun at noon and at 4 PM. Children's fares are discounted, and packages and discount fares are offered. They also offer service from Red Hook (35 min.) at 8 AM, 11 AM, 2:30 PM, and 5:45 PM.
http://www.roadtownfastferry.com

Smith's Ferry Services (☎ 775-7292) and *Native Son* (☎ 774-8685) depart from Mon. to Fri. for West End and Road Town daily from 8 AM to 5:30 PM. Sat., Sun, and Wed. Schedules are different from the other days. Fares are $45 RT adults, $35 children under 12.

http://www.smithsferry.com
http://www.nativesonbvi.com

BEACHES: The finest beaches are all on the N side of the island. Set at the westernmost end, **Smugglers Cove** offers good snorkeling. Smugglers has a bar now and a stand that sells drinks. The beach is well worth the trip.

GETTING HERE: Secluded, difficult to reach, and calm, it's reached by an unpaved but passable road. The dirt road (less than ten min., passable without four-wheel-drive during the dry) leads here from Long Bay Beach Resort. (Take the very first R; turn just before the sign for the exclusive Belmont Estates). Follow the "road," such as it is, through the forest, drive inland around a salt pond, and turn R where you'll see "parking." (Remember to bear L when you return). Taxi drivers (natch) want to see this stretch paved. Nearby residents treasure the way things are. There was a threat of development, but now it will become a national park:
http://www.bvihcg.com/smugglers.shtml

Long Bay is a mile-long white sand beach. The home of Long Bay Beach Resort, it is one of the Caribbean's most beautiful beaches. Its W end is skirted by seagrapes and palms. It has a lot of dead coral and rocks in the water, so it's not one of the better swimming beaches.

Just over the hill from Long Bay is **Apple Bay,** popular with surfers, where the Bomba Shack is located as well as the Apple and Sebastian's. Nearby are **Little Apple Bay** (good surfing) and **Carrot Bay.**

The beautifully curved **Cane Garden Bay** is popular with yachtspeople, and any water sport you can name is available at the

hotels here. If a cruise ship is in the harbor, expect crowds.

Named after the refineries which once flourished there, **Brewers Bay** is the home of the campground of the same name and offers some of the island's best snorkeling or (when the water is turgid) body surfing.

Josiahs Bay (home of several small hotels), offers **good surfing** but may have strong undertows at times. To get to it, follow Little Dick's Rd. from the Long Look Police Station and take a R before the hill.

Only made accessible by car in recent years, **Elizabeth Bay** (now called **Lambert Bay** is past **Josiahs Bay** to the E. Cuter than the Queen, Elizabeth/Lambert offers good swimming (but strong undertows!). To get here, head for the Long Look Police Station, turn onto Blackburn Hwy., then turn R onto Greenland Rd., and head up a hill and watch for an entrance gate on the L.

Long Bay East is on Beef Island. It is a great place to go. To get here, head in the direction of the airport but turn L at the salt flats, where you follow the dirt road to the R. (Do not drive *across* the flats!)

TRANSPORT, TOURS, AND CAR RENTALS: For shared taxi rates see the Introduction. You can walk (the hills are steep and the sun hot), and you can hitch.

At Wickhams Cay I, the **BVI Taxi Association** (☎ 494-2875/2322, 495-2378) offers tours and transport.

Another choice is the United **BVI Taxi Federation** (☎ 495-5539) which has six members.
http://www.unitedbvitaxi.com

Scato's Bus Service (☎ 494-2365) provides some public transportation, special tours, and airport and boat pickups. They run open-air buses around the island on an irregular schedule.

In the Romasco Building, **Travel Plan Tours** (☎ 494-2872) features every manner of car rentals, water sports rentals, diving, and tours.
http://www.aroundthebvi.com

Linked to the Brewers Bay Campground, **Style's Tour Operator** (☎ 494-2260, day; 494-3341, eve.) operates out of Wickhams Cay. They'll arrange tours, park trips, and diving.

Fly BVI (☎ 495-1747) will take you over the water and give you great photo opportunities.
http://www.fly-bvi.com

Ultralight Flight Adventures (☎ 495-2311, pager 496-5520) offers scenic flights and flight training to Anegada and Eustasia in a seaplane.

CAR RENTALS: Expect to spend from $45 pd on up, and you must pay $10 for a temporary permit. (Rates can be $35/day off season). For current rates check with the operators or see *The Welcome.*

Alphonso Car Rentals (☎ 494-8746, 494-8756, ✆ 494-8736) at Fish Bay. Rates run from around $40 pd.
http://www.alphonsocarrental.com
alphonso_ent@email.com

Avis (☎ 494-3322, 494-2193, ✆ 494-4128, 800-228-0668) is near the Botanic Gardens.
nibbscarrental@surfbvi.com

Courtesy Car Rentals (☎ 494-6443, ✆ 494-2162), Wickhams Cay I., rents four-door sedans, jeeps, and scooters from $40 pd.

Del's Jeep and Car Rental (☎ 495-9356), Cane Garden Bay, offers Suzuki Sidekicks.

Denzil Clyne Car Rentals (☎ 495-4900) at West End and offer a free day with weekly rentals.

Dollar Rent a Car (☎ 494-6093, ✆ 494-7837) rents Suzukis with 4WD and a/c.
dollar@surfbvi.com

D&D Car Rentals (☎ 495-7676, 495-4765, ✆ 494-8241) have two- and four-door Suzuki Sidekicks from $55/day.
d&dcarrental@surfbvi.com

Hertz Car Rental (☎ 495-5803) is at West End and Road Town. Cars rent from $50 pd.
http://www.hertzbvi.com
hertzbvi@hotmail.com

International Car Rentals (☎ 494-2516, ✆ 494-4713) offers cars and jeeps of all sizes. Rates start at $30 pd. They're at International Motors in Road Town.
http://www.carrentals.vg
intercar@surfbvi.com

Itgo Car Rental (☎ 494-5150, ✆ 494-4975), Wickhams Cay I., rents cars from $35 pd.
http://www.itgobvi.com
info@itgobvi.com

Jerry's Car Rental (☎ 495-4111, 494-4652, ✆ 495-4114, 800-430-7648), West End, offers pickup and delivery. Rates start at $50/day.
http://www.info-res.com/jerryjeep
islandride@surfbvi.com

National Car Rental (☎ 494-3197, ✆ 494-4085; Long Bay: 495-4877), set in the Towers in the West End, rents jeeps with unlimited mileage. Rates start at $50 pd.
national@surfbvi.com

TORTOLA

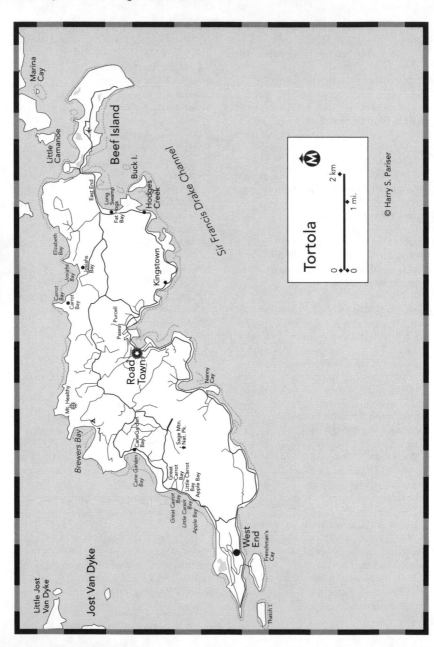

Tortola

© Harry S. Pariser

Tortola Taxi Fares

Charter rates are for maximum of 3 persons. Rates in parentheses are for each additional person in excess of 3. Tours (2.5 hrs.) are $50 (1 to 3); $15 add'l person

From Beef Island Airport to	Per Person	taxi charter	(more than 3)
East End/Long Look	3.00		
Hodge's Creek/Paraquita Baadventure Brandywine Bay/Hope/Josiah's Bay`	4.00	12.00	(4.00)
Kingstown/Fish Bay/Jean Hill/Baughers Bay/Port Purcell/Free Bottom	5.00	15.00	(5.00)
Wickhams Cay II./Road Town/Prospect Reef/ Huntum's Gut/Lower Estate	6.00	18.00	(6.00)
Sea Cow's Bay/Nanny Cay/Palestina	8.00	24.00	(8.00)
Doty/Harrigan's	10.00	30.00	(10.00)
Smuggler's Cove/West End/Little Apple Bay/Long Bay/Carrot Bay/Cane Garden Bay/Brewer's Bay	8.00	24.00	(8.00)
From Road Town to			
Prospect Reef/MacNamara/Port Purcell Roundabout/Lower Estate/Treasure Isle/ Wickhams Cay	3.00		
Upper Huntum's Ghut/CSY/Fort Hill/ Bougher's Bay/Purcell/Free Bottom	4.00		
Pieces of Eight/Duff's Bottom/Sea Cow's Bay Fish Bay/Kingstown	4.00	10.00	(4.00)
Harrigan's	4.00	12.00	(4.00)
Meyer's/Belle Vue/Brandywine/Colonial Manor/Chalwell/Fahie Hill/Long Trench/ Sky World	4.00	12.00	(4.00)
Sage Mountain	6.00	18.00	(6.00)
Nanny Cay/Pleasant Valley/Palestina	5.00	12.00	(5.00)
Havers/Coxheath/Pock Wood Pond/Doty Soldier's Hill/Hodge's Creek/Lower Hope	5.00	14.00	5.00
East End/Long Look	5.00	15.00	5.00
Brewer's Bay/Cane Garden Bay/West End/ Little Apple Bay/Beef Island Airport/ Trellis Bay/Frenchman's Cay/Long Bay Hotel/ Carrot Bay/Ballast Bay/Windy Hill	6.00	18.00	(6.00)
Smuggler's Cove	8.00	24.00	(8.00)

TORTOLA

From West End Jetty to	Per Person	taxi charter	(more than 3)
Frenchman's Cay/Fort Recovery/Zion Hill/ Lower Romney Park	3.00		
Cappoon's Bay/Little Carrot Bay/Sugar Mill Long Bay Hotel/Upper Romney Park	4.00	12.00	(4.00)
Ballast Bay/Windy Hill/Great Carrot Bay/ Pockwood Pond	4.00	12.00	(4.00)
Cane Garden Bay/Smuggler's Cove Nanny Cay/Palestina/Sea Cow's Bay/ Duff's Bottom	5.00	15.00	(5.00)
Burt/Prospect Reef/Huntum's Ghut/Road Towri/Joe's Hill/Treasure Isle/Wickhams Cay I./Baugher's Bay/ Purcell/ Free Bottom	6.00	18.00	(6.00)
Harrigan's/Great Mountain/Kingstown/ Meyers/Belle Vue/Fahie Hill/Hope Estate	8.00	24.00	(8.00)
Brewers Bay/Long Look/East End	9.00	27.00	(8.00)
Beef Island	12.00	36.00	(12.00)

Tola's Rentals (☎ 494-8652, ℮ 494-8654), Fish Bay, offers free mileage and packages. Rates start at $45 pd.
http://www.tolarentals.com
tolasales@surfbvi.com

BIKE RENTALS: Last Stop Sports Bike Rentals (☎ 494-1120, ℮ 494-0593), Port Purcell Rd., rents mountain bikes for $20 pd. They are open daily and will deliver.
http://www.laststopsports.com

Road Town

Road Town, named after its port of Road Harbour, is the only settlement truly worthy of the description "town." Small but charming, this administrative capital lies sandwiched between the island's foothills and the sea. Over the decades it has grown, and the Wickhams Cay developments and the main road through town have been constructed on reclaimed land.

Despite the opening of a disco or two, not much happens here except a bake sale on Saturdays. Roosters and hens, a goat or two, and an occasional herd of cattle still supplement the pedestrian population.

GETTING AROUND: It's easy and comfortable to walk everywhere in town. The reclaimed land along the waterfront has changed the town's face dramatically. Once, it could take an hour to drive along Main St. through the town. These days, Main Street has been preserved as a bastion of tranquility: the picture postcard West Indies as it once was. The main road is noisy and ugly, but Main Street still conjures up remembrances of a time when one came into town and hitched up your mule and there were only sixteen telephones on the entire island. Unfortunately, however, the Concrete Box

The view from Sky Bar & Restaurant is, from L to R, the S end of Virgin Gorda, Fallen Jerusalem, tiny Round Rock, Ginger Island, Cooper Island, Salt Island, Peter Island, Norman Island, and Pelican Island (a blip). Flanagan's Island is a small USVI-owned islet to your far R.

school of architecture has taken over the better part of town and is threatening to consume Main Street as well. Enjoy it while you can.

Road Town Sights

The old part of town is all along Main St. which, believe it or not, backed directly onto the harbor until 1968. The town's area has been expanded through landfill. Because influences from outside the islands are so pervasive, many old structures have been pulled down in a misguided attempt to modernize the islands.

The best place to begin a walking tour is Road Town's small **Virgin Islands Folk Museum** (☎ 494-37001, ext. 5005) on Main Street. (It's generally open Mon. to Fri., 8:30 AM–4:30 PM). Look for it next to the Beacon Bible Bookstore; it's up some steps and easy to miss.

The old **Administration Building,** facing Sir Olva Georges Plaza, was constructed in 1866 from local stone.

The century-old **De Castro Building** is a bit farther on; it contains an unusual brick circular staircase.

Down the street to the L stands **Britannic Hall,** built by a surgeon in 1910. A bit farther and also on the L is the early 19th-C **St. Georges Church**. The Anglican and Methodist churches are nearby.

Sandwiched between two churches, the **H. M. Prison** is the oldest building in town. Across the street is a workshop which markets tee shirts and other items. It may be visited. A convicted Columbian marijuana smuggler (10 tons!) and a Puerto Rican cocaine smuggler (10 kg) walked out of a workshop across for the prison and on to freedom in March 1996. The new prison is in East End and is much more secure. While the prison was once scheduled for transformation into a museum, prisoners rioting at the new facility forced its reopening as inmates were transferred to ease overcrowding.

Just past the corner of Fleming St. and Joe's Hill Rd. lies the **Sunday Morning Well,** where the Emancipation Act was reportedly read on Aug. 1, 1834. The Legislative Council sits in session and court hearings are held in the **Courthouse** or Legislative Council Chamber nearby.

The **Survey and Planning Building,** near the Police Headquarters, was originally a cotton factory.

Government House, the fomer governor's residence, stands at the other end of town near Peeble's Hospital. It is the most representative example of colonial architecture in Road Town and now has a small but fantastic new museum. The house, which replaced an earlier structure destroyed by a hurricane in 1924, dates from 1926; it closed in 1996 and reopened in late 2003. Hugh Whistler MBE, the man behind the transformation, helped save this historic structure from demolition and replacement.

As you enter the premises, you find a history of the home. The governor general's uniform, worn by Gov. Frank Savage who served from 1998–2002, is on display here. Furnishings include period pieces ranging from the late 1800s to the 1930s. Murals on the dining room walls depict life in 19th-century Tortola. The breezy outdoor patio was built for Princess Margaret's stay here in 1972, and the dining table was brought here especially for her stay. Government

Great meals are offered at the **Royal BVI Yacht Club**. Although it is a member's club, visitors are welcome.
If you are on a budget, **Bobby's Marketplace** and **Riteway** (on Fleming St.) offer excellent low cost ($3–$8) lunches and dinners to take away.

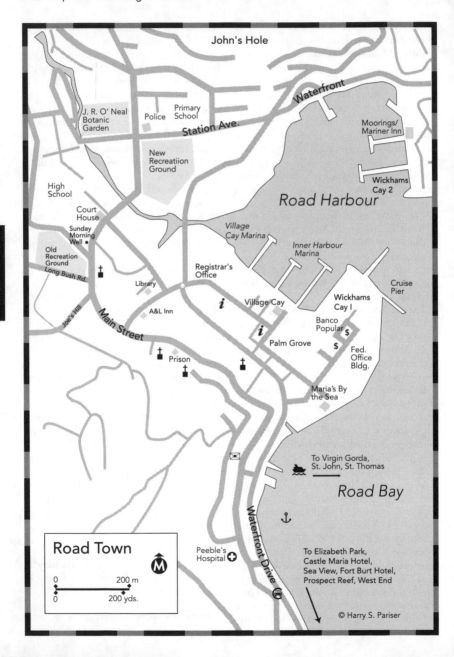

John's Hole

Waterfront

J. R. O' Neal Botanic Garden

Police

Primary School

Station Ave.

Moorings/ Mariner Inn

New Recreatiion Ground

Wickhams Cay 2

High School

Road Harbour

Court House

Sunday Morning Well •

Village Cay Marina

Old Recreation Ground

Long Bush Rd.

Inner Harbour Marina

Library

Registrar's Office

i

Cruise Pier

A&L Inn

Village Cay

Wickhams Cay I

Banco Popular

$

Joe's Hill

Main Street

i

Palm Grove

$

Fed. Office Bldg.

Prison

Maria's By the Sea

To Virgin Gorda, St. John, St. Thomas

Road Bay

Road Town

⚓

Peeble's Hospital ✚

Waterfront Drive

To Elizabeth Park, Castle Maria Hotel, Sea View, Fort Burt Hotel, Prospect Reef, West End

0   200 m
0   200 yds.

© Harry S. Pariser

TORTOLA

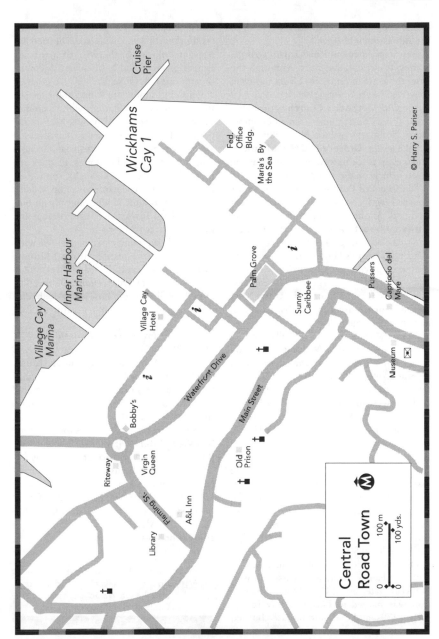

TORTOLA

**Central
Road Town**

Cruise Pier

Wickhams Cay 1

Fed. Office Bldg.

Maria's By the Sea

Inner Harbour Marina

Village Cay Marina

Palm Grove

Village Cay Hotel

Pussers

Capriccio del Mare

Sunny Caribbee

Waterfront Drive

Bobby's

Main Street

Museum

Riteway

Virgin Queen

Old Prison

Fleming St.

A&L Inn

Library

100 m
100 yds.

House is open from 9 AM–2 PM, Mon. to Sat. Admission is charged.

Four forts surround Road Town: George, Shirley, Charlotte, and Burt. Although the latter three are in ruins, **Fort Burt** has been converted into a boutique hotel.

The **Old Methodist Church** is probably Road Town's finest timber-framed building. Other landmarks include **Niles rum shop** and the unique **Grocery and Meat Market.** The pickup truck parked out in front is the oldest vehicle on the island.

The so-called **Purple Palace** is the most unusual and conspicuous architectural landmark on the island. It now houses the **Fifteen Abbott Lane** restaurant in addition to a plastic surgery clinic.

Atop Harrigan's Hill in the MacNamara section of town, **Fort Charlotte** was once one of the island's largest fortifications, built by the Royal Engineers in 1794. Now all that remains are a few walls, a cistern, and an underground magazine.

During your visit, you'll likely stop at something or other at **Wickhams Cay**. Its name stems from the fact that it was once a palm-grove-and-mangrove swamp separated from the mainland by a wide channel.

The newest museum is the **1780 Lower Estate Sugar Works Museum** which is across from the Treasure Isle Hotel. Donations are requested.

PARKS: The four-acre **J. R. O'Neal Botanic Gardens** (☎ 494-4557) provide a peaceful refuge and an introduction to the islands' flora. Maintained by the National Parks Trust and the BVI Botanical Society, the gardens are on the grounds of the town's original Agricultural Station.

The first station was established here in 1902 by Henry Steel, who was followed two years later by W. C. Fishlock. The station was moved to Parquita Bay in the early 1970s, and the building later burned

down. Support for the gardens, which were established in 1986, was spearheaded by Margaret Barwick, the wife of a former British governor and businessman and conservationist J. R. O'Neal.

On the grounds you'll find the ruins of the old Agricultural Station (with its colony of turtles), a variety of palms, herbs, and orchids. The squawking caged parrots add an edge of realism to the tropical gardens. Watch for red-footed tortoises. Plaques are everywhere: "Ms. Jane C. Taylor sponsored this tree. 1986." The gardens are open daily from dawn to dusk. If you can only go one place in Road Town, come here! Foreign visitors are charged $3 for admission.

A small community park bordered with white cedars (the territorial tree) **Queen Elizabeth Park** stands near Government House. An expanded version, due to open in 2009, will have gazebos, benches, shaded area, jogging paths and other features.

Road Town Accommodations

LOW BUDGET: The best deal in town is 30-room **Way Side Inn Guest House** (☎ 494-3606; Box 258, Road Town), which has all-year rates of around $50 s or d and caters to down-islanders. Most of the rooms share cold-water baths.

Next up on the price scale is the 38-room **Sea View Hotel** (☎ 494-2483, ✉ 494-4952; Box 59, Road Town); it offers 28 rooms for around $75 s or d plus 10% service charge. More expensive ($145) studios/ efficiencies are available. The Sea View is just out of the town's center to the S by the turnoff for Hotel Castle Maria.
seaviewhotel@surfbvi.com

National Educational Services Bookstore sells cheap postcards and has a good selection of Caribbean literature.

CENTRALLY-LOCATED HOTELS: Providing 14 a/c rooms with phone and television, **A & L Inn,** (☎ 494-6343/6344/6345, ☏ 494-6656; Box 403, Road Town), Fleming St., is two blocks in from the sea. High season rates run from around $105 s or d. Weekly and monthly rates are available. A 12% service charge is imposed. **alguesthouse@hotmail.com**

Hummingbird House (☎ 494-0039) is a bed and breakfast set in the tree lined estate of Pasea, a quiet suburb only minutes from restaurants and conveniences. All rooms have a/c (additonal surcharge applies), bath, TV, refrigerator, and coffeemaker. No smoking inside. Internet access is additional, but WiFi is free. There's a large terrace with pool, an 'honor bar" and a library lounge . Complimentary breakfast is served. **http://www.hummingbirdbvi.com yvonnelr@surfbvi.com**

Centrally located **Paradise Suites** (☎ 494-3525, ☏ 494-2162; Box 395, Road Town) offers 24 attractive rooms with phones, cable TV, a/c and fans, and refrigerators. There's also a full-sized Jacuzzi as well as 24-hour concierge service. Rates are from around $95 d. (Triples and suites are also offered). It's set in One Stop Mall where you can dine in a cafeteria with the locals, have your hair done here, and even buy clothes. Read the reviews on tripadvisor.com before booking. **http://www.paradisesuitestortola.com paradisesuitesbvi@yahoo.com**

On Wickhams Cay and in the vicinity of the marina, motel-style 40-unit **Maria's By The Sea** (☎ 494-2595, ☏ 494-2420; Box 2364, Road Town) has a bar/restaurant and a pool. Some units have kitchenettes with refrigerator, hotplate, and toaster. Rooms start at $160 d. A 10% service charge is imposed.

http://www.mariasbythesea.com mariasbythesea@surfbvi.com

Offering 19 elegant suites, **Village Cay Resort Marina and Hotel** (☎ 494-2771, ☏ 494-2773, Box 145, Road Town) is set amidst a complex of shops. This marina/hotel has a long history. It was built in 1974 and was completely renovated in 1996. Jimmy Buffet may have written his immortal celebratory carnivore ballad "Cheeseburgers in Paradise" while moored at one of the piers here. (Stanley's in Cane Garden Bay is thought to be another possibility).

It also hosts a number of prestigious nautical events including the Caribbean 1500, a cruising rally which runs from Virginia to Tortola. Its standard rooms rent for $175–$405 d. Some rooms have balconies. Facilities include a pool, restaurant, secretarial service, cable TV, a/c, and in-room refrigerators. **http://www.igy-villagecay.com vc@igy-villagecay.com**

Village Cay Gardens (☎ 494-4389, ☏ 494 6864; Box 396 Road Town) rents one-bedroom and two-bedroom apartments and villas.

HEADING NORTH OUT OF TOWN: On a hillside overlooking the harbor at Road Town, the **Treasure Isle Hotel** (☎ 494-2501, ☏ 494-2507; Box 68, Road Town) has rooms ranging from 50 motel-style rooms to three suites. The hotel is painted in attractive pastel shades.

Gourmet dining is offered on the covered terrace in its restaurant. It has a pool, tennis courts, bar, and marina. Rates are $250 d (plus 10% service and tax) during the high season. They offer a free daily shuttle to Cane Garden Bay, home of a popular beach. **http://www.treasureislehotel.net treasureislebvi@yahoo.com**

Located on the outskirts of town, the **Moorings Mariner Inn** (☎ 494-2332, ✉ 494-2226, 800-535-7289; Box 216, Road Town) lacks a beach itself. It has 39 rooms plus two suites in two blocks of two-storey buildings. Nearly all guests stay here for the boating. The Moorings Charter Boat operation here encompasses Treasure Isle Hotel. Diving and sailing package holidays are offered. Contact them for rates.
http://www.moorings.com

HEADING SOUTH FROM TOWN: Overlooking Road Town, peaceful and private **Hotel Castle Maria** (☎ 494-2553/2515/4255 ✉ 494-2111; Box 206, Road Town) is close to town but is far enough out of the way to be quiet. The hotel offers 30 units with a/c or fan, some with kitchenettes and sea views, a bar, and a large pool. Lush and carefully tended gardens border the entrance. Its Thai restaurant is open for lunch and dinner. Rates start at $95 s (garden view) and $99 d; triples and quads are offered. Weekly rates are obtainable on request. To find this hotel, turn R when you reach the Sea View and head on to the R. Keep in mind that this is a budget option: roosters crow at the break of dawn. Local Alfred Christopher is in charge here. Before booking, read the reviews at tripadvisor.com.
http://www.islandsonline.com/
  hotelcastlemaria
hotelcastlemaria@surfbvi.com

Set on the W edge of Road Town, **Prospect Reef Resort** (☎ 494-3311/3773, ✉ 494-7800, USA: 800-356-8937, Canada: 800-463-3608; Box 104 Road Town) first opened in the 1970s. Plans were to sell the apartments here, a plan that never materialized.

The 122 rooms are close-set and offer a/c (in some units), kitchen, and phone. On the premises are charter boats, snorkel and scuba, deep-sea fishing, pools, seven tennis courts, shops, hairdressing salon, and health spa (with "thalassotherapy" seaweed treatments). Rates begin at around $150 d. A 10% service charge is added. A number of packages are available, and a special children's program "Pals of Prospect Reef," offers environmental adventures. They also offer transport to Tortola beaches.

Dolphin Discovery here offers visitors a chance to meet and swim with captive dolphins. The dolphins are kept in a small lagoon, and the operating company is owned by expat Americans who operate a similar (but much larger) business in Mexico. "Swimming with dolphins" is a big business, and many environmental groups oppose the practice, claiming that it is injurious to the dolphins to keep them captive. The facility does not enjoy the most salubrious of reputations among BVI residents.
http://www.prospectreefbvi.com
info@prospectreefbvi.com

VILLAS, CONDOS, AND OTHER ACCOMMODATIONS: The **New Happy Lion Apts.** (☎ 494-2574/4088; Box 402, Road Town) offers two housekeeping units with kitchen and TV from $65–$100; it has a restaurant.
wpearl@hotmail.com

TOWARDS WEST END FROM ROAD TOWN: Set at a marina on the W coast S of Road Town, **Nanny Cay Resort and Marina** (☎ 494-2512, ✉ 494-0555, 8888-BVI-HOTEL; UK: 181-940-3399; Box 281, Road town) offers weekly rentals, although many are rented out long-term. Facilities include restaurants, adult and children's pools, training schools, laundromat, boutique, car rental, volleyball court, mountain bikes, windsurfing, and diving. A/c rooms have a private balcony/patio, kitchenette, coffee machine, phone, radio, and TV. From the property you can see Guana Island on one side and St. John on

the other. **Captain Mulligan's Golf Driving Range** (☎ 499-1513, 496-7219) is also here as are **Blue Water Divers** (☎ 494-2874; also at Sopers Hole), **Arawak Boutique, D&S Sewing Center** (video rentals), and **Bamboushay** (pottery). The ruins of Fort Chalwell are under excavation nearby. Rates for standard studios start at $200 d; tax and 10% service charge are applied. Dive packages are offered.
http://www.nannycay.com
hotel@nannycay.com

Farther on towards the West End and near Havers Estate, **Hall's Haven** (☎ 494-3946). Manuel Reef offers a fully equipped main house and a guest house. Call (902) 275-5022 or write Box 464, Chester, Nova Scotia, Canada BOJ 1JO.
arjaymarine@ns.sympatico.ca

Road Town Dining and Food
In town, there are a variety of small restaurants, a bakery, and some supermarkets.
Other restaurants are listed under the specific areas concerned.

LOCAL FOOD: You shouldn't leave the BVI without at least sampling the local food. Breakfast, at the classic **Midtown Restaurant** (☎ 494-2764), near the center of Main Street, costs $6; sandwiches are $2.50 and up; and fish and chips are around $6. They also serve local cuisine like conch fritters ($4 for a very small portion).

Located off of Main Street and near the bakery, the inexpensive **Roti Palace** offers a variety of *rotis* (*chapati*-wrapped curries), along with other Indian delicacies, in an attractive atmosphere. It has good hot sauce.

Rita's, in the Omar Hodge building (near the roundabout), is open for lunch and dinner and features authentic West Indian dishes.

Simply Delicious, in the Cutlass Building, serves traditional Caribbean dishes such as curried goat, jerk chicken and patties.

One of the least expensive places to eat in Road Town, **Bobby's Supermarket** has a great take-out cafeteria/bakery. Locals love this place to death, and the prices are quite affordable. The food is not bad at all for the price. If you are picking up picnic food and are on a budget, this is a good choice. **Rite Way** also offers sandwiches and other food at its location on the edge of town.

☞ Greg Gunter, owner of Sunny Caribbee, recommends **Jerk Station**, open nightly (next to Pussers warehouse in Lower Estate) which has "authentic Jamaican jerk chicken, pork, and ribs at moderate prices....a real local scene."

SNACKS, BAKERIES, AND LIGHT DINING: If you're on a budget or a diet, try a conch patty or other quick snack at one of these places.

The best place in the BVI for baked goods is the **Roadtown Bakery** near Sunny Caribbee on Main St. It employs students from New England Culinary Institute which has a school at the H. Lavity Stoutt Community College. The different bread and rolls here are a sheer delight to sample. It's open Mon. to Fri. 7 AM–6 PM, Sat. 7 AM–2 PM.

The **Courtyard Cafe** is a charming coffee shop on Main Street near Little Denmark. Its only downside are the smokers.

Across from Road Reef Marina, **Crandall's Pastry Plus** serves cakes, tarts, lobster and conch patties, and other light food.

The **New Happy Lion** offers breakfast and lunch; dinner is by request.

In The Cutlass Bldg. in the town center near the water, **M & S Pastry Plus** offers cafeteria-style food (spinach, rice, quiches) at very reasonable prices as well as pastries and pizza.

Across from Riteway, the comfy **Mellow Moods Cafe** charges $7 for a veggie plate; it serves local juices. It's open Mon. to Sat. from 8:30 AM–7 PM.

CHINESE: In Mint Mall, budget **Ceto's Chinese Food** serves authentic greasy Chinese fare at low prices. **Tropic Orient Garden** (☎ 494-4634) is at Wickhams Cay I and offers similar fare for lunch and dinner. There are others around.

OTHER RESTAURANTS: Overlooking the harbor, **Maria's By the Sea** is centrally located. Their special dining events, held a few times per year, are worth checking out.

In Palm Grove Shopping Centre, a/c **Palm Groov'n Restaurant** (☎ 494-4802) serves gourmet-style local food; dishes range from pancakes for breakfast and sandwiches for lunch to conch in butter sauce for dinner.

Stylish **Le Cabanon** (☎ 494-8660), Main St. next to Pussers, serves continental cuisine (lunch and dinners) on covered patios.

The Virgin Queen (☎ 494-2310), Fleming St. near the roundabout and across and upstairs from Rite Way, offers dining amidst antique and Tiffany lamp decor. West Indian and international dishes are offered along with their pizza ($15). This is a reasonably-priced and comfortable choice.

An open-air restaurant in the Columbus Centre, **Nexus Café** (☎ 494-3626) specializes in Italian, Mediterranean, and Asian dishes. It is open for three meals daily.

Run by chef Neil Tomes, who honed his culinary skills by working restaurants rated by Michelin, **Fifteen Abbott Lane** (☎ 494-2482) offers a special selection of dishes ("thoroughly modern food"); you may also dine on the balcony. Bread is baked on the premises.
http://www.fifteenabbottlane.com

Castaways Bar, Sir Oiva Georges Plaza, features a wooden sailboat converted into a full-service bar complete with a strip pole; it has an observation platform.

Listing French and continental cuisine on the menu, the **Captains Table** (☎ 494-3885) is at Inner Harbour Marina (near Village Cay and behind Mint Mall); dishes include fresh fish, live lobster from the tank, and escargot in puff pastry. Lunch (Mon.–Fri.) and dinner are served.

The Dove (☎ 493-0313) is a wine bistro located on Old Main Street in a traditional West Indian House, on old Main Street. They offer international cuisine and host a nightly happy hour from 5–7 PM.

Table Talk, on Waterfront Drive in front of the Little Denmark building, serves West Indian food. A lively bar scene here on weekends.

Near George's Plaza and across from the ferry terminal, **Pusser's Country Store and Pub** has dishes for as low as $10; the downstairs pub features sandwiches and pizza as well as their line of drinks.

At the Village Cay Marina, the **Village Cay Dockside Restaurant** (☎ 494-2771) serves three meals daily; dishes include lobster and local fish. It also has a deli, a dining room, and a sushi bar. A Happy Hour on Fri. (5–7 PM) features snacks.

Near the Moorings Marina, the **Mariner Inn** (☎ 494-2332) serves contemporary American fare including a "Yachtsman's Special." Candlelit dinners feature entrées such as jumbo gulf shrimp.

The **Royal BVI Yacht Club** (☎ 494-3567), Road Reef Marina, serves gourmet meals on a breezy open-air deck. (Try the fish cooked in beer batter). They serve a "traditional Sunday Roast" from noon–3 PM. They have many special events including a "sushi night."

TORTOLA

Atop Ridge Rd., **Sky Bar & Restaurant** (☎ 494-3567) serves lunch and dinner fare ranging from onion rings to conch fritters or pasta. Even if you aren't eating here, be sure to stop for the view!

The **Fort Burt Restaurant** was undergoing a change of management at press time. Inquire locally as to its current status.

The Pub (☎ 494-2608), scenically situated at Fort Burt Marina, serves dishes such as local lobster, fish, and sauteed shrimp over linguini.

ITALIAN FOOD: Capriccio di Mare (☎ 494-5369), Waterfront Drive, serves gourmet Italian food, including pizzas, *focacce,* and salads. It's open for three meals daily. Vegetarian choices are available. No reservations.

In the eastern part of town at Baughers Bay, **Spaghetti Junction** (☎ 494-4880; reservations necessary) has fare which blends the cuisine of both North and South; portions are generous, and the Canadian owner/manager is very friendly. Their *chioppino* (saffron, lobster, scallops, shrimps, and mussels in a spicy fish stock served over fetuccine) is well executed and popular. Vegetarian dishes (*spaghetti marinara, eggplant parmigiana, lasagna, vegetali,* and *fettucine vegetali*) are also served. There's a comprehensive wine list as well as some unusual bar drinks. The favorite dessert is chocolate mousse. Many of the people you'll find dining here actually live on the island.

La Dolce Vita, Waterfront Drive, sells Italian ices and other delights.

OUTSIDE OF TOWN: BVI Steak & Pasta House is at Duff's Bottom, just outside of Road Town five min. to the W of town.

In Purcell Estate, the **C & F Bar & Restaurant**, one of the best local restaurants, serves dinner including BBQ and curried dishes. This restaurant is a favorite with many locals including taxi drivers.

OUTSIDE OF TOWN: To the E of town, **Brandywine Bay** (☎ 495-2301) offers Italian fare in a former private hilltop home. Dishes range from grilled salmon with avocado and mango salsa to lobster Catalana. It has a good wine list and famous for its fine fare. Entrées run around $25 on up. There's also a small pavilion within the restaurant which serves appetizers. It is generally closed from early-Aug. to mid-Sept. and on Sun. There's also a beach here. **http://brandywinebay.com**

SEA COWS BAY/NANNY CAY DINING: Featuring local dishes, the colorfully named **Struggling Man's Place** (☎ 494-4163) serves everything from lobster *rotis* to curried mutton to fish & chips. It's worth a stop for a drink to soak in the views.

Set above the water's edge here, **Peg Leg's Landing** (☎ 494-0028) also serves international dishes including seafood, pizza, soups, and salads. It has a happy hour from 4.30–7 PM.

MARKET SHOPPING: There is a public market in Road Town, but there never seems to be a hell of a lot in it. (The best time to visit is Sat. 6 AM to noon). One of the main supermarkets in town is **Bobby's Marketplace** which is a great place to shop. It is open daily from 6 AM to midnight. **http://www.bobbysmarketplace.com islands@surfbvi.com**

SupaValu is a wholesale outlet near the roundabout at Wickhams Cay I., and **Riteway Super Market** is on Main Street, at Pasea Estate, and at Road Reef Marina. The best supermarket is the Riteway in Purcell Estate. It has some takeout food available.

Dorothy's Superette is on Main Street.

The Port Purcell shopping area near the deepwater dock boasts **ONE-Mart.**

Nature's Way (☎ 494-6393), Mill Mall at Wickham's Cay I, carries a complete line of health food and beauty aids. It also sells tofu sandwiches ($3.50) and vegetable burgers ($4).

If you can pry yourself out of bed in order to arrive between the hours of 4:30–7:30 AM on a Sat., you can visit the weekly **farmer's market** at RFG Plaza near the roundabout.

BOOZE: Alcohol is available at all the supermarkets, and at **The Ample Hamper** at Wickhams Cay I., **TICO** at Wickhams Cay I., **Esme's Shoppe** at Sir Olva Georges Plaza, the **Caribbean Centers** at Port Purcell, and **Caribbean Cellars** in the O'Neal Complex at Port Purcell.

The BVI's only widely marketed indigenous brew is the Tortola Spiced Rum Pirates' Blend which is available around Road Town for a pricey $13 a bottle. A distillery operatse in Cane Garden Bay.

EVENTS: See the list of events in the "Introduction."

ENTERTAINMENT: Not exactly downtown Manhattan, to say the least. Much of the entertainment happens out of town at Cane Garden Bay or other locales. The *Drinking Man's Guide to the B.V.I.* by Julian Putley contains a number of discount coupons inside which more than pay for the price of the book. Check the *Limin' Times,* which has a calendar.
http://www.limin-times.com

The Pub, at Fort Burt Marina, often has live bands (reggae, calypso, rock) on weekend evenings. Guitarist Ruben Chinnery is a frequent performer on Fri. nights.

Treasure Isle Hotel (☎ 494-2501) features music including a *fungi.*

The Moorings, Wickhams Cay I, has fungi and steel bands.

Pusser's Landing at Soper's Hole has a BBQ and band on Sundays. They also have a "dinner with movie night" for $15. If nothing is going on there you can always deposit a quarter and have your future analyzed by a fortune teller in a glass box.

Out at Prospect Reef Resort, **Scuttlebutt** offers live music.

Peter Island Resort also features live music including steelbands.

OUTLYING AREAS: The Sugar Mill at Little Apple Bay presents local music from 8 PM on Saturdays.

At **Tamarind Country Club,** in East End off of Ridge Road, you'll find entertainment on Sat. nights and Sun. brunch.

At Cane Garden Bay, balladeer Quito Rhymer holds forth solo at **Quito's Gazebo** (☎ 495-4837) on Tues. and Thurs, and he and his band play here on Fri. and Sat. nights.

Myett's usually has live music on Fridays. **The Wedding** (☎ 495-4022) has reggae on weekends in season.

In Apple Bay, **Sebastian's** (☎ 495-2412) shows movies and presents live music.

And **The Bomba Shack** (☎ 495-4148) has nightly entertainment as well as a monthly "Full Moon Party" where mushroom tea is dispensed for hallucinogenically inclined. While the tea is free, you must purchase a mug ($10) or mug and tee shirt ($25) in order to imbibe. If you stay up late, you'll be able to see a circle form around Noelle Bush-types who later leave the bras and panties behind that Bomba so proudly displays on his vehicle. Needless to say, this event is best shunned by militant feminists and Mormons, and it's not suitable for the early-to-bed set. The place is packed with vendors selling drinks and overpriced shrumes. Taxi drivers love it bcause they do an incredible business, and they can tell you some crazy stories. This is *the* wild event in the BVI! If you stay at Sebastian's, you can walk here. *A more family-oriented alternative is the full moon party at Trellis Bay on Beef Island.*

Long Bay Beach Resort (☎ 495-4252) has a steel band on Tues. and a fungi band on Thurs. **Bing's Drop in Bar and Restaurant** (☎ 495-2627) has after hours dancing and a late night menu. Much more happens at these places (in the way of barbecues and live bands) during the height of the winter season.

CONCERTS: The **Lavity Stout Community College** has a Classic series each Feb. and March. Jazz bassist Christian McBride and a number of jazz and classical performers have appeared here in the past.

Shopping

A variety of goods (many of them from the "down islands" located to the S) are available along with tee shirts ("Get Hooked on a Virgin") and other such touristic items. *(Nanny Cay, Sopers Hole, and Trellis Bay have shops listed under those locations.)*

The majority of stores are on Main Street and in Wickhams Cay. These days, the two are running together into one large shopping area. **Esme's Shop**, Sir Olva Georges Plaza, sells magazines, books, imported newspapers, and alcoholic beverages.

Samarkand, Main St., sells handcrafted jewelry and gems, and **The Jewelry Box**, 101 Main St., offers jewelry made from the sandbox tree as well as gems.

In the Abbot Bldg., **Sea Urchin** sells beachwear and other accessories, and **Kaunda's Kysy Tropix** has jewelry, TVs, and other such ridiculously overpriced equipment. They also sell CDs.

Cane Garden Bay Surf Shop, across from the Banco Popular sells surf gear and rents boards.

The **Pusser's Company Store**, one of the largest shops around, sells the famed local rum and other memorabilia.

Offering gold and silver jewelry, **Felix Silver and Gold** also has items which use coral and shell.

Set in a traditional house and one of the most attractive shops found anywhere in the Caribbean, **The Sunny Caribbee Herb and Spice Company** offers attractively packaged selections of spices from all over the Caribbean; they also sell a wide range of unusual and high quality Caribbean arts and crafts. They have a wonderful intimate **Gallery** which sells local and Caribbean art. (Copies of this book should be obtainable there). Pick up their catalog or write for one (Box 286, Main St., Tortola or Box 3237 VDA, St. Thomas 00803-3237), fax them at 494-4039, or call 494-2178.

☞ An added incentive to visit here is that free but vibrant WiFi signal is available just outside the premises. Owner Greg Gunter points out that the building housed the Social Inn, the island's first hotel, and three 17th-C cannon are on the premises.
http://www.sunnycaribbee.com
sunnycaribbee@surfbvi.com

Mon Cheri sells fashion and lingerie.

The Carifta Store sells women's clothes, gold chains, perfumes, china and crystal.

Little Denmark sells a selection of gold and silver jewelry, watches, snorkeling and fishing gear, and other items.

The **Serendipity Bookshop** is open from 9:30 AM–5 PM from Mon. to Sat. and on Sun. from 10 AM–4 PM. They have a good if small selection.

Selling brand name clothing at outlet prices, **Caribbean Outlet Store** is in Sir Georges Plaza in the center of town.

At the end of Main St., **Creque's Department Store** sells shoes and clothing.

Finally, you'll spot a **Crafts Alive Village** which sells the usual collection of souvenirs right on the main drag.

WICKHAMS CAY SHOPPING: In an old house across from Wickhams Cay, the **Shirt Shack** sells casual clothing.

Bolo's Record and Leather Shop has a wide selection of music as well as shoe repairs.

Flamboyance offers in duty-free perfume.

Clovers sells shoes, sewing accessories, and fabrics.

At the Mill Mall is another branch of the **Sea Urchin**.

The Carousel Gift Shop sells crystal, crafts, ceramics, and embroidered tablecloths.

La Gregg's sells books as well as snacks and refreshments.

The Globe has everything from cosmetics to souvenirs to swimware.

Dawn's Shoe Shop sells shoes from Italy, Spain, and Brazil, as well as handbags and hosiery.

Pace Setter sells shoes, accessories, and clothing.

OTHER ITEMS: Stamps are available from the new **philatelic bureau** located near the PO on Main St., while authentic coins (80 cents' worth for $1) are sold at a window to the left outside the G.P.O. on Main Street.

SERVICES AND INFORMATION: Above Fedex on Wickhams Cay II, the **BVI Tourism Board** is open Mon. to Fri. 9 AM–4:30 PM.

The **General Post Office,** Main Street, is open Mon. to Fri. 8 AM–4 PM, Sat. 9 AM–1:30 PM. Faxes can be sent here.

Banks include **First Caribbean Bank, Banco Popular, FirstBank,** and **The Bank of Nova Scotia.** Most have ATMs.

Free internet access is offered at the **Road Town Public Library** is on Fleming Street up from the old prison and above Riteway. Access is limited to a half hour, and the connection is sometimes slow, but it's available daily except Sun. And you can browse the collection while you wait. (The BVI Community College also has a small **library** on Main St.)

Who Are the Quakers?

In 1657, a young George Fox (1624-1691) had a call from God and became a wandering preacher. He went on to found the Society of Friends (from "Friends of Truth," John 15:15). Fox was persecuted for his beliefs. He suggested to one judge that he "tremble at the word of the Lord." The judge called him a "Quaker," and the name gained favor from there.

The Quakers or Friends believe that every individual has direct access to God, that no churches or priests are needed, that every person is of equal worth, and that one should follow an "inward light" towards spiritual development and individual perfection.

Quakers speak at meetings when moved by the spirit. Doctrine stresses simple living and pacifism. Their American Friends Service Committee has done much to further the cause of world peace. There are now some 300,000 members worldwide. There is no universal creed, and there are as many definitions of the belief as there are members.

Quakers have a long history in the BVI. The first mission was established in 1727. Prominent local Quakers have included John Pickering, first native-born lieutenant-governor; Dr. John Coakley Lettsom, founder of the London Medical Society; and William Thornton, designer of the United States Capitol who served as the first U.S. Commissioner of Patents. The Quaker presence lasted until the late 1700s. Their pacifism made their residence problematic. ∎

Bits and Pieces (☎ 494-5954; $20/hr.) is at Mill Mall and open weekdays. **Cyber Corner** (☎ 494-2974) is at Wickhams Cay. The **Java Connection** is out at Leverick Bay, and there are a few other places.

Bless Hands Health Spa (☎ 494-8156) is at Wickhams Cay 2, **Golden Palms Health Spa** (☎ 494-0138 or 494-3311, ext. 245), Long Bay, has a massage service, workout equipment, and daily spa packages.

OTHER SERVICES: Travel Plan Tours (☎ 494-2347/5720) is a competent travel agent which also offers island tours.

Tortola Travel Services (☎ 494-2215 /2216/2672) is another alternative.

For underwater camera rental and instruction, **Rainbow Visions Photography** (☎ 494-2749, ✆ 494-6390, VHF Ch. 16; Box 680, Road Town), Prospect Reef, rents equipment and offers instruction and processing. This is an excellent place to go if you would like to learn underwater photography. http://www.rainbowvisionsbvi.com rainbow@surfbvi.com

LAUNDRY: **Sylvia's Laundromat** (☎ 494-2230), Fleming St., offers dry cleaning as well. **Speed Clean** at Baughers Bay offers washers, dryers, and laundry service. Other laundries include Freemans, the one at Village Cay Marina, and at Cane Garden Bay (behind Rhymer's).

VIDEOS: Caribbean Video is next to Freemans laundry at Palm Grove Square.

PAY/CARD TELEPHONES: Phones in the center of Road Town are in front of the Cable and Wireless office and at other locations. international calls may be made and telegrams may be sent from inside the main office. Office hours are Mon. to Fri., 7 AM–7 PM, Sat. 7 AM–4 PM, and Sun. 9 AM–noon.

Pay/card phones are also at the Recreation Ground (near the police station); Village Cay Marina, The Moorings, Peebles Hospital, Nanny Cay Marina, Port Purcell, West End Jetty, and Beef Island Airport.

The pay phones have digital readouts and take either quarters (call everywhere) or phone cards, which come in denominations of $5, $10, and $20. Cards can be purchased at any phone card agency. A good place to go is to the B Mobile office just off the main roundabout.

DRUGSTORES: Qwomar Trading (☎ 494-1298, 494-5398) has a drugstore and is recommended for prescriptions and other items. It is on Blackburne Road, the main road heading W from Road Town and near the Port Purcell roundabout.

Next to the PO on Main St., **J. R. O'Neal** sells drugs, gifts, film, and other items.

Medicure in in the Hodge Bldg. near the roundabout.

Vanterpool Enterprises is near the roundabout.

Driving in the BVI brings with it some unique road hazards.

CAR RENTALS: *See the list earlier in this chapter.*

Tortola Outdoor Activities

DAY SAILS: Lunch and drinks are generally included, and rates vary but run around $60 for a half-day sail and $100 for a full-day sail. Children generally pay half-price.

Aristocat Charters (☎ 499-1249, ☎/☎ 495-4087; PO Box 4217, Road Town) offers a day sail (with drinks, buffet lunch, and snorkel equipment) aboard a 48-ft. catamaran for $110 pp; children under ten are $55 pp.
http://www. aristocatcharters.com
aristocat@surfbvi.com

Cane Garden Bay Pleasure Boats (☎ 495-9660) supplies snorkeling gear and rents seafaring crafts ranging from power-boats to kayaks.

The **Cuan Law** (☎ 494-2490, ☎ 494-5774, 800-648-3393; Box 362, Road Town) is the world's largest trimaran. "Cuan" is the Scottish-Gaelic word for ocean and "Law" is Scottish for mountain. Geared towards divers, it includes activities for the non-diver such as sailing Hobie cats, kayaking, water skiing, wake and knee boarding, snorkeling, island exploration, and beach barbecues.
http://www.bvidiving.com
cuanlaw@surfbvi.com

At the Nanny Cay Marina, **King Charters, Ltd.** (☎ 494-5820, ☎ 494-5821; Box 3454, Road Town) has day charters and powerboat rentals.
http://www.kingcharters.com
king@kingcharters.com

Island Surf and Sail BVI (☎ 494-0123. cell: 541-1404) rents all manner of boards, kayaks, snorkeling gear, and fishing equipment.
http://www.bviwatertoys.com

Black Sam Bellamy

Presently immortalized by the small island bearing his name, this Englishman began his plundering apprenticeship with fellow Anglo Ben Hornigold on the *Mary Anne*. Unfortunately for him, Hornigold made a decision not to continue to rob English ships, a decision that—while commendable from a patriotic standpoint—caused the crew to revolt and allowed Bellamy to seize command. He found a comrade-in-arms in the person of French captain Louis Lebous, and the two stationed themselves on the E side of Tortola.

Trading in ships like yuppies trade in cars, Bellamy moved from the *Mary Anne* to the larger *Mary Sultana*. Following this he captured the slaver *Whydah*, an 18-gun, 300-ton dreamboat in Feb. 1717. This craft came with some 20,000–30,000 silver and gold-filled chests as well as jewelry and other goods.

Continuing to plunder, Bellamy headed home to jolly old England in April of that year. All good things must come to an end, and, for Bellamy, the end came that April when a severe storm brought him and his crew to their doom. Two survived to tell the tale. The craft was raised from its watery tomb only in 1985. ∎

Jolly Mon Boat Rentals (☎ 495-9916, cell 443-3313, Box 471, East End) offers day-sails (from $275 half-day) and charters.
jollymon@surfbvi.com

A 50-ft. luxury catamaran, the **Kuralu** (☎/☎ 495-4381; Box 609, West End), sails from West End to Jost Van Dyke, Sandy Cay, and other locations with a four-person minimum; children are half-price.
http://www.kuralu.com
kuralucharters@surfbvi.com

M&M Powerboat Rental (☎ 495-9993), Nanny Cay, rents ridged-hull inflatables

(around $125 pd) and 22-ft contenders (around $250 pd).
http://www.powerboatrentalbvi.com
mljbvi@surfbvi.com

Blue Sail Sports (☎ 494. 6300, 866-978--4464) runs a 48-ft. catamaran out of its own marina. They offer nine different trips and are available for charter as well.
http://www.bsbvi.com/bluesail

Ppalu (☎ 494-0609), a large and fast 75-ft. catamaran, sails daily to various locations from the Village Cay Marina. Built in 1978, it's named after the title of the traditional Micronesian navigator who was always sure of his location on the seas. This impressive, comfortable, sailing vessel has a large lounge and dining area and lots of deck space above for you to lounge about.

Based on Peter Island, ***Silmaril*** (☎ 495-9225, ☏ 495-2500), a 41-ft. sailing yacht, will plan a trip (including overnight charters) which will suit your needs. Two-person minimum.
http://www.charteraboat.com/silmaril

Sunshine Power Boat Rentals (☎ 494-8813), Inner Harbour Marina, runs sportsfishing and charter trips.

Running charters and day trips to the Baths (Virgin Gorda) as well as to The Caves (Norman Island), the *White Squall II* (☎ 494-2564, ☏ 494-9753; Box 145, Road Town), an 80-ft. schooner, is berthed at "A" dock at the Village Cay Marina.
http://www.whitesquall2.com
whitesquall2@surfbvi.com

?!¢ For years the Beef Island toll was collected by a an elderly gentleman bearing a coconut shell suspended at the end of a long stick.

DIVING: There are are a number of well-run operations. Rates start at around $70–$75 for a one-tank dive and at $90–$105 for two-tank dive. Most operators offer packages.

A good resource is:
http://www.bviscuba.org

Aqua Venture Scuba Services (☎ 494-4320, ☏ 494-5608), Inner Harbour Marina, offers a variety of dives. They boast on their website that: "Our VIP guest list is extensive, including moguls from the World of Business and celebretries [sic] from the Entertainment Industry and from the Media."
http://www.aquaventurebvi.com
aquavent@surfbvi.com

Blue Water Divers (☎ 494-2847, ☏ 494-0198, VHF CH. 16; Box 846, Road Town) have operated out at Nanny Cay Marine Center since 1980. They offer introductory and certification courses as well as guided tours; packages and rentals are available.
http://www.bluewaterdiversbvi.com
bwdbvl@surfbvi.com

Dive Tortola (☎ 494-9200, 800-353-3419) is out at Prospect Reef. Instruction and rentals are offered.
http://www.divetortola.com
diving@divetortola.com

Paradise Watersports ☎ ☏ 495-9941, ☏ 495-2500), Peter Island Resorts, offers diving and a "discover scuba" course.
http://www.bviwatersports.com
peterislanddivers@hotmail.com

Rainbow Visions Photo Center (☎ 494-2749, ☏ 494-6390, VHF Ch. 16; Box 680, Road Town) is a dive operator based at Prospect Reef. They also rent video and other cameras and offer instruction and processing.

The owner is a well known photographer and writer about the BVI's marine treasures.
http://www.rainbowvisionsbvi.com
rainbow@surfbvi.com

Sail Caribbean Divers (☎ 495-1675, cell: 496-8663, ☏ 495-3244, VHF Ch. 16), is at Hodges Creek Marina and on Cooper Island.
http://www.sailcaribbeandivers.com
sailcaribbean@surfbvi.com

The **Trimarine Boat Co., Ltd.** (☎ 494-2490, ☏ 494-5774, 800-648-3393; Box 362, Road Town) operates two trimarans which offer diving and snorkeling.
http://www.bvidiving.com
cuanlaw@surfbvi.com

UBS (Underwater Boat Services) Dive Center and Lounge (☎ 494-0024, ☏ 494-0623, pager 496-5933; Box 3283, Road Town) is in Harbour View Marina in the East End. They offer personalized diving and snorkeling trips with instruction.
http://www.scubabvi.com
mail@scubabvi.com

SNORKELING: A number of operations, including some of the diving operations and day sails (including most trips) offer snorkeling, so check these sections. Count on spending around $50 for a half-day and $75 and up for a full-day trip.

Out at Prospect Reef Resort, **Caribbean Images Tours** (☎ 494-1147, ☏ 494-8599; Box 826, Road Town) offer snorkeling trips with gear and instruction.
caribimages10@hotmail.com

High Seas Adventures (☎ 495-1300, ☏ 495-1301) offers family-friendly and custom trips with experts. Snorkeling gear is *gratis*.
http://www.highseabvi.com
highsea@surfbvi.com

TORTOLA MARINAS: These generally have a full range of facilities. Check a current issue of *The Welcome* or contact the marina concerned for specifics.

Baughers Bay Marina (☎ 494-2393, ☏ 494-1183, Box 3028, Road Town) offers docks, supplies, repair shop and hotel.

The **Fort Burt Marina** (☎ 494-4200; Box 243, Road Town) offers overnight and permanent berths.

Inner Harbour Marina (☎ 494-4502; VHF Ch. 16; Box 472, Road Town) is at Wickhams Cay I.

The **Moorings-Mariner Inn** (☎ 494-2332; Box 139, Road Town), Wickhams Cay I, permits dockage for up to 90 boats. At the same marina, **Tortola Yacht Services** (☎ 494-2124, ☏ 494-4107; Box 74, Road Town), Wickhams Cay II, operates a repair and maintenance service.
http://www.tysbvi.com
tys@tysbvi.com

Nanny Cay Resort (☎ 494-3288, ☏ 494-3288), 1.5 mi. W of town, has a full-service marina.

At the West End, **Soper's Hole-Sunsail Marina** (☎ 495-4740, ☏ 494-5595; Box 609, West End) provides 36 slips and moorings.

Hodges Creek Marina (☎ 495-1178, ☏ 495-4301) opened this marina at Hodges Creek in 1996. It has a restaurant, bar, pool, hotel, as well as 82 berths which allow dockage for boats of up to 120 ft. There's also a hotel, dive shop, supplies, yacht charters (32–52 ft.), and repair services.

Penn's Landing Marina (☎ 495-1134, ☏ 495-1352; Box 2926, East End), Fat Hog's Bay, offers moorings, dockage, and yacht management and maintenance.

The **Village Cay Resort Marina** (☎ 494-2771; Box 145, Tortola; VHF Ch. 71) provides dockage for 106 boats up to 150 ft.

TORTOLA

Wheatley's Harbour View Marine Centre (☎ 495-1775) offers dockage, moorings, and other facilities.

Offlying **Peter Island Resort** and **Marina Cay** also have small marinas.

SPORTFISHING: Caribbean Fly Fishing (☎ 495-2447, ☻ 495-1626), Nanny Cay, offers guided bone and tarpon fishing. **caribbeanflyfishing@surfbvi.com**

BOARDSAILING: Boardsailing BVI (☎ 499-1590), Trellis Bay, offers rentals, lessons, clinics, surfboard and kayak rentals, and even DSL and wireless internet access ($20 ph).
http://www.windsurfing.vi
jwright@surfbvi.com

SURFING: HIHO (☎ 494-7694, ☻ 494-5595) offers surfboard rentals.

OTHER RENTALS: Try Last Stop Watersports Rentals ☎ 494-1120, ☻ 494-0593) rents kayaks, windsurfers, waterskis, body boards, and fishing rods.
http://www.laststopsports.com
info@laststopsports.com

TENNIS: Six courts may be found at **Prospect Reef Resort** (☎ 495-3311) and three courts are at the **Long Bay Beach Resort** (☎ 495-4252).

From Road Town To The East

St. Phillips Church, or the "African Church," is at Kingstown. This church was built in 1833 for the use of 600 Africans who had been removed from the bowels of a slave ship around 1815 (after the abolition of the slave trade, but before emancipation on the island). Known as the Kingstown Experiment, these slaves were placed in a freed reservation after serving an apprenticeship with the planters. While

the roof is gone, its walls — sporting faded scriptural excerpts painted by an Anglican priest — still stand.

Hub of Quaker activities and seat of government for a while after it had been transferred from Spanish Town on Virgin Gorda, **Fat Hogs Bay** still contains a ruined Quaker cemetery. (Stop at the **Mangrove Bakery and Snack Bar** for refreshments).

The **Long Look-Look East End** area is Tortola's most populated area, but it has fewer services than in Roadtown. The area was first settled in 1776 when the first slaves freed were granted land here. Subsequently, any slave that making it here would be granted freedom. From just before Long Look a road heads up to secluded **Josiahs Bay** on the N coast.

JOSIAHS BAY ACCOMMODATIONS: This relatively remote bay is slowly growing in popularity. Birdwatchers will love the pond here where you may see black-necked stilts and white-cheeked pintail ducks. Umbrella huts have been installed for sheltering visitors. There are several restaurants and gear-rental places before the secluded beach. Snorkeling is best out by the rocks. Locals catch crabs here, and cockfights take place most Sundays. **The Grape Tree Bar & Grill** (☎ 495-2818) has surfboard and beach chair rentals.

The **Serendipity House** (☎/☻ 495-1994, 494-5774; Box 925, Road Town) is an attractive villa with a pool and five bedrooms with baths. It may be rented in part or whole (holds ten).
http://serhouse.com
serhouse@surfbvi.com

The Tamarind Club Hotel (☎ 495-2477, 800-313-5662; ☻ 495-2795; Box 509, East End) is a small nine-room inn centered around a gazebo with pool, swim-up bar, gardens, and restaurant. It's set ⁹⁄₁₀ of a mi. from the beach. The comfortable and attractive a/c rooms have refrigerators, fans, and phone. There are also two three-bedroom villas. Internet hookup is available, and TV/VCR is available in some of the rooms. Rates range from $130–$200 d). Weekly rates are available, and diving, sailing, windsurfing, and adventure packages are available.

The Tamarind Club (☎ 495-2477, reservations suggested), its congenial restaurant, is set by a pool. While sandwiches and Mexican dishes are served for lunch, dinner features *cordon bleu* cuisine. Lunch entrées run $10 and up, dinner entrées start at $18, and there's a Sunday Brunch (which includes a complimentary Mimosa or Bloody Caesar).
http://www.tamarindclub.com
tamarind@tamarindclub.com

Josiahs Bay Plantation (☎ 494-6168, ☺ 494-2000), near the beach, is a home on a former sugar plantation which has been converted to art gallery, souvenir shop, and "frozen bar." Its **The Secret Garden** is a great restaurant.
http://www.bviwelcome.com/ads/
josiahsbay/index.html

Josiah's Bay Inn (☎ 495-782-4086; 407-782-4086) a variety of sizes of apartments for around $599–$1500 pw. They own the Grape Tree Bar and Grille located on the beach.
http://www.bviwelcome.com/josiahbay
josiahsbayinn@hotmail.com

LAMBERT BEACH: The **Elizabeth Beach Villas** (☎/☺ 495-2538; Box 478, East End) have a/c three-bedrooms with phone, TV/VCR, stereo, kitchen, and washer/dryer. Rates are $1,500 pw summer and $2,200 pw winter. The owners also have the **Mermaid Villa** on Beef Island.
http://dmchislop.home.comcast.net/~dmchislop
mermaid@surfbvi.com

EAST END: Emile's Mexican Cantina (☎ 495-1775), across the from Harbor View Marina, offers good Mexican food and pizza at reasonable prices. It hosts a lively weekend bar scene.

In Fat Hog's Bay, **Bing's Drop in Bar and Restaurant** (☎ 495-2627) provides the local fare which made it popular originally. It's open from 7 PM–2 AM Wed. and Thurs. and from 7 AM–4 PM on Fri. and Sat. There's a DJ every evening and art by Bing adorns the walls. Reservations are advised.

Also at Fat Hog's Bay, **De' Cal's Restaurant and Catering** (☎ 495-1429) serves three meals daily featuring pizza, and local food such as *rotis*.

Fat Hog Bob's (☎ 495-2126; dinner reservations suggested), Hodge's Creek, is open for three meals daily and features a late-night menu which is served "until the last man falls." Fresh fish, pasta, and lobster are among the offerings. There's a large-screen satellite TV. It also provides internet access and hosts a happy hour.

Hodges Creek Marina Hotel (☎ 494-5000, ☺ 494-7676; Box 633, Road Town) is associated with the yacht charter operation. It has a pool and 24 a/c rooms with satellite TV, two double beds, and phones. Winter rates run around $200 d.
http://www.hodgescreek.com
info@hodgescreek.com

Set in East End's Fat Hog's Bay at Penn's Landing Marina, romantic **Eclipse**

?!? Up until 1966. when the road from Roadtown to West End was completed, it might take all day to travel from there to Roadtown.

(☎ 495 1646) offers vegetarian dishes, lobster ravioli, tempura, swordfish, and appetizers such as tuna carpaccio. Bouillabaisse and paella can be had if you give them 24 hrs. notice. It's open Mon. to Sat. 5–10 PM and offers a Sun. brunch. It's really hopping on many an evening.
http://www.eclipse-restaurant.com

EAST END SIGHTS: Local farmers raise livestock and cultivate crops on plots leased from the Dept. of Agriculture at the **Paraquita Bay Agricultural Station** (☎ 495-2447). Farmers are present early morning and late afternoon. Follow the paths.

The Center For Applied Marine Studies at Paraquita Bay, a division of H. Lavity Stout Community College, has a sculpture portraying a traditional sloop and some displays (on the second floor). The visitors center at its **Mangrove Wetlands Preservation Project** was dedicated by Princess Anne in 2005. The project is still under development.

Beef Island

This small island, virtually an extension of Tortola, has become increasingly popular as a destination in itself. Beef Island's name stems from the period when it provided beef for buccaneers, so-named because they would smoke the beef (*boucan*). Other imaginative explanations for the name have been proposed in the past. Some claimed it came from the cows a solitary old lady used to bring to pasture here. Another explanation maintained that Quakers raised indigo and cattle here during the 18th C. A final

 For the sunset, ascend to Soldier's Hill above Cane Garden Bay. A good bar to hit is the one at Bananaquit at Heritage Villas.

story maintains that it was used as a transshipment point for cattle from Anegada.

The island remained virtually uninhabited up until 1939 when a Polish sailor arrived in Trellis Bay. Returning after the war, he erected the Trellis Bay Club, a set of stone buildings. Local legend insists that the island hosts a coterie of *duppies* (spirits).

A 300-ft. channel, which separates the island from Tortola, is spanned by the **Queen Elizabeth Bridge**, the original of which her Imperial Majesty herself dedicated in 1966. A new two-lane version opened in 2001. Crossing the bridge, the road to the L leads to the remains of a cattle estate house. This must be one of the smallest islands ever to boast an international airport. The new T. B. Lettsome International Airport opened in 2002.

Long Beach, near the 3,600-ft. runway, is is suitable for a dip before departure or after arrival. Unless you are a birdwatcher, leave nesting terns in peace by entering the beach from behind rather than through the salt pond.

A multi-million dollar resort is planned for the island. It will cover 690 acres (e.g. most of the island). It will include a marina, a 50-acre resort and hotel around Trellis Bay, a golf course, and a residential area. Quorum International, a Hong Kong-based version of Amway, has purchased the land and is funding the project. They've sold a 51% share to IYG (International Yachting Group) who own many of Tortola's marinas. The VIEC (Virgin Islands Environmental Council) is taking the government and developer to court over the Hans Creek area of the proposed development, as it is a marine protected area.

TRELLIS BAY: A well protected anchorage (which once served as a pirate's haven) and one of the best windsurfing spots (see below), Trellis Bay houses a number of restaurants and facilities.

If you visit the hill above the bay, you can see the remains of a house, now incorporated in Little Mountain Estate. This once belonged to the Widow George, a devout 18th C Quaker, who—in retaliation for pirate raids on her cattle—is said to have invited them up to the house and poisoned them with punch. After she confessed her crime to Gov. Pickering, he made her head of the first Quaker meeting house, the remains of which can also be seen here.

PRACTICALITIES: **Beef Island Guest House** (☎ 495-2303, ℮ 495-1611, VHF Ch. 16; Box 494, East End) bills itself as "a casual bed and breakfast on the beach." has four comfy rooms priced at around $100 d summer and around $120 d winter; weekly rates are available, and a 10% service charge is added. Its **De Loose Mongoose Restaurant & Bar** serves sandwiches, salads, dolphin burgers, vegetarian omelettes, and like fare. (If driving, watch out for the tethered mule near here who sometimes stretches his rope across the road while in hot pursuit of verdant mule munchies). Their website is very complete and includes restaurant menus.
http://www.beefislandguesthouse.com
info@beefislandguesthouse.com

Boardsailing BVI (☎ 495-2447), *the* place to go for boardsailing, offers internet access ($20 ph) as well as snacks at its **Trellis Bay Cybercafé**.
http://www.windsurfing.vi
jwright@surfbvi.com

"D" Besst Cup sells ice cream and coffee, which goes for up to $5 a cuppa!
The Last Resort (☎ 495-2520) is an English-style restaurant on the nearby islet of **Bellamy Cay** (named for the pirate

Mt. Healthy National Park

Tortola's only remaining windmill stands on Mt. Healthy, and the ruins of this 18th-C. structure provides the centerpiece for this 0.9-acre national park. This was once the Anderson Plantation which operated from 1798 until the abolition of slavery in 1834. Owner James Anderson perished in 1819 when his home collapsed in a hurricane.

Established in 1983 and restored in 1994, the ruins don't offer much in the way of facilities, but there is a short trail. Take a seat on the bench and try to imagine a functioning 250-acre estate which once flourished here. The surrounding slopes were covered with cane; slaves carried in cane through the openings to feed the animal- and wind-powered mill. Crushed cane was carried to the boiling house which is on private property nearby. The mill ruins were depicted on a 1991 postage stamp commemorating the 30th anniversary of the National Parks Trust. ∎

Black Sam Bellamy: *see sidebar*). Once run by local one-man cabaret entertainer Tony Snell, it once served roast-beef buffets. Tony started out on Jost Van Dyke. After a mysterious fire required them to find new digs, he and his wife saw the island's potential. For years they paid only a minimal rent. One evening the owner showed up, and, after seeing how packed the place was, decided to up the rent. Tony still returns from his UK retirement once a year for gigs, and the sole remaining 'singing' dog has been known to still chime in. His daughter and her husband have brought the place into the 21st century. Dinners (with daily specials presented table-

> "We take pride in keeping this piece of paradise clean, tidy and attractive." — Elvet Meyers, owner/ operator of Elm Beach Suites on Cane Garden Bay.

side on blackboards) are some of the finest gourmet cuisine on Tortola. Entrées range from pan-fried red snapper in an orange-and-ginger butter sauce to fresh, char-grilled tuna fillet steak (both $22). Drinks range from a bucket of Red Stripes to the tasty "Banana Mama." For dessert, you can try a "Vodka Mousse." There're also selections for vegetarians and inexpensive selections for the younger set. The resident donkey pokes his head out of his abode (in a stall next to the restaurant) from time to time. After dinner, the impromptu entertainment starts up, so be sure to bring your rock and roll shoes with you. They currently offer a "singing chef" from Wed. through Sat. From Trellis Bay, a hotline can be used to call the ferry. It's a quick and free ride across.

SHOPPING: At Trellis Bay, **Flukes** sells maps, prints and handpainted tee shirts. **Aragorn's Studio** offers an amazing range of Arawak crafts, artwork by Aragorn, and tee shirts.

At Bellamy Cay, **The Last Resort** has a boutique.

The Trellis Bay Market sells food items.

GREAT CAMANOE: Near Bellamy Cay, this island has the ruins of a great house on it. Parts of this island (19.6 acres) were donated to the National Trust by businessman Herbert C. Lee in 1999. The reserve's **Cam Bay** has good snorkeling.

SCRUB ISLAND: Scrub Island has The Estates at Scrub Island, a gated community, and **Mainsail Resort Marina and Spa** (☎ 813-254-3110 ext. 102, ☏ 813-259-9576).
http://www.mainsailbvi.com
http://www.scrubisland.com/resort

PUSSER'S MARINA CAY: Located to the N of Beef Island (five min. by launch from Trellis Bay) and sandwiched between Great

Camanoe and Scrub Island, this six-acre resort features two restaurants (beach BBQ on Fri.), boutique, and rooms with private balconies. Watersports (including scuba) abound here. It is notable as the setting for the book *Our Virgin Island* by Rob White; the film version starred Sidney Poitier and John Cassavetes. Rates (MAP) range from $195–$450 CP during the high season. There's a ferry running here from 10:30 AM; late returns are available for restaurant guests. Contact: Pusser's Marina Cay, PO Box 626, Road Town; ☎ 494-2174, ☏ 494-4775, VHF Ch. 16.
http://www.pussers.com

☞ Singer Michael Bean performs here in season.
http://www.beansmusic.com

From Road Town To West End
Bordering the Caribbean, the road was built only in the 1960s. The sea wall was wiped out by Hurricane Hugo and has been replaced by boulders.

A red-and-white sign to the R a few miles out of town marks the site of **Pockwood Pond Fort.** Built by the Dutch in 1648 to protect island shipping, it was later rebuilt by the English Royal Engineers. Its nickname "The Dungeon" stems from the underground cell (with antique graffiti carved into its walls) which may have held prisoners.

Fort Recovery, erected by the Dutch in 1660, is a small circular fort which now faces the seaside in the middle of **Fort Recovery Estate Beachfront Villa Resorts,** a private resort complex.

?!¿ Jimmy Buffet's tune *Manana* was written in the harbor of Cane Garden Bay, and *Cheeseburgers in Paradise* may have been written in Stanley's.

At Soper's Hole, a deep anchorage sheltered on the SW by Frenchman's Cay, stands the small village of **West End** with its houses painted in pastel shades, along with immigration and customs offices. Boats leave here regularly for St. John (See "From Tortola"). See the small mahogany framed sailboats under construction at The Woodworks.

West End
Accommodation and Dining

If you're arriving or leaving the West End by boat, you can eat at the **Jolly Roger** ; the other choice is informal **Zelma's Courtesy,** one of the two small restaurants across from the ferry. It sells sweet cakes, johnny cakes, fried fish, patties, lottery tickets, and newspapers (including *The New York Times*).

The casual six-room **Jolly Roger Inn & Restaurant** (☎ 495-4559, ✆ 495-4184; Box 437, Road Town) charges from $40 d (for a room with a shared bath in low season) on up; winter rates are from $66 d on up; weekly rates are available. Its pub-like restaurant serves Asian and fresh-fish dishes. (Show your children the tarpon you can see from the dock). It also has live bands, Caribbean jerk prime rib on Saturdays, and a BBQ on most weekends.
http://www.jollyrogerbvi.com
info@jollyrogerbvi.com

A few minutes on foot from the pier at the West End, the **BVI Aquatic Apartments** (☎ 495-4541, 494-2114; Box 605, West End) is a two-storey set of 14 units with kitchenettes. Prices start at around $25 s, 40 d; weekly rates available.

The gourmet **Oscar's** (☎ 495-4844, Frenchman's Point on Frenchman's Cay, serves Mediterranean dishes and tapas.

The 12-acre **Frenchman's Cay Resort** is closed for refurbishment until 2009 or so.

Soper's Hole Marina (☎ 495-4553, ✆ 495-4560. Box 601, West End) here is a full-service marina with a five-star dive center, charter yacht company, restaurant, and boutiques including **Island Treasures** (a fine art gallery and shop at Soper's Hole Marina), **Pusser's Company Store** (which is similar to the one in Road Town), **Sea Urchin** (beach ware), and the **Ample Hamper** (food, alcohol, and deli items). **Caribbean Jewellers** sell a variety of gemstones and coins, and **Samarkand Jewellers** sell maps, coins, and other items. **Latitude 18** is a hip clothing store. **Pusser's Landing** serves fish and lobster as well as other dishes in a restaurant inside the store. They're open for breakfast and lunch, and serve dishes such as pizza, fish and chips, and *roti*. **Pisces** is a friendly and attractive restaurant serving local food. It has good prices and offers good breakfasts.

Soper's Hole has a great website:
http://www.sopershole.com
erin@surfbvi.com

Bay View Inn (☎ 494-0740, ✆ 494-0741) rents four a/c rooms with refrigerator, phone, cable TV, and views. It is associated with Voyage Charters.

OTHER NEARBY ACCOMMODATION: Near the junction of the roads heading to the N Coast and to Road Town, and built around a 17th-C. Dutch fort, **Fort Recovery Estate Beachfront Villa Resorts** (☎ 495-4354, 495-4970, 800-367-8455 9 (wait for ring), ✆ 495-4036; Box 239, Road Town or Box 11156, St. Thomas 00801) offers a variety of villas which include maid service. Yoga and meditation classes, massages, babysitting service, water sports, commissary, DSL connection (66 cents/min.) and other services are available as is their gourmet room service. A car is advised if staying here. Rates start at around $160 d for a two-person villa off-season and range from $250 up to $797 for a four-bedroom luxury house (sleeps eight); continental breakfast is included. Packages

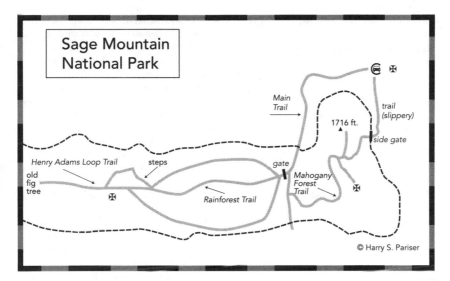

Sage Mountain
National Park

Main
Trail

trail
(slippery)

1716 ft.
▲

side gate

Henry Adams Loop Trail   steps

gate

old
fig
tree

Mahogany
Forest
Trail

Rainforest Trail

© Harry S. Pariser

are available. A 10% service charge is added along with 7% tax, and each additional person is $50. A complimentary dinner as well as a boat excursion is included in the seven-night-stay rates.
http://www.fortrecovery.com
villas@fortrecovery.com

Sage Mountain

Take a left turn at Meyers, then drive a few miles on down the road, following the base of a hill containing communications towers, to reach the trailhead leading to the top of **Mt. Sage** (1,780 ft.), the highest mountain in the Virgin Islands. This attractive area contains the remains of old houses. Orchids peek out from the primeval forest. It has been declared a protected area. Its 92 acres are under the administration of the National Park Trust. From visiting the park, you can get an idea of how the island must have looked when the Europeans first arrived. **note:** *A $3 admission fee is now charged.*

FLORA AND FAUNA: The 15–20-ft.-tall fern trees are "living fossils," virtually unchanged since the Coal Age. The bulletwood trees can be identified by their straight trunk and thick brown cracked bark. West Indian mahogany, silk cotton, white cedar (the colony's national tree), and broadleaf mahogany trees are found here. Cocoplums (related to the rose), mountain guavas (small white blossoms and green edible fruit), and red palicoureas (small red flowers blooming on a red stalk with black fruit) are among the flowering plants found here. There are also a number of species of anthurium on the ground. Among the birds are Antillean crested hummingbirds, pearly-eyed thrashers, American kestrels, mockingbirds, and Caribbean martins. Soldier crabs (hermit crabs) may be spotted on the trails.

TOURING THE PARK: *Try to obtain a brochure from the National Parks Trust before arriving.* A beautiful view of Jost Van Dyke may be had from the parking lot. To enter, take the path straight ahead, unhook the gate, and follow the gravel path until you come to an immense strangler fig. On your return, take the loop trail, which branches off to your left and then returns to the main trail. Exit through the gate again and then unlatch and enter another gate to your right. This takes you through stands of mahogany to a fork in the path.

One path marked "view" leads to a place where there would be a view if you were eight feet tall! The other path leads to the summit of Mt. Sage, which has no view at all. Take the "exit," along a grassy slope punctuated by tree ferns, back to your point of origin. Allow at least an hour for this part of your visit. You may also wish to explore the newer trails. There are now two loop trails, a second trail to the peak, and two additional trails from the gate to the fig tree.

Brewers Bay

A steep and winding road from Road Town leads over the hills and down to this secluded campground and beach. From the top of the road leading down, there's a majestic view of Jost Van Dyke with Little Jost and Sandy Cay in the background. Dark reefs shine through the crystal-clear water. The road leads down to a rustic campsite after passing by the ruins of an old sugar oven.

Above the bay along the way up to Ridge Rd. are the remains of an old sugar mill, the only extant example on the island, which lies within **Mt. Healthy National Park**, a beautiful picnic area (see sidebar on p. 282))

The 18.4 acres of **Shark Point**, to the E of Brewers Bay, were donated to the National Trust in 2000. **The Alexander H. & Gaby Nitkin Nature Reserve** is a woodland and cactus area with boulders similar to the ones found at The Baths on Virgin Gorda. American Roger Nitkin donated the land on behalf of his mother and father. "My father always considered the land at Brewer's Bay to be the most beautiful spot on earth" maintains son Roger Nitkin.

ACCOMMODATIONS: Run by Noel Callwood, **Brewers Bay Campground** (☎ 494-3463) only starts to fill around mid-Dec.; between April and then you'll have the place virtually to yourself. This is a very special way to experience Tortola. There is *great* snorkeling out on the reefs, and this is a good place to base yourself for island walks. A rental car will come in handy.

Bare sites below the coconut trees rent for $15 per night ($1.50 per extra person). Already erected tents are $40 d (extra persons $3 each). Showers are available; a terrace near the office has chairs and tables. Read the reviews on tripadvisor.com.

Two two-bedroom cottages next to the beach at Brewers Bay, **Ronneville Cottages** (☎ 494-2260/3337; Box 185, Road Town) offer kitchens, living/dining areas, terraces, TV, and maid services. Rates run from $475–525 pw summer to $675–725 pw winter for two to four persons.

Near the beach, **Icis Vacation Villas** (☎ 494-6979, ✉ 494-6980; Box 383, Road Town) have a/c units with kitchenettes. There is an open-air restaurant on the peaceful grounds. Rates run from around $125–230 summer to $145–290 winter. **http://www.icisvillas.com icisvillas@direcway.com**

Greenbank Villa and **Emerald Crest** (☎ 494-7931, ✉ 494-7132; Box 14, Road Town) are two villas with all the amenities. Rates by request. **http://www.greenbankvillas.com**

Set atop Soldier's Hill, the **D&E Vacation Home** (☎ 494-2673, ✉ 495-9805) offers one- and three-bedrooms with amenities. Rates run from $850 pw. **http://www.devacation.com info@devacation.com**

Set at Little Bay near Mt. Healthy on the North Shore, **Over the Hill** (☎ 495-1300, 800-952-9338) is a set of secluded beachside guest houses. Rates are $875–$1,575 winter pw and $525–$1050 summer pw for a house, and the off-season discount is 40%. For more information write the Bakewell Family, 12 Magnolia, St. Louis, MO 63124. **http://www.highseabvi.com cottages@highseabvi.com**

FOOD: Expensive food is sold at the commissary. Bring your own from town or St. Thomas. There's a sandwich and refreshment bar, but it's closed off-season. Coconuts drop at your feet; bring along your own machete to hack them open.

Cane Garden Bay

Home to one of the island's most beautiful beaches, Cane Garden's palm-tree-lined white crescent is a locus for tourism on the north coast.

Well into the 1950s, Cane Garden Bay depended on fishing and sugarcane cultivation for its livelihood. The settlement was cut off from the rest of the island: travel was by donkey, horse, on foot, or by sloop. The road became suitable for vehicular traffic only in the late 1950s.

Stanley's opened in the 1960s and swiftly became symbolic of the BVI laid back lifestyle. The area has been on its way up ever since. Besides the white sand, the major attraction here is the offlying coral reef.

Mercifully, the area has been spared large development, and the Rhymers and other locals own most of the tourist industry here. The beach has become even more popular now that hordes of cruise ship passengers regularly taxi it over here. However, funds from cruise ships have been used to build public showers and toilets and to construct a new sewage plant.

A surf report is here: **http://magicseaweed.com/ Cane-Garden-Bay-Surf-Report/480/**

ACCOMMODATIONS: The 27-rm. **Rhymer's Beach Hotel** (☎ 495-4639, 495-4215, ✆ 495-4820; Box 570, Road Town) has 24 rooms with daily maid service and private balconies. Some have a/c, phone, and TV. Attractive murals by Jerome Brown grace the hallways. Rates start at around $75 d off-season and rise to $100 during the high season. Complete water sports are available on the premises. It commands a three-night minimum during the high season (but they recommend you to call close to the date to check for availability for one or two-night stays). **http://www.rhymersbeachhotel.com myettent@surfbvi.com**

Located on the beach, **Elm Beach Suites** (☎ 494-2888, 494-9240, 718-217-3717; Cane Garden Bay PO), yet another Rhymer family concern, consists of five deluxe one-bedrooms with kitchenettes; some have a/c. The Sugar Apple unit has the best view. Winter rates are $140 with weekly rates available. Summer rates are 40% lower.

☞ Geared towards diners, their craft, the *Dubloon*, departs from Manuel Reef Marina at 10 AM and 4:30 PM returns at 4 PM and between 10-midnight daily. Make advance arrangements at 496-7827. **http://www.intheislands.com/elmsuites elm@candwbvi.net**

Myett's Garden Inn (☎ 495-495-9649, ✆ 495-9579) offers comfortable, large a/c rooms surrounded by tropical gardens. Rooms have king size bed, fridge, wet bar, coffeemaker, and phone. Winter rates run around $195 d. Its **Garden & Grille Restaurant** is popular so reservations are recommended.

http://www.myettent.com
myettent@surfbvi.com

Myett's also run the **Indigo Beach House** (☎ 494-2550; Box 556, Road Town) which has a phone and rents for around $2,000 pw. The informative web page tells you everything you need to know.
http://www.indigohouse.org
myettent@surfbvi.com

Set in a converted 300-yr.-old sugar factory right above Cane Garden Bay, **Ole Works Inn** (☎ 495-4837, ✆ 495-9618; Box 560, Cane Garden Bay) offers 18 a/c rooms with bath, refrigerator, TV, patios, and set in the midst of coconut groves. The mill is the reception area: it has been in the hands of owner Quito Rhymer's family for five gen-

erations. It's near the bar, so things may not always be placid and quiet. Rates run from $70–175 summer and $95–$200 winter season; weekly rates are available.
http://www.oleworksinn.com
oleworks@candwbvi.net

A luxury house set right on the beach, the **Cane Garden Bay Beach House** (☎/✆ 610-346-7695) has three bedrooms with TV, phone, and other amenities. It rents for $3,900 pw summer, $4,900 pw winter.
http://www.tortolabeach.com
tortolacgb@aol.com

Set next to the church, **Jip's** (☎ 495-4543, ✆ 495-9736) has a single unit for around $75 d.
jipsbvi@hotmail.com

Visit the eclectic Shell Museum and get a free history lesson.

A set of one-bedrooms, **Mongoose Apartments** (☎ 495-4421, ℮ 495-9721; Box 581, Cane Garden Bay) rent for $195 d; a discount is offered off-season and for weekly stays. Units are near the beach and have overhead fans and a/c.
http://www.mongooseapartments.com
hideaway@mongooseapartments.com

Perched up in the hills above town, **Carrie's Comfort Inn** (☎ 495-9220, ℮ 495-9316) has attractive units for around $100 pn. All are fully equipped with kitchen, ceiling fans, refrigerators, private bath, color TV, cable, small laundry, and maid service.
http://www.mongooseapartments.com
bobby@caribsurf.com

On Luck Hill, **Arundel Villa** (☎ 202-554-8880, 800-862-7863, 877-862-7863, ℮ 202-554-8887, ℮ 202-363-8986) offers three elegant four-bedroom homes which can hold up to six. Rooms have a phone and kitchen, and there's a pool and an ocean view. Rates run between $6,900–$7,400 pw during the winter season.
http://www. www.arundelbvi.com
arundelbvi@aol.com

Agapé Cottages (☎ 495-4825) are one- and two-bedroom units with a/c bedrooms. Breakfast is available at the owner's home, and rates start at $1100 pw.
http://www.agapecottages.com
agapecottages@aol.com

Another set of housekeeping cottages, **Cane Garden Bay Cottages** (☎ 495-9649, ℮ 495-9579) have TV, kitchen, and babysitting service. Winter rates are from $180 d; off-season and weekly discounts are available.
http://www.virginislandsholiday.com
info@virginislandsholiday.com

Sunset Vacation Apartments (☎ 495-4751; Cane Garden Bay PO) offers four one- and two-bedroom apartments with kitchens and balconies. Rates run from $350-$490 d (summer) to $560–$910 pw winter with a 25% off-season discount. It has many repeat clients.

FOOD: Rhymer's Beach Bar & Restaurant in front of the hotel, has beach chairs and public showers ($2). It's open for three meals daily. Offerings include breakfast specials and seafood specialties. A store is next to the restaurant and under the hotel.

Nephew Quito has built his **Gazebo** to the far right. Meals here are varied and range from burgers and *rotis* for lunch to a fish fry on Wed. night. The Gazebo also offers a Sunday Brunch with live steel band music as well as performances by Quito himself. It's closed on Mon. (You can buy his CDs and other sundry items at **Jan's Potpourri**).

Thee Wedding is a bar and restaurant.
Netty's Diner (☎ 495-9001, 495-4633) has great local food.

Further down the road are **Columbus Sunset Bar & Variety Store** which serves meals (local food) for reasonable prices.

At the rear of Rhymer's Beach Hotel is **Rhymer's Beauty Salon and Laundromat**.

Stanley's Welcome Beach Bar is a popular, laid-back, unpretentious venue. Down-to-earth right down to the tire swing, no one would accuse Stanley of grooming up for yuppies.

Myett's (☎ 495-9649) is a restaurant, music spot and boutique run by Kareem "Jabbar" Rhymer and his brother, Leon "Sandman" Rhymer. Kareem—who lived, studied, and worked for 14 years in San Francisco—has fulfilled a long-held dream in opening this facility. It has a battery of TVs and hosts events ranging from volleyball games to swimwear fashion shows.

TORTOLA

In addition to their Garden Inn, they also run Olivia's Corner Store and Myett's Communication Center.
http://www.myettent.com
myettent@surfbvi.com

The Paradise Club, a bar and restaurant, offers good breakfasts and hosts **Distinctively Natural**, a gift shop.

FOOD SHOPPING: **Callwood's Superette**, just a little farther on, has prices and stock similar to Rhymer's Store. **Cline's Bakery**, across the main drag from the hotel, sells a limited variety of baked goods. **Bobby's Superette** is the local branch of the Road Town enterprise.

SIGHTS: Lying across a dingy moat with a tuckered out old horse that sleeps standing up, **Callwood's Distillery**, has some of the most potent rum in the Caribbean. Fifths, quarts, and half gallons are available, and the Arundel Spiced Rum is made from rum produced here. This is one of the last functioning distilleries left on the island. Sometimes they are happy to see you, sometimes not. They've never come to groove on the tourism thing.

The Bomba Shack is party central for the North Coast.

TRIPS: Glen Henley's **Cane Garden Bay Pleasure Boats** (☎ 495-9660) supplies snorkeling gear and will do you up with seafaring crafts ranging from powerboats to kayaks.

Larry's Land and Water Taxi (☎ 495-4606, 9455, cell: 496-7435) offers fishing trips, charters, and a sunset cruise each Wed. and Sat.

SHOPPING AND SERVICES: Myett's Business Center offers internet access as well as fax and phone services. Their cosy **Olivia's Corner Store** is an attractive gift and clothing shop.

ENTERTAINMENT: Local youths delight in parking in front of the gas station and jacking up the volume on their car stereos to as high a level as possible.

At his **Quito's Gazebo** on the beach, Quito Rhymer sings his island folk tunes most evenings with selections by the likes of Bob Marley, Jimmy Cliff, and Jimmy Buffet. Quito, who traveled widely in the US before settling down back home in the BVI, has also penned his own tunes like "All God's Children Got Soul" and "My Daddy's Calloused Hands."

The Paradise Club has live bands as does **Myett's**. Music at both ranges from reggae to steel band.

Wack Attack is a two 9-hole putt course which must be the only miniature golf course that also offers snorkeling rentals. It's open 3–8 PM daily.

EVENTS: A **BVI Music Festival** is held in Cane Garden Bay around the end of May. **http://www.bvimusicfest.com**

A **Bacardi Rum Beach Party** (☎ 495-4639 for info) is held in conjunction with Territory Day on July 1.

Heading West
From Cane Garden Bay

A rough road leads on to Ballast Bay and then the Great and Little Carrot Bays. Across from the Isabella Morris Primary School and E of Sugar Mill is the home of **Mrs. Scatliffe** (☎ 495-4556) who serves dinner ($15-22; reservations essential) made with garden grown vegetables from 7 PM nightly. After dinner, she entertains guests with a gospel tune. Daytimes you may find her selling vegetables by the road near her home.

Down the road is **Clem's By the Pier** which has cassava cakes, local confections, and sandwiches. Clem and his steelband perform at his Sun. night BBQ. **Palms** serves delicious local meals most evenings. Also here are the Seventh Day Adventist Church, Dawson's Variety Store, and the Tripple "A" Bar.

LITTLE APPLE BAY: It's then another climb and descent to Little Apple Bay. **Chateau Relaxeau Caribe** (☎ 707-938-3835) is a housekeeping cottage on the beach in Little Apple Bay. It rents for $650 pw (summer) and $950 pw (winter).
http://www.virginbeer.com/chateau.htm
crc@vom.com

Certainly the most unusual structure on the entire island (and perhaps in the entire Caribbean), **The Bomba Shack** (☎ 495-4148) is the closest thing Tortola has to a modern art museum. With its graffiti, hanging painting of a psychedelic mushroom, suspended life jacket, deteriorated Canon camera body, rusted blender base, and more, Bomba is one pretty explosive little bar! Don't miss one of their "Full Moon Party" events.

 Be sure to check out Bomba's each and every full moon eve when there's always a party! Mushroom tea is dispensed at 9 and midnight. However, it does not come for free....

Cetta's Restaurant, down the road, has plates of local food for around $6.

Cameron's Place has a Bar-B-Q and a live steel band on Thurs. from 7 PM; a fish fry is held here on Saturday nights from 8 PM.

Set on the NW coast E of Sebastian's and Long Bay at Little Apple Bay, the intimate **Sugar Mill Hotel** (☎ 495-4355, 800-462-8834, Canada 800-209-6874; ☎ 495-4696; Box 425, Road Town) is one of the island's most attractive resorts, and is centered around the ruins of a 17th-C. sugar mill which was once part of the Appleby Plantation. Its 18 bedrooms come with with kitchenettes and balconies. It has a pool and is near the beach. Rates start at $255 d (summer), $340 d (winter) and range up to $695 for a two-bedroom villa during the winter. Adventure and honeymoon packages are offered. A 10% service charge is added, and there's also a spring and fall set of rates. MAP is additional. Rooms range from the poolside "standard twins" to the beachside Plantation House Suites.

The resort's highly-rated **Sugar Mill Restaurant** has dishes (around $40 for three-courses) which range from "chilled mango and champagne soup" to "lobster cornucopia with banana chutney." Lunch and an a la carte dinner is served at the **Islands** beach bar. "Honeymoon" and "Adventure" packages are available. It also has "Islands," a small beachside restaurant.
http://www.sugarmillhotel.com
sugmill@surfbvi.com

At Little Apple Bay, **Bananas on the Beach** (☎ 495-4318, ☎/☎ 495-4628; Box 2, West End) has housekeeping villas along with a beach bar and babysitting service for around $875 d (summer) and $1,155 d (winter). They also have a place at Long Bay.
beachrentals@surfbvi.com

TORTOLA

At Little Apple Bay, **Casa Caribe** (☎ 495-4318, ☏ 860-693-9482) rents two deluxe fully-equipped waterfront villas. Rates run from around $1,100 pw. **casacaribe@comcast.net**

North Shore Cottages (☎ 495-4430, ☏ 495-4070; Box 11, West End), a set of cottages with a total of 12 beds, is on Long Bay Hill. Rates run from $200 pn winter.

Between Cane Garden Bay and Carrot Bay to the SW, the overgrown ruins of **St. Michael's Church** lie atop Windy Hill. Only the stone walls of the church remain. It is said that its rector, circa 1785, was both priest and pirate. He would spy on approaching craft and then pillage them. The main road leads on to Great Carrot Bay and beyond.

Set on Windy Hill overlooking Carrot Bay along the N coast, **Heritage Inn** (☎ 494-5842, ☏ 495-4100; 877-831-7230; Box 2019, Carrot Bay) offers three two-bedroom and six one-bedroom units with maid service, kitchen (with gas range), bar, and complimentary coffee and tea. The management prides itself on catering to guests. Rates run from $ 120–175 d during the summer with a winter high of $185–$280 d.

Its **Bananakeet** restaurant was called "Bananaquit" (the name for a small Caribbean bird) at first before being changed to suit the locals. Caribbean Fusion" cuisine is served for (weekend only) lunch and (daily) dinner. Entrées run from $18 but average around $26. Live jazz is presented on Fri. nights, and it's a spectacular place to watch the sunset during its "happy hour" from 5–6 PM. Complete menus are on the website.
http://www.heritageinnbvi.com
info@heritageinnbvi.com

At Carrot Bay, the **North Shore Shell Museum** (☎ 495-4714) is quite an experience. This restaurant and "museum" is the brainchild of Egberth Donovan. Approaching, you come across a row of ships which demarcate the entrance. The museum is on the ground floor below the restaurant and consists of a wide variety of shells adorned with colorful slogans and pieces of information. All of the shells found in the museum come from Jost Van Dyke; take a shell you like and leave a donation in a box by the door. The restaurant also has a *fungi* band play some nights.

LONG BAY AREA: Overlooking Long Bay, the five-bedroom **Sunset House** (☎ 494-5864, ☏ 494-7626; Box 263, Road Town) is a Spanish-Mediterranean style villa with five baths, and Jacuzzi. Rates depend upon the size of your group but start at $6,000 pw.
http://www.areanavillas.com
info@areanavillas.com

Long Bay has an absolutely gorgeous beach panorama. A small resort set on 50 acres, the **Long Bay Beach Resort & Villas** (☎ 495-4242, 954-481-8787, 800-858-4618, ☏ 954-481-1661) offers a total of 155 units, including hillside rooms and studios along with beachside cabanas. Rooms include a/c, telephone, refrigerator, and TV. There are a number of three- and four-bedroom villas with breathtaking views which are set on the slopes above the resort.

The resort centers around a "club" which has a pool and three restaurants. Vegetarian food is available, and dietary preferences can be catered to. (Other restaurants are a short drive away.) The **Beach Restaurant** is built on the ruins of a two-century-old rum distillery; a second is the more formal gourmet **Garden Restaurant**. The informal **1748**, set on a a beachfront deck, was once part of an 18th-century sugar mill; it offers buffet breakfasts and lunches and dinners. Special weekly events include the "Barbecue

Cook-out" and a "Taste of Tortola" buffet; both evenings featuring live entertainment; it also has a popular Sunday brunch. One of the most panoramic (albeit rocky) beaches is here, as is the world's smallest non-miniature golf course and a "Wellness Spa and Salon." No-see-ums proliferate at dusk. Road Town is a half-hour drive and the airport about an hour. Rates run from $285 d (summer) to $380 d (winter). Packages are available. Call 44 (0) 870 160 9645 in the UK. Read the reviews on tripadvisor.com before booking.
http://www.longbay.com
reservations@longbay.com

Grape Tree Vacation Rentals (☎ 495-4229, ☏ 495-4491; Box 3328, Road Town) are a set of deluxe and fully-equipped one- and two-bedroom apartments with kitchen, living, dining area, patio, and cable TV. It's right on Long Bay Beach. Rates range from $600–$1,400 pw during the summer to $700–$1,800 pw during the winter.
melo@surfbvi.com

At Long Bay, **Amberjack House** is a luxurious four-bedroom villa which holds up to six. It has a kitchen equipped with a microwave, a phone, TV, and a pool. It rents for $4,400 pw during the high season with around a 25% reduction off season. For more information call (617) 868-5340, ☏ (617) 661-4580, or write 17 Berkeley St., Cambridge, MA 02138.
ieroth@aol.com

At Long Bay, **Pelican Villa** (☎ 494-3186, ☏ 494-4386) rents for around $1,700 pw with two bedrooms, two baths, and complete facilities.
http://www.go-bvi.com/pelicanvilla
pelicanvilla@go-bvi.com

At Long Bay, deluxe and fully equipped **Sunset View Vacation Rental** (☎ 495-

4315, 609-624-0062; Box 612, West End) rents for $600–$1,000 pw summer and $1,200–$2,000 pw winter. It has cable TV.
eos@surfbvi.com

Also at Long Bay, **Oleander House BVI** (☎ 495 4142) is a three-bedroom, three-bath home which rents from $2,457 pw during the high season.
http://www.oleanderhousebvi.com
info@oleanderhousebvi.com

On Zion Hill at Apple Bay, **Coco Plums** (☎ 495-4672) is a popular restaurant which serves pasta and other dishes; portions are generous.

A 15-min. drive from town in Apple Bay, **Sebastian's On the Beach** (☎ 495 4212, ☏ 495-4466, 800-336-4870; Box 441, Road Town) is at the junction of a steep road leading up and down to the West End side of the island. In order of increasing quality, rooms are tropical yard units (set 150 ft. from the beach), four rear units or two inn units, and eight beachfront rooms with balcony or porch. Rooms have fans and refrigerators. Watersports and a restaurant (seafood and West Indian) are available. Rates range from $100–$170 (summer) and from $150–$300 (winter). MAP is around $35 additional, and a 10% service charge (15% if on MAP) is included. A variety of packages are offered. They also rent **Sebastian's Seaside Villa**. Its **restaurant** serves three good meals daily. You may dine on conch stew, fritters, lobster, grilled fish, and vegetarian dishes. Watch pelicans dive for fish from the terrace.
http://www.sebastiansbvi.com
sebhotel@surfbvi.com

Beyond Sebastian's, the main road deteriorates and leads past Long Bay to **Belmont** and then on to secluded **Smuggler's Cove**. At Belmont Estates to the N of the West

End, **Equinox House** (☎ 494-5864, 941-945-12394, ☏ 941-945-4918) offers luxurious three-bedrooms with a pool which rent for $2,400–$4,100 pw during the summer and $5,100–$5,800 pw during the winter. The same management runs Villa Taino along with other properties.
http://www.areanavillas.com
info@areanavillas.com

Belmont House (☎ 495-4477, ☏ 495-4476) is a rental which has two bedrooms and two baths. Overlooking Smuggler's Cove Beach, it offers comfortable rattan furniture and has gingerbread woodwork. Families and honeymooners are welcome. Rates run around $1,800 pw in the winter.
http://www.belmont-house.com
belmont@surfbvi.com

Palm Grove Villa (☎ 495-4651), a two-bedroom, two-bath villa renting for $1,800 pw (winter), is also at Belmont.
http://www.palmgrovevilla.com
str@tranters3.fsnet.co.uk

From Tortola

There is an $15 international departure tax (air) plus $5 "security fee," and a $5 tax if you depart by ferry; cruise ship passengers pay $7. Times listed here are current at the time of publication. Ferry times are listed below; consult the latest issue of *The Welcome* to see if departure times have changed.

FOR VIRGIN GORDA: Unless you charter a flight, the only way to get here is with the excellent ferry services.

BY BOAT: *Speedy's* (☎ 495-5240, 495-5235) leaves Road Town Mon. to Sat. at 9, noon, 1:30, and 4:30; on Tues. and Thurs. also at 10:10 AM and 6:15 PM; and on Sun. *only* at 9 AM and 5:15 PM. Adults are $15 OW; $25 RT. Children (over 5) are $10 OW, $20 RT.

http://www.speedysbvi.com
speedysbvi@surfbvi.com

Smith's Ferry Services (☎ 495-4495, 494-2355) departs Road Town Mon. to Fri. at 7, 8:50, 12:30, and 3:15; on Sat. at at 7, 8:50, 12:30, and 4:15; and at 8:50, 12:30, and 4:15 on Sun. Adults are $12 OW; $20 RT. Children (over 5) are $7 OW, $11 RT.

FOR THE NORTH SOUND: You need to catch this one if you are headed for Biras Creek or the Bitter End. Make reservations. The *North Sound Express* runs from Beef Island (the island the airport is located on) to Spanish Town and on to the North Sound. The *North Sound Express* departs from Beef Island daily at 8:15, 11:15, 1, 3:45, 5:30, and 7:30 PM. All stop in Spanish Town. Rates for adults (from age 12) are $15–$20 OW; $30–$40 RT.

FOR PETER ISLAND: From the **Peter Island Ferry Dock** (☎ 495-2000) ferries leave daily at 7, 8:30, 10, noon, 2, 3:30, 5:30, 7, 8, and 10:30.

FOR JOST VAN DYKE: The *Jost Van Dyke Ferry Service* (☎ 494-2997) leaves West End at 7:30, 9:45, 1:30, and 4 on Mon to Sat. and at 9:30, 1:30 and 4 on Sun. Its craft is the *When*, as in *when* it is leaving or *when* is it leaving? If you arrive early, savor the delights of the area.

The **New Horizon Ferry Service** (☎ 495-9477) runs the *Paradise Express* and *Paradise Sunshine* from West End to Jost, Mon. to Fri., at 8, 10, 1, 4, and 6. On Sat. and Sun. it leaves at 9, 10, 1, 4, and 6. Rates are $20 RT, $12 OW; children 5–12 are free; children under five ride free.

Enroute, you'll pass Green Cay and Sandy Cay (both national parks) which will be to your R as you approach Jost.
http://www.jostvandykeferry.com

FOR ANEGADA: Smith's Ferry Services (☎ 495-4495, 494-2355) goes to Anegada on Thurs. from Road Town. It leaves at 7 AM and 3:30 PM and returns at 8:30 AM and 5 PM. A charter flight with **Fly BVI** (☎ 495-1747) is the only other way to get back and forth.

FOR ST. THOMAS: Air Sunshine (☎ 495-8900, 800-327-8900) and **Cape Air** (☎ 800-352-0714, 800-635-8787) fly daily. **American Eagle** (☎ 800-327-8900) also flies to St. Thomas.

BY FERRY: *The Road Town Fast Ferry* (☎ 494-2323), a high-speed catamaran ($55RT, 50 min.), departs at Road Town at 7 AM, 10 AM, and 2:30 PM from Mon. to Sat. and on Sun at 9 AM and 4 PM.
http://www.roadtownfastferry.com

Smith's Ferry Services (☎ 495-4495, 494-2355) depart Road Town from Mon. to Fri. at 6:15 AM, on Wed. at 2:15, and from from the West End at 7, 10, and 3. On Sat. it leaves Road Town at 6:15, 9, noon, 2, and 5:30 and West End at 7, 10, 2:30, and at 6. On Sun. it departs West End at 9:15, 12:20, 3:35, and 4:05. Fares are $45 RT adults, $35 children under $12.

Native Son (☎ 495-4617) leaves Road Town from Mon. to Fri. at 6:15 AM with an add'l trip on Wed. at 2:15; and on Mon. to Fri. from the West End at 7, 10, and 3. On Sat it runs at 6:15, and 2 from Road Town, and at 7, 10, 2:30, and 5:45 from West End. On Sun. it runs at 9:30 and 3:50 from West End and at 3:15 from Road Town. An add'l trip runs daily from the West End (via Cruz Bay and Red Hook) at 6:45, 8:30, and 4. Fares are $45 RT adults, $35 children under $12.
http://www.nativesonbvi.com

FOR ST. JOHN AND RED HOOK, ST. THOMAS: From the West End, *Smith's Ferry Services* (☎ 495-4495; $40 RT, 30 min.) heads out for Cruz Bay and on to Red Hook, St. Thomas. Ferries leave daily at 6:30, 8:50, 12:20, and at 3:45. Adults are $25 OW; $44 RT. Children (7–12) are $18 OW, $38 RT and (4–6) are $18 OW, $28 RT.

Inter-Island Boat Services (☎ 495-4166) runs from West End to Cruz Bay from Mon. to Sat. at 9:15, 12:15, and 4:15, with an add'l trip on Fri. at 5:30; and on Sun. at 9:15, 12:15, and 5:15.

The *Nubian Princess* (☎ 495-4999) sails from West End to St. John and then on to Red Hook. It departs on Sun. to Fri. from West End at 11:30 and 3:30 and from Road Town at 10:45, 2:30, and at 4:30.

FOR ST. CROIX: Air Sunshine (☎ 495-8900, 800-327-8900) flies daily. **Cape Air** (☎ 800-352-0714) flies via St. Thomas.

FOR SAN JUAN, PUERTO RICO: American Eagle (☎ 495-2559, 800-327-8900) flies as does **Air Sunshine** (☎ 495-8900, 800-327-8900), and LIAT (☎ 495-1197, 495-2577, 888-844-5428; USVI/PR: 866-549-5428; Antigua: 268-480-5601/2).

FOR THE SOUTHERN CARIBBEAN: LIAT (an acronym some maintain stands for "Leave At Any Time") flies daily to Antigua, St. Kitts, Barbados, St. Lucia, St. Maarten and Dominica. **Winair** (☎ 494-2347) flies on Fri., Sat., Sun. and Mon.
http://www.fly-winair.com

Jost Van Dyke

Less than four miles N of St. John, **Jost Van Dyke** (pop. 200) retains a distinctly rural West Indian character. Named after a Dutch pirate, this long, narrow island has hills running like a camel's humps from head to tail.

Although the island once had no paved roads, electricity, and only a few vehicles, things have changed; the island now has rental cars, internet access, and even a microbrewery. The main town is **Great Harbour** where customs, facilities, school, and a church are located.

To the W of Great Harbour is **White Bay,** which contains a long white sand beach. Unlike Great and Little Harbour, which are well protected and calm anchorages, White Bay may be subject to winter swells.

The island is generally quiet, save when restaurateur and musician Foxy Callwood stages one of his massive parties. The most popular are held during New Years, the Wooden Boat Regatta in September, and at Halloween.

One encouraging new development is **The Jost Van Dyke Preservation Society** which is working to preserve the island's natural environment.
http://www.jvdps.org
Besides the accommodations listed here, other villa rentals are listed at:
http://www.bvitourism.com/jostvan-dyke/jvd-villas.htm

GETTING HERE: Jost Van Dyke can only be reached by private boat (many yachts run day trips here) or by ferry.

The **New Horizon Ferry Service** (☎ 495-9477) runs the *Paradise Express* and *Paradise Sunshine* from West End to Jost, Mon. to Fri., at 8, 10, 1, 4, and 6. On Sat. and Sun. it leaves at 9, 10, 1, 4, and 6. Rates are $20 RT, $12 OW; children 5–12 are free; children under five ride free.

Enroute, you'll pass Green Cay and Sandy Cay, which will be to your R as you approach Jost.
http://www.jhostvandykeferry.com

Ferries also ply between Red Hook (St. Thomas) Cruz Bay (St. John) and Great Harbour on Fri. and Sat. *Inter-Island Boat Services* (☎ 495-4166) departs **Red Hook** at 8 AM and 2 PM and from **Cruz Bay** at 8:30 AM and at 2:15 PM.

GETTING AROUND: While it is possible to walk, hills are steep. Taxis will take you around (fixed rates), or you can rent a car from **Paradise Car Rental** (☎ 495-9477) or **Abe's** (☎ 495-9477). Some of the taxi drivers include friendly **Bon Chinnery** (☎ 499-8871), **Claude** (☎ 443-4178), and **JVD Safari Service** (☎ 495-9267; cell: 443-3832). The last also offers tours for $20 pp.
http://www.bviwelcome.com/jvdsafari

ENTERTAINMENT: Check out Foxy Tamarind's calypso ballads, and Foxy's also has live bands most Fri. and Sat. evenings. **Rudy's** has live entertainment on some evenings. **Ruben Chinnery** is a good local guitarist who plays at the **Soggy Dollar Bar** on Sun. afternoons.

Foxy's Wooden Boat Regatta

Vintage wooden vessels from throughout the Virgins gather each and every Labor Day for **Foxy's Wooden Boat Regatta**. This thirty-year-plus tradition has been growing over the years, its appeal enhanced by its laid-back image. It is held over each Labour Day Weekend. The Saturday competition is the Single-handed Race, and Sunday's event is the Wooden Boat Race. ∎

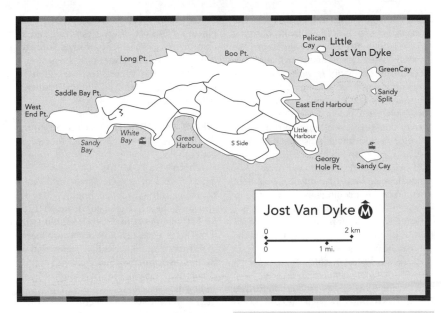

WATER SPORTS: Jost Van Dyke Watersports (☎ 495 0271, 24 hr. cell. 496-7603; VHF Ch. 16) near Foxy's in Great Harbour, offer scuba trips to more than 30 unmarked sites, certification courses, snorkel trips, internet access, dinghy and kayak rentals, and sport fishing.
http://www.jvdwatersports.com
jvdwatersports@hotmail.com

BVI Sea and Land Adventures (☎ 495-4966, cell: 499-2269), White Bay, rent a wide variety of equipment—ranging from mountain bikes to snorkeling equipment—and offer tours, beach parties, and packages. They're open daily from 9AM–5PM.
http://www.bviadventure.com
bviadventures@yahoo.com

Great Harbour Practicalities

On the beach at Great Harbour, **Foxy's Tamarind Bar** (☎ 495-9258; dinner reservations by 5 PM) is run by calypsonian Feliciano "Foxy" Callwood and is the island's oldest and most famous watering hole. Dinner features "Calypso Caribbean Lobster" and filet mignon. Large parties take place here on New Year's Eve, St. Patrick's Day, April Fool's Day, Memorial Day's Wooden Boat Race (three decades old now), and at Halloween. Foxy relates that the whole bar grew out of the needs of the 1967 Harvest Festival.

Foxy is a talented guitarist and conservationist who is working to preserve the island as it is. He's known far and wide; John Kerry was interviewed while wearing a Foxy's tee-shirt in 2004. Stories have him eating in the finest restaurants in Europe in bare feet, and he is legendary for incorporating personal characteristics of his guests into whatever song he is singing at the time. Foxy is a fearless polemicist. His calypsos take on everything from Michael Jackson, to the evils of smoking tobacco, to the difference between Northern and Southern California. He performs on a stool set in front of a realistic dummy of Foxy playing guitar. Foxy maintains that the dummy, unlike himself, doesn't offend anybody.

Foxy bottles his own brand of rum, has a microbrewery on the premises, and runs his own desalinization plant.

BBQ buffets are offered on Fri. and Sat. nights. Live and recorded music is presented when Foxy is not rolling his eyes and spouting one of his famous calypsos.

NOTE: This restaurant is generally closed from mid-Aug. through mid-Oct., but the bar may be open.
http://www.foxysbar.com

Set at the other end of the harbor, **Rudy's Bar and Restaurant** (☎ 495-9282, 775-3558, VHF Ch. 16) is owned by Rudy George and his wife. Prices in the restaurant are in the $10–$30 range. A lobster buffet ($30) is held on Thursday nights. They have modern apartment with kitchenette for around $150 pn.

Between the Foxy's and Rudy's are a number of places including the casual **Ali Baba's** (☎ 495-9280) which serves three meals and hosts a happy hour (conch fritters, *rotis*). It has a U-shaped mahogany bar and beach lounges and hammocks. It also has fishing tournaments.

The **Sea Crest Inn**, Great Harbour, offers studios from $130 pd ($90 pd summer); reduced weekly rates are available.
http://www.bviwelcome.com/seacrestinn
seacrestinn@hotmail.com

The **Southside Villas** (☎ 495-9263, ℂ 718-825-4464) has one- and two-bedroom apartments.
wewe2kof@aol.com

SHOPPING AND FOOD SHOPPING: **Nature's Basket** offers fresh fruit and an assortment of other items. **Rudy's Suprette** sells a good assortment of basic items including fresh vegetables; they also do provisioning for yachts. **Foxy's Boutique** sells souvenirs.

WHITE BAY PRACTICALITIES: Set to the W, this bay can be reached on foot or by boat or taxi.

White Bay Villas (☎ 626-7722, ℂ 626-7222) offers one-, two-, and three-bedroom fully-equipped luxury villas set above the beach. Rates run from $1,120–$3,120 (summer) to $1,400–$3,900 (winter). This is a great choice for those in search of self-catering higher-end accommodation. Rooms are attractive, and the views are tremendous. You wake to the sound of goats and birds.
http://www.jostvandyke.com
jkwhitebay@aol.com

Pink House on White Bay (☎ 319-533-1281) is a two-bedroom, two-bath home.
http://www.pinkhousebvi.com
info@pinkhousebvi.com

The next L turn heads to **White Bay Campground** (☎ 495-9358, c/o General Delivery, West End PO). This is a superb choice for adventurous, low key travelers. The owner is friendly local musician Ivan Chinnery, and the campground was the fulfillment of Ivan's long-held dream. He

 Moor a dinghy at a small jetty at the E end of Jost. Then walk N until you come to a salt pond. Passing through scrub and mangroves, follow a goat track around the perimeter to the W where you'll find a blow hole in a clearing. Tune in to its haunting melody.

proposed the idea to the property owner, a cousin visiting from NYC, and he opened it in 1993. A communal kitchen features a range and two refrigerators, and you may store your food in your own (numbered) plastic storage bin. A BBQ area is in the back. The campground charges $25/tent and $35/cabin during the low season and $40/tent and $50–$70/cabin during the winter high season. Bare sites are $15/night. The cabins are niftier than one might expect, and they have fans and small refrigerators. Some have two beds. Everyone hangs out at Ivan's **Low-Stress Bar** where you pour your own drinks.

Right on the beach at White Bay, **The Sandcastle** (☎ 495-9888, ℰ 495-9999) is a low-key hotel run by friendly Tish and Jerry O'Connell. It has two beach cottages, two garden cottages and two a/c units start at $245 pn, $295 pn during the high season ($160–$220 pn off-season). The attractively furnished two-room and bath cottages are directly on the beach and have ceiling fans. A weekly "7 day plan" is also offered. Guests often return year after year. Its informal restaurant (reservations required) serves dishes such as stuffed grouper. Its **Soggy Dollar Bar** specializes in its trademark drink, the **painkiller**, a potent rum drink invented on the premises. It serves casual lunches. The bar's name comes from boaters, who would swim to shore during winter swells, and then plop their dollars down for a drink. Romantic reservation-only gourmet dinners feature soup, salad, entrée, and a scrumptious selection of desserts served with coffee or tea. A wine list completes the picture. (The hotel is closed for the month of Sept.)
http://www.soggydollar.com
relax@soggydollar.com

Gertrude's Beach Bar and Boutique (☎ 495-9104; Box 485, Cruz Bay, St. John, VI 00801) is both bar and tee-shirt empo-

rium. Gertrude also has several attractive units to rent in the back which go for around $120 d; she is also an agent for the Perfect Pineapple (see below).

The **Perfect Pineapple** (☎ 495-9401) has deluxe one-($150) and two-bedroom ($250) suites.
http://www.perfectpineapple.com
perfectpineapple@surfbvi.com

White Bay Suprette and **Jewels Snack Shack** are also on the beach.

LITTLE HARBOUR: A paved road leads from the hill above Great Harbour and down eastward to Little Harbour, where you'll find a number of restaurants along with some accommodations.

Sidney's Peace and Love Bar (☎ 495-9271, night: 495-8655) offers three meals and features seafood; it has an all-you-can-eat (around $20) every evening save Wed. and Fri. Captains are offered free dinner. In keeping with the name, Sidney's bar operates on the honor system. The rum is cheaper than the mix, so Sidney doesn't sweat the proportions. Hanging tee shirts adorn the premises.

Harris' Place (☎ 495-9295, ℰ 495-9296) is open for three meals and happy hour daily. It features a Mon. night all-you-can-eat lobster special as well as a selection of roast meats every evening. Daily lunch specials are available, and dinner entrées range from lobster ($25 and up) to conch ($16.95). All-you-can-eat lobster dinners are $40 on Mon. nights.; a Thurs. night all-you-can-eat seafood buffet is $22.

Gerald Chinnery (☎ 495-9835, VHF Ch. 12) has a fuel dock and a small marina, and offers internet service, gasoline, pizza, and cold drinks.

Supplemented by a grocery store, **Abe's** (☎ 495-9329, ℰ 495-9529) has a daily happy hour from 5 to 6 ($1 per drink/can beer) and serves three meals daily. They also have a car rental service, and they have their own private cove with its own small sandy beach. If you would like to get to know West Indian culture and get away from it all, this would be a good choice.

Their **Abe's By the Sea Vacation Apartment** (☎ 495-9329, ✆ 495-9529) offers a three-bedroom unit with kitchen for $80–$225 high season. Rates here are negotiable depending upon how long you will stay. This is a great place to stay if you want to get away from it all.

Set on the island's E end farther on, **Sandy Ground Estates** (☎ 494-3391, ✆ 495-9379; Box 594, West End, Tortola) offers eight beachfront villas with terracotta floors and an 800-ft. beach. Prices start at $1,000 pw. (summer) and ($1,400 pw (winter).
http://www.sandyground.com
sandygroundjvd@surfbvi.com

From Sandy Ground it's possible to hike along the island's E edge, skirting mangroves and ruins facing Jost Van Dyke. Offshore are Green Cay (popularly known as "Snake Island") and other cays. It's possible to swim or wade across to reach these. Continuing, the trail narrows and passes above steep bluffs, from which it's possible to spot sea turtles. It's dangerous to climb down to the beaches along this stretch. It's possible to return to Great Harbour by hiking through thick brush and over several ridges.

DIAMOND CAY: Established in 1991, this 1.25-acre island reserve serves as a nesting site for boobies, terns, and pelicans. Diamond Cay is located off Long Bay, Jost Van Dyke. It is part of a protected area

You may rent a dinghy and visit Sandy Cay or Green Cay. Both are uninhabited small islands with great beaches and snorkeling.

which combines the privately-owned islands of Sandy Spit, Sandy Cay, and Green Cay, as well as parts of Jost Van Dyke and the surrounding marine area. The leatherback nests on Sandy Cay, and Sandy Spit hosts two species of lizard.

The volcanic nature of the island is more pronounced on Diamond Cay's E windward side which has bare, rocky cliffs which reveal its volcanic nature; the leeward side offers sandy beaches.

The place to base yourself is the breezy **Taboo Restaurant.** Lunches here feature dishes such as pizza ($13), fresh fish ($14) and vegetarian ($12) sandwiches. From here you can go for a number of short hikes, including one to the ruins of a brothel on Little Jost Van Dyke (ten min.), one to a bubbling pool, and a trail to Diamond Cay.

FROM JOST VAN DYKE: The **New Horizon Ferry Service** (☎ 495-9477) runs the *Paradise Express* and *Paradise Sunshine* from Jost to West End from Mon. to Fri., at 7, 9, noon, 2, and 5. On Sat. and Sun. it leaves at 8, 9:30, noon, 2, and 5. Rates are $20 RT, $12 OW; children 5–12 are free; children under five ride free.
http://www.jostvandykeferry.com

FOR THE USVI: *Inter-Island Boat Services* (☎ 776-6597) departs, Fri. Sat., and Sun. at 9:15 AM and 3 PM. Fare is $40 RT; it takes 45 min.

Virgin Gorda

Virgin Gorda is the third largest British Virgin Island. This spectacular island was dubbed the "fat virgin" by the Spanish because its mountainous profile, when approached by boat from the S, is reminiscent of a woman lying on her back. Eight square miles in area, its 10-mile length naturally divides itself into two parts. While the NE is mountainous, the SE is flat.

All lands above 1,000 ft. are part of the National Park; the highest point, Gorda Peak, is 1,370 ft. At the top, accessible by road, is an observation tower. The trailhead is off the main road on the way from Spanish Town (The Valley) to Gun Creek.

The island is bordered by splendid beaches, strewn with large boulders, and characterized by the ubiquitous bleating goat. **Spanish Town**, more a settlement than a town, is a pretty but otherwise totally unremarkable place. Modern amenities (roads, phones, electricity) have come here only recently. Tourism has grown immensely, to the point where The Baths, the island's chief attraction, has become overcrowded—thereby losing part of its charms. (Visit early or late to avoid daytrippers).

While Virgin Gorda has a small permanent population, many internationals are employed in hotels and restaurants. Friendly Vincentians and Grenadans are among the expats that you may find serving you at your restaurant table. They're always happy to talk about their homes and share their experiences.

HISTORY: During the late 1600s, while ownership of Tortola was disputed between the English and Dutch, Puerto Rican Spaniards occasionally raided settlements here. The original seat of the colonial government was located at Spanish Town around 1710. Although population exceeded 7,500 in the early 17th C, currently only around 1,500 people live on Virgin Gorda. Population declined after the introduction of the sugar beet to Europe and the emancipation of slaves in 1834.

In modern times, the island has grown because of the late Laurance Rockefeller's personal interest in it. In the early 1950s, the island had no electricity, telephones, sewers, doctor, paved road, or adequate educational facilities. Only when construction at Rockefeller's Little Dix Bay began in the 1960s did the island begin to enter modern times. Because the resort required a massive influx of capital in order to create the needed infrastructure, the project was dubbed "the British Virgin Islands' Red Cross."

In 1989, Fanta spared no expense in shooting a 30-second spot underwater near Devils Bay. In 1994, the Virgin Islands National Police found 29 bales containing 1914 lbs (870 kg) of cocaine stashed behind a rock in same bay. (No further incidents have been reported, but cocaine continues to be intercepted in British Virgin Islands waters). Clearly, Virgin Gorda has come a long way!

The Baths are one of the most famous attractions in the BVI. Negotiating them means slipping through boulders and climbing ladders.

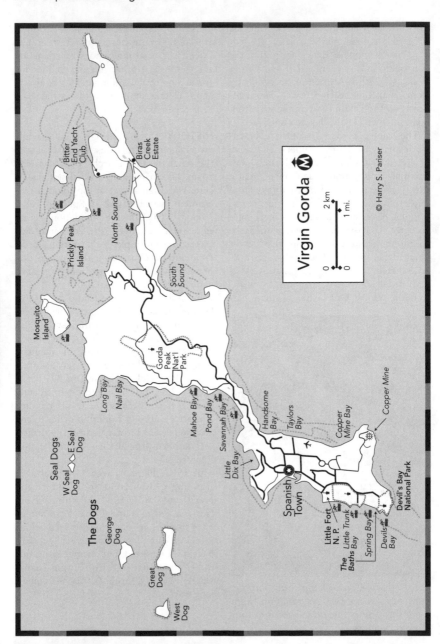

Virgin Gorda

© Harry S. Pariser

VIRGIN GORDA

Bitter End Yacht Club

Biras Creek Estate

North Sound

Prickly Pear Island

South Sound

Mosquito Island

Gorda Peak Nat'l Park

Long Bay

Nail Bay

Mahoe Bay

Pond Bay

Little Savannah Bay

Little Dix Bay

Handsome Bay

Taylors Bay

Copper Mine Bay

Copper Mine

Seal Dogs

W Seal Dog   E Seal Dog

The Dogs

George Dog

Great Dog

West Dog

Spanish Town

Little Fort N. P.

The Little Trunk Baths Bay

Spring Bay

Devils Bay

Devil's Bay National Park

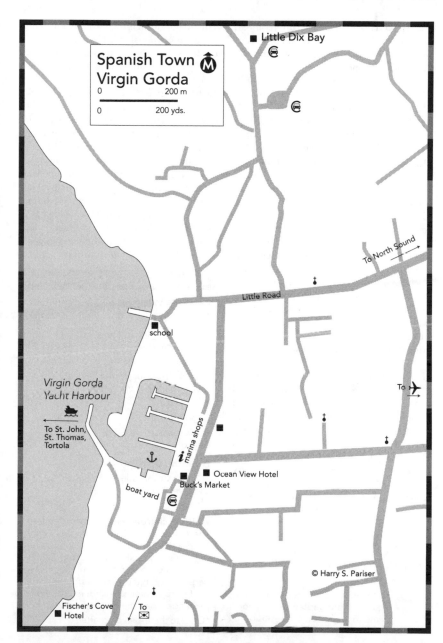

Spanish Town
Virgin Gorda

0   200 m

0   200 yds.

■ Little Dix Bay

To North Sound →

Little Road

school

Virgin Gorda
Yacht Harbour

← To St. John,
St. Thomas,
Tortola

To ✈

marina shops

boat yard

Ocean View Hotel
Buck's Market

Fischer's Cove
Hotel

To
✉

© Harry S. Pariser

VIRGIN GORDA

GETTING HERE: Ferries run from St. Thomas, St. John, and Tortola. For specifics check the "from" sections under the particular islands concerned.

BY AIR: Air Sunshine (☎ 495-8900, 800-327-8900) and **Fly BVI** fly here from St. Thomas as does **American Eagle; M & N Aviation** (☎ 495-5553), **American Eagle**, and **Vieques Air Link** (☎ 777-4055, 888-901-9247) fly from San Juan.
http://www.vieques-island.com/val

BY AIR TO NORTH SOUND: Seaborne Airlines (☎ 773-6442; ✆ 713-9077, 888-359-8687) offers a convenient flight between downtown St. Thomas and North Sound on Virgin Gorda. *However, each passenger may carry only up to 30 pounds of baggage for free; after that, it's $1 per pound You will be charged for your carry on!* Children age two or under are free. Special Internet and weekend fares are offered, as are ferry and seaplane combination packages. Check in 45 min. before your flight.
http://www.flyseaborne.com

BEACHES: There are 16 of them-enough for a week's exploring. Although Little Dix and Biras Creek have been developed, Savannah Bay and Pond are excellent for shell hunting.

Other beaches include Spring Bay Beach near The Baths, Berchers Bay Beach, St. Thomas Bay Beach, Pond Bay Beach, Mahoe Bay Beach, Devil's Bay Beach, Leverick Bay Beach, and North Sound's Deep Bay Beach. Honeymoon Beach is on Mosquito Reef which is just behind the Bitter End.

THE BATHS AND VICINITY: The premier tourist site in the British Virgin Islands, **The Baths** are truly this island's calling card.

This magnificent beach area is located at the S tip of the island. Here, huge granite boulders the size of houses topple over one another above underlying grottos of clear turquoise water. Enter the dim caverns to bathe. Light enters between the cracks, giving each grotto a different atmosphere, one which changes continually as the tide pounds in and out. You have to navigate a series of stairwalks and a ropewalk through the grottos to get from one side to another.

These granite boulders probably were born during the Tertiary Period some 70 million years ago. Magma (molten rock) formed huge sections of granite which contained large quantities of feldspar and quartz. Some 15–25 million years ago, the granite was exposed through faulting and uplifting of the sea floor

Virgin Gorda Taxi Fares	
From the Valley to	**(third person+)**
Any church, grocery store, or clinic in the Valley	3.00 (2.00)
Baths/Devil's Bay/Spring Bay	4.00 (3.00)
Savanna/Trunk Bay/Pond Bay	6.00 (3.50)
Mango Bay/Mtn. Trunk Bch./ Mahoe Bay	6.00 (5.00)
Copper Mine	5.00 (4.00)
Gun Creek/Leverick Bay/ Galleon Beach/Turtle Bay	*24.00 (6.00)
From the Dock to	
Fischer's Cove/Olde Yard Village/ Little Dix BayAirport/ Church in Village	4.00 (3.00)

Waiting charges First 10 minutes free. Thereafter, every 15 minutes, $4. Grand Tours (1½-2 hours: Valley, Coppermine, Baths, Gorda Peak, Leverick Bay) $45 for one to three; $15 per extra person. Two bags of luggage pp are free. Fares listed are for each three passengers. Additional passengers pay fares in parentheses.

*One- to three-person charter.

Keep in mind that Virgin Gorda is quiet during September, a good time to visit if you like seclusion.

and squared boulders were exposed. Over the course of millions of years, they eroded, broke and fell on top of each other, and became rounded.

One important source of erosion has been rainfall, which reacts with carbon dioxide as it falls to form a weak carbonic acid. This reacts with the feldspar and granite but not the quartz. The rough spots on the flaking area are caused by the quartz particles, which are exposed yet are still held in place by the surrounding rock. The hollows in the boulders were formed by easterly and southerly winds which accelerate the erosion on these rock faces.

ORIENTATION: To get here, turn R from the Yacht Harbour and follow the road which turns L and then straightens. Follow the road to The Baths. The hills of Ginger Island and Salt Island frame the foreground. After 1.5 mi. you will reach Spring Bay and the Crawls on the R. Continue on to the end to find The Baths entrance. *Foreign visitors are charged $3 for admission.*

The Poor Man's Bar here sells drinks, burgers, and tee shirts. As its entrepreneurial owner charges $1.25 for water, and as the other prices are comparable, he certainly won't remain impoverished for long.

The area offshore to the L has fine snorkeling. Crouch and waddle to enter the Baths. Some of the boulders resemble animals such as a lion and a whale. In the area surrounding the Baths, you can find pitch apple, frangipani, white cedar and turpentine trees as well as different species of cactus, wild tamarind, box briar, and wild sage.

A 15-min. walk from The Baths to the S brings you to 58-acre **Devil's Bay National Park,** set around a secluded coral sand beach; the somewhat rugged trail through the boulders from The Baths terminates here. *Foreigners are charged a $3 admission fee.*

Another trail leads to **Stoney Bay** on the island's tip which offers spectacular views of

Fallen Jerusalem and the surrounding islands.

The 36 acres of **Little Fort National Park,** just S of the Yacht Harbour, comprise boulder-strewn forest and are a wildlife sanctuary. Once the site of a Spanish fortress, some masonry walls (including the remains of the "Powder House") still stand on the hillside. Established in 1978, much of the park is inaccessible. Vegetation includes enormous silk cotton trees as well as pitch apple, bromeliads, and epiphytes.

Set between Little Fort and The Baths, **Spring Bay** is a recreational beach area comprising 5.5 acres.

There's good snorkeling off of its small but beautiful boulder-covered beach at **The Crawl.** This is the place to go when the cruise ships are in port and hordes of taxis are parked at The Baths. It is also a good location to practice your snorkeling techniques.

It's possible (albeit difficult) to clamber over the rocks back and forth between the two. There's no water here so — as is true throughout the area — bring your own!

OTHER SIGHTS: The **Methodist Chapel,** Crab Hill Rd., dates from 1823 and is the island's oldest building. **St. Mary's Church,** Church Hill Rd., dates from 1875. Conch shells here mark many of the older graves.

While The Baths are certainly worth a visit, you won't find the uncrowded beach you see on picture postcards unless you arrive at the crack of dawn. On any given day scores of yachts anchor offshore and cruise ship passengers are now being ferried over and then truck bused in from Tortola. What's a snorkeler to do? The best alternative is to tour The Baths and then either clamber over the rocks to less frequented Devil's Bay or to visit one of the island's other gorgeous and generally still nearly deserted beaches.

More than a century old, **Oliver Peaker's House** is the oldest home.

Nearby town at **Copper Mine Point** stand the ruins of a copper mine first mined by Spaniards from Puerto Rico during the 16th century. Its last spate of operation, under the control of Cornish miners, was from 1838–67. The ruins of the chimney, boiler house, a large cistern, and mine shaft entrances can still be found here. The National Trust is funding stabilization; send them a donation at Box 1089, Virgin Gorda. The ruins themselves are not as spectacular as is their juxtaposition with the churning, tempestuous sea below it. With a little effort, you can imagine yourself at some faraway place or time.

To get here turn R from the Yacht Harbour, follow a curve to the L, and then turn to the L and stay on the road to its termination at a "T" where you turn R and follow that rutted road to the end. A visit here is something of a short adventure.

Grub is to be had at the proximate **Mine Shaft Cafe** which has unforgettable sun-

The Bo Peep

The BVI's most famous frog is the **bo peep**, (*Eluterodactylus swarthier*), a member of the family of whistling frogs which includes Puerto Rico's emblem the coqui. Named after its colorful call, this one-inch frog has a penetrating voice which belies its size. Found only on Tortola and Virgin Gorda, this tree frog is one of three species found in the BVI. ∎

sets. Get there a bit early to savor the cool breeze and enjoy the last flights landing at Virgin Gorda airport before sundown. If you arrive a bit early, you can check out its miniature golf course.

Nail Bay, on the E coast, contains the 18th-C remains of a stone, coral, and brick sugar mill.

GORDA PEAK NATIONAL PARK: Reaching 1,370 ft., **Virgin Gorda Peak** is one of the highest in the Virgins. In 1974, the late Laurence Rockefeller donated this

Virgin Gorda's The Crawl offers hiking and snorkeling amidst barrel cacti and boulders.

At Gorda Peak National Park, climb up the ladder of the lookout tower for a spectacular view of North Sound. Anegada looms high on the horizon. The US Virgins are in the rear and St. Croix is to the SE.

tract of high-elevation dry forest, and it became a National Park. The 265-acre area surrounding the peak includes a self-guiding nature trail leading to a lookout point which joins with a paved road leading to Little Dix Bay.

HIKING: The main trail is the most direct route to the summit. Watch for orchids on the way up. In the evening they secrete a sweet perfume that attracts moths.

Found nowhere else in the VI, the bill-bush is a leafless shrub which appears to have leaves. Close inspection shows that its 7.5-in. long leaves are, in fact, modified stems. Its scarlet flowers exude an odor akin to boiling potatoes. Pinguins are found further up the trail as are mangos.

The lower trail returns to the main road and is a tad longer. Climb up and cross the small peak and head for large boulders and savor the flavor of bay rum trees. Watch for rare quail doves. Listen for their bittersweet, pensive call. Emerging in the mahogany grove, you must head back up the road about a third of a mile to find the main entrance. Along the way, watch out for the Christmas bush, a poison ivy cousin with a similar modus operandi.

Portions have been extensively reforested with mahogany. In 1999, two rare plants (*Calyptranthes thomasiana* and *Zanthoxylum thomasiana*, the *St. Thomas Prickly Ash*) were found on the peak. They are on the US Federal Endangered Species List.

Under the auspices of the North Sound Heritage Project, hiking trails are also under development at North Sound. These trails will follow the originals which ran up hills and to distant flatlands during the sugar era.

DIVE SITES NEAR VIRGIN GORDA: Nearest and most accessible is **"The Blinders."** Near The Baths, it is a mirror image of them but is 30 ft. underwater. Virgin Gorda shares some of the same dive sites as Tortola, such as **"Alice in Wonderland"** and *The Rhone*. Other Virgin Gorda sites include **"Wall to Wall," "the Chimney," "Oil Nut Bay," "Van Ryan's Rock," "Two Ray Bay," "Tiger Mountain,"** and **"Tow Rock."** The last is a pinnacle which rises from 70 ft. to 15 ft. below the water's surface.

YACHT MARINAS: The **Virgin Gorda Yacht Harbour** (☎ 495-5500, ✆ 495-5706; Box 1005, Virgin Gorda), St. Thomas Bay, gives the first hour of moorings for free and offers dockage for 100 yachts of up to 120 ft. Complete facilities including showers are offered. Their website is very informative. http://www.igy-virgingorda.com

The **Bitter End Yacht Club & Resort** (☎ 494-2746; Box 46, Virgin Gorda) can

The mine ruins at Copper Mine Point

hold 18 yachts of up to 170 ft. There are also 70 moorings and complete facilities.
http://www.beyc.com

Biras Creek Estate (☎ 495-3555; Box 54, Virgin Gorda), North Sound, has a marine railway for do-it-yourself repairs. It can hold ten yachts of up to 60 feet.

YACHT CHARTERS AND SAILING SCHOOLS: Euphoric Cruises (☎ 495-5542, 494-5511; Box 55, Virgin Gorda) offers charters; day and other trips (including a catered sunset cruise) are available.
http://www.bviboats.com
caribband@aol.com

Also at the Yacht Harbour, **Double "D" Charters** (☎ 495-6150, cell: 499-2479) is at the Yacht Harbour and offers full- and half-day sails.
doubledcharters@surfbvi.com

Pure Passion Charters (Stanford: ☎ 543 3984), in the Valley, offers day charters to surrounding islands and to and from Beef Island airport.
sandraharrigan@hotmail.com

The *Spirit of Anegada* (☎ 496-6825, 495-5937) offers daytrips to Anegada and other locales. Trips combine snorkeling with local lore and history aboard a small schooner which is also available for private charters.
http://www.spiritofanegada.com
info@spiritofanegada.com

SPANISH TOWN/THE VALLEY ACCOMMODATION: Bayview Vacation Apts (☎ 495-5329; Box 1018, Virgin Gorda) is set in a quiet garden just off of Main St. in The Valley. The atmosphere is pleasant, and your hosts are amiable locals. Bayview is a set of three attractive two-bedroom apartments with living and dining rooms, 2½

baths, kitchens and and TVs. A spiral staircase leads to the roof for private sunbathing. Rates are $680–$880 pw. during the winter and $420–$650 (summer).
http://www.bayviewbvi.com
nora@bayviewbvi.com

In The Valley and near the Yacht Harbour, 20-room **Fischers Cove Beach Hotel** (☎ 495-5252/5253, ✆ 495-5820; Box 60, Virgin Gorda) is a small beachfront cottage colony-style resort. Run by a local family, it has the charming feel of yesteryear. Guests here come back year after year. Rooms are studio cottages (standard and beachfront), efficiency cottages (family-sized with kitchenette and refrigerator, coffee maker, and microwave), and hotel rooms (equipped with refrigerator; coffee makers and microwaves available upon request). Rates start at $125 d (winter) and range to up to $315 for a family-size efficiency cottage during the high season. MAP is $40 pp add'l. There's also a 10% service charge, government tax is added; weekly rates are available. The hotel has a pleasant open-air sitting lounge; its charming beach overlooks the Dog Islands. Its restaurant **The Water's Edge** is well known. Also here is the **Rum Barrel Bar.**
http://www.fischerscove.com
fishchers@candwbvi.com

The 12-room a/c **Ocean View Hotel**, (☎ 495-5230, 800-621-1270; Box 66, Virgin Gorda) is conveniently located in town. Rooms have phone and cable TV. Rates are $60–75 d, with $85–95 d charged during the winter; long term rates available. A 10% service charge is added.
http://www.bviguide.com
butu@surfbvi.com

Virgin Gorda's most famous hotel is the 98-room Rosewood Resort's **Little Dix Bay Hotel** (☎ 495-5555, 800-928-3000, ✆ 495-

5661; Box 70, Virgin Gorda). Constructed in 1964 as a RockResort at a cost of $9 million, this resort—at $136,000 per room —is the most expensive of its size ever built! The employee-to-guest ratio is three-to-one, and it includes 500 acres of land. There are seven tennis courts here and three restaurants.

The atmosphere is one of refined gentility. Lawns are manicured, and open-air pavilions contain the restaurants as well as a library (which includes a wide screen TV with nightly movies). A children's center offers a resident nanny and every type of musical instrument and plaything you could imagine, including a walk-through playhouse. Even (or, perhaps most especially) childless adults will enjoy a visit here. One could only wish that all children, everywhere, had access to these fantastic facilities.

There are three restaurants. **The Beach Grill**, the more formal **Pavilion Dining Room**, and the exclusive **Sugar Mill Restaurant**. Food is plentiful and excellent. The beach is magnificent. A variety of sports and excursions are available, as are a variety of packages.

Rooms are comfortable, somewhat secluded, and do not have TVs. Rates run from $395 to $3,500 (summer) and from $595 to $4,500 (winter). MAP is available on request.

CONDOS: **Olde Yarde Village** (☎ 495-5544) has 30 one- to three-bedroom condos, fitness center, pool, tennis courts, and spa. Rates run from $250.
http://www.oldeyardvillage.com

HIKING There are a few hiking trails which run near the resort. *The Cowhill Trail* (15 min.) and the *Sunset Trail* (20 min.) are recommended for short jaunts. The *Little Savannah Trail* leads to **Savannah Bay**. Allow an hour or so (including swim time) to go and return. This is one place that's def-initely worth going to. Bring water, a swimsuit, and snacks.
http://www.littledixbay.com
ldb@caribsurf.com

OUTLYING ACCOMMODATION: *The following are near Spanish Town.*

AT LITTLE TRUNK BAY: **Island Time** (☎ 495-5227, 914-834-8637) is a five-bedroom/bath house with kitchen, tennis, TV/VCR, babysitting service, and phone. It rents for $4,950 pw summer and $7,625 pw winter.
http://www.islandtimevilla.com
gsbhomes@surfbvi.com

On-the-Rocks (☎ 495-5227), Little Trunk Bay, is a two-bedroom villa housing a maximum of four. There's a phone and babysitting service, and it rents for $1,650 pw summer and $2,200 pw winter. Daily rates are available.
http://wwwontherocksvilla.com
gsbhomes@surfbvi.com

Southern Gables (☎ 495-5201, 804 325-2186; Box 747, Wintergreen, VA) is a three-bedroom with babysitting service.

> **?!** Found only here, the **Virgin Gorda gecko** (*Spaerodactylus parthenopian*) measures only half an inch and is believed to be the world's smallest lizard and resides in the boulders. It is rare and a bit shy of humans, so only a few lucky visitors will see one.
>
> More common is the **"man lizard"** (*Anolis cristaellus*). The male of the species can grow to seven inches and sputs a dragonlike ridge down its back. Females and offspring have a white stripe down their spine.
>
> The common or tree iguana is found only at the North Sound area around Biras Creek here and on Peter Island.

Rates are $1,500–$2,200 pw summer and $2,000–$3,000 pw winter.
priorityproperty@hotmail.com

NEAR SPRING BAY: The **Casa Rocalta** (☎ 495-5227, 203-457-1367), a luxury three-bedroom house with phone, is managed by Guavaberry-Spring Bay Vacation Homes Property Management and charges $3,584 pw summer and $4,704 pw winter. A 20% discount is available for a rental by four or fewer persons, and a fourth bedroom is also available.
http://www.casarocalto.com
gsbhomes@surfbvi.com

The Pink House (☎ 495-5368, ⌨ 495-5669; Box 1020, Virgin Gorda) Spring Bay, is a two-bedroom/bath with living/dining room, deck, TV, phone, and babysitting service. Rates run $1,400 pw summer and $2,150 pw winter; there's a three-day minimum, and a 10% discount for stays of two weeks or more. They also have **Crosswinds,** another villa.
pinkhouse@surfbvi.com

NEAR THE BATHS: **Toad Hall** (☎ 495-5397, ⌨ 495-5708; Box 7, Virgin Gorda) is a three-bedroom/bath villa which rents for $3,500 summer and $4,500 winter.
http://www.toadhallvg.com

Guavaberry Spring Bay Vacation Homes (☎ 495-5227, ⌨ 495-5283; Box 20, Virgin Gorda) has a group of 12 modern fully-equipped one- and two-bedroom wood-faced octagonal cottages which have living, dining and cooking facilities, and patios with views are available. It's a five-minute drive to town. There's a commissary, nearby beach, and a babysitting service is available. The friendly manager is always smiling. Rates run from $140–$190 (summer) to $210–$275 during the winter season.

http://www.guavaberryspringbay.com
gsbhomes@surfbvi.com

MANGO BAY: The **Mango Bay Resort** (☎ 495-5672, 877-626-4622, ⌨ 495-5674; Box 1062, Virgin Gorda) is a set of luxury a/c one- to four-bedroom villas and studios with kitchens (including dishwasher) and patio. E-mail service and phones are available in rooms. A private jetty is provided at Mahoe Bay. Cooks are available, and you can snorkel at the beach. **Giorgio's Table,** an Italian restaurant, is on the premises. Rates range from $115–$680 (summer) to $132–$920 (winter).
http:// www.mangobayresort.com
mangobay@surfbvi.com

Villa Aquamare (☎ 787-461-2638) offers luxurious weekly rentals for $18,500.
http://www.villaaquamare.com
info@villaaquamare.com

Sea Fans (☎ 495-7421, ⌨ 495-7367) are a set of luxurious seafront villas with four separate a/c bedrooms. A pool and tennis courts are provided also. Rates run around $8,500 pw.
http://www.seafans.com
seafansbvi@cox.net

To get to **Savannah Bay Beach** and **Pond Bay Beach**, turn L from the Yacht Harbour, turn R at the "T," and follow the main road which curves L. After passing the Barracuda Restaurant, you'll go over the hill and then spy beaches to your L. Park at the turn off (which may be in the brush). Pond Bay is farther on. Pass the sign to your L to Mango Bay and Paradise and then find a parking spot.

Long Bay Beach is accessed by following the road to Mango. You will also pass the Diamond Beach Club to your R. Water is calm, and there are nearby reefs.

Katitche Point Greathouse
(☎ 495-6274, ℮ 495-6275) is an extraordinary villa with an infinity pool, and a range of amenities including a jeep. A maid and gardener are on the property. The least expensive rate is $6,000 for two for a week. Special "theme weeks" offer activities such as photography, "healing arts," and classical music instruction. The highest is $21,700 pw for the entire villa for ten.
http://www.katitchepoint.com
rentals@katitchepoint.de

AT NAIL BAY: Nail Bay Resort and Villas
(☎ 494-8000, 800-871-3551, ℮ 495-5875; Box 69, Virgin Gorda) offers one- to three-bedroom villas ranging in price from $99–$525 (summer) to $125–$750 (winter).
http://www.nailbay.com
info@nailbay.com

NORTH SOUND: One of the most popular places with yachtspeople, this area offers a wide variety of food and accommodation. Boats for locations such as The Bitter End depart from **Gun Creek** which has an information booth. **Cyril's Bar**, at Gun Creek, provides local food, drink, and atmosphere, and owner Cyril is one of the most affable taxi drivers around. **Twin House Grocery and Snack Bar** also serves good local food.

Found on the island's E tip, the N Sound is shielded by surrounding Mosquito, **Prickly Pear** (lovely **Vixen Point** here is a white sand beach with beach bar; VHF CH. 16; overnight moorings available; see sidebar for information on the national park), Eustatia, and other islands. Boats over five ft. in draft should enter from the NE at Calquhoun Reef. Otherwise, in calm weather, you can use the Anguilla Point entrance.

The island is home to the **Sand Box Seafood Grille** (☎ 495-9122) which offers dishes such as mahi mahi and swordfish. Various evening specials (such as Mexican night) are offered. A boat will run you over here from Gun Creek or Leverick Bay.

North Sound's largest resort is the 100-unit **Bitter End Yacht Club & Resort** (☎ 494-2745, ℮ 494-4756; Box 46, Virgin Gorda). The casual resort's name comes because it was the last point of New World land sailors returning to Europe would pass. Started by Basil Symonette, it began as a five-cottage "resort" with primitive facilities. He sold it to Myron and Bernice Hokin who have developed it over the decades into one of the Caribbean's best-known resorts — one which doubles as a yacht club. It may be reached by boat from the Gun Point Dock on the North Sound (be sure to imbibe at the Last Stop Bar if you have the chance) or by the North Sound Express which connects with flights from Beef Island, Tortola. The Bitter End also runs charter flights from St. Thomas and San Juan. (This may be a reasonable way to arrive if you are in a group).

Facilities include two restaurants, pool, sailing school, a full range of watersports including scuba, and a fitness trail. There's also a deli and store. A conference center will hold up to 80 people. A casual atmosphere prevails. Although not specifically designed as an "eco-resort," the Bitter End does its part to try to conserve power, decrease trash, and recycle garbage.

Their "Fast Tack Sailing Festival" runs from late Oct. to mid-Dec. and includes regattas, beach picnics, lectures, sailing clinics and the chance to join up with the greatest stars in sailing.

The view from the entrance to Mango Bay may seem to be of one large island. However, it is of a number of Virgins. The Dogs are in front and what you see depends upon where you stand. From N to S, the islands are Great Camanoe, Scrub, Tortola, and Beef.

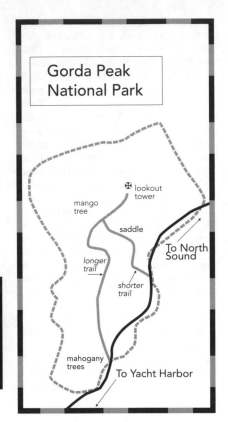

ROOMS: The Beachside Villas and Hillside Villas are accessed by wooden stairs and walkways. The attractively designed units blend right into their environment. Room facilities include a hot water dispenser (with instant coffee and tea bags supplied), a welcome gift of rum and coke, and a hammock out on the veranda.

Dubbed the "Commodore Suites," the best (and quieter) rooms here — which include a/c villas and chalets — are set a bit off from the resort center. (They were actually once part of a competing resort called Tradewinds). This "Premium Resort" consists of a set of 39 secluded hillside bun-

galows which rent in daily and eight day/seven night all-inclusive packages; rates run around $470–$595 pd (depending upon the season). Transport on golf carts is provided; otherwise it's a ten-minute walk. Also here is the Estate House — a two-bedroom villa. There are also eight live-aboard Freedom-30 yachts available for stay in the resort's harbor ($450 d FAP and up).

The lowest summer rates for any room are around $430 d FAP. There are four *other sets* of rates as well as innumerable types of packages.

DINING: Meals are served in **The Clubhouse** and **The English Carvery** (fixed-price, meat oriented meals with two seatings). The Clubhouse serves three meals daily; breakfast and lunch are basically buffet: waitpersons arrive to take your order for a selected entrée. Its dinner menu features a variety of lobster dishes as well as freshly-caught fish. Buffet dinners are $24; complete dinners (which include entrée) are $30. The only downside is the lack of a non-smoking section, a defect which hopefully will have been remedied by the time of your arrival. (Many European guests are tobacco fiends.) The non-uniformed people you see helping out on busy nights are upper-level management.

The **English Pub** at The Emporium sells snacks, but these are not included in your meal plan. Entertainment ranges from reggae and steel bands to solo guitar to movies and sporting events in the **Sand Palace**.

A day excursion here includes pickup at the dock, use of watersports equipment, and lunch for around $50. Add-ons to the Admiral's Package include the "Freedom 30 Day Charter Adventure," the "Windsurfing Adventure," the "Scuba Adventure," and the "Learn to Sail Adventure." To get here you take the North Sound Express from Beef Island or the Potter's Taxi over the mountain to Gun Creek where you meet the *Club Launch.*

If you have time, be sure to explore the hiking trails, bird sanctuary, and lookout point. It's best in late afternoon or before breakfast. At your disposal are a fleet of 20 Boston Whalers, ocean kayaks, Lasers, Rhodes 19s, J-24 Keelboats, and Mistral Sailboards. A sunset sail on the catamaran *Paranda* takes you way out to sea, serves you champagne in glorious surroundings, and then brings you back again. For more information (and they have a *lot* available!) on the resort call (800) 872-2392 or 305-468-0168.
http://www.beyc.com
binfo@beyc.com

OTHER NORTH SOUND RESORTS: Set on 140 acres, seductively attractive **Biras Creek Estate** (☎ 494-3555/3556, ✆ 494-3557; Box 54, Virgin Gorda) at North Sound was originally the creation of a Norwegian fishing magnate. The resort has 34 rooms, including 15 two-suite units running along the shore here, as well as a main building which contains the dining room, commissary, and bar. There's a pool, and a beach at Deep Bay is a short walk away. There's a bird sanctuary (with a series of well marked trails: see Bitter End above) and marina. Tennis, scuba, snorkeling, and sailing are available as are a large number of special packages. High season rates run from $810–$1,500 MAP depending upon the digs and no. of people. Low season rates are from $585–$1,000. A 25% discount prevails during Sept. In the US and Canada call 800-223-1108; in Europe call 800-373-742. Its restaurant, **The Castle** serves casually elegant meals. Great views of the sunset from here.
http://www.biras.com

Leverick Bay Hotel and Marina (☎ 495-7421/7365, US: 800-848-7081, Canada: 800-463-9396, ✆ 495-7367; Box 63, Virgin Gorda) is a North Sound resort reached by its own road. The brightly-colored hillside rooms all command ocean views. It's divided into a/c resort rooms, resort one-bedroom apartments, and two-bedroom resort condominiums. Facilities include restaurant, beach, tennis, marina, shops, and laundry. Unlike at the Bitter End, concessions are run by individuals. You'll find **The Spa** (☎ 495-7375) — which has excellent massages, facials, etc., the **Java Connection** (☎ 495-7421), which offers internet access, the **Palm Tree Gallery**, a gift shop, **Leverick Bay Watersports** (☎ 495-7376), and a branch of **Dive BVI** (☎ 495-5513). The breakfast bar doubles as an internet café. Uninhabited islands are within reach of kayak or dinghy. Leverick Bay also has a beach BBQ on Fri. nights, and a piano player entertains in the restaurant some evenings. There's also fishing and sightseeing by boat. Rates run from a low of $119 d for a resort room to a high of $149 during the high season with tax and service charge included. The *North Sound Xpress* takes you from here to Beef Island.

The associated **Virgin Gorda Villa Rentals** (☎ 495-7421, ✆ 495-7367, 800-848-7081) has efficiencies, one-, two-, and three-bedrooms ranging in price from $600–$4,900/wk (summer) to $700–$10,000 (summer). Prices include tax and maid service. They also have a tie-in with Dive BVI, and it is the home of North South Charters.
http://www.virgingordabvi.com
leverick@surfbvi.com

At Leverick Bay, **Seascape Villa** (☎ 202-337-6820, ✆ 202-337-4136) is a two-bedroom/bath villa which rents for $1,550 pw summer and $2,450 pw winter.
http://www.mcarrow.com/seascape
info@mcarrow.com

The **Saba Rock Resort** (☎ 495-7711/9966, Box 67, the Valley) has units from $175 d on a small island near the Bitter End. There's a restaurant and small museum.
http://www.sabarock.com
sabarockfun@aol.com

Food and Dining

THE VALLEY/SPANISH TOWN FOOD:
The casual mariner-oriented **Bath & Turtle** (☎ 495-5239, VHF Ch. 16) at the Yacht Harbour serves pub-style dishes for lunch and dinner as well as pizza ($13 and up), daily specials, and a Sunday brunch. Entrées range from ahi seared tuna ($20) to grilled local fish of the day ($17). Hearty breakfasts are served.

Dixie's Ice Cream Parlour, near the Yacht Harbour, is good for light dining.

Affordable **De Goose** (☎ 495-5641), opposite the Yacht Harbour, serves up *rotis*,

Roadless North Sound's traffic hazards are different than those you may be accustomed to.

salads, fish burgers, saltfish patties, and local drinks.

Set in The Valley near the Virgin Gorda Yacht Harbour, **Chez Bamboo Restaurant** (☎ 495-5752, reservations) serves French and creative international dishes for dinner. There's often music on Friday evenings.

De Beer Garden & Grill, just S of the Yacht Harbour, serves local food in a patio atmosphere with Dominican music.

One of the best (but very expensive) seafood places is **Fischer's Cove** (☎ 495-5252), which is on the beach near the harbor. Three meals are served daily. In season, a dinner buffet is served from 7–10 PM.

Now also known as **The Cotton Tree Restaurant & Sam's Piano Bar,** the **Rock Café** (☎ 495-5482) offers gourmet evening meals, and a piano player and other entertainment. Its menu was put together by the owner's Italian wife and includes Italian as well as local specialties. Dishes include such entrées as spaghetti with mussels. Be sure to try their giant margaritas, but don't try to drink one alone. They have an extensive wine list. The back patio is a romantic place to dine. Open daily from 4 PM, it is seven min. on foot from the Yacht Harbour in the direction of The Baths.

The **Little Dix Bay Hotel** (☎ 495-5555, ext. 174) offers gourmet international dining including a buffet lunch.

Thelma's Hideout, Little Dix Road, serves good, hearty meals with dishes like salt fish and boiled fish. It is open for lunch.

Verla's Hotspot also serves local food for lunch.

Anything Goes (☎ 495-5062, VHF Ch. 16) is a simple but expensive local restaurant (curries and seafood) which is on the way into town.

With West Indian dishes and a selection of international dishes every Wed., **The Valley Inn** (☎ 495-5639) serves lunch and dinner.

Friendly **Andy's Ice Cream Parlour** serves local snacks such as johnny cakes and fried fish. A small unnamed boat made into a bar stands next door.

Set by the sea (great views) and across from the PO, **Andy's Chateau de Pirate/ Sea Dog Restaurant** (☎ 495-5987) serves lunch and dinner and offers specials. it has friendly service and good food.

The **LSL Bake Shop**, South Valley on the road to The Baths, has a small selection of treats for around $2 each. Its **LSL Restaurant** (☎ 495-5151) serves good food in a very friendly atmosphere. Fresh baked bread is on hand as are the great desserts you would expect from a bakery. Caribbean jerk crab cakes with tamarind class is among the tasty appetizers. Local fish ($20), garlic shrimp ($22), and vegetarian plate ($17) are among the offerings.

At Princess Quarters, **Teacher Ilma's** (☎ 495-5355, reservations needed) serves hearty West Indian homestyle dinners at moderate prices.

The Flying Iguana (☎ 495-5277) is a combination art gallery, bar and restaurant; it serves a Sun. brunch and is near the airport. It serves pasta, grilled, and seafood dishes as well as salads and sandwiches. It's open for lunch and dinner from 10 AM "till close." Breakfasts start at 7AM.

The Barracuda (☎ 495-5350), a gourmet restaurant at Olde Yard Village, serves fresh seafood, has a good wine list, and offers afternoon and evening tapas. It's open Tues. to Sun for three meals daily; no dinner served on Mon.
http://www.barracudabvi.com

In the South Valley, **The Crab Hole** (☎ 495-5307) serves local dishes including callalou, fish, and conch in an informal, homelike atmosphere.

The Mineshaft is set near the copper mine; it has a miniature golf course.

Set in a gorgeous location next to the Mango Bay Resort, **Giorgio's Table** (☎ 495-5684) brings an Italian atmosphere to Virgin Gorda. It brings a pastiche of the nation's cuisine: Dishes range from *Pesce Fresco alla Livornese* (fresh fish coooked in tomato sauce) to *Penne All' Arrabbiata* (*penne* with tomato sauce and porcini mushrooms).

Out at The Baths, the **Mad Dog** serves sandwiches and drinks. They make a mean bushwacker.

The **Top of the Baths Restaurant** (☎ 495-5497) has a freshwater pool, great views, and good food, including lunchtime specials. Homegrown herbs are used in cooking. It's open daily from 8 AM–10 PM.

FOOD SHOPPING: **Buck's Food Market**, a medium-sized market in the Yacht Harbour right behind the Tourist Board, sells groceries ranging from fresh fish to vegetables. It has a small deli.

The Wine Cellar and Bakery sells a wide variety of alcohol, cheese, bread and pastries.

On the road to the Baths, **RTW Wholesale & Cash & Carry** sells everything from bulk peanuts to alcohol to orange juice. In addition to gas for around $2 a gallon, Delta has a minimart with snacks and cold beers ($1.50). You can sit at the counter and watch the 700 Club on TV.

Rosy's Supermarket is a friendly, medium sized market with a wide range of items. It's in The Valley.

Grocery items can also be found at the **Commissary and Ship Store** run by the Little Dix Bay Hotel. **The Chef's Pantry** at Leverick Bay is the North Sound's food store.

Ocean Delight sells ice cream and such.

OTHER SHOPPING: **Paradise Gifts & Herbs** is a combination health food and religious shop. It shares a building with **South Sound Records** which has local recordings, such as those of the Sensations band, and other Caribbean music. **Pussers Company Store** is at Leverick Bay.

NORTH SOUND DINING: Overlooking North Sound, **Biras Creek** (☎ 494-3555) provides gourmet dining at **The Castle**. Three meals are served; dinner is a five-course fixed-price menu and has a dress code. The casual **Fat Virgin's Cave** (☎ 495-7052) is on the dock.

At the Bitter End Yacht Club & Resort overlooking Gorda Sound, **The Clubhouse** (☎ 494-2746) serves three meals daily. Dinner includes steak, seafood, and local specialties.

Set at Leverick Bay on the North Sound, **The Lighthouse** (☎ 495-7154) will pick you up around the Yacht Harbour for their lunch and evening meals; they offer specials and a happy hour.

TRANSPORT, TOURS, AND RENTALS: Rates run around $40–$50 pd. Some offer free pick-up and drop-off as well as weekly rates.

The **Mahogany Taxi Service and Car Rental** (☎ 495-5469, ✆ 495-5072) operates guided tours, offers packages for day trippers, rents jeeps, and runs fishing trips.
http://www.mahoganycarrentalsbvi.com
mahoganycarrentals@surfbvi.com

Andy's Jeep and Taxi Rental (☎ 495-5511, ✆ 495-5162) has a/c taxis, open-air safari buses, tours, and rents out everything from jeeps to Daihatsus to Wranglers for around $50 pd plus other expenses; they also offer guided tours.

Hertz (☎ 495-5803) rents jeeps and cars.

In South Valley, **L & S Jeep Rental** (☎ 495-5297) has 4-, 6-, and 10-passenger jeeps.

Island Style Car Rental (☎/✆ 495-6300) rents Geo Trackers and other vehicles from $40 pd.

Speedy's Car Rental (☎/✆ 495-5240, 495-5235,✆ 495-5755), in The Valley and at Leverick Bay, rents Suzuki Sidekicks (around $60 pd) and offers Speedy's ferry passengers a discount.
http://www.speedysbvi.com
speedysbvi@surfbvi.com

Back up in The Valley, **Honda Scooter Rental** (☎ 495-5212) rents scooters by the hour or by the week.

Anything Goes (☎ 495-5811) also rents scooters as do **3P Scooters** (☎ 495-6580, cell: 499-2344).

BOAT CHARTERS AND EXCURSIONS: **Power Boat Rentals** (☎ 495-5511, ✆ 494-3867) has 15- to 24-footers for lease.

At Biras Creek Marina in North Sound, **Virgin Gorda Villa Rentals Watersports** (☎ 495-7376; Box 63, Virgin Gorda) offers instruction in water skiing and other sports, as well as dinghy rental, by the day or week

At Leverick Bay, **Spice Charters** (☎ 496-6633, ✆ 495-7688, cell: 496-6633) has trips (including diving and snorkeling) to Anegada and other locales.
http://www.spicebvi.com
info@spicebvi.com

Out at Leverick Bay, the **Water Sports Center** (☎ 495-7376) runs trips out to Anegada in a cigarette boat.

The **Bitter End** also runs a number of trips. Contact them for details.

SERVICES: A branch of **FirstBank** is located next to the Wine Cellar and Bakery in the shopping complex at the Yacht Harbour. Its machine will accept most but not all ATM cards. If you have a problem, check inside. First Caribbean International Bank is another nearby alternative. Also here is a friendly branch of the **Tourist Board** (☎ 495-5181).

Prickly Pear National Park

Named after the cactus, this North Sound park was established in 1988 and covers 234 acres. Its four salt ponds host white and black mangroves as well as both visiting and native birds. Red mangroves are found along the S shore. Sea turtles next on the N and E shore. The best beaches are on the N and E while the best snorkeling is at Cactus Point and off the NW shore. ■

Cable and Wireless (☎ 495-5444) offers long distance and fax services.

Jammin (☎ 495-7013) at Leverick Bay offers internet access for $20 ph. Or try **Java Connection** (☎ 495-7154).

The Chandlery (☎ 495-5628), at the Yacht Harbour, also offers internet service as does **Trinity Financial Services** (☎ 495-5537).

Rush It Courier Service has photocopies (25 cents/sheet) and mail forwarding.

For travel arrangements contact **Travel Plan Tours** (☎ 495-5568) which you'll find in the courtyard at the Wheel House.

Post offices are at The Valley and North Sound. **Pay telephones** are found at the airport and Yacht Harbour.

O'Neal and Grandson offers guided horseback riding as well as underwater camera rentals.

Tropical Nannies (☎ 495-6493) will take your tiny tots off your hands.

http://www.tropicalnannies.com

Beauty Therapy Services (☎ 495-5437/7375) has a range of services-from massage therapy to electrolysis to waxing.

Providing everything found in the average US drugstore, the **Island Drug Centre** can be found at the Yacht Harbour and also next to the police station.

The **Virgin Islands Community Library** (☎ 495-5516) is set opposite the clinic on

a ridge near the airport. It has only a small collection but is a great place to get out of the heat.

Steven's Laundromat (☎ 495-5525) is the place to go to wash clothes.

The Spa (☎ 495-7375) is out at Leverick Bay on the North Sound and offers massage, aromatherapy, and other beauty treatments. They have an international staff and do a great job.

VILLA RENTAL SERVICES: McLaughlin Anderson Vacations, Ltd. (☎ 693-0635, 800-537-6246, ☎ 777-4737; 100 Blackbeard's Hill, St. Thomas 00802) represents a number of villas around the island.

ENTERTAINMENT: It can be quiet here.

Set just across from the Yacht harbour, the **De Goose Night Club** (☎ 495-5641) features a live reggae band on Sat. evenings. There's a weekend disco at **Andy's Chateau** across from the PO.

You can find live music at **The Bath and Turtle** and at **Little Dix Bay**.

In the S part of The Valley, **The Crab Hole** features a DJ every Sat. evening.

At the **Pirate's Pub** and **Bitter End,** there's live music and/or DJs.

EVENTS: The music and food festival known as the **Virgin Gorda Easter Festival** or **Musical City** takes place in April.

The **Bitter End Yacht Club** (☎ 800-872-2392) sponsors the **Fast Track Sailing Festival** and the **Pro-Am Regatta** in October and the **Women's Sailing Week** in October.

For current information on major yachting, angling, and rugby events in the BVI, write to the **BVI Yacht Club** (☎ 494-3286), PO Box 200, Road Town, Tortola, BVI.

SHOPPING: The greatest variety of goods may be found at the Yacht Harbour in

town where you'll find a number of shops. Resorts also have gift shops. For the most current list, pick up a free copy of the flier *Guide to Virgin Gorda.*
http://www.vgyh.com

The following are at the Yacht Harbour: **Next Wave** sells tropical fashion items. **Blue Banana Boutique** offers casual clothes and swimwear. **Dive BVI Ltd.** sells jewelry, sundry items, and sportswear. **Thee Artistic Gallery** sells crafts and books. The **Virgin Gorda Craft Shop** sells local crafts. **Kaunda's Kysy Tropix** sells electronic goods as well as jewelry. **Flamboyance** specializes in perfumes. **Margo's Jewelry Boutique** offers an international selection of jewelry as well as batiks and handicrafts. **Misty Isle** offers tee shirts, maps, charts, and has phone service. There's also a small shop in the **Bath and the Turtle Pub** which sells tee shirts, post cards, and the like.

Featuring works by island artists, **Island Silhouette** is in Flax Plaza near Fischer's Cove. At Little Dix Bay Hotel, the **Pavilion Gift Shop** sells sportswear and other accessories.

At The Baths, the imaginatively-named **Nauti-Virgin Beachtique** sells beachwear, jewelry, and the like.

At North Sound, Bitter End's **Emporium** sells jewelry, sportswear, and gift items. They also have the **Trading Post**.

DIVING AND WATER SPORTS: A second PADI five-star center, **DIVE BVI LTD.** (☎ 495-5513, 800-848-7078; Box 1040, Virgin Gorda) operates out of Virgin Gorda Yacht Harbour (☎ 495-5513), Leverick Bay (☎ 495-7328), and Marina Cay (☎ 495-9363), and has a variety of boats. It will meet sailors with its dive boat. Special rates for snorkelers and groups are offered.
http://www.divebvi.com
info@divebvi.com

Dive Tortola (☎ 494-9200, 800-353-3419) is out at Prospect Reef.
http://www.divetortola.com
diving@divetortola.com

With a 10% discount if you bring your own gear, **Kilbride's Sunchaser Scuba** (☎ 495-9638, ℮ 495-7549, 800-932-4286), North Sound, offers dives and instruction.
http://www.sunchaserscuba.com
info@sunchaserscuba.com

Leverick Bay Water Sports (☎ 495-7376) has water skiing, boat rentals of all sorts, sailing excursions, and other activities.
http://www.watersportsbvi.com
watersports@surfbvi.com

Leverick Bay Charter Services (☎ 495-7421, ℮ 495-7367, 800-848-7081) offers charters, fishing, and private trips.
http://www.virgingordabvi.com
leverick@surfbvi.com

North Sound Powerboat Services (☎ 495-7612, cell: 499-2257; Box 2524, North Sound) offers powerboats and boat charters.
North Sound Watersports (☎ 495-7335, ℮ 495-7131; Box 2524, North Sound), rents a 26-ft. glass-bottom and a 30-ft. Bertram.
ginny@biras.com

DIVE SITES: **The Aquarium** or **Fischer's Rocks** is a 15–30 ft. beginner's site set off of Fort Point, less than a mi. from Spanish Town. Peer into anemones to find arrow crabs and cleaner fish doing their stuff. Amidst gorgonians, sea fans, and hard corals, you may find reef squid, morays, barracuda, eels, and nurse shark.

SPORTFISHING: At Biras Creek in North Sound, **Classic** (☎ 494-3555; Box 14, Virgin

Gorda) has a 38-ft. fully equipped Bertram; rates run from $450/half-day.

From Virgin Gorda

Departure schedules *may change* so be sure to check with your hotel or the ferry company to reconfirm well before departure.

There is an $15 international departure tax (air) plus $5 "security fee," and a $5 tax if you depart by ferry; cruise ship passengers pay $7.

FOR ROAD TOWN: *Speedy's Fantasy/ Speedy's Delight* (☎ 495-5240/5235) departs from Virgin Gorda for Road Town Mon. to Sat. at 8, 10, 11:30, 12:30, and 3:30 (add'l trips on Tues. and Thurs. at 6:30 and at 2:45) and on Sun. at 8 AM and 1 and 4:30 PM.
http://www.speedysbvi.com
speedysbvi@surfbvi.com

Smith's Ferry Services (☎ 494-4430/2355, 495-4495) leaves for St. John and St. Thomas (via West End) Mon. to Fri. at 7:50, 10:15, 2:15 and 4 (Road Town only); on Sat. at the same times (but not at 4); and on Sun. (Road Town only) at 10:15, 3, and 5. RT is $44 adults, $36 children (7–12).

FOR BEEF ISLAND: The *North Sound Express* (☎ 495-2138) operates between the North Sound and Beef Island ($35 OW, $65 RT) daily at 6:45, 8:45, 11:45, 2:45, 3:15 and 4:15.

It also runs between Spanish Town and Beef Island daily at 8:30, 11:30, 4, and 5:45.

FOR ST. THOMAS: *Speedy's Fantasy/ Speedy's Delight* (☎ 495-5240/5235) departs from Virgin Gorda for St. Thomas on Tues. and Thurs. at 6:30 and 2:45; and on Sat. at 8:30. RT is $60 adults, $40 children.
http://www.speedysbvi.com
speedysbvi@surfbvi.com

FOR ST. JOHN: Inter-Island Boat Services (☎ 776-6597) on St. John) operates a ferry on Tues., Thurs., and Sun. at 3 PM.

BY AIR: Air Sunshine (☎ 495-8900, 800-327-8900) flies daily to St. Croix and St. Thomas.

Anegada

The small island of **Anegada** ("drowned land") received its name because the surf pounding its reefs rises so high that it threatens to engulf the entire island. Every rule that applies to other Virgin Islands is contradicted here. It's neither steep nor craggy, and there are no mongooses, Anglican churches, or New Age bookshops. Several major tourist development schemes have been proposed for the island but, happily for the sake of the natural environment, have never materialized. Locals are delighted that they have been spared the plague of cruise ships. They like the island just the way it is.

A single government agent handles all the administrative functions and a Kindergarten to 12th grade school has 50 students and 8 teachers.

The Settlement, a collection of unremarkable frame buildings along with a few rusting pickup trucks and garage-sized churches, is home for most of the island's 180-strong population. Besides fishing, most people make a living by working on other islands. It is typically West Indian in that it boasts three churches and many bars. There have been some big changes in recent years. A new administration building has been built, the power grids are being extended.

Of the many beautiful beaches, **Loblolly Bay Beach** is the most well known.

Set at the island's southern extension, **Horseshoe Reef** is one of the Caribbean's largest reef systems and is a protected area.

ANEGADA

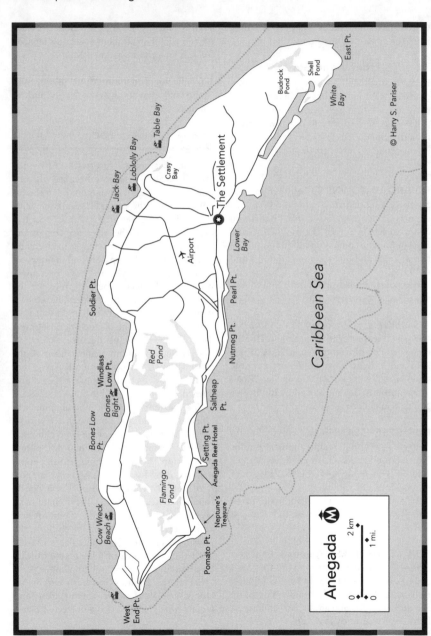

© Harry S. Pariser

East Pt.

Shell Pond

White Bay

Budrock Pond

Table Bay

Loblolly Bay

Crasy Bay

Jack Bay

The Settlement

Lower Bay

Airport

Pearl Pt.

Soldier Pt.

Nutmeg Pt.

Windlass Low Pt.

Red Pond

Bones Low Pt.

Bones Bight

Saltheap Pt.

Setting Pt.

Anegada Reef Hotel

Flamingo Pond

Cow Wreck Beach

Neptune's Treasure

Pomato Pt.

West End Pt.

Caribbean Sea

Anegada

2 km

1 mi.

0

0

THE LAND: Only 28 ft. (8.5 m) above sea level at its highest point, the 15-sq-mi. (39-sq-km) island is nine miles long and one to four mi. wide and easily affected by rising and falling tides. Consisting of limestone grating, it is completely flat in the S, and central portions have scattered lagoons, salt ponds, and marshes, as well as glorious beaches. Anegada resembles a Pacific atoll set in the Caribbean and is most similar to islands found in the Bahamas to the N; its surrounding reefs are its most spectacular feature. It is the only British Virgin Island with freshwater springs of any size.

FLORA AND FAUNA: A great variety of animal and plant life thrives here, some of which cannot be found elsewhere in this island group. The monotony of the bracken and mangrove vegetation is punctuated by spreads of lilac-colored wild orchids (*petramicra elegans*) which grow in profusion along Red Pond's salt flats. There are plenty of century plants as well as epiphytes (air plants) and lots of loathesome machineel trees. Other trees include tamarind, turpentine fir, and the ubiquitous coconut. There're also two varieties of wild sage as well as a thorny bush, the "fishing rod tree," which is collected and used as a Christmas tree, a custom unique to Anegada.

Island birds include roseate spoonbills, snowy and reddish egrets, nesting willers, great blue herons, ospreys, little blue, tri-color and green-backed herons, northern water thrushes, Antillean nighthawks, and the more commonplace frigates, plovers, and pelicans. Sandwich, roseate, and gull-billed terns come to visit during the summer months. Flamingoes (see sidebar) have also been re-introduced.

A lesser creature, but no less significant, is the Anegada Rock Iguana (*Iguana pinguins*) of which about 400 remain. This endangered lizard may reach five feet in length and weigh 20 lbs. They are most commonly seen on the island's N coast where certain trees have been banded with orange paint to denote where they live. Another place you can see them is at the breeding station next to the administration building in The Settlement.

In former times, legend has it that huge swarms of enormous mosquitos, known as "gallon nippers," roamed the island, appearing and disappearing at 10-year intervals. Their bites, in large concentration, were said to have proved fatal to sheep and sent wild goats fleeing into villages for human protection. These goats, as well as small wild horses, donkeys, and a special Spanish strain of cattle, still roam freely and greatly outnumber bipeds.

The most popular underwater creatures with visiting gourmands are its lobsters which are being taken in such tremendous quantities that overharvesting is becoming a real possibility. The conch has already been overharvested, and now small conches are being used to bait traps to supplement the customary fish guts and cowhide. Controls are in place but enforcement is difficult. For example, there is now a season on green turtle, yet some locals continue to dine on them.

HISTORY: Used first by the Indians who left heaps of conch shells behind them on the E end, the island's maze of reefs afforded protection for pirates like Kirke, Bone, and the French pirate Normand (now known as "Norman"). Although the first settlers did grow some food and cotton, they came here expecting to profit from the spoils of the frequent shipwrecks. No sooner was the cry of "vessel on the reef!" heard than the residents, sidearms in hand, would be off and running, competing to be first aboard.

The shipwrecks, which occurred with alarming frequency, were occasionally helped along by unscrupulous residents who would set out lamps to lure unsuspecting ships onto the treacherous reef.

Even though the reefs were well marked on charts, shipwrecks still occurred because of a powerful and unknown NW current which prevails from March to June. More than 300 ships met their doom here. Today 138 wrecks are charted. These include the *Paramatta*, a British steamship which hit Horseshoe Reef in 1853 in the dead of night; the HMS *Astrea*, a 32-gun British frigate which sank in 1808; and the *Rocus*, a Greek freighter carrying the unusual cargo of animal bones, which went down off the E coast of of the area now known as Cow Wreck Beach.

Horseshoe Reef claimed some modern-day pirates when a boat sank here in Oct. 1994. The boat contained three Colombians and a cargo of 10 kg of cocaine which was to have been sold in Puerto Rico.

These days there's still a land dispute raging. Most of the island is Crown land with what belongs to everyone else in dispute. A few decades ago a British contractor/developer allegedly slipped some money under the table to the government and damn near bought the entire island. He had plans for major development (with the locals confined in the best apartheid-like style to one portion of the island) but these fell through and a huge marina (planned on the site of Flamingo Pond!) was never constructed. The island has been attracting more and more attention, and the tourist board is pushing for development.

☞ George Brown, owner of the Lavenda Breeze rental villa, has some great photos of the island here:
http://www.pixadilly.com

GETTING HERE: Don't plan on sailing here unless you have good charts; more than 13 miles of barely penetrable reef surround this island. The worst time to visit is in Sept. and Oct. when the sand flies are out.

BY BOAT: Smith's Ferry Services (☎ 495-4495, 494-2355) goes to Anegada on Thurs. from Road Town. It leaves at 7 AM and 3:30 PM and returns at 8:30 AM and 5 PM.
http://www.smithsferry.com

A charter flight with **Fly BVI** (☎ 495-1747) or another charter airline is the only other way to get back and forth.
http://www.flybvi.com

The Bitter End offers snorkeling trips from their yacht club/hotel on North Sound Virgin Gorda to Anegada on Wed. and Fri. While the Wed. trip includes a meal at Neptune's Treasure, the Fri. trip offers a beach BBQ.

A **freight boat** leaves from the gas station on Anegada in the morning on Tues. (sometimes) and Fridays. It returns in the afternoons from Tortola. This is a good way to arrive with your food from Tortola if you are self-catering.

FROM ST. JOHN: High Performance Charters (☎ 340-777-7545) offers trips.

KAYAKING: Arawak Expeditions (☎ 340-693-8312; 800-238-8687; Box 853, Cruz Bay) run trips to the BVI from St. John, including five-day expeditions to Anegada (around three per year; generally in May).
http://www.arawakexp.com
arawak@att.global.net

GETTING AROUND: The roads are being paved, and the process may be completed sometime during the century. There are a number of taxi drivers including the Smith family: (☎ 443-4118).

ABC Car Rentals (☎ 495-9466) rents jeeps and 4WD vehicles. It offers free pick-up and drop-off. Rates run from around $60 pd.

The **Anegada Reef Hotel** (☎ 495-8002, ℰ 495-9362) offers daily rentals for ten-seater jeeps.

D.W. Jeep Rentals (☎ 495-9677) offers free pick up and drop off service and offers daily (around $40 pd), weekly, and monthly rates.

The **J & L Jeep Rental** (☎ 495-3138, 495-8047, 496-4275, ℰ 495-9461) rents vehicles from around $50 pd on up. The affiliated **T&A's Bike Rental** rents bikes for $15/day.
j&l@surfbvi.com

You can rent **bicycles** from the Anegada Reef; they also offer **taxi service**: return times are fixed, and you must buy tickets in advance. Bicycling may be slow going, however, as the roads are frequently sand covered.

SIGHTS: Anegada is a delightful island to explore both above and below the water. The endangered rock iguanas are best seen near Bones Bight, but you'll have to trek inland. However, there's an easy way to see them. The West Indian Iguana Group has instituted a program which captures hatchlings. Because feral cats, kestrels, and the Puerto Rican racer, a garden snake, love to feast on the crunchy young iguanas, the goal is to keep them protected until they can fend for themselves.

Funded through the BVI National Park Trust, the "Head Start" project, next to the administration building/ PO in town, holds some 50 caged iguanas. If you arrive in the morning, you may be fortunate enough to see them feeding. The project began in 1997 with three iguanas. The first release was in the fall of 2003. Some 120 or more have been released. They may live as long as 40 or 50 years.

The flamingos (see sidebar) are elusive and may be seen from afar with good binoculars; they resemble orange sacks. You'll see the occasional wild donkey as well as cows. If a cow should do some damage, no one will know who owns it. However should you chance to hit one with your car, there will be instant cognizance!

The elusive and endangered Anegada Rock Iguana

Anegadans do not lack for humor.

Around the island you'll note old coral stone walls; these are hundreds of years old. Other features are of more recent origin. The Settlement has several churches worth photographing as well as a fish pier which is best visited in the wee hours of the morning. There are gulls circling overhead, as well as small mountains of conch shells. You can see that the conch has been overfished by the small size of the most recent shells. Out at the West End you can see the remains of a British Navy helicopter landing pad near a magnificent beach. (Hike to Walkover Beach from the main road).

The Navy was stationed here for reasons best known to themselves, and their telltale droppings may be found hither and thither.

SNORKELING: The best snorkeling is on the island's N where you can try Cow Wreck Beach, Loblolly Bay and Loblolly Bay East as well as a number of other points (but these lack facilities). Offshore and underwater by Flash of Beauty at Loblolly Bay East, it's not unusual to see a live lobster crawl across the sand.

. The best way to get to these is to rent a jeep, but alternatives include taxis, bicycles and walking (possible by trail from Loblolly to The Settlement). You can head on down the beach here; it's a magnificent stretch of sand! If you head over to the E from Loblolly Bay East, you can find all sorts of shells.

ACCOMMODATIONS AND FOOD: Because everything must be imported, prices are high but often not that appreciably higher than elsewhere in the US or British Virgins. Reservations are recommended everywhere for dinner. Menus tend to be nearly identical at many restaurants.

Hotels are listed going around the island clockwise beginning with The Settlement.

About the only place to eat in The Settlement, basic and friendly **Dotsy's Bakery** (☎ 495-9667) is open from 8AM–8PM and offers fresh baked goods including pies ($5), French bread ($2.50), and coconut-and-chocolate-chip cookies. Dotsy also offers inexpensive lunches and dinners including fish sandwiches ($5).

The **Ocean Range Hotel** (☎ 495-2019, ✆ 201-782-9030; VHF CH. 16: Big Bamboo) which has studio apartments available for daily, weekly, and long-term rates

Bonefish Villa (☎ 495-8045) is a very attractive two-bedroom, two-bath villa with cable and other amenities. A lot of thought and effort has gone into furnishing this place and it shows. It holds a maximum of six. Friendly owner New Yorker Laura, who is married to a fishing guide, will provide a cell phone with a $20 card ($4 per minute to call the states) and will stock provisions for you. The beach in back is suitable for wading. It's set near Pat's Pottery between the airport and the Anegada Reef. **bonefishvilla@hotmail.com**

Potter's By The Sea (☎ 495-9182), Setting Point, Anegada, British Virgin Islands serves seafood (caught by owner Liston Potter) among other dishes. It's open for lunch and dinner.

The oldest hotel, the **Anegada Reef Hotel** (☎ 495-8002, ✆ 495-9362; Setting Point, Anegada), offers 16 comfortable but simple a/c rooms; 10 of these face the

⚑ Anegada's Flamingos ⚑

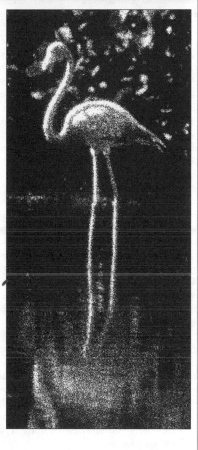

Anegada is known for many things, but the island has once again gained notice for its flock of flamingos. Although its Flamingo Pond had once hosted great flocks of the birds it had been entirely depopulated of them for nearly a half century. Roseate Flamingos were once found throughout the VI. Many were sold, and others were hunted for their feathers. The few remaining in Anegada disappeared on their own.

Dr. James Lazell studied the island's ecosystem in the 1980s and approached the National Parks Trust with a plan to re-introduce the birds. A charter flight brought eight birds from the Bermuda Aquarium and Natural History Museum and Zoo to the island in 1987. They were first released on Guana Island where four of the birds flew off, while the remaining four (who had had their wings clipped while in the zoo) died off.

In 1992, 20 birds were released. While this was short of the normal flock size of hundreds of birds, it was an improvement. However, procreation did not occur until the winter of 1995 when four wild flamingos arrived and chicks hatched in the spring. There are now many birds. The hope is that flamingos will eventually once again flourish in the BVI.

There are seven flamingo species of flamingos; roseates are the largest and may reach up to five ft. in length. The mud-built nests generally hold only one egg which both parents take turns sitting on. The chicks are born white and mature sexually after three years.

They mainly feed on miniscule aquatic creatures (such as brine shrimp) which contain carotene, the ingestion of which gives the birds their characteristic color. Flamingos feed by straining water through plates in their bills. Flamingos are shy creatures and need their privacy so be sure to keep well away from them. You wouldn't want to be responsible for the flock's extinction. ■

garden. Rooms also have fans, hot pot for coffee and tea, and sliding screened doors. You need to purchase drinking water, as the room water is not potable. Rates run from around $160–$250 (summer) to $180–$275 (winter). They also run the Anegada Reef Cottages and Villa; rates by request. Its restaurant offers American-style breakfasts supplemented by fresh fruit and fruit juices; sandwiches, salads; soups, and vegetarian platters for lunch; and a menu which includes freshly caught seafood dishes (including roast lobster) for dinner. They offer a ticketed taxi service with fixed pickup times; a run into town is $3 each way.
http://www.anegadareef.com
aneghtl@surfbvi.com

One of the island's mainstays is the Soares family whose compound has become a major center for tourism. Of Portuguese origins, the family came to the BVI from the Azores via Bermuda. Their **Neptune's Treasure Seaside Restaurant** (☎/℅ 495-9439; VHF Ch. 16 or 68) serves fresh seafood as well as inexpensive fare; a pair of gigantic shark jaws hangs above the bar.

Their **Neptune's Guest House** is perhaps the island's most comfortable hotel accommodations. Comfy a/c rooms have refrigerators, king-size beds, and face the yard. Coffeemakers are supplied upon request. Their rates are $80–110 d; weekly and off-season rates are available. The family also offers taxi service. A family-style atmosphere prevails here.
http://www.neptunestreasure.com
neptunestreasure@surfbvi.com

The Pomato Point Beach Restaurant (☎ 495-9466, VHF Ch. 16) serves seafood and other dishes for lunch and dinner; it also has a champagne breakfast. Owner Wilfred Creque also owns the **Lobster Trap** down the road near Neptune's Treasure. His

Anegada Sea Side Villas rent for around $200 pn.

An added bonus here is a small display of artifacts Included are indigenous artifacts such as stone tools, pottery shards, and zemis — pyramid-shaped rocks which served as religious representations of spirits. (Tainos once lived on the island's E end).

The bulk of the collection, however, comes from shipwrecks. There are nails, numbers from ships, timbers, and cannons and musket balls. The gin bottles date from the 1700s, and the Bellamine jug from the Rhineland was manufactured between 1550 and 1699.

Assembled pottery shards vary from pieces from the Royal Mail Steam Packet Company, the parent firm of the ill-fated Rhone to shards displaying the crest of the Pacific Steam Company.

Coins include a silver Four Real piece from the Mexican national mint; it is likely booty obtained from a Spanish galleon. Other coins are from as far afield as Brazil, Denmark, and Guatemala. You can also see several 19th-C. US coins. A few pieces even show African influences: witness the large wood-carved mortar and pestle. The best time to view the collection is in the evening when it is open before dinner.

Also at Pomato Point, the **Anegada Beach Cottages** (☎ 495-9234; Box 2733, Anegada) are comfortable, clean, and have a full kitchen with electric range. They are run by McKenzie, who used to live in Sacramento, CA, and rent for around $125–$200 pn.
http://www.anegadabeachcottages.com
mckenzie@surfbvi.com

Continuing around the island to the NW, you'll find **Cow Wreck Beach Bar & Grill** (VHF Ch. 16) which offers delicious local-style lunches and dinners; your host is a local. Their beach is one of the most beautiful on the island. Their comfortable **Cow**

Wreck Beach Villas ☎ 495-8047, ☏ 495-9461) are right next to the restaurant. They rent for around $175–$275 pn summer and $200–$300 winter. Water here is not potable, so you need to secure a supply for your stay.
http://cowwreckbeach.com
cowwreck@surfbvi.com

Keel Point Cottages (☎ 495-8019/8048, 441-0296) offers one- and two- bedroom, spacious yet simple cottages for rent.
http://www.keelpointcottages.com
keelpointcottages@yahoo.com

Lavenda Breeze (☎ 495-8045, 888-868-0199) is a villa near Loblolly which rents for around $3,500 and up per week. This beautiful and attractively furnished home is managed by Laura who also has the Bonefish Villa. One of the nicest features here is the outdoor showers.
http://www.lavendabreeze.com
george@lavendabreeze.com
laura@lavendabreeze.com

At Loblolly Bay East, **Flash Of Beauty** (☎ 495-8014, VHF Ch. 16) serves sandwiches and seafood dishes. *This is one of the best places to snorkel.*
Loblolly Beach Cottages (☎ 495-8359) rent from $1,225 pw winter.
http://www.loblollycottages.com
loblolly@loblollycottages.com

SHOPPING: V&J's sells souvenirs as does Henny's Gift Shop (on the south road), ad the Purple Turtle.

FOOD SHOPPING: The selection here isn't the best as all veggies must be imported, and the population is so small. If you wish to cook your own lobster, you must make prior arrangements; expect to spend around $10/lb. (The season runs from Dec. to around May).

Little Bit Taz Cash & Carry (☎ 495-9932) sells produce and other goods. Other places with food items include Faulkner's Store, Cap's store, Vanterpool's store, and The Purple Turtle.

SERVICES: You should bring with you what you need because you can't count on finding it here. Sticking out like a sore thumb in The Settlement, the **Administration Building** can be recognized by the BVI government shield above its door. It houses the post office, police, and the office of the District Officer. There's also a laundromat with a soft drink machine in front. The first and only gas station is right near the Anegada Reef. Sadly, the owner has cut down mangroves behind the station to build a dock for his freight boat.

ENTERTAINMENT: The best thing do is enjoy the quiet. Sex on the beach here is not a drink but a pastime for honeymooners who think no one is watching; they are kidding themselves. (Nudism is illegal).

DIVE SITES AROUND ANEGADA: With an estimated 17 wrecks per sq mile — some lying atop one another—the area should be a diver's paradise. However, many are disintegrated and lie buried in silt, thus limiting their visibility.

Settled 35 ft down, the *Parmatta* lies broken into two parts and is now overgrown with elkhorn coral.

Animal bones litter the deck of the *Rocus*, which lies 40 ft. down. There's also a noose which marks the spot where her captain, unable to face Greek authorities, hung himself. This is an intermediate dive, and the 380-ft. Greek freighter sunk in 1929 while enroute to exotic Baltimore from Trinidad. The cow bones might have been made into bone meal fertilizer, but then we would not have place names such as Cow Wreck beach. The atmosphere can be downright

As the stem is in shallower water, it's more suitable for snorkelers, as is the Rhone Reef— a fringing reef located to the S of the wreck which has two coral caves at a depth of 25 ft., as well as colorful marine life.

"**Blond Rock**," which resembles a natural amphitheater, lies submerged in 12 ft. of water. Accessible only in calm water, it lies between Dead Chest and Salt Island. (See "Dive Sites Near Tortola.")

Included in the park boundaries, the 34-acre **Dead Chest Island** is to the W. It is reputed to be the island where Blackbeard abandoned his crew: "Fifteen men on a Dead Man's Chest —Yo Ho Ho and a bottle of rum." This song is seemingly nonsensical unless you realize that a dead man's chest is a coffin (which the island, viewed in silhouette, does resemble). Seabirds (including bridled terns and noddies) nest on the 214 ft.-high cliffs facing its SW side.

The island's N slopes are covered with dry forest, salt ponds fringed with machineel and mangroves sit in a flat expanse in the N. Cactus scrub— including organ pipe and red-topped barrel cactus —grow along the steep slopes on its S side.

To its SE are the **Painted Walls**, a series of submerged rocks which form 20–50 ft. canyons. Their name comes from the colorful sponges, algae, and corals that cover their surfaces.

REGULATIONS: You may not remove any marine or terrestrial plant, animal or historical artifact. Fishing without a license is prohibited. Dispose of garbage only at correct garbage disposal points. Building fires and waterskiing are prohibited activities within park waters.

Smaller Islands

Besides the larger and better-known islands, there are numerous small islands and cays. Many are imaginatively named: Cockroach, Asbestos Point, Great Dog, The Indians, King Rock, Lizard Point, The Invisibles. Some of the more interesting are described below.

Norman Island

Norman Island is said to have been named after a French buccaneer named Normand who settled here along with his booty. Some claim Norman is Stevenson's Treasure Island. Reportedly, treasure from the *Nuestra Señora* was recovered here in 1750. It In 2007, a group illegal migrants (47 Haitians and two Dominicans, including two babies) were set ashore by smugglers.

Adventurous mariners may anchor S of Treasure Point, where there are four caves with excellent snorkeling. (Many boats run excursions here).

Row into the southernmost cave with a dinghy and see where Stevenson's Mr. Fleming supposedly took his treasure: the cave is eerie and dark, except for phosphorescent patches on the ceilings. Bats fly overhead and the only sound is the whoosh of the

Entrance to The Caves at Norman Island

eerie, but the fishlife is plentiful. A guide is needed.

Although nothing is left of the **Astrea** itself, stocks of cannonballs, cannons, iron ballast, and anchors remain.

Humpback whales migrating from S. America to Greenland are commonly sighted in the Anegada Passage between mid-Feb.. and mid-April.

FISHING: People come from all around the world to bonefish here. **Daniel Vanterpool** ☎ 495-8045) and **Kevin** and **Garfield Faulkner** will take you out.

Other Islands

Rhone National Marine Park

Extending over an 800-acre area, this marine park's most famous feature is **The Rhone**, a British mail packet ship which went down in the hurricane of 1867 and was smashed in two on the sharp rocks at Black Rock Point. The remains of the 310-ft. two-masted steamer now lie at depths of 20–80 ft. Viewed in the crystal-clear water, it's a veritable underwater museum and one of the most famous dive sites in the entire Caribbean.

HISTORY: The pride of the Royal Mail Steam Packet Company, *The Rhone* was at anchor outside of Peter Island's Great Harbour and planning to return to England when the storm commenced. The captain planned on moving to a safer spot during a lull, but the anchor chain split off. He then gunned the motors and headed for open seas with the intention of riding the storm out. Instead, the storm forced her onto the rocks at Salt Island. Almost the entire crew (some 125 people) perished. Weighing 2,738 tons, the boat was 310 ft. long and 40 ft. wide. The wreck achieved a measure of fame after being used as a location in

some scenes from the film adaptation of Peter Benchley's novel, *The Deep*.

VISITING THE PARK: Anchor at moorings provided at Lee Bay or at Salt Pond Bay; the moorings directly above the wreck are reserved for commercial dive boats which have permits. Anchors have damaged the marine life as well as the park itself. The wreck is usually visited in two dives; bow and stem sections are located near Salt Island.

Thickly covered with coral, the bow section lies 80 ft. down, while the stern—containing the remains of engine and propeller—lies at 30 feet. Both host brilliantly colored coral and myriad varieties of fish. You should watch for eels, barracuda, turtles, parrotfish, snapper, and others. You can locate the bow section, condenser, engines, prop shaft, and propeller.

The **anchor** is outside Great Harbour off Peter Island at a depth of 55 ft. (It can be hard to find; a guided tour is recommended).

Scuba divers plunge down to visit the Rhone.

OTHER ISLANDS

sea being sucked in and out. It would be easy to spend an entire day out here. Watch out for tides and the wild cattle (temperamental at times) which roam the land above.

On the island, there's a small salt pond here where birds congregate. Climb the half-hour path to the top of **Spyglass Hill**, a viewpoint once used by pirates searching for Spanish galleons. Popular dive sites Pelican Island (Rainbow Canyon, suitable for beginners) and the Indians lie nearby.

DIVING: Angelfish Reef, as its name intimates, is alive with fish. Near Treasure Point and The Caves, its maze of narrow canyons offer coral galore and depths range from 30–90 ft. You might see rays, schools of grunts, and, of course, French and your standard Angelfish.

Rainbow Canyon ranges in depth from 20–50 ft. and offers an outstanding assortment of colored beauties including trumpetfish, and angelfish and great expanses of coral.

To the W, **Ringdove Rock**, a beginner's dive, runs from 12–60 ft. Great coral and plenty of sea fans, sponges, and fish such as sergeant majors, striped parrotfish, and butterflyfish.

The Indians are four large rocks whose tips protrude near Pelican Rock. Soft and hard corals prosper in the canyons and

The Anchor of The Rhone

grottoes of these formations. You'll find sea fans, elkhorn, brain, and other corals in the 15-50 ft. depths. On the E side, a cave, reached by a short tunnel, is filled with colorful fish. Exceptionally calm, this site is suitable for both scuba and snorkeling. Avoid the area when a strong breeze hits.

Set about a mile from Norman Island in the direction of St. Croix, **Santa Monica Rock** is another underwater pinnacle. Its location makes it an ideal site to see spotted eagle rays, nurse sharks, and barracudas. Whereas the pinnacle's top is around 100 yds. in diameter, its base is 400 yds. at a depth of 70 ft. There is so much to see in the area that you may need to return. If you are lucky, you may spy a hawksbill turtle hiding under a ledge towards the bottom. The top layers reveal corals and gorgonians galore.

FOOD AND ENTERTAINMENT: Pirates Bight (☎ 446-7827) serves standard American and W Indian fare. *http://www.normanislandpirates.com*

William Thornton, a Baltic trader converted into a floating restaurant, is anchored off of Norman Island. Lunch (mahi mahi sandwiches, veggie rotis, and other light stuff) is served noon–3 and dinner (shrimp creole, *rotis*) is served 7 AM–10 PM. For more information call 494-2564 or reach them via VHF Ch. 16 or Tortola Radio. **http://www.williamthornton.com**

Peter Island

Accessible by sailboat or by private ferry from Tortola, the island is dominated by **Peter Island Hotel and Yacht Harbour.** (PO Box 211, Road Town; ☎ 495-2000; ☞ 495-2500: US: ☎ 800-346-4451, ☞ 770-476-4979).

Jay Van Andel, co-founder of Amway Corporation, who administers the resort, own the entire island, save the 16 acres owned by fisherwoman Estelle La Fontaine. She has steadfastly refused to sell out despite substantial pressure. The beach at Deadman's Bay, just five min. downhill from the units on the island's E tip, has been acclaimed the best in the British Virgins. According to local lore, the shining pink shells on the graves in the nearby cemetery serve to stave off evil spirits.

It's a popular anchorage, and you'll see the most unbelievably humongous crafts anchored here. Yachtspeople are requested to anchor in the extreme SW corner and to be wary of swells, particularly during the winter months. While the beach at Little Deadman's is near its parent, Spring Bay is a stiff half-hour hike away. (Shuttle service provided for guests). While on the island be sure to keep your eyes peeled for the common or tree iguana which is only found here and at Biras Creek on Virgin Gorda.

The anchor of *The Rhone* can be found outside Great Harbour off Peter Island at a depth of 55 ft. (A guided tour there is recommended).

Ecology minded visitors might want to check out the former landfill which has been transformed into a composting and recycling area. An industrial chipper breaks down wood products, a compost blender mushes it all up, a tractor spreads it around, and a ventilation system infuses the oxygen necessary for speedy decomposition.

GETTING HERE: The **Peter Island Boat** (☎ 494-2561) connects Baugher's Bay on Tortola with the island. Trips are daily at 8, 9, noon, 2:30, 4:30, 6, 10, and 11:30. RT is free for guests, $15 for visitors. Pickup by boat at Beef Island is also available.

ACCOMMODATION: The resort offers A-frame Scandanavian-built houses which are supplemented by beachfront rooms. These have a/c, fans, and phones. And,

of course, you get large bottles of Amway shampoo and conditioner.

A three-bedroom, two-bath private villa — with its own boat, two maids, gardener, and minimoke vehicle — is for rent (around $10,000 for six nights; it holds eight). Another rental is Sprat Bay, a smaller cottage which houses six. Two six-bedroom villas opened in 2004.

Tennis courts, a pool, darts, billards, ping pong, and other games are offered. There are several beaches, spa, a pool, and windsurfing, scuba and snorkeling are offered. It's tied in with an Ashore/Afloat plan. Hobie Wave sailboats, windsurfers, and bicycles are available free to all guests. There are a variety of room plans available. Room rates range from $540–$9,000 FAP d (summer) to $865–$12,000 FAP d (winter).

DINING: Peter Island Resort has a good reputation for food and service. The restaurant serves gourmet food and has a great wine list. A great idea is to go to Peter's Island on a day trip, enjoy the beach at Deadman's, and eat lunch there as well.

The Deadman's Bay Bar & Grill serves lunch and dinner (Tues. to Sun. "formally casual;" around $40 dinner, $20 lunch with unlimited salad bar). The rotating menu at the elegant **Tradewinds Restaurant** offers continental and West Indian dishes for lunch and dinner (evening dress code).

ENTERTAINMENT: Steel band or fungi music can be found in the Yacht Club lounge every evening.
http://www.peterisland.com

Salt Island

Salt Island is appropriately named. Off the NW point of Salt is a small settlement where the entire population (of one, an aging stalwart known as Henry) resides. He collects salt from the three salt ponds as locals have been doing for the past 150 years. The gathering season is in April and May. Formerly, these ponds supplied salt for the Royal Navy. They're still owned by the illustrious British queen whose representative comes over once a year to collect a bag of salt for the rent! Moorings are provided at Lee Bay which is just N of the Rhone wreck.

Yachtspeople can also anchor at Salt Pond Bay off the settlement. Both of these anchorages can be rough and are recommended for day use only. Very few visitors venture to step ashore. If you see Henry or another local, let him or her know why you're there. Salt Island is the number-one diving destination in the BVI. owing to the wreck of the *Rhone.*

Cooper Island

This island (pop. nine) is the home of the intimate **Cooper Island Beach Club** (☎ 494-3721 (messages), 800-542-4624; Box 859, Road Town] at Machioneel Bay on the NW; the 20 moorings in the marina are $20 for overnight. There's also good swimming and snorkeling on the beach.

Cooper makes a good lunch stop for those sailing upwind to Virgin Gorda. Food offerings in the casual oceanfront restaurant (open daily for lunch and dinner) include grilled mahi-mahi, lobster, and mixed salad. Prices range from $7-$10.

In operation for over two decades, this is hardly your typical resort. Each villa, named after an island ("Barbados," "Fallen Jerusalem" are two) has two rooms which are equipped with kitchenette, shower, rattan furniture, and a selection of books and games. Water comes from cisterns underneath the buildings, and lighting and ceiling fans are powered by 12 V DC. Rates start at $75-95 d summer and rise to $135-$175 winter. A 10% service charge is added. Write Box 859, Road Town; call 800-542-4624. A

variety of packages (including diving) are also available.
http://www.cooper-island.com
info@cooper-island.com

Offering three one- to three-bedroom cottages along the beach, **Cooper Island Hideaways** has kitchens and other facilities; they rent from $875 pw summer and $1,330 pw winter. For more information call (513) 232-4126 or write 1920 Barg Lane, Cincinnati, OH 45230-1702.
http://www.cooperisland.com
info@cooper-island.com

DIVING: Sail Caribbean Divers (☎ 495-1675) offer diving. They also operate from Hodges Creek.
http://www.sailcaribbeandivers.com

Carrot Rock, a dive site fronted by large pillar corals, lies offshore.

An intermediate-level site set 25–40-ft. deep, **Dry Rocks West** or "Vanishing Rocks" are set off the NE of Salt I. Strong currents make for plenty of life below water. Great pillar coral, butterflyfish, and a plethora of sergeant majors are among the highlights.

Fallen Jerusalem National Park

When viewed from the sea, the 12 acres of **Fallen Jerusalem** resemble the ruins of an ancient city to its gigantic granite boulders. It excites the imagination of all who see it.

Now a national park, the island's goats have been removed in order to protect the vegetation, and birds such as the pearly-eyed thrasher, common ground-dove, scaly-naped pigeon, and the Zenaida dove are found here. Nesting seabirds here (and on neighboring Round Rock and Broken Jerusalem) include brown boobies, laughing gulls, terns, brown pelicans, noddies, and red-billed and white-billed tropicbirds. Its stretch of beach may be visited on calm days.

Sandy Cay National Park

Located to the E of Little Jost Van Dyke, **Sandy Cay**, an uninhabited islet once owned by the late Laurence Rockefeller, sports a white sand beach and hiking trails. This 14-acre island, made a national park in 2008, boasts nearly 90 plant and tree species in an environment that might best be described as a miniature version of a tropical coastal dry forest. The water is deep until you are very near the shore. The area is subject to swells, so it does not make a good anchorage year round.

The Dogs

The Dogs, a miniature archipelago, covers 165.5 acres of land and 4,435 acres of sea. The Dogs are named after the little monk seals which were once plentiful here. The British called them "sea dogs" and the Spanish as "lobos marinas" ("sea wolves"). The last one was executed in 1954.

Occupying 24 acres, **West Dog National Park** is a critical refuge for laughing gulls, bridled terns, sooty terns, roseate terns, red-billed tropic birds, and nesting doves. It is to be part of a proposed protected area which will include neighboring consanguinal canines Great West Dog, East Seal Dog, and West Seal Dogs as well as Cockroach walk and underwater pinnacles Tow Rock and Van Ryan's Rock.

Justifiably popular with divers, snorkelers, and yacht people alike, the best anchorages here are at **George Dog** to the W of Kitchen Point and on the S side of **Great Dog**.

Dive site moorings near West Dog mark Joe's Cave, Wall to Wall, and Flintstones. The area is a good place to stop when sailing from North Sound to Jost Van Dyke.

Great Tobago

There are some 210 acres on **Great Tobago**, the most westerly of the BVI. It is a sanctuary for the magnificent frigatebird.

Necker Island

Necker Island is owned by Richard Branson, the British multimillionaire whose other properties include Virgin Records, Virgin Cola, and Virgin Atlantic Airways. (He recently purchased tiny 125-acre Mosquito (Moskito) Island which he intends to transform into a similar private "eco" resort). The Balinese-style house on this 74-acre island may be rented and ensures complete privacy. Aside from the 22 staff members, no one else will be allowed on this island during your stay. You'll have your own snooker table (the only one in all of the British Virgins), a private pool and Jacuzzis, outdoor and indoor dining tables, spectacular views, private beach, and tennis courts. All water sports are provided.

Guests here have included the late Princess Di and her family. Google co-founder Larry Page was married here in 2007. (Reportedly, he spent a total of US$15 million on the bash. Rates run from $24,000-$38,000 pd depending upon the number of guests (1–24). Included in this are all meals and drinks, helicopter transfer from St. Thomas (for a stay of a week or more; otherwise transfer is by launch from Beef Island, the location of Tortola's airport). Extras include scuba, sailing, and deep sea fishing.

In the US contact Resorts Management Inc. (☎ 800-557-4255, 212-696-4566, ✆ 212-689-1598). In Canada call 800-387-1201 or call 416-968-2374 in Ontario. In Britain, call 011-44-208-600-0496.
http://www.neckerisland.com

Guana Island

This privately-owned upscale resort and nature reserve is run by the **Guana Island**

Club (☎ 494-2354, 800-544-8262; 10 Timber Trail, Rye, NY 10580; 914-967-6050, ✆ 914-967-8048). Guana, an 850-acre island, offers gourmet dining, miles of scenic hiking and walking, white sand bathing beaches, two tennis courts, and water sports. The whitewashed stone walled cottages were constructed as a private club in the 1930s on the foundations of a Quaker estate house which had been abandoned by its owners after they found sugar cane slavery to be morally unconscionable. (Quaker ruins can still be seen around the island.)

The main building and all cottages are set on a hilltop and command beautiful views of the Atlantic and Caribbean. The remainder of the island, including its seven beaches, remains undeveloped. Although most beaches can be reached on foot, two are accessible only by boat. As yachties are unwelcome, an atmosphere of serenity and privacy prevails. There are 20 trails, some of which climb the 825-ft. Sugarloaf Mountain. A few are easy, many are challenging, most offer superb views and serenity.

If you're lucky, you may be able to see such endangered species as the Masked Booby, the barefoot screech owl, the bridled quail dove, the red-legged tortoise, the white crowned pigeon—which have been returned to thrive on Guana and the rock iguana, which has been rescued from the blink of oblivion. (Guana boasts that it's "the only wildlife sanctuary in the world with a cocktail hour"). If arranged in advance, a boat will meet guests at Tortola's airport on Beef Island from 9–5. Rates (AP) for the 15 rooms are divided into four rate seasons and range from $775 d on up (for the off season) to a high of $7,500 pn for a two- or three-bedroom villa (which comes with many extras). "Rent The Island" rates are available upon request.
http://www.guana.com
reservations@guana.com

Most Romantic Places to Kiss

The BVI has no lack of great places

➤ In Mt. Sage National Park on Tortola

➤ At the ruins at Mt. Healthy on Tortola

➤ In Road Town's Botanical Gardens

➤ On the trails above the Bitter End on North Sound, Virgin Gorda

➤ In the caves at The Baths on Virgin Gorda

➤ At dusk at a beach on Anegada

?!¢ The ghosts of numbers of extinct species ply the land and water of the Virgins. Manatees, giant tortoises, enormous large rodents, parrots, and flightless birds are among the casualties of human rapacity.

John Lettsome

Born on Little Jost Van Dyke, John Coakley Lettsome (1744–1815) got off to a remarkable start. He was one of two twins, the seventh such set of twins, and the only twin to survive. Sent to medical school in England, he returned to the VI. As a Quaker, he freed all his slaves.

After doctoring in these parts, he returned to England to found the British Medical Society and the Royal Humane Society. Lettsom was one of the principal advocates for the "dispensary movement" which fought the smallpox epidemic and paved the way for the health clinics and specialty hospitals you find all over the world today.

The British Medical Society, in association with Royal Society of Medicine, has established an essay prize in honor of Dr. Lettsome. ■

Glossary

bareboat — A charter boat which comes without crew.

calabash (*calabaza*)— Small tree native to the Caribbean whose fruit, a gourd, has multiple uses when dried.

callaloo — Caribbean soup made with callaloo greens.

Caribs — Original people who colonized the islands of the Caribbean, giving the region its name.

cassava — Staple crop indigenous to the Americas. Bitter and sweet are the two varieties. Bitter must be washed, grated, and baked in order to remove the poisonous prussic acid. A spongy cake is made from the bitter variety as is cassareep, a preservative which is the foundation of West Indian pepperpot stew.

cays — Indian-originated name which refers to islets in the Caribbean.

century plant— also known as *karato*, *coratoe*, and *maypole*. Flowers only once in its lifetime before it dies.

conch — Large edible mollusk usually pounded into salads or chowders.

cutlass — The Caribbean equivalent of the machete. Originally used by buccaneers and pirates.

duppy — Ghost or spirit of the dead which is feared throughout the Caribbean. Derives from the African religious belief that a man has two souls. One ascends to heaven while the other stays around for a while or permanently. May be harnessed by good or evil

through *obeah*. Some plants and birds are also associated with *duppies*.

escabeche — Spanish and Portuguese method of preparing seafood.

Johnkonnu — Festivities dating from the plantation era in which bands of masqueraders, dressed with horse or cow heads or as kings, queens or as devils. Now a dying practice throughout the Caribbean, it is preserved largely through tourism.

love bush— Orange-colored parasitic vine, found on Jamaica, St. John, and other islands. Resembles nothing so much as the contents of a can of spaghetti.

machineel — Small toxic tree native to the Caribbean. Its fruit, which resembles an apple, and milky sap are lethal. See clearly marked specimens near the Annaberg ruins on St. John.

obeah — Caribbean black magic imported from Africa.

sea grape — West Indian tree, commonly found along beaches, which produces green, fleshy, edible grapes.

sensitive plant — also known as mimosa, shame lady, and other names. It will snap shut at the slightest touch.

star apple — Large tree producing segmented pods, brown in color and sour in taste, which are a popular fresh fruit.

woman's tongue — Asian plant whose name comes from its long seed pods. Dry when brown, they flutter and rattle in the breeze, constantly making noise.

Booklist

Travel and Description

Carter, Dorene E. *Portraits of Historic St. Croix: Before and After Hurricane Hugo.* Frederiksted, St. Croix: Caribbean Digest Publishing, 1991.

Creque, Darwin D. *The US Virgins and the Eastern Caribbean.* Philadelphia: Whitmore Publishing Co., 1968.

Dammann, Arthur E. and David W. Nellis. *A Natural History Atlas to the Cays of the United States Virgin Islands.* Sarasota, FL: Pineapple Press.

Hamsun, Knud. *From Denmark to the Virgin Islands.* New York: Dormance and Co., 1947.

Hart, Jeremy C. and William T. Stone. *A Cruising Guide to the Caribbean and the Bahamas.* New York: Dodd, Mead and Company, 1982. Description of planning and plying for yachties. Includes nautical maps.

Hartman, Jeanne Perkins. *The Virgins: Magic Islands.* New York: Appleton Century, 1961.

Hayward, Du Bose. *Star Spangled Virgin.* New York: Farrar and Rhinehart, 1939.

Holbrook, Sabra. *The American West Indies, Puerto Rico and the Virgin Islands.* New York: Meredith Press, 1969.

Kurlansky, Mark. *A Continent of Islands.* New York: Addison-Wesley, 1992. One of the best books about the Caribbean ever written, a must for understanding the area and its culture. Although the Virgin Islands are only touched upon, it provides an excellent backdrop to understanding.

Morrison, Samuel E. *The Caribbean as Colombus Saw It.* Boston: Little and Co.: 1964. Photographs and text by a leading American historian.

Naipaul, V.S. *The Middle Passage: The Caribbean Revisited.* New York: MacMillan, 1963. Another view of the West Indies by a Trinidad native.

Radcliffe, Virginia. *The Caribbean Heritage.* New York: Walker & Co., 1976.

Robertson, Alan H. and Fritz Henle. *Virgin Islands National Park: The Story Behind the Scenery.* Las Vegas: KC Publications, 1974.

Van Ost, John R. and Harry Kline. *Yachtsman's Guide to the Virgin Islands and Puerto Rico.* North Miami, Florida: Tropic Isle Publishers, Inc. Where to anchor in the area.

Ward, Fred. *Golden Islands of the Caribbean.* New York: Crown Publishers, 1967. A picture book for your coffee table. Beautiful historical plates.

Wood, Peter. *Caribbean Isles.* New York: Time Life Books, 1975.

Wouk, Herman. *Don't Stop the Carnival.* Glasgow: Fontana Books, 1979. The classic novel of expatriate life in the Virgin Islands.

Zucker, Eric. *The Virgins: Places and People.* St. Thomas: FLICKS Productions, 1992

Flora and Fauna

Ackerman, James D. *The Orchids of Puerto Rico and the Virgin Islands*. San Juan, PR: University of Puerto Rico Press, 1992. A beautifully illustrated and well written tome.

Humann, Paul. *Reef Fish Identification*. Jacksonville: New World Publications, 1989. This superb guide is filled with beautiful color photos of 268 fish. Information is included on identifying details, habitat and behavior, and the reaction of various species to divers.

Humann, Paul. *Reef Creature Identification*. Jacksonville: New World Publications, 1992. The second in the series, this guide covers 320 denizens of the deep. Information is given on relative abundance and distribution, habitat and behavior, and identifying characteristics.

Humann, Paul. *Reef Coral Identification*. Jacksonville: New World Publications, 1993. Last in this indispensable series (now available as a boxed set entitled "The Reef Set"), this book identifies 240 varieties of coral and marine plants. The different groups are described in detail.

Kaplan, Eugene. *A Field Guide to the Coral Reefs of the Caribbean and Florida*. Princeton, NJ: Peterson's Guides, 1984.

MacLean, Dr. William P. *Reptiles and Amphibians of the Virgin Islands*. London: 1982.

University of the Virgin Islands. *Island Peak to Coral Reef: A Field Guide to the Plant and Marine Communities of the Virgin Islands*. St. Thomas: University of the Virgin Islands, 2005. A superb guide.

Raffaele, Herbert A. *A Guide to the Birds of Puerto Rico and the Virgin Islands*. Princeton, NJ: 1989, Princeton University Press.

de Oviedo, G. Fernandez. (trans./ed. S.A. Stroudeniire. *Natural History of the West Indies*. Chapel Hill: University of North Carolina Press, 1959.

Sutton, Lesley. *Fauna of the Caribbean: The Last Survivors*. London: Macmillan Caribbean, 1993.

History

Boyer, William W. *America's Virgin Islands*. Durham, North Carolina: Carolina Academic Press, 1983. A superb overview of the political and social history of the islands.

Deer, Noel. *The History of Sugar*. London: Chapman, 1950.

Dookhan, Issac. *A History of the Virgin Islands of the United States*. St. Thomas: College of the Virgin Islands, Caribbean Universities Press, 1974.

Gooding, Bailey W. and Justine Whitfield. *The West Indies at the Crossroads*. Cambridge, MA: Schenkmann Publishing Co., Inc., 1981. A political history of the British Caribbean during the 1970s.

Hill, Valdemar A., Sr. *Rise to Recognition, An Account of Virgin Islanders from Slavery to Self-Government*. St. Thomas: St Thomas Graphics, 1971.

Mitchell, Sir Harold. *Caribbean Patterns*. New York: John Wiley and Sons, 1972. Dated but still a masterpiece. The best reference guide for gaining an understanding of the history and current political status of nearly every island group in the Caribbean.

O'Neill, Edward A. *Rape of the American Virgins*. New York: Praeger, 1972. Scathing history and revealing account of trouble in American Paradise.

Willocks, Harold W. L. *The Umbilical Cord: A History of the United States Virgin Islands from Pre-Columbian Era to the Present*. Christiansted, St. Croix: 1995. This book, by a local attorney and historian, serves as an excellent historical introduction to the Virgin Islands.

Sociology and Anthropology

Abrahams, Roger D. *After Africa*. New Haven, CT: Yale University Press, 1983. Fascinating accounts of slaves and slave life in the West Indies.

Horowitz, Michael H. (ed) *People and Cultures of the Caribbean*. Garden City, New York: Natural History Press for the Museum of Natural History, 1971. Sweeping compilation of social anthropological essays.

Art, Architecture, and Archaeology

Buissert, David. Historic *Architecture of the Caribbean*. London: Heinemann Educational Books, 1980.

Gosner, Pamela. *Historic Architecture of the USVI*. Durham, NC: Moore Publishing Company, 1971.

Goaner, P. *Caribbean Georgian*. Washington DC: Three Continents, 1982. Well illustrated guide to "Great and Small Houses of the West Indies."

Lewisohm, F. *The Living Arts & Crafts of the West Indies*. Christiansted, St. Croix: Virgin Islands Council on the Arts, 1973. Local crafts illustrated.

Willey, Gordon R. *An Introduction to American Archeaology, Vol. 2, South America*. Englewood Cliffs, New Jersey: Prentice-Hall, Inc., 1971.

Music

La Motta, Bill and Joyce. *Virgin Islands Folk Songs*. St. Thomas: Joyce La Motta's Tuskimaro VI. Tunes by the late composer and his wife.

Language

Highfield, A. R. *The French Dialect of St. Thomas, Virgin Islands: A Descriptive Grammar with Text and Glossary*. Ann Arbor: Karoma Publishers, Inc., 1979.

Literature

Anderson, John L. *Night of the Silent Drums*. New York: Scribner, 1976. Fictional narrative of a Virgin Islands slave rebellion.

Whitney, Phyllis A. *Columbella*. New York: Doubleday, 1966. Mystery romance set in St. Thomas.

Index

D

E

F

G

H

I

J

Manatee Press Vacation Reading Suggestions

Here's some unusual vacation reading selections for your trip to the Virgin Islands. These are all books we've either read recently and loved or are time-honored classics you may have overlooked. Happy reading!

Nonfiction
Fast Food Nation by Eric Schlosser
The Sorrows of Empire by Chalmers Johnson
Ghost Wars by Steve Coll
A People's History of the United States by Howard Zinn
Nickel and Dimed by Barbara Ehrenreich
Deer Hunting With Jesus by Joe Bageant
The Wrecking Crew by Thomas Frank

Novels
The Buddha of Suburbia by Hanif Kureishi
A House for Mr. Biswas by V. S. Naipau
A Bend in the River by V. S. Naipaul
Don't Stop the Carnival by Herman Wouk
Welcome to the Monkey House by Kurt Vonnegut
Love Warps the Mind a Little by John Dufresne
Catch 22 by Joseph Heller
Brave New World by Aldous Huxley
Digging to China by Anne Tyler
Sellevision by Augusten Burroughs
A Confederacy of Dunces by John Kennedy Toole
All The King's Men by Robert Penn Warren
A Fine Balance by Rohinton Mistry
The Abstinence Teacher by Tom Perrotta
Rabbit is Rich by John Updike
The God of Small Things by Arundhati Roy
Drop City by T. C. Boyle
Tortilla Curtain by T. C. Boyle
Martin Chuzzlewit by Charles Dickens
A Free Life by Ha Jin
The Space Between Us by Thirty Umrigar